CROSSWORDS

CROSSWORDS

ARCTURUS

ARCTURUS

This edition published in 2013 by Arcturus Publishing Limited
26/27 Bickels Yard, 151–153 Bermondsey Street,
London SE1 3HA

ISBN: 978-1-78212-578-5
AD003711EN

Printed in the UK

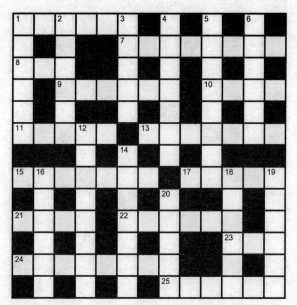

1

Across

1 Probable (6)
7 Eastern (8)
8 Section of a play (3)
9 Passage through or under something (6)
10 Melt (4)
11 Slumbered (5)
13 Leisure time away from work (7)
15 Deep red (7)
17 Acute pain (5)
21 In a lofty position (4)
22 Electronic messages (6)
23 High rocky hill (3)
24 Done again and again (8)
25 Floor of a house (6)

Down

1 Acquires knowledge (6)
2 Water boiler (6)
3 In an early period of life (5)
4 One who spoils other people's fun (7)
5 Needlework created by interlacing yarn (8)
6 Central American canal (6)
12 Brochure (8)
14 Ornament made of ribbon, given as an award (7)
16 Bankrupt (6)
18 Pearl-producing shellfish (6)
19 Annually, every twelve months (6)
20 Stripes (5)

2

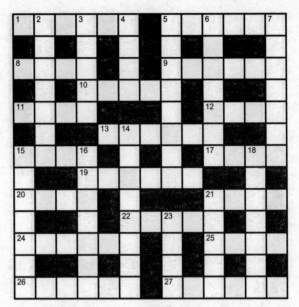

Across

1 Seen, looked at (6)
5 British political party (6)
8 Untamed (4)
9 Mounts for the lenses of sunglasses (6)
10 Flavour (5)
11 Item of crockery (4)
12 Male sovereign (4)
13 Indigenous person (6)
15 Went by plane (4)
17 Makes a knot (4)
19 Twelfths of a foot (6)
20 Chest bones (4)
21 Use a keyboard (4)
22 Trench (5)
24 Within (6)
25 Waterside plant (4)
26 Zero (6)
27 Most up-to-date (6)

Down

2 First letter of a name (7)
3 Distance across (5)
4 Canine creatures (4)
5 Period of existence (8)
6 Thick bedcover (7)
7 Hands in one's notice (7)
14 Mishap (8)
15 Belonging to another country (7)
16 Having a desire for (7)
18 Fast train that makes a limited number of stops (7)
21 Projected through the air (5)
23 Urban area (4)

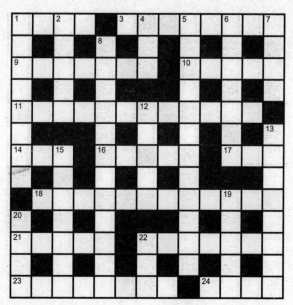

Across

1 Washtub (4)
3 Owned up to (8)
9 Authorise (7)
10 Outer layer on bread (5)
11 Reference work containing articles on various topics (12)
14 Centre of a storm (3)
16 Depends on (5)
17 As well (3)
18 Standing in for (12)
21 Grown-up (5)
22 Set free (7)
23 Going very fast (8)
24 Optical organs (4)

Down

1 Ornament worn around the wrist (8)
2 Subject (5)
4 Pass from physical life (3)
5 More and more (12)
6 Sightseer (7)
7 Palm fruit (4)
8 Condensed (12)
12 Follows orders (5)
13 Legislative assembly of the USA (8)
15 Carry out a killing (7)
19 Country, capital Rome (5)
20 Flexible containers (4)
22 Directed or controlled (3)

4

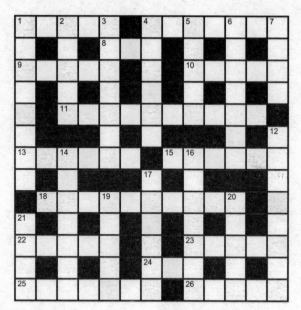

Across

1 Roman god of love (5)
4 Of the heart (7)
8 Fish eggs (3)
9 Female relative (5)
10 Paris underground railway (5)
11 Clinic where medicine is handed out (10)
13 Put into cipher (6)
15 Odd or fanciful idea (6)
18 Disagreeable (10)
22 Goes in front (5)
23 Male deer (5)
24 Large monkey (3)
25 Takes into custody (7)
26 Military vehicles (5)

Down

1 Yellow songbirds often kept as pets (8)
2 Beg earnestly (5)
3 Put on clothes (7)
4 Stopped (6)
5 Plays boisterously (5)
6 Time between one event and another (7)
7 Cut with an axe (4)
12 Mental state induced by suggestion (8)
14 Mythical being, half man and half horse (7)
16 Pair of earphones (7)
17 Maria ___, opera singer (1923–77) (6)
19 Inventories (5)
20 Educate in a skill (5)
21 Italian sports car manufacturer, ___ Romeo (4)

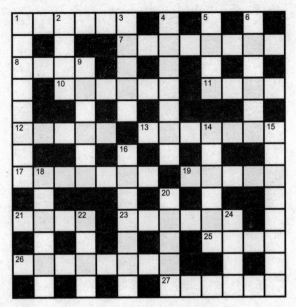

Across
1 Permits (6)
7 Wheeled heavily or clumsily (8)
8 Idiots (4)
10 Beat hard (6)
11 Corrosive compound (4)
12 Robber (5)
13 Slim, supple and graceful (7)
17 Line on a map connecting points of equal height (7)
19 Consume (3,2)
21 Layer of dirt or froth on the surface of a liquid (4)
23 Offbeat (6)
25 Dress worn primarily by Hindu women (4)
26 Move towards (8)
27 Person who is in charge (coll) (3,3)

Down
1 Fragrant (8)
2 Elevate, raise (4)
3 Drinking tube (5)
4 Salman ___, British author (7)
5 Thought (4)
6 Light gas often used to fill balloons (6)
9 Most timid (6)
14 Makes an orderly pile (6)
15 Discharging (8)
16 Small oval citrus fruit with a thin sweet rind (7)
18 Inhabit (6)
20 Ability to see (5)
22 Female horse (4)
24 Back garden (4)

6

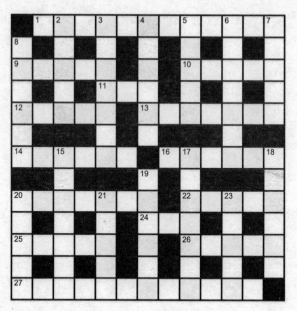

Across

1 Arm of the Atlantic Ocean between North and South America (9,3)
9 Book of maps (5)
10 Up to the present time (2,3)
11 Fluid used for writing (3)
12 Prongs of a fork (5)
13 Expressing sorrow, mournful (7)
14 Enclose in (6)
16 Chaos (6)
20 Rotating shaft (7)
22 Vertical part of a stair (5)
24 *Much ___ about Nothing*, Shakespeare play (3)
25 Use to one's advantage (5)
26 Roofing material (5)
27 Mirror (7,5)

Down

2 Woody ___, US film-maker and comic actor (5)
3 Takes a firm stand (7)
4 Sponsored (6)
5 Wide open (5)
6 Fashionable (7)
7 Trick (5)
8 Bovine animals (6)
15 The USA's Windy City (7)
17 Spray can (7)
18 Combined (6)
19 Small porous sachet containing leaves for infusion, making a drink (3,3)
20 Cloak, often knitted (5)
21 Indian city (5)
23 Crustlike surfaces of healing wounds (5)

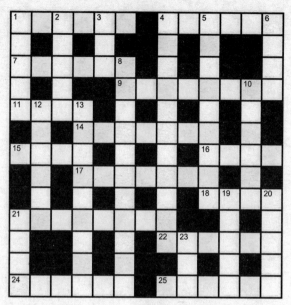

Across

1 Earlier in time (6)
4 Wide road (6)
7 Unwell (6)
9 Heated building for growing tender plants (8)
11 Joy Adamson's lioness in *Born Free* (4)
14 Secures, fixes (7)
15 Turned-back hem at the end of a sleeve (4)
16 ____ Blyton, author (4)
17 Anarchical (7)
18 Eye infection (4)
21 ____ XVI, pope who resigned in 2013 (8)
22 Ironic parody (6)
24 Make attractive or lovable (6)
25 Military trainees (6)

Down

1 Accuse of being responsible (5)
2 Drops down (5)
3 Dashed (3)
4 Resolutions (11)
5 Claim back (9)
6 Slab found on a roof (4)
8 One who gives the credit of authorship to someone else (11)
10 Sound powers of mind (6)
12 Living room (6)
13 Abundant wealth (9)
19 Clan (5)
20 Pitchers (5)
21 Live-action film about a piglet (4)
23 Ms Gardner, Hollywood actress (1922–90) (3)

8

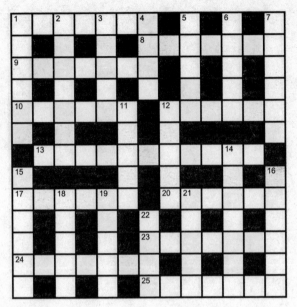

Across
1 Walks with a lofty proud gait (7)
8 Located in the open air (7)
9 Place of complete bliss, delight and peace (7)
10 Wandered (6)
12 Cleared of uncultivated plants (6)
13 Quality of having no practical purpose (11)
17 Freshwater carnivorous mammals (6)
20 Break free (6)
23 Dissimilar (7)
24 Present as worthy of regard or confidence (7)
25 Came out (7)

Down
1 Foodstore (6)
2 State of being behind in payments (7)
3 Discontinue (5)
4 Submerge in a liquid (4)
5 Make up for past sins (5)
6 Expected and wished (5)
7 Large fleet, especially of Spanish warships (6)
11 Eats sparingly, in order to reduce weight (5)
12 Squander (5)
14 Gliding on ice (7)
15 Intimation of dismissal (6)
16 Decapitate (6)
18 Ms Wynette, country music singer (1942–98) (5)
19 Insurrectionist (5)
21 Protect from light (5)
22 Dandy (4)

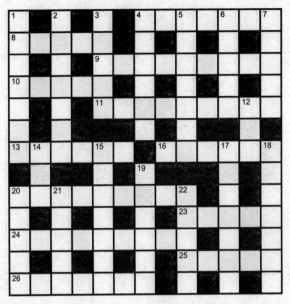

Across

4 Shrink back (7)
8 Give a speech (5)
9 Act of putting one thing into another (9)
10 Pieces of potato fried in deep fat or oil (5)
11 Wares sold in a hat shop (9)
13 Cut in two (6)
16 Rich and fashionable people who travel widely for pleasure (3,3)
20 Period during which there is no war (9)
23 Priory residents (5)
24 Entertainment venue (9)
25 Creepy (5)
26 Hearing distance (7)

Down

1 Conceited, empty-headed person (7)
2 Assorted (7)
3 Form of theological rationalism (5)
4 In a hasty manner (6)
5 White, ant-like insect (7)
6 Tolerate (5)
7 Bitter, aromatic plant (5)
12 Fish eggs (3)
14 Frozen water (3)
15 World's swiftest cat (7)
17 Remove moisture by making use of centrifugal forces (4-3)
18 Ballroom dance (3-4)
19 Colour of the rainbow (6)
20 Pasta in short tubes (5)
21 Fury (5)
22 Glowing fragment of wood or coal left from a fire (5)

10

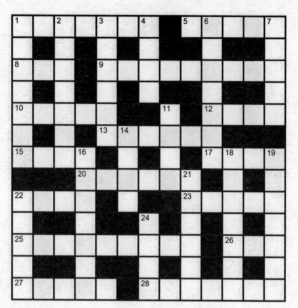

Across

1 Hobby (7)
5 Traditional pantomime tale, ___ in the Wood (5)
8 Girl's name (3)
9 Metal object sounded to warn of danger (5,4)
10 Teatime sweet bread roll (5)
12 Diminutive (4)
13 Corrupt morally (6)
15 Has sight of (4)
17 Request on an invitation (inits) (4)
20 Dental decay (6)
22 Skim (4)
23 Loses fluid from an accidental hole (5)
25 Gas used in welding (9)
26 Notice of intent to pay (inits) (3)
27 Tall stories (5)
28 Feel distaste towards (7)

Down

1 Expresses approval of (7)
2 Capital of Costa Rica (3,4)
3 Envisioned (6)
4 Mild yellow Dutch cheese (4)
6 Umpire (7)
7 Aunt ___, game played by throwing sticks at a doll (5)
11 Sum charged for riding in a bus (4)
14 British nobleman (4)
16 Ceremonial or emblematic staff (7)
18 Official language of Tanzania (7)
19 Arrangement of the body and its limbs (7)
21 Slumbers (6)
22 Respond to a stimulus (5)
24 Small ball with a hole through the middle (4)

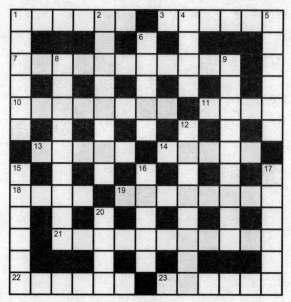

Across

1 Abhor (6)
3 Capital of Austria (6)
7 Scary (11)
10 Stringed instrument (8)
11 Blackthorn fruit (4)
13 Eight singers who perform together (5)
14 Twilled woollen fabric (5)
18 Black bird with a raucous call (4)
19 Haberdasher (8)
21 Attempt to anticipate or predict (6-5)
22 Come to the fore (4,2)
23 Hostility (6)

Down

1 Charge falsely or with malicious intent (6)
2 Glass for sherry (8)
4 Egyptian deity (4)
5 Became less intense (6)
6 Jeans fabric (5)
8 Harmless (9)
9 Explosive substance (9)
12 Seven-sided shape (8)
15 People in a play (6)
16 Walked stealthily (5)
17 Dependable, loyal (6)
20 Colour of unbleached linen (4)

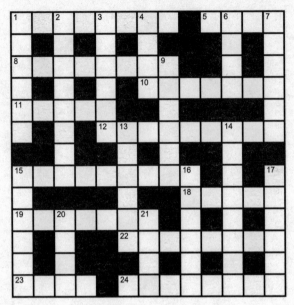

Across

1 Someone injured or killed in an accident (8)
5 Bazaar (4)
8 Of land cultivation (8)
10 Go down (7)
11 Crockery (5)
12 Young birds not yet fledged (9)
15 Cradle songs (9)
18 US state, capital Boise (5)
19 Brickwork (7)
22 Fighter plane used for suicide missions (8)
23 Fill to satisfaction (4)
24 Short-legged flightless birds (8)

Down

1 Accident, fate (6)
2 Relating to a medical operation (8)
3 Pilot of a plane (6)
4 Stout-bodied amphibian (4)
6 Republic of Ireland (4)
7 Second book of the Old Testament (6)
9 Stinging plant (6)
13 Go on board (6)
14 City in southern Japan on Kyushu (8)
15 Boundaries (6)
16 Fathering (6)
17 Blankets (6)
20 River deposit (4)
21 Renowned lock-making company (4)

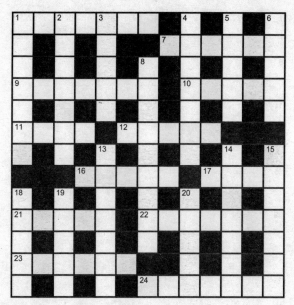

Across
1 Premonitions, intuitive feelings (7)
7 Thomas ____, US inventor (1847–1931) (6)
9 Repair provisionally (5,2)
10 Having the same measure as another (5)
11 Walking stick (4)
12 Two-winged insects characterised by active flight (5)
16 Happen again (5)
17 Relieve (4)
21 Compounds capable of turning litmus red (5)
22 Sound excluder (7)
23 Weariness after a flight (3-3)
24 Absorbs (knowledge or food) (7)

Down
1 Nag, bother persistently with trivial complaints (3-4)
2 Puts things in order (7)
3 Disorderly outburst or tumult (coll) (3-2)
4 Sticks like glue (7)
5 Deplete (3,2)
6 Fireplace (5)
8 Clapped (9)
13 Animal product used as a furniture polish (7)
14 Proceeds at great speed on horseback (7)
15 Mongolian emperor, ____ Khan (1162–1227) (7)
18 Stringed instrument of the guitar family (5)
19 Clenched hands (5)
20 Incorrect (5)

14

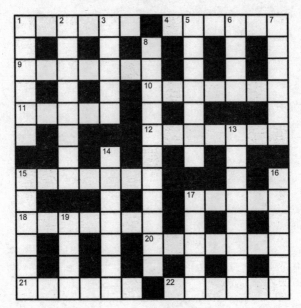

Across
1 Cook (vegetables) briefly (6)
4 Think highly of (6)
9 Strong feeling (7)
10 Admit one's guilt (7)
11 Military blockade (5)
12 Nobility (7)
15 Highly contagious avian virus such as H5N1 (4,3)
17 Bring dishonour upon (5)
18 Daphne du Maurier novel (7)
20 Period of the afternoon when a light meal is taken (7)
21 Physically strong (6)
22 Refuse to accept or acknowledge (6)

Down
1 Bosom (6)
2 Higher than average (5,3)
3 Country, capital Santiago (5)
5 Tool used to hold or twist a nut (7)
6 Otherwise (4)
7 Foam used in hair styling (6)
8 Put in a short or concise form (11)
13 Scratchy (8)
14 Waste pieces left over after sawing wood (7)
15 Boundary line (6)
16 Waterless, empty area (6)
17 Dry white Italian wine from Verona (5)
19 Rear-facing point on an arrow (4)

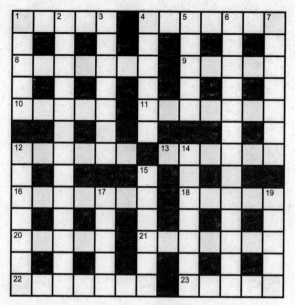

Across

1 Blue semi-precious stone, ___ lazuli (5)
4 Compress into a wad (7)
8 Mythical being, half man and half horse (7)
9 Ran easily (5)
10 Male bee (5)
11 Cut of meat (7)
12 Farewell remark (3-3)
13 Backing singers (6)
16 Sleeping room (7)
18 Mass of eggs deposited by frogs (5)
20 Professional cooks (5)
21 First in rank or degree (7)
22 Retailer selling on the internet (1-6)
23 Sound practical judgment (5)

Down

1 Coherent (5)
2 Item of photographic equipment without a lens (7,6)
3 Elegant, imposing (7)
4 Dead body (6)
5 Grinding tooth (5)
6 Deliberate act of acquisition (13)
7 News (7)
12 Two-wheeled vehicle (7)
14 Woman who invites guests to a social event (7)
15 Dealer in fabrics (6)
17 Aromatic herb (5)
19 Care for sick people (5)

16

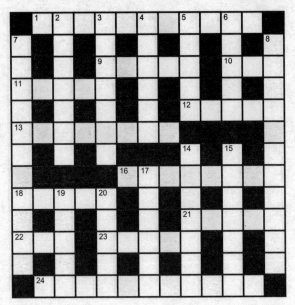

Across

1 Sweet-smelling climbing plant (11)
9 Pedestrianised public square (5)
10 Sound made by a cow (3)
11 Loop formed in a cord or rope (5)
12 Wheel coverings (5)
13 Building used to store frozen water (3,5)
16 Wide view (8)
18 Presentation, briefly (5)
21 Popular literary genre (abbr) (3-2)
22 Little rascal (3)
23 Clumsy (5)
24 Recklessness in politics or foreign affairs (11)

Down

2 Autumn month (7)
3 Male ruler (7)
4 Shoes with wheels attached (6)
5 Graph (5)
6 Madagascan primate (5)
7 Painful inflammation of the upper throat (11)
8 Plant grown for its pungent, edible root (11)
14 Sheath for a handgun (7)
15 Lunatics (7)
17 Miserable (6)
19 Lukewarm (5)
20 Cocktail fruit (5)

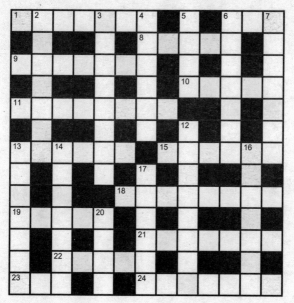

Across

1 Put on clothes (7)
6 Bunkum (3)
8 Condensed but memorable saying (5)
9 Symbolic objects used as distinctive badges (7)
10 Perspiration (5)
11 Restricted computer network (8)
13 Fraudulence (6)
15 Bread shop (6)
18 Turned aside from a direction or course (8)
19 Limited periods of time (5)
21 Make or become happy (7)
22 Hanging cloth used as a blind (5)
23 Gaming cube (3)
24 Emit heat (7)

Down

2 Love affair (7)
3 Situation, set-up (8)
4 One of Santa's reindeer (6)
5 Heating elements in an electric fire (4)
6 Government income due to taxation (7)
7 Bear witness (7)
12 Radio frequency (8)
13 Become wider (7)
14 Deteriorate due to the action of water or acid (7)
16 Vote back into office (2-5)
17 Hang around (6)
20 Expectorated (4)

18

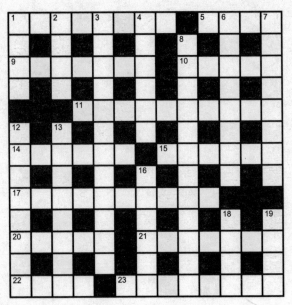

Across

1 Apprehension about what is going to happen (8)
5 Freezes over (4)
9 Item given to partly pay for a new one (5-2)
10 Last letter of the Greek alphabet (5)
11 Fall back to a worse condition (10)
14 Young nightbirds (6)
15 Russian wolfhound (6)
17 Country, capital Pyongyang (5,5)
20 Lightweight triangular scarf (5)
21 Removing hair with a razor (7)
22 Stare at lustfully (4)
23 Fireproof material (8)

Down

1 Location (4)
2 Drench (4)
3 Latest possible moment (8,4)
4 Miscellaneous (6)
6 Sideboard or buffet (8)
7 Spacecraft, especially in science fiction (8)
8 Group of diverse companies run as a single organisation (12)
12 Back and forth (2,3,3)
13 Relating to office work (8)
16 Deprivations (6)
18 Cotton or linen fabric (4)
19 Matures (4)

19

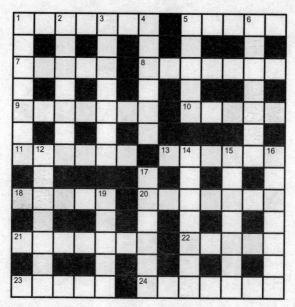

Across
1 Design device (7)
5 Ten-limbed mollusc (5)
7 Implied (5)
8 Division of a book (7)
9 Alleviate (7)
10 Large natural stream of water (5)
11 Assert to be true (6)
13 (Of an anchor) just clear of the bottom (6)
18 Turned-back hems at the ends of sleeves (5)
20 Associate who works with others (7)
21 Large hemispherical brass or copper percussion instruments (7)
22 Clemency (5)
23 Censure severely (5)
24 Makes fun of, parodies (5,2)

Down
1 Japanese warrior (7)
2 Renders capable for some task (7)
3 Makers of knives, forks, etc (7)
4 Sycophant (6)
5 Step (5)
6 Large mass of frozen water (7)
12 Feed (7)
14 Team of manual labourers (7)
15 Entrails (7)
16 Get a move on! (5,2)
17 Physical science relating to light (6)
19 Stone writing tablet (5)

20

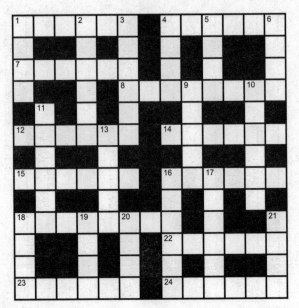

Across
1 Stops (6)
4 Agree (6)
7 Timber structure made in the shape of a capital letter (1-5)
8 Non-professionals (8)
12 Showing determination and a lack of fear (6)
14 Keg, cask (6)
15 Cooking in an oven (6)
16 Clandestine (6)
18 Exceptionally famous person (8)
22 Hun king nicknamed the 'Scourge of God' (6)
23 Origin (6)
24 Reaping hook (6)

Down
1 Lake in north central Africa (4)
2 Burns with steam (6)
3 Being wet with perspiration (6)
4 Swedish pop group (4)
5 Coffee shop (4)
6 Hearing organs (4)
9 Commerce (5)
10 Stank (6)
11 Mind out (6)
13 Melodies (5)
16 Scatters in a mass of droplets (6)
17 Family of languages including Gaelic (6)
18 Creeping low plant (4)
19 Plant family which includes the maple (4)
20 Remove (4)
21 Possess (4)

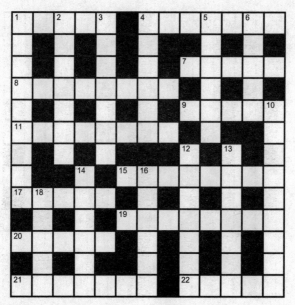

Across

1 Welsh breed of dog (5)
4 Beneficiary of a will (7)
7 Compass point at 0 or 360 degrees (5)
8 Edible item often roasted on an open fire (8)
9 Remove a lid (5)
11 Ornamental climbing plant (8)
15 In the open air (8)
17 Lawn flower (5)
19 Food stores, larders (8)
20 Ocean-going vessel (5)
21 Capable of being stretched (7)
22 Observed (5)

Down

1 Become infected with a common virus (5,4)
2 Restored, freshened (7)
3 As an alternative (7)
4 Lapis ____, azure blue semi-precious stone (6)
5 Circa, close to (6)
6 Crowd actor (5)
10 Fastener used on clothing (5,4)
12 Issue of a newspaper (7)
13 Aviator who assists the captain of a plane (2-5)
14 Things of value or usefulness (6)
16 Fit for service, functional (6)
18 Line spoken by an actor to the audience (5)

22

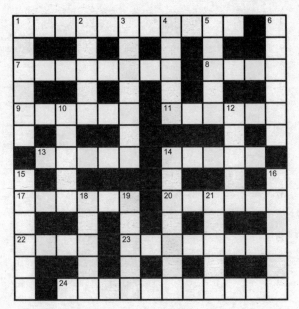

Across

1 Of eggs, fried only on one side (coll) (5,4,2)
7 Changing, amending (8)
8 'Lady' whose real name is Stefani Joanne Angelina Germanotta (4)
9 Instance of misfortune (6)
11 Declare (6)
13 Biblical shepherd who slew Goliath (5)
14 Skin disease affecting domestic animals (5)
17 Countrified (6)
20 Uniform worn by chauffeurs (6)
22 Humble request for help (4)
23 Chart with rectangular blocks of varying proportional height (3,5)
24 Near what? (11)

Down

1 Economise (6)
2 Horse's sound (5)
3 Accidentally slid or fell (7)
4 Religious doctrine (5)
5 Impulses (5)
6 ___ and the Beast, famous fairy tale (6)
10 Hits with an open hand (5)
12 Bird of prey (5)
14 Disease transmitted by the mosquito (7)
15 Hollow under the upper limb where it is joined to the shoulder (6)
16 Infectious disease transmitted by lice (6)
18 Rubbish (5)
19 Heavy wooden pole tossed as a test of strength (5)
21 Sign of the zodiac (5)

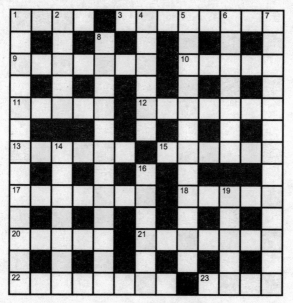

Across

1 Allude to (4)
3 Inflammation of a bone (8)
9 Educational institution (7)
10 Mixer drink (5)
11 Poisonous (5)
12 Inspiring admiration or wonder (7)
13 Make less effective (6)
15 Has faith in (6)
17 Throw into great confusion or disorder (7)
18 Country, capital Niamey (5)
20 Boredom (5)
21 Huge destructive wave (7)
22 Wisdom or understanding (8)
23 Palm fruit (4)

Down

1 Smart frock suitable for formal social occasions (8,5)
2 Printer connected to a telegraph that operates like a typewriter (5)
4 Children's outdoor toy (6)
5 Capitalist (12)
6 Flimsy (7)
7 Government department concerned with espionage (6,7)
8 Interval between stimulus and reaction (8,4)
14 Root vegetable (7)
16 Infected with bacteria (6)
19 Tropical fruit having yellow skin and pink pulp (5)

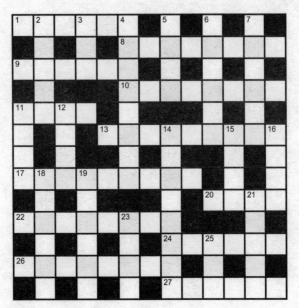

Across

1 Sea-girt territory (6)
8 Popular frozen dessert (3,5)
9 Straightens out (6)
10 Having more than one spouse at a time (8)
11 Most fitting (4)
13 Above comparison (9)
17 Element from which an alchemist was expected to make gold (4,5)
20 Plenty (4)
22 Less lengthy route to a destination (5,3)
24 Mad (6)
26 Extremely hungry (8)
27 Lay bare (6)

Down

2 Sweeping stroke or blow (5)
3 ___ Baba (3)
4 Uproot (8)
5 Hollow metal device which rings when struck (4)
6 Avoiding waste (6)
7 Scottish quarter day (28 August) (6)
11 Tell tales (coll) (4)
12 Adult female hogs (4)
14 Censure severely (8)
15 Reverberate (4)
16 Soap froth (4)
18 Place of religious retreat for Hindus (6)
19 Breadwinner (6)
21 Hinged lifting tool (5)
23 Compact mass (of earth) (4)
25 Concession given to mollify (3)

Across

1 Medicated lozenge for the throat (8)
5 Wash with a mop (4)
8 How a result is obtained or an end achieved (5)
9 Seek people's votes (7)
10 Ardently serious (7)
12 Believe to be true (7)
14 Substance taken to counter indigestion (7)
16 Perfumed (7)
18 Paper-folding art (7)
19 Broadcast (a programme) on radio or television (5)
20 Name by which Thailand was formerly known (4)
21 Look like (8)

Down

1 Bicycle accessory (4)
2 Deliberately causes a delay (6)
3 Inverted (6,3)
4 Small ornamental case worn on a necklace (6)
6 Craftsman who makes cloth (6)
7 Infatuated (8)
11 Say again (9)
12 Cutting implement (8)
13 Part of the eye (6)
14 Specialised opinion (6)
15 Little angel (6)
17 Slight competitive advantage (4)

26

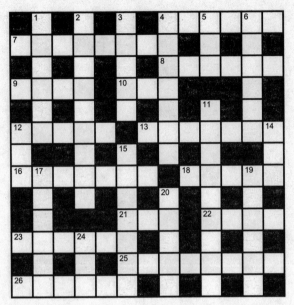

Across
- **4** Most recent (6)
- **7** US state (8)
- **8** Bell of the clock associated with the Houses of Parliament (3,3)
- **9** Small biting fly (4)
- **10** Of a thing (3)
- **12** Tempest (5)
- **13** Made up one's mind (7)
- **16** Indian Ocean island, capital Saint-Denis (7)
- **18** Paris underground railway (5)
- **21** Nothing (3)
- **22** Harangue (4)
- **23** Score of one stroke under par in golf (6)
- **25** Sailing vessel used in former times (8)
- **26** Game associated with Wimbledon (6)

Down
- **1** Large stinging paper wasp (6)
- **2** Impression left by the sole in walking (9)
- **3** Fanatical (5)
- **4** Edible crustacean (7)
- **5** Label (3)
- **6** Involuntary expulsion of air from the nose (6)
- **11** Impervious to damage by flames (9)
- **12** Title of a baronet (3)
- **14** Singing couple (3)
- **15** Affectation of being demure in a provocative way (7)
- **17** Beguile (6)
- **19** Rivulet (6)
- **20** Hawaiian greeting (5)
- **24** Hideout (3)

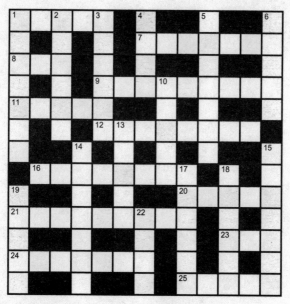

Across

1 Establish (3,2)
7 Hair cleanser (7)
8 Venomous snake (3)
9 Slide of snow from a mountainside (9)
11 Screws, rivets (5)
12 Income (8)
16 People who escape into a world of fantasy (8)
20 Basic unit of money in Iceland (5)
21 Tenaciously unwilling to yield (9)
23 Vehicle test (inits) (3)
24 Concentrated extract (7)
25 Easy to reach (5)

Down

1 Crate used as a makeshift stand by a public speaker (7)
2 Tumble, collapse (6)
3 Expression (6)
4 Region regularly afflicted by monsoons (4)
5 Noted, distinguished (7)
6 Quantity of twelve items (5)
10 Person who avoids the company of others (5)
13 Capital of Jordan (5)
14 Unbeliever, infidel (7)
15 Shockingly repellent (7)
17 Preliminary drawing (6)
18 Archer (6)
19 One stroke over par in golf (5)
22 In one's sleeping place (4)

28

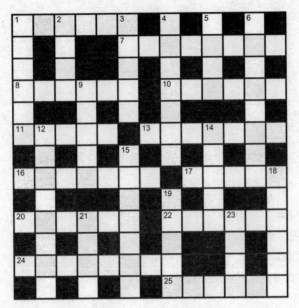

Across

 1 Automatons (6)
 7 Listed individually (8)
 8 Pays out (6)
 10 Gnawed (6)
 11 Experiment (5)
 13 Covered cistern (7)
 16 Female spirit of Irish folklore, whose wailing warns of death (7)
 17 Media personality, ___ Street-Porter (5)
 20 *The* ___ *Queene*, epic poem by Edmund Spenser (6)
 22 Number indicated by the Roman XI (6)
 24 Marked by excessive self-indulgence and moral decay (8)
 25 Nap in the early afternoon (6)

Down

 1 Brown with a reddish tinge (6)
 2 Cattle shed (4)
 3 Unassertive man or boy (5)
 4 Saved (7)
 5 Presidential assistant (4)
 6 Give a new meaning to (8)
 9 Approaches (5)
 12 Rouse once again (8)
 14 Empty area (5)
 15 Greek goddess of fertility (7)
 18 Treeless Arctic plain (6)
 19 Tailed amphibians (5)
 21 Highway (4)
 23 Open barrels or casks (4)

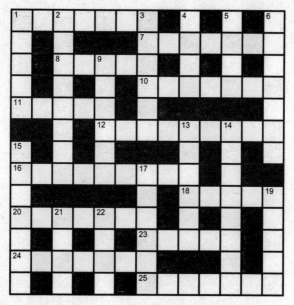

Across

1 Matrimony (7)
7 Enter uninvited (7)
8 Brittle fragment (5)
10 Money set by for the future (4,3)
11 Portly (5)
12 Ad lib (9)
16 Irrational (9)
18 Celtic language (5)
20 Watch (7)
23 Dined at home (3,2)
24 Male demon believed to lie on sleeping persons (7)
25 Composer who once teamed with Lake and Palmer (7)

Down

1 Country called Cymru in its own language (5)
2 Treacherous, unpatriotic (8)
3 Abduct, usually for a ransom (6)
4 Mr Redding who sang (Sittin' on) The Dock of the Bay (4)
5 Remedy (4)
6 Country, capital Brussels (7)
9 Performing (6)
13 Connected to a computer network (6)
14 People undergoing medical treatment (8)
15 Capital of Cyprus (7)
17 Wrinkle (6)
19 One of the Great Lakes (5)
21 Draw into the mouth by creating a vacuum (4)
22 Gown (4)

30

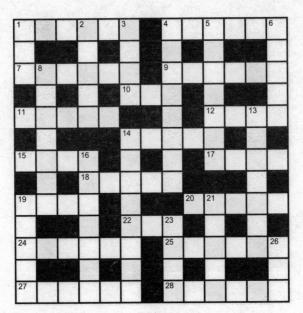

Across

1 Shuts (6)
4 Is unable to (6)
7 Small smooth stone (6)
9 Walked with long steps (6)
10 Food in a pastry shell (3)
11 Instrument played
   with a bow (5)
12 State of the USA (4)
14 Lance (5)
15 Tibetan oxen (4)
17 Nymph who fell in love
   with Narcissus (4)
18 Crisp bread (5)
19 Greek letter (4)
20 Snooped (5)
22 Form of transport,
   double-decker (3)
24 Set a match to (6)
25 Inner part of a nut (6)
27 Remind (6)
28 Stripped of rind or skin (6)

Down

1 Ceiling (3)
2 Roman prophetess (5)
3 Dance move (4)
4 Hinged window sash (8)
5 Help to develop
   and grow (7)
6 Biting tools (5)
8 Lift (7)
13 Gain with effort (7)
14 Protective strap
   in a car (4,4)
16 Large structure for
   open-air sport (7)
19 Barrage balloon (5)
21 Money container (5)
23 Cut, miss (4)
26 Boy (3)

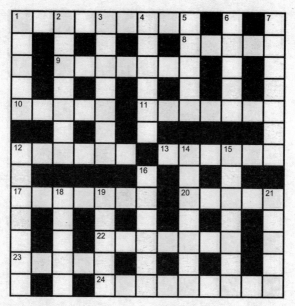

Across
1 Multiply by four (9)
8 Give expression to feelings (5)
9 Shoemaker (7)
10 Edge tool used in shaving (5)
11 Industrial plant for extracting metal from ore (7)
12 Quaggy (6)
13 Makes law (6)
17 Fawning in attitude or behaviour (7)
20 Principal river of Pakistan (5)
22 Cut of meat (7)
23 Former province of western France, on the Loire (5)
24 Mexican tortilla (9)

Down
1 Country, capital Doha (5)
2 Spanish fortress or palace built by the Moors (7)
3 Renaissance (7)
4 Most deficient in colour (6)
5 Suggestive of the supernatural (5)
6 Be sick, retch (5)
7 Documents providing permanent information of past events (7)
12 Play featuring singing and dancing (7)
14 Capital of Kenya (7)
15 Solo passage near the end of a piece of music (7)
16 Decimal system (6)
18 Dry red Spanish wine (5)
19 Bring out an official document (5)
21 Capital of Bulgaria (5)

32

Across

1 Printer's mark, indicating an insertion (5)

7 Fugitive, escapee (7)

8 Highest female voice (7)

9 Mounted (7)

10 Lacking zest or vivacity (8)

14 Flexible pipe for conveying a liquid (4)

16 Travel by foot (4)

18 Former sweetheart (3,5)

21 Draws back, as with fear or pain (7)

23 Railway building (7)

24 Cocktail of vermouth and gin (7)

25 Emblem representing power (5)

Down

1 Proportion of revenue over outlay in a given period of time (4,4)

2 Parts of a river where the current is very fast (6)

3 Semi-aquatic creature (4)

4 Flower, the source of saffron (6)

5 Beautiful mausoleum at Agra, northern India (3,5)

6 Daily news publications (6)

11 Pay close attention to (4,4)

12 Inflated pride (3)

13 Mournful (3)

15 Grace, style (8)

17 Television receiver (6)

19 Canine film star (6)

20 Hurting (6)

22 Destiny (4)

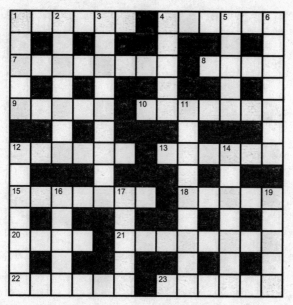

Across
1 Capital of Colombia (6)
4 Spherical objects (6)
7 Taking (territory) as if by conquest (8)
8 At another time (4)
9 Judged (5)
10 Act passed by a legislative body (7)
12 Verse (6)
13 On the go (6)
15 Goggling, as in surprise (3-4)
18 Moral principle (5)
20 Female sheep (4)
21 Write carelessly (8)
22 Full in quantity or extent (6)
23 Brings together (6)

Down
1 Explosion (5)
2 Person who is not a Jew (7)
3 Art of mounting the skins of animals so they have a lifelike appearance (9)
4 Lamb leg suitable for roasting (5)
5 Family of languages widely spoken in southern Africa (5)
6 Heartfelt (7)
11 Increase by natural growth or addition (9)
12 Capital of French Polynesia, on the north-west coast of Tahiti (7)
14 Limit the range or extent of (7)
16 Gather into a ruffle (5)
17 End in a particular way (5)
19 Masticates (5)

34

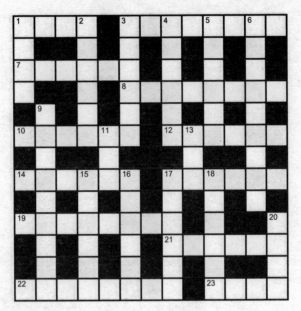

Across

1 Collides with (4)
3 Exact correspondence of form on opposite sides of a dividing line or plane (8)
7 Listener (6)
8 Destined, meant (8)
10 Produce incisors, molars, etc (6)
12 Constricted (6)
14 Pungent root eaten as a salad vegetable (6)
17 New Testament book telling the story of Christ (6)
19 Explosive device hidden in the ground (8)
21 Correspond to (6)
22 Extremely poisonous (8)
23 Expel (gases or odours) (4)

Down

1 Ditch used to divide lands without hiding the view (2-2)
2 Screenplay (6)
3 Endeavour (6)
4 Meat from a mature domestic sheep (6)
5 Breadwinner (6)
6 Someone worthy of imitation (4,5)
9 Capable of being disproved (9)
11 Features (3)
13 Fuss (3)
15 Anil (6)
16 Coiffure (6)
17 Any leafy plants eaten as vegetables (6)
18 Coniferous tree (6)
20 One-hundredth of a dollar (4)

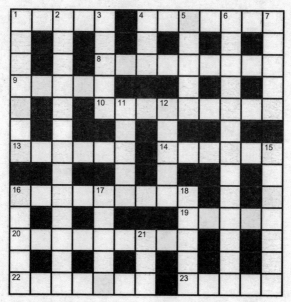

Across

1 Not flexible or pliant (5)
4 Self-importance (7)
8 Constitutional capital of The Netherlands (9)
9 Colour of wood or earth (5)
10 Full agreement between a number of people (9)
13 Sits on one's heels (6)
14 Scattered wreckage (6)
16 Lazy, unambitious (9)
19 Glacial (5)
20 Italian word for a woman loved or loving (9)
22 Colonist (7)
23 In a softened tone (5)

Down

1 Contagious skin infection (7)
2 Without the means to be in verbal contact (13)
3 Former French coin (5)
4 Units (1/6 inch) used in printing (3)
5 Wayside plant with daisy-like flowers (2-3)
6 Person involved in the ownership of manufacturing concerns (13)
7 Contagious viral disease (5)
11 Blackbird (5)
12 Faces (5)
15 In close-packed rows (7)
16 Economise (5)
17 Treasure of unknown ownership (5)
18 Muscle cramp (5)
21 Scottish port (3)

36

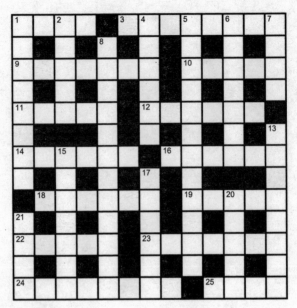

Across

1 For certain (4)
3 Maybe (8)
9 Itemised statement of money owed (7)
10 Easily agitated or alarmed (5)
11 Imperial measures of capacity (5)
12 In a single direction (3-3)
14 Beads used in prayer (6)
16 School for training horses (6)
18 Savoury appetiser (6)
19 Forbidden (5)
22 Native of Basra, for example (5)
23 Appease (7)
24 Commercial enterprise (8)
25 Drum, pound (4)

Down

1 Evasive (8)
2 Bird associated with the Tower of London (5)
4 Nocturnal wildcat of Central and South America (6)
5 Port and resort in northern Spain (3,9)
6 Bombardment (7)
7 Child's stringed toy (2-2)
8 Thesis required for an advanced academic degree (12)
13 Aromatic (8)
15 Beetles considered divine by ancient Egyptians (7)
17 Entices, lures (6)
20 Make a strident sound (5)
21 Tree branch (4)

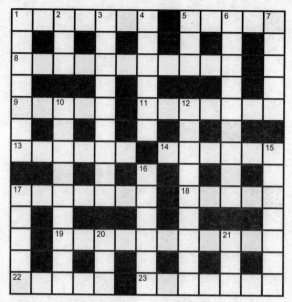

Across

1 Outlined, incomplete in detail (7)
5 Propels with the foot (5)
8 Large company or group of businesses acting as single entity (11)
9 Distinctive spirit of a culture or an age (5)
11 Bird otherwise known as the peewit (7)
13 Submerged (6)
14 Ornamental band around the outside of a building (6)
17 Be uncomfortably hot (7)
18 Assists in wrongdoing (5)
19 Megalithic monument (5,6)
22 Garden barrier (5)
23 Edible shellfish generally (7)

Down

1 Victory (7)
2 Sin (3)
3 Platform for a lookout near the top of a mast (5-4)
4 Annually, every twelve months (6)
5 Colourful ornamental carp (3)
6 Many-legged insect (9)
7 Lean end of the neck (5)
10 People who persistently follow along (7-2)
12 Latin phrase meaning for each person (3,6)
15 Part of London that includes Bow and Spitalfields (4,3)
16 Natives of Athens, eg (6)
17 Fill completely (5)
20 Be indebted to (3)
21 Sound made by a dove (3)

38

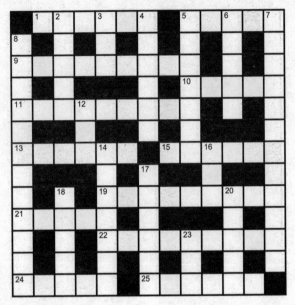

Across
1 Narrow backstreets (6)
5 Less than the correct amount (5)
9 Deliberately (2,7)
10 Head of a religious order (5)
11 Having branches or flower heads that droop (9)
13 Make unhappy (6)
15 Twelfths of a foot (6)
19 Cosmic (9)
21 Unusual and typically rather shocking (5)
22 Small rounds of water that fall from the sky (9)
24 Easily irritated (5)
25 Forever (6)

Down
2 Showy garden plant (5)
3 Fruiting spike of a cereal plant (3)
4 Exactly right (4,2)
5 Male child of your spouse and a former partner (7)
6 Blacksmith's block (5)
7 Vacuum container for hot or cold drinks (7,5)
8 Marking on a direction finder (7,5)
12 Papa (3)
14 Personal attendant of the royal family (7)
16 Low-breed dog (3)
17 Mineral such as quartz (6)
18 Minute particles of matter (5)
20 Flamboyant (5)
23 Condensed water vapour (3)

Across

4 Small and pulpy edible fruits (7)

7 Artist's workroom (7)

8 Limbless reptile (5)

9 Carry on a romantic relationship with more than one person (3-4)

10 Plaything that moves back and forth (5)

11 Disagreeing, especially with a majority (9)

14 Inflammation of the stomach lining (9)

18 Cloudless (5)

19 Plot something harmful (7)

20 Implant (5)

21 Shoulder ornament (7)

22 Comforted in a time of great distress (7)

Down

1 Brine-cured (6)

2 Projections used with mortises (6)

3 Stick used for dowsing (8,3)

4 Light wind (6)

5 Sloping kind of print (6)

6 Vehicle for travelling on snow (6)

8 Female to whom one is related by marriage (6-2-3)

12 Admission (6)

13 Plant-derived (6)

15 Drew in by a vacuum (6)

16 Rotates rapidly (6)

17 Case for a knife (6)

40

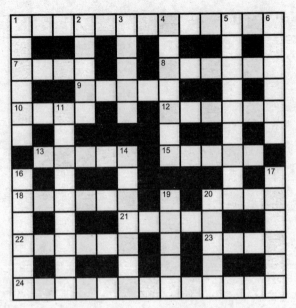

Across

1 European nation (6,7)
7 Walk through water (4)
8 Package (6)
9 Find repugnant (5)
10 Pip (4)
12 Evaded (6)
13 Form of musical entertainment (5)
15 Beauty parlour (5)
18 Jostles (6)
20 Pale grey (4)
21 Consumers (5)
22 Brainteaser (6)
23 Bird of New Zealand (4)
24 From that time onwards (13)

Down

1 Foolhardy (6)
2 Horizontal part of a stair (5)
3 Russian country house (5)
4 Make an impact on (7)
5 Shedding foliage in the autumn (9)
6 Illness (6)
11 Volatile (9)
14 Satisfy (thirst) (7)
16 Upward movement (6)
17 Large indefinite number (6)
19 Japanese form of fencing (5)
20 Cockeyed (5)

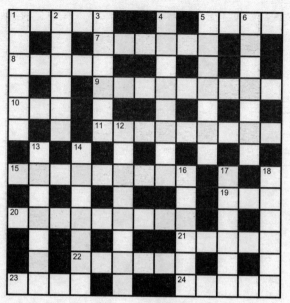

Across

1 Muffler (5)
5 Basic monetary unit of Mexico (4)
7 Set of eight notes (6)
8 Articles of commerce (5)
9 Offered advice (9)
10 Time period (3)
11 Idle person (9)
15 Dog that can be trained to fetch game (9)
19 Append (3)
20 False opinions or impressions (9)
21 Imbecile (5)
22 Baby birds (6)
23 Unemployment benefit (4)
24 Large cat (5)

Down

1 Communicate silently (6)
2 Shorebird with slender upward-curving bill (6)
3 Palaeontological relic (6)
4 Grotesquely carved figure (8)
5 Regular payment to a retired person (7)
6 Add sugar (7)
12 Pre-dinner drink (8)
13 Reminder of past events (7)
14 Beat severely (7)
16 Express opposition (6)
17 Going out with, romantically (6)
18 News chief (6)

42

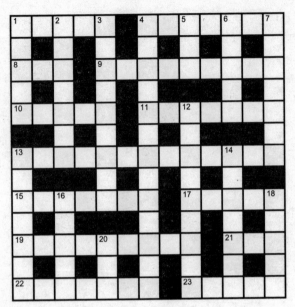

Across

1 Bad habits (5)
4 Officer of the court (7)
8 Small sharp bite (3)
9 Compartment for post (9)
10 Fire a gun (5)
11 With the least fat (7)
13 Aircraft accommodation between first and economy (8,5)
15 Plant valued for its fragrant tubular flowers (7)
17 Craggy, mountainous (5)
19 Occurring at a formal investiture or induction (9)
21 Large African antelope (3)
22 Burdened (7)
23 Cuts into pieces (5)

Down

1 Second planet from the sun (5)
2 Ample, plentiful (7)
3 Damaged tips of a person's hair, usually due to dryness (5,4)
4 Blemished by conflict (6-7)
5 Anger (3)
6 Permeate (5)
7 Causes an obsessive attachment to someone or something (7)
12 Dipsomaniac (9)
13 Research scientists (slang) (7)
14 Brisk and lively tempo (7)
16 Large antelope (5)
18 ___ truly, letter ending (5)
20 Mousse (3)

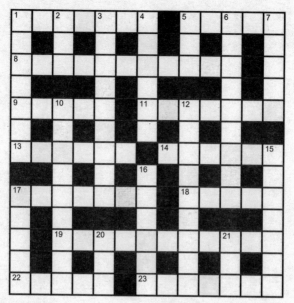

Across

1 Eight-armed sea creature (7)
5 Desert animal (5)
8 Wrongdoer (11)
9 Prefix meaning 'above' (5)
11 Extreme mental distress (7)
13 Make numb (6)
14 Fiends (6)
17 Prickly plant (7)
18 Kingdom in the South Pacific (5)
19 Having unattractive thinness, weedy (11)
22 Woolly ruminant (5)
23 Swift pirate ship (7)

Down

1 Fought back (7)
2 Flammable liquid distilled from wood or coal (3)
3 Rife, especially at the present time (9)
4 Successive (6)
5 Incision (3)
6 Undertaker (9)
7 Walk as if unable to control one's movements (5)
10 Trite or obvious remark (9)
12 Constellation of Ursa Major (5,4)
15 Dash a liquid against (7)
16 Relating to or containing iron (6)
17 North African port and capital city (5)
20 Duck (3)
21 Indian state, capital Panaji (3)

44

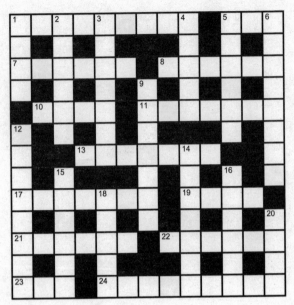

Across

1 Narrow buoyant plank for riding the waves (9)
5 Topple, overturn (3)
7 Rhododendron-like shrub (6)
8 Catlike (6)
10 Equipment for the reproduction of sound (2-2)
11 Remark (7)
13 Prepared by a compositor for printing (7)
17 Stretchy fabric (7)
19 Prophet (4)
21 Threw a ball towards the batsman (6)
22 Whitish 'meal' drunk before an X-ray (6)
23 Manipulate in a fraudulent manner (3)
24 Heir (9)

Down

1 Confidence trick (4)
2 Person who handles equipment for travelling entertainers (6)
3 Briefness (7)
4 Cherished desire (5)
5 Lavatory (6)
6 Plucking implement (8)
9 Any domain of knowledge accumulated by systematic study (7)
12 Month with 30 days (8)
14 Catch in a trap (7)
15 Common garden insect (6)
16 Mastermind (6)
18 Woodland plants (5)
20 Independent ruler or chieftain (4)

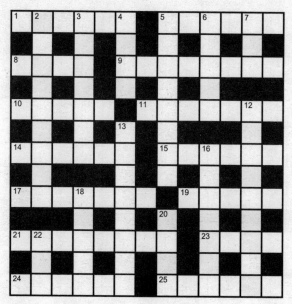

Across

1 Newborn children (6)
5 Underground passage (6)
8 Duelling sword (4)
9 Flush with water (8)
10 Beautiful young woman (5)
11 Implore (7)
14 Knitted or woven with a diamond-shaped pattern (6)
15 Rain-bearing cloud (6)
17 Son of Zeus who slew the Medusa (7)
19 Thin meat soup (5)
21 Holiday (8)
23 Shed blood (4)
24 Speaker (6)
25 Game played in an enclosed court (6)

Down

2 Orchard plant (5,4)
3 In a perfect way (7)
4 Mix (4)
5 Military rank (8)
6 Framework of a railway carriage (5)
7 Pertinent (3)
12 Innumerable (9)
13 Queer, strange (8)
16 Carrion-eating, black and white stork of Africa (7)
18 Hard slap (5)
20 Burden of responsibility (4)
22 Expression of surprise or sudden realisation (3)

46

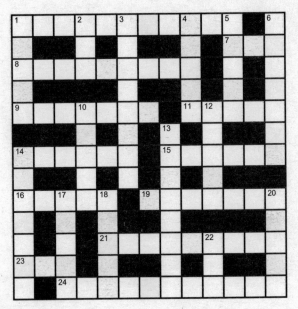

Across

1 Methods of self-defence such as karate and kung fu (7,4)
7 Metal cooking vessel (3)
8 Choice (9)
9 Musician and artist who married John Lennon in 1969 (4,3)
11 Purloin (5)
14 Has the same value (6)
15 Be present at (6)
16 Distinguish oneself (5)
19 One who denies the existence of God (7)
21 Be a part or attribute of (9)
23 Zodiacal Lion (3)
24 Parasite such as the flea (11)

Down

1 Stale and unclean smelling (5)
2 Definite article (3)
3 Affect with wonder (8)
4 Ladder steps (5)
5 Reproductive body produced by plants such as the fern (5)
6 Drew in by breathing (7)
10 Egg-shaped (5)
12 Identifying appellation (5)
13 Serving woman (8)
14 Green gem (7)
17 Tree with edible pods used as a chocolate substitute (5)
18 Large grassy plain (5)
20 Apparatus for receiving radio signals (5)
22 Nervous twitch (3)

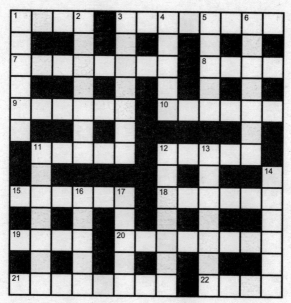

Across

1 Prefix denoting half (4)
3 Strong line connecting a weight to a sliding window (4,4)
7 Plant with soothing juice used to treat burns (4,4)
8 Red gemstone (4)
9 Jubilant (6)
10 Tomboy (6)
11 Walk heavily (5)
12 Short simple song (5)
15 Madman (6)
18 Vipers (6)
19 Invoice (4)
20 Administrative district of a nation (8)
21 Convince (8)
22 Person's manner of walking, pace (4)

Down

1 Formed (6)
2 Popular chilled beverage (4,3)
3 Go faster (5,2)
4 Space created by the swing of a scythe (5)
5 Bear, convey (5)
6 Violent theft (7)
11 Shore next to the coast (7)
12 Give, sell, or transfer to another (7)
13 Drawing an outline (7)
14 Express agreement (6)
16 Small areas of land surrounded by water (5)
17 Coconut meat (5)

48

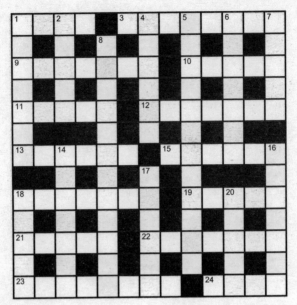

Across

1 Mixer drink (4)
3 Dots in a text showing suppression of words (8)
9 Russian empress (7)
10 Outer layer on bread (5)
11 English composer whose works include *The Planets* (5)
12 Rushed (7)
13 Marine gastropod found clinging to rocks (6)
15 Someone who makes an offer (6)
18 Region of central Spain (7)
19 Acts to arouse action (5)
21 Norwegian composer (1843–1907) (5)
22 Artist's paint-mixing board (7)
23 Disfigured, misshapen (8)
24 Clothed (4)

Down

1 Schoolbag (7)
2 Slow speech with prolonged vowels (5)
4 Despise (6)
5 Impervious to correction by punishment (12)
6 Analysed (7)
7 Located (5)
8 Small digit on the hand (6,6)
14 Powerful deep-chested dog (7)
16 Remoulded car tyre (7)
17 Sentimental movie (coll) (6)
18 Cooped up (5)
20 Colourful part of a flower (5)

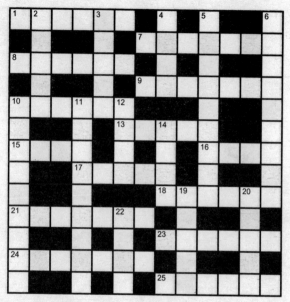

Across

1 Underweight (6)
7 Feel of a surface (7)
8 King who tried to hold back the tide (6)
9 Wine merchant (7)
10 Small wave on the surface of a liquid (6)
13 Glisten (5)
15 Church benches (4)
16 Basic monetary unit of Bangladesh (4)
17 Aromatic herb (5)
18 Fortified wine mainly from southern Spain (6)
21 Daybreak (7)
23 Brownish hair colour (6)
24 Eighth planet from the Sun (7)
25 Twine (6)

Down

2 Yellowish-brown colour (5)
3 Region of South Africa, KwaZulu-___ (5)
4 Type of food shop (abbr) (4)
5 Figurine (9)
6 Assistant who handles correspondence (9)
10 Stand for, symbolise (9)
11 All future generations (9)
12 Catch sight of (4)
14 *The ___ of March*, 2011 film (4)
19 Pursue like a ghost (5)
20 Repeat performance (5)
22 Mentally healthy (4)

50

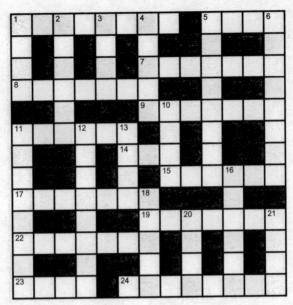

Across

1 Text of an opera (8)
5 Exhaled with force (4)
7 Taken undue advantage of (3,4)
8 Take to be the case (7)
9 Advocate of political reform (7)
11 Dough used in making pies (6)
14 Lamb's mother (3)
15 Determines the direction of travel (6)
17 City in western Israel (3,4)
19 Archaeological period (4,3)
22 Showing nervous apprehension (7)
23 One of a pair (4)
24 Most distant or remote (8)

Down

1 Spring up (4)
2 Short underpants (6)
3 Light fawn colour (4)
4 Narrow towards a point (5)
5 Shop that sells women's clothes and jewellery (8)
6 Winch on a ship or in a harbour (8)
10 Chopping tools (4)
11 Draw out, prolong (8)
12 Government levy (8)
13 Abominable snowman (4)
16 Empower (6)
18 Prospect (5)
20 Building for drying hops (4)
21 Get out (4)

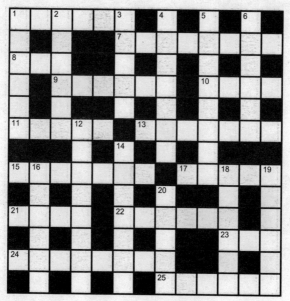

51

Across

1 Lays bare (6)
7 Collarbone (8)
8 Raises (3)
9 Ghost (6)
10 Decorated with frosting (4)
11 Burn with steam (5)
13 Climbing plant (7)
15 Sharp-cornered (7)
17 Flexible twig of a willow (5)
21 Curved gateway (4)
22 Light informal meals (6)
23 Desired result (3)
24 Produce (energy) (8)
25 Salt used especially in baking powder (6)

Down

1 Rejects with contempt (6)
2 Country, capital Moscow (6)
3 Dandruff (5)
4 Catch (7)
5 Without mercy (8)
6 Arm covering (6)
12 Sound of amusement (8)
14 Hitter of a baseball, cricket ball, etc (7)
16 Looked after during an illness (6)
18 Ant or beetle, for example (6)
19 Peruser of text (6)
20 Gentleman's gentleman (5)

52

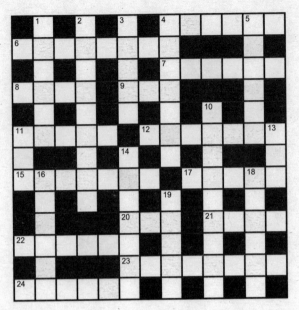

Across

4 High-kicking dance of French origin (6)
6 Royalist supporter of Charles I (8)
7 Not mature (of fruit) (6)
8 Flip (a coin, for example) (4)
9 Forest tree (3)
11 Love intensely (5)
12 Period of 100 years (7)
15 Rumbling sound associated with lightning (7)
17 Confronts bravely (5)
20 ___ King Cole, jazz pianist and singer (3)
21 Compass point (4)
22 University honour (6)
23 Obtain by cadging (8)
24 Universe (6)

Down

1 King who died at the Battle of Hastings (6)
2 One of the five tendons at the back of the knee (9)
3 Vital organ of the body (5)
4 Griddle cake (7)
5 Foreign home help (2,4)
10 Misted over (7,2)
11 Astern (3)
13 Affirmative answer (3)
14 Novelty (7)
16 Up until this time (6)
18 Regimental flag (6)
19 Bird mythically supposed to deliver babies (5)

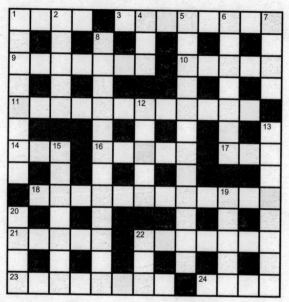

Across

1 Master Simpson, cartoon character (4)
3 Pants (8)
9 Coalminer (7)
10 Pertaining to the nose (5)
11 The internet, generally (5,4,3)
14 Disencumber (3)
16 Asian country (5)
17 Holy sister (3)
18 Board resting on supports useful when pasting wallpaper (7,5)
21 Mother-of-pearl (5)
22 Extinguish (a candle) (4,3)
23 Groping, irresolute (8)
24 Unwanted plant (4)

Down

1 In reverse (8)
2 Measuring stick (5)
4 Not either (3)
5 Annulment (12)
6 British sculptor, Sir Jacob ___ (1880–1959) (7)
7 Part of a window frame (4)
8 Burial garment in which a corpse is wrapped (7-5)
12 Force (5)
13 Not having been warmed (8)
15 Commands with authority (7)
19 Intoxicating liquor (coll) (5)
20 One-twelfth of a foot (4)
22 Bread roll (3)

54

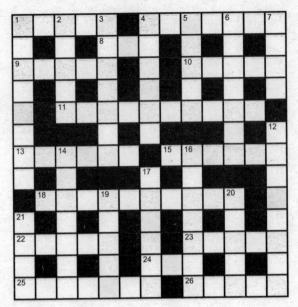

Across

1 Alloy of iron and carbon (5)
4 Prevention or interruption due to rain (4-3)
8 Large nation (inits) (3)
9 Lubricated (5)
10 Put out, as of a candle (5)
11 Highly contagious disease of pigs (5,5)
13 ____ Pepys, famous diarist (1633–1703) (6)
15 Species of fly that transmits sleeping sickness (6)
18 Disagreeable (10)
22 At a distance (5)
23 Deceive (5)
24 Calm central region of a cyclone (3)
25 Run away (7)
26 Oozes (5)

Down

1 Martin ____, US film director (8)
2 ____ Island, New York Bay area (5)
3 Opponent of technological progress (7)
4 German composer of operas (1813–1883) (6)
5 Grasslike marsh plant (5)
6 Sumptuous (7)
7 Items worn about the neck (4)
12 Lets air out of (8)
14 US state (7)
16 Spiritualists' meetings (7)
17 Hazard (6)
19 Pause during which things are calm (3-2)
20 In that place (5)
21 Prevents from speaking out (4)

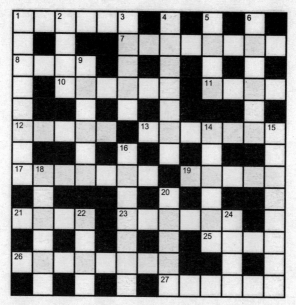

Across
1 Placard (6)
7 Blessing (8)
8 Gaffe (4)
10 Hard deposit on the teeth (6)
11 Vegetable, emblem of Wales (4)
12 Barbarous (5)
13 Swathe (7)
17 Former province of northern Ethiopia (7)
19 Capital of Bangladesh (5)
21 Left side of a ship (4)
23 One who rides breaking waves (6)
25 Source of illumination (4)
26 Murder of a king (8)
27 Parasitic plant (6)

Down
1 Work of art that imitates the style of some previous work (8)
2 Short theatrical episode (4)
3 Irritable, peevish (coll) (5)
4 Frank and honest (7)
5 Painful sore (4)
6 Small, roofed building affording shade and rest (6)
9 Document granting an inventor sole rights (6)
14 Substance covering the crown of a tooth (6)
15 Duck-billed creature (8)
16 Caused by an earthquake (7)
18 Begin again, as with negotiations (6)
20 Short-lived (5)
22 Lacking excess flesh (4)
24 Called on the phone (4)

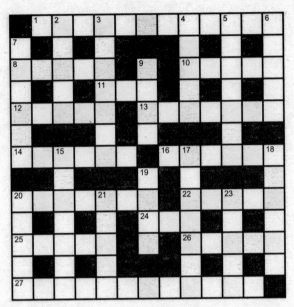

Across

1 Judicial capital of South Africa (12)
8 Au revoir (5)
10 Rise to one's feet (3,2)
11 Dressmaking aid (3)
12 Check accounts (5)
13 In an abrupt manner (7)
14 Make a disguised reference to (6)
16 Japanese woman trained to entertain men (6)
20 Say out loud for the purpose of recording (7)
22 Mountain ash tree (5)
24 Historical period (3)
25 Puppet character, one of Jim Henson's Muppets (5)
26 Slightly sticky to the touch (5)
27 World's largest body of water (7,5)

Down

2 Scottish landowner (5)
3 Spewed forth lava and rocks (7)
4 Landlocked republic in West Africa (5)
5 Holds in high regard (7)
6 Item worn by a baby (5)
7 Capital of Cuba (6)
9 Archaic word meaning 'in the direction of' (4)
15 Brief and to the point (7)
17 Fickle (7)
18 Vexes (6)
19 Cattle reared for their meat (4)
20 Excavate (3,2)
21 Remote in manner (5)
23 Religion of modern witchcraft (5)

Across

1 Ring for sealing a pipe joint (6)
4 Wax drawing stick (6)
7 Central area in a building which is open to the sky (6)
9 Concept or idea not associated with any specific instance (8)
11 Brass instrument (4)
14 Elects to office (5,2)
15 Prima donna (4)
16 Stretched out (4)
17 Invasions or hostile attacks (7)
18 Celebrity (4)
21 Tranquilliser (8)
22 Highly seasoned fatty sausage (6)
24 Harsh, stern (6)
25 Toxin (6)

Down

1 Colossus (5)
2 Bush (5)
3 ___ de Cologne, perfume (3)
4 Narrow escapes (5,6)
5 Consciousness (9)
6 Not diluted (4)
8 Most outstanding work of a creative artist (11)
10 Equipment for taking pictures (6)
12 One of a kind (6)
13 Accessible (9)
19 Ruptures (5)
20 Govern (5)
21 Stitches together (4)
23 Gone by (3)

58

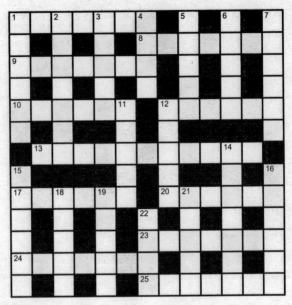

Across

1 Artist (7)
8 Attempt to equal or surpass (7)
9 Go forward (7)
10 Mistakes (6)
12 Offer for sale from place to place (6)
13 Wares (11)
17 Acid found in vinegar (6)
20 Chair of state of a monarch (6)
23 Prior to a specified time (7)
24 Stately, refined (7)
25 Saddam ____, former Iraqi leader (7)

Down

1 Toyed (6)
2 Opposite in nature (7)
3 Article of faith (5)
4 Marsh plant (4)
5 Citation (5)
6 Acted presumptuously (5)
7 Young cow (6)
11 Concerned with one specific purpose (2,3)
12 Variety of grape used in wine making (5)
14 Depository for goods (7)
15 Upward slope in the centre of a road (6)
16 Native of Nairobi, eg (6)
18 Throw out (5)
19 Peruvian tribe at the time of the Spanish conquest (5)
21 Plants used in cookery (5)
22 Town in England on the River Avon (4)

Across

4 Endeavour (7)
8 Perfume (5)
9 Nocturnal insect, a domestic pest (9)
10 Compulsory military service (5)
11 Association organised to promote art, science or education (9)
13 Distress signal (6)
16 Forbid the public distribution of (6)
20 Setting down in permanent form (9)
23 Eagle's nest (5)
24 Proximity (9)
25 Ejects with force (5)
26 Very fast (7)

Down

1 Tympanic membrane (7)
2 In the vicinity (7)
3 Prickly desert plants (5)
4 Confront, solicit (6)
5 Rotary engine (7)
6 Sound made by a cat (5)
7 Lake and popular resort area of Nevada, USA (5)
12 Number in a brace (3)
14 Top card (3)
15 Flighty scatterbrained simpleton (slang) (7)
17 Blood-red (7)
18 Discharge (7)
19 Feeling of intense unhappiness (6)
20 Coarse sieve used for forming soft food into strands (5)
21 Chew noisily (5)
22 Carbonated, frothy (5)

60

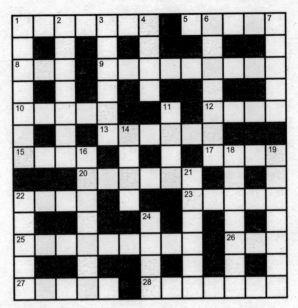

Across
1 Insects with pincers at the rear of the abdomen (7)
5 Country, capital Cairo (5)
8 Bulgarian monetary unit (3)
9 One who extracts fuel from a pit (4,5)
10 Garments of a jockey (5)
12 Track (4)
13 Arm joints (6)
15 Wooden vehicle on runners (4)
17 Extremely wicked (4)
20 Bars of metal (6)
22 Weight units of 2240 lbs (4)
23 Projection shaped to fit into a mortise (5)
25 Listen secretively (9)
26 Section of a play (3)
27 Antarctic explorer (5)
28 Beer-making establishment (7)

Down
1 Signs up to join the military (7)
2 Turn around (7)
3 Make a cut (6)
4 Large bodies of water (4)
6 Brief view (7)
7 Flashlight (5)
11 Vessel for travel on water (4)
14 Manufacturer of toy bricks (4)
16 Express opposition (7)
18 Place affording a good view, ___ point (7)
19 Protracted (7)
21 Metal paper fastener (6)
22 Lock of hair (5)
24 Decapod crustacean (4)

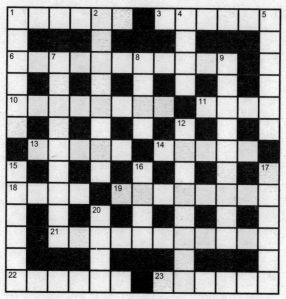

Across

1 Ambush (6)

3 Editions of a magazine or newspaper, for example (6)

6 Stone coffin (11)

10 Stimulating (8)

11 Recess in a church (4)

13 Identification tab (5)

14 Hair on the chin (5)

18 Put one's name to (4)

19 Underground cemetery (8)

21 Kill on a large scale (11)

22 Muslim form of salutation (6)

23 Start a computer again (6)

Down

1 Flat disc used as a seal to prevent leakage (6)

2 Disciples chosen by Christ to preach his gospel (8)

4 Aromatic grey-green herb (4)

5 Small pouch for shampoo, etc (6)

7 Parallelogram (9)

8 Extremity of the arm (4)

9 Star that explodes (9)

12 Proportional (8)

15 Evaluate (6)

16 Travelling show (4)

17 Not in a specified place (6)

20 Highest volcano in Europe (4)

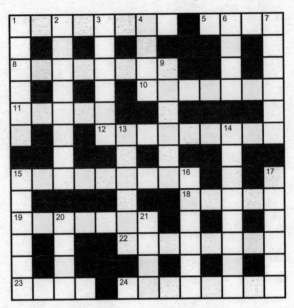

Across
1 Raze to the ground (8)
5 Brandy made from the residue of grapes after pressing (4)
8 Symbol used as an emblem by the medical profession (8)
10 Period which starts on 1 January (3,4)
11 Low humming sound (5)
12 Contest in which a baton is passed between runners (5,4)
15 Before the expected time (9)
18 Birthplace of Mohammed (5)
19 Egg white (7)
22 Light (8)
23 Posing no difficulty (4)
24 Relating to books (8)

Down
1 Resolve (6)
2 Moderate to inferior in quality (8)
3 Storage cabinet (6)
4 Eschew (4)
6 Last Stuart monarch, Queen of England (4)
7 Price for some article (6)
9 Bracing atmosphere by the coast (3,3)
13 Alternative – this or that (6)
14 Huge South American snake (8)
15 Flatfish with distinctive orange spots (6)
16 Dominion (6)
17 Obtained, especially accidentally (4,2)
20 Creeping or crawling invertebrates (4)
21 Follower of Hitler (4)

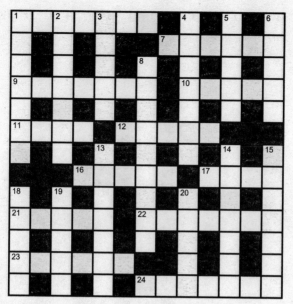

Across

1 Country, capital Vienna (7)
7 Sale of miscellanea, often for charity (6)
9 Official language of Bangladesh (7)
10 Cut thinly (5)
11 Stained with a colourant (4)
12 Show appreciation (5)
16 Honesty (5)
17 Period of 52 weeks (4)
21 Submerged ridges of coral (5)
22 Elementary particle (7)
23 Black eye (slang) (6)
24 Small dynamo with a secondary winding (7)

Down

1 No-one in particular (7)
2 Stroll (7)
3 Location detector (5)
4 Platform projecting from the wall of a building (7)
5 Capital of Egypt (5)
6 Carrying weapons (5)
8 Resist (9)
13 Cut of beef from the chest (7)
14 Impoverish (7)
15 Major river of Colombia and Venezuela (7)
18 Sprang up (5)
19 Plant exudation (5)
20 Prompting (5)

64

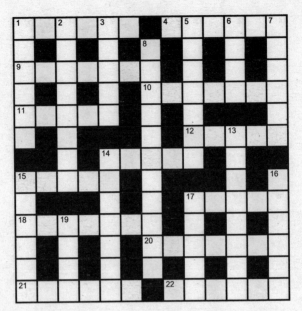

Across

1 The courage to carry on (6)
4 Conventional (6)
9 Sailor (7)
10 Motivate (7)
11 No longer new, uninteresting (5)
12 Storehouse (5)
14 Ms Minogue (5)
15 Feel (5)
17 Wound made by cutting (5)
18 Love story (7)
20 Assign a duty to (7)
21 Poem of fourteen 10- or 11-syllable lines (6)
22 Slang (6)

Down

1 Yellow-flowered tropical tree (6)
2 Web-footed turtle living in fresh or brackish water (8)
3 Make a thrusting forward movement (5)
5 In football, beyond a prescribed line or area (7)
6 Very short skirt (4)
7 Express grief verbally (6)
8 Powerful mammal native to North America (7,4)
13 Giving delight and satisfaction (8)
14 Principal theme in a speech (7)
15 Similar things placed in order (6)
16 Bleach, make paler (6)
17 Dark reddish-brown (5)
19 Principal (4)

Across

1 Acute (5)
4 Filled with bewilderment (7)
8 Hospital social worker (7)
9 Gets bigger (5)
10 Of sound (5)
11 Outfit (clothing and accessories) for a new baby (7)
12 Shoves (6)
13 Moved with a sudden jerky motion (6)
16 Weakening or degeneration (especially through lack of use) (7)
18 Portable shelters (usually of canvas) (5)
20 Communion table (5)
21 Spare time (7)
22 Hibernating (7)
23 In an unfortunate manner (5)

Down

1 Neuters (an animal) (5)
2 Manager of a business or school (13)
3 Style, flair (7)
4 Hardly, sparsely (6)
5 Humid (5)
6 Artfully persuasive in speech (6-7)
7 Come down (7)
12 Sign posted in a public place as an advertisement (7)
14 Gets (7)
15 Cord hole (6)
17 Hooded jacket (5)
19 Sleazy or shabby (5)

66

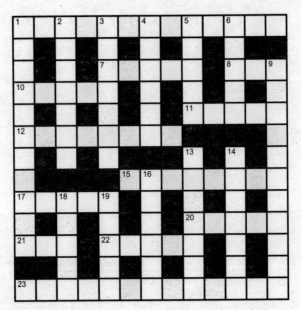

Across

1 In a reflex manner (13)
7 Capital of Oregon, USA (5)
8 Dry (wine) (3)
10 Gives off (5)
11 Beaver-like animal (5)
12 Property in a family for generations (8)
15 Enquire as to the wellbeing of (3,5)
17 Primitive (5)
20 Scottish valleys (5)
21 Force by impact (3)
22 Joint in the leg (5)
23 One of a series of slabs placed in a stream as an aid to crossing (8-5)

Down

1 Large entrance, reception room, or waiting area (11)
2 Republic in north-western Africa (7)
3 Projectile (7)
4 Spanish city famous for steel and swords (6)
5 Child's magazine (5)
6 Hearty (5)
9 Rural regions (11)
13 Generosity (7)
14 Shakespearean play set in Venice (7)
16 Oral (6)
18 Battleground of World War I (5)
19 Car wheel immobilising device (5)

67

Across
1 Sterile (7)
6 Drinking vessel (3)
8 Existing (5)
9 Assembles, gets together (7)
10 Have in common (5)
11 Worthy of being chosen (8)
13 Hallowed (6)
15 Counterpane (6)
18 Artificially produced jet of water (8)
19 Holds fast (5)
21 Concentration (7)
22 Rise or move forward (5)
23 H Rider Haggard novel (3)
24 Breathe (7)

Down
2 Turner with a narrow flexible blade (7)
3 Adolescent (8)
4 Fortress, stronghold (6)
5 Touch with the lips (4)
6 Mixture (7)
7 Rotten, decayed (4,3)
12 Apertures, holes (8)
13 Methods (7)
14 Wash (7)
16 Aircraft pilot (7)
17 Reflect deeply on a subject (6)
20 Channel Island (4)

71

68

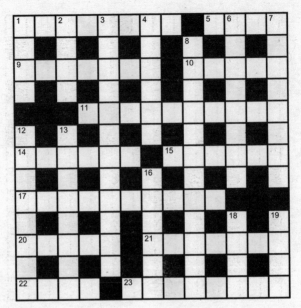

Across

1 Customary way of operation (8)

5 Metal food containers (4)

9 Absurd pretence (7)

10 Grovel (5)

11 Eating house (10)

14 Immature insects (6)

15 Combatant who is able to defeat rivals (6)

17 Shorten, condense (10)

20 Three-dimensional (5)

21 Give moral or emotional strength to (7)

22 Row or layer (4)

23 Minor celestial body composed of rock and metal (8)

Down

1 Heavy iron tool used to break up rocks (4)

2 Indian nursemaid (4)

3 Establishment specialising in the selling of holidays (6,6)

4 Swindles (6)

6 Items listed individually on a menu (1,2,5)

7 Beneficial (8)

8 Relationship less intimate than friendship (12)

12 Sharply defined to the mind (5-3)

13 Likely (8)

16 Female relatives (6)

18 Company emblem (4)

19 Despatch (4)

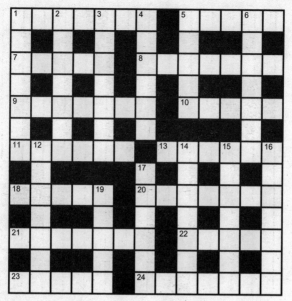

Across

1 Gave a raucous clucking cry (7)
5 Religious building (5)
7 Natives of Iraq or Jordan, for example (5)
8 Lack of proper care and attention (7)
9 Look for a specific person or thing (4,3)
10 Radioactive gas (5)
11 Part of a meal (6)
13 Attach, do up securely (6)
18 Fake (5)
20 Giacomo ____, composer of *Madame Butterfly* (7)
21 Enclosed heat-producing chamber (7)
22 Presentation, briefly (5)
23 Short descriptive poem of rural life (5)
24 Shake with fear (7)

Down

1 Creation of the highest excellence (7)
2 French castle (7)
3 Periods of instruction (7)
4 Signify (6)
5 Predict from an omen (5)
6 Surround completely (7)
12 Pompous, grandiloquent (7)
14 Depository containing historical records (7)
15 Washing machine with one drum for washing and another for spin drying (4-3)
16 Offensively malodorous (7)
17 Pleasantly optimistic (6)
19 Will (5)

70

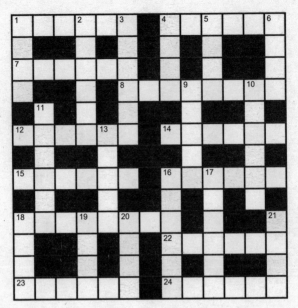

Across

1 Deserving regret (3,3)
4 Pail (6)
7 Is identical to in quantity (6)
8 Example (8)
12 Go bad or sour (6)
14 Occupation for which one is trained (6)
15 Relating to or similar to bears (6)
16 Artist's crayon (6)
18 Strong black coffee (8)
22 Stuffed with soft material (6)
23 Paying customer (6)
24 Wander about aimlessly (6)

Down

1 Makes a knot (4)
2 Prejudiced (6)
3 Want strongly (6)
4 Curtsies (4)
5 Unconscious state (4)
6 Covering for a wheel (4)
9 Head ornament (5)
10 Intelligent (6)
11 Overbearing pride or presumption (6)
13 Jessica ____, Oscar-winning actress who featured in *Grey Gardens* (5)
16 Correct (6)
17 Infrequently (6)
18 Large-scale (4)
19 Memorisation by repetition (4)
20 Table condiment (4)
21 Edge tool used to cut and shape wood (4)

Across

1 Prices (5)
4 Sales slip (7)
7 Pulse vegetables (5)
8 Action by a landlord that compels a tenant to leave the premises (8)
9 Downy juicy fruit (5)
11 Type of cosmetic (8)
15 Without foundation in reason or fact (8)
17 Standoffish (5)
19 Inflammation of a nerve accompanied by pain (8)
20 First letter of the Greek alphabet (5)
21 Unattractively thin and weedy (7)
22 Blockade (5)

Down

1 Self-service restaurant (9)
2 Wither, especially due to loss of moisture (7)
3 Russian artificial satellite, the first to orbit the Earth (7)
4 Inaccessible and sparsely populated (6)
5 Made level or straight (6)
6 Overwhelming feeling of anxiety (5)
10 Equine footwear, considered lucky (9)
12 Relating to iron (7)
13 Point at which to retire for the night (7)
14 Israelite leader who destroyed Jericho (6)
16 Bureau (6)
18 Bush with fragrant flowers (5)

72

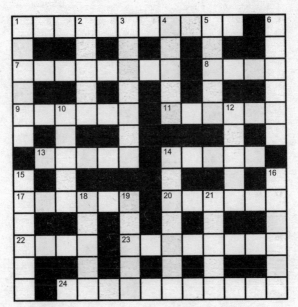

Across

1 Sun with the celestial bodies that revolve around it (5,6)

7 Italian sponge cake, coffee and brandy dessert (8)

8 Encourage to do wrong (4)

9 Motive (6)

11 Marked by hardheaded intelligence (6)

13 Become rotten, as of an egg, for example (5)

14 Gasps for breath (5)

17 Lessen the density or solidity of (6)

20 Calm, with no emotional agitation (6)

22 Short note (4)

23 Standards of judgment (8)

24 Basic French dressing for salads (11)

Down

1 Surgical stitch (6)

2 Victoria Beckham's former surname (5)

3 Study of the physical world (7)

4 Steam bath (5)

5 Glorify (5)

6 Swimmer (6)

10 Tree with rot-resistant wood (5)

12 Remove a knot (5)

14 Going by (7)

15 Prepared (a gun) for firing (6)

16 Supply with oxygen (6)

18 Species of bacteria which can threaten food safety (1,4)

19 Popular Mexican palm-like plant (5)

21 Minor parish official (5)

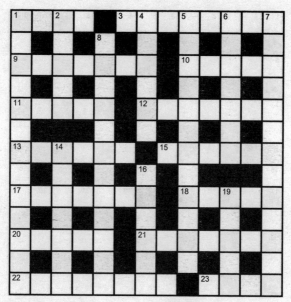

Across

1 Tear violently (4)
3 Street with only one way in or out (3-2-3)
9 Cook in very hot water for a short time (7)
10 Superior (5)
11 Bring into play (5)
12 Localised ulcer or sore (7)
13 Agents which assist colonic irrigation (6)
15 Pattern in music (6)
17 Ceremony of religious worship (7)
18 Pools of standing water (5)
20 Curry dish cooked and served in a flat-bottomed metal pot (5)
21 Girl's name (7)
22 Keen or close watch (coll) (5,3)
23 Join metal (4)

Down

1 Deserving severe rebuke or censure (13)
2 Dentist's assistant (5)
4 Set down cargo (6)
5 Former German monetary unit (12)
6 Acutely insightful and wise (7)
7 Form of greeting sent towards the end of the year (9,4)
8 With the order reversed, perversely (12)
14 Noise excluder (7)
16 Conforming to propriety or good taste (6)
19 Wash off soap (5)

74

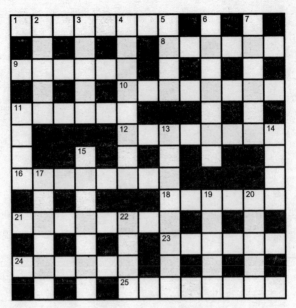

Across

1 Accidental collision that is narrowly avoided (4,4)
8 Antipathetic (6)
9 Aviators (6)
10 Garments worn by members of the same group (8)
11 Small carnivore with short legs and an elongated body (6)
12 Bonding substance (8)
16 Temple to all the gods (8)
18 Abandonment, decay (6)
21 Black treacle (8)
23 In an overt way (6)
24 Money returned to a payer (6)
25 Ultimately following (8)

Down

2 Group considered superior (5)
3 Protective coverings of buildings (5)
4 Protect from heat, cold, noise, etc (8)
5 Hindu woman's garment (4)
6 Exceptional courage when facing danger (7)
7 Science fiction author (1920–92) (6)
11 Distort, buckle (4)
13 Good-looking (8)
14 Fencing sword (4)
15 One of several parallel layers of material (7)
17 Point in orbit (6)
19 Item of bed linen (5)
20 Spicy sauce to accompany Mexican food (5)
22 Align oneself with (4)

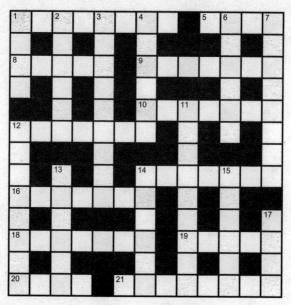

Across

1 Personal magnetism (8)
5 Draw slowly or heavily (4)
8 Oozes slowly (5)
9 Exceed (7)
10 Squeeze out (7)
12 Bank employee (7)
14 Goddess of retribution (7)
16 One of the three superpowers in *Nineteen Eighty-Four* (7)
18 Beasts of burden (7)
19 Plant also known as the century plant (5)
20 Contest of speed (4)
21 ___ figure, rough estimation (8)

Down

1 Yield (4)
2 Foreigners (6)
3 Beguiling but harmful (9)
4 Usual form of address for a man (6)
6 Counting frame (6)
7 US city famous for entertainment and gambling (3,5)
11 Small version of a larger image (9)
12 Record of annual dates (8)
13 Humorously sarcastic (6)
14 Sickness (6)
15 Musical composition of three or four movements of contrasting forms (6)
17 Jaws of a bird (4)

76

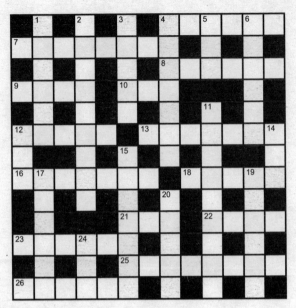

Across

4 In short supply (6)
7 Small, slender long-tailed parrot (8)
8 Within the confines of a building (6)
9 Charitable gifts (4)
10 Pocket (3)
12 Proficient (5)
13 Go backwards (7)
16 Affianced (7)
18 Type of pistol (5)
21 Female deer (3)
22 Marine mammal (4)
23 Performer who moves to music (6)
25 Step-up (8)
26 Doghouse (6)

Down

1 Narrative song (6)
2 Pouched mammal (9)
3 Hermann ____, author of *Steppenwolf* (5)
4 Adhesive label (7)
5 Be of service (3)
6 Part of a song repeated after each verse (6)
11 Requisition forcibly, as of enemy property (9)
12 Alcoholic beverage (3)
14 Make a mistake (3)
15 Plant's climbing organ (7)
17 Invalidate (6)
19 Slip away (6)
20 Shore (5)
24 Dupe, swindle (3)

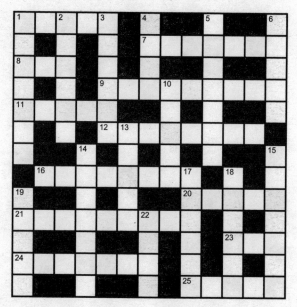

Across

1 Cut the wool from (5)
7 One who has had a limb removed (7)
8 Choose or show a preference (3)
9 Feeling of thankfulness and appreciation (9)
11 Move smoothly and effortlessly (5)
12 Foolhardy (8)
16 Large cool star (3,5)
20 On your own (5)
21 Contagion (9)
23 Posed for artistic purposes (3)
24 Disposed to please (7)
25 Combine (5)

Down

1 Double-barrelled firearm (7)
2 Have as a logical consequence (6)
3 Forest fire fighter (6)
4 Daddy (4)
5 Gesture of respectful greeting, for women (7)
6 Rise in bodily temperature (5)
10 Souvenir (5)
13 Expel, eject (5)
14 Relating to glands near to the kidneys (7)
15 Take air in and out (7)
17 Bicycle for two riders (6)
18 Waker (6)
19 Roll of tobacco (5)
22 Mountain goat (4)

78

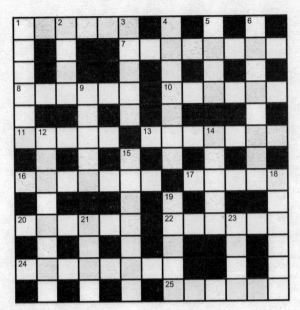

Across

1 Seed often used on bread rolls (6)
7 Logically valid (8)
8 Hired (6)
10 Participant in a race (6)
11 Spiral, coil (5)
13 Limp, flabby (7)
16 Biblical wife of Ahab (7)
17 Written work (5)
20 Opening move in chess (6)
22 European mint with aromatic and pungent leaves (6)
24 Exercises authoritative power over (8)
25 Seven people considered as a unit (6)

Down

1 Burn superficially (6)
2 Examine hastily (4)
3 Become ground down (5)
4 Cylindrical containers for liquids (7)
5 Having started life (4)
6 Branch of biology that studies heredity and variation in organisms (8)
9 Lining of the stomach of a ruminant used as food (5)
12 Lifting device (8)
14 Shows concern (5)
15 Decorate with strings of flowers (7)
18 Specialist (6)
19 Popular board game (5)
21 Washtub (4)
23 Pimple (4)

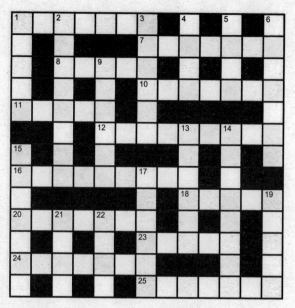

Across

1 Pieces of cloth used to mend a hole (7)
7 Solution used as a cleanser for the organs of sight (7)
8 Whole range (5)
10 Nominal (7)
11 Metal-shaping machine (5)
12 Sad (9)
16 Attacker (9)
18 Acknowledge (5)
20 Musical effect produced by rapid alternation of tones (7)
23 German submarine in World War II (1-4)
24 Replies (7)
25 Goes on board (7)

Down

1 Group of people summoned for jury service (5)
2 Constrains (8)
3 Compositor (6)
4 Departed, went (4)
5 Lavish formal dance (4)
6 In a little while (7)
9 Breakfast food (6)
13 Size of a book (6)
14 Famous cinema performer (4,4)
15 Relating to reality (7)
17 Stimulate (6)
19 Lone Star State of the USA (5)
21 Direction of the rising sun (4)
22 Call used three times by a Town Crier (4)

80

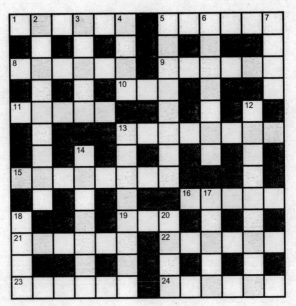

Across

1 Shrewdness shown by keen insight (6)
5 Pastoral (6)
8 Bowl-shaped vessels (6)
9 Victim of ridicule or pranks (6)
10 Young newt (3)
11 Place of safety or sanctuary (5)
13 Cadaverous (8)
15 Reduces the worth of (8)
16 Cider fruit (5)
19 Forty winks (3)
21 Sympathetic compatibility (6)
22 Tree and shrub species (6)
23 Tobacco user (6)
24 Country, capital Stockholm (6)

Down

2 Property that defines one's individual nature (9)
3 Indian corn (5)
4 Organ of smell (4)
5 Constantly in motion (8)
6 Buyer, purchaser (7)
7 Restaurant cook (4)
12 Celestial body orbiting another (9)
13 Waste (8)
14 Type of model made by Madame Tussaud (7)
17 Location, whereabouts (5)
18 Divisions of a week (4)
20 Exceed (4)

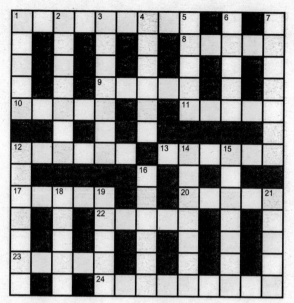

Across

1 Need of mending (9)
8 Board used with a planchette (5)
9 Wife of a rajah (5)
10 Banishment (5)
11 Spicy tomato sauce (5)
12 Small stamp or seal on a ring (6)
13 Peninsula between the Red Sea and the Persian Gulf (6)
17 Frameworks for holding objects (5)
20 Employment (5)
22 Frenzied (5)
23 Locations (5)
24 Item used to mark a grave (9)

Down

1 Move to music (5)
2 Going by boat (7)
3 Pass from the body (7)
4 Retaliate (6)
5 Strong cords (5)
6 Polite (5)
7 Musical setting for a religious text (7)
12 Proverbially, the lowest form of wit (7)
14 Rowdy, strident (7)
15 Bluster (7)
16 Crescent-shaped yellow fruit (6)
18 Coagulates (5)
19 Pulverise (5)
21 Lofty nest of a bird of prey (5)

82

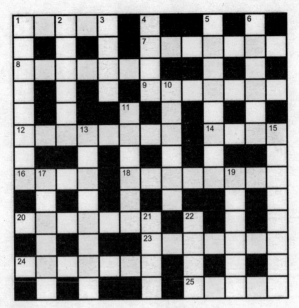

Across

1 Breed of dog used for hunting (5)

7 In the middle (7)

8 Carnivorous freshwater fish of South America (7)

9 Items of neckwear in the form of a knot with two loops (3,4)

12 Time of year when the sun is at its greatest distance from the equator (8)

14 Garments, clothes generally (4)

16 Milk-pudding ingredient (4)

18 Horizontal rod between two vertical posts (8)

20 Twist out of shape (7)

23 Pasta 'cushions' (7)

24 Hunt cry telling that the fox has been sighted (5-2)

25 Destitute (5)

Down

1 Mental state induced by suggestion (8)

2 Imaginary or illusory (6)

3 Basic unit of money in Vietnam (4)

4 Crust-like surface of a healing wound (4)

5 Laws (8)

6 Person who comes to no good (coll) (3,3)

10 Spotted wildcat (6)

11 Nipper at the end of a claw (6)

13 Evenly (8)

15 Critical examination (8)

17 Beast (6)

19 Turn into (6)

21 Ancient city in Asia Minor (4)

22 River which flows through Bristol (4)

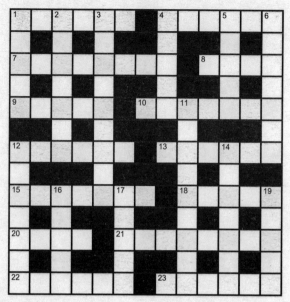

Across

1 Ignore or overlook (4,2)
4 Arranges so as to be parallel or straight (6)
7 Popular coffee-flavoured liqueur (3,5)
8 Pros and ____ (4)
9 Dress or groom with elaborate care (5)
10 Body of water into which the River Jordan flows (4,3)
12 Visitor (6)
13 Make plump (6)
15 Marked by peace and prosperity (7)
18 Two times (5)
20 Man-eating giant (4)
21 Order that is served with a main course (4,4)
22 Carnivorous marine fishes (6)
23 Fully developed people (6)

Down

1 Raise, erect (3,2)
2 Sporting dog (7)
3 Offence of speaking sacrilegiously about God (9)
4 Slacken off (5)
5 Give a shine to (5)
6 Provide with nourishment (7)
11 Social policy of racial segregation (9)
12 Collusion (7)
14 Trifling (7)
16 Insect grub (5)
17 Desert watering hole (5)
19 Distinctive spirit of a culture (5)

84

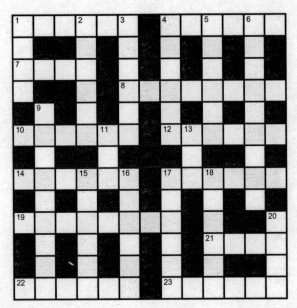

Across

1 Frozen celestial objects that travel around the sun (6)
4 ___ Cole, footballer and ex-husband of Cheryl Cole (6)
7 Certain (4)
8 Decorative item (8)
10 Abnormally deficient in colour (6)
12 Small river (6)
14 Woman often 'in distress' in stories (6)
17 Tray for serving food or drinks (6)
19 Early Christian church (8)
21 Portend (4)
22 One who voluntarily suffers death (6)
23 Repair shop where vehicles are serviced (6)

Down

1 Example, instance (4)
2 Good look (coll) (6)
3 In next to first place (6)
4 Sports stadia (6)
5 Hand tool with a heavy rigid head (6)
6 Extended by pulling and stretching (9)
9 Russian musical instrument (9)
11 Slang term for diamonds (3)
13 Afternoon meal (3)
15 Small and compactly built upright piano (6)
16 Dawdle (6)
17 Old or experienced sailor (coll) (3,3)
18 Wood that has been prepared for building (6)
20 Festival, celebration (4)

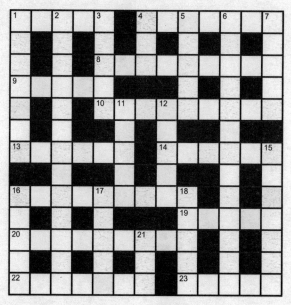

Across

1 Sybil Fawlty's husband in *Fawlty Towers* (5)
4 Make level (7)
8 Rebuke formally (9)
9 Girl who features in Lewis Carroll's famous stories (5)
10 Chemist (9)
13 Attraction (6)
14 Revised before printing (6)
16 Institution providing labour and shelter for the poor (9)
19 From that time (5)
20 Uneducated person (9)
22 Plant also known as erica (7)
23 Racing vessel (5)

Down

1 Sudden happening that brings good fortune (7)
2 Psychotic mental illness (13)
3 Enticed (5)
4 Dandy (3)
5 Burning (5)
6 Crossing the sea between Britain and the USA (13)
7 Point directly opposite the zenith (5)
11 Inuit dwelling (5)
12 Jetties (5)
15 Eat away from home (4,3)
16 Determine the heaviness of (5)
17 Unkind or cruel (5)
18 Literary composition (5)
21 Make imperfect (3)

86

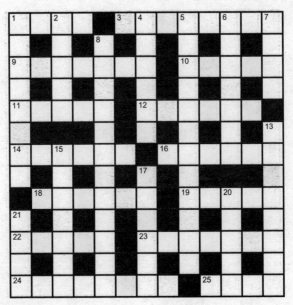

Across

1 George ____, footballer who died in 2005 (4)

3 Writer of music (8)

9 Fighter (7)

10 Display stand for a painting (5)

11 Bloodsucking parasite (5)

12 Arrangement (6)

14 Ocean floor (6)

16 Lag behind (6)

18 Sweet, dark purple plum (6)

19 Island of central Hawaii (5)

22 Country in which Mumbai is situated (5)

23 Cocktail (7)

24 Change from a gaseous to a liquid state (8)

25 Computer memory unit (4)

Down

1 Mythical reptile with a lethal gaze or breath (8)

2 Ointment (5)

4 Forceful military attack (6)

5 Area (sometimes in a balcony) set aside for reporters (5,7)

6 Hang freely (7)

7 Depend (4)

8 Former table of earthquake intensity (7,5)

13 Expressing contempt or ridicule (8)

15 Desert, leave (7)

17 Feeling of ill-will arousing active hostility (6)

20 Cacophonous (5)

21 Bluish-white metallic element (4)

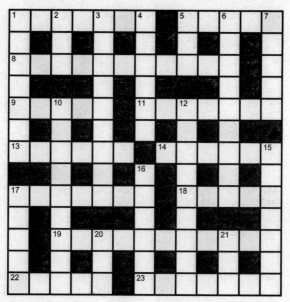

Across
1 Horse's bit (7)
5 Informal term for US dollars (5)
8 Imprison (11)
9 Foods made from flesh (5)
11 Immediate (7)
13 Harvester (6)
14 Disappearing gradually (6)
17 Capital of Iraq (7)
18 Greta ___, film star (1905–90) (5)
19 Hypothesis that is taken for granted (11)
22 Fill quickly beyond capacity (5)
23 Potato slice cooked in batter (7)

Down
1 Shine with a weak or fitful light (7)
2 Joan of ___, French heroine (3)
3 Agricultural dwelling, buildings and land (9)
4 Protective fold of skin (6)
5 Constricting snake (3)
6 Maurice ___, French actor and cabaret singer (9)
7 Supply sparingly (5)
10 Absence of pain without loss of consciousness (9)
12 Place of complete bliss (7-2)
15 Adult (5-2)
16 Fools (6)
17 Public announcement of a proposed marriage (5)
20 Drivel, trash (3)
21 Ailing (3)

88

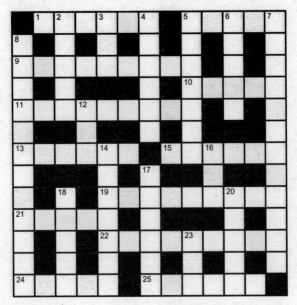

Across

1 In a slumber (6)
5 Cause fear in (5)
9 Become one (9)
10 Punctuation mark (5)
11 Continue steadfastly (9)
13 Fruit with yellow flesh (6)
15 Leave (6)
19 Onyx marble (9)
21 Clothes drier (5)
22 Kind of gelatin used for fining real ale (9)
24 Platform (5)
25 Trough from which cattle or horses feed (6)

Down

2 Indian lute (5)
3 Ovum (3)
4 Puts into position (6)
5 Come before (7)
6 Ms Campbell, model (5)
7 Lively and competitive (atmosphere or environment) (3,3,6)
8 Thick-skinned herbivorous animal of Africa (12)
12 Plant juice (3)
14 Extreme greed for material wealth (7)
16 Step in dancing (especially in classical ballet) (3)
17 Marie Curie's discovery (6)
18 Plays, theatre (5)
20 Banter (5)
23 Firearm (3)

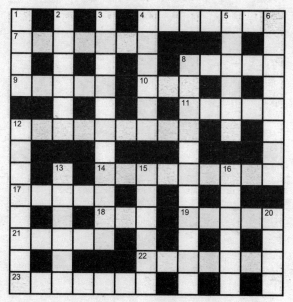

Across
4 Knife used in dissection (7)
7 Flower seller (7)
8 In line with a length or direction (5)
9 Bind again or anew (5)
10 Circuit (3)
11 Balance (5)
12 Onlooker (9)
14 Seeds which produce an edible oil (4,5)
17 In Hinduism, an ascetic holy man (5)
18 Rim (3)
19 Main part of the human body (5)
21 Entertain (5)
22 Characterised by strong feelings (7)
23 Carry out in practice (7)

Down
1 A long way off (4)
2 Unborn vertebrate in the later stages of development (6)
3 Container for preserving historical records to be discovered in the future (4,7)
4 Obtuse (6)
5 Disorder characterised by fear (6)
6 Woody (8)
8 Confirmation, proof (11)
12 Country, capital Gaborone (8)
13 Alter or regulate so as to achieve accuracy (6)
15 Exclamation of joy or victory (6)
16 Ingenious (6)
20 Domesticated bovines (4)

90

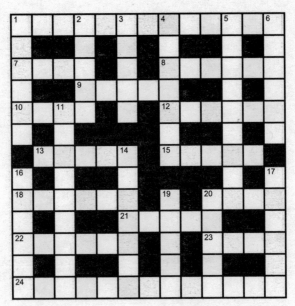

Across

1 Name given to 15 July (2,8,3)
7 Similar (4)
8 Long narrow flag or streamer (6)
9 Province of eastern Belgium (5)
10 Being in a tense state (4)
12 Become more distant (6)
13 Use a dragnet (5)
15 Pale yellow colour (5)
18 Planetary paths (6)
20 Expression of incredulity (2,2)
21 Sharp point on a plant (5)
22 Superior in quality (2,4)
23 Ms Turner, whose hits include *Simply The Best* (4)
24 Emperor of Ethiopia (1892–1975) (5,8)

Down

1 Distributed equally (6)
2 In a weak, pale or languid manner (5)
3 River which flows through Rome (5)
4 Endanger (7)
5 Life-threatening (9)
6 Jerked (6)
11 Giuseppe ___, Italian patriot whose conquest of Sicily and Naples led to the formation of the Italian state (9)
14 Hears (7)
16 Seat carried on an elephant's back (6)
17 Blazing (6)
19 Intestine (5)
20 Poker stakes (5)

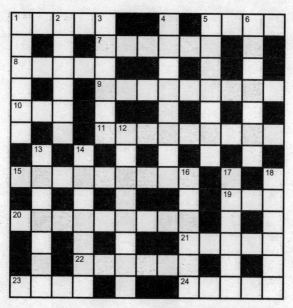

Across

1 Primary (5)
5 Muslim of the former Ottoman empire (4)
7 Seem (6)
8 Hospital rooms with more than one bed (5)
9 Chinese gooseberry (4,5)
10 Before, poetically (3)
11 Handling, management (9)
15 Infectious liver disease (9)
19 21st letter of the Greek alphabet (3)
20 Drug that temporarily quickens some vital process (9)
21 Ugly evil-looking old woman (5)
22 Italian operatic tenor (1873–1921) (6)
23 Published volume (4)
24 Wed (5)

Down

1 Water tanker (6)
2 Frozen fruit-flavoured dessert (6)
3 Small box for holding valuables (6)
4 Japanese dish (8)
5 Ancient Greek or Roman warship (7)
6 Areas, districts (7)
12 Light teasing repartee (8)
13 Hitchcock film of 1958 (7)
14 Hanging bed of canvas (7)
16 Humorous TV drama based on real life (coll) (6)
17 State of commotion and noise (6)
18 Four score and ten (6)

92

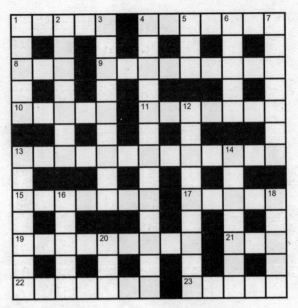

Across

1 Scarf bandage (5)
4 Egyptian paper reed (7)
8 Beast of burden (3)
9 Army officer rank (9)
10 Cleave (5)
11 Settle or put right (4,3)
13 Clandestine (13)
15 Alien (7)
17 Keyboard instrument (5)
19 City in northern Scotland (9)
21 Strong anger (3)
22 Very cold waterproof bag applied to the body to reduce swelling (3,4)
23 Country on the Iberian Peninsula (5)

Down

1 Lines where pieces of fabric are sewn together (5)
2 Narrow-minded (7)
3 Mediator (2-7)
4 Bothersome annoying person (coll) (4,2,3,4)
5 Green vegetable (3)
6 Powerful herbivore with a horned snout (abbr) (5)
7 Large dark low cloud (7)
12 Eight-tentacled sea creatures (9)
13 Japanese dish of thinly sliced raw fish (7)
14 Musical toy (7)
16 Variety show (5)
18 Huge sea (5)
20 Scandinavian type of knotted pile rug (3)

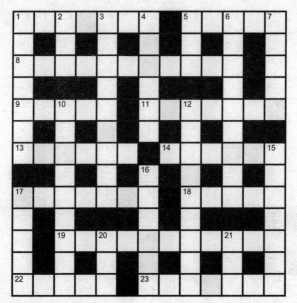

Across

1 Speech disorder (7)
5 Leans (5)
8 Noisy quarrel (11)
9 Devout (5)
11 Vulcanised rubber (7)
13 Somewhat (6)
14 Next to (6)
17 Container for coal (7)
18 Food often named the 'staff of life' (5)
19 Sensuous and exotic Eastern female entertainer (5,6)
22 Exhausted (5)
23 Young woman who behaves in a boisterously assertive or crude manner (coll) (7)

Down

1 Large-headed turtle with powerful hooked jaws (7)
2 Behave (3)
3 Discovery which proves to be illusory (5,4)
4 Travelled aimlessly over a wide area (6)
5 Garland of flowers (3)
6 Able to feel or perceive (9)
7 Animal prized for its fur (5)
10 Be larger in quantity (9)
12 From a vessel into the water (9)
15 Certify (7)
16 Gertrude ____, renowned English gardener (1843–1932) (6)
17 Canonised person (5)
20 Directed (3)
21 Crib (3)

94

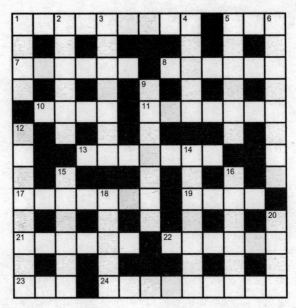

Across

1 Study of the physical properties of sound (9)
5 Deep groove (3)
7 Shred (6)
8 Units of weight for precious stones (6)
10 Close one eye quickly as a signal (4)
11 Merciful (7)
13 Dictionary (7)
17 Spectacles (7)
19 Optical organs (4)
21 Ceremonial (6)
22 Small rooms on a ship (6)
23 Device used to propel a boat (3)
24 Animal of Arctic regions (5,4)

Down

1 High male voice (4)
2 Beat through cleverness (6)
3 Dapple (7)
4 Discoloured appearance (5)
5 Harvested (6)
6 Glass cylinder closed at one end (4,4)
9 Oval (7)
12 Australian marsupial (8)
14 Outdoor (4-3)
15 Component (6)
16 Give up work (6)
18 One who is playfully mischievous (5)
20 Russian monarch (4)

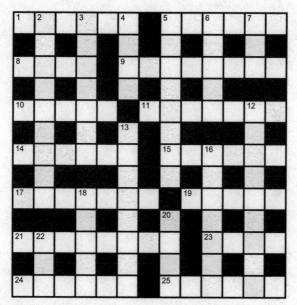

Across
1 Scratch repeatedly (6)
5 Annoyed, resentful (6)
8 Marshes (4)
9 Dazzlingly beautiful (8)
10 Humorist (5)
11 Give evidence (7)
14 Warning or proviso (6)
15 Induce to commit perjury (6)
17 Holding under a rental agreement (7)
19 Aladdin's spirit (5)
21 Natural bright daylight (8)
23 Shallow basket used when gardening (4)
24 Small growths on a mucous membrane (6)
25 Set up, incriminated (coll) (6)

Down
2 Cocoa (9)
3 Severely simple (7)
4 Boundary, rim (4)
5 Marked by a disposition to oppose and contradict (8)
6 Mission (5)
7 World's second-largest living bird (3)
12 Items placed in a home, making it ready for occupancy (9)
13 People who act as substitutes (5-3)
16 Drink given to people who are ill (4,3)
18 Impertinent (5)
20 Organ of photosynthesis and transpiration in plants (4)
22 Vehicle from another world (inits) (3)

96

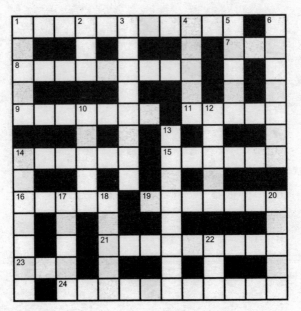

Across

1 Evil said to be inherited by all descendants of Adam (8,3)

7 Egg cells (3)

8 Hard brittle greyish-white metallic element (9)

9 Public transport vehicles (7)

11 Appreciation (5)

14 Uses jointly (6)

15 Travelling show (6)

16 Fowl's perch (5)

19 Strong post for attaching a mooring line (7)

21 Native of Manhattan or Brooklyn, for example (3,6)

23 Expert (3)

24 Impoverished, destitute (11)

Down

1 Relating to odours or the sense of smell (5)

2 Muzzle (3)

3 Drivel (8)

4 Paid out money (5)

5 Words used to refer to people, places or objects (5)

6 Annuls (7)

10 Coagulated milk used to make cheese (5)

12 Month with 30 days (5)

13 Words formed by the initial letters of other words (8)

14 Resembling a dream (7)

17 Of time long past (5)

18 Loose-fitting cloak (5)

20 Repairs a worn or torn hole (5)

22 Informer (3)

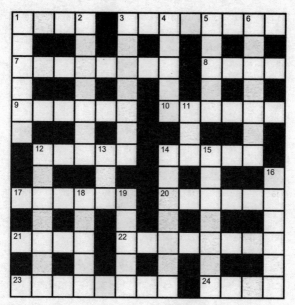

Across

1 Raised platform (4)
3 Legal action where the outcome is likely to set a precedent (4,4)
7 Change, amendment (8)
8 Gelling agent (4)
9 Engraves with acid (6)
10 Prison official (6)
12 Morose, churlish (5)
14 Concentrate (5)
17 Malignant growth or tumour (6)
20 Terminal section of the alimentary canal (6)
21 Vegetable known as lady's fingers (4)
22 Decorated with heraldic arms (8)
23 Uncharged particle with zero mass when at rest (8)
24 Rabbit's tail (4)

Down

1 Make or become dimmer (6)
2 Slide unobtrusively (7)
3 Desirous of a drink (7)
4 Tendon (5)
5 Position of professor (5)
6 Ability to walk steadily on the deck of a pitching ship (3,4)
11 Flurry (3)
12 Restrain with fetters (7)
13 Side sheltered from the wind (3)
14 Motley assortment of things (7)
15 Greek mythological giant with a single eye in the middle of his forehead (7)
16 Amongst (6)
18 Move effortlessly (5)
19 Jewish scholar (5)

98

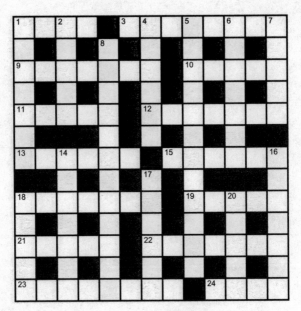

Across

1 Lady (4)
3 Captain Nemo's submarine (8)
9 Of marriage (7)
10 Revolving arm of a distributor (5)
11 Harmonious sounds (5)
12 Avoiding waste (7)
13 Sliced (of meat) (6)
15 Protective head covering (6)
18 Self-annihilation (7)
19 Greek letter (5)
21 Prove to be false or incorrect (5)
22 Isolate (7)
23 Recently married person (8)
24 Consistency (4)

Down

1 Vigorous (7)
2 Moves aimlessly and listlessly (5)
4 Finally (2,4)
5 Mayonnaise dressing often served with fish (7,5)
6 Metallic element (7)
7 Gesture involving the shoulders (5)
8 Science of the physiological processes of living things (12)
14 Coloured arc of light in the sky (7)
16 Catastrophe (7)
17 Tenant (6)
18 Alarm (5)
20 Cartoon character created by Walt Disney (5)

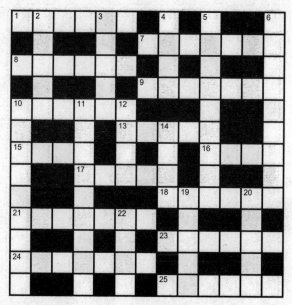

Across

1 Fragrant oily resin used in perfumes (6)
7 Unspecified person (7)
8 Reel, spool (6)
9 Insensitive or heartless (7)
10 Flamboyantly elaborate, showy (6)
13 Take as one's own (5)
15 Further, additional (4)
16 At rest (4)
17 Narrow paddle boat (5)
18 Off, sour (6)
21 Expert who studies data (7)
23 One living temporarily in a tent (6)
24 Shallow depression in the ground in which brine evaporates to leave a deposit (7)
25 Hound dog (6)

Down

2 Love affair (5)
3 Farewell remark (5)
4 ___ Parks, African-American civil rights activist (4)
5 Satisfaction of a desire or want (9)
6 Counterpane (9)
10 Small coffee cup (9)
11 Hypothesise (9)
12 Fine cord of twisted fibres (4)
14 Above, beyond (4)
19 Humble (5)
20 Paragon (5)
22 Blackleg (4)

100

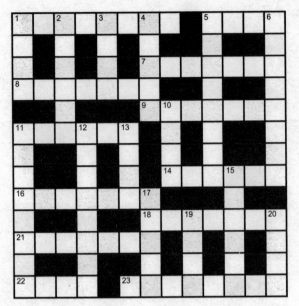

Across

1 Shamefaced (8)
5 Exchange (4)
7 Insignificantly small (7)
8 Flat upland (7)
9 Manual dexterity (7)
11 Pleasure obtained by inflicting harm on others (6)
14 Impels (6)
16 Derived from living matter (7)
18 Certain of (7)
21 Small edible crustaceans (7)
22 Study intensively for an exam (4)
23 Meant (8)

Down

1 Cock-a-leekie, for instance (4)
2 Mission (6)
3 Gait (4)
4 Air cavity in the skull (5)
5 Curved oriental sword (8)
6 Profession devoted to governing (8)
10 Hinged section of a table (4)
11 Summary (8)
12 Dreamer (8)
13 Medium-length dress (4)
15 Abundant non-metallic element (6)
17 Hindu social class (5)
19 Edible fat (4)
20 Expired (4)

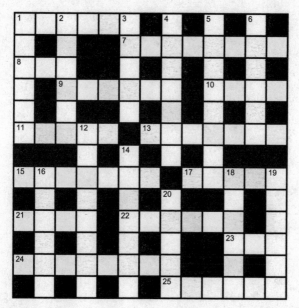

Across

1 Forest gods (6)
7 Vigilant (4-4)
8 Cereal grass (3)
9 Inn (6)
10 In a murderous frenzy (4)
11 Atomiser (5)
13 Odontologist (7)
15 Appropriate (7)
17 Group containing one or more species (5)
21 Group of countries in special alliance (4)
22 Field on which a university's buildings are situated (6)
23 Explosive initials! (3)
24 Pincers (8)
25 Emphasis (6)

Down

1 Ladles used to serve out ice cream (6)
2 Walk unsteadily (6)
3 Not affected by alcohol (5)
4 Move in a sinuous, or circular course (7)
5 Adroitness and cleverness in reply (8)
6 Lures (6)
12 Fastened together (8)
14 Device affixed to a door, rapped to gain attention (7)
16 Relatives by marriage (2-4)
18 Snuggle (6)
19 Provinces (6)
20 Wrong (5)

102

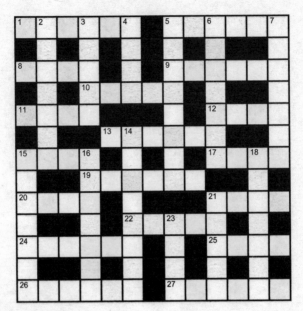

Across

1 Render unable to hear (6)
5 Approaching (6)
8 Stout rounded pole used to support rigging (4)
9 To the opposite side (6)
10 Irritates, annoys (5)
11 Departed (4)
12 The smallest quantity (4)
13 Ludicrous acts (6)
15 Ship's company (4)
17 Consequently (4)
19 Dry gully (6)
20 Word denoting a particular thing (4)
21 Longitudinal beam of the hull of a ship (4)
22 Frequently (5)
24 Precious red gemstones (6)
25 All right (4)
26 Wealth (6)
27 Financier (6)

Down

2 Endow with strength (7)
3 Boat used to transport people and cars (5)
4 French word for Christmas (4)
5 Arrange or order by categories (8)
6 Square hole made to receive a tenon (7)
7 Nazi secret police (7)
14 Unconsciousness induced by drugs (8)
15 Food provider (7)
16 Very irritable (7)
18 Hand-thrown bomb (7)
21 Recognised (5)
23 Sepulchre (4)

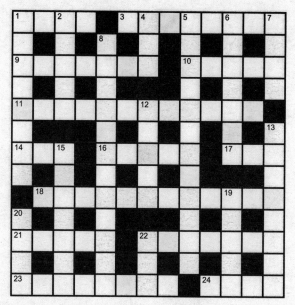

Across

1 Knock senseless (4)
3 Puzzled (8)
9 City and lake in central Switzerland (7)
10 Cloth woven from flax (5)
11 Method of removing unwanted hair (12)
14 Feline mammal (3)
16 Move on hands and knees (5)
17 Gunge (3)
18 Object used in playing a popular table game (8,4)
21 Organisation for people with high IQs (5)
22 Protective shoe-coverings (7)
23 Brief intensive course for a small group (8)
24 French for 'father' (4)

Down

1 Ability to meet financial obligations as they become due (8)
2 Brother of one's father (5)
4 Lyric poem (3)
5 Having a complete set of adult plumage (5,7)
6 Producing musical notes with the voice (7)
7 Unpleasantly cool and humid (4)
8 Minimum amount of material needed to maintain a nuclear reaction (8,4)
12 Port city of Japan (5)
13 Fuse or cause to grow together (8)
15 Diluting agent (7)
19 Semi-precious stone (5)
20 Fish-eating diving duck (4)
22 In addition (3)

104

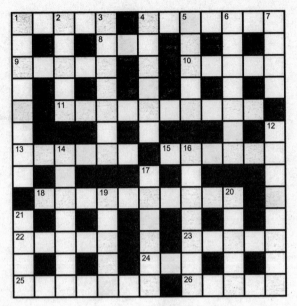

Across

1 Dart (5)
4 Make amorous advances towards (7)
8 Each and every (3)
9 Bart Simpson's father (5)
10 Instant (5)
11 Use of numbers in counting and calculation (10)
13 Hydrophobia (6)
15 Intrigue (6)
18 People who inhabit a territory or state (10)
22 Growth on the surface of a mucous membrane (5)
23 Large pill used in veterinary medicine (5)
24 Girl's name (3)
25 Release (3,4)
26 Angry dispute (3-2)

Down

1 Palace of the Moorish kings of Granada, Spain (8)
2 Cuban dance (5)
3 Bellicose, militant (7)
4 Of delicate or slender build (6)
5 Underworld river (5)
6 Culinary art (7)
7 Tall perennial woody plant (4)
12 Throw overboard (8)
14 Pamphlet (7)
16 One who ascends on foot (7)
17 Overnight case (6)
19 Higher in position (5)
20 Synthetic fabric (5)
21 Musical composition (4)

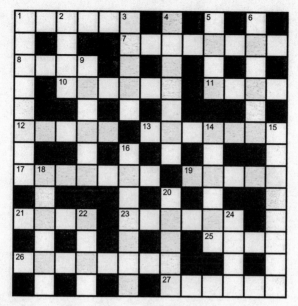

Across

1 Part of the eye (6)
7 Shipwrecked person (8)
8 Skimpy, thin (4)
10 Grand and imposing entrance (6)
11 Large brown seaweed (4)
12 Boasts (5)
13 Furtiveness (7)
17 Descriptive word or phrase (7)
19 Popular game played with pieces of stiffened paper (5)
21 Strong wind (4)
23 Devastated (6)
25 Duck's feathers (4)
26 Earmarked, reserved (3,5)
27 Substance that turns red in acid (6)

Down

1 Blameworthy (8)
2 Gather, as of crops (4)
3 Extremely sharp (5)
4 Set apart (7)
5 Position in a social hierarchy (4)
6 Mattress filled with straw (6)
9 Nothing (6)
14 Astonished (6)
15 Meeting at which election candidates address potential voters (8)
16 Resist doing something (7)
18 Supplication (6)
20 Dot on a computer screen (5)
22 Academic test (abbr) (4)
24 Disastrous destiny (4)

106

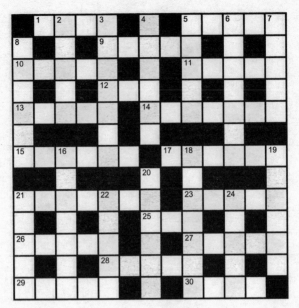

Across

1 Official symbols of a family, state, etc (4)
5 Belonging to a nobleman (5)
9 Cetacean mammal (5)
10 Make speeches (5)
11 Adult male elephants (5)
12 Consume (3)
13 Gusset (5)
14 Vainglorious conduct (7)
15 Tilt to one side (6)
17 Consequence (6)
21 Card game, a form of rummy (7)
23 Dryad (5)
25 Charge (3)
26 Dwelling (5)
27 Echo sounder (acronym) (5)
28 Depends on (5)
29 Italian poet (1265–1321) (5)
30 Constant (4)

Down

2 Carriageways (5)
3 Term of endearment (7)
4 Hearty and lusty, crude (6)
5 Prevent from entering (5)
6 Meet head-on (7)
7 Inventories (5)
8 Astrological region of constellations (6)
16 Dilapidated (3-4)
18 Skill (7)
19 Close-fitting pullover or vest (1-5)
20 Roof-supporting beam (6)
21 Vegetable used as a substitute for spinach (5)
22 Prospect (5)
24 Finely chopped meat (5)

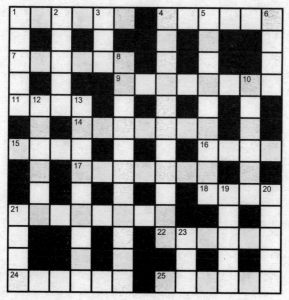

Across
1 Heaviness (6)
4 Wonder (6)
7 Alleviation (6)
9 All existing matter and space considered as a whole (8)
11 Asian plant widely cultivated for its oily beans (4)
14 Male ballet dancer (7)
15 Rivet (4)
16 Withered (4)
17 Red eruption of the skin (7)
18 Deprivation (4)
21 Dried aromatic fruit of a Caribbean tree used in cooking (8)
22 Figurine (6)
24 Sugary confections (6)
25 Free (6)

Down
1 Labours (5)
2 Filling (5)
3 Weeding tool (3)
4 House trailers, such as caravans, etc (6,5)
5 Practice session (9)
6 Entice (4)
8 Accessories (curtains, carpets, etc) for a room (11)
10 Tempests (6)
12 Popular flavour of soup (6)
13 Person to whom an envelope is written (9)
19 Eightsome (5)
20 Fertilised plant ovules (5)
21 Painting, sculpture, music, etc (4)
23 Seaman (3)

108

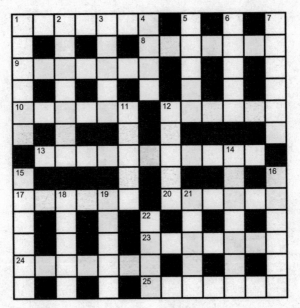

Across

1 Sent out unsolicited emails (7)
8 Reproduction (7)
9 Dressing for a wound (7)
10 Long, thin cake filled with cream (6)
12 From that place (6)
13 Principal character in a work of fiction (11)
17 Dodges (6)
20 Rich Black Forest cake (6)
23 Marriage ceremony (7)
24 Trade stoppage (7)
25 Female wild cat (7)

Down

1 Wept convulsively (6)
2 Shaped like a ring (7)
3 ___ *Vice*, TV series (5)
4 Depicted (4)
5 Unit of geological time (5)
6 Large wild ox with shaggy hair (5)
7 Kidney-shaped nut (6)
11 Interprets words (5)
12 Flexible part of a whip (5)
14 Aseptic (7)
15 Fireplace frame (6)
16 Raymond Briggs's Bogeyman (6)
18 Sun-dried brick (5)
19 ___ board, used to shape fingernails (5)
21 Relating to sound (5)
22 Not having permission to desert one's post (inits) (4)

Across

4 Live together (7)
8 Structure for open-air sports (5)
9 Set of steps (9)
10 Eighth letter of the Greek alphabet (5)
11 Popular game played on a rink (3,6)
13 Distributor of playing cards (6)
16 Not yet put into service (6)
20 Volunteer force for the defence of a country (4,5)
23 Single entities (5)
24 Ill-famed (9)
25 Relating to them (5)
26 Female stage performer (7)

Down

1 Combatted (7)
2 Biblical wife of Isaac and mother of Jacob and Esau (7)
3 Ethnic group of Kenya and Tanzania (5)
4 Place of worship (6)
5 Hunting spear (7)
6 Colour of least lightness (5)
7 Very small (coll) (5)
12 Augment (3)
14 Former name of Tokyo, Japan (3)
15 Congest (7)
17 Microchip element (7)
18 Written account (7)
19 Small, lightweight boats (6)
20 Reddish-brown hair dye (5)
21 Choral work (5)
22 Covered with a layer of fine powder (5)

110

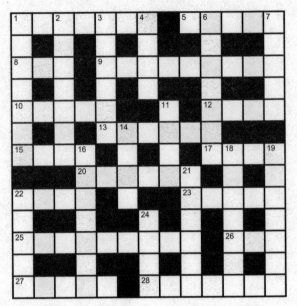

Across

1 Item made with meat and a raised pastry crust (4,3)
5 Port in southern Iraq (5)
8 Move the head up and down (3)
9 Ephemeral (9)
10 American raccoon (5)
12 Islamic ruler (4)
13 Muffle, suppress (6)
15 Boy's name (4)
17 Slightly wet (4)
20 Mainstay (6)
22 Barley used in brewing (4)
23 Open and observable (5)
25 Ride a bicycle with the pedals at rest (9)
26 Umberto ____, author of *Foucault's Pendulum* (3)
27 Throbs dully (5)
28 Muscular weakness caused by nerve damage (7)

Down

1 Hypothetical remedy for all ills or diseases (7)
2 Bureaucratic procedure (3,4)
3 Regional dialect (6)
4 Panache (4)
6 Liquorice-flavoured herb (7)
7 Later on (5)
11 Rounded thickly curled hairdo (4)
14 Short, sharp nail with a broad head (4)
16 Reflective road stud (4-3)
18 Perpetually young (7)
19 Inciting sympathy and sorrow (7)
21 Hair curler (6)
22 Secret criminal group in Sicily (5)
24 Honk (4)

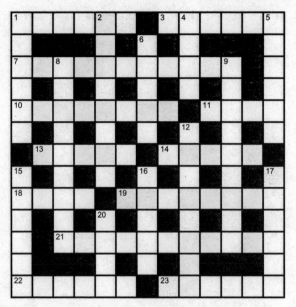

Across

1 Security, sanctuary (6)
3 Trousers for casual wear (6)
7 Science or practice of building or flying aircraft (11)
10 Not free to move about (8)
11 Attention (4)
13 Give way (5)
14 Biblical tower intended to reach to heaven (5)
18 Drizzle (4)
19 At a regular rate or pace (8)
21 One who does not live in a particular place (3-8)
22 One employed to make written copies of documents (6)
23 Automatic response (6)

Down

1 Try to locate (6)
2 Palpable (8)
4 Placed in position (4)
5 Tool similar to a spade (6)
6 Hand tool for boring holes (5)
8 Performance of a musical composition (9)
9 Drink, a mixture of lager and cider (9)
12 Mild cathartic (8)
15 German composer, Johannes ___ (1833–1897) (6)
16 Alternative (5)
17 Phrase structure (6)
20 Handle (4)

112

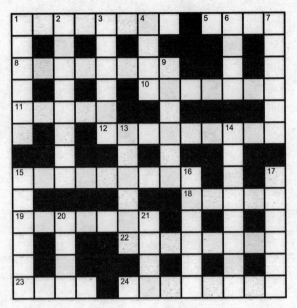

Across

1 Decorate with heraldic arms (8)
5 Male children, sons (4)
8 Fail to take into account (8)
10 Ask earnestly (7)
11 Racecourse at which the Derby and the Oaks are run (5)
12 Flag hoisted when a ship is about to sail (4,5)
15 Compass point at 225 degrees (5-4)
18 Friendship (5)
19 To sum up, concisely (2,5)
22 Fashion business, colloquially (3,5)
23 Red eruption of the skin (4)
24 Unable to appreciate music (4-4)

Down

1 Guided anti-ship missile (6)
2 Traditional words used when hearing someone sneeze (5,3)
3 Great coolness and composure (6)
4 Musical instrument (4)
6 Erstwhile (4)
7 Man who courts a woman (6)
9 Rests on bended legs (6)
13 Attorney (6)
14 Make neat, smart, or trim (8)
15 Sharpshooter (6)
16 Chatter (6)
17 Me (6)
20 Small pieces (4)
21 Portuguese city in the Algarve (4)

Across

1 Medical instrument used to inject (7)
7 Rat or mouse, for example (6)
9 Earth and water creations made by children (3,4)
10 Of the countryside (5)
11 Skim along swiftly and easily (4)
12 Manufacturer (5)
16 Chill out (5)
17 Rent (4)
21 Parts of a plant typically found under the ground (5)
22 Mineral source (3,4)
23 Strike against forcefully (6)
24 Woven floor coverings (7)

Down

1 Conjecture (7)
2 Metallic element of the platinum group (7)
3 Lowest point (5)
4 Bird which inhabits ponds and lakes (7)
5 Hair on the chin (5)
6 Showing deterioration from age, as with bread for example (5)
8 Moving staircase (9)
13 Infectious viral disease (7)
14 Varied (7)
15 Painfully desirous of another's advantages (7)
18 Snatches (5)
19 Largest artery of the body (5)
20 American ____, poisonous shrub (5)

114

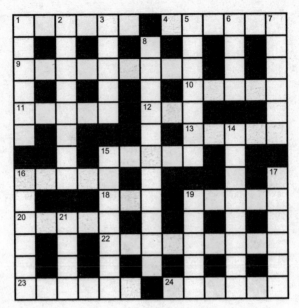

Across

1 Fawning dependant (6)
4 Loud confused noise from many sources (6)
9 Viewing comprehensively and extensively (9)
10 Beginning of an offensive (5)
11 Ordered series (5)
12 Bring to a close (3)
13 Sufferer from Hansen's disease (5)
15 Came to terms with (3,2)
16 Purchaser (5)
18 Hostelry (3)
19 Frame of iron bars to hold a fire (5)
20 Conduits for fluids (5)
22 Chatty (9)
23 Farm implement used to break up soil (6)
24 Dire warning (6)

Down

1 Apply badly or incorrectly (6)
2 As a rule (8)
3 Abnormally fat (5)
5 Iniquitous, sinful (7)
6 Establishments where alcoholic drinks are served (4)
7 Gentle teasing (6)
8 Extricate, free from complications or difficulties (11)
14 Animal or plant that lives in or on a host (8)
15 Cartilage (7)
16 Monetary plan (6)
17 Most recent (6)
19 Grate (teeth) (5)
21 Monk's cubicle (4)

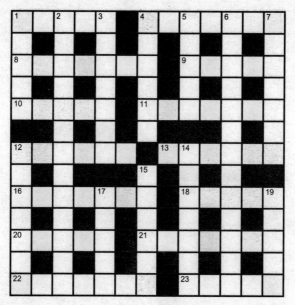

Across

1 Bus garage (5)
4 Pillars (7)
8 Islands of the Pacific and adjacent seas, collectively (7)
9 Heave, regurgitate (5)
10 Beach, strand (5)
11 Assistance in time of difficulty (7)
12 Grabbed forcefully (6)
13 Superior monks (6)
16 Greek currency unit prior to the euro (7)
18 Footwear (5)
20 Flexible appendages of animals (5)
21 More clamorous (7)
22 Innocent, without fault (7)
23 Supple (5)

Down

1 Sag (5)
2 Avoidance of plain dealing (13)
3 Tax imposed on ships (7)
4 Rough (6)
5 Meant to be sung (5)
6 Specialist in the study of weather and climate (13)
7 Globes, orbs (7)
12 Tranquillises (7)
14 Resembling an animal (7)
15 City on the French Riviera, the site of an annual film festival (6)
17 Careless speed (5)
19 Dish out (5)

116

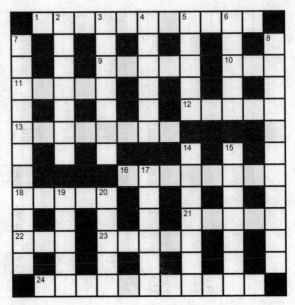

Across

1 Rapid and intense programme of training (5,6)
9 Women's quarters (5)
10 Moldovan monetary unit (3)
11 Same again (5)
12 Swellings, protuberances (5)
13 Separately priced items from a menu (1,2,5)
16 Plentiful (8)
18 Exchanges for money (5)
21 Norwegian dramatist (5)
22 Ms Herzigova, supermodel (3)
23 Kindly endorsement and guidance (5)
24 Printing from a plate with raised characters (11)

Down

2 Device for catching rodents (3,4)
3 Learned person (7)
4 Three-valved brass musical instrument (6)
5 Cause to lose one's nerve (5)
6 Three-dimensional shape (5)
7 Children's search and find game (4-3-4)
8 Marginal resources for existence (11)
14 Front tooth (7)
15 Dried grapes (7)
17 Carnivorous burrowing mammal (6)
19 Depart, go (5)
20 Column, of light for example (5)

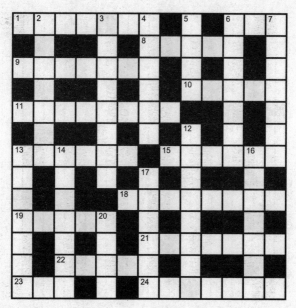

Across
1 Fast-running bird (7)
6 Speck (3)
8 Liquorice-flavoured seeds (5)
9 Open-topped glass flasks used for serving wine or water (7)
10 Ceremonial elegance and splendour (5)
11 Velocipedes (8)
13 Traps for birds or small mammals (6)
15 Humour (6)
18 Restore confidence in (8)
19 Kitchen appliance used for cooking food (5)
21 Fleshy pendulous part of the hearing organ (7)
22 Avowed (5)
23 Relax in a chair (3)
24 Plucked (7)

Down
2 Large, ocean-dwelling mammal (3,4)
3 Contaminated with a virus (8)
4 Hurry (6)
5 Sagacious (4)
6 Express strong disapproval of (7)
7 Leon ____, Russian revolutionary associated with Lenin (7)
12 Fruit preserved by cooking with sugar (8)
13 Distilled alcoholic beverages (7)
14 In the middle of (7)
16 Hard-wearing (7)
17 One who rules during the absence of a monarch (6)
20 Very dark black (4)

118

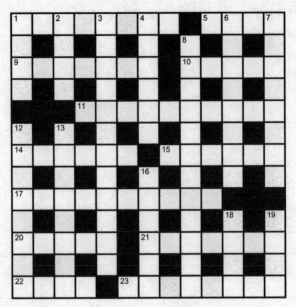

Across

1 Too self-assertive, boastful (8)
5 Hoots with derision (4)
9 Land area, especially of a farm (7)
10 Off the cuff (2-3)
11 Cold dessert baked in a crumb crust (10)
14 Borough of New York City, ___ Island (6)
15 Living, independent things (6)
17 Building where musical dramas are performed (5,5)
20 Contort (5)
21 Basic unit of currency in Nicaragua (7)
22 Collection of facts (4)
23 Crystalline rock that can be cut for jewellery (8)

Down

1 Muslim prayer leader (4)
2 Mother of Jesus (4)
3 Capital punishment (5,7)
4 Israeli monetary unit (6)
6 Medium used by artists (3,5)
7 Put under water (8)
8 Flexible rulers (4,8)
12 Miscellaneous (8)
13 Procedure carried out by a cosmetic surgeon (8)
16 Yarn of looped or curled ply (6)
18 Ms Chanel, fashion designer (4)
19 Bundle of straw or hay (4)

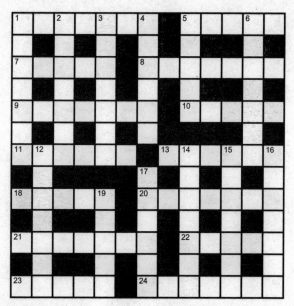

Across
1 Street plan (4,3)
5 Relish served with food (5)
7 Cultivates by growing (5)
8 Having a cigarette (7)
9 Variety of mandarin orange (7)
10 Brook (5)
11 Diminish (6)
13 Large heavy rope for nautical use (6)
18 Decorate to make more attractive (5)
20 Ancestry (7)
21 Island country, capital Nassau (7)
22 Sophisticated, smooth (5)
23 Roost (5)
24 Kitchen appliance (7)

Down
1 Denial (7)
2 Impregnates with oxygen (7)
3 Bad or disorderly government (7)
4 Relating to the system for delivering mail (6)
5 Unemotional person (5)
6 Call together (for a meeting) (7)
12 Final stages of an extended process of negotiation (7)
14 Loss of memory (7)
15 Material used to form a hard coating on a porous surface (7)
16 Graceful woodland animal (3,4)
17 Clothes cupboard (6)
19 Minor goddess of nature (5)

120

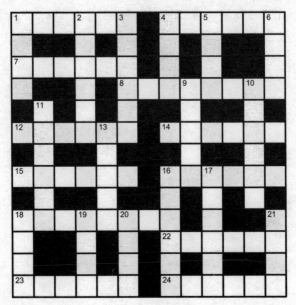

Across

1 Made illegal payments to, in exchange for favours or influence (6)
4 Be preoccupied with something (6)
7 Rectifies (6)
8 Till where money is taken for goods purchased (4,4)
12 Women (6)
14 Radio antenna (6)
15 Aircraft shed (6)
16 Reference point to shoot at (6)
18 Make again (8)
22 Helix (6)
23 Tool used for bending wire (6)
24 Drowsy (6)

Down

1 Obnoxious child (4)
2 Tiny Japanese tree (6)
3 Object thrown in athletic competitions (6)
4 ___ and ends (4)
5 Wearing footgear (4)
6 Hessian bag (4)
9 Dog-like nocturnal mammal (5)
10 Electric razor (6)
11 Capital of Zimbabwe (6)
13 Dodge (5)
16 Dissertation (6)
17 Experience again, often in the imagination (6)
18 Inclined surface (4)
19 Ill-mannered (4)
20 Gives assistance (4)
21 Fine-grained soil which becomes hard when fired (4)

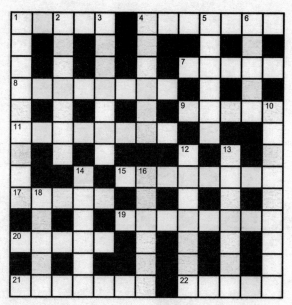

Across

1 Bout, period of indulgence (5)
4 J D Salinger novel, *The ___ in the Rye* (7)
7 Light brown colour (5)
8 Style that draws the hair back so that it hangs down (8)
9 Fourth letter of the Greek alphabet (5)
11 Colander (8)
15 Mischievous adventure (8)
17 Judge's hammer (5)
19 State of inactivity or stagnation (8)
20 Noise (5)
21 Alter (a document or statement) fraudulently (7)
22 Saline (5)

Down

1 Conjecturing (9)
2 Conventional nickname for a fox (7)
3 Image boost (3-4)
4 Appealing to refined taste (6)
5 Bordeaux wine (6)
6 Discharge (5)
10 Small item carried or worn to complement an outfit (9)
12 Parts by which things are picked up (7)
13 Non-synthetic (7)
14 Court game (6)
16 Without much speed (6)
18 Hawaiian greeting (5)

122

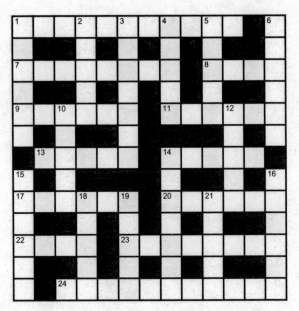

Across

1 Sensible and practical (4-2-5)
7 Arm of the North Atlantic to the west of Wales (5,3)
8 Roman cloak (4)
9 Put down by force (6)
11 Fodder harvested while green (6)
13 Emblem worn like a brooch (5)
14 Edible smooth-skinned fruits with a single hard stone (5)
17 Young cattle (6)
20 Light shoe with straps (6)
22 Faucets (4)
23 Enough (8)
24 Loose, licentious (11)

Down

1 Most lacking in moisture (6)
2 Pried (5)
3 Designed to incite to indecency (7)
4 John Quincy ____, sixth president of the United States (5)
5 Absolute (5)
6 Lacking even the rudiments of courage (6)
10 Noisy altercation (5)
12 Targeted (5)
14 Advertising signs (7)
15 Implement for cutting grass (6)
16 Extraterrestrial beings (6)
18 Peak of a cap (5)
19 Group of many insects (5)
21 Island republic in the South Pacific Ocean (5)

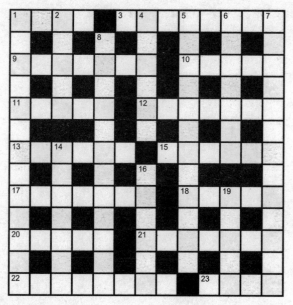

Across

1 Nautical term used in hailing (4)

3 Aversion (8)

9 Display of bad temper (7)

10 Divisions of a pound sterling (5)

11 Broker (5)

12 Deluge (7)

13 Sprinted (6)

15 Large shrimps cooked in breadcrumbs (6)

17 The act of coming together again (7)

18 Historical object (5)

20 Bringing death (5)

21 Motionlessness (7)

22 Continually complaining or finding fault (8)

23 Uncastrated male hog (4)

Down

1 Creations of decorative design and handiwork (4,3,6)

2 One sixteenth of a pound (5)

4 Prisoner (6)

5 Apparatus for setting down and playing back sounds (4,8)

6 Ray of natural light (7)

7 Instrument of execution in the USA (8,5)

8 Husband of one's sister (7-2-3)

14 Mechanical device on a camera (7)

16 Slow-moving molluscs (6)

19 Bingo (5)

124

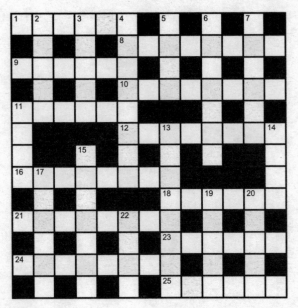

Across

1 Depletes (4,2)
8 Roused (8)
9 Arctic canoes (6)
10 Australian state, capital Hobart (8)
11 One who grants a tenancy (6)
12 Responded (8)
16 Surpassing what is common (8)
18 Designate (6)
21 Declares an objection (8)
23 Become set (6)
24 Conference attendee (8)
25 Reached the highest point of (6)

Down

2 Line on which music is written (5)
3 Totters (5)
4 Highly seasoned cut of smoked beef (8)
5 Empty spaces between things (4)
6 Periods of ten years (7)
7 Country formerly known as British Honduras (6)
11 Racing sled for one or two people (4)
13 Dashes a liquid against (8)
14 Wish harm upon (4)
15 Climate (7)
17 County in southern England (6)
19 Country, capital Damascus (5)
20 Domestic birds (5)
22 Card game (4)

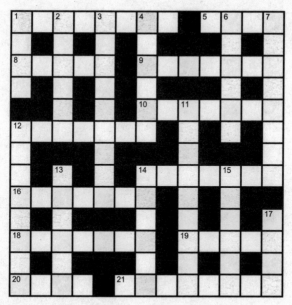

Across

1 Portable travelling bag for carrying clothes (8)
5 Public passenger vehicle (4)
8 Man-made fibre (5)
9 Declined (7)
10 Central part of an atom (7)
12 Dessert (7)
14 Brief statement that presents the main points (7)
16 Schematic or technical drawing (7)
18 Strait (7)
19 Belonging to them (5)
20 Gyrate (4)
21 Group of persons gathered together for a common purpose (8)

Down

1 Disappeared beneath the waves (4)
2 Away from the coast (6)
3 Holder (9)
4 Leapt (6)
6 Passages between rows of seats (6)
7 Organised action of making of goods for sale (8)
11 Group delegated to consider some matter (9)
12 Brings out for display (8)
13 USA state, capital Honolulu (6)
14 Odours (6)
15 Part of speech (6)
17 Military land force (4)

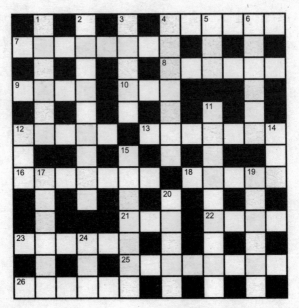

Across

4 Kidnap (6)
7 Small sacks of dried seeds used in children's games (8)
8 Medicinal pill (6)
9 Celebrity (4)
10 ___ Tolstoy, Russian writer (3)
12 Look at intently (5)
13 Let loose (7)
16 Noisy talk (7)
18 Burial chamber (5)
21 Common rodent (3)
22 Indian bread, baked in a clay oven (4)
23 Appliance that corrects dental irregularities (6)
25 Person with a record of successes (8)
26 Overly sweet and sugary (6)

Down

1 Pour from a bottle into one more ornate (6)
2 Moral soundness (9)
3 In a poor way (5)
4 Amaze (7)
5 Present a knighthood (3)
6 Shouts of approval (6)
11 Oddment (9)
12 Hollow, flexible, bag-like structure (3)
14 Conspicuous success (3)
15 Rumour (7)
17 Every sixty minutes (6)
19 Lent out (6)
20 Deserving of a scratch (5)
24 French vineyard or group of vineyards (3)

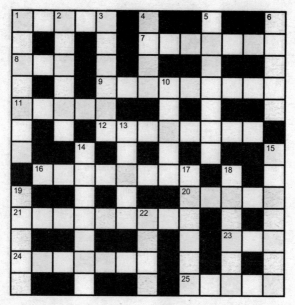

Across

1 Old Testament prophet (5)
7 Natural height of a person (7)
8 Destiny (3)
9 Congenial (9)
11 Stairs (5)
12 Royal title (8)
16 Disease caused by lack of thiamine (4-4)
20 American raccoon (5)
21 Sparkling citrus fruit drink (9)
23 Shack (3)
24 Saliva, especially as ejected from the mouth (7)
25 Premature (5)

Down

1 Spiritless man or youth (7)
2 Cotton fabric with a shiny finish (6)
3 Game played in an enclosed court (6)
4 Person who employs something (4)
5 Wandered away (7)
6 Central pillar of a circular staircase (5)
10 Gas formerly used as an anaesthetic (5)
13 Suffuse with colour (5)
14 Three people considered as a unit (7)
15 Very holy or virtuous (7)
17 Glacial period in Earth's history (3,3)
18 Collect together (6)
19 Brag (5)
22 Pinnacle (4)

128

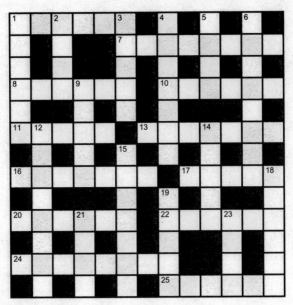

Across

1 Person who carries equipment on an expedition (6)
7 Bête noire (8)
8 Land on which food is grown (6)
10 Refusal to admit something (6)
11 Enquired (5)
13 Hot and spicy (7)
16 Difficult, entangling situation (3,4)
17 Repairs (5)
20 Shakespearean play (6)
22 "Open ____", magic words used by Ali Baba (6)
24 Oil used as fuel in lamps (8)
25 Shelled, aquatic reptile (6)

Down

1 Yellow fruit (6)
2 Primitive chlorophyll-containing, mainly aquatic organism (4)
3 One who drives cars at high speeds (5)
4 Encrusted with sugar (7)
5 Part of the lower jaw (4)
6 Diminished in strength or quality (8)
9 Noise made by a sheep (5)
12 Brine (8)
14 Machine used for printing (5)
15 New Testament book (7)
18 Hold back to a later time (6)
19 Thing of value (5)
21 King of the beasts (4)
23 Assist in doing wrong (4)

129

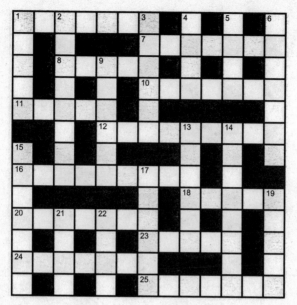

Across

1 Anton ____, Russian dramatist (1860–1904) (7)
7 Carry out a killing (7)
8 Couples (5)
10 Compress (7)
11 Fruits of the blackthorn (5)
12 Unsure and constrained in manner (3,2,4)
16 Resolutely courageous (9)
18 Loved (5)
20 Causes harm or hurt (7)
23 Particular items (5)
24 Sticky substance made from sugar (7)
25 Childhood disease caused by deficiency of vitamin D (7)

Down

1 Missives used as birthday or Christmas greetings (5)
2 Put to work (8)
3 Craft designed for water transportation (6)
4 Dandy (4)
5 Naked (4)
6 Official who is expected to ensure fair play (7)
9 Being in the original position (2,4)
13 Walk unsteadily, as a small child (6)
14 Not deficient in intellect (coll) (3,5)
15 Collide violently with an obstacle (3,4)
17 Sample (6)
19 Fruits of the palm tree (5)
21 Scoff (4)
22 Large stone (4)

130

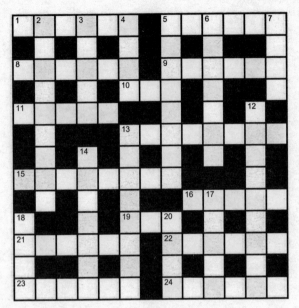

Across

1 Close of day (6)
5 Front of a building (6)
8 Stoneworkers (6)
9 Grasp eagerly (6)
10 Outfit (3)
11 Boarding-house for holidaymakers (5)
13 Placed very near together (5-3)
15 Elaborate (8)
16 Become less intense (5)
19 ___ City, 2005 film (3)
21 Failing in what duty requires (6)
22 Expenditure (6)
23 Austin ___, movie character played by Mike Myers (6)
24 Cut into small pieces (6)

Down

2 Not decorated (9)
3 Push roughly (5)
4 Chore (4)
5 Meal which can be prepared and served quickly (4,4)
6 Climb awkwardly (7)
7 Reverberation (4)
12 Sink in (9)
13 Person of exceptional importance and reputation (8)
14 Overturn (a boat) accidentally (7)
17 Conducting stick (5)
18 Stage item (4)
20 Standard (4)

Across
1 Devoted to a cause or purpose (9)
8 Approximate (5)
9 Prefix meaning recent or modern
10 Cut into pieces (5)
11 Despatches (5)
12 Cattle farm (5)
13 Most broad (6)
14 Semi-liquid mixture of flour, eggs and milk, used in cooking (6)
18 Striped animal (5)
21 Give form to (5)
23 Above average in size (5)
24 And not (3)
25 Public dance hall (5)
26 Division of the week (9)

Down
1 Ridges of sand created by the wind (5)
2 Killed by submerging in water (7)
3 X marks (7)
4 Removing (6)
5 Appliance that removes moisture (5)
6 Relating to a person (5)
7 Conjunction expressing a doubt or choice between alternatives (7)
13 Sorcerers (7)
15 Non-attendance (7)
16 Instructed (7)
17 Compelled (6)
19 Sweep (5)
20 Permit (5)
22 Before the expected time (5)

132

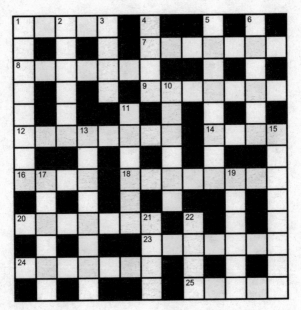

Across
1 Facing of a jacket (5)
7 Remainder (7)
8 Country dwelling (7)
9 Cherubic (7)
12 Loose-fitting white ecclesiastical vestment (8)
14 Brings to a close (4)
16 Basic unit of currency in Germany (4)
18 Not registered (8)
20 As a minimum (2,5)
23 Whip used to inflict punishment (7)
24 Seedless raisin (7)
25 Small heron (5)

Down
1 Ball game played with long-handled racquets (8)
2 Maker of earthenware vessels (6)
3 Metallic element, symbol Pb (4)
4 Waste product useful as a fertiliser (4)
5 Enduring (8)
6 Hidden underground (6)
10 Pine leaf (6)
11 Causes to feel resentment or indignation (6)
13 Possessions (8)
15 Matter deposited at the bottom of a lake, for example (8)
17 False (6)
19 Extreme fear (6)
21 Russian emperor (4)
22 Elect (4)

133

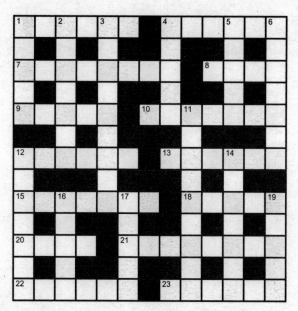

Across

1 Offer suggestions (6)
4 Satellite of Jupiter (6)
7 Psychological disorder characterised by delusions of persecution or grandeur (8)
8 Salve, ointment (4)
9 Fragrant resin used as incense (5)
10 Analgesic substance (7)
12 Held responsible (6)
13 Mistakes (6)
15 Relating to the eye socket (7)
18 Be important (5)
20 Caustic (4)
21 Illegal action inciting resistance to lawful authority (8)
22 Glutinous (6)
23 More orderly (6)

Down

1 Abundant (5)
2 Plant also known as vervain (7)
3 Feeling, often of nostalgia (9)
4 Greek muse of lyric poetry (5)
5 Giraffe-like creature (5)
6 Adrift (7)
11 Pronouncement encouraging or banning some activity (9)
12 Organic matter used as fuel (7)
14 Eye doctor (7)
16 Russian pancake (5)
17 Put to the test (5)
19 Radio set (5)

134

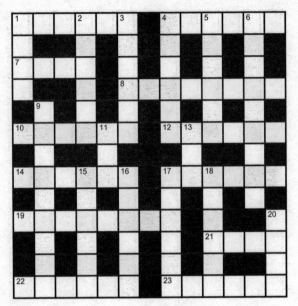

Across

1 Give in (6)
4 Small pleasure boat powered by cycling (6)
7 Tori ___, singer (4)
8 Person who runs at speed over a short distance (8)
10 Swim like a dog in shallow water (6)
12 Sacredly obscure (6)
14 Invasion by pathogenic bacteria (6)
17 Envelop (6)
19 Proprietary trademark of a popular soft drink (4-4)
21 Halo of light (4)
22 Small pieces of bread, for example (6)
23 Walk with long steps (6)

Down

1 Stony waste matter (4)
2 Disguised (6)
3 Paper handkerchief (6)
4 Organised persecution of an ethnic group (6)
5 Takes in fluid (6)
6 Focus of public attention (9)
9 One who arrives after the expected time (9)
11 Floral garland (3)
13 Coniferous tree (3)
15 Ski race over a winding course (6)
16 Hits with a missile (6)
17 Humiliates (6)
18 Liaison, romantic intrigue (6)
20 Donated (4)

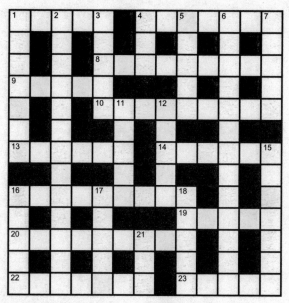

135

Across

1 Firm and hearty (5)
4 Enthusiastic approval (7)
8 Surgical procedure (9)
9 Wears out (5)
10 Free from disorder (9)
13 Haphazard (6)
14 Put together two or more pieces (4,2)
16 Formal separation from an alliance or federation (9)
19 Had better (5)
20 Woodworker (9)
22 Emanating from stars (7)
23 Songs of praise (5)

Down

1 Disperse (7)
2 Rate at which experience is acquired (8,5)
3 Worthless material (5)
4 Bladed chopping tool (3)
5 Gambling game using two dice (5)
6 Major division of the natural world (6,7)
7 Cut into small pieces (5)
11 Organic component of soil (5)
12 Debilitating viral disease (5)
15 Social gatherings (7)
16 Religious orders (5)
17 Carapace (5)
18 Compass point (5)
21 Pitch (3)

136

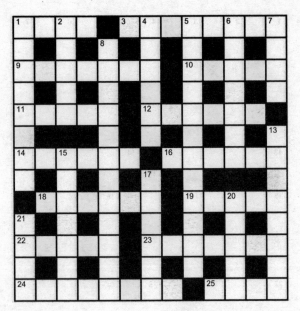

Across

1 Site of the famous Leaning Tower (4)
3 Telephone switchboard assistant (8)
9 Going well with, complementing (7)
10 Civilian clothing (5)
11 Land surrounded by water (5)
12 Converted to leather (6)
14 Bedding material (6)
16 March in a procession (6)
18 Capital of Mali (6)
19 Estate to which a wife is entitled on the death of her husband (5)
22 Close-fitting (5)
23 Enfold (7)
24 Lipstick, for example (8)
25 God of love, also known as Cupid (4)

Down

1 Capable of happening or existing (8)
2 Pig food (5)
4 Home for a hog (6)
5 Cylindrical fireworks (5,7)
6 Lustrous material (7)
7 Sudden attack (4)
8 Gossip (6-6)
13 Intrepid (8)
15 Lachrymator (4,3)
17 Art of growing miniature trees (6)
20 Basic drink (5)
21 Of or relating to the ear (4)

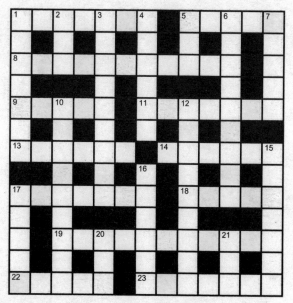

Across

1 Athletic competition in which a heavy metal ball is hurled (4,3)
5 Slender, graceful young woman (5)
8 Hate coupled with disgust (11)
9 Capital of Vietnam (5)
11 Slanted letters (7)
13 Season of the year (6)
14 Insusceptible (6)
17 Unbearable physical pain (7)
18 Slumber (5)
19 Document of credentials (11)
22 Pass along (5)
23 Latticework used to support climbing plants (7)

Down

1 Breaks violently into pieces (7)
2 Yoko ____, widow of John Lennon (3)
3 Special advantage or benefit not enjoyed by all (9)
4 Deeply sad (6)
5 Travel across snow (3)
6 Angular distance of a place east or west of the Greenwich meridian (9)
7 Bristles (5)
10 Digital (9)
12 Truce (9)
15 Female ruler of many countries (7)
16 Exacting (6)
17 Photocopier ink (5)
20 Beam (of light) (3)
21 Completely (3)

138

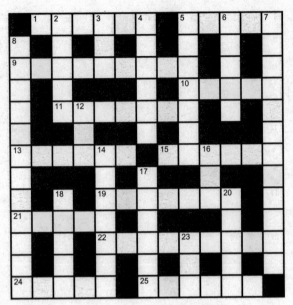

Across

1 Pressure line on a weather map (6)
5 Sharp projections on the paws of an animal (5)
9 Time between midday and evening (9)
10 Someone who works underwater (5)
11 Exhaust, use up (7)
13 Not elegant or graceful (6)
15 Chivalrous nobleman (6)
19 Hone (7)
21 Hits with a flat object (especially of flies) (5)
22 Given to copying (9)
24 Murdered (5)
25 Oesophagus (6)

Down

2 Replete (5)
3 Exclude (3)
4 Greek island in the Aegean Sea (6)
5 Censure (7)
6 Higher up (5)
7 Infectious bacterial disease affecting especially children (7,5)
8 Tool used for manicure (4,8)
12 Deciduous tree (3)
14 Meeting devoted to a particular activity (7)
16 Coat a cake with sugar (3)
17 Maxim (6)
18 Sweat room (5)
20 Racket (5)
23 Be unwell (3)

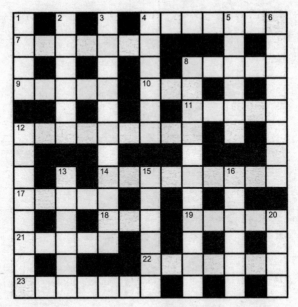

Across

4 Crash helmet, colloquially (4,3)
7 London football club (7)
8 Left over, superfluous (5)
9 Native of Muscat, eg (5)
10 Expression of disapproval (3)
11 Correct (text) (5)
12 Indigestion (9)
14 Exposing human folly to ridicule (9)
17 Indian side dish of yogurt and chopped cucumbers (5)
18 Male sheep (3)
19 Immature insect (5)
21 Boxer's return punch (5)
22 One who interprets text, especially scripture (7)
23 Fishing boat that uses a dragnet (7)

Down

1 Lower part of an interior wall (4)
2 Written stories (6)
3 Day of remembrance (11)
4 Thin layers of rock used for roofing (6)
5 Guide (6)
6 Exceptionally bad (8)
8 Road construction vehicle (11)
12 Lacking physical strength or vitality (8)
13 Long jagged mountain chain (6)
15 Moderate (6)
16 Foundation garment (6)
20 Chief port of Yemen (4)

140

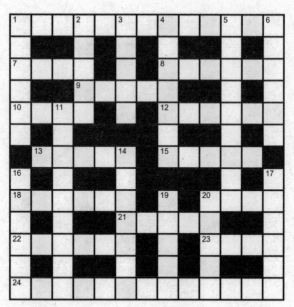

Across

1 Too small to make a significant difference (13)
7 Units of work or energy (4)
8 Modernise (6)
9 Long journeys on foot (5)
10 Weedy annual grass (4)
12 Restrains from moving or operating normally (4,2)
13 Felt concern or interest (5)
15 Oarsman (5)
18 Private party in the evening (6)
20 Consciousness of one's own identity (4)
21 Sheltered from light or heat (5)
22 Units of length (6)
23 Tidings (4)
24 Officer ranking immediately below the head of an organisation (4,9)

Down

1 Form a mental image (6)
2 Ski run densely packed with snow (5)
3 Jolly ____, pirates' flag (5)
4 Clump, bundle (7)
5 Woman's undergarment (9)
6 Excepted (6)
11 Lifelike (9)
14 Chest of drawers (7)
16 Isaac ____, science fiction author (6)
17 Compensate for (6)
19 Gives one's support or approval to (5)
20 Church council (5)

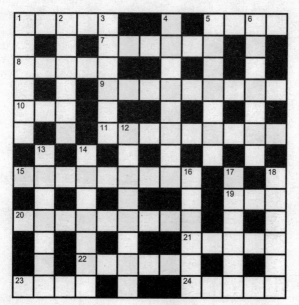

Across
1 Digit of the hand (5)
5 Villein (4)
7 Disquiet (6)
8 Santa ____, Father Christmas (5)
9 Period within which something must be completed (4,5)
10 Chap (3)
11 Capable of seeing to a great distance (5-4)
15 Criminal who smashes a shop window with a vehicle (3-6)
19 Immoral act (3)
20 Integral to a plan of action, especially in war (9)
21 Call to mind (5)
22 Goes in (6)
23 Gas used in lighting (4)
24 Casts off (5)

Down
1 Fishing gear (6)
2 Country, capital Kampala (6)
3 Commotion (6)
4 Military wake-up call (8)
5 Banded with pieces of contrasting colour (7)
6 Lived (7)
12 Liquorice-flavoured sweet liqueur (8)
13 Prisoner (7)
14 Make wider (7)
16 Cove (6)
17 On land (6)
18 Not if (6)

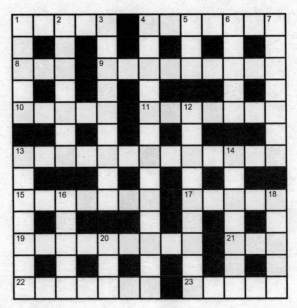

Across

1 Strong sweeping cut (5)
4 Breastbone (7)
8 Belonging to us (3)
9 God-fearing (9)
10 Exhaust-driven engine compressor, in short (5)
11 Staying power (7)
13 Cultured, appealing to those having worldly knowledge and refinement (13)
15 Masses of snow permanently covering the land (7)
17 Growing older (5)
19 Raising (bread, etc) with yeast (9)
21 Her (3)
22 Greatly feared (7)
23 Illuminated (3,2)

Down

1 Pathfinder (5)
2 Delivery from a plane or helicopter (7)
3 Mouth organ (9)
4 Smugly complacent (4-9)
5 Hen's produce (3)
6 Old Testament mother-in-law of Ruth (5)
7 Popular hot condiment (7)
12 Heavenly being of the highest rank (9)
13 Expert (7)
14 Matching cardigan and pullover worn at the same time (7)
16 Wipe off (5)
18 Urge a horse to go faster (3,2)
20 Conclusion (3)

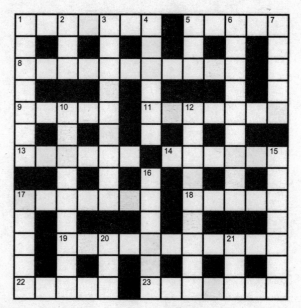

Across

1 Do away with (7)
5 Bored, having had enough (3,2)
8 Shaving tool with a guard to prevent deep cuts in the skin (6,5)
9 Not in any circumstances (5)
11 Interlace (7)
13 Large edible predatory eel (6)
14 Traditional Christmas songs (6)
17 Native of Eilat, for example (7)
18 Short poem of rural life (5)
19 State of being suitable or opportune (11)
22 Chirp (5)
23 Monetary unit of Malaysia (7)

Down

1 Poisonous metallic element (7)
2 No longer attached (3)
3 Happen or take place between other events (9)
4 Courageous men (6)
5 Felt cap of Morocco (3)
6 Large sleeping room containing several beds (9)
7 Military chaplain (5)
10 Chamber of the heart (9)
12 Custom (9)
15 Outstanding (7)
16 One-dimensional (6)
17 Block of metal (5)
20 Hard-shelled seed (3)
21 Henpeck (3)

144

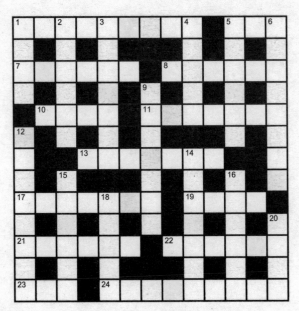

Across

1 Restore to life (9)
5 Limb (3)
7 Italian brandy made from residue of grapes after pressing (6)
8 Endured (6)
10 Lairs (4)
11 Chemical used in reactions (7)
13 Truth (7)
17 Raised in rank (7)
19 Laugh loudly and harshly (4)
21 Locations (6)
22 Directions for cooking something (6)
23 Large monkey (3)
24 Disorderly outburst or tumult (9)

Down

1 Feeling of intense anger (4)
2 Drool (6)
3 Quick-witted retort (7)
4 Jewelled headdress (5)
5 Deer's horn (6)
6 Reflect deeply on a subject (8)
9 Overture (7)
12 Climbing garden plant with fragrant flowers (5,3)
14 Group of people attractively arranged (7)
15 Roof of the mouth (6)
16 List of fixed charges (6)
18 Adjust finely (5)
20 Give up, relinquish (4)

145

Across

1 Noisy quarrel (6)
5 Taken dishonestly (6)
8 Flexible containers (4)
9 Roomy (8)
10 Thick sugary liquid (5)
11 Turn aside (7)
14 Manage with what one has (4,2)
15 Not certain (6)
17 Start out on a sea voyage (3,4)
19 Terrace (5)
21 Type of neuralgia which affects the hips (8)
23 Abreast of (4)
24 American biscuit (6)
25 Plant with spiny bracts (6)

Down

2 Commercially produced for immediate use (5-4)
3 Dress (7)
4 Girdle (4)
5 Distribute, allocate (5,3)
6 Projecting bay window (5)
7 Flightless Australian bird (3)
12 Meat-eating animal (9)
13 Murder (8)
16 Kitchen utensil used for spreading (7)
18 Crude dwelling (5)
20 Food used in a trap (4)
22 Make the sound of a dove (3)

146

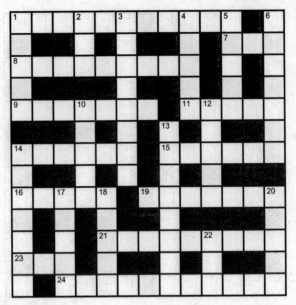

Across

1 Child of an aunt or uncle (5,6)

7 Judo belt (3)

8 Acute spasmodic nerve pain (9)

9 Skinny (7)

11 Cut in two (5)

14 Block the passage through (6)

15 Increase twofold (6)

16 Military dictators (5)

19 Mail (7)

21 Manner of existing (9)

23 Hour at which something is due (inits) (3)

24 Take apart (11)

Down

1 Hollow teeth of a venomous snake (5)

2 Man's title (3)

3 Chamber within which a piston moves (8)

4 Secret store (5)

5 Book-length story (5)

6 Bishop's see (7)

10 Dexterous (5)

12 Grown-up (5)

13 State of inactivity (8)

14 Wounded (7)

17 Wanderer (5)

18 Shafts on which wheels rotate (5)

20 Sift (5)

22 Woollen cap of Scottish origin (3)

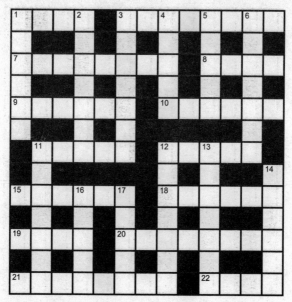

Across

1 Highland dagger (4)
3 Male shop assistant (8)
7 Be earlier in time (8)
8 Rise upward into the air (4)
9 Solemn and wise in appearance (6)
10 Rope or canvas headgear for a horse (6)
11 Marinate (5)
12 Primly out of date (5)
15 Greek 'L' (6)
18 Mariner (6)
19 Ailments (4)
20 Horse-drawn vehicle with four wheels (8)
21 Immaculately clean and unused (8)
22 Respiratory organ of a fish (4)

Down

1 Fabulous monster (6)
2 Turkish viceroy who ruled Egypt (7)
3 Serious collision (especially of motor vehicles) (5-2)
4 Bloodsucker (5)
5 Fibre used for making rope (5)
6 Place of study (7)
11 Machine that inserts metal fasteners into sheets of paper (7)
12 Be worthy of (7)
13 Putting words on paper (7)
14 Severe or trying experience (6)
16 Foundation (5)
17 Computer code representing text (inits) (5)

148

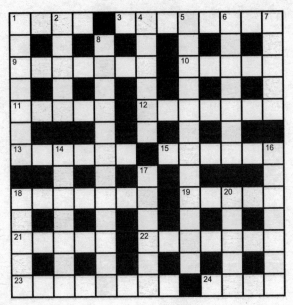

Across

1 Taunt (4)
3 Friendly (8)
9 Point of view (7)
10 Assortment (5)
11 Capital of Japan (5)
12 Arctic sled dogs (7)
13 Malleable odourless plastic explosive (6)
15 Fist fighters (6)
18 Outer adjacent area of any place (7)
19 Quietly in concealment (coll) (5)
21 Complete change of direction (1-4)
22 Of the appetites and passions of the body (7)
23 Frenzy (8)
24 Sean ____, US film actor and director (4)

Down

1 Organ of speech (7)
2 Briefly shut the eyes (5)
4 Parts of the year (6)
5 Defendant charged with adultery in a divorce proceeding (2-10)
6 Outdoor blaze (7)
7 Fencing swords (5)
8 Failure to do as one is told (12)
14 Nobleman (in various countries) ranking above a count (7)
16 Bloated (7)
17 Breakfast food of untoasted dry cereals and fruits (6)
18 Sac (5)
20 Measuring instrument (5)

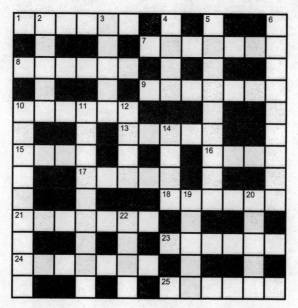

Across

1 Verbally report or maintain (6)
7 In any case (7)
8 Cut or impressed into a surface (6)
9 Cross-brace that supports a rail on a railway track (7)
10 Appraise (6)
13 Artificial gems (5)
15 Bean curd (4)
16 Capital of Latvia (4)
17 Garden tool for cutting grass on lawns (5)
18 Dreamlike state (6)
21 Make amends for, remedy (7)
23 Grade or level (6)
24 Producing a sensation of touch (7)
25 Improved, mended (6)

Down

2 Yoga position (5)
3 Judge tentatively (5)
4 Toll of a bell (4)
5 Contrariwise (4,5)
6 Early form of sextant (9)
10 Power or right to give orders or make decisions (9)
11 Determine the amount of (9)
12 Eject in large quantities (4)
14 Type (4)
19 Female ruff (5)
20 Thin pancake (5)
22 Underside of a shoe (4)

150

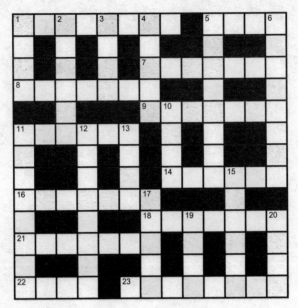

Across

1 Unceremonious and disorganised struggle (8)

5 Egyptian goddess of fertility (4)

7 Ancient city buried when Vesuvius erupted (7)

8 Marsh gas (7)

9 Filled pasta cases (7)

11 Filter out (6)

14 Sealed in a tin (6)

16 Aerial (7)

18 Not accurate (7)

21 Apparel (7)

22 Actor's portrayal of someone (4)

23 Graveyard (8)

Down

1 Former name of Thailand (4)

2 Member of a crowd causing a violent disturbance of the peace (6)

3 Aluminium silicate mineral (4)

4 Person afflicted with Hansen's disease (5)

5 Lock up in jail (8)

6 Feisty (8)

10 ____ Guinness, actor (4)

11 Police vehicle (5,3)

12 One who is not present (8)

13 Naming word (4)

15 Subtle difference in meaning (6)

17 Long, narrow passageway (5)

19 Facilitate (4)

20 People in general (4)

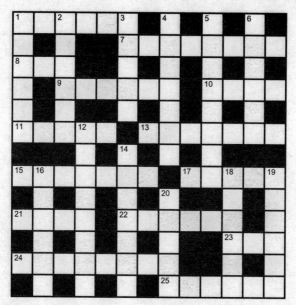

Across

1 Skilled trades (6)
7 Knitted jacket (8)
8 Rubbish dump (3)
9 Live on, persist (6)
10 Barrier consisting of a horizontal bar and supports (4)
11 Scatter in a jet of droplets (5)
13 Put under a military blockade (7)
15 Hither and ____, here and there (7)
17 Prime minister of India from 1947 to 1964 (5)
21 Broad smile (4)
22 Cover for a corpse (6)
23 Present a knighthood (3)
24 Intense (8)
25 Marked by excessive self-indulgence (6)

Down

1 Juicy fruit, such as lemon, orange, etc (6)
2 Materialise (6)
3 Clean with hard rubbing, scrub (5)
4 Person who mates and sells the offspring of animals (7)
5 Severe recurring headache (8)
6 Howling like a hound (6)
12 Person who is present and participates in a meeting (8)
14 Becomes angry (coll) (4,3)
16 Crowds (6)
18 Crowd or draw together (6)
19 Incapable (6)
20 Banal (5)

152

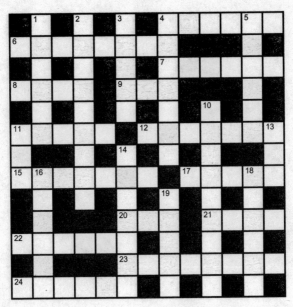

Across

4 Reject on oath (6)
6 Bald (8)
7 Run at full speed over a short distance (6)
8 Long fishes (4)
9 French vineyard or group of vineyards (3)
11 Increased, raised (5)
12 Unit of area equal to 10,000 square metres (7)
15 Whole number (7)
17 Social position or status (5)
20 Promissory note (inits) (3)
21 Heredity unit (4)
22 Horse's pace between a trot and a gallop (6)
23 Ecstatic (8)
24 Surprise attack (6)

Down

1 Fabricated (4,2)
2 Squinting, having convergent strabismus (5-4)
3 Area of sand sloping down to the water (5)
4 Adopted in order to deceive (7)
5 Campanologist (6)
10 In an odd manner (9)
11 Israeli submachine-gun (3)
13 Female sheep (3)
14 Revival of learning and culture (7)
16 Highly incendiary liquid used in fire bombs (6)
18 Becomes stretched or taut (6)
19 Asian dish eaten with rice (5)

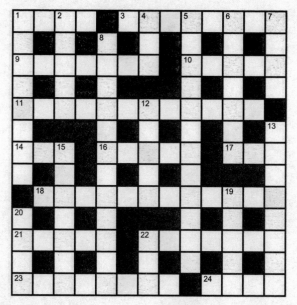

Across

1 Junk email (4)
3 Dutch spirit distilled from potatoes (8)
9 Criticising harshly on a web site (coll) (7)
10 Rich cake (5)
11 Having an appearance of solidity or relief (12)
14 Ignited (3)
16 Mischievous fairies (5)
17 Hawaiian garland of flowers (3)
18 Perusing and correcting printed matter (12)
21 Small drum played with the hands (5)
22 Person whose job it is to dust and vacuum, etc (7)
23 Writer of literary works (8)
24 Impulse (4)

Down

1 Suggestive or persuasive advertising (4,4)
2 Plant used in the making of tequila (5)
4 Part of a gearwheel (3)
5 Sovereign countries united by factors such as a common language (6,6)
6 Incomplete (7)
7 Egyptian canal (4)
8 Fiscal system of both private and state enterprise (5,7)
12 Set or keep apart (5)
13 Women's underwear and nightclothes (8)
15 Multitudes (7)
19 Closer to the centre (5)
20 Slender double-reed instrument (4)
22 Type of lettuce (3)

154

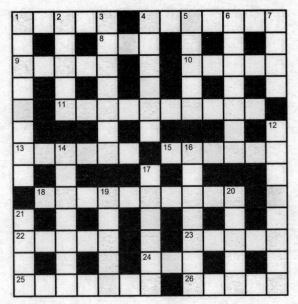

Across

1 Clump-forming perennial plant (5)
4 Marine fowl (7)
8 US TV corporation (inits) (3)
9 Large showy flower (5)
10 Indian currency unit (5)
11 Moving onward (10)
13 Chief port of Australia (6)
15 Venerate (6)
18 Colouring of a person's face (10)
22 Rental contract (5)
23 Mexican comrade (5)
24 Clairvoyance (inits) (3)
25 Malicious gossip (7)
26 Fence made of shrubs (5)

Down

1 Desperate (8)
2 Crouch, bow (5)
3 From now on; usually used with a negative (3,4)
4 Thin top layer on a solid floor (6)
5 Harsh or corrosive in tone (5)
6 Encroach (7)
7 Feat (4)
12 Grape sugar (8)
14 Series of pictures representing a continuous scene (7)
16 Inscription on a tombstone (7)
17 Doghouse (6)
19 Beg earnestly (5)
20 Fountain nymph (5)
21 In addition (4)

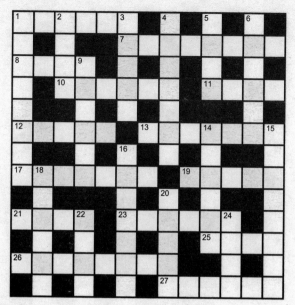

Across

1 Leave in the lurch (6)
7 Distinguish (8)
8 Jump lightly (4)
10 Clergyman (6)
11 Water falling in drops (4)
12 Covered with small pieces of rock (5)
13 Flat highland (7)
17 Shattered, broken into pieces (7)
19 Subtraction sign (5)
21 Increased in size (4)
23 Pictures (6)
25 Hackney carriage (4)
26 Was given (8)
27 Feels (6)

Down

1 Maladies (8)
2 Sea-going vessel (4)
3 Periodic rises and falls of the sea (5)
4 Marked by great fruitfulness (7)
5 Celestial body (4)
6 Continent (6)
9 Publishes (6)
14 Bathroom fixture (6)
15 On a higher floor (8)
16 Take to be true (7)
18 Branded (6)
20 Stripes (5)
22 Period of seven consecutive days (4)
24 Tells (4)

156

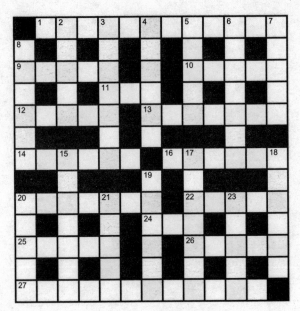

Across

1 Sweet fleshy red fruits (12)
9 Beat, pound (5)
10 Wobble (5)
11 Piece of scrap material (3)
12 Relative magnitudes of two quantities (5)
13 Very unfriendly (7)
14 Method (6)
16 Stripe (6)
20 Pharmacist (7)
22 Yaps (5)
24 Popular drink (3)
25 Fastened with a thick cord (5)
26 Lead to (5)
27 Out of date (3-9)

Down

2 Have faith in (5)
3 Commend, sanction (7)
4 Lustrous (6)
5 Relaxes (5)
6 Fancy (7)
7 Subdivision of an act of a play (5)
8 Repositories (6)
15 Trod (7)
17 Leaves dried and prepared for smoking (7)
18 Osculated (6)
19 Connect (6)
20 Consignment (5)
21 Asian country (5)
23 Course (5)

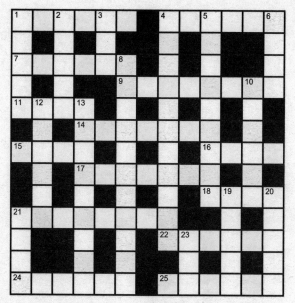

Across

1 Group of words (6)
4 Filament (6)
7 Sour-tasting (6)
9 Taken in marriage or betrothal (8)
11 Neither good nor bad (2-2)
14 Worried unnecessarily or excessively (7)
15 Musical notation written on a stave (4)
16 Towards the side sheltered from the wind (4)
17 Wearing away (7)
18 Short-term worker (abbr) (4)
21 Sweat (8)
22 Stabbing weapon (6)
24 Large streams (6)
25 Extremely poisonous or injurious (6)

Down

1 Applauds (5)
2 Operatic airs (5)
3 ___ Lanka, country (3)
4 Showed compassion (11)
5 Superfluous (9)
6 Passed away (4)
8 Appropriate to grand and formal occasions (11)
10 Hold in high regard (6)
12 Recently (2,4)
13 Loathsome (9)
19 Bordered (5)
20 Convivial gathering (5)
21 Couple (4)
23 Mature (3)

158

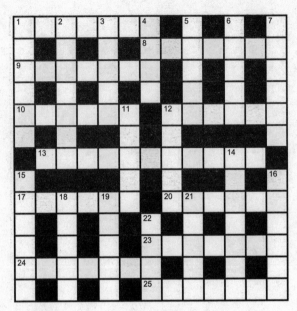

Across

1 Fruit resembling a small peach (7)

8 Horizontal plant stem with shoots above and roots below (7)

9 Scholarly life (7)

10 Obtain by coercion or intimidation (6)

12 Baby's bed (6)

13 Brought low in spirit (11)

17 Lacking in insight (6)

20 Irrigation conduit (6)

23 At no particular moment (7)

24 From the Orient (7)

25 Glut, excess (7)

Down

1 Astounds (6)

2 Nuclear plant (7)

3 Shout of approval (5)

4 Long arduous journey (4)

5 Motorcycle rider (5)

6 Committee having supervisory powers (5)

7 Insect's antenna (6)

11 Designation (5)

12 Uncouth (5)

14 Large imposing building (7)

15 Pass on, of information (6)

16 Authoritative command (6)

18 Gene Pitney song, *Twenty-four Hours from* ___ (5)

19 Mixture of rain and snow (5)

21 Coating (5)

22 Enthusiastic devotees (4)

Across

4 Long flag, often tapering (7)
8 Treat badly (5)
9 Distribute according to a plan (9)
10 Goes in front (5)
11 Pleasure (9)
13 Room in a roof space (6)
16 "Hey ___," said by a magician (6)
20 Method of writing rapidly (9)
23 Nimble, spry (5)
24 Natural and unavoidable catastrophes (4,2,3)
25 Hands out playing cards (5)
26 Put into code (7)

Down

1 Shouting for (7)
2 Custodian of a museum (7)
3 Dog's lead (5)
4 Forms of internet advertising (3-3)
5 More jumpily excitable (7)
6 *A Town like* ___, Nevil Shute novel (5)
7 Military vehicles (5)
12 Occupied a chair (3)
14 Fire's remains (3)
15 Measure of energy available for doing work (7)
17 Alike (7)
18 Side of a coin bearing the Queen's head (7)
19 Captured (6)
20 Relative magnitude (5)
21 Spirit dispenser (5)
22 Informal term for a father (5)

160

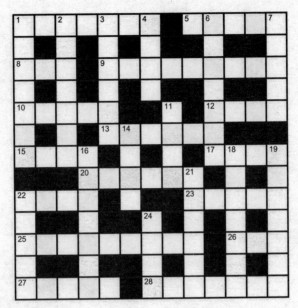

Across
1 Bondage (7)
5 Loose garment worn by Muslim women (5)
8 Electrical resistance unit (3)
9 Person skilled in telling anecdotes (9)
10 Understood (5)
12 Religious painting (4)
13 Deals with (6)
15 Antlered animal (4)
17 Words of a book (4)
20 Greek "I have found (it)" (6)
22 Decoratively tied strips of ribbon (4)
23 Daughter of a sibling (5)
25 Member of an irregular armed resistance force (9)
26 Curious (3)
27 Attempted (5)
28 Puzzle (7)

Down
1 Aghast (7)
2 Opening to which a sleeve can be attached (7)
3 Straying from the right course (6)
4 Expression of disgust (4)
6 Undo from a spiralled state (7)
7 Protective garment (5)
11 Endorse (4)
14 Uncommon (4)
16 Set aside for future use (7)
18 Ugly sight (7)
19 One division of a week (7)
21 Chronological records (6)
22 Biblical term meaning 'fathered' (5)
24 Poor and dirty dwelling (4)

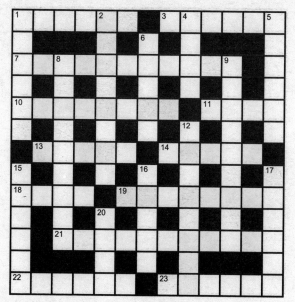

Across

1 Inclined to plumpness (6)
3 Powdered type of sugar (6)
7 Muscular stiffness occurring after death (5,6)
10 Indian or African animal (8)
11 Flows back (4)
13 Grilled food on a skewer, served with peanut sauce (5)
14 Detector used to locate distant objects (5)
18 Zealous (4)
19 Explosive, fickle (8)
21 Transducer used to detect and measure light (8,3)
22 Easy, uncomplicated (6)
23 Technique (6)

Down

1 Arched (6)
2 Annual occasion of celebration (8)
4 Motor vehicle (4)
5 Study for an examination (6)
6 In an early period of life (5)
8 Syrup made from pomegranates (9)
9 Underwater warship (9)
12 Place of complete bliss (8)
15 Extensive treeless plains of South America (6)
16 Value (5)
17 Myth, fable (6)
20 Repast (4)

162

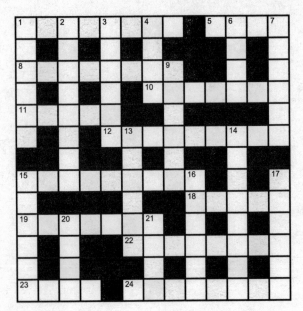

Across

1 Location (8)
5 Completed (4)
8 Blind alleys (4,4)
10 Fulfil the requirements of (7)
11 Come up (5)
12 Elaborate and remarkable display on a lavish scale (9)
15 Person of imagination or foresight (9)
18 Aquatic mammal (5)
19 Bottle up (feelings, for example) (7)
22 Rubble which acts as a bed for cement (8)
23 Bridge (4)
24 Personality disturbance characterised by a state of unconscious conflict (8)

Down

1 One who travels about selling his wares (6)
2 Thin slices, especially of planed wood (8)
3 City of ancient Egypt, now part of Luxor (6)
4 Chances (4)
6 Lubricates (4)
7 Protein which acts as a catalyst (6)
9 Dish for holding a cup (6)
13 Impose a penalty (6)
14 Timid, fearful (8)
15 Against (6)
16 Distant but within sight (6)
17 Commands given by a superior (6)
20 Mountain lion (4)
21 Free from the risk of harm (4)

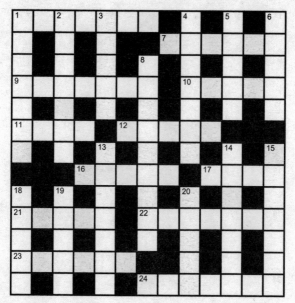

Across
1 Small rounded boat made of hides stretched over a wicker frame (7)
7 Collection of star systems (6)
9 Swing used by circus acrobats (7)
10 Fragrance (5)
11 Ringlet (4)
12 Change (5)
16 Having existence (5)
17 Region bordering Israel and Egypt (4)
21 Happen (5)
22 Experiencing illness aboard a ship (7)
23 Provided with a particular motif (6)
24 Ornament made of ribbon, given as an award (7)

Down
1 Get in touch with (7)
2 Wed again (7)
3 Meeting of witches (5)
4 Device for opening several locks (7)
5 One of the four countries of the UK (5)
6 Recurring series of events (5)
8 Fill something previously emptied (9)
13 Having hair on the chin (7)
14 Natural home of an animal or plant (7)
15 Parcel (7)
18 Compass point at 180 degrees (5)
19 Measures of land (5)
20 Addition, subtraction, division, multiplication, etc (abbr) (5)

164

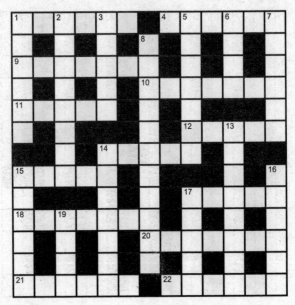

Across

1 Leave, depart (3,3)
4 One who owes money (6)
9 Insistent (7)
10 Concentrated (7)
11 Stage (5)
12 Digit written as VIII in Roman numerals (5)
14 Foreigner, stranger (5)
15 Painful eyelid swellings (5)
17 Very steep, almost vertical (5)
18 Go back over (7)
20 Cup, goblet (7)
21 Abrupt (6)
22 Economical (6)

Down

1 Tending to speak irritably (coll) (6)
2 Semi-formal afternoon social gathering (3,5)
3 Accepted practice (5)
5 Made of clay (7)
6 Mountain lake (4)
7 Mr De Niro, actor (6)
8 Creature with a long, twig-like body (5,6)
13 Salutation, especially on meeting (8)
14 With a side or oblique glance (7)
15 Thin strips, parings (6)
16 Pen-name of author Eric Arthur Blair, George ____ (6)
17 Ringo ____, former Beatle (5)
19 Incline (4)

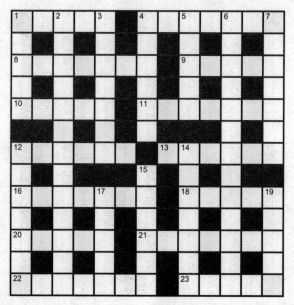

Across

1 Cause to feel resentment or indignation (5)
4 Sorrow (7)
8 Person who cuts and sets window panes (7)
9 Gather, as of natural products (5)
10 French river (5)
11 Country, capital Dakar (7)
12 Vessel in which water is heated for circulation (6)
13 Semi-precious gemstone (6)
16 Hold under a lease agreement (7)
18 Lovers' assignation (5)
20 Deviating from the truth (5)
21 Extensions (7)
22 Bible book (7)
23 Nocturnal winged creatures (5)

Down

1 Leaves of a book (5)
2 Attribute that fits a person for something (13)
3 Look which is believed to have the power to inflict harm (4,3)
4 Strain (6)
5 Begin eating heartily (coll) (3,2)
6 Way out to be used in case of fire, etc (9,4)
7 Vest (7)
12 Accumulation of jobs yet to be dealt with (7)
14 Word opposite in meaning to another (7)
15 Lays out in a line (6)
17 Roman cloaks (5)
19 Examinations (5)

166

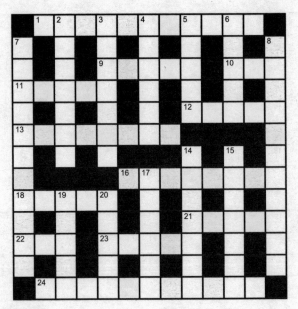

Across

1 Tape used to clean the teeth (6,5)

9 Stupid, foolish person (coll) (5)

10 Rowing pole (3)

11 Snares (5)

12 Country roads (5)

13 Showing good spirits (8)

16 Upright pole on which a hinged barrier is hung (8)

18 Drama which is sung (5)

21 Bay or cove (5)

22 Equip (3)

23 Squeeze (5)

24 Murder, especially a socially prominent person (11)

Down

2 Runs away (7)

3 Shaved crown of a monk's head (7)

4 Four-wheel covered carriage (6)

5 Patriotic (5)

6 Look down on with disdain (5)

7 Wall-mounted bulletin display panel (11)

8 Type of embroidery (5-6)

14 Meat from a deer (7)

15 Set of carpenter's implements (4,3)

17 Mother superior (6)

19 Boundaries (5)

20 First letter of the Greek alphabet (5)

167

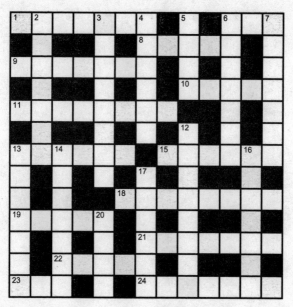

Across

1 Large green long-horned grasshopper of North America (7)
6 Brief swim (3)
8 Quickly (5)
9 Complacently or inanely foolish (7)
10 Well turned-out (5)
11 Metallic element used to make light-bulb filaments (8)
13 Court clown (6)
15 Dense woodland (6)
18 Publican (8)
19 Small, open pies (5)
21 Thrift (7)
22 Takes part in an informal conversation (5)
23 Timid (3)
24 Large drinking vessel (7)

Down

2 Usually (2,1,4)
3 Thick slice of bread (coll) (8)
4 Darted (6)
5 Felines (4)
6 Reduce in worth or importance (7)
7 Shield from danger (7)
12 Place where a person grew up (4,4)
13 An uneasy state (7)
14 Concealment (7)
16 Cooking utensil (7)
17 Absorb food (6)
20 Box lightly (4)

168

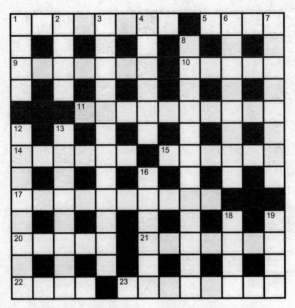

Across

1 Amount that can be contained (8)

5 Foreman (4)

9 Short-legged flightless bird of Antarctic regions (7)

10 Machine tool (5)

11 Marked by pomp or formality (10)

14 Edible part of a nut (6)

15 Caps made of soft cloth (6)

17 Moderation in eating and drinking (10)

20 Interior (5)

21 Boat seen on the canals of Venice (7)

22 Exhibiting vigorous good health (4)

23 Disciple (8)

Down

1 Manage, make do (4)

2 Section of glass (4)

3 Issue that attracts great public attention (5,7)

4 Travelling repairman who mends pots, pans, etc (6)

6 One who is not a member of a group (8)

7 Without pips (8)

8 Visible radiation (12)

12 Unpredictably excitable (8)

13 Crook (8)

16 Drooped (6)

18 Bird symbolising peace (4)

19 Breathe noisily, as when exhausted (4)

Across
1 Brilliant, excellent (6)
4 Sever (3,3)
7 Turkish lord (3)
8 Impinge (upon) (4,2)
9 Split (6)
10 Subject (5)
13 Drum held between the knees (5)
15 Drivers' resting place (3-2)
17 Final Greek letter (5)
18 Mature (5)
20 Jovial (5)
23 Become more exciting (coll) (3,2)
26 Draw out (6)
27 Hereditary (6)
28 Decide, make a choice (3)
29 Mint-like herb used in perfumery (6)
30 Shouted loudly (6)

Down
1 Outer area of a city (6)
2 Medicinal beverage (6)
3 Stringed instrument (5)
4 Island in the Bay of Naples (5)
5 Commotion (6)
6 Difficult to handle (6)
10 Fang (5)
11 Garment fold (5)
12 Gripping device (5)
14 Former, previous (3)
16 Prohibit (3)
18 In a new or different way (6)
19 Opens (trousers or a skirt) (6)
21 Shrink back (6)
22 Opened wide (6)
24 ___ of, in close proximity to (2,3)
25 State of being one (5)

170

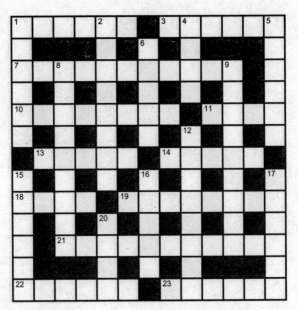

Across

1 Ring road (6)
3 Keeping a secret or furtive watch (6)
7 Having a good effect on the body or mind (11)
10 Drive out an evil spirit (8)
11 Poke or thrust abruptly (4)
13 Automobile race run over public roads (5)
14 Pen made from a bird's feather (5)
18 Zealous (4)
19 Coalition (8)
21 Defile by touching or mixing with (11)
22 Main meal of the day (6)
23 Armoured hat (6)

Down

1 Dairy product (6)
2 Hardly at all (8)
4 Pavement (4)
5 Grimy (6)
6 Untidy (5)
8 Person with an abnormal sense of self-importance (9)
9 Autonomous region of Spain, capital Barcelona (9)
12 One who flees (8)
15 Sealed in a tin (6)
16 Primitive plant forms (5)
17 Dislike intensely (6)
20 Leg joint (4)

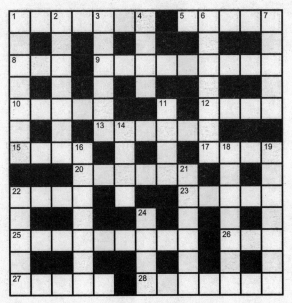

Across

1 Church tower (7)
5 Bony skeleton of the head (5)
8 Overworked horse (3)
9 Using again after processing (9)
10 Common amphibians (5)
12 Month of the year (4)
13 Dinner jacket (6)
15 Ridge of rock, coral, etc (4)
17 US university (4)
20 Consume, absorb (6)
22 Belonging to that woman (4)
23 Medieval musical instrument (5)
25 Fantastic but vain hope (4,5)
26 Sharp knock (3)
27 Country bumpkin (5)
28 Wreath of flowers (7)

Down

1 US legislator (7)
2 Etch into a surface (7)
3 Stickler (6)
4 Every one (4)
6 Spoilsport (7)
7 Long-shanked (5)
11 Female birds (4)
14 Compulsion (4)
16 Type of wide-angled lens (7)
18 Canadian province (7)
19 Broke loose (7)
21 Involuntary vibration (6)
22 Euphoric (5)
24 Mass of ice (4)

172

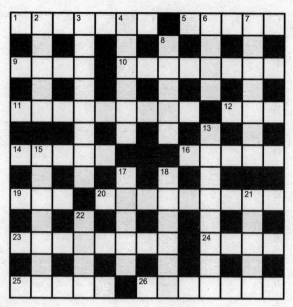

Across

1 Scratched (shoes) (7)
5 Explosives (5)
9 Former coin of India and a girl's name (4)
10 Official report of news or progress (8)
11 Nasty, sly and spiteful behaviour (9)
12 Travel regularly over a route (3)
14 Cliffs (5)
16 Covers with gold (5)
19 Stuffiness (3)
20 Conjectures (9)
23 Dense blizzard (5-3)
24 Hankering (4)
25 Excessive rate of interest (5)
26 Highway robber (7)

Down

2 South American dance of African origin (5)
3 Lavishes insincere praise on (8)
4 Receding (6)
6 Is indebted (4)
7 Checked (7)
8 Half-melted snow (5)
13 Forming a link (between) (8)
15 Overwhelms (7)
17 Young leaf or bud signifying the coming of spring (5)
18 Maker of clay vessels (6)
21 Former offender (abbr) (2-3)
22 Leading performer (4)

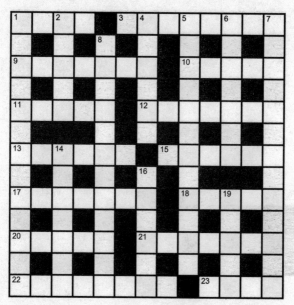

Across
1 Orchard fruit (4)
3 Place to wash (8)
9 Herb used in cooking (7)
10 Held back, as of breath (5)
11 Attain (5)
12 Italian sculptor and architect of the Baroque period (7)
13 Frightens (6)
15 Elongated cluster of flowers (6)
17 Slight suggestion (7)
18 More active than normal (coll) (5)
20 Conform (5)
21 Trips taken to perform tasks (7)
22 Imaginary place of great wealth and opportunity (2,6)
23 Mandibles (4)

Down
1 Postpone or delay needlessly (13)
2 Battleground (5)
4 Single-celled, water-living protozoon (6)
5 Shop that sells sewing and dressmaking materials (12)
6 Larger than normal for its kind (7)
7 Period of doubt and anxiety experienced in middle age (3-4,6)
8 Till which calculates a bill in a shop (4,8)
14 Clumsy (7)
16 Consented (6)
19 Bamboo-eating mammal (5)

174

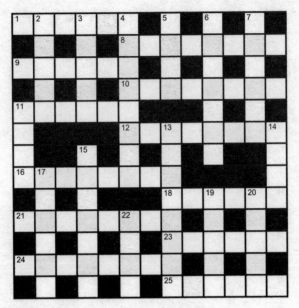

Across

1 Is on the edge of (6)
8 The world of scholars (8)
9 Outdoor meal (6)
10 Reticent (8)
11 Native of Kathmandu, for example (6)
12 A stopping (8)
16 Words with opposite meanings (8)
18 Of a sphere, flattened at opposite sides (6)
21 Practising abstention from alcohol (8)
23 Spoken (6)
24 Song sung beneath a lady's window (8)
25 Half asleep (6)

Down

2 Outcast (5)
3 Port in north-west Italy (5)
4 Room in a church where a priest prepares for a service (8)
5 Succeed in an examination (4)
6 Criticised as worthless (7)
7 Muscle that flexes the forearm (6)
11 Star which ejects material (4)
13 Explained or answered (8)
14 If not, then (4)
15 Within a glass container (7)
17 Necessary for relief (6)
19 Very slow in tempo (5)
20 Small short-necked dabbling river ducks (5)
22 Strap with a crosspiece on the upper of a shoe (1-3)

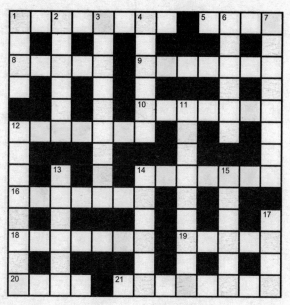

Across

1 Briefly giving the gist of something (8)
5 Musical work (4)
8 Fragrant rootstock of various irises (5)
9 Swimmers (7)
10 Give the right to (7)
12 In the direction of the ocean (7)
14 Wealthy and privileged people (coll) (3,4)
16 Innovator (7)
18 Stuffy (atmosphere) (7)
19 Everyone except the clergy (5)
20 Knotted (4)
21 Penitent (8)

Down

1 Smut from a fire (4)
2 Eye part (6)
3 Promise of reimbursement in the case of loss (9)
4 Sent a telegram (6)
6 Abundance (6)
7 Defendants in a court of law (8)
11 Aviator hired to fly experimental aeroplanes in designed manoeuvres (4,5)
12 Take the place of (8)
13 Stock exchange in Paris (6)
14 Picture painted on a plaster wall (6)
15 Italian town, birthplace of St Francis (6)
17 Drainage ditch (4)

176

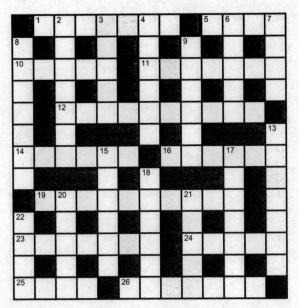

Across
1 Very shaken (7)
5 Proclaim (4)
10 Really (5)
11 Tinning plant (7)
12 Second glance, of surprise (6,4)
14 Contemporary (6)
16 Thin pieces (6)
19 Mythical marine snake (3,7)
23 Raise (a matter) for discussion (5,2)
24 Grate (5)
25 Infants (4)
26 Ugly offensive object (7)

Down
2 Stalked relentlessly (7)
3 Soft fur, also known as nutria (5)
4 Is good (at) (6)
6 Angular front opening of a sweater (1-4)
7 Systems (4)
8 Pours (out) (7)
9 Slowly get into the mind (6)
13 Climbs (7)
15 Quit a job (6)
17 Supplier of refreshments (7)
18 Mobile phone system where talk time is bought ahead (6)
20 Remove (from a building) (5)
21 Relieves (5)
22 Adjoin, border (4)

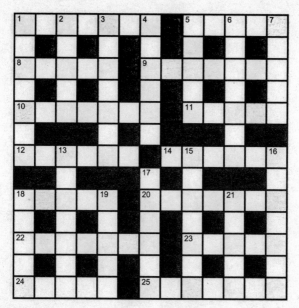

Across
1 Thrive, do well (7)
5 Just made (5)
8 Small terrestrial lizard (5)
9 Enlarges, like the pupil of an eye (7)
10 Breaks down (computer) (7)
11 Back of a ship (5)
12 Constraint, imprisonment (6)
14 Accedes (6)
18 Increase the running speed of a car's engine (coll) (3,2)
20 Sustain (7)
22 Practice of cleanliness (7)
23 Indian ball, often of onions (5)
24 Petty officer on a ship (5)
25 Following closely on the heels of (7)

Down
1 Frolicked, capered (7)
2 Largest city in Nebraska, USA (5)
3 Takes (game) illegally (7)
4 Salad vegetable (6)
5 Information stores (5)
6 Most remote (7)
7 Kids, hoaxes playfully (coll) (3,2)
13 Devastates (7)
15 Compost container (4-3)
16 Expelling a long breath (7)
17 Proliferate (6)
18 Course of therapy following addiction or illness (abbr) (5)
19 Tidy and clean feathers with the beak (5)
21 Animal related to the giraffe (5)

178

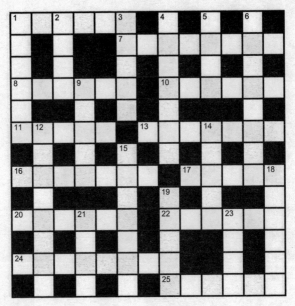

Across

1 Relative position (6)
7 In no particular place (8)
8 Make a dry crackling sound (6)
10 Arch of the foot (6)
11 Go in (5)
13 Compactness (7)
16 Speak haltingly (7)
17 Removes the central part of an apple (5)
20 Dismissed from the mind (6)
22 Substance similar to stucco (6)
24 Humidity (8)
25 Conditional release from prison (6)

Down

1 Change direction abruptly (6)
2 Unfortunately (4)
3 Sugary (5)
4 No longer active in one's profession (7)
5 Large brown mushrooms (*Boletus edulis*) (4)
6 Move to a different place (8)
9 Behave towards (5)
12 Across the whole country (8)
14 Item of cutlery (5)
15 'Fab' group associated with the 1960s (7)
18 Tap forcefully (6)
19 Pleasantly cold and invigorating (5)
21 Yawn (4)
23 Extinct bird of Mauritius (4)

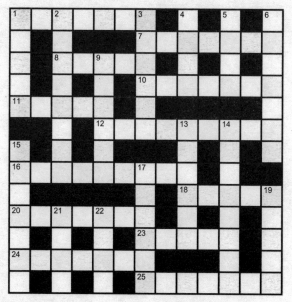

Across

1 Small pools of rainwater (7)
7 Shirt, blouse (7)
8 French goodbye (5)
10 Hit without restraint (4,3)
11 Sailing vessel with a single mast (5)
12 Having made no legally valid will before death (9)
16 Type of make-up (9)
18 Turn inside out (5)
20 Gruelling (7)
23 Thrown into a state of disarray (5)
24 Anarchical (7)
25 Hold spellbound (7)

Down

1 Causes emotional distress (5)
2 Conversation between two persons (8)
3 Engrave (6)
4 Obtains (4)
5 Floor covering (abbr) (4)
6 British manufacturer of luxury motor cars (7)
9 Naughtily or annoyingly playful (6)
13 Conduits for carrying off waste products (6)
14 Spiny insectivore with a long tongue (8)
15 Fiasco (7)
17 Neglect (6)
19 Mountainous province of western Austria (5)
21 Daybreak (4)
22 Be compliant (4)

180

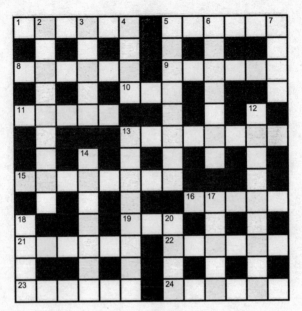

Across

1 Loan shark (6)
5 Part of a dress above the waist (6)
8 Splits down the middle (6)
9 Twisting force (6)
10 Hitherto (3)
11 Nimble (5)
13 Two-yearly (8)
15 Death of part of the living body (8)
16 Demon (5)
19 Lick up (3)
21 Narcotic drug (6)
22 Without remuneration (6)
23 Country bumpkins (6)
24 Organ of the body between the stomach and the diaphragm (6)

Down

2 Kill (animals) for food (9)
3 Make merry (5)
4 Pink-tinged (4)
5 Support for the wall of a building (8)
6 Beloved (7)
7 Divisible by two (4)
12 Sweetheart (9)
13 Unwarranted, without foundation (8)
14 Army unit (7)
17 Urge or force to an action (5)
18 Half asleep (4)
20 Informal name for a cat (4)

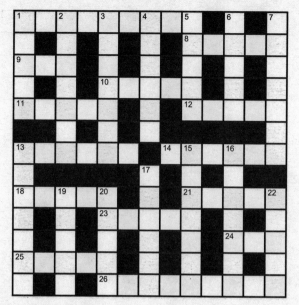

Across

1 Carnival held on Shrove Tuesday (5,4)
8 Country, capital Beijing (5)
9 Outer edge of a plate (3)
10 Ability (5)
11 Hi (5)
12 The two in a pack of playing cards (5)
13 Surface on which pictures can be projected (6)
14 Freewheels (6)
18 Fastens with a key (5)
21 Defect (5)
23 Vacillate (5)
24 Cooking vessel (3)
25 Authoritative declaration (3-2)
26 As fast as possible (4-5)

Down

1 Spring month (5)
2 Walker (7)
3 Tedious (7)
4 Repeat aloud from memory (6)
5 Tell off (5)
6 Small and delicately worked item (5)
7 Financiers (7)
13 Unaccompanied musician (7)
15 Give new strength or energy to (7)
16 Socially awkward or tactless act (4,3)
17 Tiers (6)
19 Sepals of a flower (5)
20 Swift descent through the air (5)
22 Name of a book (5)

182

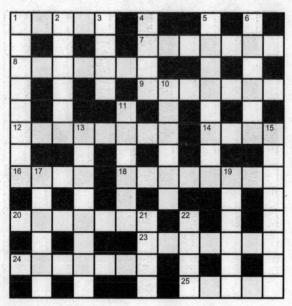

Across

1 Anthem (5)
7 Word spelled the same but with a different meaning to another (7)
8 Funeral procession (7)
9 Thrown out (7)
12 Plausible but false (8)
14 High tight collar (4)
16 Not any (4)
18 Split up (8)
20 Dancer's one-piece costume (7)
23 Currency used in Kabul, for example (7)
24 Wholly occupy (7)
25 Position (5)

Down

1 Soft leather shoe (8)
2 Three times (6)
3 Digits of the foot (4)
4 Clarified butter used in Indian cookery (4)
5 Magician (8)
6 Me in person (6)
10 Jesus, Mary and ___, the Holy Family (6)
11 Water diviner (6)
13 Animal (8)
15 Marked by mania uncontrolled by reason (8)
17 Vast seas (6)
19 Relaxed (2,4)
21 Hyphen (4)
22 Ova (4)

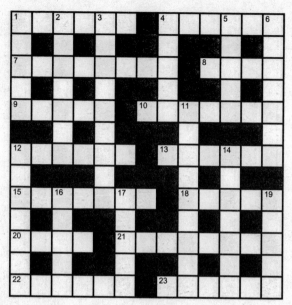

Across

1 Naval flag (6)
4 Unsullied (6)
7 Innocuous (8)
8 Live in a tent (4)
9 Skid (5)
10 Attribute (7)
12 Separates by sifting (6)
13 Sharp hooked claws (6)
15 Ask for (7)
18 Worked into an emotional fever (coll) (3,2)
20 Part of an animal (4)
21 Cherished desire (8)
22 Edible black marine bivalve (6)
23 Be contingent upon (6)

Down

1 Attitude, beliefs (5)
2 Continue to live, despite adversity (7)
3 First James Bond film in which Pierce Brosnan starred (9)
4 Instances (5)
5 Hindu religious teacher (5)
6 Put into words (7)
11 Rapid descent by a submarine (5-4)
12 One of several parallel layers of material (7)
14 External (7)
16 Gives up (5)
17 Common gastropod (5)
19 Yearned for (5)

184

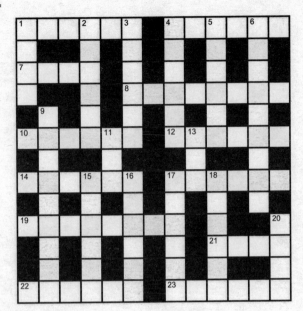

Across

1 On a plane (6)
4 Wealth regarded as an evil influence (6)
7 Leak through (4)
8 Heavy textile with a woven design (8)
10 Preliminary coat of paint (6)
12 Decisive moment in a novel or play (6)
14 Bag containing a small amount of ointment or shampoo, etc (6)
17 Common seasoning (6)
19 Cunning (8)
21 Transparent optical device (4)
22 Be in an agitated emotional state (6)
23 Shot or scene that is filmed again (6)

Down

1 Succulent plant (4)
2 Discrimination against a person in the latter part of life (6)
3 Physician (6)
4 Shortsighted (6)
5 Breakfast food (6)
6 Excessively keen (9)
9 Expose (food) to gamma rays to kill micro-organisms (9)
11 To stretch out (3)
13 Caustic washing solution (3)
15 Elevation (6)
16 High-pitched (6)
17 One who behaves affectedly in order to impress others (6)
18 Young hen (6)
20 ___ of Man or Wight, for example (4)

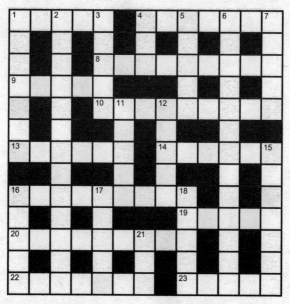

Across

1 Foot lever (5)
4 Person given the task of keeping watch (7)
8 Pirate (9)
9 Espresso coffee with milk (5)
10 Handling of an operation (9)
13 Abstain from (6)
14 Passé (slang) (3,3)
16 Blue-green colour (9)
19 Absolutely necessary (5)
20 Bias (9)
22 Remorse for conduct in the past (7)
23 Now (5)

Down

1 Goods carried by a large vehicle (7)
2 Tooth doctor (6,7)
3 Defamatory writing (5)
4 Resin-like substance secreted by certain insects (3)
5 Opaque gems (5)
6 Relationship lasting for a single evening (3-5,5)
7 Slabs of grass and grass roots (5)
11 Get the better of (5)
12 Religious paintings (5)
15 Basket on wheels (7)
16 Refill (3-2)
17 Complete reversal of direction (1-4)
18 Something that happens at a given place and time (5)
21 Decorate with frosting (3)

186

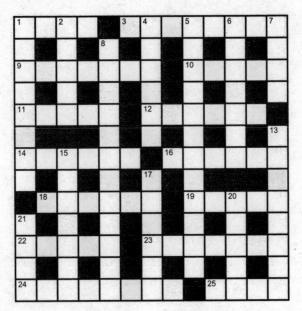

Across

1 Sir ____ Bogarde, British actor (1921–1999) (4)
3 Colloquial name for New York City (3,5)
9 Comforted, consoled (7)
10 Rid of impurities (5)
11 Set of recordings, especially musical (5)
12 Large gun (6)
14 Native American tents (6)
16 Scolding or domineering woman (6)
18 Peninsula of Ukraine, on the Black Sea (6)
19 Pastorale (5)
22 Bars of rolled steel making a track (5)
23 Coiffure (7)
24 Demonstrate to an interested audience (8)
25 Go out with (4)

Down

1 Feeling of intense dislike (8)
2 Parallelogram with four equal sides (5)
4 Cause to occur rapidly (6)
5 Inflammation of part of the abdomen (12)
6 Framework that supports climbing plants (7)
7 Biblical garden (4)
8 Instrumental entertainment played by a small ensemble (7,5)
13 Act of washing and dressing oneself (8)
15 Covered and often columned entrance to a building (7)
17 Feeling of sympathy for the misfortunes of others (6)
20 Popular house plant (5)
21 Goddess of the rainbow (4)

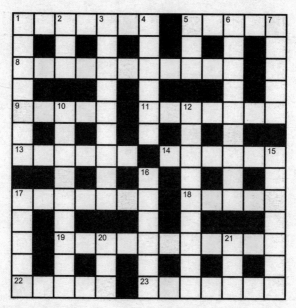

Across

1 Preparing food by heating it (7)
5 Swift, quick (5)
8 Dessert fruit suitable for consuming raw (6,5)
9 ___ Wilde, dramatist (5)
11 Betrayal of a trust (7)
13 Tough synthetic resin chiefly used to coat non-stick cooking utensils (TM) (6)
14 In operation (6)
17 Engage in hand-to-hand combat (7)
18 Coming next after the eighth (5)
19 Trial of ability between opponents (11)
22 Containing nothing (5)
23 Woodland flower (7)

Down

1 Type of cigar (7)
2 Frequently, poetically (3)
3 Deepest (9)
4 Seizes and holds firmly (6)
5 Tear apart (3)
6 Exactness (9)
7 Daily written record of events (5)
10 Container for a popular hot drink (6,3)
12 Little known, abstruse (9)
15 Add something extra to make more intense (7)
16 Groups containing one or more species (6)
17 Dispense with, forgo (5)
20 Month with 31 days (3)
21 Artificial language, a simplification of Esperanto (3)

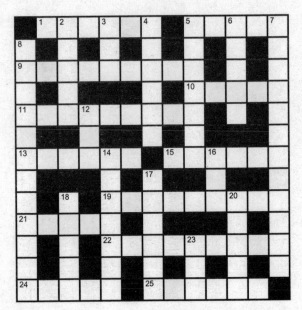

Across

1 Edible decapod (6)
5 Having a hemispherical vault (5)
9 Combat aircraft (9)
10 Military fabric (5)
11 Rebel, guerrilla (9)
13 Produces water vapour (6)
15 Plug for a bunghole in a cask (6)
19 Spring flower (9)
21 One's ancestry (coll) (5)
22 Incite (9)
24 Enter (3,2)
25 Sprinter (6)

Down

2 Causes pain (5)
3 Not well (3)
4 Give in to, indulge (6)
5 Area of a computer monitor on which icons and windows appear (7)
6 Type of parrot (5)
7 Shop selling ready-to-eat food products (12)
8 Arousing wonder (3-9)
12 Country, capital Washington DC (inits) (3)
14 Grand house (7)
16 ___ and buts, objections (3)
17 Pencil rubber (6)
18 Slightly wet (5)
20 Trap for birds or small mammals (5)
23 Forename of golfer, Mr Woosnam (3)

Across

4 Relating to the motion of material bodies (7)
7 Go on too long (7)
8 Mound of stones piled up as a memorial (5)
9 Section of an orchestra (5)
10 Light mid-afternoon meal (3)
11 Scrub (5)
12 Sport with few restrictions on the moves that competitors employ (9)
14 Archetypes (9)
17 Tree which produces berries in autumn (5)
18 Expire (3)
19 Cavalry unit (5)
21 Looks for (5)
22 Side by side (7)
23 Make tidy (5,2)

Down

1 Explosive device (4)
2 Period of ten years (6)
3 Have an argument or dispute (coll) (5,6)
4 Hard to solve, complex (6)
5 Three-legged support (6)
6 Legislative assembly of the USA (8)
8 Detailed record of the background of a person under study (4,7)
12 Relating to scientific methods in the investigation of crime (8)
13 Stick to (6)
15 Polar feature (6)
16 Unprincipled (6)
20 Savoury meat paste (4)

190

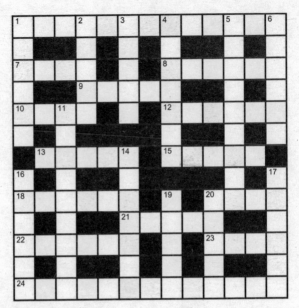

Across

1 Shame felt when a guilt is made public (13)

7 Insincere talk about religion or morals (4)

8 Referee (6)

9 Airport in Chicago (5)

10 Large jug (4)

12 Text of a popular song (6)

13 Yields, surrenders (5)

15 Headscarf worn by Muslim women (5)

18 Remove packaging (6)

20 Office note (4)

21 West Indian dance (5)

22 Capital of Taiwan (6)

23 Monk's hood (4)

24 Small adhesive tokens stuck on letters or packages (7,6)

Down

1 Surpass (6)

2 Stage-player (5)

3 Basic unit of money in Saudi Arabia (5)

4 Make a sucking sound, as when walking through mud (7)

5 Do away with (9)

6 Belief in the existence of God (6)

11 Alpine perennial plant (9)

14 Young tree (7)

16 Serious quarrel, especially one that ends a friendship (coll) (4-2)

17 Planets (6)

19 Excludes (5)

20 Coffee-chocolate drink (5)

Across

1 Army doctor (5)
5 Caramel brown (4)
7 Apprehension (6)
8 Cooks slowly and for a long time in liquid (5)
9 Bully (9)
10 Shortened forename of US president Lincoln (3)
11 Courier (9)
15 Predominant (9)
19 Unit of electric current (abbr) (3)
20 Don't look this in the mouth! (4,5)
21 Daughter of one's brother (5)
22 Damaged irreparably (6)
23 Grotto (4)
24 Early period of development (5)

Down

1 Lose (6)
2 Slimmer (6)
3 Tradition (6)
4 Fortified place where troops are stationed (8)
5 Relevant relation or interconnection (7)
6 Cause to be nervous or upset (7)
12 Yielding a profit (8)
13 Popular flavour of ice cream (7)
14 Ecstasy (7)
16 In accord with the latest fad (6)
17 Elaborate cake (6)
18 Lecture (6)

192

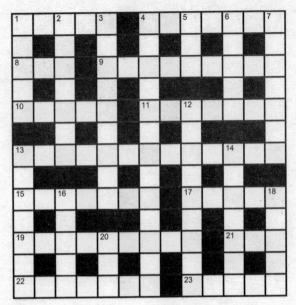

Across

1 Looped edging on a ribbon (5)
4 Indian bread (7)
8 Intent (3)
9 Number of contestants coming close behind the winner (7-2)
10 Elevations of the land (5)
11 Region of northern Europe (7)
13 Conspicuous or noteworthy (13)
15 Internal organs collectively (7)
17 Caricaturing (5)
19 Armistice, truce (9)
21 Leguminous plant (3)
22 Close of day (7)
23 Orders (5)

Down

1 Cook in a simmering liquid (5)
2 Type of cloud (7)
3 Gate consisting of a post that acts as a pivot for rotating arms (9)
4 Intense and uncontrolled fire (13)
5 Period of time (3)
6 In a state of uncertainty, perplexed (2,3)
7 Made difficult or slow (7)
12 Pirate ship (9)
13 Contraptions, tools (7)
14 Sharp bend (7)
16 Country, capital Madrid (5)
18 Plant grown as a lawn (5)
20 Inflated feeling of personal worth (3)

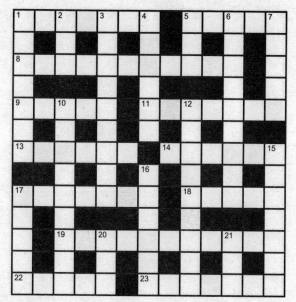

Across

1 Itinerant Australian labourer (7)
5 Young person attending school (5)
8 Furnace for burning refuse (11)
9 Leisurely walk (5)
11 Young foreign people who help with housework or childcare (2,5)
13 Made a noise like a snake (6)
14 Criticised harshly, usually online (coll) (6)
17 Disordered (7)
18 Order of Greek architecture (5)
19 The act of watching (11)
22 Unstable (5)
23 Painted structures of a stage set (7)

Down

1 Popeye's favourite vegetable! (7)
2 The alphabet (inits) (3)
3 Spiced mixture of chopped raisins, apples, etc (9)
4 Standard (6)
5 Animal kept for companionship (3)
6 Sweet edible fruit that resembles a large tomato (9)
7 Comes down to earth (5)
10 Lively Brazilian dance (5,4)
12 Beat rapidly (9)
15 Quality of being polite and respectable (7)
16 Fruits produced by an oak tree (6)
17 Gateaux (5)
20 Crafty (3)
21 Extreme anger (3)

194

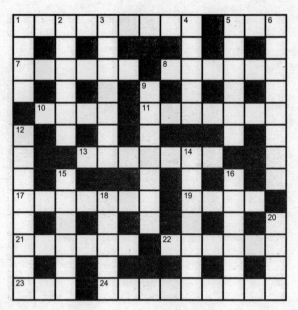

Across

1 Recovering readily from adversity (9)
5 Earlier in time than, poetically (3)
7 Fervent proponent of something (6)
8 Detest (6)
10 Desert of Mongolia and China (4)
11 Gift (7)
13 Metal used in thermometers (7)
17 Official who signals the beginning of a race (7)
19 Thomas ___, German writer (1875–1955) (4)
21 Detestable (6)
22 Narrow steep-sided valley (6)
23 Duvet warmth rating (3)
24 Admit defeat (9)

Down

1 Level to the ground (4)
2 Umbra (6)
3 Resembling a lion (7)
4 Plural of that (5)
5 Starter course of a meal (6)
6 Action-packed (8)
9 Person devoted to the enjoyment of food (7)
12 Official travel permit (8)
14 Storm around (7)
15 Placing horizontally (6)
16 Pitiless (6)
18 Tie the limbs of a bird before cooking (5)
20 Low dam built across a stream (4)

Across

1 Superficial (6)
4 Deep-water floor (6)
8 Baby's knitted footwear item (6)
10 Urged (6)
11 Steering organ of a fish (3)
12 Conclude (3)
13 Nought (3)
14 Metal found in nuggets (4)
16 Beach grains (4)
19 Alongside (4)
21 Rich-looking, upper-class (coll) (4)
24 Be in the red (3)
25 Ram's mate (3)
26 Smallest whole number (3)
27 Wheel cover (6)
29 Looked for custom (6)
31 Infer from what precedes (6)
32 Opening part (4-2)

Down

1 Make excuses to (someone) (3,3)
2 Sounding like a dove (6)
3 False statement (3)
5 Flightless bird (3)
6 Aft (6)
7 Deprive of by deceit (coll) (6)
9 Observed suspiciously (4)
10 Pea-shells (4)
15 Fair few? (3)
17 In the past (3)
18 Bludgeoned (coll) (6)
19 Like ducks' feet, for instance (6)
20 Cannabis plant (4)
21 Shower (with missiles) (4)
22 Gave an owl's call (6)
23 Endured, lasted out (4,2)
28 Part of a circumference (3)
30 Material from which metal is extracted (3)

196

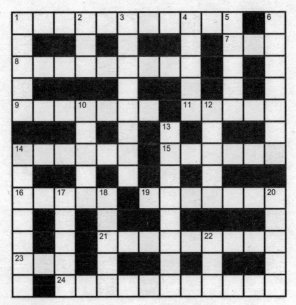

Across

1 Bursary (11)
7 Nickname of US president Eisenhower (3)
8 Great European painter prior to the 19th century (3,6)
9 Moving to music (7)
11 Finely powdered tobacco (5)
14 Breathes noisily in sleep (6)
15 Direction leading to the centre (6)
16 Violent impact (5)
19 It begins after 31 December (3,4)
21 Rising upward (9)
23 Anoint or lubricate (3)
24 Acid-base indicating substance (6,5)

Down

1 Rapier (5)
2 Unit of electrical resistance (3)
3 Fire-raiser (8)
4 Hurts, injures (5)
5 Colourful rice (5)
6 Properly nourished (4-3)
10 Heavy open wagons (5)
12 Very recently (5)
13 Similarity in appearance or character (8)
14 Divide into segments (7)
17 Coral reef (5)
18 Blood pump (5)
20 Helicopter propeller (5)
22 Chemical which carries genetic information (inits) (3)

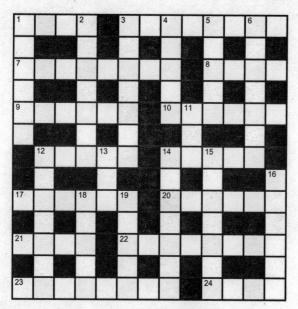

Across

1 Norse god of mischief (4)
3 Superior skill, prowess (8)
7 Start using a gun (4,4)
8 Private box or enclosure in a theatre (4)
9 Fertilised egg (6)
10 Become less light (6)
12 Finicky (5)
14 Counters used to represent money when gambling (5)
17 Burrowing animal (6)
20 Sacred word repeated in prayer (6)
21 Assistant (4)
22 Three-sided figure (8)
23 Evaluates, quantifies (8)
24 Sprinkled with seed (4)

Down

1 Slacken (6)
2 Refuses to acknowledge (7)
3 Court-ordered support paid by one spouse to another (7)
4 Pace (5)
5 Relating to the Sun (5)
6 Return to a former state (7)
11 Deciduous tree (3)
12 Delicate, frail (7)
13 ___ Lanka, republic (3)
14 Makes a pledge, promises (7)
15 Batting turn of a cricket player (7)
16 Large underground chamber (6)
18 Makes beer (5)
19 Coach (5)

198

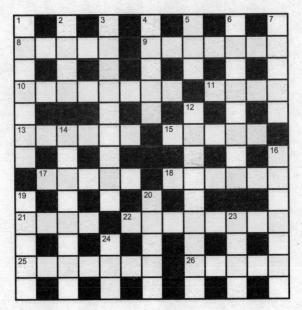

Across

8 Welsh breed of long-bodied, short-legged dog (5)

9 Feels angry (7)

10 Schemed (8)

11 Musical piece (4)

13 Complains (coll) (6)

15 Junior (5)

17 Says positively (5)

18 Out of ___, lacking balance (6)

21 Athletic breed of horse from the Middle East (4)

22 Trying hard (8)

25 Hinders (5,2)

26 Transcend (5)

Down

1 Block of frozen water for cooling drinks (3,4)

2 Smile broadly (4)

3 Clergymen (9)

4 Poplar (5)

5 Gaelic word meaning a mountain peak (3)

6 Produce routinely in large quantities (5,3)

7 From the Orient (5)

12 Makes less barbaric (9)

14 Likely to provoke jealousy (8)

16 Evasive (7)

19 Municipal swimming pool (5)

20 Prevents, halts (5)

23 Very short distance (4)

24 Invite (3)

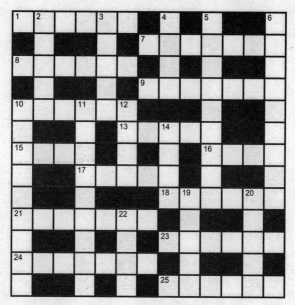

199

Across

1 Oddments (6)
7 Small flute (7)
8 Solid part of the Earth's surface (6)
9 Knocked unconscious by a heavy blow (7)
10 Football (6)
13 Defence plea of being elsewhere (5)
15 Tatters (4)
16 Animal's den (4)
17 Velvety leather (5)
18 Stings (6)
21 Right (7)
23 Ice cream container (6)
24 Develops (7)
25 Determines the heaviness of (6)

Down

2 Goods carried by a large vehicle (5)
3 One-hundredths of a pound (5)
4 Prescribed selection of foods (4)
5 Scarcely detectable amount (9)
6 Repairs to the highway (9)
10 Litter used as a means of transporting sick people (9)
11 Oven-cooked stew (9)
12 People who belong to the same genetic stock (4)
14 "Beware the ___ of March", advice given to Julius Caesar (4)
19 Large northern deer (5)
20 Molars, for example (5)
22 Professional cook (4)

203

200

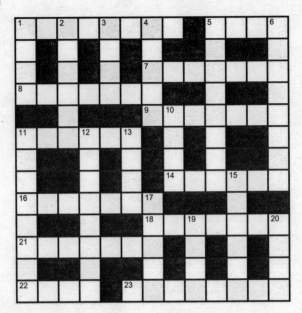

Across

1 Exercise that increases the need for oxygen (8)
5 Young sheep (4)
7 Confirmed the truth or accuracy of (something) (7)
8 Difference of opinion (7)
9 Habitual method of procedure (7)
11 Cinnamon-yielding tree (6)
14 Scorches (6)
16 Locally prevalent (7)
18 Leftover (7)
21 Put in the shadow (7)
22 Lone (4)
23 Check printed material for errors (4-4)

Down

1 ___ *Lang Syne*, Scottish song (4)
2 Type of monkey, macaque (6)
3 Capital of Azerbaijan (4)
4 Blanket (5)
5 Site (8)
6 Financial obligations that are unlikely to be repaid (3,5)
10 Poems (4)
11 Marked by lack of attention (8)
12 At an unfixed or unknown moment (8)
13 Opposed to (4)
15 Looked at with a fixed gaze (6)
17 Statement of beliefs (5)
19 Numerous (4)
20 Diplomacy (4)

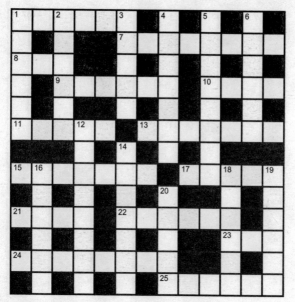

Across

1 Removes facial hair (6)
7 Animal that lives by preying on others (8)
8 Adult male person (3)
9 Let know (6)
10 Uncouth ill-bred person (4)
11 Garbage (5)
13 Motor vehicles specially modified to give high power and speed (3,4)
15 Casks, kegs (7)
17 Ravioli, for example (5)
21 Metallic element, symbol Fe (4)
22 New World vulture (6)
23 ___ and outs, details of a situation (3)
24 With unflagging vitality (8)
25 Small piece of cloth or paper (3,3)

Down

1 Peak (6)
2 Medicinal plant (6)
3 Bobbin, reel (5)
4 Celestial object seen as a narrow waxing crescent (3,4)
5 Microscopic organisms (8)
6 Divided into two branches (6)
12 Person unknown to you (8)
14 Momentary flash of light (7)
16 Frightened (6)
18 Place of worship associated with a sacred thing or person (6)
19 Entertained (6)
20 Acute insecurity (5)

202

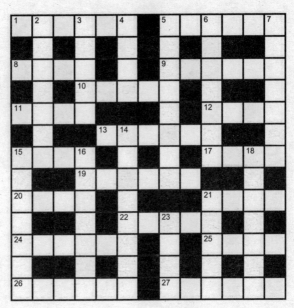

Across

1 Vocation (6)
5 Repartee (6)
8 Pilgrimage to Mecca (4)
9 Steam baths (6)
10 Start, commencement (5)
11 Small bunch of flowers (4)
12 Keen on (4)
13 Rough area on the skin (6)
15 Sediment in wine (4)
17 Pay close attention to (4)
19 Does business (6)
20 No longer here (4)
21 Cut-price event (4)
22 Country, capital Sana'a (5)
24 Owns up to (6)
25 Well-ventilated (4)
26 Restaurant customers (6)
27 Cashier (6)

Down

2 In the latest fashion (1,2,4)
3 Relish (5)
4 Steals (4)
5 Notorious French prison (8)
6 Nurture (7)
7 Answer (7)
14 Investigation (8)
15 Dawdler (7)
16 Germ-free (7)
18 Make bigger (7)
21 Growl (5)
23 Ditch around a castle (4)

Across

1 Affectedly prim (coll) (6)
4 Gait (6)
9 Plant with flowers on long spikes (5)
10 Device for connecting non-matching plugs and sockets (7)
11 Judo level (3)
12 Small mouselike mammal (5)
13 ___ flu, stomach ailment (7)
14 Coarse cotton cloth (6)
15 Bivalve mollusc (6)
18 US hotel worker (7)
20 Passive (5)
22 Give permission to (3)
23 Portable light (3,4)
24 Restless, fidgety (5)
25 Put into cipher (6)
26 Item used for writing (3,3)

Down

1 Ends of the Earth (5)
2 Put in jeopardy (7)
3 Advertisement carried on the shoulders (8,5)
5 Process of changing the order of something (13)
6 Place in a grave (5)
7 Aural pain (7)
8 Shabby, seedy (5)
14 Small kitchen on the deck of a ship (7)
16 Patella (4-3)
17 Slight woman or girl (5)
19 Mauve-flowered shrub (5)
21 Test-wear (a garment) before buying it (3,2)

204

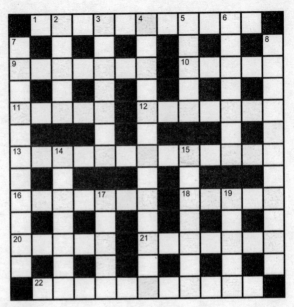

Across

1 Building for viewing the heavens (11)
9 Growing less (7)
10 Adjust again after an initial failure (5)
11 Religious mendicant (5)
12 Minding, nursing (7)
13 Form of art intended to present an unromanticised view of the world (6,7)
16 Falls on the Canada/US border (7)
18 Fire-raising (5)
20 Biblical region with an unnamed queen (5)
21 Object that sank the *Titanic* (7)
22 As a rule (11)

Down

2 ___ *Beauty*, Anna Sewell's only novel (5)
3 North-east African state that gained independence in 1993 (7)
4 Non-consumption of meat (13)
5 Italian city on the river Po (5)
6 Composer of *The Barber of Seville* (7)
7 Attractive but slightly disreputable quality (11)
8 Oversee the lighting and other technical aspects of a play (5,6)
14 Continental country house (7)
15 Inexpert (7)
17 "Man's love is of man's life a thing ___", line by Byron (5)
19 Hard outer covering (5)

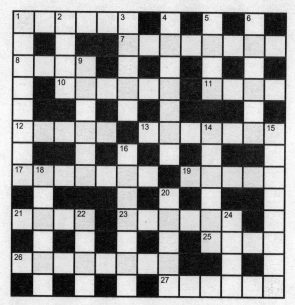

Across

1 Furnished room with a sleeping area and some plumbing (6)
7 Ruffian, yob (8)
8 Relaxation (4)
10 Orange root vegetable (6)
11 Pretentious (4)
12 Frolic, cavort (5)
13 Dissent (7)
17 Force produced by a pressure difference (7)
19 Church instrument (5)
21 Proficient (4)
23 Made warm (6)
25 Heavy book (4)
26 Soak in a seasoned stock (8)
27 Most uncivil (6)

Down

1 Buildings used to house military personnel (8)
2 Phonograph record (4)
3 Prickle, barb (5)
4 Twist and press out of shape (7)
5 Female operatic star (4)
6 Prickly desert plant (6)
9 Special skill (6)
14 Small tower (6)
15 Block of flats (8)
16 Proceed (2,5)
18 Optimistic (6)
20 Thin biscuit often eaten with ice cream (5)
22 Arabian ruler (4)
24 Give a narcotic to (4)

206

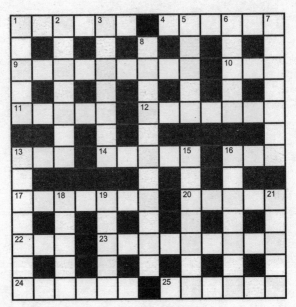

Across

1 ___ Mahler, composer, 1860–1911 (6)
4 Breakfast food holder (3,3)
9 Informal occasion for dropping in (4,5)
10 Night bird (3)
11 ___ out, dwindle (5)
12 Grieves (7)
13 Go fast (3)
14 Believes (5)
16 Egg-laying fowl (3)
17 Obtained, originated (from) (7)
20 Extracts the best (5)
22 Science workshop (abbr) (3)
23 Vast and dark (9)
24 Interrogates (6)
25 Handy to have (6)

Down

1 Band (5)
2 Stayed longer in bed (5,2)
3 Held fast (7)
5 Lustre (5)
6 Headdress for a monarch (5)
7 Drives off the road (5,2)
8 Chicory (5,6)
13 Danger signal (3,4)
15 Fastens (7)
16 Repulse (4,3)
18 Jewish teacher (5)
19 Sung part of a piece of music (5)
21 Rope-making fibre (5)

Across

1 Place on top of, overlay (11)
7 German physicist who discovered X-rays (8)
8 Landscaped complex of shops (4)
9 Total (6)
11 Intercede (6)
13 Desert garden (5)
14 Provide a brief summary (5)
17 Song of devotion or loyalty (6)
20 Be earlier in time, precede (6)
22 Temporary provision of money (4)
23 Disposition to be patient and long-suffering (8)
24 Mercury (11)

Down

1 Dished up (6)
2 Tedium (5)
3 The act of entering (7)
4 Committee (5)
5 Group of islands, capital Apia (5)
6 Missile fired from a gun (6)
10 Grilled bread (5)
12 Mental representation (5)
14 Inclined beams supporting a roof (7)
15 Disreputable or vicious person (coll) (3,3)
16 Less tight (6)
18 Believer in a major religion (5)
19 Imitate (5)
21 Of the kidneys (5)

208

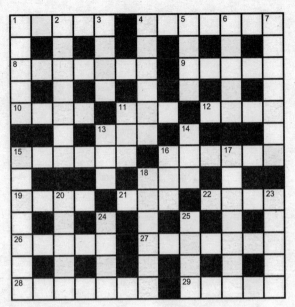

Across

1 Greenfly, for instance (5)
4 Return from a trip (3,4)
8 Chuckled (7)
9 Excavated (3,2)
10 Uses a needle (4)
11 Baffle, deceive (3)
12 Stalk (4)
13 Decree that prohibits something (3)
15 Hot spring (6)
16 Sea depth measure (6)
18 Tent-bracing rope (3)
19 Heading (4)
21 Trot (3)
22 Plant used for flavouring (4)
26 Sharp instrument (5)
27 Term describing a substance that can be dispersed in a liquid (7)
28 Midriff-baring garment (4,3)
29 Marketplace (5)

Down

1 Aberdeen ____, cattle (5)
2 Road (7)
3 North-country valley (4)
4 Boy at a christening? (6)
5 Clear up (4)
6 Slang of thieves (5)
7 Stayed silent (coll) (4,3)
11 At a great distance (3)
13 Wager (3)
14 Reddish-brown horse (3)
15 Unpatented (drug) (7)
16 Stuffiness (3)
17 Shop where shoes are mended (4,3)
18 Chat (6)
20 Female singing voice, between soprano and contralto (5)
23 Freshwater fish (5)
24 Be anxious (4)
25 Musical notation written on a stave (4)

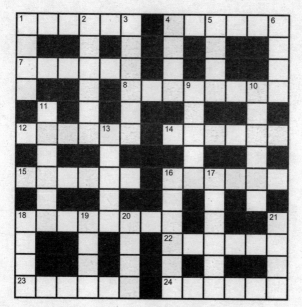

Across

1 Celebrated (6)
4 Express astonishment or surprise (6)
7 Finger-shaped cream cake (6)
8 Etch into a material or surface (8)
12 Solve crime (6)
14 Rolls of tobacco prepared for smoking (6)
15 Domestic ass (6)
16 Tool resembling a hammer (6)
18 Academic term (8)
22 Relating to the backbone (6)
23 Confidential (6)
24 Official emissary of the Pope (6)

Down

1 Feast upon (4)
2 Not clear (6)
3 Go at top speed (6)
4 Kate ___, celebrity model (4)
5 Stand up on the hind legs (4)
6 Emotion of strong affection (4)
9 High-quality porcelain (5)
10 Hairdresser (6)
11 Far off (6)
13 Board game (5)
16 Small piece of food (6)
17 Existing (6)
18 Solidifies (4)
19 Always (4)
20 Nipple (4)
21 Sticky paste (4)

210

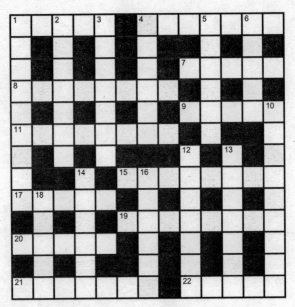

Across

1 Dish on which food is served (5)
4 Tranquillised (7)
7 Small portable timepiece (5)
8 Celibacy (8)
9 Asian pepper plant (5)
11 Long-tailed game bird (8)
15 Spicy pasta steamed with a meat and vegetable stew (8)
17 Showing keen interest or intense desire (5)
19 Product that removes dirt, etc (8)
20 Might (5)
21 Holy war (7)
22 Lit by twilight (5)

Down

1 Very steep cliff (9)
2 Attire (7)
3 Overwhelming happiness or joyful excitement (7)
4 Church officer in charge of sacred objects (6)
5 Rouse from slumber (6)
6 Person who acts as host at formal occasions (coll) (5)
10 In an unhurried way (9)
12 Embarrassed (7)
13 Lymph glands at the root of the tongue (7)
14 Domains (6)
16 Provide a favour for someone (6)
18 Secretive or illicit relationship (5)

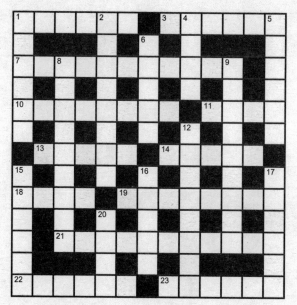

Across

1 Bicycle seat (6)
3 Joined by treaty or agreement (6)
7 Blasé (11)
10 Forceful and insistent advertising (4,4)
11 Run away quickly (4)
13 Berkshire town, famous for its racecourse (5)
14 Tall tower referred to in the Bible (5)
18 Land measure (4)
19 Popular pond creature (8)
21 Australian musical instrument, played by holding in both hands and flexing (6,5)
22 Stabbing weapon (6)
23 Population count (6)

Down

1 Looked for (6)
2 Venture involving risk but promising great rewards (4,4)
4 Queue (4)
5 Make moist (6)
6 Hands out playing cards (5)
8 Device used to open bottles (9)
9 Italian for 'the sweet life' (5,4)
12 Lower jawbone (8)
15 Source of danger (6)
16 Cast off hair, skin or feathers (5)
17 Shelters from light (6)
20 Double-reed woodwind instrument (4)

212

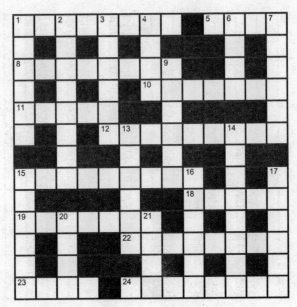

Across

1 Bring to light, reveal (8)
5 Professional charges (4)
8 Insignia used by the medical profession (8)
10 Large heavy knife (7)
11 Use a divining rod in search of underground water (5)
12 Having an exceedingly bad reputation (9)
15 Steward (9)
18 Evil or corrupt practice (5)
19 Covered against loss (7)
22 Drool (8)
23 Girdle (4)
24 Showing profound esteem (8)

Down

1 Make up one's mind (6)
2 Obliquely (8)
3 Fungal, mossy growth (6)
4 Film of impurities on the surface of a liquid (4)
6 Border (4)
7 Fasteners with threaded shanks (6)
9 Small meat and vegetable turnover of Indian origin (6)
13 Loads, an abundance (coll) (6)
14 Stubborn (8)
15 Emergency (6)
16 Indigenous person (6)
17 Begrudge (6)
20 Male children (4)
21 Native of Copenhagen, for example (4)

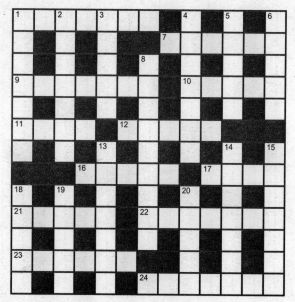

Across

1 Windstorm that lifts up clouds of dust (7)
7 Front of a building (6)
9 Everlasting (7)
10 Made a written record of (5)
11 Move in large numbers (4)
12 Castrated bull (5)
16 Artist's tripod (5)
17 Give up (4)
21 Has in mind (5)
22 Brochure (7)
23 One who takes spoils or plunder (as in war) (6)
24 Firecrackers (7)

Down

1 Three score and ten (7)
2 Cervine mammal (3,4)
3 Highland pole (5)
4 Wash clothes (7)
5 Coat in fat (5)
6 Prepared for action (5)
8 Winged creature that transmits sleeping sickness (6,3)
13 Soft wool fabric with a colourful swirled pattern of curved shapes (7)
14 Substitute (7)
15 Alphabetic characters (7)
18 Grin (5)
19 Breakfast rasher (5)
20 Heathen (5)

214

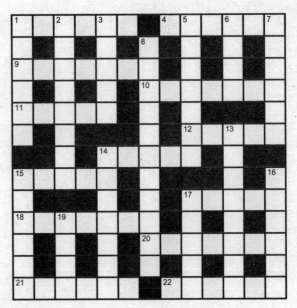

Across

1 Without danger (6)
4 Intense dislike (6)
9 Price of a plane ticket (3,4)
10 Style of design popular in the 1920s and 1930s (3,4)
11 Entice (5)
12 Abrupt (5)
14 Matching set of furniture (5)
15 Capture (5)
17 Relative magnitude (5)
18 Defensive mound (7)
20 Consider in detail (7)
21 CD player (6)
22 Give in, as to influence or pressure (6)

Down

1 Lacking in quantity (6)
2 Most notable or prominent (8)
3 Slightest (5)
5 Transparent plastic (7)
6 Went on horseback (4)
7 Force out of office (6)
8 Myopic (4-7)
13 Member of one's family (8)
14 Enfold (7)
15 Stroke lovingly (6)
16 Authoritative command (6)
17 Judder (5)
19 Spice made from the covering of the nutmeg (4)

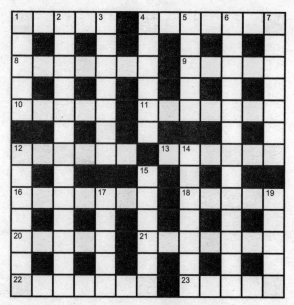

Across

1 Common crustaceans (5)
4 Have (7)
8 Allure or entice (7)
9 Cinema attendant (5)
10 Pathfinder (5)
11 Walk by dragging one's feet (7)
12 Covering for the ankle, fitting over the upper of a shoe (6)
13 Strip fixed to something to hold it firm (6)
16 Comparison in order to show a similarity (7)
18 Scent (5)
20 Mexican comrade (5)
21 Making warm (7)
22 Pyrogenic (7)
23 Person with no fixed residence (5)

Down

1 Caste (5)
2 Expecting unquestioning obedience (13)
3 Cause to jump with fear (7)
4 Compound often used in agriculture and industry (6)
5 Finnish steam bath (5)
6 Extravagant behaviour intended to attract attention (13)
7 Doctor (7)
12 Basic unit of currency in Paraguay (7)
14 Decline to vote (7)
15 Disease transmitted by body lice (6)
17 Convex moulding with a cross section of a quarter of a circle (5)
19 Inflexible (5)

216

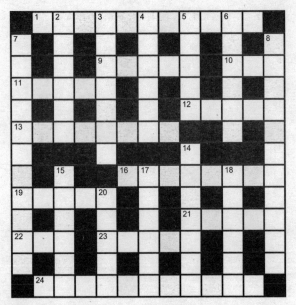

Across

1 River or stream (11)
9 Remedy (5)
10 Bustle (3)
11 Functions (5)
12 Fasten by passing rope through a hole (5)
13 Combination of lenses at the viewing end of optical instruments (8)
16 With the side towards the spectator (8)
19 Skin covering the top of the head (5)
21 Male duck (5)
22 Mr Garfunkel, singer-songwriter (3)
23 Bedlam (5)
24 Supposition (11)

Down

2 Accumulate (6)
3 Rubbery (7)
4 Churchman (6)
5 Cow's milk-gland (5)
6 Afraid (6)
7 First of January (3,5,3)
8 Not having actual being (3-8)
14 Pair of earphones (7)
15 Substance (6)
17 Defuse (6)
18 Slowly, in musical tempo (6)
20 Bundles (5)

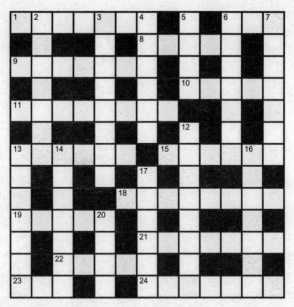

Across

1 Tool used to cut metal (7)
6 Association of criminals (3)
8 Bouquet (5)
9 Type of dog (7)
10 Agent used in fermenting beer (5)
11 Thin flexible tube inserted into the body (8)
13 Former Spanish monetary unit (6)
15 Area set back or indented (6)
18 Ribbon-like intestinal parasite (8)
19 Protective secretion of bodily membranes (5)
21 Biological (7)
22 Frighten away (5)
23 Common type of tree (3)
24 Educator (7)

Down

2 So-so (7)
3 Narrow, pointed shoe heel (8)
4 Network of rabbit burrows (6)
5 Punch and Judy dog (4)
6 Gruesome (7)
7 Hard-cased, winged creatures (7)
12 Mental deterioration (8)
13 Advance, advertise (7)
14 Ironical language (7)
16 Facet (7)
17 Large heavily built seabird (6)
20 One who works during a strike (4)

218

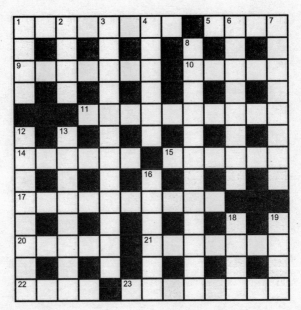

Across

1 Scenery intended to stand alone (3,5)

5 Blonde (4)

9 Slanted letters (7)

10 Facing of a jacket (5)

11 Help (10)

14 Women's stockings (6)

15 Very small (6)

17 Without flaws or loopholes (10)

20 Public acts of violence and disorder (5)

21 Cyclone (7)

22 Grandeur (4)

23 Genetic endowment (8)

Down

1 Expressed in words (4)

2 Native of Bangkok, for example (4)

3 Quirk (12)

4 Characteristic of the universe (6)

6 Narrow blind tube in the intestine (8)

7 Alleviated (8)

8 Framework on which to hang garments to dry (7-5)

12 White, early spring flower (8)

13 Dais (8)

16 Largest digit of the foot (3,3)

18 Wise Men who brought gifts to Jesus (4)

19 Warm and snug (4)

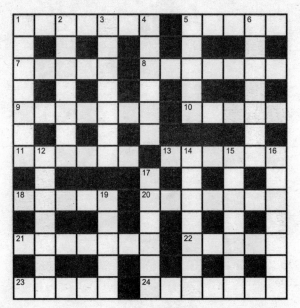

Across

1 Vehicle framework (7)
5 Lads (5)
7 Transmitting live (2,3)
8 Hone (7)
9 Receive a share of (7)
10 Cold vegetable dish (5)
11 Death (6)
13 Largest province of Canada (6)
18 Round objects used in games (5)
20 Be relevant to (7)
21 Type of long-grained rice (7)
22 Native of Baghdad, for example (5)
23 Small, round and gleaming (of eyes) (5)
24 Perfumed (7)

Down

1 Cut into pieces (7)
2 Word of transposed letters (7)
3 Do something to a greater degree (7)
4 County of southern England (6)
5 Uncouth (5)
6 Short introductory essay preceding the text of a book (7)
12 Issue forth (7)
14 Country, capital Kiev (7)
15 Without any attempt at concealment (7)
16 Encrusted with sugar (7)
17 Mars, ruins (6)
19 Sheltered from light or heat (5)

220

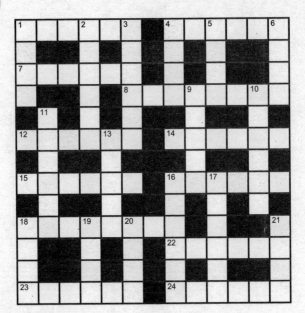

Across

1 Full of exultant happiness (6)
4 Positive declaration (6)
7 Moral principles (6)
8 Herbivorous land turtle (8)
12 Light tanker for supplying water or fuel (6)
14 Sponsor, investor (6)
15 Trade by exchange (6)
16 Small and often ornate box for holding valuables (6)
18 Valuer, estimator (8)
22 Italian square surrounded by buildings (6)
23 Close of day (6)
24 "Open ___", magic words used by Ali Baba (6)

Down

1 Australian term for a young kangaroo (4)
2 Egyptian god of the underworld (6)
3 Female sibling (6)
4 At a great distance (4)
5 Anise-flavoured Greek liqueur (4)
6 Delicate, woven and decorative fabric (4)
9 Diadem (5)
10 Meat pin (6)
11 Wandering tribesmen (6)
13 Level betting (5)
16 Main body (6)
17 Gardening scissors (6)
18 Becomes older (4)
19 Stretches (out) (4)
20 Condiment, sodium chloride (4)
21 Cook in an oven (4)

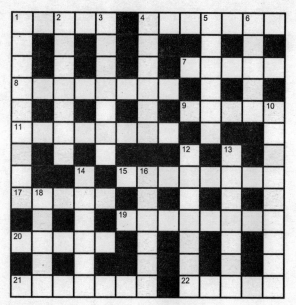

Across

1 Japanese rice dish (5)

4 Enduring strength and energy (7)

7 Bathroom fixture (5)

8 XIX in Roman numerals (8)

9 Closely crowded together (5)

11 County in southern England (8)

15 Increase in extent or intensity (8)

17 Fling (5)

19 Daughter of a sovereign (8)

20 Projecting edge of a roof (5)

21 Person who rides a bicycle (7)

22 Coil of knitting wool (5)

Down

1 Catapult (9)

2 Family appellation (7)

3 Awaiting (2,5)

4 Withdraw from an organisation (6)

5 Cricket over in which no runs are scored (6)

6 Demands (5)

10 Annexe (9)

12 Insanity (7)

13 Graceful antelope of Africa and Asia (7)

14 Toward or located in the north (6)

16 Actor's lines (6)

18 Of great weight (5)

222

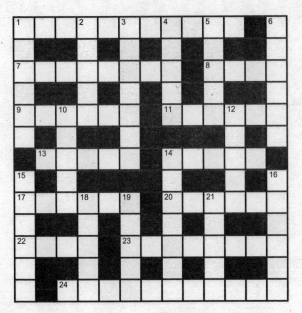

Across

1 Organic compound having powerful soporific effect (11)
7 Antipathy (8)
8 Eject in large quantities (4)
9 Dreamlike state (6)
11 Chase (6)
13 Earnings (5)
14 Church associated with a convent (5)
17 Appraise (6)
20 Disarrange or rumple (6)
22 Archaic form of the word 'you' (4)
23 Madmen (8)
24 Fluid circulating through the body (11)

Down

1 Loveliness (6)
2 Member of the peerage (5)
3 Skeletal muscle having three origins (7)
4 Approach (3-2)
5 Weapon that delivers an electric shock (5)
6 Maker of archery equipment (6)
10 Accumulate (5)
12 Vehicles used to travel over snow (5)
14 Pays heed (7)
15 Any of various small breeds of fowl (6)
16 Part of a ship's equipment or cargo that is thrown overboard (6)
18 Evenly matched (5)
19 Barrage (5)
21 Express (5)

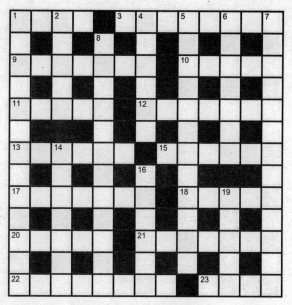

Across

1 Neither good nor bad (2-2)
3 Come together for a meeting (8)
9 Partly coincide (7)
10 Grows from, originates (5)
11 Impurities left in the final drops of a liquid (5)
12 Trucks (7)
13 Spite (6)
15 Hindu deity (6)
17 Former capital of China (7)
18 Foxhole (5)
20 Voluptuously beautiful young woman (5)
21 US 'Heart of Dixie' state (7)
22 Line of descent of a pure-bred animal (8)
23 Informal conversation (4)

Down

1 Skill in fencing (13)
2 Panorama (5)
4 Lithe (6)
5 Former member of the armed forces (2-10)
6 Flaw that spoils the appearance of something (7)
7 Compass point at 112.50 degrees (4,5-4)
8 Indistinct yet unmistakable barrier on the career ladder (5,7)
14 Lackadaisical (7)
16 Related on the father's side (6)
19 Freshwater fish (5)

224

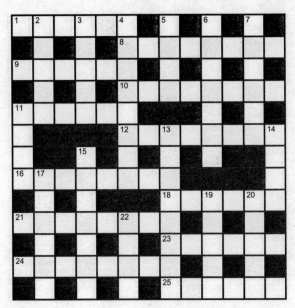

Across
1 Caused to stop (6)
8 Kept apart (8)
9 Quagmire (6)
10 Marked by quiet, caution and secrecy (8)
11 Small informal restaurant (6)
12 Tepid (8)
16 Source of oil, also used as food (4,4)
18 Refuse to acknowledge (6)
21 Religious zeal (8)
23 Sharp-eyed birds (6)
24 Taking delight in beauty (8)
25 Weighing machine (6)

Down
2 Garlic mayonnaise (5)
3 Characteristic (5)
4 Cause to go into a solution (8)
5 Give medicine to (4)
6 Instrument from which a person is executed by hanging (7)
7 Gentle wind (6)
11 Implores (4)
13 Generosity (8)
14 Chief (4)
15 Engage in boisterous, drunken merrymaking (7)
17 Device for loosening or removing the tops of bottles, cans, etc (6)
19 18th letter of the Greek alphabet (5)
20 In what place? (5)
22 Graphic symbol (4)

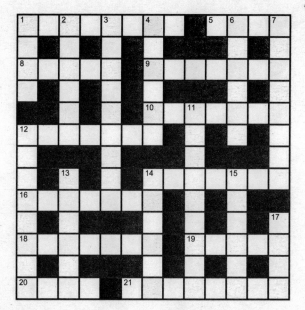

Across
1 Filaments from a web spun by a spider (8)
5 Taxis (4)
8 Expect (5)
9 Plant which is the source of tapioca (7)
10 Cause the downfall of (rulers) (7)
12 Traditions (7)
14 Obedient (7)
16 Body of water between Israel and Jordan (4,3)
18 Nobleman (in various countries) ranking above a count (7)
19 Ice house (5)
20 Manufactured (4)
21 Placed very near together (5-3)

Down
1 Cogwheel (4)
2 Beams of light (6)
3 Regions on diametrically opposite sides of the Earth (9)
4 Overabundance (6)
6 Plant similar to the rhododendron (6)
7 First courses (8)
11 Portable power packs (9)
12 Aromatic seed used as seasoning (8)
13 Implement used to clean the barrel of a firearm (6)
14 Maiden (6)
15 Female germ cells of a plant (6)
17 Sea vessel (4)

229

226

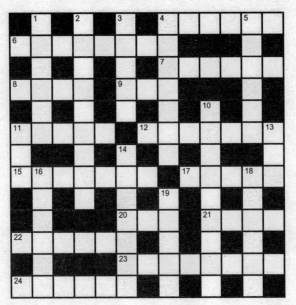

Across

4 Reverberated (6)
6 In these times (8)
7 Consortium of companies formed to limit competition (6)
8 Act presumptuously (4)
9 Epoch (3)
11 Jelly based on fish or meat stock (5)
12 Marked by refinement in taste and manners (7)
15 Very drunk (slang) (3-4)
17 Light wood (5)
20 Tap lightly (3)
21 At the summit of (4)
22 Comfort in disappointment or misery (6)
23 Height of the ocean's surface (3,5)
24 Piously earnest (6)

Down

1 Determines the sum of (6)
2 Range oneself with one party or another (4,5)
3 Widely known and esteemed (5)
4 Someone who breaks free (7)
5 Appear (6)
10 Gambit, ploy (9)
11 High mountain (3)
13 Field covered with grass (3)
14 Storm (7)
16 Compel to behave in a certain way (6)
18 Plain dough cakes, often griddled (6)
19 Cut of meat (5)

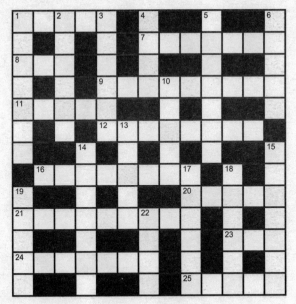

Across

1 Covers the surface of (5)
7 Bring forward (7)
8 Cut part of a tree trunk (3)
9 Confidently aggressive (9)
11 Perfume (5)
12 Alienate (8)
16 Land and the buildings on it (8)
20 Connections (5)
21 Sum total of many miscellaneous things (9)
23 Shoddy or tasteless articles (3)
24 Driving force (7)
25 Popular web portal (5)

Down

1 Percussion instrument (7)
2 Fisherman (6)
3 Dignified and sombre in manner (6)
4 Contains the flow of (usually water) (4)
5 Requiring (7)
6 Instrument for measuring a quantity (5)
10 Eagle's nest (5)
13 Catapult (5)
14 Question after a military operation (7)
15 Italian rice dish (7)
17 Sordid (6)
18 Grab hastily (6)
19 Fundamental (5)
22 Domed recess (4)

228

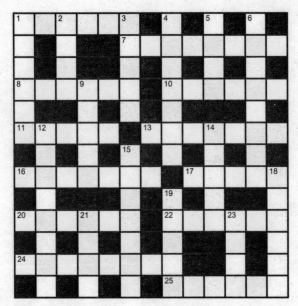

Across

1 Juicy fruit, such as lemon, orange, etc (6)
7 Urgently needed; absolutely necessary (8)
8 Not of sound mind (6)
10 Jolted (6)
11 Bride's partner (5)
13 One more (7)
16 Cause to separate and go in different directions (7)
17 Haywire (5)
20 Italian brandy made from residue of grapes after pressing (6)
22 Scour a surface (6)
24 Stay of execution (8)
25 Invasion by pathogenic bacteria (6)

Down

1 Shedding tears (6)
2 Bathroom fixtures (4)
3 Sloping mass of loose rocks at the base of a cliff (5)
4 Chinese herb believed to have medicinal powers (7)
5 Former unit of money in Italy (4)
6 Unnatural lack of colour (8)
9 At great height (5)
12 Fipple flute (8)
14 Equipment that measures periods (5)
15 After the expected or usual time (7)
18 Perspires (6)
19 Underground tunnels (5)
21 Airborne soldier (abbr) (4)
23 Social insects (4)

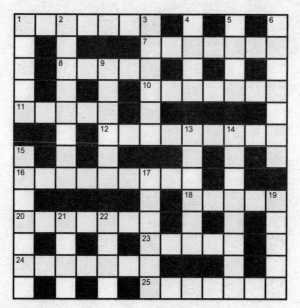

Across

1 Grave (7)
7 Sphere of vision (7)
8 Apostle who joined St Jude in Persia (5)
10 Fill to satisfaction (7)
11 Divisions of the school year (5)
12 Expectation, prospect (9)
16 Still in doubt (9)
18 Throws away as refuse (5)
20 Localised sore (7)
23 Root vegetable (5)
24 Scholarly life (7)
25 Make amends for, remedy (7)

Down

1 Lacking cash (5)
2 Puts aside, earmarks (8)
3 Detection device (6)
4 Basic rhythmic unit in a piece of music (4)
5 Spanish sparkling white wine (4)
6 Claimed, but not proved (7)
9 Someone unable to adapt to their circumstances (6)
13 Walk unsteadily, as a small child (6)
14 Rush (8)
15 Completely out of control (7)
17 Smaller (6)
19 Cut-price events (5)
21 Hitch, unforeseen problem (4)
22 Duelling sword (4)

230

Across

1 Symptom of indigestion (6)
5 Challenge aggressively (6)
8 Insurgents (6)
9 Commend (6)
10 Golfing device (3)
11 Country, capital Rome (5)
13 Short musical drama (8)
15 Impetuosity (8)
16 Light-beam amplifier (5)
19 Distressing (3)
21 Clothing (6)
22 Icon representing a person, used in internet chat and games (6)
23 Emergence (6)
24 Vocalist (6)

Down

2 Exactly alike (9)
3 Angler's basket (5)
4 Persistently annoying person (4)
5 Desperate (8)
6 Room (7)
7 Large container for liquids (4)
12 Deadlock (9)
13 In a foreign country (8)
14 Coated, frozen dessert in the shape of a brick (4-3)
17 Anew (5)
18 Female pantomime character (4)
20 Platform (4)

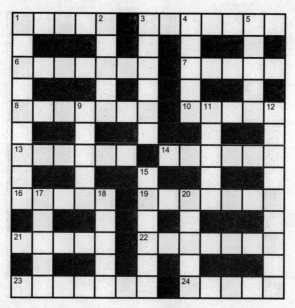

Across

1 Lives in a tent (5)
3 Musical accompaniment added above a basic melody (7)
6 Account for (7)
7 Become rotten, as of an egg, for example (5)
8 An insignificant place (7)
10 Injured by a bee or wasp (5)
13 Young swan (6)
14 Respiratory disorder (6)
16 Locations (5)
19 Affording an abundant supply (7)
21 Home of a beaver (5)
22 Active (2,3,2)
23 Devoid of practical purpose (7)
24 Military chaplain (5)

Down

1 Plain straight openings from shoulder to shoulder of sweaters (9)
2 Partial darkness (5)
3 Rich fruit cake (6)
4 Corset (5)
5 Man-made fibre (5)
9 Flexible joint (5)
11 For all (music) (5)
12 Former British prime minister (9)
15 To the opposite side (6)
17 Presses clothes (5)
18 Sift (5)
20 Raise, erect (3,2)

232

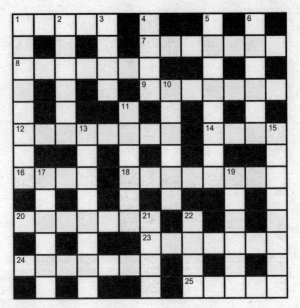

Across

1 Breathes noisily, as if exhausted (5)

7 Part of a barrier or fence (7)

8 Accomplish (7)

9 Image boost (3-4)

12 Idle (8)

14 Egg cell (4)

16 Wading bird (4)

18 On a higher floor (8)

20 Add sugar, for example (7)

23 Pop duo formed by Andy Bell and Vince Clarke (7)

24 Popular lens-shaped seeds that are soaked prior to cooking (7)

25 Oozes (5)

Down

1 Words or drawings sprayed onto walls (8)

2 North African desert (6)

3 Let fall off (4)

4 At liberty (4)

5 Extreme excess (8)

6 Being in the original position (2,4)

10 Metamorphic rock (6)

11 Water down (6)

13 Music-tape container (8)

15 Kept woman (8)

17 Player who delivers the ball to the batsman (6)

19 Invulnerable to infection, poison, etc (6)

21 Bird's home (4)

22 Heating elements in an electric fire (4)

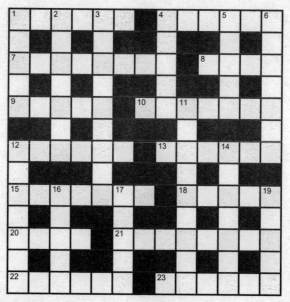

Across

1 Government of the Roman Catholic Church (6)
4 Deliberately hurts, annoys or offends (6)
7 Pilot of an aircraft (8)
8 Mother (4)
9 Desert in north-eastern Egypt (5)
10 Anticipate (7)
12 Rock fragments and pebbles (6)
13 Rush about (6)
15 Original disciple (7)
18 Takes short quick breaths (5)
20 Move through water using strokes (4)
21 Sensational in appearance (8)
22 Smiles contemptuously (6)
23 Instruction to go away (4,2)

Down

1 Crests (5)
2 Carnivorous freshwater fishes of South America (7)
3 Substance such as salt, mustard or pickle (9)
4 Fight (3-2)
5 Small short-necked dabbling river ducks (5)
6 Elegant, imposing (7)
11 Open to arguments, ideas, or change (9)
12 Spectacles (7)
14 Act wildly or without restraint (3,4)
16 Compound of oxygen with another element (5)
17 Inventories (5)
19 Ability to see (5)

234

Across

1 Separated into lots or classes (6)
4 Pays out (6)
7 Waterless (4)
8 Requiring precise accuracy (8)
10 Noisy disturbance (6)
12 Sacredly obscure (6)
14 Person fond of making over-fine distinctions (6)
17 Enveloping bandage (6)
19 Horse-drawn vehicle with four wheels (8)
21 Asian plant widely cultivated for its oily beans (4)
22 One of the Channel Islands (6)
23 Wispy white cloud (6)

Down

1 Rise upwards into the air (4)
2 Neaten, place in order (4,2)
3 Compulsory force or threat (6)
4 Muslim form of salutation (6)
5 Fills with high spirits (6)
6 So direct in manner as to be blunt (9)
9 Of a quantity that can be counted (9)
11 Large pot for making coffee or tea (3)
13 Coniferous tree (3)
15 Corresponds, tallies (6)
16 Worthless, of poor quality (6)
17 Having a beautiful natural panorama (6)
18 Maltreater (6)
20 Open barrels or casks (4)

Across

1 Brass instrument without valves (5)
4 Deprives of food (7)
8 Gave up voluntarily (9)
9 Headdress worn by a bishop (5)
10 Metamorphose (9)
13 Underground passage (6)
14 Excursion (6)
16 Having no definite form (9)
19 Month with 30 days (5)
20 Bona fide (9)
22 Typographical error (7)
23 Girl's name (5)

Down

1 Organic matter used as fuel (7)
2 Large portable hi-fi with built-in speakers (coll) (6,7)
3 Type of heron (5)
4 ___ City, 2005 film (3)
5 Lies adjacent to (5)
6 British military decoration for gallantry (8,5)
7 Biblical city known for vice and corruption (5)
11 Imperial (5)
12 Secluded corners (5)
15 Old Spanish ship (7)
16 Dry white Italian wine (5)
17 Discharge, throw out (5)
18 Fires from a job (5)
21 Woollen cap of Scottish origin (3)

236

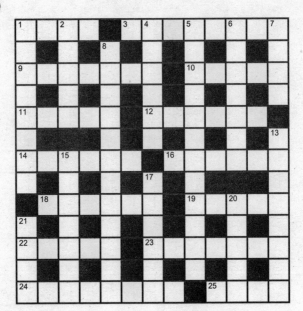

Across

1 Produce a sound expressive of relief (4)
3 Authorised, gave permission to (8)
9 Strangling (7)
10 Stir vigorously (5)
11 Noosed rope (5)
12 Cooked slowly and for a long time in liquid (6)
14 Young cat (6)
16 Building in which films are shown (6)
18 Anil (6)
19 Influenced decisively (5)
22 Fabric made from spun flax (5)
23 Sudden fit (7)
24 Climbing, flowering shrub (8)
25 Hair on a lion's neck (4)

Down

1 Of a kind specified previously (8)
2 Give a shine to (5)
4 Take up, as of knowledge (6)
5 Associated with a church (12)
6 Crush, tighten (7)
7 Clammy (4)
8 Unwillingness to comply (12)
13 Death of part of the body (8)
15 Leaseholders, occupants (7)
17 Art of growing miniature trees (6)
20 Small pendant fleshy lobe at the back of the soft palate (5)
21 Went by plane (4)

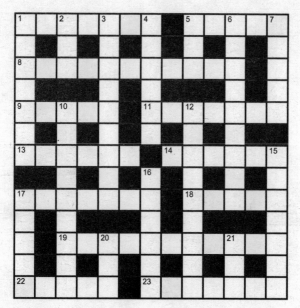

Across

1 Arena (7)
5 ____ Asimov, science-fiction writer (5)
8 Pit viper with horny segments at the end of the tail (11)
9 Barrier constructed to keep out the sea (5)
11 Makes certain of (7)
13 High-pitched and sharp (6)
14 Sealed in a tin (6)
17 Serious collision (especially of motor vehicles) (5-2)
18 Conjecture (5)
19 Suggest that someone is guilty (11)
22 Perspiration (5)
23 Marine plant (7)

Down

1 Ancient rolled documents (7)
2 Law passed by Parliament (3)
3 Poor physical or mental condition (3,6)
4 Created disorder (6)
5 Former Hollywood star, ____ Lupino (1918–95) (3)
6 Condition markedly different from the norm (9)
7 Coffee shops (5)
10 Adaptable (9)
12 Place of complete bliss (7-2)
15 Become wider (7)
16 Physical science relating to light (6)
17 Secret agents (5)
20 Reduced (3)
21 Expert (3)

238

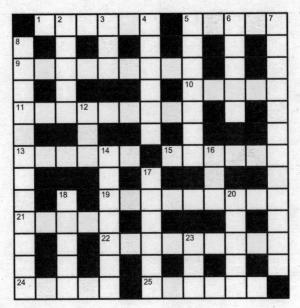

Across

1. Measure of mental ability (2,4)
5. Same again (5)
9. Having no known name (9)
10. Japanese verse form (5)
11. Paid driver (9)
13. Military action in which besieged troops burst forth from their position (6)
15. Schedule (6)
19. Portable weapons such as rifles, pistols, etc (5,4)
21. Simultaneous discharge of firearms (5)
22. Italian mathematician also known as Leonardo of Pisa (9)
24. Dispel gloom (5)
25. Blood vessel (6)

Down

2. Allotment (5)
3. Cambridgeshire cathedral city (3)
4. Small gardening tool (6)
5. Cloth used when washing-up (7)
6. Unspoken, implied (5)
7. Practice of gaining an advantage over another person (3-9)
8. Self-absorbed (12)
12. In the month preceding the present one (abbr) (3)
14. To the degree or extent that (7)
16. Ms Herzigova, model (3)
17. African country surrounded by Senegal (6)
18. Primitive plant forms (5)
20. Take place again (5)
23. Snare, trap (3)

Across

- **4** Night attire (7)
- **7** Outdoor (4-3)
- **8** Mood disorder (5)
- **9** Grasslike marsh plant (5)
- **10** Glide over snow (3)
- **11** Dirt-free (5)
- **12** Album into which items can be pasted (9)
- **14** Contest in which a baton is passed between runners (5,4)
- **17** Scottish valleys (5)
- **18** Cereal grass (3)
- **19** Detestation (5)
- **21** Make parallel (5)
- **22** Rapid rise (7)
- **23** Horizontal surfaces for holding objects (7)

Down

- **1** Head honcho (4)
- **2** Easy to eat or chew (6)
- **3** Shop assistant (11)
- **4** "Hey ___," said by a magician (6)
- **5** Cut into small pieces (6)
- **6** Stand still, cease to flow (8)
- **8** Disney cartoon character (6,5)
- **12** Small refracting telescope (8)
- **13** Italian port, a major tourist attraction (6)
- **15** Substance used as acid/alkali indicator (6)
- **16** Bee-house or collection of beehives (6)
- **20** Compliant, tame (4)

240

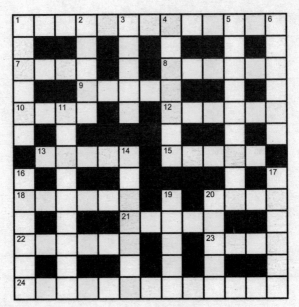

Across

1 Tropical arm of the Pacific Ocean (5,5,3)
7 Three-dimensional shape (4)
8 Hand-held piece of armour (6)
9 Mixture of rain and snow (5)
10 Yours and mine (4)
12 Develop (6)
13 Scour vigorously (5)
15 Small crane on a ship (5)
18 Temporary cessation of breathing, especially during sleep (6)
20 Partially burn (4)
21 Rolls-____, motor manufacturing company (5)
22 Mutilated, wounded (6)
23 Cobbler's stand (4)
24 European country (5,8)

Down

1 Area, zone (6)
2 Plait of hair (5)
3 System of principles or beliefs (5)
4 As an alternative (7)
5 Mollusc or crustacean, for example (9)
6 Patron saint of Scotland (6)
11 Make peace, come to terms (9)
14 Lodger (7)
16 Material used for surfacing roads or other outdoor areas (6)
17 Judgmental reviewer (6)
19 Thick sugary liquid (5)
20 Famous person (abbr) (5)

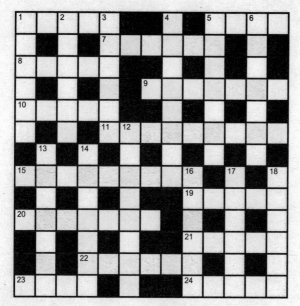

Across

1 Garment worn on the upper half of the body (5)
5 Dress worn primarily by Hindu women (4)
7 Launch an attack on (6)
8 Public announcement of a proposed marriage (5)
9 St Andrew's cross (7)
10 Measure equal to approximately 1.76 pints (5)
11 Got back, regained (9)
15 Digital (9)
19 In existence (5)
20 Unit of relative loudness (7)
21 Military trainee (5)
22 Sheen (6)
23 Ancient Greek harp (4)
24 Linger (5)

Down

1 Barely noticeable (6)
2 Catch fire (6)
3 Sample (6)
4 Conic section (8)
5 Slide unobtrusively (7)
6 Make a new request to be supplied with (7)
12 Disorder of the central nervous system characterised by convulsions (8)
13 In silence (7)
14 Car or lorry, for example (7)
16 Surgical knife with a pointed double-edged blade (6)
17 Fragment of incombustible matter left after a fire (6)
18 Watchman (6)

242

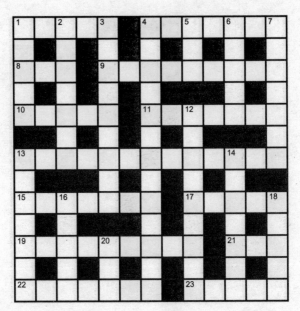

Across

1 Biblical brother of Esau (5)
4 Building where corpses or bones are deposited (7)
8 Barrier which contains the flow of water (3)
9 Artificial lake (9)
10 Inner layer of the skin (5)
11 Full to satisfaction (7)
13 Children's playthings (7,6)
15 Causes to feel resentment or indignation (7)
17 Central pillar of a circular staircase (5)
19 Without limit (9)
21 Of a thing (3)
22 Tranquillises (7)
23 Exchanges for money (5)

Down

1 Fatigued (5)
2 Finely woven type of linen (7)
3 Uncouth ill-bred person (9)
4 Tills (4,9)
5 Atmosphere (3)
6 Not a single person (2-3)
7 Pantries (7)
12 Forecast (9)
13 Parallelogram with four equal sides (7)
14 Building for the preparation of logs and lumber (7)
16 Liquid (5)
18 Endures (5)
20 Very small circular shape (3)

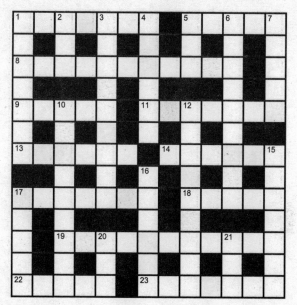

Across

1 Corroborate (7)
5 Scottish lakes (5)
8 Farming (11)
9 Clump of trees (5)
11 Bring into servitude (7)
13 Came to rest (6)
14 Tedious (6)
17 Break into many pieces (7)
18 Globe, planet (5)
19 Have superior power and influence (11)
22 Long pointed weapon (5)
23 Latticework used to support climbing plants (7)

Down

1 Area around the altar of a church (7)
2 And not (3)
3 Of weather, unpleasantly cold or wet (9)
4 Grinder of corn (6)
5 Mr Reed who took a *Walk on the Wild Side* (3)
6 Maurice ___, French actor and cabaret singer (9)
7 Military blockade (5)
10 Fleshy edible fruit with a tuft of stiff leaves (9)
12 Pantomime character (4,5)
15 Female deity (7)
16 Audition (3,3)
17 Despatches (5)
20 Make a mistake (3)
21 Every one (3)

244

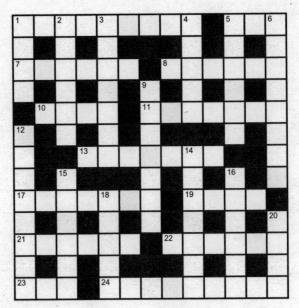

Across

1 Aviator hired to fly experimental aeroplanes (4,5)
5 Border of cloth doubled
back and stitched down (3)
7 Gazed (6)
8 Not outside a building (6)
10 Sport (4)
11 Sound excluder (7)
13 Movement of the sea
in the same direction
as the wind (3,4)
17 Representative form (7)
19 Cleansing agent (4)
21 More sluggish (6)
22 Hardy cereal with
coarse bristles (6)
23 Beard found on a
bract of grass (3)
24 Revise (a book) by
removing offensive
passages (9)

Down

1 Duty (4)
2 Doctor-priest or medicine
man working by magic (6)
3 Come before (7)
4 Powdered ink (5)
5 Fairground game of
ring throwing (4-2)
6 Loan for the purchase
of property (8)
9 Coloniser (7)
12 Beneath the surface
of the ocean (8)
14 Abandon hope (7)
15 Old World monkey (6)
16 Spanish dish made
with rice, shellfish
and chicken (6)
18 Cause to be annoyed,
irritated or resentful (5)
20 *Auld Lang* ___, popular
New Year's Eve song (4)

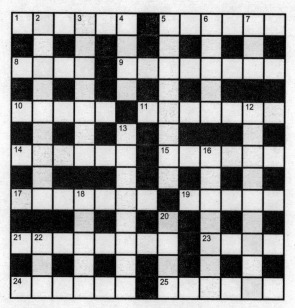

Across

1 Maintenance (6)
5 Shoes with wheels attached (6)
8 Of champagne, dry (4)
9 Every year (8)
10 One stroke over par in golf (5)
11 Instrument from which a person is executed by hanging (7)
14 ___ Reeves, singer who had a hit with *Dancing in the Street* (6)
15 Rub elbows with (coll) (6)
17 In the interval (7)
19 Leaves of a book (5)
21 Camouflage (8)
23 Abreast of (4)
24 Windcheater (6)
25 Male reproductive organ of a flower (6)

Down

2 Penetrate gradually (9)
3 Ask earnestly (7)
4 Juicy, gritty-textured fruit (4)
5 Expose one's body in order to get a tan (8)
6 Be of service (5)
7 Long and slippery fish (3)
12 Nutritious (9)
13 Independent in behaviour or thought (8)
16 Brilliant and showy technical skill (7)
18 Betting stake (5)
20 Precious stones (4)
22 Tavern (3)

246

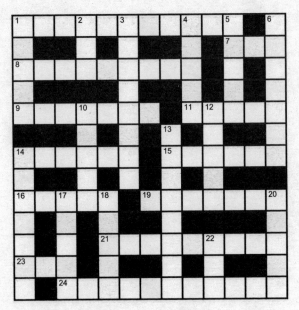

Across

1 Quick vote, with numbers being estimated rather than counted (4,2,5)
7 Motor vehicle (3)
8 Piece of rock or metal from outer space (9)
9 Scraped (7)
11 Of limited quantity (5)
14 Woven with a diamond-shaped pattern (6)
15 Become famous (6)
16 Cause to be embarrassed (5)
19 Long red pepper, milder than chilli (7)
21 Political party's declaration of intentions (9)
23 Fish eggs (3)
24 Showing concern for the rights and feelings of others (11)

Down

1 Lively ballroom dance from Brazil (5)
2 Very small (3)
3 Compelled to eat (5-3)
4 Depends on (5)
5 Aqualung (5)
6 Take air in and out (7)
10 Bottomless gulf or pit (5)
12 Evil spell (5)
13 Having a regular wage (8)
14 Relating to or causing love (7)
17 Ancient Mexican civilisation (5)
18 Enclose (3,2)
20 Conjure up in the memory (5)
22 Head of corn (3)

Across

1 Added to (4)
3 Blister near the mouth caused by a viral infection (herpes simplex) (4,4)
7 Woody (8)
8 Finishing line for a foot race (4)
9 Hold in a tight grasp (6)
10 Passage through or under something (6)
11 Multiplication (5)
12 Concentrate (5)
15 List of fixed charges (6)
18 Higher in rank (6)
19 Shaft of light (4)
20 Palpable (8)
21 Seeking advancement or recognition (8)
22 Small but useful pieces of advice (4)

Down

1 Law force (6)
2 Equivalent word (7)
3 Apparel (7)
4 Hungarian composer of classical music (5)
5 Glossy fabric (5)
6 Bottle up (feelings, for example) (7)
11 Dealers (7)
12 Open mesh fabric resembling an angling trap (7)
13 Be composed of (7)
14 Short underpants (6)
16 Two-syllable feet in poetry (5)
17 Ruling on a point of Islamic law (5)

248

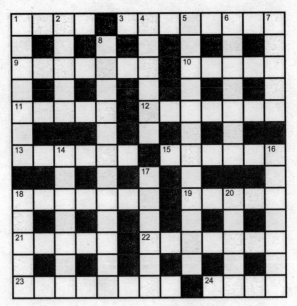

Across

1. Birthday missive (4)
3. Causing fear or dread (8)
9. Lover, suitor (7)
10. Final Greek letter (5)
11. Air cavity in the skull (5)
12. *On the Origin of* ___, work by Charles Darwin (7)
13. Buffoons (6)
15. Scottish dish (6)
18. Turkish viceroy who ruled Egypt (7)
19. Additional (5)
21. Drink alcohol to excess (coll) (5)
22. Relating to swine (7)
23. Infatuated (8)
24. Belonging to that woman (4)

Down

1. Creation of the highest excellence (7)
2. Resident of the capital of Italy (5)
4. Forceful military attack (6)
5. Chief Brazilian port, famous as a tourist attraction (3,2,7)
6. Sensation (7)
7. Packs to capacity (5)
8. Feeling of evil to come (12)
14. Not easily borne (7)
16. Ability to walk steadily on the deck of a pitching ship (3,4)
17. Folk (6)
18. Pieces of food on a skewer (5)
20. Banal (5)

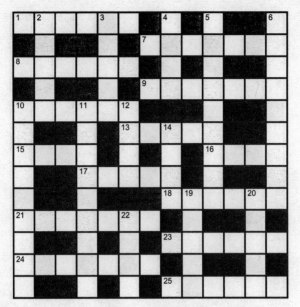

Across

1 Small, roofed building affording shade and rest (6)
7 Detonate (7)
8 Unwell (6)
9 Gist (7)
10 Arrow on a computer screen (6)
13 Later on (5)
15 Source of illumination (4)
16 Gen (abbr) (4)
17 Scene of action (5)
18 Intimation of dismissal (6)
21 Put wholehearted trust or reliance on (5,2)
23 Swimmer (6)
24 Set down (7)
25 Abode of God and the angels (6)

Down

2 Au revoir (5)
3 Drum held between the knees (5)
4 Group of countries in an alliance (4)
5 Design plan or other technical drawing (9)
6 Magnifier of distant objects (9)
10 Agreement on a secret plot (9)
11 Capable of being divided or dissociated (9)
12 Feeling of intense anger (4)
14 Conjunction used in comparatives (4)
19 Talk pompously (5)
20 Thin pancake (5)
22 Part of a necklace (4)

250

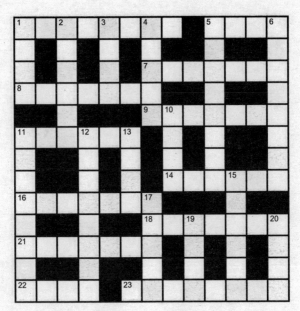

Across

1 Move from one place to another (8)
5 Collection of facts (4)
7 Romanies (7)
8 Study of the physical world (7)
9 Making small marks into the surface (7)
11 Tyre accessories that increase traction (6)
14 Touched with the lips (6)
16 Difficulty (7)
18 Items inserted in a written record (7)
21 Began (7)
22 Mats (4)
23 Disappeared from view (8)

Down

1 Playthings (4)
2 Continent of which Libya is a part (6)
3 Cut, as of wood (4)
4 Boundaries (5)
5 Psychological suffering (8)
6 Appointed to a post or duty (8)
10 Prepare food by heating (4)
11 Writer of music (8)
12 Large floating masses of frozen water (8)
13 Not all (4)
15 Changeover (6)
17 Means for communicating information (5)
19 Hackney carriage (4)
20 Small hard fruit (4)

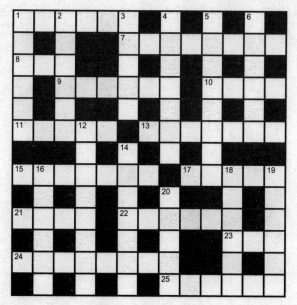

Across

1 Unit of electric current (6)
7 Point in time at which something must be completed (8)
8 Male child (3)
9 Calculating machine (6)
10 French word for Christmas (4)
11 Rub out (5)
13 Flask for carrying water (7)
15 Contract, abridge (7)
17 Annoyed (5)
21 ___ and ends (4)
22 Splits down the middle (6)
23 Case containing a set of articles (3)
24 Military wake-up call (8)
25 Position of a person in society (6)

Down

1 Take for granted (6)
2 Central American canal (6)
3 Formal proclamation (5)
4 Hitter of a baseball, cricket ball, etc (7)
5 Microscopic oceanic organisms (8)
6 Involuntary expulsion of air from the nose (6)
12 Emphasised (8)
14 Part of a door fastener (7)
16 Concealed (6)
18 Ring for sealing a pipe joint (6)
19 Young people (6)
20 State of depression (5)

252

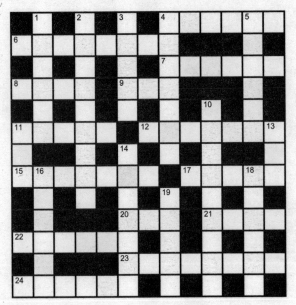

Across

4 Country, capital Oslo (6)
6 Turtle's shell (8)
7 Foolish (6)
8 Corrode, as with acid (4)
9 Not at home (3)
11 Slaver (5)
12 Phlegm (7)
15 Undying (7)
17 Consecrate (5)
20 Vehicle from another world (inits) (3)
21 Smallest particle in an element (4)
22 Spanish dance in triple time (6)
23 Not yet unsealed (8)
24 Stems of plants (6)

Down

1 Jailor (6)
2 Device consisting of a corrugated surface to scrub clothes on (9)
3 Inhibition or ban resulting from social custom (5)
4 Having no personal preference (7)
5 Solution (6)
10 Decoration hung in a home (9)
11 Gaming cube (3)
13 Features (3)
14 Complacently or inanely foolish (7)
16 Part of the neck (6)
18 Hand tool for lifting loose material (6)
19 Non-metallic element, atomic number 5 (5)

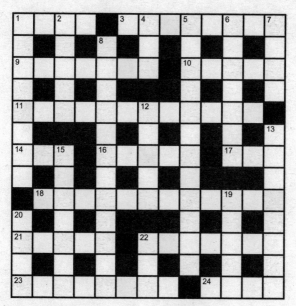

Across
1 Statement of verified information (4)
3 Fireproof material (8)
9 Animal skin which has been tanned (7)
10 Sign of the zodiac (5)
11 Organised opposition to authority (12)
14 Biblical character whose wife was turned into a pillar of salt (3)
16 Relating to odours or the sense of smell (5)
17 Observe (3)
18 Medium (12)
21 Become less in amount or intensity (3,2)
22 Popular alcoholic beverage (3,4)
23 Perturbing (8)
24 Fluid-filled sac (4)

Down
1 Cavity containing the root of a hair (8)
2 Edible shellfish (5)
4 Form of address (3)
5 Narrow rubber loops used to hold objects together (7,5)
6 Makers of fitted clothes such as suits, trousers and jackets (7)
7 Window frame fitted with a pane of glass (4)
8 Stage dancing (12)
12 Insect such as an ant (5)
13 Consciously perceiving (8)
15 Betting adviser (7)
19 In a cold manner (5)
20 Sluggish (4)
22 Went faster (3)

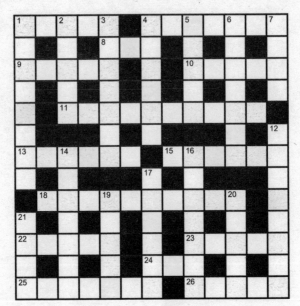

Across

1 Supply food ready to eat (5)
4 Looked after a small child in the absence of a parent (7)
8 Water in a solid state (3)
9 Titled peers of the realm (5)
10 Impudent aggressiveness (5)
11 Following on from (10)
13 Leash (6)
15 Draw back (6)
18 Loops of soft yarn, cut to give a tufted pattern (10)
22 Sightless (5)
23 Tolerate (5)
24 Lick up (3)
25 Bondage (7)
26 Conforming to Islamic dietary laws (5)

Down

1 Slices of chilled meat (4,4)
2 Rolls (5)
3 Arousing or provoking laughter (7)
4 Cup without a handle (6)
5 Family of languages widely spoken in southern Africa (5)
6 Out of the ordinary (7)
7 Golfing pegs (4)
12 Film report (8)
14 Russian empress (7)
16 Inscription on a tombstone (7)
17 Extremely poisonous or injurious (6)
19 Avoid by a sudden quick movement (5)
20 Shrimp-like planktonic crustaceans (5)
21 Flows back (4)

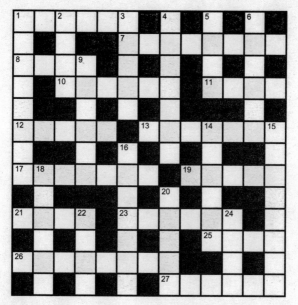

Across

1 Title given to a nun (6)
7 Suddenly and unexpectedly (8)
8 Roman love poet, born in 43 BC (4)
10 Pick out (6)
11 Group of three (4)
12 Muslim name for the one and only God (5)
13 Pitiable (7)
17 Made of clay (7)
19 Vapour produced by fire (5)
21 Article (4)
23 Small and compactly built upright piano (6)
25 Carry (4)
26 Ability to notice small details (coll) (5,3)
27 In next to first place (6)

Down

1 State of inactivity following an interruption (8)
2 Runners used for gliding over snow (4)
3 First stomach of a cow (5)
4 Device for catching rodents (3,4)
5 Immense (4)
6 Similar things placed in order (6)
9 Pour from a bottle into one more ornate (6)
14 Marine gastropod found clinging to rocks (6)
15 Sheep watcher (8)
16 Becomes angry (coll) (4,3)
18 Real (6)
20 Married women (5)
22 Capital of the Maldives (4)
24 Tortilla rolled around a filling (4)

256

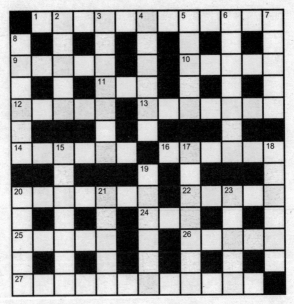

Across

1 Forcible indoctrination into a new set of attitudes and beliefs (12)
9 Melts, as of ice (5)
10 Cover with cloth (5)
11 Equality (3)
12 Ethnic group of Kenya and Tanzania (5)
13 Christian recluse (7)
14 Dental decay (6)
16 Things of value or usefulness (6)
20 Army unit (7)
22 Come to pass (5)
24 Is able to (3)
25 Pointed projection on a fork (5)
26 Ignominy (5)
27 Break into parts, fall apart (12)

Down

2 Scans written words (5)
3 Urge on or encourage (7)
4 Person dressed in a specified garment (6)
5 Creep (5)
6 Form a mental picture (7)
7 Web-footed, long-necked birds (5)
8 Nuclear (6)
15 Calamitous (7)
17 Patron (7)
18 Rode the waves on a board (6)
19 Turn into (6)
20 Animal with two feet (5)
21 Gas used to fill light bulbs (5)
23 Recite with musical intonation (5)

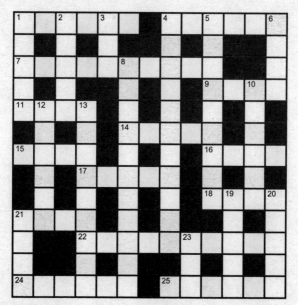

Across

1 Fabric for a painting (6)
4 Roof extension accommodating a window (6)
7 Act of taking something that is offered (10)
9 Young, unmarried woman (4)
11 Dance move (4)
14 Legerdemain (5)
15 Cheats, swindles (4)
16 Mountain lake (4)
17 Father Christmas (5)
18 Twilight (4)
21 Sleeping places (4)
22 Large panel showing the results of a contest (10)
24 Cheap and nasty, inferior (6)
25 Uncompromising in discipline (6)

Down

1 Applauds (5)
2 Alcove (5)
3 Type of cobra (3)
4 Item of furniture (6,5)
5 Voted back into office (2-7)
6 Moulders (4)
8 Jargon (11)
10 Counties (6)
12 Organisation of theatrical performers (6)
13 Had ownership (9)
19 Accepted practice (5)
20 Small anchor (5)
21 Purchases (4)
23 Four-winged insect (3)

258

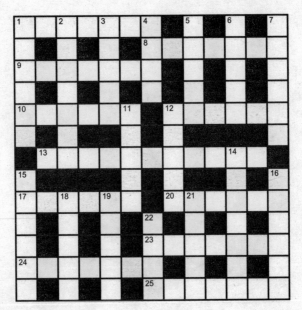

Across

1 Military unit (7)
8 Make amends for, atone (7)
9 Axle (7)
10 Quantity (6)
12 Plod, footslog (6)
13 Commemoration of meritorious service (11)
17 Without justification (6)
20 Thin layer of mineral (6)
23 Extreme greed for material wealth (7)
24 Made up of famous top performers (3-4)
25 State of being poorly illuminated or lacking contrast (7)

Down

1 Programming language (6)
2 Composed of animal fat (7)
3 Of time long past (5)
4 At no time (poetically) (4)
5 Higher in position (5)
6 Devoid of clothing (5)
7 Equipment-carrier on an expedition (6)
11 Ms Wynette, country music singer (1942–98) (5)
12 Mountainous province of western Austria (5)
14 Culinary art (7)
15 Agency, department (6)
16 Ring-shaped bread rolls (6)
18 Passed out playing cards (5)
19 All except the clergy (5)
21 Clock that wakes a sleeper at a preset time (5)
22 Measure of 36 inches (4)

259

Across
4 Overshadowed (7)
8 Condensed but memorable saying (5)
9 Relating to plants (9)
10 Supple (5)
11 Angular distance of a place east or west of the Greenwich meridian (9)
13 Israeli monetary unit (6)
16 European mint with aromatic and pungent leaves (6)
20 Sharp-eyed (9)
23 Farewell remark (5)
24 Thoughtlessly hasty (9)
25 Time of life between the ages of 13 and 19 (5)
26 Slight and subtle variations (7)

Down
1 Love songs (7)
2 Confined, imprisoned (7)
3 Insurrectionist (5)
4 Very fond (6)
5 Income from investment paid regularly (7)
6 Lightweight triangular scarf (5)
7 Dig deeply into (5)
12 Singing couple (3)
14 Central part of a car wheel (3)
15 Having no fixed course (7)
17 Banded with pieces of contrasting colour (7)
18 Persevere, endure (7)
19 Regional slang (6)
20 The Hunter constellation (5)
21 Reddish-brown colour (5)
22 Appetising (5)

263

260

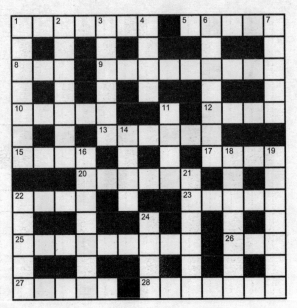

Across

1 Heartfelt (7)
5 Kindly endorsement and guidance (5)
8 Objective (3)
9 General activity and motion (9)
10 Respiratory organs (5)
12 Deficient in beauty (4)
13 Begrudges (6)
15 Old-fashioned form of the word 'you' (4)
17 Large-scale (4)
20 Papal legate (6)
22 Go by (4)
23 Stylistic talent (5)
25 Seabird with a massive wingspan (9)
26 Be unwell (3)
27 Place of safety or sanctuary (5)
28 Draw back (7)

Down

1 Small mild-flavoured onion (7)
2 Candidate (7)
3 Slip by (6)
4 Make changes in text (4)
6 Utter with excitement (7)
7 Bright and pleasant (5)
11 Equipment for the reproduction of sound (2-2)
14 Ms Myskow, TV celebrity (4)
16 Catch in a trap (7)
18 Mollify (7)
19 Decorated metal band worn around the head (7)
21 Counterbalance (6)
22 Hunt illegally (5)
24 Male pig (4)

2

261

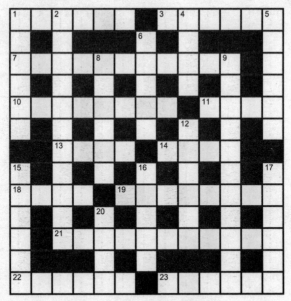

Across

1 Dark purplish-red wine (6)
3 Tools used for sweeping (6)
7 Combination (11)
10 Thin Mexican pancake (8)
11 Marine mammal (4)
13 Fellow (4)
14 By word of mouth (4)
18 Opaque gem (4)
19 Cooking utensil (8)
21 Ominous (11)
22 Wood prepared for use as building material (6)
23 Seven people considered as a unit (6)

Down

1 Marked by skill in deception (6)
2 Style of painting representing ideas in geometric form (8,3)
4 Sudden short attack (4)
5 Building for horses (6)
6 Ahead of time (5)
8 Semiaquatic reptile resembling an alligator (6)
9 Embroidery resembling tapestry (11)
12 Day nursery for young children (6)
15 Label listing the contents of a consignment (6)
16 Maritime (5)
17 Chivalrous nobleman (6)
20 Slope or hillside in Scotland (4)

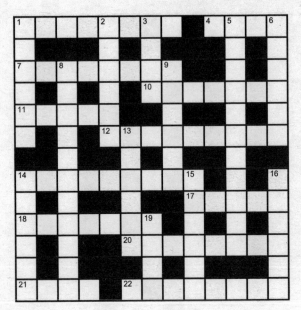

Across

1 Reprimand (8)

4 Expression used at the end of a prayer (4)

7 Had an influence on (8)

10 Docking (7)

11 Boredom (5)

12 Squeeze or press together (9)

14 Unable to be washed away or erased (9)

17 African venomous snake (5)

18 Explorer and journalist who found David Livingstone at Lake Tanganyika (7)

20 Characteristic of a particular area (8)

21 Fine specks of detritus (4)

22 Short tube attached to the muzzle of a gun (8)

Down

1 Scratched at, as if with talons (6)

2 Manoeuvre (6)

3 Tube of a tobacco pipe (4)

5 Tribal healer (8,3)

6 Solid lump of a precious metal (6)

8 Exciting or amusing goings-on (coll) (3,3,5)

9 Fin on the back of a fish (6)

13 ___ Twist, Dickens character (6)

14 Brought out (6)

15 Group of countries with one ruler (6)

16 Prison guard (6)

19 Creature said to live in the Himalayas (4)

263

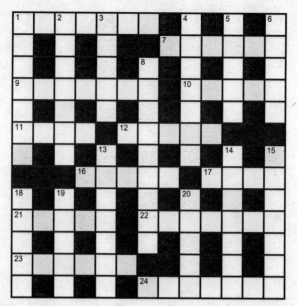

Across

1 Male child of your spouse and a former partner (7)
7 Common root vegetable (6)
9 Mark to indicate a direction (7)
10 Sound (5)
11 Regular, level (4)
12 Having an unchanging value (5)
16 Formal title used when addressing a woman (5)
17 Decoratively tied strips of ribbon (4)
21 Prices (5)
22 Merciful (7)
23 Participant in a game (6)
24 Hot and spicy (7)

Down

1 Machine that inserts metal fasteners into sheets of paper (7)
2 Worked up, stimulated (7)
3 Saline (5)
4 Suffering from physical injury (7)
5 Sudden strong fear (5)
6 Tailed heavenly body (5)
8 Bad-tempered (9)
13 Herb with aromatic finely cut leaves (7)
14 Ornament made of ribbon, given as an award (7)
15 Receptacle used by smokers (7)
18 Range (5)
19 Muslim religion (5)
20 Spy (5)

264

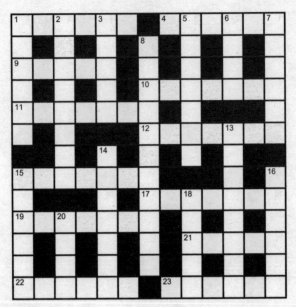

Across

1 Sudden (6)
4 Deviates from a course (6)
9 Adult male domestic cattle (5)
10 Mutual empathy (7)
11 Interconnected system (7)
12 Ungentle (7)
15 Musical setting for a religious text (7)
17 Wife-to-be (7)
19 Pungent gas (7)
21 Picture recorded by a camera (abbr) (5)
22 Treeless Arctic plain (6)
23 Giving a signal by a movement of the hand (6)

Down

1 Lacking in pigmentation (6)
2 Person with whom one is associated by blood or marriage (8)
3 Sauce typically served with pasta (5)
5 Giving a gratuity (7)
6 Rounded thickly curled hairdo (4)
7 Resolve (6)
8 Country formerly known as Upper Volta (7,4)
13 Green vegetable (8)
14 Artist (7)
15 Swiss cottage (6)
16 Have a place (6)
18 First letter of the Greek alphabet (5)
20 Cut with a blade (as of grass) (4)

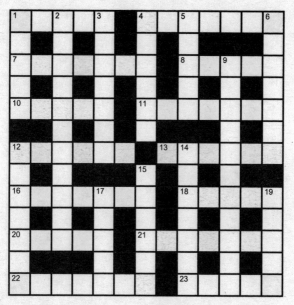

Across

1 Mayhem (5)
4 One who habitually doubts accepted beliefs (7)
7 Bloodline (7)
8 Acidic fruit (5)
10 Popular literary genre (abbr) (3-2)
11 Waterfall (7)
12 Country, capital Ankara (6)
13 Time to come (6)
16 Specialist assigned to the staff of a diplomatic mission (7)
18 Cooks slowly and for a long time in liquid (5)
20 Rise as vapour (5)
21 Cut in three (7)
22 Newspaper with half-size pages (7)
23 Come to terms with (3,2)

Down

1 Removes the calyx of a strawberry (5)
2 Basic French dressing for salads (11)
3 Extremely poisonous substance (7)
4 Unpleasant odour (6)
5 ___ Island, New York Bay area (5)
6 Call together (for a meeting) (7)
9 Amount, of distance for example (11)
12 Passage (7)
14 Improving or increasing trend (7)
15 Occupying a chair (6)
17 Raised medallion (5)
19 Grilled food on a skewer, served with peanut sauce (5)

266

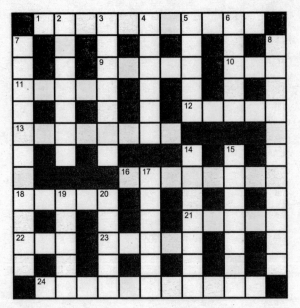

Across

1 Wheel-shaped Dutch dairy product (5,6)
9 Twilled woollen fabric (5)
10 Yoko ___, widow of John Lennon (3)
11 Biblical wife of Abraham and mother of Isaac (5)
12 Mr Mosimann, famous chef (5)
13 Intensity (8)
16 Great in quantity (8)
18 Shore of a sea (5)
21 Freedom from disputes (5)
22 Umberto ___, author of *Foucault's Pendulum* (3)
23 Declares or affirms as true (5)
24 Central American capital city (3,8)

Down

2 Method of delivery of a cricket ball (7)
3 Smart and stylish (7)
4 Floor covering (6)
5 Liquid used to stimulate evacuation (5)
6 Call out (5)
7 Not believed likely (11)
8 Expert in art, food or drink (11)
14 Relating to the lowest parts of the ocean (4-3)
15 Leaves dried and prepared for smoking (7)
17 Untwist (6)
19 Hawaiian greeting (5)
20 Snares (5)

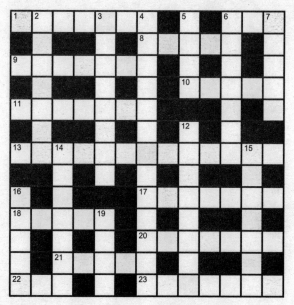

Across

1 Distilled alcoholic beverages (7)
6 Informal term for a mother (3)
8 Musical drama (5)
9 Upstart (7)
10 Unrelaxed, taut (5)
11 Vainglorious, extravagant or melodramatic conduct (7)
13 Lacking in courage (13)
17 Device for an announcer to read from while looking into a television camera (3,4)
18 Scrutinise accounts (5)
20 Prehistoric metalworking period (4,3)
21 Capital of Jordan (5)
22 Canine creature (3)
23 Small racing vehicles with lightweight bodies (2-5)

Down

2 Flat highland (7)
3 Unfit for consumption (8)
4 Self-analysis (4-9)
5 County known as the Garden of England (4)
6 Small dynamo with a secondary winding (7)
7 Creator (5)
12 Colourful explosive device (8)
14 Filled sack used to protect against floodwater (7)
15 Vertical (7)
16 Founded (5)
19 Subdue (4)

268

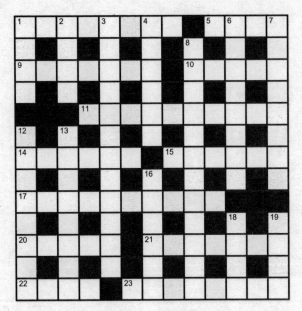

Across

1 Basis for comparison (8)
5 Young men (4)
9 Damaging, likely to cause injury (7)
10 Common viper (5)
11 Entire range of skills used in a particular field (10)
14 Tweezer (6)
15 Admittance (6)
17 Operating with microchips (10)
20 Dry red Spanish wine (5)
21 Instalment (7)
22 Feat (4)
23 Playing repeatedly in the same kind of rôle (8)

Down

1 District of London noted for restaurants and nightclubs (4)
2 Askew (4)
3 Varying according to circumstances (12)
4 Alleviation (6)
6 Experienced person who has been through many battles (3-5)
7 A stopping (8)
8 Culinary art (5,7)
12 Came into view (8)
13 Container for a letter, thin package, etc (8)
16 Humour (6)
18 Settee (4)
19 Not diluted (4)

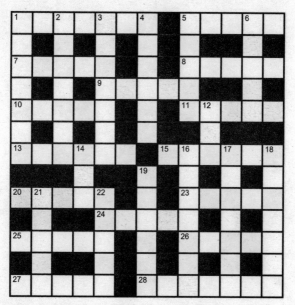

Across

1 Arid regions of the world (7)
5 Sleazy or shabby (5)
7 Florida resort (5)
8 Precise (5)
9 Glisten (5)
10 Draws back the lips in a smile (5)
11 Vile, despicable (5)
13 One who transmits a message (6)
15 Against (6)
20 Lost moisture (5)
23 Nimble, spry (5)
24 Single entities (5)
25 Beautify (5)
26 Fool (5)
27 Vine fruit (5)
28 Knitted jumper (7)

Down

1 Causes harm (7)
2 Railway building (7)
3 Print anew (7)
4 Contract, become smaller (6)
5 Alloy of iron and carbon (5)
6 Common waterbirds (5)
12 Belonging to us (3)
14 Colouring agent (3)
16 Skilful at eluding capture (7)
17 Powered conveyance that carries people up a mountain (3,4)
18 Be uncomfortably hot (7)
19 Fried potato slices (6)
21 Measuring instrument which uses echoes (5)
22 Classroom fool (5)

270

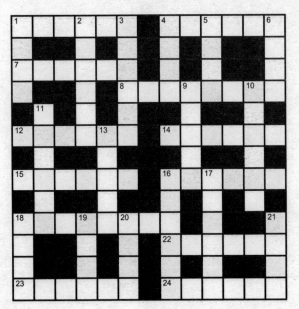

Across

1 Piled (6)
4 Pale (of colour) (6)
7 Women (6)
8 State of motionlessness (8)
12 Diminish (6)
14 Sizeable hole (6)
15 Bread shop (6)
16 Boil slowly (6)
18 High fur hat worn by the Guards in the UK (8)
22 Acid associated with ants (6)
23 Any leafy plants eaten as vegetables (6)
24 Find, trace (6)

Down

1 Frame or body of a ship (4)
2 Gripping hand tool with two hinged arms (6)
3 Blueprint (6)
4 Mountain lion (4)
5 Pimple (4)
6 Grassy garden area (4)
9 American raccoon (5)
10 Stableman or groom at an inn (historically) (6)
11 Do as you are told (6)
13 Monetary units of Italy, Portugal, Austria, etc (5)
16 Wicked, unholy (6)
17 Decimal measurement system (6)
18 Sudden very loud noise (4)
19 Strong cord (4)
20 Expression of love (4)
21 Dull pain (4)

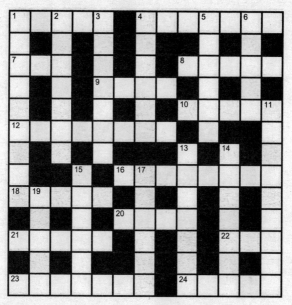

271

Across

1 Suspended loosely or freely (5)
4 Learned person (7)
7 Animal kept as a domestic pet (3)
8 Take one's ease (5)
9 Bridge (4)
10 Called (5)
12 Excessively agitated (8)
16 Known widely and usually unfavourably (8)
18 Literary composition (5)
20 Mixture of fog and smoke (4)
21 In a poor way (5)
22 Geological period of time (3)
23 'Fab' 1960s group (7)
24 County (5)

Down

1 Ritual killing (9)
2 Not yet proved (7)
3 Ground together, of teeth (7)
4 Highly seasoned fatty sausage (6)
5 In a single direction (3-3)
6 Humble (5)
11 Cause to separate and go in different directions (9)
13 Aircraft storage sheds (7)
14 Ancient city buried when Vesuvius erupted (7)
15 Mattress filled with straw (6)
17 Dark grey cloud (6)
19 Line on which music is written (5)

272

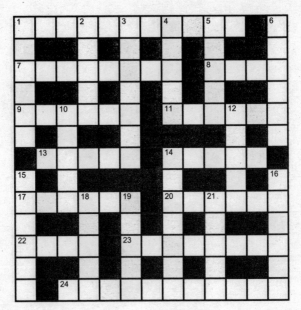

Across

1 Any undertaking that is easy to do (coll) (5,2,4)
7 End-user (8)
8 Large, edible marine fish (4)
9 Rents out (6)
11 Disorderly fighting (6)
13 Cultivates by growing (5)
14 Wall hanging of heavy handwoven fabric (5)
17 Tenant (6)
20 Sickness (6)
22 Was present, is now gone (4)
23 Natives of Teheran, for example (8)
24 Murder, especially a socially prominent person (11)

Down

1 Preserve in vinegar (6)
2 Kegs (5)
3 Diffusion of liquid through a porous membrane (7)
4 Measure of gold's purity (5)
5 Stringed toys flown in the wind (5)
6 Cloth seller (6)
10 John Quincy ___, sixth president of the USA (5)
12 Remains in place (5)
14 Plants that flower once in a year, then die (7)
15 All over the world (6)
16 Bother (6)
18 Musical compositions with words (5)
19 Heather (5)
21 Coupling (5)

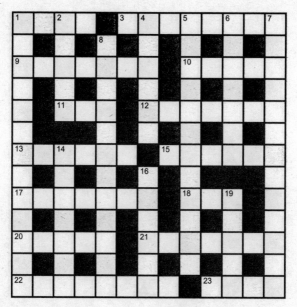

Across
1 High male voice (4)
3 Capital of Finland (8)
9 Cattle plague such as foot-and-mouth disease (7)
10 Beg earnestly (5)
11 Grass used as fodder (3)
12 Open-topped glass flasks used for serving wine or water (7)
13 Defeat some challenge or person (3,3)
15 Visitor (6)
17 Feels remorse (7)
18 Exclamation expressing disgust (3)
20 Motif (5)
21 Lessons (7)
22 Electrical device used to limit current flow (8)
23 Group noun for quails or larks (4)

Down
1 Manager of a business or school (13)
2 Flashlight (5)
4 Harem guard (6)
5 Not subject to explanation according to the established order of things (12)
6 Necessary for relief or supply (7)
7 In a productive and hard-working manner (13)
8 Alternative name for the vegetable called gumbo or okra (5,7)
14 Female ruler of many countries (7)
16 Hitchcock film (6)
19 Hermann ___, author of *Steppenwolf* (5)

274

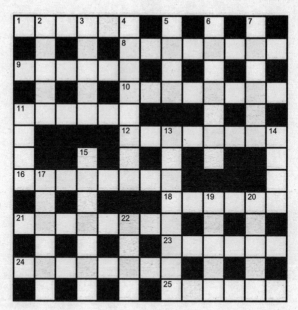

Across
1 Stoneworkers (6)
8 Disencumber (8)
9 Loud confused noise from many sources (6)
10 Delighted (8)
11 One who suffers for the sake of principle (6)
12 Person with a record of successes (8)
16 Fabled island that was swallowed by an earthquake (8)
18 Gruff, husky (6)
21 Small raised red spots caused by inflammation of the sweat glands (4,4)
23 Set down cargo (6)
24 Unmelodious (8)
25 Mad ____, character in *Alice's Adventures in Wonderland* (6)

Down
2 Caribbean island, capital Oranjestad (5)
3 Celestial path (5)
4 Take away (8)
5 Strap with a crosspiece on the upper of a shoe (1-3)
6 Body of water between Kazakhstan and Uzbekistan (4,3)
7 Strike out (6)
11 Aluminium silicate mineral (4)
13 Highly secret or confidential (coll) (4-4)
14 Eastern staple foodstuff (4)
15 New Testament book (7)
17 Restrains from moving or operating normally (4,2)
19 Distribute (5)
20 Dais (5)
22 Imitated (4)

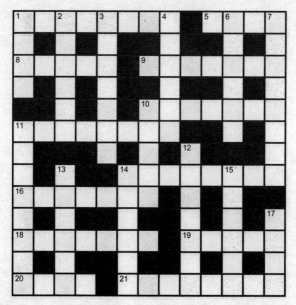

Across

1 Unable to appreciate music (4-4)
5 Not in action (4)
8 Adult female (5)
9 Woman who invites guests to a social event (7)
10 Sentence which uses every letter of the alphabet (7)
11 Treacherous, unpatriotic (8)
14 Male voice between bass and tenor (8)
16 Lacking depth (7)
18 Mollify (7)
19 Step (5)
20 British nobleman (4)
21 Places of political unrest and potential violence (3,5)

Down

1 Administrative division of a county (4)
2 Minor goddesses of nature (6)
3 Castle cellar (7)
4 Associated with flowers (6)
6 Dingy (6)
7 Group of musicians (8)
10 Fruit with yellow flesh (5)
11 Equestrian display (8)
12 Absorbs (knowledge or food) (7)
13 Covered picnic basket (6)
14 Russian soup, with a beetroot juice base (6)
15 Size of a book (6)
17 Weapons (4)

276

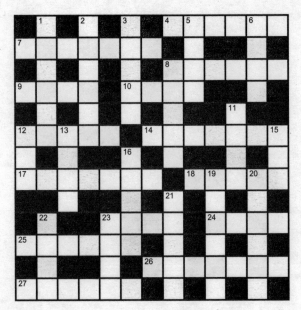

Across

4 Patron saint of England (6)
7 US legislator (7)
8 Kitchen appliance, oven (6)
9 Waistband (4)
10 Word denoting a particular thing (4)
12 Dirty and disorderly (5)
14 City of ancient Mesopotamia famed for its Hanging Gardens (7)
17 Boat seen on the canals of Venice (7)
18 Quarrel (5)
23 Successor (4)
24 Stitched (4)
25 Battle (6)
26 Very holy or virtuous (7)
27 Rook in the game of chess (6)

Down

1 Calm, unagitated (6)
2 Flavours (6)
3 Largest artery of the body (5)
5 Greek love god (4)
6 Jubilant delight (4)
8 Tobacco product (5)
11 Device that prevents the escape of water from a sink (4)
12 Drinking vessel (3)
13 Produce tones with the voice (4)
15 Maiden name indicator (3)
16 Group of warships (5)
19 Despatch again (6)
20 Sickly (6)
21 Orderly arrangement (5)
22 Roman cloak (4)
23 Large and imposing manor (4)

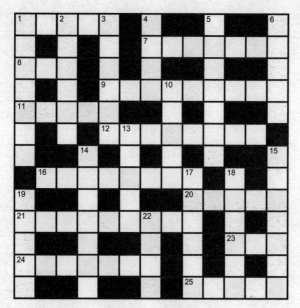

Across

1 Merits, deserves (5)
7 Surface over which business is transacted (7)
8 Attila the ____ (3)
9 Attack made by planes (3,6)
11 Gambling game using two dice (5)
12 Slow Cuban dance and song in duple time (8)
16 Catered for completely, without any need for effort on the part of the recipient (5-3)
20 In advance (5)
21 Fleece rug (9)
23 Mr Geller, spoon-bender (3)
24 Annual publication giving weather forecasts, etc (7)
25 Seek information from (5)

Down

1 Moral (7)
2 Landing strip (6)
3 Flatten (6)
4 Mark left by a wound (4)
5 Underwater breathing device (7)
6 Laundering appliance that removes moisture (5)
10 Garden tool (5)
13 Sisters of one's parents (5)
14 Person who exercises control over workers (7)
15 More dizzy or disorientated (7)
17 Hazard (6)
18 Snub (6)
19 US Academy Award (5)
22 Deliver a blow with the foot (4)

278

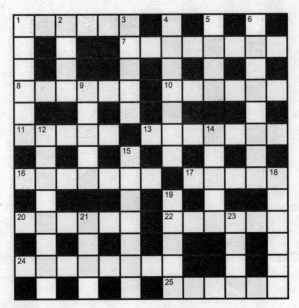

Across

1 Sofa, couch (6)
7 Native of the USA (8)
8 Slender (6)
10 Reached the highest point of (6)
11 Lady Nancy ___, first woman MP (5)
13 Erased (7)
16 Put out of action (by illness) (4,3)
17 Taunts, teases (5)
20 State capital of Tasmania (6)
22 ___-Herzegovina, European country (6)
24 Without good sense or judgment (8)
25 Frightens (6)

Down

1 Afternoon nap (6)
2 Melody (4)
3 Dined (5)
4 Acute and highly contagious viral disease (7)
5 Verdi opera with an Egyptian theme (4)
6 Walkway (8)
9 Surname of Colin, champion professional darts player (5)
12 Used on the ocean (8)
14 Exercises evaluating skill or knowledge (abbr) (5)
15 Baby's soft woollen shoes (7)
18 External forms (6)
19 Follows orders (5)
21 Bitter (4)
23 Approach (4)

279

Across
1 Acrobat's swing (7)
8 Entails (8)
9 Vogue (5)
11 Sugar frosting (5)
12 Not flexible or pliant (5)
13 Tall perennial grasses (5)
14 Musical form consisting of a repeated theme (5)
15 Large wading bird (5)
16 Boxes (5)
17 Country roads (5)
19 Damp (5)
20 Planetary satellites (5)
22 Barack ____, US president (5)
24 Kingdom in the South Pacific (5)
25 Caused to show discomposure (8)
26 Person with bright auburn hair (7)

Down
1 Flexible appendages of animals (5)
2 State of being achievable (13)
3 Bluish-white metallic element (4)
4 Finishing (6)
5 Member of the US House of Representatives (11)
6 Excessively embellished (4-9)
7 Helps (7)
10 Landmark located on the Champ de Mars in Paris (6,5)
15 Obtains, especially accidentally (5,2)
18 More orderly (6)
21 Ten-tentacled sea creature (5)
23 Fashion (4)

280

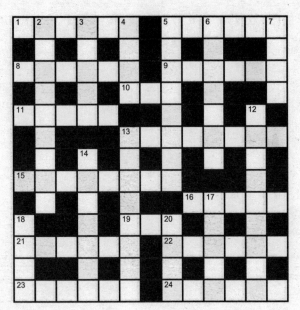

Across

1 Mythological god of light and day (6)
5 Destructive relative of the grasshopper (6)
8 Go back to a previous state (6)
9 Deprive of food (6)
10 Imaginary monster (3)
11 Writing material (5)
13 Hero-worshipped (8)
15 People who are not thankful or appreciative (8)
16 Floor consisting of open space at the top of a house (5)
19 Common type of rodent (3)
21 Herb with leaves valued as salad greens (6)
22 Inspired (6)
23 Put forth shoots (6)
24 Antenna (6)

Down

2 Rife, especially at the present time (9)
3 Province of eastern Belgium (5)
4 Upon (4)
5 Deliciously juicy (8)
6 Mortification, humiliation (7)
7 Long journey (4)
12 Many-legged insect (9)
13 Sense of concern or curiosity (8)
14 Stipulated condition (7)
17 Item of furniture (5)
18 Street of dwellings that were originally private stables (4)
20 Quarrel about petty points (4)

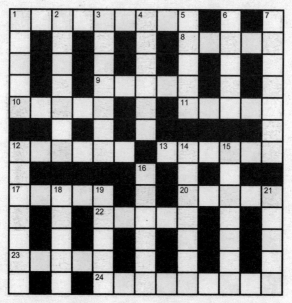

Across
1 Tall pole on which ensign is raised (9)
8 Former Nigerian capital (5)
9 Staggers (5)
10 Gradient (5)
11 Mr Davis, former Snooker World Champion (5)
12 Overtook, went by (6)
13 Interruption in the intensity or amount of something (6)
17 Fencing swords (5)
20 Repairs (5)
22 Lake and popular resort area of Nevada, USA (5)
23 Asp, for example (5)
24 Skilful in movements of the hands (9)

Down
1 Imposes a monetary penalty (5)
2 Showing apprehension (7)
3 Greatest in status (7)
4 Mother superior (6)
5 *The Mill on the* ___, George Eliot novel (5)
6 Plant used in the making of tequila (5)
7 Futile (7)
12 Assumption (7)
14 Soak in a liquid (7)
15 Hybrid between grapefruit and mandarin orange (7)
16 Statue with the body of a lion and the head of a man (6)
18 Ceremonial elegance and splendour (5)
19 Warhorse (5)
21 Chairs (5)

282

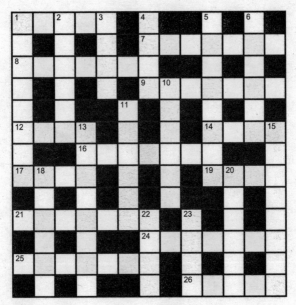

Across

1 Livid (5)
7 Descriptive word or phrase (7)
8 Fawning in attitude or behaviour (7)
9 Went down on bended knee (7)
12 Sense organs for hearing and equilibrium (4)
14 Compass point (4)
16 Capital of Georgia, USA (7)
17 Slender (4)
19 Tibetan or Mongolian priest (4)
21 Tooth doctor (7)
24 Radio or TV antennae (7)
25 Most tidy (7)
26 Nettlesome (5)

Down

1 Marked by casual disrespect (8)
2 More spacious and well ventilated (6)
3 First name of authoress Blyton (4)
4 Period of seven consecutive days (4)
5 Characterised by lightness and insubstantiality (8)
6 Jemmies (6)
10 Subtle difference in meaning (6)
11 Permits (6)
13 Holiness (8)
15 Farce, charade (8)
18 Took notice of (6)
20 Ever (6)
22 London art gallery (4)
23 Troublesome child (4)

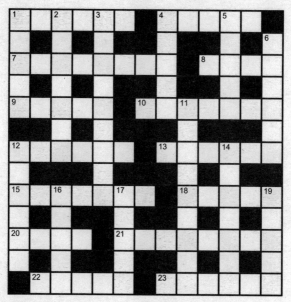

Across

1 Roof in the form of a dome (6)
4 Big boats (5)
7 Edible flatfish (8)
8 Roster of names and tasks (4)
9 Prophets (5)
10 Matching cardigan and pullover (7)
12 Seedy (6)
13 Person who is very poor (6)
15 Cul-de-sac (4,3)
18 Criticism disguised as praise (5)
20 One of two or more contesting groups (4)
21 Groove between a woman's breasts (8)
22 Articles of commerce (5)
23 Say's Law: Supply creates its own ___ (6)

Down

1 Turned-back hems at the ends of sleeves (5)
2 Innovator (7)
3 Slip of a large mass of dirt and rock down a mountain (9)
4 Spirally threaded cylindrical rod (5)
5 Devoutly religious (5)
6 Encrustation that forms on the teeth and gums (6)
11 Lifeless (9)
12 Pleasure obtained by inflicting harm on others (6)
14 Proportionately (3,4)
16 Relating to sound (5)
17 Notches (5)
19 End resistance (5)

284

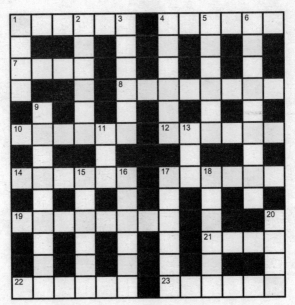

Across

1 Muddle, miscellany (6)
4 Armed fight (6)
7 Go by boat (4)
8 Endowed with natural abilities (8)
10 Second book of the Old Testament (6)
12 First day of the working week (6)
14 Service of china or silverware, used at table (3,3)
17 Small padded envelope (6)
19 Enjoyable (8)
21 Book of the Old Testament (4)
22 Emphasis (6)
23 Protective head covering (6)

Down

1 Make jokes (4)
2 Protruded outwards (6)
3 Fills with optimism (6)
4 State of extreme confusion and disorder (6)
5 Substance found in tea (6)
6 Set free (9)
9 Of the highest quality (9)
11 Application (3)
13 Female reproductive cells (3)
15 Metal paper fastener (6)
16 Expresses gratitude (6)
17 Attempt at political revolution (6)
18 Breakfast food made from grains (6)
20 Treaty (4)

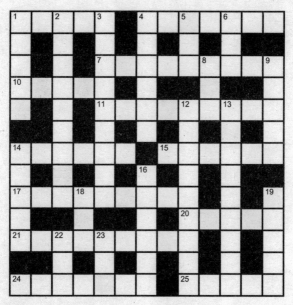

Across

1 Factions (5)
4 Water jug (7)
7 Depiction (9)
10 River which flows through Paris (5)
11 Taciturnity (9)
14 Block of text at the top of each page of a book (6)
15 Athletic (6)
17 Need of mending (9)
20 Perfect type (5)
21 Towards the centre of a sailing vessel (9)
24 Canine symbol of Britain (7)
25 Pieces of paper money (5)

Down

1 Half-melted snow (5)
2 Those not in the armed forces (9)
3 Take the place of, supplant (9)
4 Functional equality (6)
5 Seaman (3)
6 Orkney island (3)
8 Alcoholic beverage (3)
9 Suspicious, untrusting (5)
12 Ornamental covering for a horse (9)
13 Compass point at 45 degrees (5-4)
14 Greek mythological monster (5)
16 Cooking in an oven (6)
18 Flushed (3)
19 Assumed name (5)
22 Sick (3)
23 Melancholy (3)

286

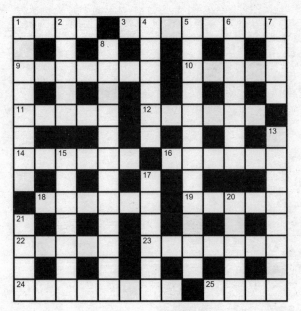

Across

1 Chopped meat mixed with potatoes (4)
3 Special importance or significance (8)
9 Dilapidated (3-4)
10 Cause to lose one's nerve (5)
11 Hold on tightly (5)
12 In a level and regular way (6)
14 Children's outdoor toy (6)
16 Thin, scanty (6)
18 Equipment for taking pictures (6)
19 Stout twists of fibre (5)
22 Powerful herbivore with a horned snout (abbr) (5)
23 Saying (7)
24 Lifting device used for hauling or hoisting (8)
25 Computer memory unit (4)

Down

1 Money in the form of bills or coins (4,4)
2 One of the two main branches of orthodox Islam (5)
4 Trough from which cattle or horses feed (6)
5 Common British bird (5,7)
6 Piece of embroidery demonstrating skill with various stitches (7)
7 Performs an act of transgression (4)
8 Nocturnal bird of prey with two tufts on top of the head (4-5,3)
13 Workable, possible (8)
15 Dodging, non-payment (7)
17 South American plains (6)
20 Religious righteousness (5)
21 Make beer (4)

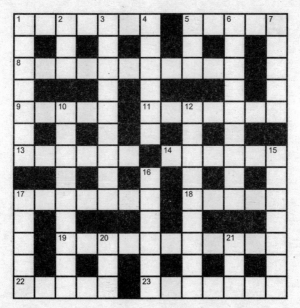

Across
1 Short, curved sword (7)
5 Exists (5)
8 Portable device which warms the air in a room (5,6)
9 In a peculiar manner (5)
11 Bird otherwise known as the peewit (7)
13 Secure (6)
14 Russian vehicle drawn by three horses abreast (6)
17 On the other hand (7)
18 Closer to the centre (5)
19 Junior (11)
22 Murdered (5)
23 Athletes who compete in foot races (7)

Down
1 Make the last row of stitches when knitting (4,3)
2 Drink made by infusing dried leaves (3)
3 Gas used chiefly in welding (9)
4 Decorous or proper (6)
5 Ignited (3)
6 Brilliant red, scarlet (9)
7 Gesture involving the shoulders (5)
10 Indigestion (9)
12 Vertical structure that divides or separates (9)
15 Stuffy (atmosphere) (7)
16 Loan shark (6)
17 Gives notice of impending danger (5)
20 Garbage container (3)
21 ___ Maria, prayer to the Virgin Mary (3)

288

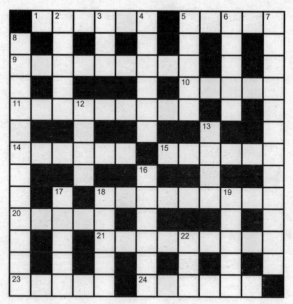

Across

1 Economise (6)

5 Citizen sworn to give a true verdict in a court of law (5)

9 Conventional expression of farewell (9)

10 Eighth letter of the Greek alphabet (5)

11 Twenty-four hours ago (9)

14 Country, capital Kampala (6)

15 Nonetheless (4,2)

18 Exceptionally bad (9)

20 Faithful (5)

21 Arturo ____, Italian orchestra conductor (1867–1957) (9)

23 Person or thing beyond hope or help (coll) (5)

24 Hypothesis (6)

Down

2 Cuts into pieces (5)

3 Charged particle (3)

4 Asian temple (6)

5 Pier, breakwater (5)

6 Measuring stick (5)

7 State of connectedness between people (12)

8 *The* ____, Hans Christian Andersen's tale of a cygnet (4,8)

12 Collapsible shelter (4)

13 Type of food shop (abbr) (4)

16 Determined in advance (6)

17 Tower supporting high-tension wires (5)

18 Communion table (5)

19 Flexible twig of a willow (5)

22 Bladed chopping tool (3)

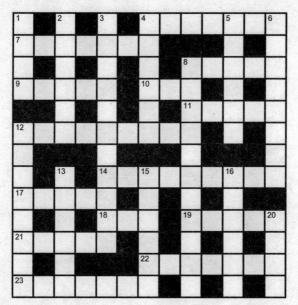

Across

4 Sorrow (7)
7 Insistent (7)
8 Open, observable (5)
9 Equine animal (5)
10 Gossip (3)
11 Interjection instructing someone to be silent (5)
12 Bold outlaw (9)
14 Us (9)
17 Eats sparingly, in order to reduce weight (5)
18 Little rascal (3)
19 Army unit of two or more divisions (5)
21 German submarine in World War II (1-4)
22 Hard dense tissue forming the bulk of a tooth (7)
23 Moves text or graphics on a computer screen (7)

Down

1 German composer (1685–1750) (4)
2 Former name of the Indian city of Chennai (6)
3 Strongroom in which valuables may be securely stored (4-7)
4 Mark of disgrace (6)
5 Good look (coll) (6)
6 Schoolbags (8)
8 Going out of production (11)
12 State of inactivity or stagnation (8)
13 Diversion (6)
15 Parts of a river where the current is very fast (6)
16 Small animals or insects that are pests (6)
20 Moved very fast (4)

290

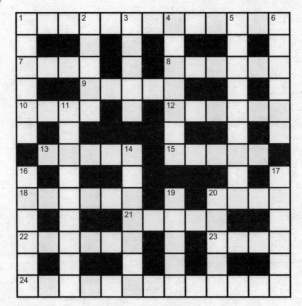

Across

1 Person who deals in goods of little value (3-3-4,3)
7 Quick look (4)
8 Legendary (6)
9 Afterwards (5)
10 Departed (4)
12 Bureau, place of work (6)
13 Stripes (5)
15 Went out with, courted (5)
18 Greek 'L' (6)
20 Greenish-blue colour (4)
21 Nigerian monetary unit (5)
22 Ancient (3-3)
23 Twinge (4)
24 Archipelago off the south-western coast of England (5,2,6)

Down

1 Annul by rescinding (6)
2 Make a request (5)
3 Fatality (5)
4 Relating to vehicles for use on rough terrain (3-4)
5 Wares sold in a hat shop (9)
6 Prods (6)
11 Metal object sounded to warn of danger (5,4)
14 Person deemed to be despicable or contemptible (2-3-2)
16 Compound capable of turning litmus blue (6)
17 Warmly and comfortably (sheltered) (6)
19 Fowl (5)
20 Island in the Bay of Naples (5)

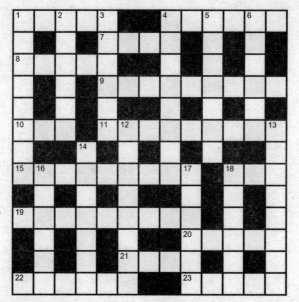

Across
1 Former French coin (5)
4 Deep ditch (6)
7 River which flows through York (4)
8 Natives of Iraq, eg (5)
9 Give a brief statement of the main points (9)
10 Move the head in agreement (3)
11 Change the order or arrangement of (9)
15 Deliberately (2,7)
18 Male sheep (3)
19 Lacking conscious awareness of (9)
20 Terminate before completion (5)
21 Expel (gases or odours) (4)
22 Flat metal tumblers which revolve in locks (6)
23 Divided into regions (5)

Down
1 Pink wading bird (8)
2 Became less intense (6)
3 Treat with excessive indulgence (6)
4 Either end of a bus route (8)
5 Measure of amount of energy available for doing work (7)
6 French sweet blackcurrant liqueur (6)
12 Cold-blooded vertebrates such as tortoises and snakes (8)
13 Swiss cheese with large holes (8)
14 Able to be heard (7)
16 Bite off tiny pieces (6)
17 Inferior substitute or imitation (6)
18 Spiritually converted (6)

292

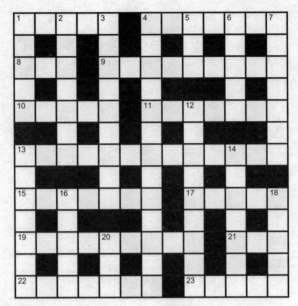

Across

1 Fertilised plant ovules (5)
4 Ballroom dance in double time (3-4)
8 Gentle blow (3)
9 Person who uses insincere praise (9)
10 Be worthy or deserving (5)
11 Defendant in a court of law (7)
13 Bacterium which can cause scarlet fever, pneumonia, etc (13)
15 Small crown (7)
17 Tartan (5)
19 Insert commas, full stops, etc (9)
21 Adult males (3)
22 Longest river of Asia (7)
23 Rise rapidly, rush (5)

Down

1 Scarper (5)
2 Ruler (7)
3 Metal fastener in the form of a clasp, with a guard (6,3)
4 Roadside restaurant catering mainly for long-distance lorry drivers (9,4)
5 Decide, make a choice (3)
6 Number in a trio (5)
7 Maritime robbers (7)
12 Late news inserted into a newspaper (4,5)
13 Salary given to an employee who is ill (4,3)
14 Smooth talker (7)
16 Angry dispute (3-2)
18 Move to music (5)
20 Small insectivorous bird (3)

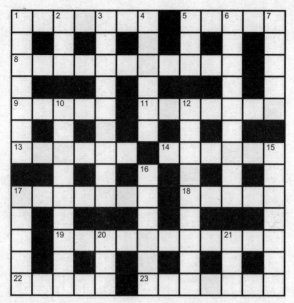

Across

1 Very distant (3,4)
5 Short (5)
8 Typical of Europe (11)
9 Tennis stroke that puts the ball into play (5)
11 Precious gem (7)
13 Impair in force or sensation (6)
14 Newspaper chief (6)
17 Expand by lengthening or widening (7)
18 Financial institutions (5)
19 Night of 31 December (3,5,3)
22 Complete and without restriction or qualification (5)
23 This evening (7)

Down

1 Concentrated into a sharp beam (7)
2 Master Weasley, friend of Harry Potter (3)
3 State of intense passion or activity (5,4)
4 Gives way (6)
5 Club (3)
6 Obtained illegally or by improper means (3-6)
7 Compound leaf of a fern (5)
10 Place in a different order (9)
12 Brightest star in the constellation Taurus (9)
15 Admiration or esteem (7)
16 Dire warning (6)
17 Fabric sheets used on a yacht (5)
20 Period of conflict (3)
21 Product of a hen (3)

294

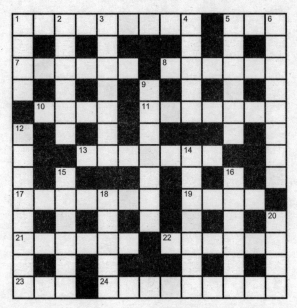

Across

1 Witty remark (9)
5 Carbon dioxide, for example (3)
7 Covered with a waterproof coating (6)
8 Decanter (6)
10 Brought into existence (4)
11 Chemical used in reactions (7)
13 Disappointment (3-4)
17 Tramp about (7)
19 Saturate (4)
21 Impelled (6)
22 *Two Gentlemen of* ___, comedy by Shakespeare (6)
23 Overworked horse (3)
24 Identification of the nature or cause of a phenomenon (9)

Down

1 Black and yellow stinging insect (4)
2 Time of year (6)
3 Wash (7)
4 Australian marsupial which feeds on the eucalyptus (5)
5 Pointed beard (6)
6 Band of colours, as seen in a rainbow (8)
9 Pressed down with the feet (7)
12 Extinct elephant-like mammal (8)
14 Cowboy film (7)
15 Expressing in words (6)
16 Beauty parlours (6)
18 Implore (5)
20 Minstrel songs (4)

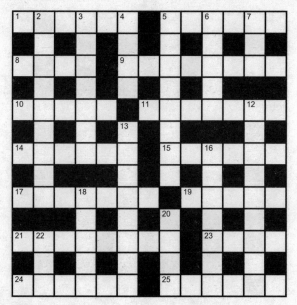

Across
1 End product (6)
5 Artist of consummate skill (6)
8 Estimation (4)
9 Storyteller (8)
10 Plait hair (5)
11 Loosely woven fabric used for flags, etc (7)
14 Inclined beam supporting a roof (6)
15 Elongated cluster of flowers (6)
17 Plume (7)
19 Clumsy (5)
21 Tending to cure or restore to health (8)
23 In the quickest time (inits) (4)
24 Item that fastens together two ends of a belt (6)
25 Flat disc used as a seal to prevent leakage (6)

Down
2 Promise to do or accomplish (9)
3 Keyboard player (7)
4 Savoury taste experience (4)
5 Place for the temporary storage of dead bodies (8)
6 Tip at an angle (5)
7 Inflated feeling of self-worth (3)
12 Door sign (9)
13 Presenting matters as they are (4-4)
16 Seek people's votes (7)
18 Adjust finely (5)
20 Exhaled with force (4)
22 ___ de Cologne, perfume (3)

296

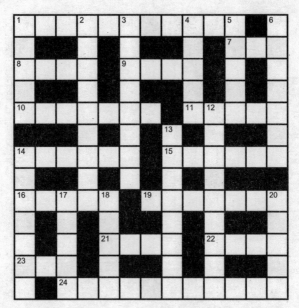

Across

1 Chief Tanzanian port (3,2,6)
7 Notice of intent to pay (inits) (3)
8 Skewer for holding meat over a fire (4)
9 As well (4)
10 The Devil (coll) (3,4)
11 Climbing plant supporter (5)
14 One who obtains pleasure from inflicting pain (6)
15 Seed of the pea family (6)
16 Cautious, wary (5)
19 Tract of land (7)
21 Hardy cabbage (4)
22 Exhibiting vigorous good health (4)
23 French vineyard (3)
24 Drama representing the suffering of Christ (7,4)

Down

1 Public dance hall (5)
2 Broad in scope or content (9)
3 Separating the notes, in music (8)
4 Nuclear weapon (1-4)
5 Sound made by a cat (5)
6 Ceremony at which a dead person is buried or cremated (7)
12 Proprietary rights (9)
13 Very close and trusted friend (5,3)
14 Concealment (7)
17 Rise to one's feet (3,2)
18 Exclamation of surprise (5)
20 Very poor, impoverished (5)

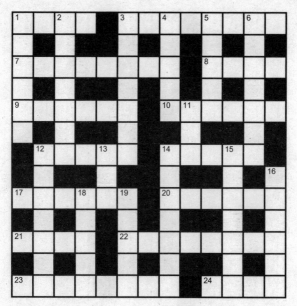

Across

1 Padlock fitting (4)
3 Made allowances for, overlooked (8)
7 Causing worry (8)
8 Enemies (4)
9 Contaminates (6)
10 Strand of yarn (6)
12 Common cinema name (5)
14 Slender, graceful young woman (5)
17 Deliberately causes a delay (6)
20 Not corresponding to acknowledged facts or criteria (6)
21 Mature male antelope (4)
22 Internal organs, collectively (8)
23 Greenland caribou (8)
24 Second letter of the Greek alphabet (4)

Down

1 Fireplace (6)
2 Fowl that frequents coastal waters (7)
3 Deep red (7)
4 Dark period (5)
5 Volunteer (5)
6 Solution used as a cleanser for the organs of sight (7)
11 Fodder (3)
12 Thrust out (7)
13 Grease (3)
14 Mechanical device on a camera (7)
15 Command, control (7)
16 Colourless watery fluid of blood (6)
18 Compare (5)
19 Unit of volume equal to one cubic metre (5)

298

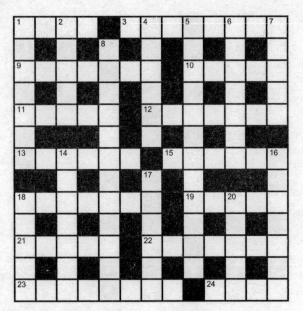

Across

1 Equipment for a horse (4)
3 Dots in a text showing suppression of words (8)
9 Feign (7)
10 Loom (5)
11 Surpass (5)
12 Item of jewellery (7)
13 Make a disguised reference to (6)
15 Male relative (6)
18 Cup, goblet (7)
19 Picture placed within the bounds of a larger one (5)
21 Assigned to a station (5)
22 Scottish biscuit (7)
23 Drivel (8)
24 Lower limbs (4)

Down

1 Milk-pudding ingredient (7)
2 Large box with a lid (5)
4 Spoons used to serve soup (6)
5 Around the middle of a scale of evaluation (12)
6 Marine creature with a long flattened snout with toothlike projections (7)
7 Branchlet (5)
8 One who serves in a subordinate capacity (coll) (6,6)
14 Involvement (7)
16 Loses freshness, vigour or vitality (7)
17 Sour-tasting yellow fruits (6)
18 Small house in the woods (5)
20 Remove body hair (5)

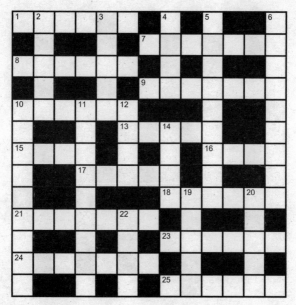

Across

1 Accident, fate (6)
7 Alcoholic beverage flavoured with the fruit of the blackthorn (4,3)
8 Asiatic wild ass (6)
9 Covered and often columned entrance to a building (7)
10 Fall down, as if collapsing (6)
13 Ardent follower and admirer (5)
15 Asian desert (4)
16 Eric ____, member of the Monty Python team (4)
17 Desire strongly (5)
18 Most cunning (6)
21 Nematode (7)
23 Interment (6)
24 Green gem (7)
25 Fish eagle (6)

Down

2 Follower of a major religion (5)
3 Wicker basket used by anglers (5)
4 Collection of miscellaneous things (4)
5 Adroitness in using the hands (9)
6 Pleasure (9)
10 Made more constricting (9)
11 Masonry (9)
12 Island associated with Napoleon (4)
14 Competes (4)
19 Sings the praises of (5)
20 Protect from light (5)
22 Rivulet (4)

300

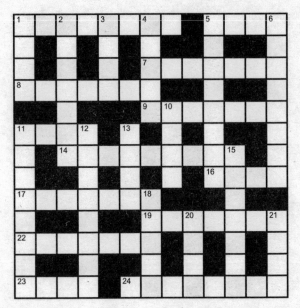

Across

1 Most free from danger or risk (8)
5 ____ Christian Andersen, storyteller (4)
7 Innumerable but many (7)
8 Most wound up (7)
9 Greets enthusiastically (7)
11 Household dirt (4)
14 Wavered (9)
16 Back end (4)
17 Sea area between Viking and Dogger (7)
19 Disentangles (7)
22 Contends for in argument (7)
23 Be unable to find (4)
24 Title of respect for a clergyman (8)

Down

1 Gentle, indulgent (4)
2 Relating to the county west of Devon (7)
3 Capital of Italy (4)
4 Compass point at 180 degrees (5)
5 Trouble (coll) (3,5)
6 Ominous (8)
10 Mild yellow Dutch cheese (4)
11 Flower associated with spring (8)
12 Legal action where the outcome is likely to set a precedent (4,4)
13 Journey in a vehicle (4)
15 Swerve (7)
18 Girl's name (abbr) (5)
20 Coffee shop (4)
21 Rivet (4)

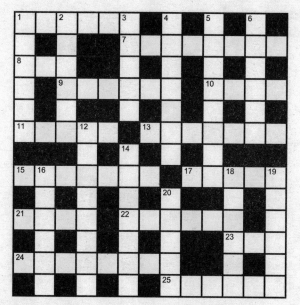

Across

1 Lumps together (6)
7 South American monkey with claws instead of nails (8)
8 Joan of ___ (3)
9 Historical woman's gown (6)
10 Largest organ of the body (4)
11 Forcibly pull (something) from a person's grasp (5)
13 Discomfort or illness (7)
15 Criticising strongly (7)
17 Consume (3,2)
21 Brightest star in the constellation Lyra (4)
22 Looks forward to (6)
23 Body of salt water (3)
24 Perennial wild plant with blue flowers (8)
25 Of the peerage (6)

Down

1 Field where grass is grown (6)
2 Wet-nurse (6)
3 English explorer said to have been saved by Pocahontas (5)
4 Armoury (7)
5 Casserole of aubergine and ground lamb in a sauce (8)
6 Exceptional creative ability (6)
12 Located (8)
14 Dispenser that produces a vapour to relieve congestion (7)
16 Elbow-room (6)
18 Bunch of cords fastened at one end (6)
19 Country, capital Warsaw (6)
20 Burial chamber (5)

302

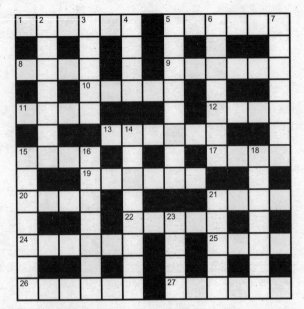

Across
1 Country, capital Lusaka (6)
5 Number: the Roman XI (6)
8 French superior of a monastery (4)
9 Stout-bodied insect (6)
10 ___ del Sol, popular Spanish resort region (5)
11 Tau cross with a loop (4)
12 Underside of a shoe (4)
13 Plantation (6)
15 Point on an arrow (4)
17 Put in order (4)
19 Mr Sayle, comedian (6)
20 Press down tightly (4)
21 Thrust (4)
22 Exhaust-driven engine compressor, in short (5)
24 Containing salt (6)
25 Mosque official (4)
26 Stands for paintings (6)
27 Ms Rantzen, celebrity (6)

Down
2 Country, capital Tirana (7)
3 Deciduous tree (5)
4 Top cards (4)
5 Mischievous adventure (8)
6 Removes by cutting (7)
7 Most close (7)
14 Protects from harm (8)
15 Thin plain-weave cotton or linen fabric (7)
16 Christen (7)
18 Form differently (7)
21 Indicate (5)
23 Actor's portrayal of someone (4)

Across

1 Cereal grain used in distilling (4)
3 Secret phrase (8)
9 Let back in (7)
10 Comes close (5)
11 Having an appearance of solidity or relief (12)
14 Liturgical vestment worn by priests (3)
16 Adult insect (5)
17 *Much ___ about Nothing*, Shakespeare play (3)
18 Establish as valid (12)
21 Indian form of address for a man (5)
22 Branch of mathematics (7)
23 Distribute loosely (8)
24 Gravel (4)

Down

1 Someone skilled in shooting (8)
2 Depart (5)
4 Perform (3)
5 Capital of the Dominican Republic (5,7)
6 Musical toy (7)
7 Move with great haste (4)
8 Not subject to destruction, death or decay (12)
12 Mass of eggs deposited by frogs (5)
13 Prediction (8)
15 Turns red, as with embarrassment (7)
19 Fossilised resin (5)
20 Employed (4)
22 Equine animal (3)

304

Across

1 Animal prized for its fur (5)
4 Querulous (7)
8 Zero (3)
9 Watery discharge from the eyes or nose (5)
10 Mistake (5)
11 Refuse to accept (10)
13 Rope or canvas headgear for a horse (6)
15 Fungus causing timber to crumble (3,3)
18 Hard natural coal that burns slowly (10)
22 Make a rhythmic sound with the fingers (5)
23 Fill with high spirits (5)
24 Range of knowledge (3)
25 First book of the Bible (7)
26 Largest satellite of Saturn (5)

Down

1 Having a rough, uncomfortable texture (8)
2 Haemorrhage (5)
3 All together, as a group (2,5)
4 Bell-bottomed (6)
5 Fragrant resin used as incense (5)
6 Eternally (7)
7 Fat used in cooking (4)
12 Large fish valued for its roe (8)
14 Period of time sufficient for factors to work themselves out (4,3)
16 Apparel (7)
17 Arctic canoes (6)
19 Organic component of soil (5)
20 Perform as if in a play (5)
21 Male deer (4)

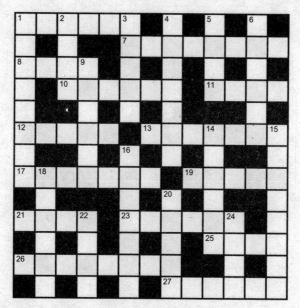

Across

1 Not in a specified place (6)
7 Pre-wedding celebration for women (3,5)
8 Mild expletive used to express vexation (4)
10 Coiffure (6)
11 Aquatic bird (4)
12 River which flows through Rome (5)
13 Arch of facial hair (7)
17 Having spots or patches of colour (7)
19 ___ Cagney, Hollywood star who died in 1986 (5)
21 Disease of the skin (4)
23 Ransacked (6)
25 Overabundant (4)
26 Tedious (8)
27 Birds associated with the Tower of London (6)

Down

1 Kidnapped (8)
2 Former hereditary monarch of Iran (4)
3 In that place (5)
4 Word opposite in meaning to another (7)
5 Lacking hair (4)
6 Ornamental plaster used to cover walls (6)
9 Absorb (4,2)
14 Lightweight single-breasted jacket (6)
15 Self-indulgent idlers (8)
16 Large, ocean-dwelling mammal (3,4)
18 Region centred on the North Pole (6)
20 Lobby, vestibule (5)
22 Female sheep (4)
24 US coin worth one tenth of a dollar (4)

306

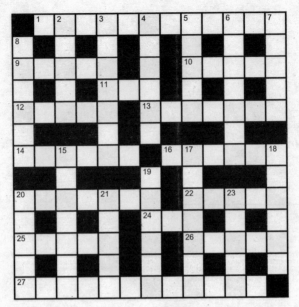

Across

1 Spoken or written accounts (12)
9 Goes in front (5)
10 Capital of Tibet (5)
11 Single-digit number (3)
12 Ms Campbell, model (5)
13 Yokels, country bumpkins (7)
14 Fashions (6)
16 Meeting of spiritualists (6)
20 Small, furry-tailed, squirrel-like rodents (7)
22 Set of beliefs (5)
24 Nineteenth letter of the Greek alphabet (3)
25 Highest peak in the Alps, Mont ____ (5)
26 Left over, superfluous (5)
27 Popular cold drink (3,5,4)

Down

2 Greek muse of lyric poetry (5)
3 Region of central Spain (7)
4 Hereditary (6)
5 Tall stories (5)
6 Enthusiastic recognition (7)
7 Crustlike surfaces of healing wounds (5)
8 Briefly shuts the eyes (6)
15 Distance measured in three-foot units (7)
17 Pardons (7)
18 Becomes ground down (6)
19 Light-sensitive membrane at the back of the eye (6)
20 City in the United Arab Emirates on the Persian Gulf (5)
21 Bring upon oneself (5)
23 Large antelope (5)

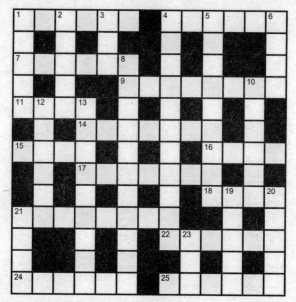

Across

1 Beefeater (6)
4 Norse dragon that was slain by Sigurd (6)
7 Skilled trades (6)
9 Engage in plotting (8)
11 Lob, pitch (4)
14 Melodious (7)
15 Bullets, etc (abbr) (4)
16 Slender double-reed instrument (4)
17 Twitter like a bird (7)
18 Put away for storage (4)
21 Destroy or injure severely (8)
22 Fixed portion that is allotted (6)
24 Elaborate party (often outdoors) (6)
25 In a feeble manner (6)

Down

1 Racing vessel (5)
2 Authorises (coll) (5)
3 Toward a ship's stern (3)
4 Smooth-textured sausage often served in a roll (11)
5 Light sandals with a thong between the big and second toe (4-5)
6 Gown (4)
8 Group of related countries in northern Europe (11)
10 Fanciful asymmetric ornamentation (6)
12 Brass that looks like gold, used to decorate furniture (6)
13 Women's hosiery items (9)
19 Dense (5)
20 Extremely breezy (5)
21 Warm tubular covering for the hands (4)
23 Affirmative word (3)

308

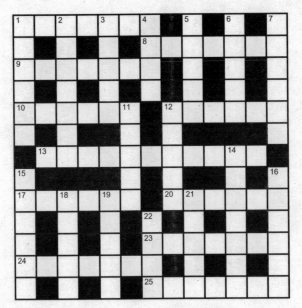

Across

1 Ethical or moral principle that inhibits action (7)
8 Cavalryman (7)
9 From the Orient (7)
10 Common songbird (6)
12 Penetrate (6)
13 Cultural rebirth from the 14th to the middle of the 17th centuries (11)
17 Dense woodland (6)
20 Tree and shrub species (6)
23 Impose something unpleasant (7)
24 Small piece of toast served in soup (7)
25 Sum of money saved for the future (4,3)

Down

1 Case for a knife (6)
2 Earmark (7)
3 Hunts for (5)
4 Highest volcano in Europe (4)
5 Welsh breed of dog (5)
6 Scent trail of an animal (5)
7 Chauffeur (6)
11 Raise (a flag, for example) (5)
12 Fusilli, for example (5)
14 Powerfully addictive narcotic (7)
15 Consequence (6)
16 Untidy, disorganised (6)
18 Android (5)
19 Sir Walter ____, British author (1771–1832) (5)
21 Informal restaurants (5)
22 Native of Helsinki, for example (4)

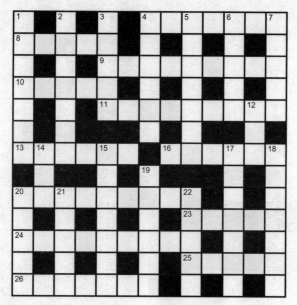

Across

4 US state on the Gulf of Mexico (7)
8 Bohemian dance (5)
9 Characterised by toilsome effort (9)
10 Make up for past sins (5)
11 Giving an overall review of a situation (7,2)
13 Red, globular salad vegetable (6)
16 Mend, fix (6)
20 Large sleeping room containing several beds (9)
23 Semi-precious stone (5)
24 Shoulder belt for carrying ammunition (9)
25 Ambition (5)
26 Quick-witted retort (7)

Down

1 Orator (7)
2 Permitted (7)
3 Strong winds (5)
4 Musical records (6)
5 Flight company (7)
6 In line with a length or direction (5)
7 Fable writer (5)
12 Israeli submachine-gun (3)
14 Gone by (3)
15 Ship's crew members (7)
17 Substance taken to counter indigestion (7)
18 Official who is expected to ensure fair play (7)
19 Part of a dress above the waist (6)
20 Prevent from entering (5)
21 Make by sewing together quickly (3,2)
22 Back gardens (5)

310

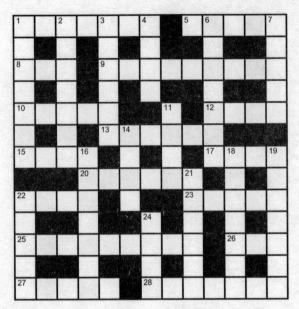

Across
1 Mail (7)
5 Deflect, fend off (5)
8 Cloth hat (3)
9 Container holding flint, etc, for kindling fires (9)
10 Man who brought back the Golden Fleece (5)
12 Galls, vexes (4)
13 Military personnel (6)
15 Clean with soap and water (4)
17 Track down (4)
20 In a new way (6)
22 Move back and forth (4)
23 Speedily (5)
25 Gaining with effort (9)
26 Append (3)
27 Piece of cloth used for wiping the nose (abbr) (5)
28 Beer-making establishment (7)

Down
1 Tetanus (7)
2 Keyboard operators (7)
3 Degree (6)
4 Bathroom fixture (4)
6 Paint that provides a hard glossy transparent coating (7)
7 Lone Star State of the USA (5)
11 Crash out (4)
14 Underdone (4)
16 Stack of dried grass for use as fodder (7)
18 Oblivious (7)
19 One division of a week (7)
21 Bargain over a price (6)
22 Space created by the swing of a scythe (5)
24 Jointed appendage (4)

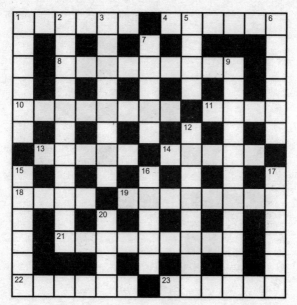

Across

1 Portable computer (6)
4 Stroll (6)
8 Being in force (9)
10 Widespread outbreak of disease (8)
11 Daze (4)
13 Washing fixture found in a bathroom (5)
14 Facial hair (5)
18 Utter a pig-like cry (4)
19 Highly decorated earthenware with a glaze of tin oxide (8)
21 American state, capital Baton Rouge (9)
22 Unstintingly extravagant (6)
23 Act against an attack (6)

Down

1 Pantry (6)
2 Temporary (11)
3 Vigilant (4-4)
5 Entrance passage into a mine (4)
6 Travelling on horseback (6)
7 Distinctive attire worn by a nun (5)
9 Kill on a large scale (11)
12 Providing no shelter or sustenance (8)
15 Relating to the system for delivering mail (6)
16 Spicy sauce to accompany Mexican food (5)
17 Narrative poem of popular origin (6)
20 Humorous plays on words (4)

312

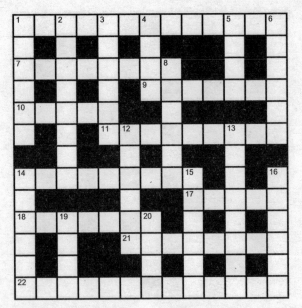

Across
1 Person who spreads malicious gossip (13)
7 Capital of Syria (8)
9 Entertainment venue (7)
10 Prime minister of India from 1947 to 1964 (5)
11 Member of the faculty at a college or university (9)
14 Institution providing labour and shelter for the poor (9)
17 Empty area (5)
18 Looked up to (7)
21 Advocate of the principles of monarchy (8)
22 Period of the French Revolution marked by extreme repression and bloodshed (5,2,6)

Down
1 Short stretch of railway track used to store rolling stock (6)
2 Large comfortable seat (8)
3 Serve out (4,2)
4 Awkward stupid person (4)
5 Person's pace (4)
6 Try a court case anew (6)
8 Moves position slightly (6)
12 Member of a crowd causing a disturbance of the peace (6)
13 More furtive or sly (8)
14 Craftsman who makes cloth (6)
15 Break free (6)
16 Clergyman assisted by a curate (6)
19 Country, capital Bamako (4)
20 Raise (a hat), especially in respect or greeting (4)

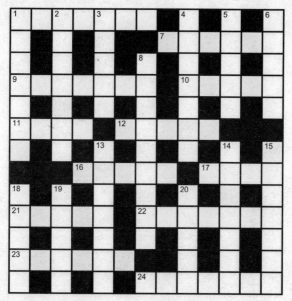

Across

1 Separate into parts (5,2)
7 Digestive fluid (6)
9 Of the greatest possible degree (7)
10 Rod which forms the body of an arrow (5)
11 Division of a dollar (4)
12 Method of producing designs on cloth by covering with wax, then dyeing (5)
16 Tree with rot-resistant wood (5)
17 Supreme god of the Romans (4)
21 Inquiry into unfamiliar or questionable activities (5)
22 Country, capital Zagreb (7)
23 Murderer (6)
24 Give someone wrong directions or information (7)

Down

1 Peace and quiet (7)
2 Plundering during riots (7)
3 Piece of absorbent cloth (5)
4 Legal case (7)
5 Holy war waged by Muslims (5)
6 Glue made of flour and water (5)
8 Degeneration (9)
13 Cross-brace that supports a rail on a railway track (7)
14 Arrangement of the body and its limbs (7)
15 Animal with six feet (7)
18 Long sharp-pointed implement (5)
19 Fungus which thrives in damp conditions (5)
20 Sturdy footwear that covers the lower legs (5)

314

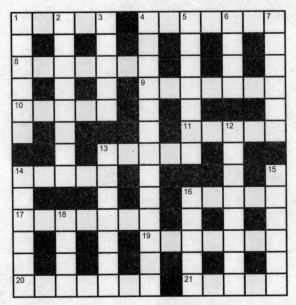

Across

1 Morsel (5)
4 Fortune (7)
8 Come into possession of (7)
9 Long, narrow deposit of beach material (4,3)
10 Moon-related (5)
11 Pigpens (5)
13 Second planet from the sun (5)
14 Panache (5)
16 Work very hard (5)
17 Meeting for boat races (7)
19 Most direct route (7)
20 Unspecified person (7)
21 Extremely ornate (5)

Down

1 Piercingly high-pitched (6)
2 Of late (8)
3 Head of a religious order (5)
4 Item of bedroom furniture (8,5)
5 Timidity (7)
6 Metrical unit with unstressed-stressed syllables (4)
7 Pines (6)
12 Encroachment by an enemy (8)
13 Hitchcock film of 1958 (7)
14 Bushes (6)
15 Salad vegetable (6)
16 Projecting ridge on a mountain (5)
18 Pacific island, capital Hagåtña (4)

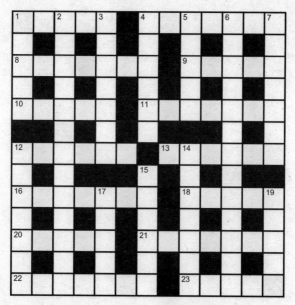

Across

1 Loose-fitting garment (5)
4 Study of language structure (7)
8 Shaped like a ring (7)
9 Roofed with thin rectangular slabs (5)
10 Run off to marry (5)
11 Copy (7)
12 Looted (6)
13 Series of arches supported by columns (6)
16 Land area, especially of a farm (7)
18 Pig, hog (5)
20 Item (5)
21 Acquired knowledge (7)
22 No longer active in one's profession (7)
23 Mark (~) placed over the letter 'n' in Spanish (5)

Down

1 Make fun of (5)
2 Maverick (13)
3 Educational institution (7)
4 Mr Depardieu, French film star (6)
5 Misbehave badly (3,2)
6 Involving several countries (13)
7 Send out or emit (7)
12 Nuclear plant (7)
14 Begin again (7)
15 Cut down (a tree) (6)
17 Predict from an omen (5)
19 Give qualities or abilities to (5)

316

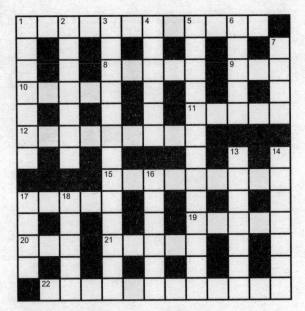

Across

1 Appliance in which garments can be hung and wrinkles ironed out (7,5)

8 Send or drive out (5)

9 Acid present in all living cells (inits) (3)

10 Latin phrase meaning 'in itself' or 'intrinsically' (3,2)

11 Diminutive form of Elizabeth (5)

12 Moving staircase (9)

15 Serialised TV programme (4,5)

17 Outer surfaces of an object (5)

19 Young leaf or bud signifying the coming of spring (5)

20 Tit for ____, getting even (3)

21 Claim as due or just (5)

22 Shine in the dark (12)

Down

1 Induced into action by using one's charm (7)

2 Fast-running African flightless bird (7)

3 Insomnia (13)

4 Happen or occur again (6)

5 Elevated railway in an amusement park (13)

6 Garments worn primarily by Hindu women (5)

7 Humorous anecdote or remark intended to provoke laughter (4)

13 Divisions of a minute (7)

14 Island linked with Principe (3,4)

16 County of Northern Ireland (6)

17 Satisfy completely (4)

18 People of the Netherlands (5)

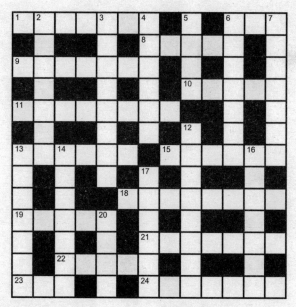

Across

1 Relating to the motion of material bodies (7)
6 Seedcase (3)
8 Mouth sore (5)
9 Relating to the stomach (7)
10 Send (payment) (5)
11 Parts of a tree that are no longer alive (4,4)
13 Journalist's attribution (6)
15 Overly diluted (6)
18 Pair of matching single divans (4,4)
19 Animal with two feet (5)
21 Speak in a low voice (7)
22 Darkest part of a shadow (5)
23 Crystalline rock that can be cut for jewellery (3)
24 Either end of the sail support of a square-rigged ship (7)

Down

2 Mental pictures collectively (7)
3 Chucking (8)
4 Bird which lays eggs in other birds' nests (6)
5 Blemish, indication of damage done (4)
6 Statement from which a conclusion can be drawn (7)
7 Annihilate (7)
12 More lively and self-confident (8)
13 Theory of the origin of the universe (3,4)
14 Single amount of money (4,3)
16 City north of Calgary, Alberta (3,4)
17 Involving movement or communication in opposite directions (3-3)
20 Financial obligation (4)

318

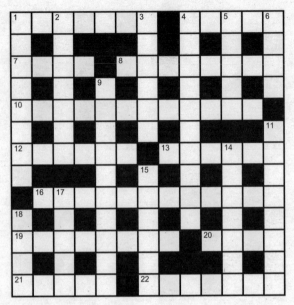

Across

1 Stop the flow by closing a valve (4,3)
4 Cheat by avoiding payment of a gambling debt (5)
7 Clothing (4)
8 Relating to the arts and to intellectual achievements (8)
10 Most prominent or important position (5,2,5)
12 Appeared (6)
13 Cipher used in WWII (6)
16 Charge for converting currencies (8,4)
19 Person who doubts the truth of religion (8)
20 Comes to the assistance of (4)
21 Projection shaped to fit into a mortise (5)
22 Japanese warrior (7)

Down

1 Guide which shows the way (8)
2 Resurrect (7)
3 Soft and downy (6)
4 Gloomy person who stifles others' enjoyment (coll) (3,7)
5 Characteristic of song (5)
6 Cargo space in a ship (4)
9 Short leather trousers worn in Austria, eg (10)
11 Skim over the sea whilst being towed by a speedboat (5-3)
14 Person who cuts and sets panes into windows or doors (7)
15 Ludicrous acts done for fun (6)
17 Noble gas (5)
18 Piece (4)

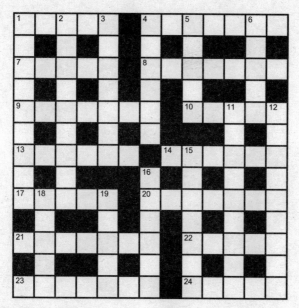

Across

1 Consternation (5)
4 Large Arctic mammal, the male having a long spiral ivory tusk (7)
7 Rich cake (5)
8 Of or relating to the skull (7)
9 ___ Stone, Egyptian hieroglyphic inscription (7)
10 Narrow to a point (5)
13 Treeless grassy plains of South America (6)
14 Stimulus or boost to an activity (6)
17 Tearful (5)
20 Sterile (7)
21 Boldly resisting authority or an opposing force (7)
22 Forbidden (5)
23 Powerful family (7)
24 Regions (5)

Down

1 Atmospheric phenomenon sometimes seen at dusk (9)
2 Industry and technology concerned with aviation, satellites, etc (9)
3 Outstanding musician (7)
4 Poetically, the drink of the gods (6)
5 Undergo a chemical change (5)
6 With the mouth wide open, as in wonder or awe (5)
11 Acceptable to the taste (9)
12 Greedy or grasping (9)
15 Disposition to remain inactive (7)
16 Support for a travelling crane (6)
18 Opponent (5)
19 William Butler ___, Irish poet (5)

320

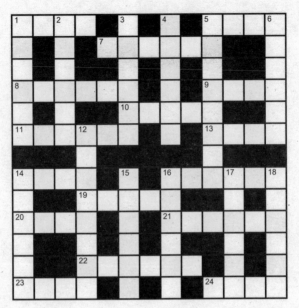

Across

1 Arrived (4)
5 Cain's brother (4)
7 Small rooms on a ship (6)
8 Scratch repeatedly (6)
9 Basic units of electric current (4)
10 One dozen dozen (5)
11 Large gathering of people (6)
13 Eyelid swelling (4)
14 Rescue (4)
16 Parasitic plant (6)
19 Controlled a vehicle (5)
20 Biblical patriarch, Jacob's third son (4)
21 Prospered, flourished (6)
22 Digit, quantity (6)
23 Common amphibian (4)
24 Genuine (4)

Down

1 Clothes cupboard (6)
2 Looking glass (6)
3 Person or scheme that comes to no good (coll) (3,3)
4 Common mineral occurring in small crystals (6)
5 Political murderer (8)
6 Canine film star (6)
12 Responsive to orders (8)
14 Grave (6)
15 Pillar (6)
16 Shackle (6)
17 Sullen or angry stare (6)
18 Hold back to a later time (6)

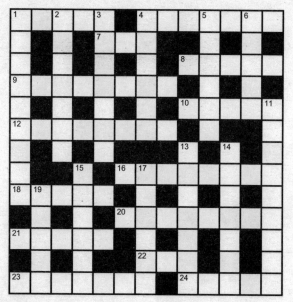

Across

1 Overexcitable (coll) (5)
4 General idea (7)
7 Fruiting spike of a cereal plant (3)
8 Ursine creatures (5)
9 Moving with short unsteady steps (8)
10 Addition, division, etc (abbr) (5)
12 Person appointed by a court to manage assets under litigation (8)
16 Honour, award (8)
18 Velocity (5)
20 Speaker of many languages (8)
21 Contributions to state revenue (5)
22 Raises (3)
23 Push down (a button) (7)
24 Link up, connect (3,2)

Down

1 Attack of violent mental agitation (9)
2 Manufactured item (7)
3 Transform from a useless or uncultivated state (7)
4 Flinch, recoil (6)
5 Type of salad (6)
6 Cause to wither (5)
11 Choice (9)
13 Scribe (7)
14 Edgar ____, English writer noted for his crime novels (1875–1932) (7)
15 Shooting star (6)
17 Flower, the source of saffron (6)
19 Woodworking tool (5)

322

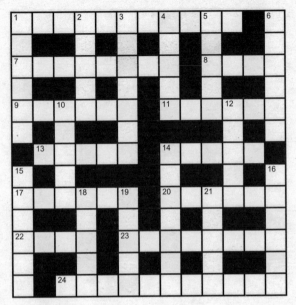

Across

1 One of the Twelve Apostles of Jesus (11)
7 Plant pigment converted to vitamin A in the body (8)
8 Endorsement made in a passport (4)
9 Father or mother (6)
11 Snuggle (6)
13 Informal term for a British policeman (5)
14 Elephant tusk substance (5)
17 One of two actors who are given the same status in a film (2-4)
20 Debacle (6)
22 Not reflecting light (4)
23 Administrative district of a nation (8)
24 Not showing proper respect, cheeky (11)

Down

1 Muscle that flexes the forearm (6)
2 Treasure of unknown ownership (5)
3 In an open manner (7)
4 Large body of salt water (5)
5 Mr Presley, rock and roll legend (5)
6 Drink to follow immediately after another drink (6)
10 Parts of a plant typically found under the ground (5)
12 Limited periods of time (5)
14 Ahead (2,5)
15 Shrewdness shown by keen insight (6)
16 Channel between England and the Isle of Wight (6)
18 ____ pole, tribal emblem (5)
19 Indian currency unit (5)
21 Foreigner, stranger (5)

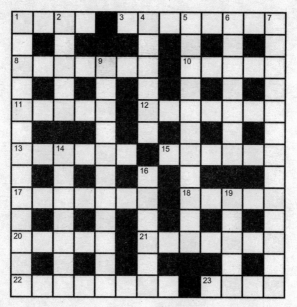

Across

1 Be wide open (4)
3 Closely trimmed cut of pork (5,3)
8 Lives in (7)
10 Map (5)
11 Nicola ___, boxer who won a gold medal at the 2012 Olympics (5)
12 Having two feet (7)
13 Device that attracts iron (6)
15 French brandy (6)
17 Product of coal tar used in dyeing (7)
18 Former province of western France, on the Loire (5)
20 Andean mammal (5)
21 Group whose members can interbreed (7)
22 Cadaverous (8)
23 Impairment resulting from long use (4)

Down

1 Rubella (6,7)
2 Civil or military authority in Turkey (5)
4 Ignore or overlook (4,2)
5 Give mutually or in return (11)
6 Native of Kigali, for example (7)
7 Type of warship (6-7)
9 Cause to become widely known (11)
14 Pull a face (7)
16 Japanese woman trained to entertain men (6)
19 Extract liquid from a fruit or vegetable (5)

324

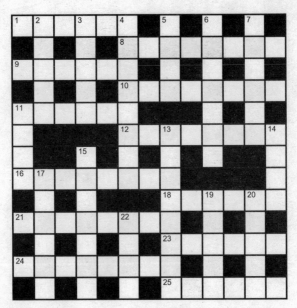

Across

1 Annoy continually or chronically (6)
8 Educator who works at a college (8)
9 Skilled handicrafts (6)
10 Island off the coast of Australia (8)
11 Safe (6)
12 Come out again (2-6)
16 Computing term: large unit of information (8)
18 Covered in turf (6)
21 Official residence provided by a church for its parson (8)
23 Native of the ancient city of Troy (6)
24 Person who is given the same appellation as another person (8)
25 Become angry (coll) (3,3)

Down

2 Acquiesce (5)
3 In Hinduism, an ascetic holy man (5)
4 In a direction towards the Orient (8)
5 Papas (4)
6 Oxygenated (7)
7 Becoming weary (6)
11 Confidence trick (4)
13 Those skilled in the interpretation of text, especially scripture (8)
14 Posing no difficulty (4)
15 Floor show at a nightclub (7)
17 Old Testament prophet (6)
19 On your own (5)
20 Debonair (5)
22 Eve's partner (4)

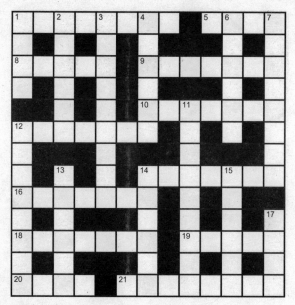

Across

1 Officers of the court employed to execute writs and processes (8)
5 Tasks, pieces of work (4)
8 Bulb, traditionally from Holland (5)
9 Collide violently with an obstacle (3,4)
10 Examine (7)
12 Adopted in order to deceive (7)
14 Athlete (7)
16 Horizontal direction of a celestial body (7)
18 Feelings of excessive pride (7)
19 Copy on thin paper (5)
20 Two singers who perform together (4)
21 Moral excellence (8)

Down

1 Washtub (4)
2 Relatives by marriage (2-4)
3 Ad lib (9)
4 Having burning desire or emotion (6)
6 Units of weight equal to one sixteenth of a pound (6)
7 Gunfight, especially to the death (coll) (5-3)
11 Presented for consideration or judgment (9)
12 High-tech (8)
13 Bridegroom-to-be (6)
14 Residential district, often run-down (6)
15 Timber structure made in the shape of a capital letter (1-5)
17 Slippery fishes (4)

326

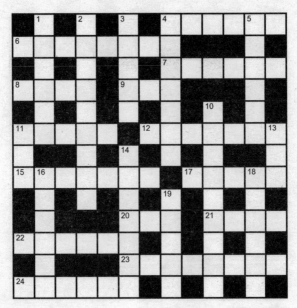

Across

4 Detective who follows a trail (6)
6 Clouding of the lens of the eye (8)
7 Somewhat (6)
8 Highland dagger (4)
9 Named before marriage (3)
11 Elizabeth ___, cosmetics company (5)
12 Gliding on ice (7)
15 Surname of Emilio, brother of Charlie Sheen (7)
17 Hole that an anchor rope passes through (5)
20 Bathing resort (3)
21 Standard monetary unit of Burma (4)
22 Addition that extends a main building (6)
23 Not deserved (8)
24 Beads made by oysters (6)

Down

1 Straight sword with a narrow blade (6)
2 Overfamiliar through too much use (9)
3 Sensations of acute discomfort (5)
4 Marked with stripes (7)
5 Makes a logical connection (4,2)
10 Assailants (9)
11 Imitate (3)
13 Unit of gravitational force (3)
14 Son of Zeus who slew the Medusa (7)
16 Lightweight item used in bathing (6)
18 Phases (6)
19 Confronted (5)

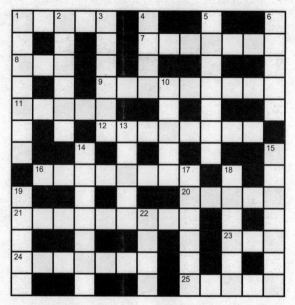

Across

1 Informal language (5)
7 Roman empress, the wife of Nero (7)
8 ___ King Cole, jazz pianist and singer (3)
9 Sepulchral monument (9)
11 Stone writing tablet (5)
12 Arboreal rodent (8)
16 Equips in advance (8)
20 Former model and ex-wife of Donald Trump (5)
21 Unhappy (9)
23 Forbid (3)
24 Largest of the central Ryukyu Islands (7)
25 Fathered (5)

Down

1 Penetrates gradually (5,2)
2 Relating to the stars (6)
3 Reduces to small shreds (6)
4 Machine for weaving (4)
5 Collection of electrical cells (7)
6 Sports (5)
10 Fabric used to cover gaming tables (5)
13 Four children born at the same time (abbr) (5)
14 Fish from which kippers are made (7)
15 Bound with linked metal rings (7)
17 Moves unobtrusively or furtively (6)
18 Slight convexity (as of the surface of a road) (6)
19 Supplement (3-2)
22 Stratum of ore or coal (4)

328

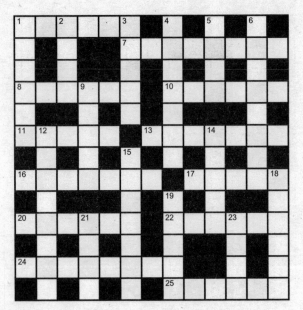

Across

1 Mineral such as quartz (6)
7 Mariner (8)
8 Slow the growth or development of (6)
10 British naval hero (6)
11 Number considered lucky (5)
13 Favouring close friends and relatives for positions of power (7)
16 Workers' dining hall (7)
17 Just made (5)
20 Unwholesome atmosphere (6)
22 *Addams Family* character played by Christopher Lloyd (6)
24 Disease caused by lack of thiamine (4-4)
25 Photographed, as of bones (1-5)

Down

1 Equal portions into which the capital stock of a corporation is divided (6)
2 Erotic desire (4)
3 Away (5)
4 Inhabited by ghosts (7)
5 Release after a security has been paid (4)
6 Sedimentations (8)
9 Dexterous (5)
12 One who administers a test (8)
14 Giants who like to eat human beings (5)
15 Discussed an issue (7)
18 Proclaim (6)
19 Stick on (5)
21 Branch of orthodox Islam (4)
23 People in general (4)

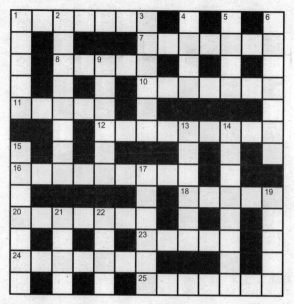

Across

1 Italian painter and architect (1483–1520) (7)
7 Edible shellfish, a source of mother-of-pearl (7)
8 Aquatic mammal (5)
10 Freezing (3-4)
11 Rose to one's feet (5)
12 Gut (9)
16 Foundation garments (9)
18 Elder brother of Moses (5)
20 Grazing land (7)
23 Gene Pitney song, *Twenty-four Hours from* ___ (5)
24 Japanese art of folding paper into shapes (7)
25 Master of ceremonies (7)

Down

1 Picture puzzle (5)
2 Produce for consideration (8)
3 Long noosed rope (6)
4 Bundle of straw or hay (4)
5 Ms Chanel, fashion designer (4)
6 Hawked around (7)
9 More neat (6)
13 Lie with one's limbs spread out (6)
14 Step-up (8)
15 Side story in a play, novel, etc (7)
17 Medicine that induces vomiting (6)
19 Sister's daughter (5)
21 Hurried swallow (4)
22 River of Russia and Kazakhstan which flows into the Caspian Sea (4)

330

Across

1 Ski race over a winding course (6)
5 Represent an incident as if in a play (3,3)
8 Thread used for sewing (6)
9 Tremble with cold (6)
10 Condensed water vapour (3)
11 Natives of Copenhagen, for example (5)
13 One whose business is to provide food or meals (8)
15 Put in working order (8)
16 Air attack (5)
19 And so forth (abbr) (3)
21 Reefs of coral (6)
22 Organism that requires free oxygen for respiration (6)
23 Country, capital Stockholm (6)
24 More miserly (6)

Down

2 Care for (4,5)
3 Metal-shaping machine (5)
4 Intellect (4)
5 Responded (8)
6 Become denser (7)
7 Weedy annual grass (4)
12 Police officer of the lowest rank (9)
13 Hard Italian cheese, often grated (8)
14 Walked in shallow water (7)
17 Insect grub (5)
18 Metal food containers (4)
20 Quiet, serene (4)

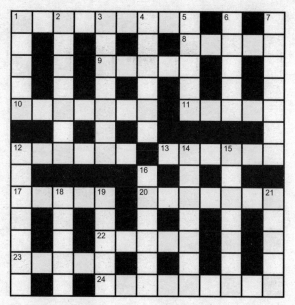

Across

1 Huge rise of water along the seashore (5,4)

8 Compass point at 0 or 360 degrees (5)

9 Bungs (5)

10 Conduct work (7)

11 Surplus to requirements (5)

12 Interior (6)

13 Socially awkward (6)

17 Professional performer who tells jokes (5)

20 Period between one event and another (7)

22 Book of maps (5)

23 Walking ___, elated (2,3)

24 Residence of a religious community (9)

Down

1 Capital city of Japan (5)

2 Makes numb (7)

3 Region one might visit to see Santa (7)

4 Lucky charm (6)

5 End in a particular way (5)

6 Magnificent, wonderful (5)

7 Movable barrier used in motor racing (7)

12 Front tooth (7)

14 Painters, sculptors, etc (7)

15 Light automatic rifle (7)

16 Write the required information onto a form (4-2)

18 Recorded background music played in public (TM) (5)

19 Allure (5)

21 Ron ___, *Oliver!* actor (5)

332

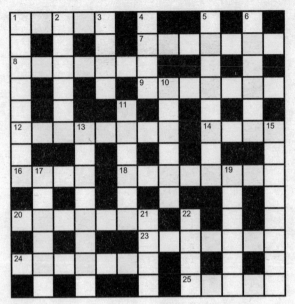

Across

1 Pound, pulse (5)
7 Generous (7)
8 Vast Asian region of Russia (7)
9 Island country in the Persian Gulf (7)
12 Agree to give up or do without (8)
14 Piece of money (4)
16 Crippled (4)
18 Having the highest rating (4-4)
20 Material used to form a hard coating on a porous surface (7)
23 Person who accepts the world as it literally is (7)
24 Porch along the outside of a building (7)
25 Frenzied (5)

Down

1 Pleasant, palatable (8)
2 Mugger (6)
3 Master Simpson, cartoon character (4)
4 Block (4)
5 Takes back, recants (8)
6 Large N American deer (6)
10 Turn up (6)
11 Render unable to hear (6)
13 Large amount (coll) (8)
15 Drug that produces numbness or stupor (8)
17 Examination generally taken after seven years of secondary education (1,5)
19 Italian painter who experimented with bright, vibrant colours (c1488–1576) (6)
21 Device used to catch animals (4)
22 Salve, ointment (4)

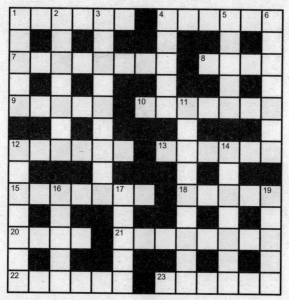

Across

1 First city to host the modern Olympic Games three times (6)
4 Dairy product (6)
7 Short tubes of pasta (8)
8 Gifted, competent (4)
9 Uruguay's second largest city (5)
10 Place out of sight (7)
12 Item used to brew a hot beverage (6)
13 Put to the test (3,3)
15 Rudolf ___, Russian-born ballet dancer (1938–93) (7)
18 Bridges (5)
20 Alight (4)
21 State of reduced excitement or anxiety (8)
22 Mr Spielberg, film director (6)
23 Native of Sana'a, eg (6)

Down

1 Enticements (5)
2 TV chef, ___ Lawson (7)
3 Study of bones (9)
4 Pale brown colour (5)
5 Set of data arranged in rows and columns (5)
6 Vote back into office (2-5)
11 Scintillate, sparkle (9)
12 Knots (7)
14 Pearlescent (7)
16 Wife of a rajah (5)
17 City in western Germany (5)
19 Mount on which Moses received the Ten Commandments (5)

334

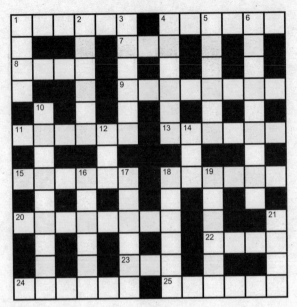

Across

1 Winner (6)
4 Vast, sandy region (6)
7 Biblical man (3)
8 Certain (4)
9 Work of art imitating the style of a previous work (8)
11 Child of one's aunt or uncle (6)
13 Hear (6)
15 Piece of material inset to enlarge a garment (6)
18 Remove an electrical device from a socket (6)
20 Conforming to set procedure or discipline (8)
22 Self-defence discipline (4)
23 Afternoon meal (3)
24 Excessively conventional and unimaginative (6)
25 Rubble, dust (6)

Down

1 Jar for flowers (4)
2 Ancient Egyptian city (6)
3 Begin again, as with negotiations (6)
4 Type of fuel used in an internal-combustion engine (6)
5 Discolourations (6)
6 Morally justified (9)
10 Soft blue cheese made from ewes' milk (9)
12 Frozen water (3)
14 Boy's name (3)
16 Gave a grin (6)
17 One score and ten (6)
18 Transfer a file to another computer (6)
19 Region of north-west India and northern Pakistan (6)
21 Cuts, as with grass for example (4)

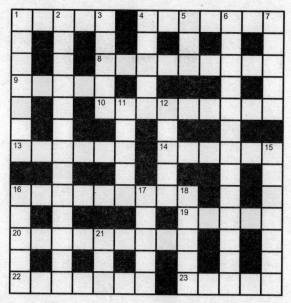

Across

1 Oxygen and nitrogen, for example (5)
4 Interpreting a written document (7)
8 Item traditionally laid down to greet important visitors (3,6)
9 Circumvent (5)
10 Wicked (9)
13 Captured (6)
14 Forceful consequence (6)
16 Undertaking, assurance (9)
19 Dave ____, Irish comedian who died in 2005 (5)
20 Variable-geometry aircraft (5-4)
22 Vest (7)
23 Country, capital Cairo (5)

Down

1 Occurring among members of a family usually by heredity (7)
2 Act of suffocating by constricting the windpipe (13)
3 Enchantress (5)
4 Done away with (3,2)
5 Sleeveless outer garment worn by Arabs (3)
6 Unlikely circumstance or thing (13)
7 Bill ____, of Microsoft fame (5)
11 Consumed (5)
12 Similar (5)
15 Bauble (7)
16 Strong currents of air (5)
17 Contaminate (5)
18 Emblem representing power (5)
21 Mousse for to the hair (3)

336

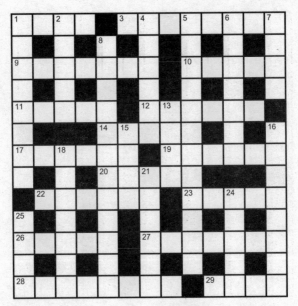

Across

1 Part of the ear (4)
3 State capital of Ohio, USA (8)
9 Discern (4,3)
10 Drops down (5)
11 Took an exam again after failing (5)
12 Set up for use (6)
14 Choral work (5)
17 Put up a tent (6)
19 Radio antenna (6)
20 Provide again with weapons (2-3)
22 Bedridden (6)
23 Anoint with oil (5)
26 ___ dish, used to grow bacterial cultures (5)
27 Act of taking by force (7)
28 Popular Italian dessert (8)
29 Not as much (4)

Down

1 Verse of five lines (8)
2 Cooks in an oven (5)
4 Beat through cleverness (6)
5 Disorganised (12)
6 Official language of Bangladesh (7)
7 Tolerable, indifferent (2-2)
8 Between noon and midnight (4,8)
13 Close to (4)
15 European river (4)
16 Uninformed (8)
18 Colossus (7)
21 Entertains or diverts (6)
24 Ooze (5)
25 Catch sight of (4)

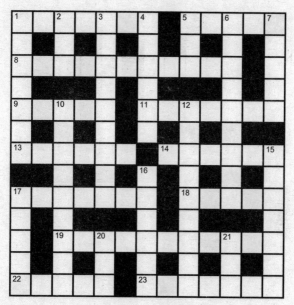

Across

1 Speech disorder (7)
5 Cart (5)
8 Genre of popular music originating in the 1950s (4,3,4)
9 Relieves (5)
11 Personal matters (7)
13 Offer (money) as payment (6)
14 Rove in search of booty (6)
17 Indirect routes (7)
18 The Devil (5)
19 Utter confusion, uproar (11)
22 Bush (5)
23 Thin varnish used to finish wood (7)

Down

1 Snake (7)
2 Part of a curve (3)
3 Enquiry into the finances of a person applying for monetary aid (5,4)
4 Having spokes (6)
5 Which person? (3)
6 Wander aimlessly in search of pleasure (9)
7 Brief written records (5)
10 Abrasive medium used to remove paint from wood (9)
12 Flat paving slab (9)
15 Vigorous (7)
16 Holdings (6)
17 Farm storage outbuildings (5)
20 Seize suddenly (3)
21 Ailing (3)

338

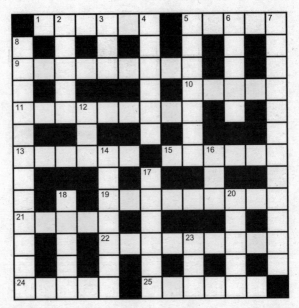

Across

1 Choose not to participate (3,3)
5 Birthplace of Mohammed (5)
9 Time of day (9)
10 Drainage channel (5)
11 Areas into which the zodiac is divided (4,5)
13 Safety device in a motor vehicle (3,3)
15 Apply stiffening agent to cloth (6)
19 Spiritual head of Tibetan Buddhism (5,4)
21 Bart Simpson's father (5)
22 Strive (9)
24 Irritates, annoys (5)
25 Talk in a desultory manner (6)

Down

2 Type of bread used as a pocket for filling (5)
3 Device used to propel a boat (3)
4 Despite the fact that (6)
5 Characteristic mental attitude (7)
6 Coagulates (5)
7 Oval large stadium with tiers of seats (12)
8 Homicide without malice aforethought (12)
12 Steal (3)
14 Location of a building (7)
16 Completely (3)
17 Engineless plane (6)
18 Aroma (5)
20 Ring of coral surrounding a lagoon (5)
23 Limb (3)

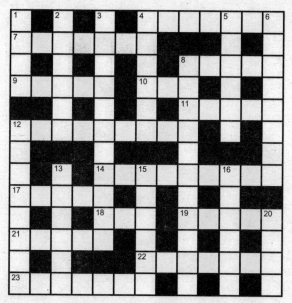

Across

- **4** Borne (7)
- **7** Hard Swiss cheese made in rounds (7)
- **8** Compounds capable of turning litmus red (5)
- **9** End of a roof (5)
- **10** Circuit (3)
- **11** Cut in two (5)
- **12** Financial officer (9)
- **14** Exercise device consisting of an endless belt (9)
- **17** Cowboy contest (5)
- **18** Visitor from space? (inits) (3)
- **19** Astute (5)
- **21** Ecstasy (5)
- **22** Seductive stare or look at another person (slang) (4,3)
- **23** Widely-spoken language (7)

Down

- **1** Highly excited (4)
- **2** Hollow globule of gas (6)
- **3** Impoverished, destitute (11)
- **4** Basement (6)
- **5** Frozen spike of water (6)
- **6** Rumple, tousle (8)
- **8** Substance that stimulates love or desire (11)
- **12** Extremely bad (8)
- **13** Bordering (6)
- **15** A sufficient amount (6)
- **16** Envisioned (6)
- **20** Having appendages on the feet (4)

340

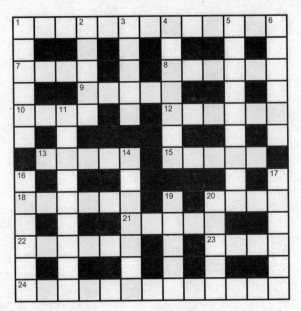

Across

1 White compound used chiefly in baking powder (5,2,6)
7 Makes a wager (4)
8 Works of fiction (6)
9 Fertile tract in the desert (5)
10 Yet (4)
12 Time of celebration in the Christian calendar (6)
13 Frown (5)
15 Physical strength (5)
18 Children's magazines (6)
20 Speck (4)
21 Elegant water-birds (5)
22 Bridge which crosses the Grand Canal in Venice (6)
23 Threesome (4)
24 Rapid informal network by which information or gossip is spread (4,9)

Down

1 Construction built by a spider (6)
2 Malicious burning of property (5)
3 Rotund, extremely chubby (5)
4 Become nervous or uneasy (5,2)
5 Handling, management (9)
6 Holiday town (6)
11 Cover (9)
14 Supple (7)
16 Beetle considered divine by ancient Egyptians (6)
17 Unruffled (6)
19 Legend (5)
20 On the move (5)

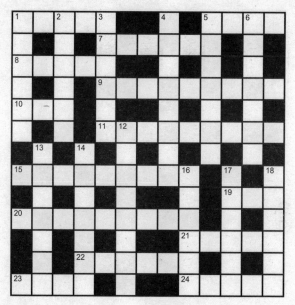

Across

1 Canal boat (5)
5 Go round and round (4)
7 Most recent (6)
8 Drinking vessel (5)
9 Layer of paint applied after the primer (9)
10 Little isle, in a river (3)
11 Sleeping place for two (6,3)
15 Arm of the Mediterranean between Greece and Turkey (6,3)
19 Overwhelming feeling of wonder (3)
20 Enchant, cause to be enamoured (9)
21 River flowing into the North Sea (5)
22 Objective (6)
23 Edge tool used to cut and shape wood (4)
24 Wise men (5)

Down

1 Pauper (6)
2 Cooks in an oven (6)
3 Resulted (6)
4 Look like (8)
5 Adhesive label (7)
6 One who enters by force in order to conquer (7)
12 Eater of meat and vegetables (8)
13 Crustacean with five pairs of legs (7)
14 Say again, repeat (7)
16 Warns of danger (6)
17 Arousing from slumber (6)
18 Caps made of soft cloth (6)

342

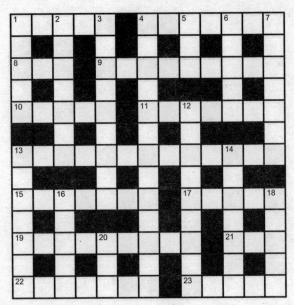

Across

1 Outerwear items (5)
4 Icy covering of a mountain peak (7)
8 Renegade (3)
9 Taxing of one's energy (9)
10 Russian pancake (5)
11 *The* ___, tragi-comic play by Shakespeare (7)
13 Canes used as supports when travelling on foot (7,6)
15 Brief and to the point (7)
17 Covered with hoar frost (5)
19 Bulbous plant with showy, trumpet-shaped flowers (9)
21 Belonging to you and me (3)
22 Fellow feeling (7)
23 Off-colour (5)

Down

1 Tree with edible pods used as a chocolate substitute (5)
2 Mound made by social insects (3-4)
3 Doubt about someone's honesty (9)
4 In a calculated manner (13)
5 Possess (3)
6 Struggle for breath (5)
7 Former Spanish coins (7)
12 Car drivers (9)
13 Provision of economic assistance to persons in need (7)
14 Chair containing a chamberpot (7)
16 Chafe at the bit, like a horse (5)
18 Grubby (5)
20 All the same (3)

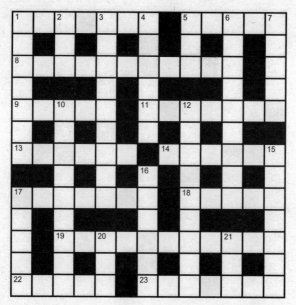

Across

1 Victory (7)
5 Energy supplied (5)
8 Somnambulist (11)
9 Contributed (5)
11 Inciting sympathy and sorrow (7)
13 Tidy up (6)
14 Contenders, challengers (6)
17 Book part (7)
18 Cut the wool from (5)
19 Endowed with the capacity to reason (11)
22 Become established (3,2)
23 Sharp piercing cry (7)

Down

1 Provide with nourishment (7)
2 Billiards stick (3)
3 Appropriate to a purpose (9)
4 Tending to speak irritably (coll) (6)
5 Irritate (3)
6 Notable public figure or celebrity (9)
7 Portable shelters (usually of canvas) (5)
10 Playwright (9)
12 More in need of a drink (9)
15 Cause friction, chafe (7)
16 Boring tools (6)
17 Burns superficially (5)
20 Bronze (3)
21 Film starring Bette Davis, *All about* ___ (3)

344

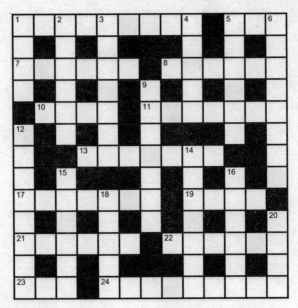

Across

1 Obviate (9)
5 Side sheltered from the wind (3)
7 Talk under one's breath (6)
8 Narcotic drug (6)
10 Cleared a debt (4)
11 Penalty or fine for wrongdoing (7)
13 Advent (7)
17 Stoppage (7)
19 Foot covering (4)
21 Air that is inhaled and exhaled (6)
22 Gender that refers to inanimate objects (6)
23 Affirmative answer (3)
24 Manner of existing (9)

Down

1 Renown (4)
2 Ceremonial (6)
3 Slim (7)
4 Person afflicted with Hansen's disease (5)
5 Weighted down with weariness (6)
6 Vote (8)
9 Member of a police force (7)
12 Done in a friendly spirit (8)
14 Localised ulcer or sore (7)
15 Guts, intestines (6)
16 Verse (6)
18 Up to a time that (5)
20 Gratis (4)

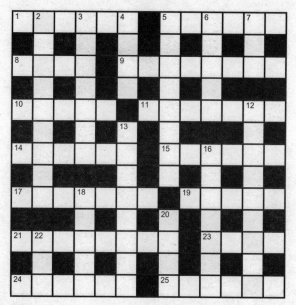

Across

1 Maltreater (6)
5 Turn inside out (6)
8 Highest level attainable (4)
9 Acted upon (8)
10 Sweeping stroke or blow (5)
11 Not devious (7)
14 Of a person: unimpressionable, inflexible (6)
15 Suppose to be the case, without proof (6)
17 Make a commitment (7)
19 Cunning (5)
21 Ruffian (8)
23 Cut off with the teeth (4)
24 Avenue (6)
25 Distance covered by a step (6)

Down

2 Region that is isolated and resists progress (9)
3 Church tower (7)
4 Genuine (4)
5 Intimate, cosy (8)
6 Spoken (5)
7 Perennial herb with grey-green bitter-tasting leaves (3)
12 Pretended, feigned (9)
13 Vision (8)
16 Sleep (7)
18 Confused scuffle (5)
20 Burden (4)
22 Available (3)

346

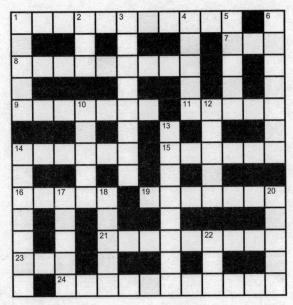

Across

1 Document of credentials (11)
7 Blend (3)
8 Impersonal, nameless (9)
9 Continue (7)
11 Check accounts (5)
14 Take in liquids, drink (6)
15 Pleasantly occupied (6)
16 Employees (5)
19 Perfumed (7)
21 Impermanent (9)
23 Umberto ____, author of *The Name of the Rose* (3)
24 Word used to connect clauses or sentences (11)

Down

1 Embrace (5)
2 Unit of weight equivalent to 2240 pounds (3)
3 Extremely hungry (8)
4 Confused or unable to decide what to do (2,3)
5 Improve, correct a text (5)
6 Raised in rank (7)
10 Rigidly formal (5)
12 Complete change of direction (1-4)
13 Cooking utensil (8)
14 Entrails, intestines (7)
17 Concerned with one specific purpose (2,3)
18 Belong, be in harmony (3,2)
20 Senior member of a group (5)
22 Bunkum (3)

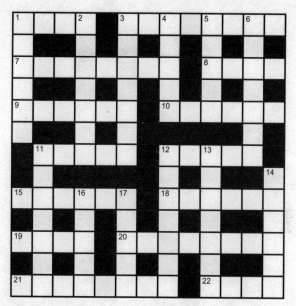

Across

1 Walk through water (4)
3 Message sent by mail without an envelope (8)
7 Most uneven or jagged (8)
8 Natural underground chamber (4)
9 Bird of prey's claws (6)
10 Annually, every twelve months (6)
11 Meditated or pondered (5)
12 Accord or comport with (5)
15 Make an error (4,2)
18 Number of lines of verse (6)
19 Soft creamy French cheese (4)
20 Warning traffic signal (3,5)
21 Captain Nemo's submarine (8)
22 Change course in sailing (4)

Down

1 Pleasant degree of atmospheric heat (6)
2 Absorb (7)
3 Delighted (7)
4 Indonesian and Malaysian dish served with a spiced peanut sauce (5)
5 Bedtime beverage (5)
6 Small stream (7)
11 Disease transmitted by the mosquito (7)
12 In any case (7)
13 Criticising harshly on a web site (coll) (7)
14 Baby's plaything (6)
16 Garment fold (5)
17 Hazard (5)

348

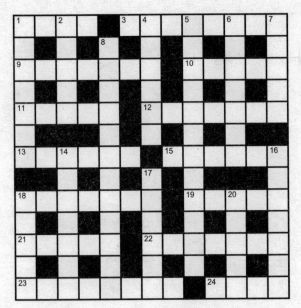

Across

1 World's largest continent (4)
3 The world of scholars (8)
9 Treachery (7)
10 Lean end of the neck (5)
11 Patty Bouvier's twin sister in TV's *The Simpsons* (5)
12 Formality in bearing and appearance (7)
13 Silvery metallic element (6)
15 Niche or alcove (6)
18 Lever that activates the firing mechanism of a gun (7)
19 Landed estate of a lord (5)
21 Lustre (5)
22 Outdoor blaze (7)
23 Writer of literary works (8)
24 Declare untrue (4)

Down

1 Skilled craftsman (7)
2 Paragon (5)
4 Country, capital Ottawa (6)
5 Quarrel (12)
6 Square hole made to receive a tenon (7)
7 Very cross (5)
8 Business that sells and rents out property (6,6)
14 Stoneworking tools (7)
16 Dentist's consulting room (7)
17 Clans (6)
18 Flavour (5)
20 Lacking experience of life (5)

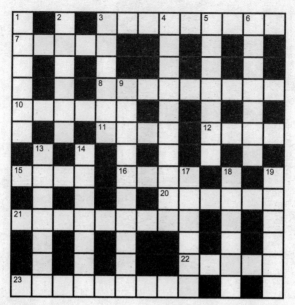

Across

3 Unit of frequency, one million cycles per second (9)

7 Last letter of the Greek alphabet (5)

8 Enchant, fascinate (9)

10 US Aloha State, famous for its volcanic mountains (6)

11 Fosbury ____, high jump manoeuvre (4)

12 Optical organs (4)

15 Fork prong (4)

16 Word denoting a person or thing (4)

20 Without breaks between notes, in music (6)

21 Without bounds (9)

22 Utter monotonously and repetitively (5)

23 Touchy (9)

Down

1 Purchased (6)

2 Fame, celebrity (6)

3 Mountainous plateau in France, ____ Central (6)

4 Admirer of England and English things (10)

5 Renders capable for a task (7)

6 Paired, coupled (7)

9 Gas jet providing a flame to ignite a larger burner (5,5)

13 Woman who is engaged to be married (7)

14 French composer of operas such as *Lakme* (1836–91) (7)

17 Entice away from principles or proper conduct (6)

18 Beauty treatment involving massage and cleansing (6)

19 Red fruit eaten as a vegetable (6)

350

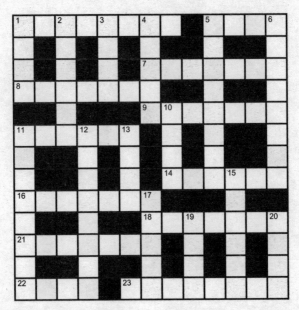

Across

1 Cook over an open fire (8)
5 Information (4)
7 Most readily to hand (7)
8 Digit (7)
9 Stretchy (7)
11 Goes by, overtakes (6)
14 Steered into a resting position (6)
16 Verify (7)
18 Very badly (7)
21 Tomato sauce (7)
22 Stated (4)
23 Relied (8)

Down

1 Outlying farm building (4)
2 Pieces of poetry or verse (6)
3 All the time (4)
4 Brother of one's father (5)
5 Catastrophe (8)
6 Fastened together (8)
10 Spring up (4)
11 Dish served traditionally on Shrove Tuesday (8)
12 Rose to the top (8)
13 Go off, as with milk (4)
15 Slaughtered (6)
17 Tree, emblem of Canada (5)
19 Front of the human head (4)
20 Back garden (4)

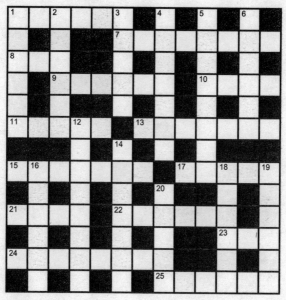

Across

1 Items of crockery (6)
7 Crested parrot of the Australian region (8)
8 Lip (3)
9 Something done (6)
10 ___ and cons (4)
11 Strong sweeping cut (5)
13 Storage locker (7)
15 Placed a bet (7)
17 Lure (5)
21 Flesh used as food (4)
22 Drool (6)
23 Travellers' pub (3)
24 Support that enables people to survive (8)
25 Wall paintings (6)

Down

1 Able to absorb fluids (6)
2 Large fleet, especially of Spanish warships (6)
3 Firm open-weave fabric used by window-cleaners (5)
4 Malicious gossip (7)
5 Precious blue gemstone (8)
6 Sullen (6)
12 Climbing garden plant with fragrant flowers (5,3)
14 Caused by an earthquake (7)
16 Acid found in vinegar (6)
18 Dock (6)
19 Game played on a court (6)
20 Capital of Oregon, USA (5)

352

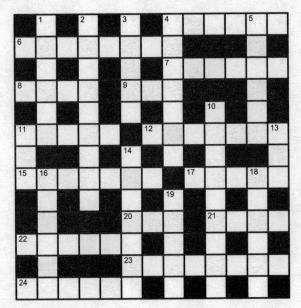

Across

4 Red Leicester or Cheddar, for example (6)
6 Wedlock (8)
7 Moved the head up and down (6)
8 Subdivisions of a play (4)
9 Feed (3)
11 Name given to a product (5)
12 Most indolent (7)
15 Sources of danger (7)
17 Political organisation (5)
20 Fixture found on a chimney stack (3)
21 Individually (4)
22 Fast gait of a horse (6)
23 Qualified for by right according to law (8)
24 Ground surrounded by water (6)

Down

1 Dish for holding a cup (6)
2 Offered as a gift (9)
3 Covered with slabs on which to walk (5)
4 In the middle (7)
5 Sugary confections (6)
10 Tube of finely ground tobacco wrapped in paper (9)
11 Morsel (3)
13 Archaic form of the word 'your' (3)
14 Ceased (7)
16 People (6)
18 Document showing that a fare has been paid (6)
19 Condition (5)

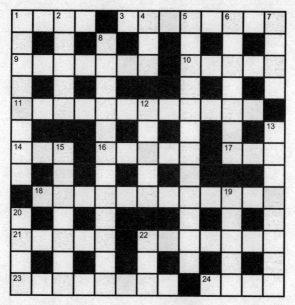

Across

1 Underwater vessels (abbr) (4)
3 Long-distance running race (8)
9 Fried ball of minced meat or fish coated in breadcrumbs (7)
10 Receives and entertains guests (5)
11 Small portable radio link (coll) (6-6)
14 Cut wood (3)
16 Egg-shaped (5)
17 Hour at which something is due (inits) (3)
18 Middle way between two extremes (7,5)
21 Burning (5)
22 Shudder involuntarily (7)
23 Location (8)
24 Court order (4)

Down

1 Continually complaining or finding fault (8)
2 Aromatic herb (5)
4 Top card (3)
5 Seemingly small but actually mortal weakness (8,4)
6 Facility caring for the terminally ill (7)
7 Bird's construction (4)
8 Consequence of one event setting off a chain of similar events (6,6)
12 Royal headdress (5)
13 Storey below ground (8)
15 Becomes tired (7)
19 Natural brown earth pigment (5)
20 Feeler attached to the mouth of a spider (4)
22 Likewise (3)

354

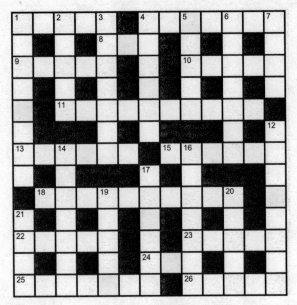

Across

1 Primary (5)
4 Implemented (7)
8 Stage or portion of a journey (3)
9 Drama which is sung (5)
10 Mindful (5)
11 Body of individuals belonging to a society (10)
13 Pleasant arrangements of musical notes (6)
15 Mode of procedure (6)
18 Limits, dividing lines (10)
22 Cool down (5)
23 Existing (5)
24 Bird which hoots (3)
25 Motors (7)
26 Appears (5)

Down

1 Blooms (8)
2 Water vapour (5)
3 Asserted one's right to (7)
4 Concurred (6)
5 Popular juicy fruits (5)
6 Native of Rome, for example (7)
7 Depicted (4)
12 Garment extending from the waist to the ankle (8)
14 Peering (7)
16 Wildlife (7)
17 Wireless sets (6)
19 Synthetic fabric (5)
20 Grab roughly (5)
21 Town and port in north-west Israel (4)

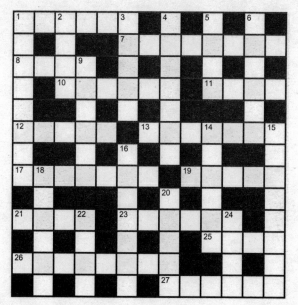

Across

1 White sheep originating in Spain (6)
7 Acting game, popular at Christmas (8)
8 Bass (4)
10 Try to stir up public opinion (6)
11 Principal (4)
12 Quizzes (5)
13 Cultivated (7)
17 Toothed wheel engaged with a pawl (7)
19 Articles to be traded (5)
21 Knowledge gained through tradition (4)
23 Ghost (6)
25 Informal greeting used on meeting or parting (4)
26 Hollow-horned ruminant (8)
27 Tension (6)

Down

1 Person who acts as a link between parties (8)
2 Ridge of rock, coral, etc (4)
3 Eight singers who perform together (5)
4 Spendthrift (7)
5 Inner surface of a hand (4)
6 Next to (6)
9 Characterised by romantic association (6)
14 Humorously sarcastic (6)
15 Having a wish for something (8)
16 Variation of something (7)
18 Exist in large quantities (6)
20 Homes for bees (5)
22 Looked at (4)
24 Periodic rise and fall of the sea (4)

356

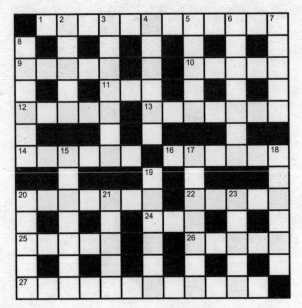

Across

1 Giant fairground rides (6,6)
9 Loft (5)
10 Serpent (5)
11 Floral garland (3)
12 Seasoned, colourful rice (5)
13 Central part of an atom (7)
14 Froth produced by soap (6)
16 US state, capital Juneau (6)
20 Weather averaged over a long period of time (7)
22 Not affected by alcohol (5)
24 And nothing more (3)
25 Bear fruit (5)
26 Legally binding command (5)
27 Predictable, expected (12)

Down

2 Praise, glorify (5)
3 One who lives in solitude (7)
4 Twine, cord (6)
5 Chaos (5)
6 Articulate (7)
7 Fathers (5)
8 Abseil (6)
15 Skeletal muscle having three origins (7)
17 Hears (7)
18 Supply or impregnate with oxygen (6)
19 One who owes money (6)
20 Soft fur, also known as nutria (5)
21 Type of snake (5)
23 ___ Mulroney, former Canadian prime minister (5)

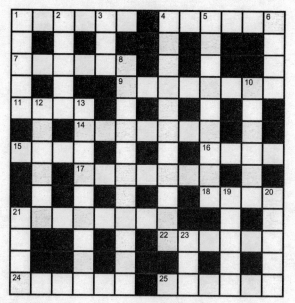

Across

1 Berthed (6)
4 Dough used in making pies (6)
7 Shrine where a god is consulted (6)
9 Produced a bloom (8)
11 Informal name for a cat (4)
14 Nervous, impatient or restless (7)
15 Spanish artist who painted *The Witches' Sabbath* (4)
16 Requirement (4)
17 Tread on and crush (7)
18 Russian emperor (4)
21 Plastic commonly used for saucepan handles (TM) (8)
22 Audacious (6)
24 Nigel ___, British actor whose films include *A Passage to India* (6)
25 Savagely cruel (6)

Down

1 Sag (5)
2 Form, category (5)
3 Slippery fish (3)
4 Engrossed in thought (11)
5 Means of protection from injury, hardship, etc (6,3)
6 Measure of three feet (4)
8 Able to produce the result intended (11)
10 Word uttered by Archimedes (6)
12 Imaginary place considered perfect (6)
13 Figurine (9)
19 Bird that resembles a swallow (5)
20 Kingly, majestic (5)
21 43rd president of the USA (4)
23 Broadcast (3)

358

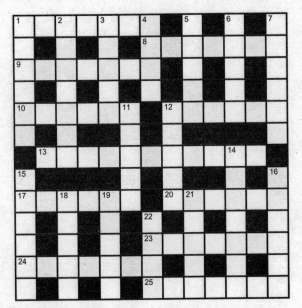

Across

1 Receptacle used for cleaning clothes or linens (7)
8 Perpetually young (7)
9 Imaginary line around the Earth (7)
10 Bionic man or woman (6)
12 Tie (6)
13 Insincerely emotional, maudlin (11)
17 Free-and-easy (6)
20 Woman often 'in distress' in stories (6)
23 Competition (7)
24 Mouldable synthetic substance (7)
25 Pike fitted with an axe head (7)

Down

1 Most miserable or pitiable person (6)
2 Trip up (7)
3 Private instructor (5)
4 Lyric poet (4)
5 Narrow shelf (5)
6 Area of sand sloping down to the water (5)
7 Towards the tail of a ship (6)
11 Cook by radiated heat (5)
12 Thick woollen fabric (5)
14 Let off the hook (7)
15 Agree to receive or do (6)
16 Toyed (6)
18 Utilising the energies of the Sun (5)
19 Extremely sharp (5)
21 Small bone in the middle ear (5)
22 Curved structure (4)

Across

4 Unbeliever (7)
8 All animal life of a place (5)
9 Deficient in alertness or activity (9)
10 Bring out an official document (5)
11 Splendid and expensive-looking (9)
13 Little crustacean (6)
16 Marked by suitability (6)
20 Disposed to believe on little evidence (9)
23 Colour slightly (5)
24 Convertible, pliant (9)
25 Construct (a building) (5)
26 Person who requires medical care (7)

Down

1 Places of business (7)
2 One who gives chase (7)
3 Cut-price events (5)
4 Eventually (2,4)
5 Praise unduly (7)
6 Quietly in concealment (coll) (5)
7 Tying cords (5)
12 Employ (3)
14 Of a female (3)
15 Canadian policeman, usually on horseback (7)
17 Property acquired violently and illegally (7)
18 Julia ___, actress in the 2004 movie *Closer* (7)
19 Frozen dessert (6)
20 Car wheel immobilising device (5)
21 Glorify (5)
22 Exorbitant (5)

360

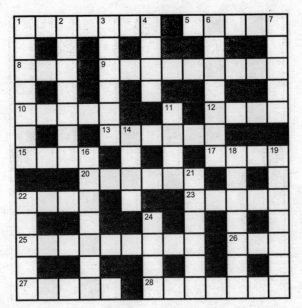

Across

1 Examiner of accounts (7)
5 Norwegian sea inlet (5)
8 ___ Khan, Islamic religious leader (3)
9 Sport played on a rink (3,6)
10 Well-known internet search engine (5)
12 In one's sleeping place (4)
13 Mimi ___, Tom Cruise's first wife (6)
15 Eye secretion (4)
17 Native of Edinburgh, eg (4)
20 Alibi (6)
22 Spreads seeds (4)
23 Powder applied to the cheeks (5)
25 Fears, worries (9)
26 Baby goat (3)
27 Garden tool for cutting grass on lawns (5)
28 Retinue (7)

Down

1 Expert who studies data (7)
2 Greek currency unit prior to the euro (7)
3 Maker and alterer of garments (6)
4 Marsh plant (4)
6 Male donkey (7)
7 Wood nymph (5)
11 Items used to secure washing to a line (4)
14 Formerly (4)
16 Reprieve (7)
18 Laugh quietly (7)
19 Foot lever (7)
21 Pencil mark remover (6)
22 Group of many insects (5)
24 Bluish-white metallic element with medicinal properties (4)

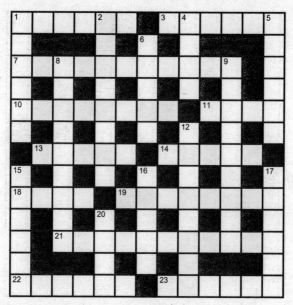

Across

1 Swim like a dog in shallow water (6)
3 Capital of Croatia (6)
7 Having a good effect on the body or mind (11)
10 New participant in some activity (8)
11 Excavates (4)
13 Jeer at (5)
14 Blacksmith's workplace (5)
18 Move in a spiral course (4)
19 Race between candidates for elective office (8)
21 Safety item worn by a motorcyclist to protect the head (5,6)
22 Fine spores borne by an anther in a flower (6)
23 Climb up (6)

Down

1 Having a strong effect (6)
2 Despising (8)
4 Poker stake (4)
5 Look around a shop casually and randomly (6)
6 Last Commandment (5)
8 Person with an abnormal sense of self-importance (9)
9 Thin transparent plastic material used to wrap food (9)
12 Crush (8)
15 Permanent mass of snow on the land (6)
16 Cleanse the entire body (5)
17 Joined together (6)
20 Movable barrier in a fence or wall (4)

362

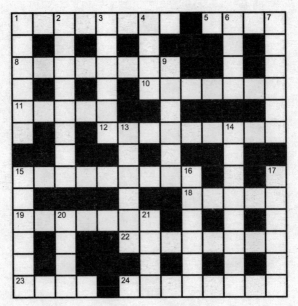

Across

1 Set again after an initial failure (8)
5 Weight units of 2240 lbs (4)
8 Native of Vienna, for example (8)
10 Move in a sinuous, or circular course (7)
11 Ballroom dance (5)
12 Plant with succulent young shoots, eaten as a vegetable (9)
15 Topics that are not clearly one thing or the other (4,5)
18 Rigid layer of the Earth's crust (5)
19 Passage selected from a larger work (7)
22 Emerging from an egg (8)
23 Badgers' den (4)
24 Unfinished business (5,3)

Down

1 Shows a response (6)
2 One who is not present (8)
3 Mouselike jumping rodent (6)
4 Unwanted email (4)
6 Was in debt to (4)
7 Tempests (6)
9 US state in which Las Vegas is located (6)
13 Angel of the highest order (6)
14 Culinary setting agent (8)
15 Natives of Athens, for example (6)
16 Gaps (6)
17 Pleaded (6)
20 Ancient Briton (4)
21 Filled tortilla (4)

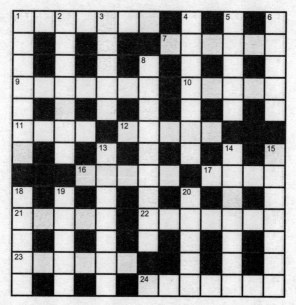

Across

1 With much sound (7)
7 Quarter (6)
9 Remoulded car tyre (7)
10 Take in fluids through the mouth (5)
11 Indian bread, baked in a clay oven (4)
12 Biblical term meaning 'fathered' (5)
16 Water-filled ditches surrounding castles (5)
17 Long detailed story (4)
21 Characteristic of a sheep (5)
22 Plate for making identical copies (7)
23 Guided anti-ship missile (6)
24 Goddess of retribution (7)

Down

1 Cell specialised to conduct nerve impulses (7)
2 First letter of a name (7)
3 Person who does no work (5)
4 Driver who won't let others pass (4,3)
5 Sweet and fleshy product of a tree or other plant (5)
6 Twilled cloth used for military uniforms (5)
8 Promote, publicise (9)
13 Notwithstanding (7)
14 God of wine, also known as Dionysus (7)
15 Instrument from which a person is executed by hanging (7)
18 Product of bees (5)
19 Bereaved wife (5)
20 Poison of snakes, etc (5)

364

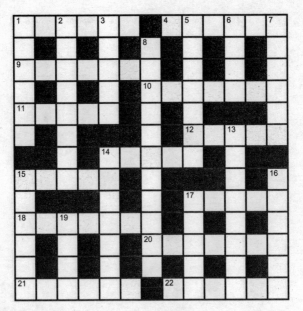

Across
1 Begin a journey (3,3)
4 Item applied to a sprain in order to reduce swelling (3,3)
9 Fleshy pendulous part of the hearing organ (7)
10 Resembling a dream (7)
11 Huge person (5)
12 Percussion instruments (5)
14 From that time (5)
15 Squeeze with the fingers (5)
17 Throw with great effort (5)
18 Lessen a load (7)
20 Projecting moulding (7)
21 Revealed (6)
22 Not if (6)

Down
1 Santa's sledge (6)
2 Herb with leaves often used in vinegar (8)
3 Drift on water (5)
5 Fellow member of the Communist Party (7)
6 Live-action film about a piglet (4)
7 Organisations of craftsmen or merchants (6)
8 State of hopelessness (11)
13 City dweller (8)
14 Travel back and forth between two points (7)
15 Structure supporting the lower limbs (6)
16 Renegades (6)
17 Wading bird with a long neck (5)
19 Banking system (4)

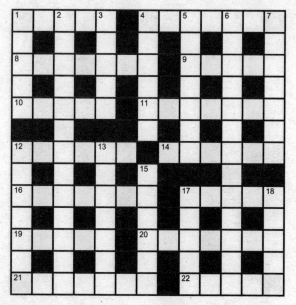

Across

1 Gave medicine (5)
4 Andiron (7)
8 Potion dispenser (7)
9 Swayed back and forth (5)
10 Kick out (5)
11 Relating to glands near to the kidneys (7)
12 Enclose in (6)
14 Rectifies (6)
16 Different form of the same thing (7)
17 Held off, kept distant (2,3)
19 Animal related to the giraffe (5)
20 Following a course likely to achieve what is required (2,5)
21 Ornamental timepiece seen in a garden (7)
22 Alpine vocal call (5)

Down

1 Evade (5)
2 Drape used in a bathroom (6,7)
3 Terminus (5)
4 Conventional (6)
5 Pulpit (7)
6 Sloping surface on which washed dishes are put to dry (8,5)
7 Spectacles worn to protect the eyes (7)
12 Jealous (7)
13 Official language of Tanzania (7)
15 Promenade, saunter (6)
17 Suitably (5)
18 Country bumpkin (5)

366

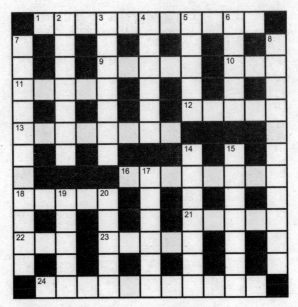

Across

1 Type of firework (5,6)
9 Kent ferry port (5)
10 Automobile (3)
11 Argentinian football manager, ____ Maradona (5)
12 Enthusiastic approval (5)
13 Star-shaped character used in printing (8)
16 Ancestor (8)
18 Ancient city mentioned in conjunction with Gomorrah (5)
21 Australian wild dog (5)
22 Augment (3)
23 Beaded counting frames (5)
24 Sitting with one limb laid over the other (5-6)

Down

2 Items (7)
3 Principality in the Pyrenees (7)
4 Blankets (6)
5 Hospital worker (5)
6 In the area (5)
7 Children's search and find game (4-3-4)
8 Members of a fellowship, collectively (11)
14 Material for animals to sleep on (7)
15 Principal theme in a speech (7)
17 Popular flavour of soup (6)
19 Dismal (5)
20 Grumbles (5)

367

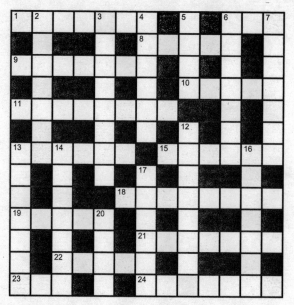

Across
1 On the whole (7)
6 Craze (3)
8 Dwelling house (5)
9 Loosen by turning (7)
10 Loose garment worn by Muslim women (5)
11 In equilibrium (8)
13 Brown with a reddish tinge (6)
15 Command with authority (6)
18 Uneconomical (8)
19 Bay or cove (5)
21 Peninsula in south-western Europe (7)
22 Wine and hot water drink (5)
23 Directly or exactly, straight (3)
24 Small axe with a short handle (7)

Down
2 Volcanic island republic in Melanesia (7)
3 Placed in a particular order (8)
4 Attorney (6)
5 Toothed implement used to disentangle hair (4)
6 Cap which protects the tip of an umbrella (7)
7 Failure to fulfil (7)
12 Medicinal lotion (8)
13 Given new electrical cabling (7)
14 Visible horizon (7)
16 Bravery (7)
17 Disappear from view (6)
20 Garments, clothes generally (4)

371

368

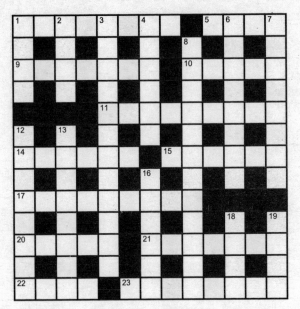

Across

1 Set apart (8)
5 Dressed skin of an animal (4)
9 Astral (7)
10 Group considered superior (5)
11 Christian missionary to the Gentiles (5,4)
14 Very cold compartment in a refrigerator (6)
15 Precious stones (6)
17 Places to much of a burden on (9)
20 Overseas telegram (5)
21 Repeat (7)
22 Muck, filth (4)
23 Velocity of a plane (8)

Down

1 Computer storage item (4)
2 Bound (4)
3 Pay no attention to, disrespect (a person) (4-8)
4 Common garden insect (6)
6 Copied (8)
7 Monocle (8)
8 Inability to relax or be still (12)
12 Having had one's marriage dissolved (8)
13 Winter month (8)
16 Island in French Polynesia, capital Papeete (6)
18 Sleeveless, cloak-like garment (4)
19 Place in the post (4)

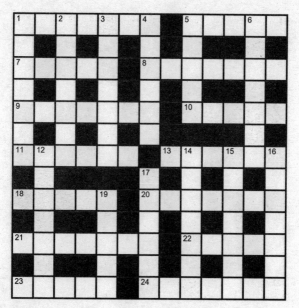

Across

1 Crops such as wheat, barley, etc (7)
5 Old name for the capital of Bangladesh (5)
7 Goes along at great speed (5)
8 Round shapes (7)
9 Encroach (7)
10 Less dangerous (5)
11 Kidney-shaped nut (6)
13 Military trainees (6)
18 Become sour (2,3)
20 Shorten, curtail (7)
21 Member of an evangelical Protestant church (7)
22 Gateway in a fence (5)
23 Aspirations (5)
24 Hands in one's notice (7)

Down

1 Of the heart (7)
2 Instructions for cooking meals (7)
3 It's said to make the heart grow fonder (7)
4 Small pouch for shampoo, etc (6)
5 Popular pub game (5)
6 Of weather or climate, physically mild (7)
12 Pear-shaped fruit (7)
14 Takes into custody (7)
15 Swirling (7)
16 Coins of Israel (7)
17 Hard deposit on the teeth (6)
19 Cooks in fat or oil (5)

370

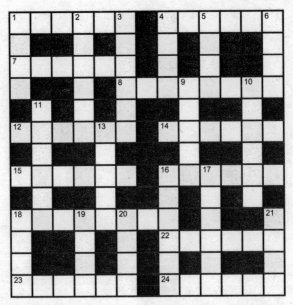

Across

1 Shouted out for (6)
4 Feel remorse for (6)
7 Preserve a dead body (6)
8 Wild headlong rush of frightened animals (8)
12 Belittle (6)
14 Plot of ground adjoining a house (6)
15 Brigand (6)
16 Musical note having the time value of an eighth of a whole note (6)
18 Resent (8)
22 Hindu god forming a triad with Vishnu and Shiva (6)
23 Barbaric, violent (6)
24 Toxic alkaloid used by South Americans as an arrow poison (6)

Down

1 Organised group of workmen (4)
2 Held legally responsible (6)
3 Sweet, dark purple plum (6)
4 Flightless bird of South America (4)
5 Stage item (4)
6 Printed characters (4)
9 Sound made by a cat (5)
10 Become more intense (6)
11 Waste matter carried away in drains (6)
13 French goodbye (5)
16 Port city of Canada (6)
17 Foreign home help (2,4)
18 Formal offers at an auction (4)
19 Capital of Latvia (4)
20 Bird symbolising peace (4)
21 Naked (4)

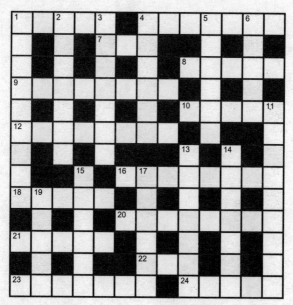

Across
1 Fabric (5)
4 Throw or cast away (7)
7 Ms Braun, Hitler's mistress (3)
8 Trap for birds or small mammals (5)
9 Social standing (8)
10 Shortest digit of the hand (5)
12 T-shaped cleaning implement with a rubber edge across the top (8)
16 Anonymous (8)
18 Electronic message (5)
20 Fashion business, colloquially (3,5)
21 Inebriated (5)
22 Belonging to him (3)
23 In a little while (7)
24 Fine net used for tutus (5)

Down
1 Blood cell (9)
2 Composed of or containing bone (7)
3 Plant also known as erica (7)
4 Hang freely (6)
5 Blanket-like cloak (6)
6 Idly play a guitar (5)
11 Small restaurant (9)
13 Most damp (7)
14 Deep-fried ball of ground dried chickpeas or broad beans (7)
15 Victorious contestant (6)
17 Absence of emotion or enthusiasm (6)
19 Ngaio ___, writer of whodunnit stories (5)

372

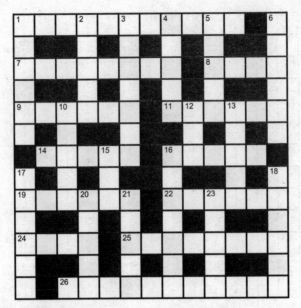

Across

1 Brief moment in time (5,6)
7 Person who assists the infirm with domestic work (4,4)
8 Expel gas from the stomach (4)
9 Right or appropriate for a particular person, purpose or situation (6)
11 Steep in, saturate (6)
14 Jester (5)
16 Curl of the lip (5)
19 Cruel dictator (6)
22 Enclose (6)
24 Persian fairy (4)
25 Jubilation (8)
26 Soft edible blue-black fruit resembling a currant (11)

Down

1 Division of a group into opposing factions (6)
2 Chemically inactive (5)
3 Slim or small (7)
4 ___ pants, cropped women's trousers (5)
5 Wealthy man (5)
6 Occur (6)
10 Graven images (5)
12 Adult male person (3)
13 Minor parish official (5)
15 Former name of Tokyo (3)
16 Apply (paint) in small touches (7)
17 Modifies for a new purpose (6)
18 Firm, stable (6)
20 Thick stew made of rice and chicken (5)
21 Pinch (5)
23 Teatime sweet roll (5)

Across

1 Inclined surface (4)
3 Examines closely and critically (8)
9 Slender tower on a mosque (7)
10 Harden to (5)
11 City in the Piedmont region of Italy (5)
12 More stony or rugged (7)
13 Settlement (6)
15 Of the backbone (6)
17 Famous (7)
18 Slowly, in music (5)
20 Indian side dish of yogurt and chopped cucumbers (5)
21 1982 film starring Dustin Hoffman (7)
22 Ineffectual or unsuccessful person or thing (coll) (4,4)
23 Kin group (4)

Down

1 Device used to work a machine from a distance (6,7)
2 Labourer who works below the ground (5)
4 Agent creating and controlling things in the universe (6)
5 Young male hero in pantomime (9,3)
6 Warning (7)
7 Native of Freetown, for example (6,7)
8 Item used when pressing clothes (7,5)
14 Metallic element (7)
16 Full of rushed activity (6)
19 Pertaining to the nose (5)

374

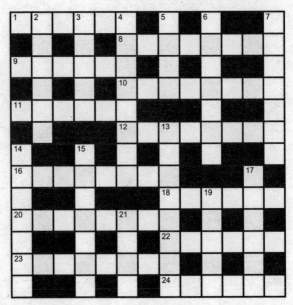

Across

1 Item used to secure headwear (6)

8 Cause to grow thin or weak (8)

9 Lee Harvey ____, assassin of US President John F Kennedy (6)

10 Something of sentimental value (8)

11 Ebb (6)

12 Text of an opera (8)

16 Ta very much! (5,3)

18 Thin top layer on a solid floor (6)

20 Provides money for (8)

22 Circumvents, dodges (6)

23 Outside (8)

24 Spit for holding meat in place (6)

Down

2 Jane ____, English novelist (1775–1817) (6)

3 Stage (5)

4 Famous 19th Century Australian bushranger (3,5)

5 Plant cultivated for seed and as a forage crop (4)

6 Pale lager with a strong flavour of hops (7)

7 Evolve (7)

13 Capital of Belgium (8)

14 Provided with employees (7)

15 Prepared dough (7)

17 Night flight on which passengers get little or no sleep (coll) (3-3)

19 Line of travel (5)

21 Ice cream container (4)

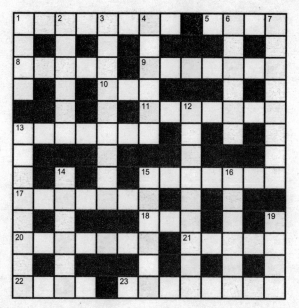

Across

1 Slow and apathetic (8)
5 State of disorder (4)
8 Missives used as birthday or Christmas greetings (5)
9 Person in an organisation who has access to exclusive information (7)
10 Number: the Roman X (3)
11 Made certain (7)
13 Person who makes garments from animal skins (7)
15 Light, plastic disk used as a plaything (7)
17 Edmund ____, English poet (1552–99) (7)
18 Self-importance (3)
20 Female stage performer (7)
21 Satisfy (thirst) (5)
22 Stained with a colourant (4)
23 Skilled equestrian (8)

Down

1 Bag made of hessian or plastic, for example (4)
2 State of commotion and noise (6)
3 Inflammation of the stomach lining (9)
4 Black eye (slang) (6)
6 Live on, persist (6)
7 Sit or stand astride (8)
12 Lung disease caused by inhaling particles of quartz or slate (9)
13 Emergency care (5,3)
14 Produce incisors, molars, etc (6)
15 Picture painted on a plaster wall (6)
16 Make steady (6)
19 Line of ore between layers of rock (4)

376

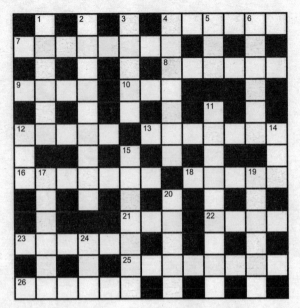

Across

4 Self-effacing (6)
7 Lengthy and aggressive lecture (8)
8 Hydrophobia (6)
9 Damaged by long use (4)
10 Number of turns in 60 seconds (inits) (3)
12 Twist into a state of deformity (5)
13 Good physical condition (7)
16 Proprietary thermoplastic resin of exceptional transparency (7)
18 Cured pig's meat (5)
21 Grazing land (3)
22 Bath powder (4)
23 Hunting expedition (6)
25 Worrying unnecessarily or excessively (8)
26 Looking directly towards (6)

Down

1 Dark brownish-red colour (6)
2 Behavioural attribute distinctive to an individual (9)
3 Forum in ancient Greece (5)
4 Imaginary water nymph (7)
5 Invest with a knighthood (3)
6 Enchantments (6)
11 Childish (9)
12 Opening (3)
14 Wickedness (3)
15 Overhead surface of a room (7)
17 Mistakes (6)
19 Connected to a computer network (6)
20 Mrs Simpson, Bart Simpson's mother (5)
24 ___ Baba (3)

Across

1 Greek letter (5)
5 Country, capital Lima (4)
7 Drill used to shape or enlarge holes (6)
8 Morsel left at a meal, crumb (3)
9 Business administrator (9)
11 Series of linked objects (5)
12 Be careful, follow advice (4,4)
16 Shamefaced (8)
20 Affect with wonder (5)
21 Cancellation of civil rights (9)
23 Mr Geller, psychic (3)
24 Continuation of the collar of a jacket or coat (6)
25 Country, capital Vientiane (4)
26 Bundle (of straw, eg) (5)

Down

1 Shaped and stuffed pasta dumplings (7)
2 Shared by two or more parties (6)
3 Enthusiastic (6)
4 Put together (4)
5 Glazed and salted cracker (7)
6 Mammary gland of bovids (5)
10 Gangs of people who work on ships (5)
13 Trembling poplar (5)
14 Causes to run off the tracks (7)
15 Wild West law officer (7)
17 Annoy continually (6)
18 Animal or plant material used to fertilise land (6)
19 Apostolic (5)
22 Squirrel's nest (4)

378

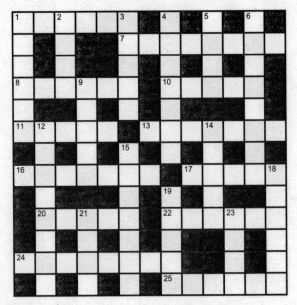

Across

1 Restriction on being outside (6)

7 Excessively devoted to a single faction (3-5)

8 Dissertation (6)

10 Count (3,2)

11 Short formal piece of writing (5)

13 Country, capital Copenhagen (7)

16 Cut of beef from the chest (7)

17 Durable (5)

20 Church cellar (5)

22 Biblical prophet, Elijah's successor (6)

24 Without equal (8)

25 Has faith in (6)

Down

1 Middle (6)

2 Contest of speed (4)

3 Inferior to another in quality (5)

4 Refunded some fraction of the amount paid (7)

5 Jenny ____, Swedish soprano (1820–87) (4)

6 Vaulting game (8)

9 Sends an unsolicited email (5)

12 Tooth on the rim of gearwheel (8)

14 Native New Zealander (5)

15 Small falcon that hovers in the air (7)

18 One of four playing-card suits (6)

19 Wild animal (5)

21 Narration, story (4)

23 Pouches (4)

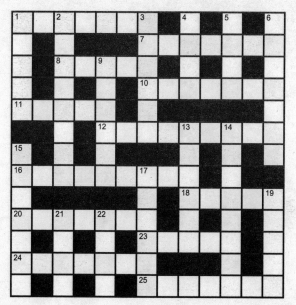

Across

1 Indication, usually of a disease (7)
7 Wolfgang ___ Mozart, composer (7)
8 Suburban residences (abbr) (5)
10 Protection (7)
11 Love affair (5)
12 Medical instrument for examining the interior of a bodily organ (9)
16 Spring-flowering shrub with yellow flowers (9)
18 Truss (3,2)
20 Abundant element, atomic number 16 (7)
23 Treats with contempt (5)
24 Having toothlike projections (7)
25 Periods of ten years (7)

Down

1 Capital of Bulgaria (5)
2 Incorrect or unsuitable name (8)
3 Lumped together (6)
4 Estimate the value (4)
5 Root vegetable from which sugar is derived (4)
6 Took the place of, seized power (7)
9 Only, just (6)
13 Motionless (6)
14 Showing excessive or compulsive concern with something (8)
15 In football, beyond a prescribed line or area (7)
17 Wounded (6)
19 Capital of France (5)
21 Short-tailed wildcat (4)
22 Cold sea fog (4)

380

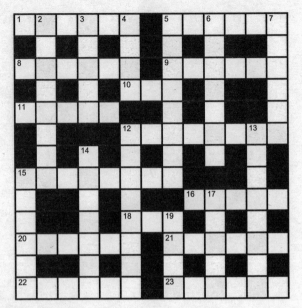

Across

1 Sloping kind of print (6)
5 Unpleasant or tedious tasks (6)
8 Country formerly known as British Honduras (6)
9 Aquatic South American rodent resembling a small beaver (6)
10 Continuing in the same way (abbr) (3)
11 Biblical tower intended to reach to heaven (5)
12 Promoted (8)
15 Reduce in rank (8)
16 Cap made of soft cloth (5)
18 Biblical prophet (3)
20 Capital of Greece (6)
21 Get back (6)
22 Remove completely from recognition or memory (6)
23 Fortified wine (6)

Down

2 Dutch city (3,5)
3 French river which flows into the North Atlantic (5)
4 Native tribe of North America and Canada (4)
5 Building material (8)
6 Porridge ingredient (7)
7 Remained (6)
12 Disappear gradually; as of emotions, for example (8)
13 Outer surface (8)
14 Plant also known as vervain (7)
15 Establish an association (6)
17 Tidal bore in a river (5)
19 Coloured part of the eye (4)

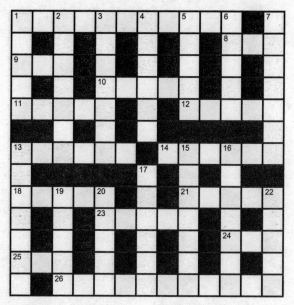

Across

1 Painful inflammation of the upper throat (11)
8 (They) exist (3)
9 Appropriate, seize (3)
10 Censure severely (5)
11 Small terrestrial lizard (5)
12 Dilate (5)
13 In the current fashion or style (6)
14 Rectangular blocks used to construct a wall (6)
18 Of the countryside (5)
21 Basic monetary units in Thailand (5)
23 Off the cuff (2-3)
24 Judo belt (3)
25 Bird similar to an ostrich (3)
26 Unrealistic prospect of future happiness (coll) (3,2,3,3)

Down

1 Bone in the leg (5)
2 Skinflint (7)
3 Masses of snow permanently covering the land (7)
4 Wolflike (6)
5 Forest plants (5)
6 Soothing ointment (5)
7 Childhood disease (7)
13 Sailor (7)
15 Refuse (7)
16 Collusion (7)
17 Migratory game fish (6)
19 Increase the running speed of a car's engine (coll) (3,2)
20 Deep serving spoon (5)
22 Gleaming (5)

382

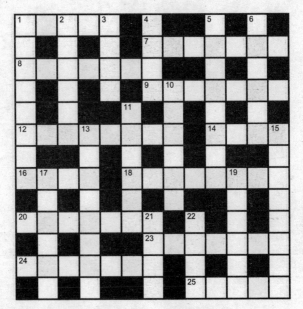

Across

1 Propeller with several angled blades (5)
7 Restricted (7)
8 Genuine (7)
9 Forceful and extreme (7)
12 Businessperson engaged in retail trade (8)
14 Pack to capacity (4)
16 Arrive (4)
18 Awesomely large (8)
20 Acutely insightful and wise (7)
23 Lacking reverence for a god (7)
24 Formerly the basic unit of money in the Netherlands (7)
25 Popular board game (5)

Down

1 Affecting the body as a whole (8)
2 Forest fire fighter (6)
3 Unwanted plant (4)
4 Ran away quickly (4)
5 Cuts apart for the purpose of examination (8)
6 Latin word for Queen, often seen on coins and in abbreviated form (6)
10 Sir Simon ___, English conductor born in Liverpool in 1955 (6)
11 High-kicking dance (6)
13 Heavy, woven fabric used in rugs and bedspreads (8)
15 Black treacle (8)
17 Not clear (6)
19 Short sleep (6)
21 Wear out, exhaust (4)
22 Long narrative poem (4)

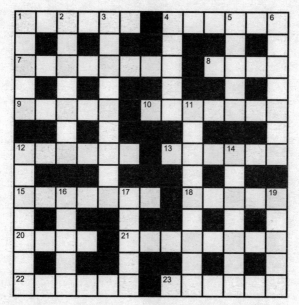

Across

1 Scours (6)
4 Paper handkerchief (6)
7 Scaremonger (8)
8 Fearless and daring (4)
9 Jetties (5)
10 Conveyance attached to a motorcycle (7)
12 Sprinted (6)
13 Provide what is desired or needed (6)
15 Instinctive motive (7)
18 Prospect (5)
20 Coat with plaster (4)
21 Give up the throne (8)
22 Breathe out (6)
23 Moves stealthily (6)

Down

1 Scallywag (5)
2 Literate people (7)
3 Very attractive woman (coll) (9)
4 Musical passage for all performers (5)
5 Unemotional person (5)
6 Getting on in years (7)
11 Lower joint of the leg of a fowl (9)
12 Become less (7)
14 Continue to exist (7)
16 Chubby (5)
17 Platform (5)
19 Large water jugs with wide spouts (5)

384

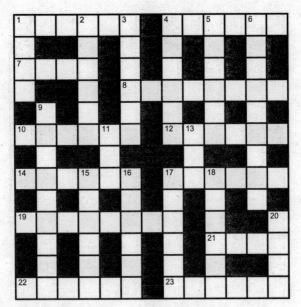

Across

1 Component (6)
4 40th President of the USA (6)
7 Tussock (4)
8 Topic which isn't clearly one thing or the other (4,4)
10 Invited visitors (6)
12 Formal agreement (6)
14 Airtight sealed metal container (3,3)
17 Shrink back (6)
19 Member of an irregular armed force that fights by sabotage and harassment (8)
21 Vegetable known as lady's fingers (4)
22 Robinson ___, hero of a Daniel Defoe novel (6)
23 Seed often used on bread rolls (6)

Down

1 Destiny (4)
2 Satellite of Saturn (6)
3 Extends over an area (6)
4 Most uncommon (6)
5 Alight, aflame (6)
6 Be a part or attribute of (9)
9 Mountainside cable railway (9)
11 Beverage (3)
13 Female sandpiper (3)
15 Units of weight for precious stones (6)
16 Dame ___ Melba, opera singer after whom Peach Melba was named (6)
17 Supplies again with weapons (6)
18 Small, lightweight boats (6)
20 Palm fruit (4)

385

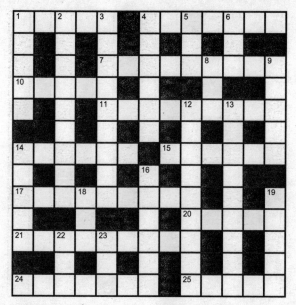

Across
- **1** Snooped (5)
- **4** Altered (7)
- **7** Sacred writings of a religion (9)
- **10** Ellipses (5)
- **11** From a vessel into the water (9)
- **14** Counting frame (6)
- **15** Healthier, especially after an illness (6)
- **17** Pleasure ground (5,4)
- **20** Norse goddess (5)
- **21** Republic in Central America (5,4)
- **24** Highest in excellence (7)
- **25** Natives of Ankara, for example (5)

Down
- **1** Footwear usually with a wooden sole (5)
- **2** Not relaxed (3,2,4)
- **3** Degenerate, debauched (9)
- **4** Tilt to one side (6)
- **5** Venomous snake (3)
- **6** Large African antelope (3)
- **8** Ultimate principle of the universe (3)
- **9** Duck valued for its soft down (5)
- **12** First meal of the day (9)
- **13** Instrument that measures the height above ground (9)
- **14** Trick (5)
- **16** Doglike (6)
- **18** Coaster (3)
- **19** Traditional pantomime tale, ___ in the Wood (5)
- **22** Plant fluid (3)
- **23** Grow old (3)

386

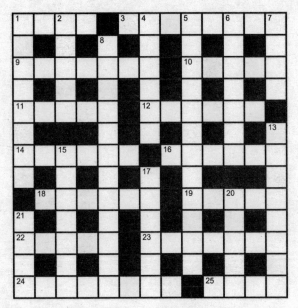

Across

1 Solid swollen underground bulb-shaped stem (4)

3 Dreadful (8)

9 Lymph glands located in the pharynx (7)

10 Framework of a military unit (5)

11 English composer whose works include *The Planets* (5)

12 Complete successfully (6)

14 Critical evaluation (6)

16 One-dimensional (6)

18 Attack (6)

19 Indian currency unit (5)

22 Swivel (5)

23 Everyday, routine (7)

24 Dole out (medication) (8)

25 Surname of Buffalo Bill (4)

Down

1 Silence by interruption (3,5)

2 Relating to the kidneys (5)

4 Become bone-like (6)

5 Marked by stubborn resistance to authority (12)

6 Point at which to retire for the night (7)

7 Fencing sword (4)

8 Gossip (6-6)

13 Fresh foliage or vegetation used for decoration (8)

15 In relation to (3-1-3)

17 Attributes responsibility to (6)

20 Keyboard instrument (5)

21 Potato (coll) (4)

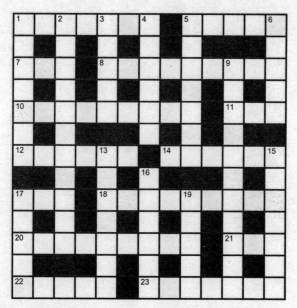

Across

1 Layer of earth lying immediately beneath the surface (7)

5 Leaves a vehicle by the side of the road (5)

7 Diminutive of Henry (3)

8 Slide of snow from a mountainside (9)

10 Seize a thing on its way (9)

11 Chaps (3)

12 Makes a rhythmic sound (6)

14 Elaborately adorned (6)

17 Narrow runner used for gliding over snow (3)

18 Set of steps (9)

20 Employee who mixes and serves alcoholic drinks (9)

21 Strong, angry emotion (3)

22 Haulage vehicle (5)

23 Most compact (7)

Down

1 Helmut ____, former chancellor of Germany (7)

2 Powerful short-haired dog (4,7)

3 Elated (2,3)

4 Primed with ammunition (6)

5 Large flat dish used for food (7)

6 Beer mug (5)

9 Based on or involving resemblance (11)

13 Great skilfulness and knowledge of some subject (7)

15 Aspect or factor (7)

16 Smoothed with abrasive paper (6)

17 Roman prophetess (5)

19 Repeat performance (5)

388

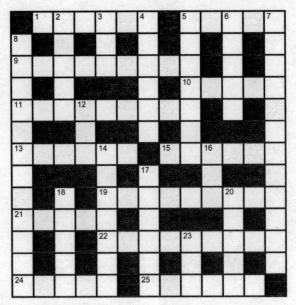

Across

1 Walk like a duck (6)
5 Native North American tribal emblem (5)
9 Italian word for a woman loved or loving (9)
10 Not dirty (5)
11 Capital of Cambodia (5,4)
13 Blazing (6)
15 Jimmy ___, former US president (6)
19 Pruning shears (9)
21 Encounters (5)
22 Given to copying (9)
24 Commercial exchange (5)
25 Make unauthorised alterations (6)

Down

2 Once more (5)
3 Two performers (3)
4 Joyful (6)
5 Windpipe (7)
6 Radio set (5)
7 Suffering from lack of adequate nutrition (12)
8 Act of moving something from its natural environment (12)
12 Egg cells (3)
14 Projectile (7)
16 *The Catcher in the* ___, J D Salinger novel (3)
17 Actor's notes (6)
18 Fourth letter of the Greek alphabet (5)
20 Bring together (5)
23 Aspire (3)

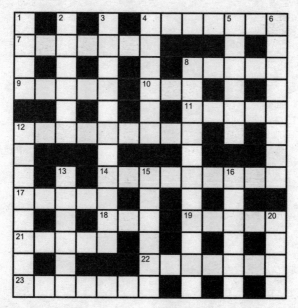

Across

4 Greek goddess of the hunt (7)
7 Leisurely, easy-going (7)
8 Red dye (5)
9 Interlace (5)
10 Artificial language, a simplification of Esperanto (3)
11 Areas within a house (5)
12 Climbing plants that produce fragrant flowers (5,4)
14 Watching (9)
17 Govern (5)
18 Scottish port (3)
19 Worthless material (5)
21 Common (5)
22 Designed to incite to indecency (7)
23 Refuse to acknowledge (7)

Down

1 Front part of a vessel or aircraft (4)
2 Separate with violence (6)
3 Surpassing what is common (11)
4 Offer suggestions (6)
5 Small, freshwater fish (6)
6 Writer's or musician's last work (4,4)
8 Plant grown for its pungent, edible root (11)
12 Encircle (8)
13 Muddles, entanglements (3-3)
15 Emotion of great sadness (6)
16 Pressed smooth with a heated implement (6)
20 Edible fat (4)

390

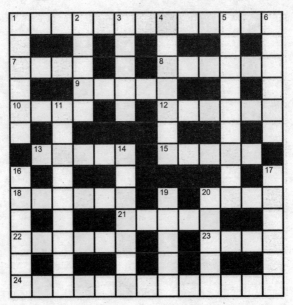

Across

1 Large carnivorous dinosaur, ___ rex (13)
7 Further, additional (4)
8 Running with great speed (6)
9 Unit of weight (1000 kg) (5)
10 Curves (4)
12 Rat or mouse, for example (6)
13 Strong, lightweight wood (5)
15 Utter a frog-like sound (5)
18 From that place (6)
20 Examine (4)
21 Ms Witherspoon, actress (5)
22 Gigantic African and Australian tree with edible fruits (6)
23 Stalk (4)
24 Plan to discredit a public figure by means of slanderous stories (5,8)

Down

1 Male domestic feline (6)
2 Assists in wrongdoing (5)
3 Childminder (5)
4 Ball-shaped (7)
5 Say again (9)
6 Visions (6)
11 One who escorts young women at social events (9)
14 Sour or bitter in taste (7)
16 Surname of Trevor Nunn's wife, Imogen (6)
17 Flower part (6)
19 Muslim lady of rank (5)
20 Olympic women's javelin gold medallist, ___ Sanderson, CBE (5)

391

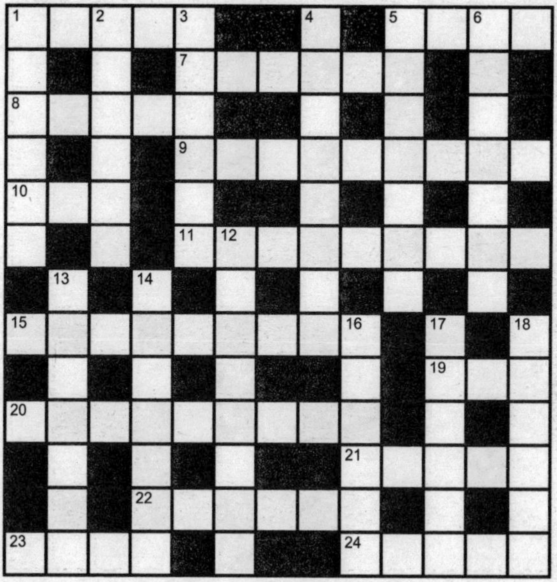

Across

1 Belonging to a city (5)
5 A great deal (4)
7 1955 Vladimir Nabokov novel of lust and love (6)
8 Slogan (5)
9 Plant such as the clove pink (9)
10 Devoured (3)
11 Just and fair to all (9)
15 Small, burrowing mammal with a body protected by horny plates (9)
19 Before, poetically (3)
20 Frolicked, larked about (9)
21 Leave or strike out, as of vowels (5)
22 City in south-western Switzerland (6)
23 Clarified butter used in Indian cookery (4)
24 Stratum (5)

Down

1 Percussion instrument (6)
2 Blackballs (6)
3 Small translucent cover for protecting plants (6)
4 Occurring every second year (8)
5 Suggesting war or military life (7)
6 Inner whorl of petals in a flower (7)
12 One who collaborates with an enemy occupying force (8)
13 Width (7)
14 Garden vegetable (7)
16 Difficult experience (6)
17 In a spooky manner (6)
18 Thin layer of superior wood glued to a base of inferior wood (6)

392

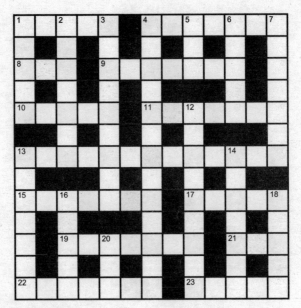

Across

1 Implied (5)
4 Chilled beverage (4,3)
8 Beard found on a bract of grass (3)
9 Aardvark (7)
10 Removes the rind from (5)
11 Signs up to join the military (7)
13 Instruments used to break down doors of fortified buildings (9,4)
15 Long, formal letter (7)
17 Epidermal pore in a leaf or stem (5)
19 *Coming to* ___, 1988 Eddie Murphy movie (7)
21 Have (3)
22 One who interprets text, especially scripture (7)
23 County that borders the Thames estuary (5)

Down

1 *Lady and the* ___, Disney movie (5)
2 Performance of music (7)
3 Ephemeral (9)
4 Being prepared but not yet ready (2,3,8)
5 Compass point at 67.5 degrees (inits) (3)
6 Small, open pies (5)
7 Bottomless gulfs (7)
12 Make or pass laws (9)
13 Workplace where people are very busy (7)
14 Inclined towards or displaying love (7)
16 Effigy (5)
18 Take illegally, as of territory (5)
20 Adam's wife (3)

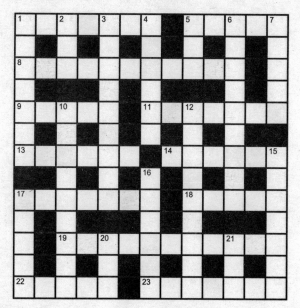

Across

1 Garden flower (7)
5 Criminal (5)
8 Complete act of breathing in and out (11)
9 Nazi peace emissary (5)
11 Professional entertainer (7)
13 Moved to music (6)
14 Crescent-shaped yellow fruit (6)
17 Strongly built, sturdy (4-3)
18 Broker (5)
19 Marital band worn on the finger (7,4)
22 Lofty nest of a bird of prey (5)
23 One of the three superpowers in *Nineteen Eighty-Four* (7)

Down

1 Sat, as on a branch (7)
2 "It is", poetically (3)
3 Without a sound (9)
4 Mountain peak on which Noah's ark came to rest (6)
5 US law enforcement agency (inits) (3)
6 Expanse of scenery (9)
7 Mother-of-pearl (5)
10 Large and showy garden plant (9)
12 1805 battle off the southwest coast of Spain (9)
15 Island group, ____ and Barbuda (7)
16 Clothing of a distinctive style (6)
17 Oscar ____, Irish writer (5)
20 British river (3)
21 Uncertainties, doubtful factors, ____ and buts (3)

394

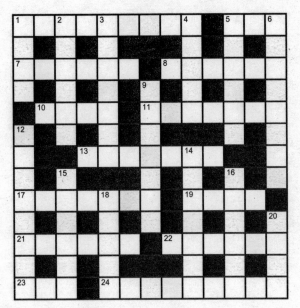

Across

1 Sewing consisting of pieces of different materials stitched together (9)
5 Riotous crowd (3)
7 Immense cloud of gas and dust in space (6)
8 Angle that resembles the hind limb of a canine (3-3)
10 Writing implements (4)
11 Move aside (4,3)
13 Written acknowledgement of payment (7)
17 Pamphlet (7)
19 Cans (4)
21 Arachnid (6)
22 Warning or proviso (6)
23 At all times, poetically (3)
24 Requisition forcibly, as of enemy property (9)

Down

1 Section of glass (4)
2 Medicinal pill (6)
3 Roman Catholic bishopric of Rome (4,3)
4 Rap (5)
5 Country, capital Lilongwe (6)
6 Imaginary evil spirit, used to frighten children (8)
9 Free pardon (7)
12 Censure severely or angrily (8)
14 Term of endearment (3,4)
15 Duplicator (6)
16 Fabricate, make up (6)
18 City on the River Aire (5)
20 Agitate (4)

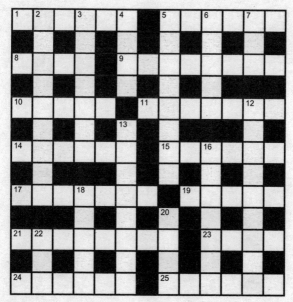

Across

1 Naughtily or annoyingly playful (6)
5 Seldom (6)
8 Former communist country (inits) (4)
9 Formal event performed on a special occasion (8)
10 Desert animal (5)
11 Oval-shaped edible nuts (7)
14 Local church community (6)
15 Disreputable wanderers (6)
17 Women's game (7)
19 Group of witches (5)
21 Lotion used in the treatment of sunburn (8)
23 Box lightly (4)
24 Howling like a hound (6)
25 Made neat and orderly (6)

Down

2 Handle badly (9)
3 Native of Eilat, eg (7)
4 Chop with rough blows (4)
5 Trait associated with the countryside (8)
6 Fictional character played by Sylvester Stallone (5)
7 System that links computers (inits) (3)
12 Belittle (9)
13 Old coin formerly worth one twentieth of a UK pound (8)
16 Wakened (7)
18 Indian dish of vegetables deep fried in batter (5)
20 Become soft or liquid, usually by heating (4)
22 Ms Gardner, Hollywood actress (1922–90) (3)

396

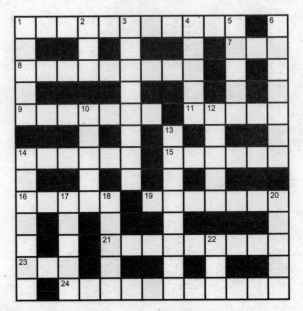

Across

1 Felines with slanting blue eyes and creamy coats (7,4)

7 Mental capacity (3)

8 Newspaper column giving opinions (9)

9 Root vegetable (7)

11 City in India (5)

14 Young nobleman attendant on a knight (6)

15 Observing (6)

16 Large and elaborate meal (5)

19 Origins (7)

21 The relation of something to the matter at hand (9)

23 Means of returning something by post (inits) (3)

24 Entertainment highlight (4-7)

Down

1 Woolly mammals (5)

2 Encountered (3)

3 Continued to live through hardship or adversity (8)

4 Sickened, was ill (5)

5 Pig food (5)

6 Engraving made with the use of acid (7)

10 Natives of Bern, for example (5)

12 Go in (5)

13 Free from guilt (8)

14 Gentlest (7)

17 Longs for (5)

18 Upper body (5)

20 Pierce with a lance (5)

22 High mountain (3)

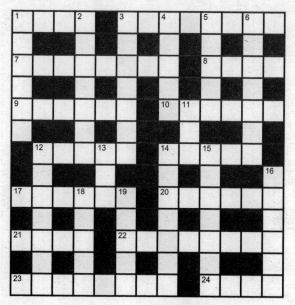

Across

1 Coagulated milk, used to make cheese (4)
3 Clothes closet (8)
7 Squid served as food (8)
8 Male of domestic cattle (4)
9 Tenant (6)
10 Navy man (6)
12 Addressed, covered (5)
14 Light sandal (5)
17 Signboard, for example, bearing shopkeeper's name (6)
20 Lay bare for all to see (6)
21 Sean ____, US film actor and director (4)
22 Be heavier than (8)
23 Throttle, asphyxiate (8)
24 Rabbit's tail (4)

Down

1 Edible mollusc (6)
2 Body of water into which the River Jordan flows (4,3)
3 Least strong (7)
4 Harnesses (5)
5 Jewish scholar (5)
6 Meat that is salted, cut into strips and dried in the sun (7)
11 Burned remains (3)
12 Local language variant (7)
13 Garland of flowers (3)
14 Supporting framework (7)
15 Tyrannise (7)
16 Glowing with heat (3-3)
18 Dance involving a long line of people (5)
19 In the centre of (5)

398

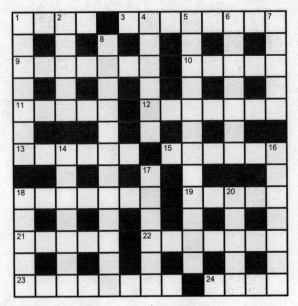

Across

1 Uninterrupted stream or discharge (4)
3 Manufactured (8)
9 Thieves (7)
10 Country on the Iberian Peninsula (5)
11 Remove a knot (5)
12 Investigate (7)
13 Happenings (6)
15 Moves effortlessly, by force of gravity (6)
18 Short periods of light rain (7)
19 Titles (5)
21 Advance (5)
22 Mediocre (7)
23 Penalised (8)
24 Second-hand (4)

Down

1 Chance or luck (7)
2 Eye socket (5)
4 Refreshed as by sleeping or relaxing (6)
5 Thwarted, let down (12)
6 Coloured sticks of wax for drawing (7)
7 Closely packed (5)
8 All the same (12)
14 Feeling (7)
16 Dangle (7)
17 Get away (6)
18 Undress (5)
20 Occasions for eating food (5)

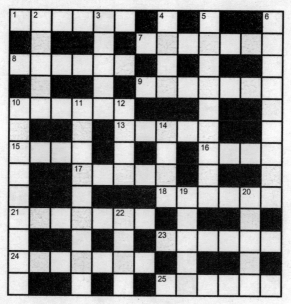

Across

1 Jesus (6)
7 Summons (4,3)
8 Assistant (6)
9 Turns back to front (7)
10 Fit for service, functional (6)
13 Transfer to another track, of trains (5)
15 Resist (4)
16 Tangerine/grapefruit hybrid (4)
17 Errol ___, swashbuckling film star (1909–59) (5)
18 Retaliate (6)
21 Amounts of time (7)
23 Barrel maker (6)
24 Leisurely walk (7)
25 Hallowed (6)

Down

2 Back parts of human feet (5)
3 Carapace (5)
4 Incline (4)
5 Escapade (9)
6 Authorise use of medicine (9)
10 Subway (9)
11 Male lover of a young woman (9)
12 Catch sight of (4)
14 Arm bone (4)
19 Alto violin (5)
20 Domestic birds (5)
22 Antlered animal (4)

400

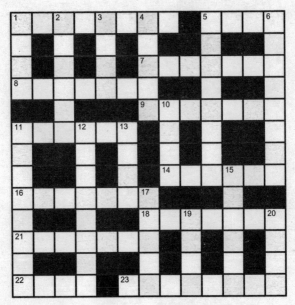

Across

1 Start (8)
5 Idiots (4)
7 Involving volcanic processes (7)
8 Henri ____, French artist (7)
9 Period between sunrise and sunset (7)
11 Rug (6)
14 Flamboyantly elaborate, showy (6)
16 Popular group associated with the 1960s (7)
18 To a higher position (7)
21 Devastates (7)
22 Table condiment (4)
23 Fills with gas or air (8)

Down

1 Buddy (4)
2 Trusted guide (6)
3 Makes a mistake (4)
4 Bawled (5)
5 Addition to regular working hours (8)
6 Having the characteristics of a female sibling (8)
10 Chopped (4)
11 Dog guarding the entrance to Hades (8)
12 Painting of a person's face (8)
13 Remove (4)
15 Run at full speed over a short distance (6)
17 Ms George, who starred in *Straw Dogs* (5)
19 Structure commonly built of masonry (4)
20 Takes to court (4)

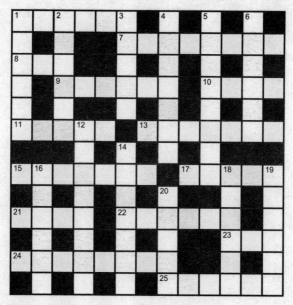

Across

1 Large shrimps cooked in breadcrumbs (6)
7 Formality in bearing and appearance (8)
8 Step in dancing (especially in classical ballet) (3)
9 Bring into the country (6)
10 Ale (4)
11 Use water to remove soap (5)
13 Hansen's disease (7)
15 Type of trout (7)
17 Urge a horse to go faster (3,2)
21 Short theatrical episode (4)
22 Extending the legs at right angles to the trunk (6)
23 Vase that usually has a pedestal or feet (3)
24 Musical squeeze-box (8)
25 Frogmen (6)

Down

1 Light evening meal (6)
2 Designate (6)
3 Inuit dwelling (5)
4 At a more distant point (7)
5 Floating on the breeze (8)
6 Stroke tenderly (6)
12 Formal and explicit approval (8)
14 Long pillow (7)
16 Ornament worn above the foot (6)
18 Make certain of (6)
19 Indicates the direction of (6)
20 Lacking taste or flavour (5)

402

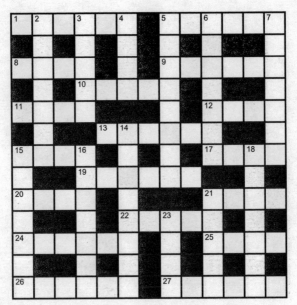

Across

1 Frowns with displeasure (6)
5 Instant in time (6)
8 Barrels (4)
9 Arch of the foot (6)
10 Varieties (5)
11 Large pond (4)
12 Yob deterrent (inits) (4)
13 Attack as false or wrong (6)
15 Withered (4)
17 Happy (4)
19 Package (6)
20 Primates (4)
21 British peer (4)
22 Clark ____, film actor (1901–60) (5)
24 Greek god of light (6)
25 Animal's neck hair (4)
26 Pressed for payment of a debt (6)
27 Stocking gauge measure (6)

Down

2 Reduce to ashes (7)
3 Fritter away (5)
4 Dish often served as a first course (4)
5 Wetness (8)
6 Small hardy range horse (7)
7 Serious infection of the intestine (7)
14 Popular garden plant with showy yellow or orange flowers (8)
15 In the direction of the ocean (7)
16 Fifth letter of the Greek alphabet (7)
18 With a side or oblique glance (7)
21 Devil (5)
23 Curve (4)

403

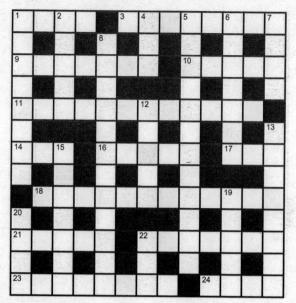

Across

1 Division between signs of the zodiac (4)
3 Ate greedily (8)
9 Enlightened (7)
10 Roman hunt goddess (5)
11 Psychological disorder affecting a large group (4,8)
14 Brownie (3)
16 Piece of music for nine instruments (5)
17 Ms Cassidy, singer whose albums include *Songbird* (3)
18 Insusceptible of reform (12)
21 Victoria Beckham's former surname (5)
22 Trade name for an adhesive bandage (4-3)
23 Affect with wonder (8)
24 Scorch (4)

Down

1 Afternoon treat associated with the West Country (5,3)
2 Moves through water (5)
4 Bring to a close (3)
5 First half of the Christian Bible (3,9)
6 Be fully aware of (7)
7 Name given to 6 June 1944 (1-3)
8 To the degree that good judgment would allow (6,6)
12 Sound practical judgment (5)
13 Aromatic shrub (8)
15 China, Korea, Japan, etc (3,4)
19 Offensively bold (5)
20 Region bordering Israel (4)
22 Form of transport, double-decker (3)

404

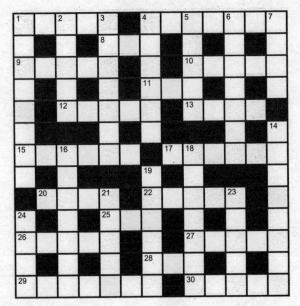

Across

1 Crouch, bow (5)
4 Deadened (a sound) (7)
8 In the past (3)
9 Asian water lily (5)
10 Country, capital Niamey (5)
11 Large nation (inits) (3)
12 Move on hands and knees (5)
13 Metallic element, symbol Pb (4)
15 Warm up in preparation for athletic activity (6)
17 Venerate (6)
20 Matures (4)
22 Beeps, as with a horn (5)
25 Moldovan monetary unit (3)
26 Assortment (5)
27 Asinine, silly (5)
28 ___ and outs (3)
29 Hair cleanser (7)
30 Faint-hearted (5)

Down

1 Doing things without the assistance of others (4-4)
2 Relating to sight (5)
3 Corridor (7)
4 Self-contained component (6)
5 Conclusive in a process (5)
6 Cases used to carry belongings (7)
7 Nearly hopeless (4)
14 Chum up with (8)
16 Dark purple-red (7)
18 Conceited, self-centred person (7)
19 Place for the teaching or practice of an art (6)
21 Slumber (5)
23 Muscle cramp (5)
24 Official symbols of a family, state, etc (4)

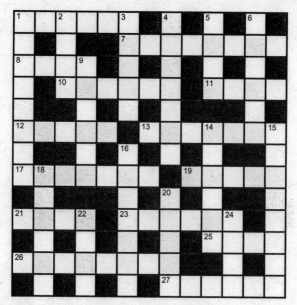

Across

1 Wrangle (over a price) (6)
7 Overcame (8)
8 Long narrow opening (4)
10 Desert of southern California (6)
11 Broad smile (4)
12 River separating Devon from Cornwall (5)
13 Small round stones (7)
17 Country, capital Monrovia (7)
19 Small vessels for travel on water (5)
21 Pale grey (4)
23 State resembling deep sleep (6)
25 Of or relating to the ear (4)
26 Period of unusually warm weather (8)
27 Verbalises (6)

Down

1 Medical institution (8)
2 Dismal, dour (4)
3 ___ Allan Poe, author (5)
4 Presented for acceptance or rejection (7)
5 Association of criminals (4)
6 Describe the meaning of (6)
9 Up until now (2,4)
14 Unbroken mustang (6)
15 Defendants in a court of law (8)
16 Strong north wind which blows in France during the winter (7)
18 Editions of a magazine or newspaper, for example (6)
20 Counterfeits (5)
22 Abominable snowman (4)
24 Sicilian volcano (4)

406

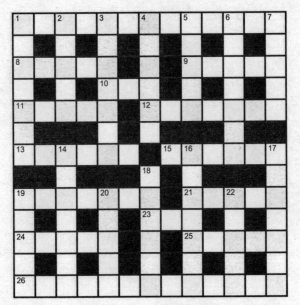

Across

1 Father Christmas (5,8)
8 Bingo (5)
9 Small concavity (5)
10 Put into service (3)
11 Protective garment (5)
12 Noted, distinguished (7)
13 Breadwinner (6)
15 Marked by the appetites and passions of the body (6)
19 Trip (7)
21 Disturbing the public peace (5)
23 Make the sound of a dove (3)
24 Range of mountains (5)
25 Search, reconnoitre (5)
26 Epidemic disease (7,6)

Down

1 Save from ruin or destruction (7)
2 Entomb (5)
3 Beat severely (7)
4 Expression of surprise or scepticism (6)
5 Capital of Vietnam (5)
6 Reading desk (7)
7 Sport of shooting at clay pigeons (5)
14 Stick vegetable, eaten as a fruit (7)
16 Spray can (7)
17 Outfit (clothing and accessories) for a new baby (7)
18 Forming a ring or series (6)
19 Biblical character (5)
20 Fine strong silky fabric (5)
22 Incorrect (5)

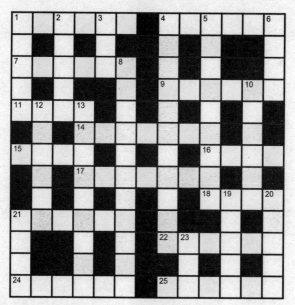

Across

1 Agriculturalist (6)
4 Soapbox (6)
7 Isaac ___, science fiction author (6)
9 Harem guard (6)
11 Capital of Ukraine (4)
14 Citizen who has a legal right to vote (7)
15 Restless or urgent desire (4)
16 Expectorated (4)
17 Look which is believed to have the power to inflict harm (4,3)
18 Squad (4)
21 Affirm by oath (6)
22 Season of the year (6)
24 Spread by scattering (6)
25 Paying customer (6)

Down

1 Roberta ___, US singer (5)
2 River which flows through Bonn (5)
3 Former name of the Japanese capital Tokyo (3)
4 Punctuation mark, bracket (11)
5 Complete collection of plates and dishes for the table (6,3)
6 Mixture of ground animal feeds (4)
8 Farewell oration (11)
10 North American nation (6)
12 Whole, unbroken (6)
13 Forcefulness of expression (9)
19 Deport from a country (5)
20 Physical strength (5)
21 Requests (4)
23 Close friend (3)

408

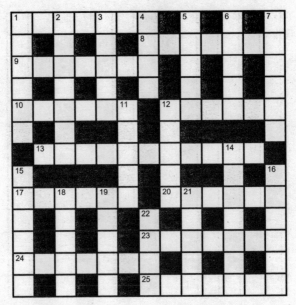

Across

1 Direction indicator (7)
8 French castle (7)
9 Place of complete bliss, delight and peace (7)
10 Compliment (6)
12 Prime minister of India from 1966 to 1977 and 1980 to 1984 (6)
13 Substitute (11)
17 Swung back and forth (6)
20 Responsibilities (6)
23 Ancient jar used to hold oil or wine (7)
24 Hold under a lease agreement (7)
25 Lawrence ____, English author (1912-1990) (7)

Down

1 Cockpit cover (6)
2 Seaside resort in Kent (7)
3 Natives of Kuwait, eg (5)
4 Fraudulent business scheme (4)
5 Iraq's second largest city (5)
6 Stitched (5)
7 Irish capital (6)
11 Large antelope (5)
12 Avarice, gluttony (5)
14 Disgusting (7)
15 Characteristic to be considered (6)
16 Country, capital Jerusalem (6)
18 Egyptian High Dam (5)
19 Third planet from the sun (5)
21 Superior (5)
22 Division of a hospital (4)

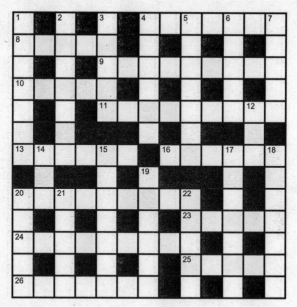

Across

4 Extremely savage (7)
8 Bamboo-eating mammal (5)
9 Ambiguous (9)
10 Flock of geese in flight (5)
11 Not counterfeit or copied (9)
13 Request for a repeat performance (6)
16 Rich and fashionable people who travel widely for pleasure (3,3)
20 Conspicuously and outrageously bad (9)
23 Colouring medium (5)
24 Consortium (9)
25 Main (5)
26 Advancers of cash (7)

Down

1 Incident (7)
2 Having a deficiency of red blood cells (7)
3 Animal life in a region (5)
4 Leave voluntarily (6)
5 Funeral procession (7)
6 Abstract form of painting (2,3)
7 Of sound (5)
12 US musician and record producer, ____ Turner (3)
14 Henpeck (3)
15 Music of the early 20th century (7)
17 Make amorous advances towards (7)
18 Give evidence in a court of law (7)
19 Natives of Italy's capital (6)
20 Artist's tripod (5)
21 Angry dispute (3-2)
22 Very small spot (5)

410

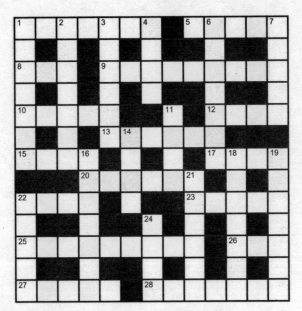

Across

1 Realised beforehand (7)
5 Small plant-sucking insect (5)
8 Deep groove (3)
9 Chronic drinker (9)
10 Girl who features in Lewis Carroll's famous stories (5)
12 Fired a bullet (4)
13 Mr De Niro, actor (6)
15 Beloved person (4)
17 Adult male deer (4)
20 Egg on (6)
22 Foolish (coll) (4)
23 Stir vigorously (5)
25 Food turner with a broad blade (4,5)
26 Yes (3)
27 Large natural stream of water (5)
28 Rubbing out (7)

Down

1 Onwards, ahead (7)
2 Greek wine (7)
3 Sharpshooter (6)
4 Tiny, common UK bird (4)
6 Christian clergymen (7)
7 Inhabited (5)
11 Departed, went (4)
14 On a single occasion (4)
16 Guy ____, Madonna's ex-husband (7)
18 Huge destructive wave (7)
19 Chinese herb believed to have medicinal powers (7)
21 Disease of the skin (6)
22 Postpone (5)
24 Presidential assistant (4)

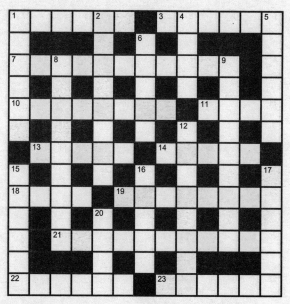

Across

1 However (6)
3 Small hand tool with a handle and flat metal blade (6)
7 Greatly desired (6,5)
10 Merchant who brings goods into the country from abroad (8)
11 Cooker (4)
13 Country, capital Nairobi (5)
14 European country (5)
18 Number represented by the Roman IX (4)
19 Hideousness, unsightliness (8)
21 Facing or experiencing financial trouble or difficulty (4-7)
22 Agile (6)
23 Freshwater carnivorous mammals (6)

Down

1 State capital of Texas, USA (6)
2 Receptacles for cigarette ends (8)
4 Roster of names (4)
5 Myth, fable (6)
6 Country called Cymru in its own language (5)
8 Last in an indefinitely numerous series (9)
9 Party-goers (9)
12 Loud (8)
15 Out of sight (6)
16 Land of the pyramids (5)
17 Lines directed to an audience (6)
20 Relating to speech (4)

412

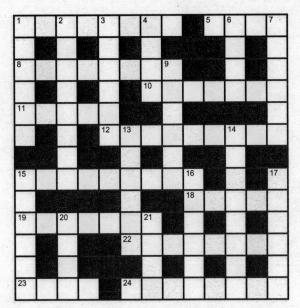

Across

1 Answer (8)
5 Celestial body (4)
8 Put together (8)
10 Riding a board on the crest of a wave (7)
11 Went down on the knees (5)
12 Eight-tentacled sea creatures (9)
15 Give up (9)
18 Happening, occurrence (5)
19 Citrus fruits (7)
22 Give an account of (8)
23 Expired (4)
24 Concern (8)

Down

1 Carnivorous marine fishes (6)
2 Hearer (8)
3 Red salad fruit (6)
4 Greases (4)
6 Cab (4)
7 Long, narrow hills (6)
9 Continent (6)
13 Sealed in a tin (6)
14 At an unfixed or unknown moment (8)
15 Gained points in a game (6)
16 Deliverance (6)
17 Thoroughfare (6)
20 Domain (4)
21 Witnessed (4)

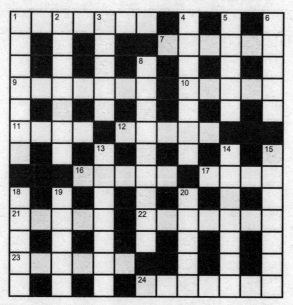

Across

1 Flavourless (7)
7 Cause extensive destruction (6)
9 Reflective road stud (4-3)
10 Quick, rapid (5)
11 Brand name of a ballpoint pen (4)
12 Woody ___, US film-maker and comic actor (5)
16 Person authorised to act for another (5)
17 Behind schedule (4)
21 Lesser (5)
22 Fierce (7)
23 Expansion (6)
24 Bring about (7)

Down

1 Lump of frozen water (3,4)
2 Natural height of a person (7)
3 Called out somebody's name over a public address system (5)
4 Female spirit of Irish folklore, whose wailing warns of death (7)
5 Bowl-shaped vessel (5)
6 Bunk in a ship, train, etc (5)
8 Without volition or conscious control (9)
13 In proportion (3,4)
14 Prehistoric human male (7)
15 Consistency (7)
18 Mexican friend (5)
19 Make angry (5)
20 Jolly ___, pirates' flag (5)

414

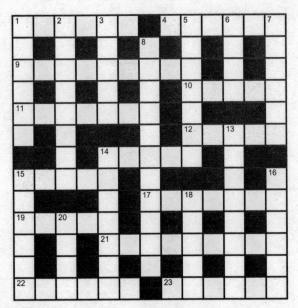

Across

1 Feel bitter or indignant about (6)
4 Heavy creamy-coloured paper resembling parchment (6)
9 Spiny-finned fish (9)
10 Aroma (5)
11 Piercing cries (7)
12 Settle (a loan) (5)
14 Money risked on a gamble (5)
15 The place at which (5)
17 Lack of agreement or harmony (7)
19 Spokes (5)
21 Message that tells the particulars of an act or occurrence (9)
22 Lacking in liveliness or charm (6)
23 Decoration along a wall (6)

Down

1 Physically strong (6)
2 Startle (8)
3 African antelope (5)
5 Pop duo whose albums include *Light at the End of the World* (7)
6 Entice (4)
7 In the main (6)
8 Falling short of some prescribed norm (11)
13 Powerful bleaching agent for the hair (8)
14 Meeting for an exchange of ideas (7)
15 Applied heat (6)
16 Resist separation (6)
18 Ringo ____, former Beatle (5)
20 Ridge of sand (4)

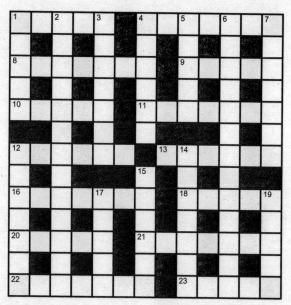

Across

1 Large parrot (5)
4 Let saliva drivel from the mouth (7)
8 Power to direct or determine (7)
9 Magnificence (5)
10 Hindu aphorism (5)
11 Fortress (7)
12 Supporting metal beam (6)
13 Fuzzy (6)
16 Dental filler (7)
18 Social position or status (5)
20 Country, capital Port-au-Prince (5)
21 Gastronome (7)
22 Admit one's guilt (7)
23 Welcome (5)

Down

1 Protective secretion of bodily membranes (5)
2 Anxiety and confusion (13)
3 Military conflict (7)
4 Choose (6)
5 Had better (5)
6 Force of fluid on the walls of the arteries (5,8)
7 Monarchy (7)
12 Computer generated image (7)
14 Deficient (7)
15 Causes to move forward with force (6)
17 Move smoothly and effortlessly (5)
19 Turn inside out (5)

416

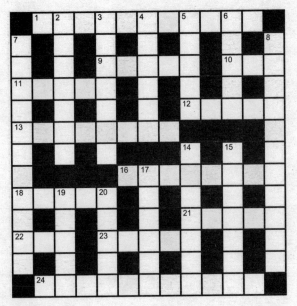

Across

1 Retail store serving a sparsely populated region (7,4)
9 Headdress for a king or queen (5)
10 Cereal crop (3)
11 Act of stealing (5)
12 No longer fashionable (5)
13 Global computer system (8)
16 Regal (8)
18 Bisect (5)
21 Species of bacteria which can threaten food safety (1,4)
22 Electrically charged particle (3)
23 Basic unit of money in Jordan (5)
24 Not the highest rank in a classification (6,5)

Down

2 Mammals such as rats, mice, etc (7)
3 Physicians (7)
4 Ribbon-like strip of pasta (6)
5 Pretty girl who works as a photographer's model (3-2)
6 Types, varieties (5)
7 Swimming costume (7,4)
8 Religious blessing (11)
14 Common, not specific (7)
15 Touches with brushing motions (7)
17 Turned away from sin (6)
19 Location at which an event is held (5)
20 Exhibition of cowboy skills (5)

Across

1 Major river of Colombia and Venezuela (7)
6 Basic monetary unit of Latvia (3)
8 City in central Japan on southern Honshu (5)
9 Coastal area of Italy and France (7)
10 Braid of hair (5)
11 Car repairmen (9)
13 On land (6)
16 Breakwater used to check erosion (6)
19 Elementary awareness of stimulation (9)
21 Depart, go (5)
22 Former kingdom in the Czech Republic (7)
23 Reproductive structure (5)
24 Prepare leather (3)
25 Country, capital Maseru (7)

Down

2 Looters, plunderers (7)
3 Outdoor (4-3)
4 Animal similar to the giraffe (5)
5 Rigid circular bands of metal, wood, etc (5)
6 In the vicinity (7)
7 Producing a sensation of touch (7)
12 Sprocket (3)
13 Cause pain or suffering (7)
14 Six-sided polygon (7)
15 Female sheep (3)
17 Attains (7)
18 Artefact from the latter part of the Stone Age (7)
19 Capital of South Korea (5)
20 Alfred ____, Swedish 'Prize' instigator (5)

418

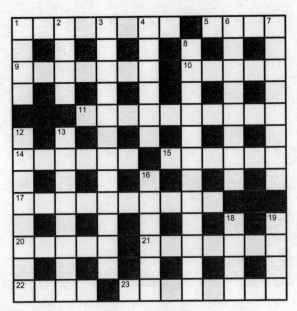

Across

1 Funny man (8)
5 Rent (4)
9 Muscular weakness caused by nerve damage (7)
10 Distressed (5)
11 Disposed to attack others (10)
14 Jam-packed (6)
15 Most deficient in colour (6)
17 Mass of calcium carbonate projecting upward from the floor of a cave (10)
20 Ethical (5)
21 Egg-shaped and flutey-toned musical instrument (7)
22 Bulge or swelling (4)
23 Germane (8)

Down

1 Emulate (4)
2 Female horse (4)
3 Not to one's liking (12)
4 Soak up (6)
6 Filled with revolutionary ideas (8)
7 Appeal (8)
8 Demonstrate or verify by evidence (12)
12 First-year university student (8)
13 Diminished in strength or quality (8)
16 Put (a restriction) in place (6)
18 Prima donna (4)
19 Flat floating platform for swimmers (4)

419

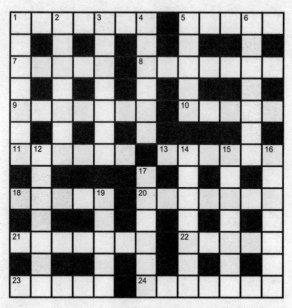

Across

1 Cross the road without regard for traffic (7)
5 Markedly masculine (5)
7 Duffer (5)
8 Search haphazardly (7)
9 Steady pace, like that of a canine (7)
10 Zodiacal constellation (5)
11 Circuit for the distribution of electricity (6)
13 Grins (6)
18 Growth on the surface of a mucous membrane (5)
20 Release from a suspended position (7)
21 Shallow depression in which brine evaporates (7)
22 Currently being employed (2,3)
23 Denim trousers (5)
24 For the most time (7)

Down

1 Common black and grey bird noted for thievery (7)
2 More immature (7)
3 Painkiller developed in Germany in the 1890s (7)
4 Martial art (6)
5 Mother (5)
6 Practice of cleanliness (7)
12 Archaeological period (4,3)
14 Special assignment (7)
15 Spare time (7)
16 Portion (7)
17 Smokestack of a ship (6)
19 Tubes (5)

423

420

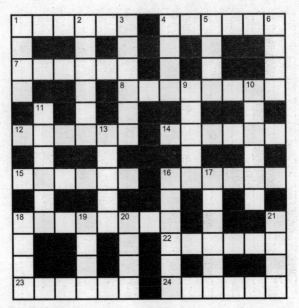

Across

1 Prejudiced (6)
4 Constituent of concrete (6)
7 Accomplish (6)
8 Contagious infection of the skin (8)
12 Form of a word used to denote more than one (6)
14 Without much intelligence (6)
15 Give birth to a litter of piglets (6)
16 Fine building stone (6)
18 Colander (8)
22 Go round and round (6)
23 Popular garden plant with a brightly coloured flower head (6)
24 Pancake Day, ____ Tuesday (6)

Down

1 Broken husks of the seeds of cereal grains (4)
2 Bracing atmosphere by the coast (3,3)
3 Old Testament book (6)
4 Harvest (4)
5 Barley used in brewing (4)
6 Country, capital Lomé (4)
9 Crowd actor (5)
10 Gruesome, revolting (6)
11 Ductile, malleable (6)
13 Garlic mayonnaise (5)
16 ____ dancers, associated with May Day (6)
17 Carnivorous bird (6)
18 Middle Eastern canal (4)
19 Prayer-ending word (4)
20 Name of the dog in *Peter Pan* (4)
21 US film star and dancer, ____ Kelly (4)

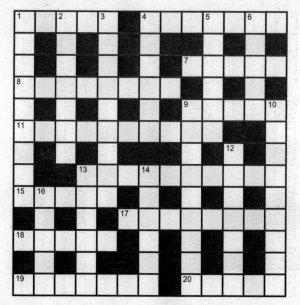

Across

1 Outstanding players in a tournament (5)
4 Covered with hair (7)
7 Side between ribs and hipbone (5)
8 Treeless grassy plains (8)
9 Fry quickly in a little fat (5)
11 The voting back into office (2-8)
13 Unrestrained by convention or morality (10)
15 Assigned a rank (5)
17 State of being disregarded or forgotten (8)
18 French queen, wife of Louis XVI, ___ Antoinette (5)
19 Says again (7)
20 Gaiters (5)

Down

1 Patron (9)
2 Lands (7)
3 Having very keen vision (5-4)
4 Truthful (6)
5 Related to wooded regions (6)
6 Article of faith (5)
9 Occasionally (9)
10 Avidity (9)
12 Wife of Prince Charles (7)
13 Contraption (6)
14 Raise in a relief (6)
16 Become less intense (5)

422

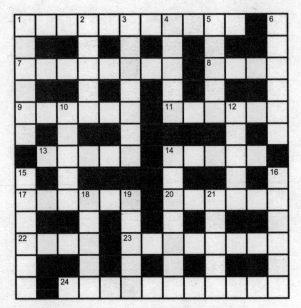

Across

1 Weapon designed to be thrown (4,7)

7 More impertinent or saucy (8)

8 Flat tableland with steep edges (4)

9 Period of instruction (6)

11 Walk awkwardly, with short, limping steps (6)

13 Construct (5)

14 Item of bed linen (5)

17 Forces open (6)

20 In golf, a score of one stroke under par on a hole (6)

22 Interweave (4)

23 Device that controls the amount of light admitted (8)

24 Nobility (11)

Down

1 Challenge aggressively (6)

2 Actions (5)

3 Ruled over (7)

4 Compass point (5)

5 Retire from military service (5)

6 School uniform jacket (6)

10 Of an Arabic ruling family (5)

12 Intermingle (5)

14 Temperature below freezing point (7)

15 Popular edible fruits (6)

16 As a result of this (6)

18 Smudge, daub (5)

19 Scorches (5)

21 Revolving blade (5)

423

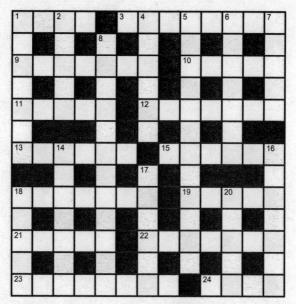

Across

1 Upper-class gent (coll) (4)
3 Period of one's existence (8)
9 Maltreaters (7)
10 Russian rulers (5)
11 Gather, as of natural products (5)
12 Provide evidence for (7)
13 Scribble (6)
15 Most broad (6)
18 Written account (7)
19 Mrs Major, wife of former UK prime minister John (5)
21 Location of something surrounded by other things (5)
22 Tiredness (7)
23 Became more intense (8)
24 French for 'father' (4)

Down

1 Lachrymator (4,3)
2 Stroke of luck (5)
4 Ant or beetle, for example (6)
5 Greatly exceeding bounds of moderation (12)
6 Confectionery made from sugar, butter and nuts (7)
7 Offensive (5)
8 Inexpensive fipple flute (5,7)
14 Remains (7)
16 Swing used by circus acrobats (7)
17 Cold dessert often served at parties (6)
18 Having a hemispherical vault (5)
20 Scoundrel (5)

427

424

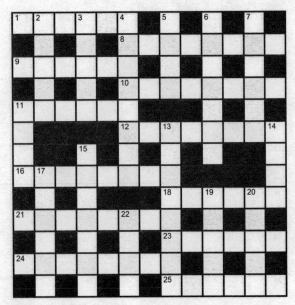

Across

1 Surgeon's stitch (6)
8 Working animal that can be trained to lead a blind person (5,3)
9 Ticking over (6)
10 Marine creature (8)
11 European language (6)
12 Outflow (8)
16 Popular frozen sweet (3,5)
18 Thin strip of covered cord used to edge hems (6)
21 Type of moist aerated Italian bread made with olive oil (8)
23 Message communicated to God (6)
24 Country, capital Harare (8)
25 Washed off soap (6)

Down

2 Beneath, below (5)
3 Organisation of employees (5)
4 Low-gloss paint texture (8)
5 Site of the famous Leaning Tower (4)
6 Propriety in manners and conduct (7)
7 Venom (6)
11 Group of islands, capital Suva (4)
13 Poisonous strip used to attract and kill airborne insects (8)
14 Offshoot of a branch (4)
15 Fictional character in the *Arabian Nights* (3,4)
17 Medical centre (6)
19 Simple (5)
20 Female relative (5)
22 Brass instrument (4)

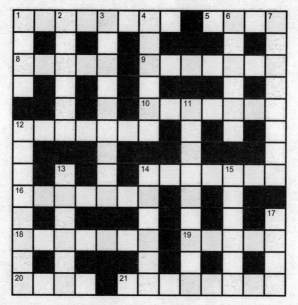

Across

1 Eroded and barren region in south-western South Dakota and north-western Nebraska (8)
5 Poke or thrust abruptly (4)
8 Region of the hips and groin (5)
9 Using a bike (7)
10 Confer dignity or honour upon (7)
12 Cravat (7)
14 Leaves (7)
16 Dry red Italian table wine (7)
18 Makes unhappy (7)
19 Organic compound (5)
20 Grains on the beach (4)
21 Stronghold (8)

Down

1 South American rope with weights, used in hunting (4)
2 Having the nature of a god (6)
3 Claim (9)
4 Official order (6)
6 Felt hat with a creased crown (6)
7 Narrow French stick loaf (8)
11 Careless, inattentive (9)
12 Unconsciousness induced by drugs (8)
13 Lime tree (6)
14 Ludicrous failure (6)
15 Uncle's wife (6)
17 Greek god of love (4)

426

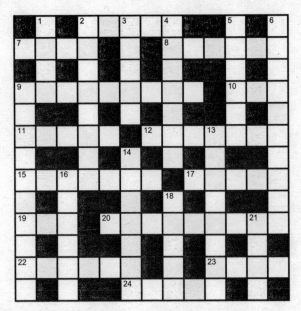

Across

2 Samuel ___, English diarist (1633–1703) (5)
7 Scottish hillside (4)
8 Pursue or resume (4,2)
9 Gain courage (4,5)
10 Sticky stuff (3)
11 Sharp, narrow ridge found in rugged mountains (5)
12 Surgeon's pincers (7)
15 Line of track providing a runway for wheels (7)
17 One sixteenth of a pound (5)
19 Boy (3)
20 Stock of pieces that a person or company is prepared to perform (9)
22 Young bird of prey (6)
23 Secure (4)
24 Goes out (5)

Down

1 Waste product useful as a fertiliser (4)
2 Support for a statue (8)
3 Walked up and down (5)
4 Fame (7)
5 Association of sports teams (6)
6 Fabrics, padding, springs, etc, used in the making of furniture (10)
9 Cart for serving light refreshments (3,7)
13 Wife of an earl (8)
14 Artist's paint-mixing board (7)
16 Colour of the rainbow (6)
18 Former monetary unit of Finland (5)
21 Narrow fissure in rock (4)

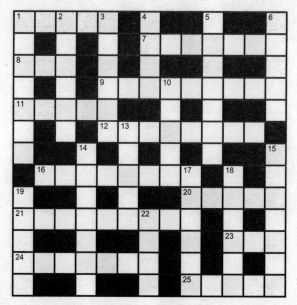

Across

1 Galas (5)
7 Square cap worn by RC clergy (7)
8 Paddle used to move a boat (3)
9 Cheap lodging place (9)
11 Blasphemed (5)
12 Withers, as with a loss of moisture (8)
16 Understands (8)
20 Crisp bread (5)
21 Not widely liked (9)
23 Type, kind (3)
24 Julie ____, star of *The Sound of Music* (7)
25 Donkeys (5)

Down

1 Floating wreckage of a ship (7)
2 Great fear (6)
3 One of four playing-card suits (6)
4 Wanes (4)
5 Turns into (7)
6 Specific points in history (5)
10 Cut into pieces (5)
13 Japanese poem (5)
14 Brickwork (7)
15 Captures again (7)
17 Several parallel layers of material (6)
18 Newborn children (6)
19 Pertaining to hearing (5)
22 Beat severely with a whip or rod (4)

428

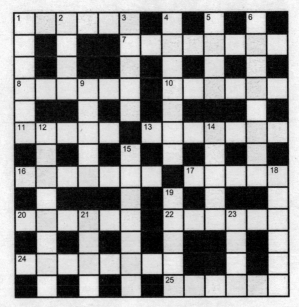

Across

1 Brilliance (6)
7 Single-reed instrument (8)
8 Beam over a doorway (6)
10 Australian currency unit (6)
11 To hinder or preclude, in law (5)
13 Wool grease (7)
16 Bring up in conversation (7)
17 Creature (5)
20 Skilful or adept in action (6)
22 Ice cream dish (6)
24 Not deficient in intellect (coll) (3,5)
25 Chair of state of a monarch (6)

Down

1 Framework of metal bars used as a partition (6)
2 Midday (4)
3 Skin that covers the top of the head (5)
4 Toothed steel belt used to cut piles of material (7)
5 Beak (4)
6 Denial (8)
9 Freshwater fish (5)
12 At a regular rate or pace (8)
14 Huge sea (5)
15 Sell illicit products such as drugs or alcohol (7)
18 Animal fat used in cooking (6)
19 Thing of value (5)
21 Expletive (4)
23 Lower part of an interior wall (4)

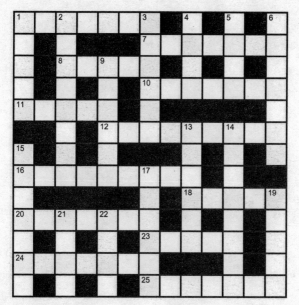

Across
1 Prisoner held as a form of insurance (7)
7 Rich stew (7)
8 Singer whose albums include *Confessions* (5)
10 Participant in some activity (7)
11 Period of darkness (5)
12 Military unit formed to accomplish a particular objective (4,5)
16 Narrow buoyant plank for riding the waves (9)
18 Particle of sand (5)
20 Musical (7)
23 Devoured (5)
24 Lion-hearted King (7)
25 Hold spellbound (7)

Down
1 One of the Great Lakes (5)
2 One who imports without paying duties (8)
3 The act of coming out (6)
4 Boat associated with Cambridge, for example (4)
5 Ditch used to divide lands without hiding a view (2-2)
6 Spicy type of relish (7)
9 Large bath for more than one person (3,3)
13 Move restlessly (6)
14 Family servant of long standing (8)
15 Basic currency unit of the former East Germany (7)
17 Agree (6)
19 Country, capital Kathmandu (5)
21 Destiny (4)
22 Actress, Cameron ___ (4)

430

Across

1 Crab apple-like fruit used for preserves (6)
5 Regimental flag (6)
8 Moorings (6)
9 Designating sound transmission from two sources (6)
10 Group which released the album *Meltdown* in 2004 (3)
11 Thin candle (5)
13 Cosmetic preparation (8)
15 Collarbone (8)
16 Savoury jelly (5)
19 Directed (3)
21 Foolhardy (6)
22 Point in orbit (6)
23 Dessert (6)
24 Happening without warning (6)

Down

2 In a graceful or stylish manner (9)
3 Strong coffee with a frothed milk topping (5)
4 ___ Parks, African-American civil rights activist (4)
5 Hold sacred (8)
6 Was in an agitated emotional state (7)
7 Gas used in lighting (4)
12 Honour (9)
13 Undiplomatic (8)
14 Greed (7)
17 Was upright (5)
18 Insect between larva and adult stage (4)
20 Raised platform (4)

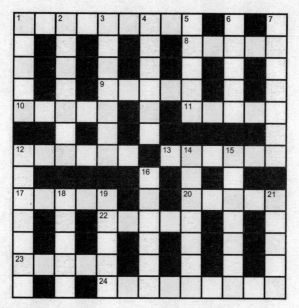

Across

1 One who obtains pleasure from receiving punishment (9)

8 Towards the stern of a ship (5)

9 By surprise (5)

10 Relating to birds (5)

11 Bout, period of indulgence (5)

12 Swine's home (6)

13 Mistakes resulting from inattention (6)

17 Puts into a letterbox (5)

20 Glaringly vivid (5)

22 Forename of Mr Agassi, tennis champion (5)

23 Vestige (5)

24 Called in an official matter, such as to attend court (9)

Down

1 Secret criminal group in Sicily (5)

2 Dismissing an employee (coll) (7)

3 Paul ____, French artist (1839–1906) (7)

4 Convict (6)

5 Discusses (5)

6 Civic leader (5)

7 Floors of a building (7)

12 Measuring instrument consisting of a graduated glass tube (7)

14 Brisk and lively tempo (7)

15 Abrades (7)

16 Total uproar (6)

18 Closed litter for one passenger (5)

19 Economises (5)

21 Celtic priest (5)

432

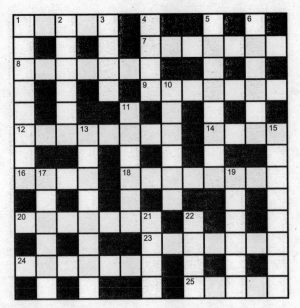

Across

1 Combination of musical notes (5)
7 Beneficiary of a will (7)
8 Of pasta, cooked so as to be firm when eaten (2,5)
9 Have within (7)
12 Pattern of symptoms (8)
14 Above, beyond (4)
16 Expression of incredulity (2,2)
18 Device regulating electrical current (8)
20 Discolouration of metal surface caused by oxidation (7)
23 Set apart from others (7)
24 Items of neckwear in the form of a knot with two loops (3,4)
25 Extract (metals) by heating (5)

Down

1 Personal magnetism (8)
2 Informal term for your father (3,3)
3 Lairs (4)
4 ___ Guinness, actor (1914–2000) (4)
5 Timid, fearful (8)
6 Formula for cooking (6)
10 Icebreaker (6)
11 Stashes away (6)
13 Precise and explicit (8)
15 Temperamentally disinclined to talk (8)
17 Lend flavour to (6)
19 Violent denunciation (6)
21 Expression of dislike (4)
22 Foreman (4)

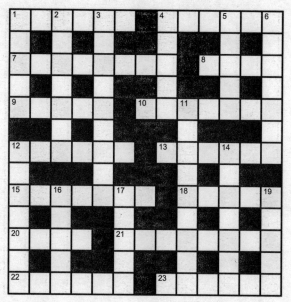

Across

1 Unpleasantly cool and humid (6)
4 Detractor (6)
7 Minor celestial body composed of rock and metal (8)
8 Scottish island, capital Portree (4)
9 Peninsula at the north end of the Red Sea (5)
10 Compel by threatening (7)
12 Reduced to small shreds, as with cheese (6)
13 One-time (6)
15 Every evening (7)
18 Light-headed (5)
20 Animal's foot (4)
21 Change, amendment (8)
22 Make do (6)
23 Area set back or indented (6)

Down

1 Uncouth (5)
2 Insect's feeler (7)
3 Jollity (9)
4 Durable aromatic wood (5)
5 Capital of Japan (5)
6 Person whose job it is to dust and vacuum, etc (7)
11 Next to (9)
12 Fabric in a plaid weave (7)
14 Woman skilled in aiding the delivery of babies (7)
16 Fully developed (5)
17 Above average in size (5)
19 Jerks violently (5)

434

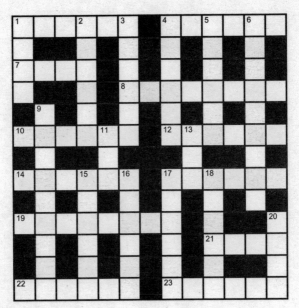

Across

1 Floating aimlessly (6)
4 Obtained, especially accidentally (4,2)
7 At the peak of (4)
8 Towards the centre (8)
10 Small active songbird (6)
12 Have on loan (6)
14 Marked by meekness or modesty (6)
17 Countries of Asia (6)
19 Glancing rebound (8)
21 Greek letter (4)
22 Seat of the faculty of reason (6)
23 Distort a message or story (6)

Down

1 Slightly open (4)
2 Pass on, reveal (information) (6)
3 Extreme care in spending money (6)
4 Spider's snare (6)
5 Reflect (6)
6 Type of pen with a small sphere at the tip (9)
9 Answers, explanations (9)
11 Not in good health (3)
13 Belonging to us (3)
15 Filmed life story (6)
16 Breathe out (6)
17 Choosing (6)
18 Pressure line on a weather map (6)
20 Story (4)

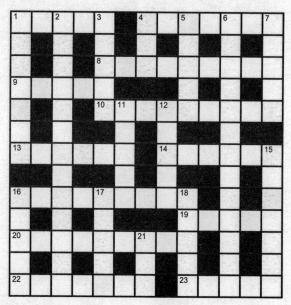

Across

1 Rounded projections of ears (5)
4 Protective cover for a leg joint (4-3)
8 Wearing down through sustained attack (9)
9 Footwear items (5)
10 Accustom (9)
13 Touching or pushing at with the end of the foot (6)
14 Tom ___, hero of novels by Mark Twain (6)
16 British statesman who served as Prime Minister four times (9)
19 Anaemic-looking (5)
20 Domesticated cavy (6,3)
22 Made small, bell-like sounds (7)
23 Muster strength for a renewed effort (5)

Down

1 Flickering with a soft radiance (7)
2 Person who shares a common ancestor (5,8)
3 Pulverise (5)
4 Equipment (3)
5 Authoritative proclamation (5)
6 Children's learning place (7,6)
7 Slow learner (5)
11 Acute insecurity (5)
12 Henrik ___, Norwegian dramatist (1828–1906) (5)
15 Act of returning to the Earth's atmosphere (2-5)
16 Lamb leg suitable for roasting (5)
17 Emit an odour (5)
18 Showing impatient expectancy (5)
21 Doctor of Philosophy (abbr) (3)

436

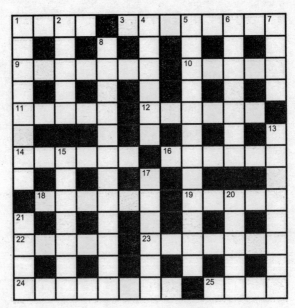

Across

1 Floor on a boat (4)
3 Organised collection of related information (8)
9 Cut of meat (7)
10 Be suspended in the air (5)
11 Beginning of an offensive (5)
12 Getting older (6)
14 Depressing, drab (6)
16 Involuntary expulsion of air from the nose (6)
18 Sculpture (6)
19 Noise (5)
22 State of being disregarded or forgotten (5)
23 Blackberry bush (7)
24 Metallic cylinder used for storage (8)
25 Caps, berets, etc (4)

Down

1 Force out from a position (8)
2 Popular game played with pieces of stiffened paper (5)
4 Yearly (6)
5 First day of Lent (3,9)
6 Move forward (7)
7 Monetary unit used by some countries of the EU (4)
8 Showing disdain, insolent (12)
13 Bawdiness, obscenity (8)
15 Stool to rest the feet of a seated person (7)
17 Unconvincing, weak (6)
20 Region of complete shadow (5)
21 Group of countries in special alliance (4)

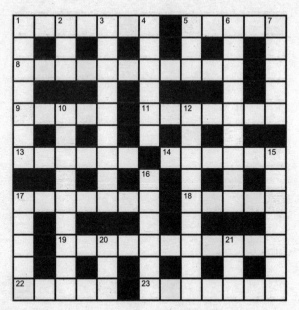

Across

1 Garbage collector (7)
5 Drop behind (5)
8 Words that read the same backwards as forwards (11)
9 Pigment prepared from the ink of cuttlefishes (5)
11 Climbs down (7)
13 Rich fruit cake, decorated with almonds (6)
14 On an incline (6)
17 Rushing stream (7)
18 Seeped (5)
19 Splendid (11)
22 Hosiery items (5)
23 Sticky substance made from sugar (7)

Down

1 Ousted (7)
2 ___ volatile, smelling salts (3)
3 Hard brittle greyish-white metallic element (9)
4 Scandinavian monarchy (6)
5 Male cat (3)
6 Nazi concentration camp during World War II (9)
7 Young sheep (5)
10 Giving an unbroken view of the whole region (9)
12 Make do with whatever is at hand (9)
15 Young woman who displays irresponsible or brash behaviour (coll) (7)
16 Stern (6)
17 Check marks (5)
20 Hydrogen, for example (3)
21 And so forth (abbr) (3)

438

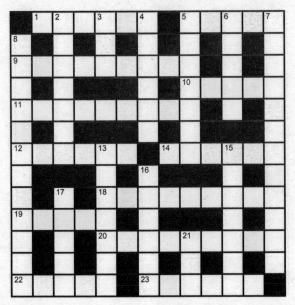

Across

1 Shuts (6)
5 Be overcome by a sudden fear (5)
9 Native Australian (9)
10 Paces (5)
11 Shaft in a building in which a series of steps is built (9)
12 Nakedness (6)
14 Farewell remark (3-3)
18 Respiratory disease (9)
19 Mr Izzard, comedian (5)
20 Obstruct or hinder any discussion (9)
22 Very small fish (5)
23 Melted (6)

Down

2 Gymnastic garment (7)
3 ___ Lanka, country formerly known as Ceylon (3)
4 Grabbed forcefully (6)
5 Elvis ___, US rock singer (7)
6 Book-length story (5)
7 Substantial, large in amount (12)
8 Methods (4,3,5)
13 Prepared by a compositor for printing (7)
15 Dressing for a wound (7)
16 Extract the essence of something by boiling it (6)
17 King of England (944–975) (5)
21 Mrs Sharples, former *Coronation Street* rôle (3)

439

Across

4 Woman's accessory (7)
7 Laugh quietly or with restraint (7)
8 Particle (5)
9 Religious doctrine (5)
10 Sense organ for hearing (3)
11 Thespian (5)
12 Extremely funny (9)
14 Engage in combat (coll) (4,5)
17 Mythical cave-dweller (5)
18 Flightless Australian bird (3)
19 Pedestrianised public square (5)
21 Point directly opposite the zenith (5)
22 Drink given to people who are ill (4,3)
23 Foams as if boiling vigorously (7)

Down

1 Compound capable of turning litmus red (4)
2 Member of Genghis Khan's clan (6)
3 Road construction vehicle (11)
4 Up until this time (6)
5 ___ and the Beast, famous fairy tale (6)
6 Willing to give (8)
8 Leaping insect (11)
12 Meeting at which election candidates address potential voters (8)
13 Dish of flavoured melted cheese (6)
15 Small pieces of bread, for example (6)
16 Property consisting of houses and land (6)
20 At a distance (4)

440

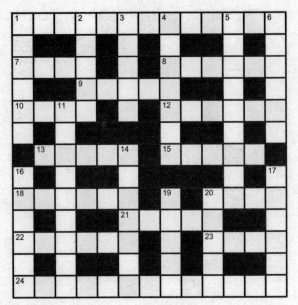

Across

1 Traditionally a date for playing tricks on others (5,5,3)
7 Bobbin (4)
8 Small purple plum (6)
9 Church passage (5)
10 Cook slowly in liquid (4)
12 Withdraw (6)
13 Upstairs storage space (5)
15 Country of the Arabian Peninsula (5)
18 Participant in a race (6)
20 Computer memory unit (4)
21 Popeye's girlfriend (5)
22 Roller on a typewriter (6)
23 Study intensively for an exam (4)
24 Outcome in which virtue triumphs over vice (6,7)

Down

1 Take into custody (6)
2 Relative by marriage (2-3)
3 Fictitious, untrue (5)
4 Hospital attendant (7)
5 Breakthrough (9)
6 A bet on four or more horses in different races (6)
11 Try to lessen the seriousness or extent of (9)
14 Habitual, inveterate (7)
16 Cause to stumble (4,2)
17 Hard-cased arthropod (6)
19 Small and delicately worked piece (5)
20 Plague, annoy continually (5)

441

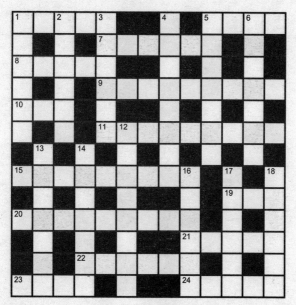

Across

1. Dish out (5)
5. Cattle shed (4)
7. Blue-flowered herb (6)
8. Measure the depth of something (5)
9. Protection against future loss (9)
10. Distinction of honour awarded by the Queen (inits) (3)
11. Brings into existence (9)
15. Looks like (9)
19. Hatchet (3)
20. Member of a widespread secret fraternal order (9)
21. Dripping wet (5)
22. Vehicle for travelling on snow (6)
23. Sum charged for riding in a bus (4)
24. Casing (5)

Down

1. Soda dispenser (6)
2. Stirred up, excited (6)
3. Receding (6)
4. Vision unassisted by microscope, telescope, etc (5,3)
5. Small sack of dried seeds used in children's games (7)
6. Cattle thief (7)
12. Hugged (8)
13. Country to the north of Armenia (7)
14. Discharge (7)
16. Detects automatically (6)
17. Knot (6)
18. Gertrude ____, renowned English gardener (1843–1932) (6)

445

442

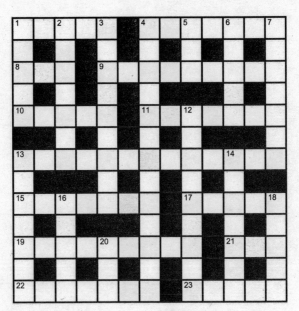

Across

1. Parson (5)
4. Evergreen conifer (7)
8. Dupe, swindle (3)
9. Compulsory (9)
10. Steam bath (5)
11. Morally strict (7)
13. Breed of cattle (8,5)
15. Balearic Island, capital Mahón (7)
17. Heather (5)
19. Tolerating without protest (9)
21. Light touch or stroke (3)
22. Detect with the senses (7)
23. High, thin in tone (5)

Down

1. Bad habits (5)
2. Eat (7)
3. Criminal who smashes a shop window with a vehicle (3-6)
4. Union by linking together in a series or chain (13)
5. Green vegetable (3)
6. Wear away by natural forces (5)
7. Skilfulness in deception (7)
12. Animal that feeds on refuse (9)
13. Inflatable plastic ring worn as a swimming aid (7)
14. Hotplate (7)
16. Head/body connectors (5)
18. Monastery (5)
20. Food in a pastry shell (3)

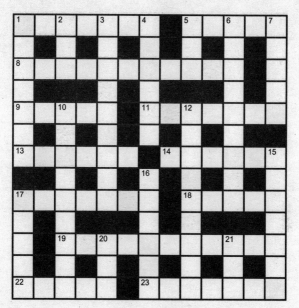

Across

1 Beetroot soup (7)
5 Colour of least lightness (5)
8 Polygraph used in interrogation (3,8)
9 Class of people enjoying superior status (5)
11 At a previous point (7)
13 Deserved by one's efforts (6)
14 Person who serves at table (6)
17 Ablution facility (7)
18 Undersides of the feet (5)
19 Ice cream containing chopped candied fruits (5,6)
22 Mike ___, former heavyweight champion boxer (5)
23 Money set by for the future (4,3)

Down

1 Take to be true (7)
2 Repent (3)
3 Most ingenious (9)
4 Swarmed (6)
5 Item used in playing cricket (3)
6 Small firearm which shoots pellets (3,6)
7 Native or inhabitant of Cambodia (5)
10 Causes annoyance in (9)
12 Confirms in a good opinion or impression (9)
15 Uttering in a grating voice (7)
16 Edna ___, Irish writer (born in 1932) (6)
17 Baked to a cinder (5)
20 Browning of the skin caused by the sun (3)
21 Quoits target (3)

444

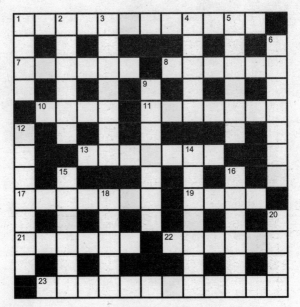

Across

1 Specialist who administers drugs during medical operations (12)
7 Insurrection, uprising (6)
8 World's largest hot desert (6)
10 Swathe (4)
11 Part of London which includes Bow and Spitalfields (4,3)
13 Stretches, draws tight (7)
17 Quiver (7)
19 ___ Marx, communist (4)
21 Four-wheeled covered carriage (6)
22 Ms Jackson, actress and MP (6)
23 Someone versed in the collection and interpretation of data (12)

Down

1 Land force of a nation (4)
2 Blood vessel leading from the heart (6)
3 Mark on the skin caused by exposure to solar rays (7)
4 Salvers (5)
5 Ocean floor (6)
6 Financial obligation unlikely to be repaid (3,4)
9 Acts in a threatening manner (7)
12 Pin used in bowling (7)
14 Forename of Gogol, Russian writer (7)
15 ___ butter, popular spread (6)
16 Sultanate in north-western Borneo (6)
18 Show off (5)
20 Farm outbuilding (4)

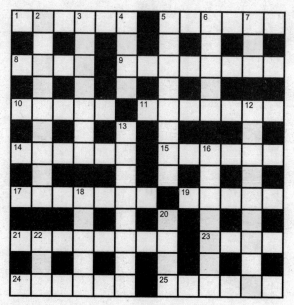

Across

1 Upward movement (6)
5 Order of business (6)
8 Hindu woman's garment (4)
9 Long-legged bird (8)
10 At no time (5)
11 Female of the black grouse (7)
14 Encounter between opposing forces (6)
15 Infectious disease transmitted by lice (6)
17 Cooking utensil (7)
19 Judge's mallet (5)
21 American state in the Rocky Mountains (8)
23 Crack in a lip caused usually by cold (4)
24 Fail to fulfil a promise (6)
25 Make unhappy (6)

Down

2 Extra component of a machine (5,4)
3 Clearly apparent (7)
4 Bean curd (4)
5 Liveliness and eagerness (8)
6 Enlighten (5)
7 Archaeological site (3)
12 Determine the amount of (9)
13 Drink (8)
16 Frolicked, capered (7)
18 Roused from slumber (5)
20 Jumps on one foot (4)
22 Metal-bearing mineral (3)

446

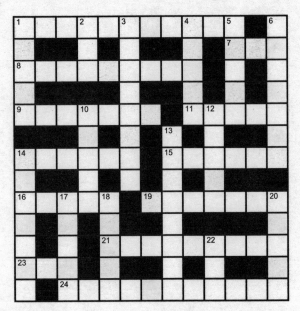

Across

1 Otherwise (11)
7 Across or above, poetically (3)
8 Continent in the southern hemisphere (9)
9 Vehicles in motion (7)
11 Leaves of a book (5)
14 Discover the site of (6)
15 Writer (6)
16 Garments (5)
19 Depository for goods (7)
21 Stand for, symbolise (9)
23 Boy child (3)
24 Operation in which the difference between two numbers is calculated (11)

Down

1 Compulsory military service (5)
2 Healthy (3)
3 Became fully aware of (8)
4 Disreputable wanderer (5)
5 Immature (5)
6 Pocket, misappropriate (7)
10 Candle light (5)
12 Behind (5)
13 Microbes (8)
14 Generosity (7)
17 Sets on fire (5)
18 Wash vigorously (5)
20 Having been consumed (5)
22 Pose (3)

Across

1 Be lazy or idle (4)
3 Mercifulness (8)
7 Case indicating the agent in passive sentences (8)
8 Fictional sea captain created by Jules Verne (4)
9 Colourful bird (6)
10 Tap for drawing water from a cask (6)
11 Lustre (5)
12 Berkshire town, famous for its racecourse (5)
15 Glowing fragments of wood left from a fire (6)
18 Shorebird with a slender upward-curving bill (6)
19 Mount ____, the highest peak in Japan (4)
20 Natives of Rome, eg (8)
21 Woman's lace scarf (8)
22 Courage (coll) (4)

Down

1 Rough shelter at the side of a house (4-2)
2 Bride-to-be (7)
3 Roll of hair worn at the nape of the neck (7)
4 Fencing swords (5)
5 Tedium (5)
6 Mixture of decaying vegetation and manure (7)
11 Italian liqueur made with elderberries and flavoured with liquorice (7)
12 US state (7)
13 Creating a copy of some biological entity (7)
14 Abnormal state in which the flow of a liquid (such as blood) is slowed (6)
16 Live, be (5)
17 Persuasive line of talk (5)

448

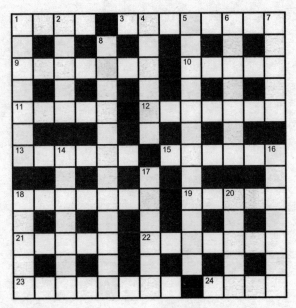

Across

1 Town in south-western England on the River Avon (4)
3 From first to last (3,2,3)
9 German measles (7)
10 Torpid (5)
11 Native of Basra, for example (5)
12 Spotted wildcat (7)
13 Call into question (6)
15 In some way or other (coll) (4,2)
18 Commanded not to do (7)
19 Small and delicate (5)
21 Member of a Mexican tribe overthrown by Cortes in 1519 (5)
22 Swills a liquid around the back of the throat (7)
23 Penitent (8)
24 Park in central London (4)

Down

1 Filled tortilla (7)
2 Bone of the leg (5)
4 Almost (6)
5 Mathematics of triangles (12)
6 Stylish, graceful (7)
7 Outmoded (5)
8 Vehicle of extraterrestrial origin (6,6)
14 Person excessively concerned about propriety and decorum (7)
16 Skill (7)
17 Heaviness (6)
18 Former French unit of currency (5)
20 Completely, entirely (5)

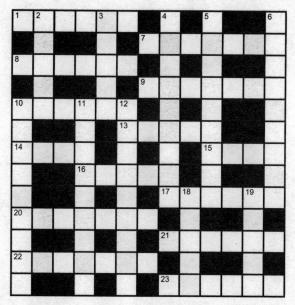

Across

1 Shrewd (6)
7 Due to, on account of (7)
8 Substance in fruit which aids in setting jam (6)
9 Fiasco (7)
10 Trousers for casual wear (6)
13 Furious (5)
14 Units of work or energy (4)
15 One of a series of graduated measurements (as of clothing) (4)
16 Lure, entice (5)
17 Provide compensation for death or damage (6)
20 Famous American waterfalls (7)
21 Small lynx of North America (6)
22 Becoming firm (7)
23 Postponements (6)

Down

2 Place the letters of a word in the correct order (5)
3 Use one's brain (5)
4 Vast plain and National Park in Tanzania (9)
5 Loss of the ability to move a body part (9)
6 Private conversation between two people (4-1-4)
10 Sugariness (9)
11 Censure severely (9)
12 Oldest independent country in Europe (3,6)
18 Not a soul (2-3)
19 Equip in advance for a particular purpose (5)

450

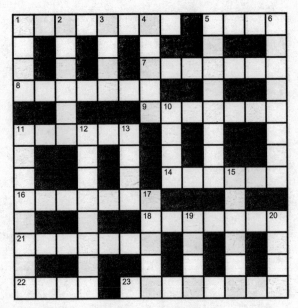

Across
1 Bedtime drink (8)
5 Rip, rend (4)
7 State of being uncooked (7)
8 Least difficult (7)
9 Atrocious (7)
11 Dedicate (6)
14 Coined (6)
16 Let loose (7)
18 Poisonous metallic element (7)
21 Hector ____, French composer (1803–69) (7)
22 Water which falls from clouds (4)
23 Spanish style of dancing (8)

Down
1 Africa's longest river (4)
2 Mineral used to make plaster (6)
3 Hollow cylinder (4)
4 Main artery of the body (5)
5 Metallic element used to make light-bulb filaments (8)
6 Explained or answered (8)
10 Lip of a hat (4)
11 Crunchy, green salad vegetable (8)
12 Navigator who commanded the first expedition to circumnavigate the world (8)
13 Tie-on labels (4)
15 Band of tissue connecting a muscle to bone (6)
17 Light brown, nut-coloured (5)
19 Former name of Thailand (4)
20 Lake in the foothills of the Alps in northern Italy (4)

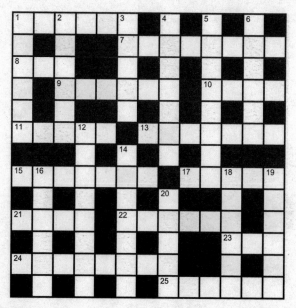

Across

1 Box in which a corpse is buried (6)
7 Obvious to the mind or senses (8)
8 Metal cooking vessel (3)
9 Foodstuff eaten for breakfast (6)
10 Gulp (4)
11 Public dance hall (5)
13 Listening (7)
15 Prosperous (7)
17 Financial obligations (5)
21 Item of footwear (4)
22 Not so warm (6)
23 Force by impact (3)
24 Plumage (8)
25 Pieces of furniture (6)

Down

1 Replicated (6)
2 Barriers serving to enclose an area (6)
3 Belly button (5)
4 Implements, puts into service (7)
5 Maintain in unaltered condition (8)
6 Native of Mumbai, for example (6)
12 Gathers together (8)
14 Investigated (7)
16 Resounded (6)
18 Keg, cask (6)
19 Adhesive postal tokens (6)
20 Most unfit (5)

452

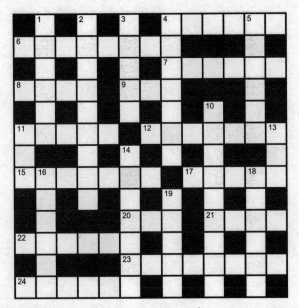

Across

4 Sailors' rhythmical work song (6)

6 Motion (8)

7 Kidnap (6)

8 Flat, thin circle (4)

9 Unit of weight equivalent to 2240 pounds (3)

11 Maurice ____, French composer (1875–1937) (5)

12 Lean back (7)

15 More worn and shabby (7)

17 Impertinent (5)

20 German city, birthplace of Albert Einstein (3)

21 Chief port of Yemen (4)

22 Greek capital city (6)

23 Example (8)

24 Soft decayed area in a tooth (6)

Down

1 Legendary 'Lady' who rode naked through Coventry (6)

2 Tall wooden containers lined with metal (3,6)

3 Pulsates (5)

4 Chief port and town of the Falkland Islands (7)

5 Business leader (6)

10 Red toadstool with white spots (3,6)

11 Common rodent (3)

13 Cambridgeshire city (3)

14 French composer, Claude ____ (1862–1918) (7)

16 ____ Christie, crime novelist (6)

18 Screens out, sifts (6)

19 Glowing fragment of wood or coal left from a fire (5)

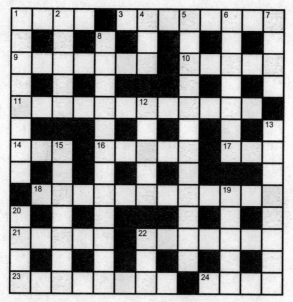

Across

1 Placed in position (4)
3 Not circulating or flowing (8)
9 Ireland's longest river (7)
10 Snare, loop in a rope (5)
11 Amount of financial gain a business has after deducting expenditure (6,6)
14 Catch sight of (3)
16 Throw out (5)
17 Hawaiian floral garland (3)
18 Not considered respectable in appearance or character (12)
21 Russian city on the Vyatka River (5)
22 Theft (7)
23 Recollections (8)
24 Adult male horse kept for breeding (4)

Down

1 Bugle call sounded at funerals (4,4)
2 US state, capital Boise (5)
4 Cardinal number (3)
5 Shop which sells a wide range of goods (7,5)
6 Inconsiderate of or hostile to others (7)
7 Woodland plant (4)
8 Operator of a railway locomotive (6,6)
12 Finish a task completely (3,2)
13 Exhibiting childlike credulity (4-4)
15 Short poem with a witty ending (7)
19 Noise made by a sheep (5)
20 Cream off (4)
22 Be prostrate (3)

454

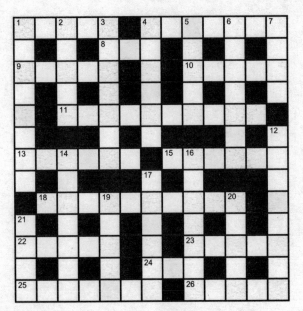

Across

1 Cut (wood) (5)
4 Narrow strip of land connecting two larger land areas (7)
8 Hostelry (3)
9 Orchard fruits (5)
10 Capital of Bangladesh (5)
11 Alliance (10)
13 Engraves with acid (6)
15 Carnivorous burrowing mammal (6)
18 Girl who attends a woman about to be married (10)
22 Having much foliage (5)
23 Adult male birds (5)
24 Rate of travel (inits) (3)
25 Filaments (7)
26 Spool-and-string toys (2-3)

Down

1 Provided (8)
2 Dock (5)
3 Feel distaste towards (7)
4 To set in from the margin (6)
5 Periodic rises and falls of the sea (5)
6 Definition (7)
7 Remain, sit tight (4)
12 US state, capital Little Rock (8)
14 Swift pirate ship (7)
16 Lawlessness (7)
17 Sacred songs (6)
19 Senior member of a group (5)
20 Fall into ruin (5)
21 Regrettably (4)

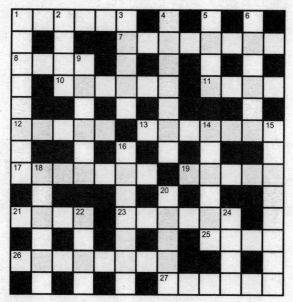

Across

1 Mob (6)
7 Deferring of a payment to later time (8)
8 Homework (4)
10 Change to ice (6)
11 Coagulated blood from a wound (4)
12 Brand name (5)
13 Griddle cake (7)
17 Cut short (7)
19 Structure for open-air sports (5)
21 Curved gateway (4)
23 River which flows through London (6)
25 Cereal thrown at weddings (4)
26 Come together (8)
27 Small stamp or seal on a ring (6)

Down

1 Country which is not a monarchy (8)
2 Cattle reared for their meat (4)
3 Made a mistake (5)
4 Mathematical system (7)
5 Instrument sounded to announce a meal (4)
6 Vehicle for carrying a coffin (6)
9 Clergyman (6)
14 Combination of two or more commercial companies (6)
15 Part of a church at right angles to the nave (8)
16 On edge, jumpy (7)
18 Displace (6)
20 Pantomime women (5)
22 Habitation for bees (4)
24 Put one's name to (4)

456

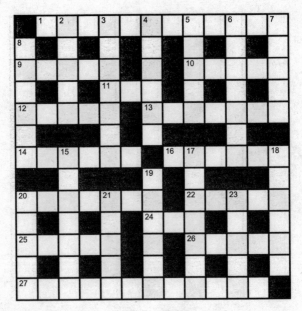

Across

1 The internet, generally (5,4,3)
9 Common cinema name (5)
10 Fruit pulp (5)
11 Behave (3)
12 Armada (5)
13 Not functioning properly (7)
14 Subtle difference in meaning (6)
16 Rehearsal, test (3,3)
20 Largest anthropoid ape (7)
22 Heavenly body (5)
24 Fluid used for writing (3)
25 Frameworks for holding objects (5)
26 Exactly matched (5)
27 Marked by imagination and a readiness to undertake new projects (12)

Down

2 Abnormally fat (5)
3 Madman (7)
4 Deserving, commendable (6)
5 One of the Seven Dwarfs (5)
6 Experienced fighter (7)
7 Mark placed over a vowel to indicate a short sound (5)
8 Scientist engaged in military research (6)
15 Juicy fruit (7)
17 Childhood disease caused by deficiency of vitamin D (7)
18 Stinging plant (6)
19 Plunderer, robber (6)
20 Deep ravine (5)
21 Light-beam intensifier (5)
23 Grieve over a death (5)

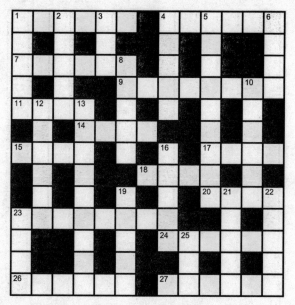

Across

1 Small box for holding valuables (6)
4 Take a firm stand (6)
7 Television receiver (6)
9 Slaughterhouse (8)
11 Villein (4)
14 Country, capital Teheran (4)
15 Beds for babies (4)
17 Sheltered and secluded place (4)
18 Unfettered (4)
20 Take a chance (4)
23 Dearth, lack (8)
24 Temple (6)
26 Airport waiting area (6)
27 Muffle, suppress (6)

Down

1 Talons (5)
2 More certain (5)
3 Epoch, age (3)
4 Religion of Muslims (5)
5 Merchant who sells writing materials (9)
6 Row or layer (4)
8 Capital of Bolivia (2,3)
10 Fools (6)
12 Adequate (6)
13 Angler (9)
16 Grovel (5)
19 Perhaps (5)
21 In snooker, to pocket the cue ball after hitting another (2-3)
22 Scoundrel (5)
23 Secure against leakage (4)
25 Little insect (3)

458

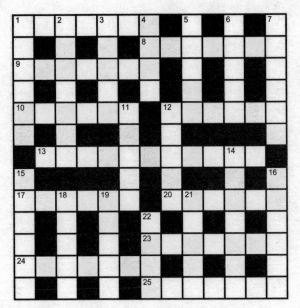

Across
1 Sanctified (7)
8 Go back over (7)
9 Marsh gas (7)
10 Engrave (6)
12 Having a highly polished surface (6)
13 Machine with a revolving drum used in making concrete (6,5)
17 Small ornamental case worn on a necklace (6)
20 Advance evidence for (6)
23 Arrogant person (7)
24 One serving a sentence in a jail or prison (7)
25 Oriental (7)

Down
1 Make utterly muddled, stupefy (6)
2 Squeeze out (7)
3 Marsh (5)
4 Sketched (4)
5 Play for time (5)
6 Solid projectiles shot by a musket (5)
7 Greek god of the west wind (6)
11 Religious doctrine proclaimed as true (5)
12 Greek letter (5)
14 Teach (7)
15 Domesticated llama with long silky fleece (6)
16 Whisked (6)
18 Sidekick (5)
19 Spooky (5)
21 Workstations (5)
22 Daintily pretty (4)

459

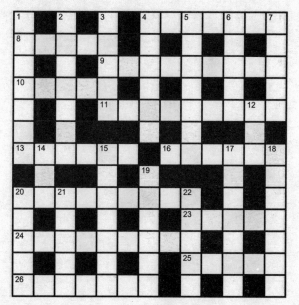

Across
- **4** Attack with artillery (7)
- **8** Old Testament mother-in-law of Ruth (5)
- **9** Focused ray of high-intensity radiation (5,4)
- **10** Extreme (5)
- **11** Science of matter (9)
- **13** Endeavour (6)
- **16** Movie theatre (6)
- **20** Compass point at 225 degrees (5-4)
- **23** Modify (5)
- **24** Habitual craving (9)
- **25** Thin mortar used between tiles (5)
- **26** Lacking sight (7)

Down
- **1** Male demon believed to lie on sleeping persons (7)
- **2** Sydney ___, film actor (7)
- **3** Bush with fragrant flowers (5)
- **4** Woven shopping bag (6)
- **5** Cocktail made of gin or vodka with dry vermouth (7)
- **6** Vigilant, awake (5)
- **7** Child's comforter (5)
- **12** Cane spirit (3)
- **14** As well (3)
- **15** Conveyance that transports people (7)
- **17** Country, capital Quito (7)
- **18** Rouse, stir up (7)
- **19** Antiquities, keepsakes (6)
- **20** Condition (5)
- **21** Unjustified (5)
- **22** Tasting sour (5)

460

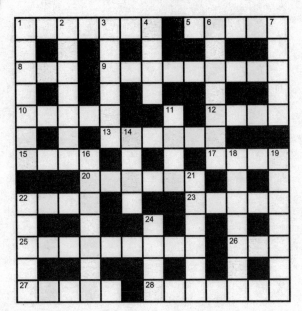

Across

1 Down payment (7)
5 Alloy of copper and zinc (5)
8 Earth's nearest star (3)
9 Brightly coloured capsicum (3,6)
10 Plea of being elsewhere (5)
12 Once ____ a time (4)
13 Deer's horn (6)
15 Pulls sharply (4)
17 Regular (4)
20 Ill-tempered (6)
22 Native of the country formerly known as Siam (4)
23 Welsh breed of dog (5)
25 Feeling of longing for something past (9)
26 Distinction of honour (inits) (3)
27 Showing self-interest and shrewdness (5)
28 Witchcraft (7)

Down

1 Far-off (7)
2 Awaiting conclusion or confirmation (7)
3 Country, capital Belgrade (6)
4 Put things in order (4)
6 State of elated bliss (7)
7 Alarm (5)
11 Charitable gifts (4)
14 Standard (4)
16 Besotted (7)
18 Containing too many words (7)
19 Artlessness (7)
21 Oblong cream puff (6)
22 Mixer drink (5)
24 Ova (4)

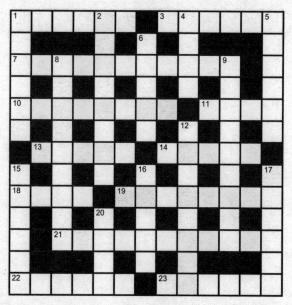

Across

1 Midnight meeting of witches (6)
3 Farm tool used to prepare the soil prior to sowing (6)
7 Unenduring, transient (11)
10 Told (8)
11 Joint protected in front by the patella (4)
13 Rolled up, as with straw or hay (5)
14 Walked through water (5)
18 Prepare for printing (4)
19 Walt Disney film of 1940 (8)
21 Thing done successfully with effort, skill or courage (11)
22 Season of the year (6)
23 Far from the intended target (6)

Down

1 Underweight (6)
2 Medium for radio and television broadcasting (8)
4 Vegetable, emblem of Wales (4)
5 Cyber-terrorist (6)
6 Thin disc of unleavened bread used in a religious service (5)
8 Latin phrase meaning for each person (3,6)
9 American state, capital Nashville (9)
12 Serving woman (8)
15 Arm of the Indian Ocean between Africa and Arabia (3,3)
16 Dog ___, tattered (5)
17 Hearty and lusty, crude (6)
20 Which person? (4)

462

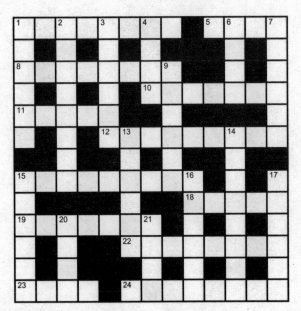

Across

1 Contrary (8)
5 Wish harm upon (4)
8 Driven crazy (8)
10 Early part of night (7)
11 Assign (5)
12 Spaceman (9)
15 Thistle-like flower head with edible fleshy leaves (9)
18 Disgrace (5)
19 Document certifying successful completion of a course (7)
22 Vulnerability to the elements (8)
23 Sharpen by rubbing (4)
24 Protective strap in a car (4,4)

Down

1 Out-of-date (slang) (3,3)
2 Having undergone infection (8)
3 Musical composition of three or four movements of contrasting forms (6)
4 Affectedly dainty or refined (4)
6 Not in favour of (4)
7 Zero (6)
9 Antonin ____, Czech composer (1841–1904) (6)
13 Plot, plan (6)
14 Rotating coil of a dynamo (8)
15 Royal prince (6)
16 Bodyguard (6)
17 Smallest in number (6)
20 Gait (4)
21 Shaft on which a wheel rotates (4)

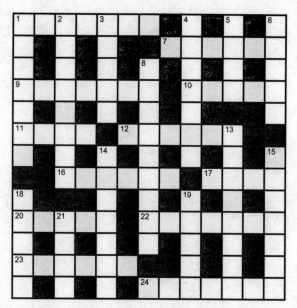

Across

1 Ancient Greek city, site of the Temple of Artemis (7)

7 Mystical belief based on Hebrew scriptures (6)

9 Combatted (7)

10 Bread-raising agent (5)

11 British peer (4)

12 Hooded waterproof jacket (6)

16 Ancient ruler of Persia (6)

17 First James Bond film (2,2)

20 Blackbird (5)

22 Farewell (7)

23 Merchant who sells foodstuffs (6)

24 Smearing with bitumen (7)

Down

1 Rendered capable for some task (7)

2 Bullied, intimidated (8)

3 Bony skeleton of the head (5)

4 Legal representatives (7)

5 Molten rock (4)

6 Careless speed (5)

8 Capital of Scotland (9)

13 Pacific island republic, capital Tarawa (8)

14 Having decorative ruffles (7)

15 Canvas receptacle from which a horse can feed (7)

18 In preliminary or sketchy form (5)

19 Grinding tooth (5)

21 Desist (4)

464

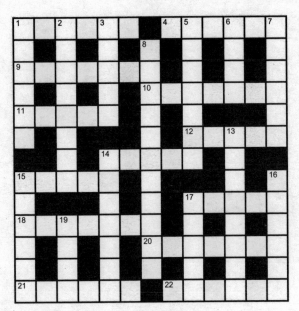

Across

1 Lessen (6)
4 Characteristic pronunciation (6)
9 Grassy plain (7)
10 Make free from confusion or ambiguity (4,3)
11 Small areas of land surrounded by water (5)
12 Sweet substance (5)
14 Band around a horse's belly (5)
15 Brood (on) (5)
17 Motorised bicycle (5)
18 Defraud (7)
20 Open framework (7)
21 Thin sliver of wood (6)
22 Secret or hidden (6)

Down

1 Fix (6)
2 Time limit (8)
3 Ringlets (5)
5 Hold dear (7)
6 Reverberation (4)
7 Salt used especially in baking powder (6)
8 With great urgency (11)
13 Black lead (8)
14 Make or become happy (7)
15 Object thrown in athletic competitions (6)
16 Season preceding Christmas (6)
17 Paris underground railway (5)
19 Material effigy worshipped as a god (4)

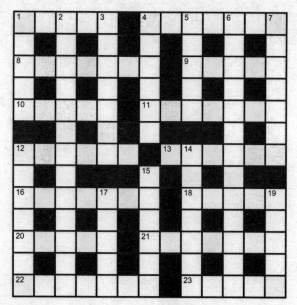

Across

1 Impersonate (5)
4 Potato slice cooked in batter (7)
8 Diacritical mark sometimes placed below the letter 'c' (7)
9 Edible crustacean (5)
10 Establish (3,2)
11 Oval (7)
12 Monster of which Medusa was a type (6)
13 Aid, be of help (6)
16 More mentally alert (7)
18 Sun-dried brick (5)
20 Group of elite soldiers (1-4)
21 More festive (7)
22 Adornment that hangs from a piece of jewellery (7)
23 Isle and county of southern England (5)

Down

1 Scorns, derides (5)
2 Large inland sea (13)
3 West Indian song (7)
4 Very frightened (6)
5 Scandalise (5)
6 Toxic condition once caused by an additive used in paint (4,9)
7 Sharply biting or acrid especially in taste (7)
12 Source of illumination that burns a fuel derived from coal (3,4)
14 Small brownish songbird (7)
15 On time (6)
17 Resort city in western Florida (5)
19 White heron (5)

466

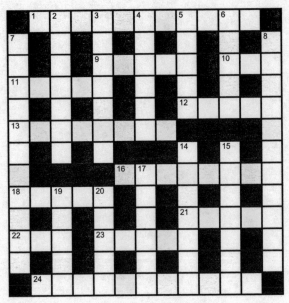

Across

1 Laundress (11)
9 Parody (5)
10 Scull (3)
11 Behaves in a sneaky and secretive manner (5)
12 Organs located in the chest (5)
13 Portable travelling bag for carrying clothes (8)
16 Native of Manila, for example (8)
18 Wanderer (5)
21 Criminal who takes property (5)
22 Add together (3)
23 Semi-precious stone with streaked colouring (5)
24 Writing implement (8,3)

Down

2 Artificial human (7)
3 Cushion for kneeling on (as when praying in church) (7)
4 Largest of the Dodecanese islands (6)
5 Edible organs of an animal (5)
6 Fruit of the oak (5)
7 Conjuror, prestidigitator (11)
8 After-dinner drink made with whiskey (5,6)
14 Water tank (7)
15 Obvious to the eye (7)
17 Herbivorous lizard of tropical America (6)
19 West Indian dance (5)
20 Deplete (of resources) (5)

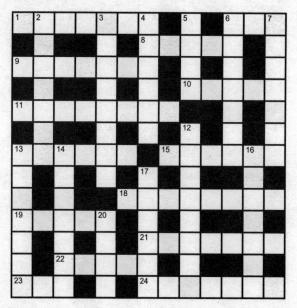

Across

1 King who unknowingly killed his father and married his mother (7)
6 Profound emotion inspired by a deity (3)
8 Changes direction (5)
9 Lady's bedroom or private sitting room (7)
10 Sharp part of a knife (5)
11 US state (8)
13 Person who lives by asking for money or food (6)
15 Brine-cured (6)
18 Not usual (8)
19 Workmanship (5)
21 Puzzles (7)
22 Golf course by the sea (5)
23 Legendary popular music pianist, ___ Charles (3)
24 Verbal defamation of character (7)

Down

2 Characterised by strong feelings (7)
3 Marked by rash extravagance (8)
4 Narrow channel of the sea joining two larger bodies of water (6)
5 Baby's bed (4)
6 Sudden attack (7)
7 Went in (7)
12 Either of two states (North and South) of the USA (8)
13 Retailer of meat (7)
14 To an extraordinary degree (7)
16 Issue from a source (7)
17 Be constantly talking or worrying about something (6)
20 Lilliputian (4)

468

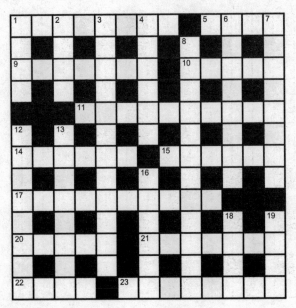

Across

1 Baked thick biscuit made from oats, syrup and butter (8)
5 Yarn arranged lengthways on a loom (4)
9 Practicality (7)
10 Further from the centre (5)
11 Contour economically or efficiently (10)
14 Insightfulness (6)
15 Heavenly beings (6)
17 Full of rough and exuberant animal spirits (10)
20 Monarch (5)
21 To put it briefly (2,1,4)
22 Cloth covering to keep a teapot warm (4)
23 Officials expected to ensure fair play (8)

Down

1 Military stronghold (4)
2 Biblical first man (4)
3 Partnership designed to share risk or expertise (5,7)
4 Upward slope in the centre of a road (6)
6 Achieved (8)
7 Marked by a disposition to oppose and contradict (8)
8 Corresponding in size or degree (12)
12 Uncivilised (8)
13 Dead skin at the base of fingernails or toenails (8)
16 Expensive white fur (6)
18 Pigmented spot on the skin (4)
19 Probabilities (4)

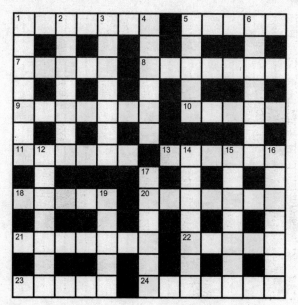

Across

- **1** Rise to one's feet (5,2)
- **5** Spicy tomato sauce (5)
- **7** Collection of maps (5)
- **8** Thin layer covering a surface (7)
- **9** Popular pub entertainment (7)
- **10** Capital of Afghanistan (5)
- **11** Give to a charity (6)
- **13** Chum (6)
- **18** Robbery at gunpoint (5)
- **20** Guarantee as meeting a certain standard (7)
- **21** Letters from devotees to a celebrity (3,4)
- **22** Correspond (5)
- **23** Legendary outlaw, ___ Hood (5)
- **24** Take back (7)

Down

- **1** Piled, one on top the other (7)
- **2** Device on an aircraft that controls lateral motion (7)
- **3** Twist and press out of shape (7)
- **4** Protester stationed outside a place of work (6)
- **5** Had a strong unpleasant smell (5)
- **6** Capital of Puerto Rico (3,4)
- **12** Aromatic Mediterranean herb used in cooking (7)
- **14** Beaming (7)
- **15** Ancient state of central Italy (7)
- **16** Most profound (7)
- **17** Distributor of playing cards (6)
- **19** Educate in a skill (5)

470

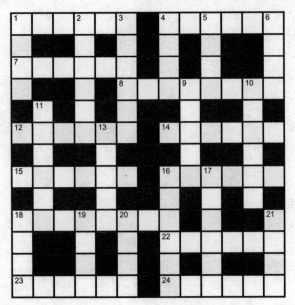

Across

1 Emotional wound or shock (6)
4 Virtuoso (6)
7 Dawdle (6)
8 Not suitable for food (8)
12 Capital of Austria (6)
14 Extensively, far and wide (6)
15 Inelastic tissues connecting muscles to bones (6)
16 Wounded with the teeth (6)
18 Head of a government department (8)
22 Person who handles equipment for travelling entertainers (6)
23 Plant with spiny bracts (6)
24 Nuts or fruit pieces in a sugar paste (6)

Down

1 Narrated (4)
2 Improvement (6)
3 Large continent (6)
4 Moon about (4)
5 House attached to another (4)
6 Ill-mannered (4)
9 City in the United Arab Emirates (5)
10 Shaped masses of baked bread (6)
11 Woman's two-piece bathing suit (6)
13 Tailed amphibians (5)
16 Infertile (6)
17 Group of coral islands in Micronesia (6)
18 Nearly all (4)
19 Printing fluids (4)
20 Cash register (4)
21 Held back, retained (4)

471

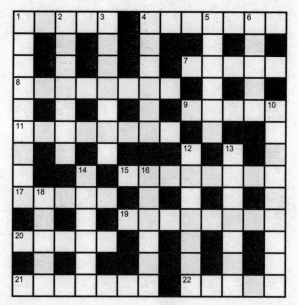

Across

1. Pulse vegetables (5)
4. Short-handled receptacle used with a brush (7)
7. Pair of game birds (5)
8. Elementary particle with a negative charge (8)
9. Three-dimensional (5)
11. Number indicated by the Roman XVIII (8)
15. Done manually, without mechanical aids or devices (8)
17. Radioactive gas (5)
19. Technician who produces moving cartoons (8)
20. Applies heat (5)
21. Homer's epic poem (7)
22. Fashion (5)

Down

1. Flag hoisted when a ship is about to sail (4,5)
2. Hypersensitive reaction (7)
3. Act passed by a legislative body (7)
4. Signify (6)
5. Make a showing (4,2)
6. Computer code representing text (inits) (5)
10. Protective covering in which plants are protected from the cold (4,5)
12. Natives of Bonn, for example (7)
13. Make-believe (7)
14. Universe (6)
16. Airstrip (6)
18. Prize (5)

472

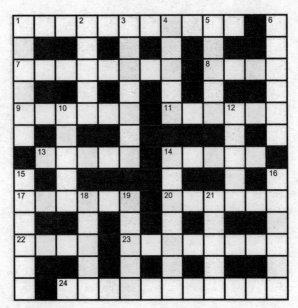

Across

1. Beasts of burden (4,7)
7. Sane (8)
8. Small slender gull with a forked tail (4)
9. Remove the bones from (6)
11. Dig up for reburial (6)
13. Having a sharp inclination (5)
14. Prince who abducted Helen of Troy (5)
17. African antelope with ridged curved horns (6)
20. Human being (6)
22. Religious picture (4)
23. Country, capital Colombo (3,5)
24. Very large or ungainly (11)

Down

1. Decontaminate (6)
2. Small creatures eaten by whales, etc (5)
3. Without taking a break (3-4)
4. Noisy riotous fight (5)
5. Spring-loaded door fastener (5)
6. Outdoor home for a dog (6)
10. Pause during which things are calm (3-2)
12. Divisions of quantity (5)
14. Capsicum spice (7)
15. Fondness (6)
16. Dangerous (6)
18. Declare invalid (5)
19. Greek author of fables (5)
21. Cook with dry heat (5)

473

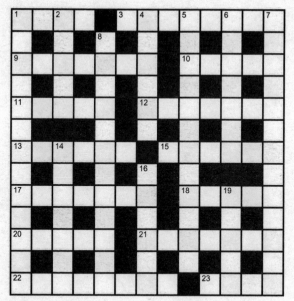

Across
1 Refuse heap (4)
3 Remarkably rapid (8)
9 Group that released *One Step Beyond* and *Night Boat to Cairo* (7)
10 Number indicated by the Roman VII (5)
11 Historical object (5)
12 Capital of Cyprus (7)
13 In a hasty and foolhardy manner (6)
15 Quarters for military personnel (6)
17 Involuntary vibration (7)
18 Stroll, saunter (5)
20 John ___, pioneering US astronaut (5)
21 Burdensome (7)
22 Went back over (8)
23 Information reported in the papers (4)

Down
1 Light brown sweetening agent originally from Guyana (8,5)
2 Metal disk awarded to a winner (5)
4 Providing relief (6)
5 Part of the Pacific Ocean (4,5,3)
6 Act of rewriting something (7)
7 Vision correctors worn directly on the eye (7,6)
8 Island to the east of Australia and north of New Zealand (3,9)
14 Pupil (7)
16 Furrow (6)
19 Separated into pieces (5)

474

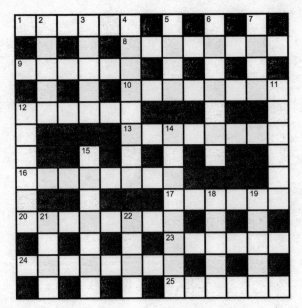

Across

1 Horse's fastest pace (6)
8 Intensified in value or beauty (8)
9 Foam used in hair styling (6)
10 Belief that all violence is unjustifiable (8)
12 Stiffening substance used on textiles (6)
13 Witness (8)
16 Summons to attend a court of law (8)
17 Examine (6)
20 Inebriate, sot (8)
23 Indifferently, carelessly (6)
24 Radio receiver (8)
25 Part by which a thing is picked up (6)

Down

2 In the air (5)
3 Unsuccessful person (5)
4 Small viewing aperture in a door (8)
5 Elegant and stylish (4)
6 Livery (7)
7 Devices which fit locks (4)
11 Of the sea (6)
12 Cooked in a marinade (6)
14 Marked by great carelessness (8)
15 Light cakes (7)
18 Synthetic fabric (5)
19 Large group of fish (5)
21 Barrier consisting of a horizontal bar and supports (4)
22 Figure-skating jump involving a turn in mid air (4)

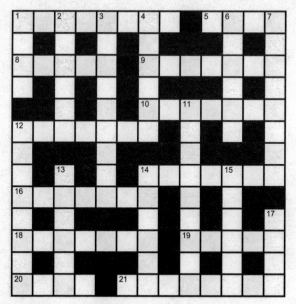

Across

1 Earmarked, reserved (3,5)
5 Capital of Norway (4)
8 Venomous hooded snake (5)
9 Transported in one's arms (7)
10 Country known as Burma (7)
12 At short range (5,2)
14 Opening giving access to a drain (7)
16 Staying power (7)
18 Took small bites (7)
19 Distinguish oneself (5)
20 Swarm (4)
21 Object of loathing (8)

Down

1 Unwell (4)
2 Island in the West Indies (6)
3 Long strings of pasta (9)
4 Flee (6)
6 Mark of infamy (6)
7 Stubbornly persistent in wrongdoing (8)
11 Expiation (9)
12 Edible item often roasted on an open fire (8)
13 Wager (6)
14 Unmarried young woman (6)
15 Prophet (6)
17 Bloodsucking parasite (4)

476

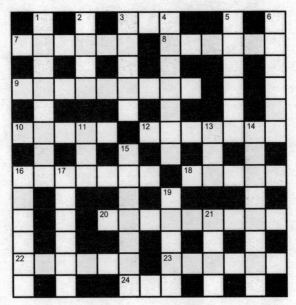

Across

3 Weapon for shooting arrows (3)
7 North American native dog (6)
8 Fit to be eaten (6)
9 Sparkling citrus fruit drink (9)
10 Scent, smell (5)
12 Made by intertwining threads in a series of connected loops (7)
16 Large water bird (7)
18 Room used for reading and writing (5)
20 Accompanying, chaperoning (9)
22 Offer to pay a higher price for (6)
23 Fastening device used on clothing (6)
24 Stretch (3)

Down

1 Soft food made by boiling oatmeal (8)
2 Earth's natural satellite (4)
3 Sloping edge on a cutting tool (5)
4 Marriage ceremony (7)
5 Missing (6)
6 Decapitate (6)
11 Israeli submachine-gun (3)
13 Yellow-coloured explosive compound (inits) (3)
14 Imperil (8)
15 Edge of a road or path (7)
16 Racing bird (6)
17 Sign attached to a car indicating that the driver is a learner (1-5)
19 Intoxicating liquor (coll) (5)
21 Cassette (4)

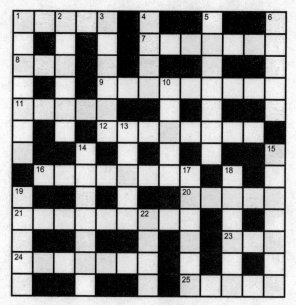

Across

1 Move to a higher point (5)
7 Egg white (7)
8 Dashed (3)
9 Anyone at all (9)
11 Skin disease affecting domestic animals (5)
12 Heating appliance (8)
16 Closing violently (8)
20 Sky-blue (5)
21 Act of putting one thing into another (9)
23 Bovine creature (3)
24 Joint of a finger when the fist is closed (7)
25 Bad-tempered and irritable (coll) (5)

Down

1 Firm chewy candy (7)
2 Period of play in cricket (6)
3 Maker of beer (6)
4 Light drawn around the head of a saint (4)
5 Period between childhood and adolescence (7)
6 Vicious angry growl (5)
10 Direct descendant (5)
13 Allow to enter (5)
14 Recurrent rhythmical series, beat (7)
15 Road for high-speed traffic in the USA (7)
17 Male goose (6)
18 Mellifluous (6)
19 Touches with the tongue (5)
22 Mountain goat (4)

478

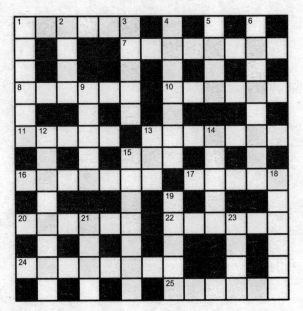

Across

1 Tortilla chips (6)
7 Concerning someone's private life (8)
8 Imperial capacity measure equal to four pecks (6)
10 Seat used by a rider (6)
11 Perspire (5)
13 Reinstate (7)
15 Ground containing a mat of grass and grass roots (3)
16 Marked by rude or peremptory shortness (7)
17 Salt water (5)
20 Prince Consort to Queen Victoria (6)
22 Sibling (6)
24 Occurring within an institution or community (8)
25 Trading place (6)

Down

1 Rain-bearing cloud (6)
2 Tight-fitting hats (4)
3 Cause to flow out or over (5)
4 Put on clothes (7)
5 Pool (4)
6 Witch's brewing pot (8)
9 Cures (5)
12 Combat aircraft (8)
13 Fish eggs (3)
14 Wears out (5)
15 Going well with, complementing (7)
18 Straying from the right course (6)
19 Religious song (5)
21 Garden of Adam and Eve (4)
23 Short, sharp nail with a broad head (4)

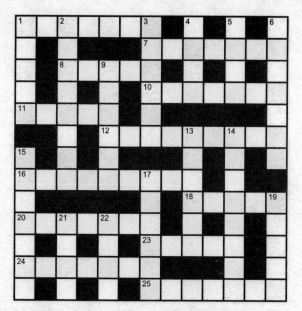

Across

1 Having a cigarette (7)
7 Do away with (7)
8 Brutal (5)
10 Make less visible (7)
11 Run off to wed (5)
12 Elaborate and remarkable display on a lavish scale (9)
16 Gluttonous seabird with a distensible pouch (9)
18 Present (5)
20 Gulp (7)
23 Not silently (5)
24 Ill-prepared (7)
25 Whip used to inflict punishment (7)

Down

1 Kitchen range (5)
2 Swift cursory examination or inspection (coll) (4-4)
3 Aplenty (6)
4 Moves the head in agreement (4)
5 Stead (4)
6 Robbers (7)
9 Agency promoting teaching and the arts (inits) (6)
13 Design marked onto the skin (6)
14 Record of annual dates (8)
15 Represents or performs as if in a play (4,3)
17 Forever (6)
19 In golf, a hole played in two strokes under par (5)
21 City, site of the Taj Mahal (4)
22 Leash (4)

480

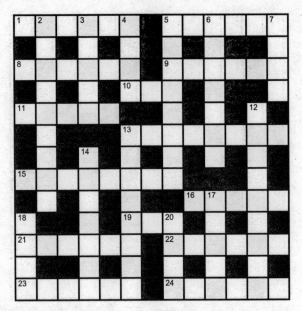

Across

1 Sudden flash (as of lightning) (6)
5 Cuts into two equal pieces (6)
8 Inn (6)
9 Edible seed (6)
10 Liquid mineral (3)
11 Italian poet famous for his *Divine Comedy* (5)
13 Luring of an internet user to reveal personal details (8)
15 Frightening (8)
16 Harsh or corrosive in tone (5)
19 Terminate (3)
21 Icon representing a person, used in internet chat and games (6)
22 Motive (6)
23 Vigour (6)
24 Bosom (6)

Down

2 Public place for light refreshment (3,6)
3 Choose by a vote (5)
4 Game also known as bingo (4)
5 Slope, geographical feature (8)
6 Tediously protracted (7)
7 Alone, unaccompanied (4)
12 In complete agreement (9)
13 Possessions (8)
14 Fried piece of food in batter (7)
17 Pursue (5)
18 Unable to walk (4)
20 Dull, dreary (4)

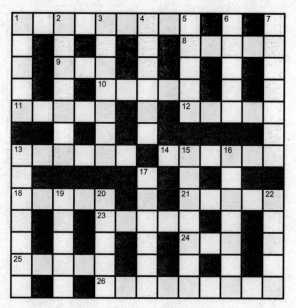

Across

1 Parasitic plant that one might be kissed under (9)
8 Garden tool for cutting grass on lawns (5)
9 Choose (3)
10 Online journal (1-4)
11 Arrangement or neatness (5)
12 Passing from physical life (5)
13 Package of several things tied together (6)
14 Body such as Mars, eg (6)
18 Produces musical tones with the voice (5)
21 German empire (5)
23 Cetacean mammal (5)
24 ____ Tolstoy, writer (3)
25 Elegance and beauty of movement (5)
26 Gloomy disposition (9)

Down

1 Oval fruit with a very large seed (5)
2 Acted as a substitute (5,2)
3 Situated at or extending to the side (7)
4 Stenographer (6)
5 Fix securely (5)
6 Hindu religious teacher (5)
7 Temporary shortage of rainfall (7)
13 Put under a military blockade (7)
15 Siren of German legend (7)
16 Capital of Kenya (7)
17 Hairy facial growths (6)
19 Landlocked Asian country (5)
20 Clean with a broom (5)
22 Living quarters for female relatives in a Muslim household (5)

482

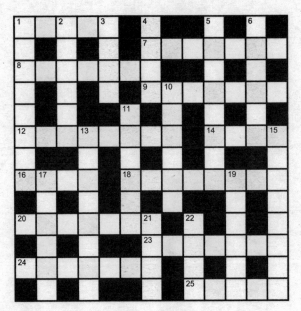

Across

1 Vertical passage into a mine (5)
7 Sale of goods in lots (7)
8 Bowmen (7)
9 Helps by becoming involved (5,2)
12 Travel past (8)
14 Container for a bird (4)
16 Spinning toys (4)
18 Object serving as a model (8)
20 Gives away, deceives (7)
23 Downwind (7)
24 Child's construction set for making mechanical models (TM) (7)
25 Cacophonous (5)

Down

1 Distribute, allocate (5,3)
2 Niche (6)
3 Long arduous journey (4)
4 Sea fish (4)
5 Uncharacteristic (8)
6 Poignant (6)
10 Film of 1991, co-starring Susan Sarandon and Geena Davis, ___ & Louise (6)
11 Larder (6)
13 Limit (8)
15 Commonplace (8)
17 Followed orders (6)
19 Compound which can turn litmus paper blue (6)
21 Blackthorn fruit (4)
22 Harness strap (4)

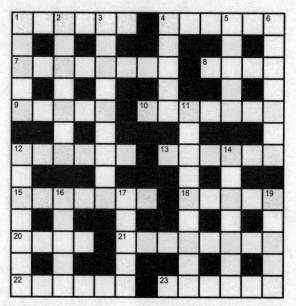

Across

1 Involuntary vibration (6)
4 Infected with bacteria (6)
7 Criminal who commits homicide (8)
8 Unable to speak (4)
9 British author of *The Grass Is Singing* (1950), ___ Lessing (5)
10 Denial (7)
12 One living temporarily in a tent (6)
13 Hairdresser (6)
15 Eight-armed sea creature (7)
18 Fine net used for veils (5)
20 Body of a ship (4)
21 Bearing flowers (8)
22 Regulate (a radio or television set) (4,2)
23 Close-fitting pullover or vest (1-5)

Down

1 Domesticated (5)
2 Tympanic membrane (7)
3 Slumber for longer than intended (9)
4 Rise or move forward (5)
5 Violent young criminals (5)
6 Shoemaker (7)
11 Divisive (9)
12 Type of needlework (7)
14 Vincenzo ___, Italian composer of operas (1801–35) (7)
16 Sharp, hooked claw (5)
17 Characteristic of a city (5)
19 Cardinal number (5)

484

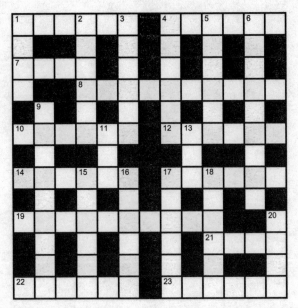

Across

1 On someone's part (6)
4 Sieved (6)
7 Hindu princess (4)
8 Prop thrown in slapstick comedies (7,3)
10 Small pleasure boat powered by cycling (6)
12 Lasso (6)
14 Thrown carelessly (6)
17 Treat with excessive indulgence (6)
19 Flying machine sustained by rotating blades (10)
21 Curved hair growing from the edge of an eyelid (4)
22 Idolised (6)
23 Bounded or limited in magnitude (6)

Down

1 Avian creature (4)
2 Ms Keyes, singer (6)
3 Wall painting (6)
4 Sudden violent wind (6)
5 Fireplace frame (6)
6 Calculated approximately (9)
9 Convalesced (9)
11 Strong washing solution (3)
13 Alias (inits) (3)
15 Machine for chopping bacon (6)
16 Fated (6)
17 Postpone (3,3)
18 Arthurian magician (6)
20 Item of footwear (4)

485

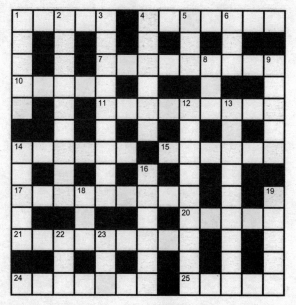

Across

1 Farewell (5)
4 Side view of a face (7)
7 Belonging naturally, essential (9)
10 Tidy and clean feathers with the beak (5)
11 Flattery, especially when persuasive or insincere (5,4)
14 Plaid associated with Scotland (6)
15 Caught sight of (6)
17 Peevishness (9)
20 Slack, lax (5)
21 Make merry (9)
24 Remuneration (7)
25 Magic charm (5)

Down

1 Proficient (5)
2 Translate (9)
3 Remove an application from a computer (9)
4 Plausible glib talk (6)
5 Kimono sash (3)
6 Of a thing (3)
8 Mesh (3)
9 Coated thickly (5)
12 Lacking flavour (9)
13 Ancient Athenian philosopher (384–322 BC) (9)
14 Theme (5)
16 Baby (6)
18 Consumption (3)
19 Substance such as iron or aluminium, for example (5)
22 Set down (3)
23 Fatal disease of cattle (inits) (3)

486

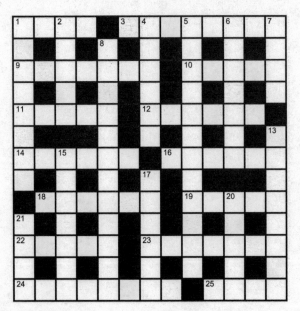

Across

1 Dark purplish-brown colour (4)
3 Egg-laying, Australian creature (8)
9 Padded cloth covering to keep a pot warm (3,4)
10 Squeeze (5)
11 Peers of the realm (5)
12 Fighting forces (6)
14 Salad vegetable (6)
16 Commonly repeated word or phrase (6)
18 March aggressively into another's territory (6)
19 Flip to a vertical position (2-3)
22 Native of Muscat, eg (5)
23 Bring up (7)
24 On the spur of the moment (8)
25 Individual unit (4)

Down

1 Card game played by one person (8)
2 Seat (5)
4 Non-professional person (6)
5 Flexible rulers (4,8)
6 Keep from happening (7)
7 Long strip of fabric (4)
8 British political party (12)
13 Reverie (8)
15 Cord worn around the neck to hold a knife or whistle (7)
17 Disclose (6)
20 Precise (5)
21 Portions of a tree used as firewood (4)

487

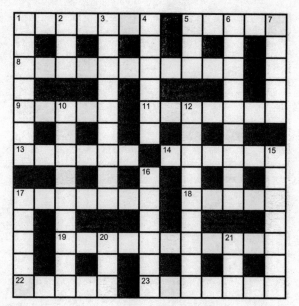

Across

1 Replenishment (7)
5 Evidence (5)
8 Not giving careful consideration (11)
9 Wayside plant with daisy-like flowers (2-3)
11 Drags (a riverbed, for example) (7)
13 Catch in a snare (6)
14 Inclined, bent (6)
17 General rule regarding moral conduct (7)
18 Bohemian dance (5)
19 Lack of thankfulness or appreciation (11)
22 Showing quick and inventive verbal humour (5)
23 Flimsy (7)

Down

1 Horizontal plant stem with shoots above and roots below (7)
2 Short sleep (3)
3 On a large scale, without careful discrimination (9)
4 Scottish landowners (6)
5 Edgar Allan ____, writer (3)
6 Eight-sided (9)
7 Perceives by touch (5)
10 Person who holds radical views (9)
12 Immunity from a duty (9)
15 Boxlike containers in a piece of furniture (7)
16 Royal family that once ruled Scotland (6)
17 Fruit with yellow flesh (5)
20 Light-hearted, carefree (3)
21 Vehicle from another world (inits) (3)

488

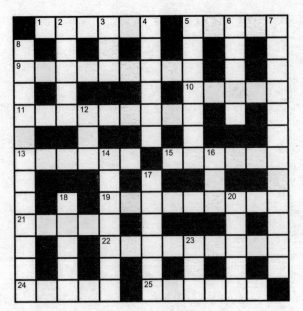

Across

1 Youngest son of Queen Elizabeth II (6)
5 Popular literary genre (abbr) (3-2)
9 Native of Lahore, for example (9)
10 Rice cooked in well-seasoned broth (5)
11 Meat-eating animal (9)
13 Without much speed (6)
15 Paragons (6)
19 Cylindrical masses of earth voided by burrowing creatures (9)
21 Piece of cloth used for drying (5)
22 Turn out in the end (9)
24 Borders (5)
25 Smile affectedly (6)

Down

2 Capital of Senegal (5)
3 Pompous fool (3)
4 Fire-breathing monster (6)
5 Clergyman's salary (7)
6 Short descriptive poem of rural life (5)
7 Body's protection against disease (6,6)
8 Reusable craft for travelling outside the Earth's atmosphere (5,7)
12 At once (3)
14 Anarchical (7)
16 Seventh Greek letter (3)
17 Varieties of domesticated animals within a species (6)
18 Plaything that moves back and forth (5)
20 Digging implement (5)
23 Woollen cap of Scottish origin (3)

Across

4 Child's two-wheeled vehicle operated by foot (7)
7 Pillow (7)
9 Plaything (3)
10 Tendency (5)
11 Inland waterway (5)
12 Centre of a storm (3)
13 Facial postures (11)
19 Applied science (11)
24 Repair (3)
25 Silence (5)
26 Proportion (5)
27 A pair of (3)
28 Cost (7)
29 Emerged from an egg (7)

Down

1 Disperse (7)
2 Slumbering (6)
3 Violin (6)
4 Light informal meals (6)
5 Names of literary compositions (6)
6 Be similar in end sound, eg cat and mat (5)
8 Aware of (4)
14 Sprint (3)
15 Travel across snow (3)
16 Coat a cake with sugar (3)
17 Neither (3)
18 Took no notice of (7)
19 Transfer abroad (6)
20 Caprine animal (4)
21 Required (6)
22 Continent in the northern hemisphere (6)
23 Mean, designate (6)
24 Get (5)

490

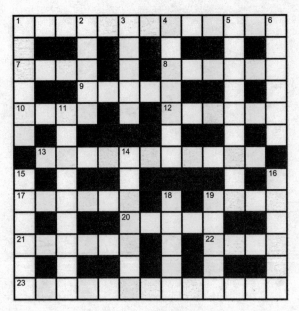

Across

1 Business, organisation (13)
7 Cougar (4)
8 Public speaker (6)
9 Returned from the dead (5)
10 Bill in a restaurant (4)
12 Warning signals that wail (6)
13 Disembowelled (11)
17 Become set (6)
19 Harp used by ancient Greeks (4)
20 Letter such as a, e or i, for example (5)
21 Come out (6)
22 In addition (4)
23 Decays, falls apart (13)

Down

1 Await, anticipate (6)
2 Separate (5)
3 Insect parasitic on warm-blooded animals (5)
4 Back, patronise (7)
5 To a high degree (9)
6 Beat the seeds out of grain (6)
11 City in northern Scotland (9)
14 Nunnery (7)
15 Showing keen practical judgment (6)
16 Courageous men (6)
18 Due (5)
19 South American animal (5)

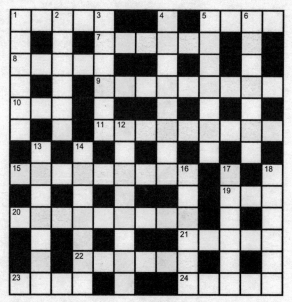

Across

1 Measures of medicine (5)
5 Very dry (4)
7 Belonging to those people (6)
8 No longer new, uninteresting (5)
9 Red wine grape variety (5,4)
10 Each and every (3)
11 Instrument for recording the number of steps taken (9)
15 Uncensored or unrestricted print media (4,5)
19 Steal from a person (3)
20 Concentrated (9)
21 Disciple of Saint Paul (5)
22 Deeply sad (6)
23 Extremely (4)
24 King of Judea who ordered the death of many children (5)

Down

1 Consternation (6)
2 Slow-moving molluscs (6)
3 Come to the fore (4,2)
4 Stringent, strict (8)
5 Into pieces (7)
6 Asked as a guest (7)
12 Rail link between the UK and France (8)
13 Fold in the skin, often as a result of ageing (7)
14 Number, LXX in Roman numerals (7)
16 Preliminary drawing (6)
17 Fissure in the earth's crust (6)
18 Humiliated, shamed (6)

492

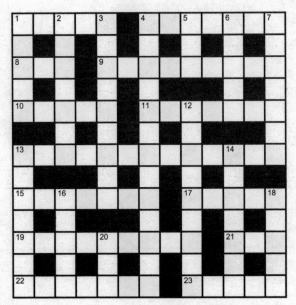

Across

1 Makes a noise like a lion (5)
4 Meantime (7)
8 Nervous twitch (3)
9 Person with an unusual or odd personality (9)
10 Pursue like a ghost (5)
11 Immense clouds of gas and dust in space (7)
13 Film (6,7)
15 Ill-fated liner (7)
17 Implement used to sharpen razors (5)
19 Looseness of the bowels (9)
21 Acquire (3)
22 Spins on an axis (7)
23 Sing the praises of (5)

Down

1 Heave, regurgitate (5)
2 Statement (7)
3 Popular cereal used as a vegetable (9)
4 Not noticeable (13)
5 Silvery metal (3)
6 Relating to the countryside (5)
7 Large heavy knife used for cutting vegetation (7)
12 Behind the scenes in a theatre (9)
13 Principal bullfighter (7)
14 Erect (7)
16 Extended area of land (5)
18 Colourful part of a flower (5)
20 Decay (3)

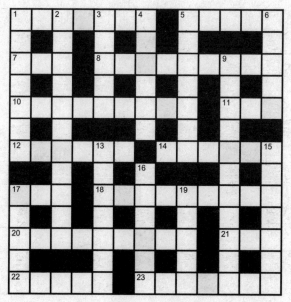

Across

1. Throw away (7)
5. Elephant's proboscis (5)
7. Yoko ___, widow of John Lennon (3)
8. Russian musical instrument (9)
10. Prepare (4,5)
11. That girl (3)
12. Plant stalks used as roofing material (6)
14. Frankfurter served in a bun (3,3)
17. Chinese cooking pan (3)
18. Kill (animals) for food (9)
20. Aristocratic (9)
21. Painting, sculpture, etc (3)
22. Take an oath (5)
23. Dapple (7)

Down

1. Small carpet placed in an entranceway to a building (7)
2. Exchange where security trading is conducted (5,6)
3. Deep yellow colour (5)
4. Soap series about the Ewing family (6)
5. Hunt cry telling that the fox has been sighted (5-2)
6. Jack in a pack of cards (5)
9. Shorter side of a curved racecourse (6,5)
13. Bank employee (7)
15. Instrument of execution (7)
16. Established customs (6)
17. Rubs gently (5)
19. Aladdin's spirit (5)

494

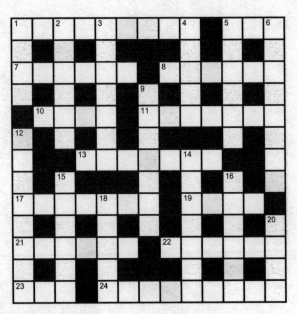

Across

1 Instance that does not conform to a rule (9)
5 Fill out (3)
7 Miscellaneous (6)
8 Misgivings (6)
10 Departs (4)
11 Savouring (7)
13 Praise enthusiastically or extravagantly (7)
17 Short preview of a film or TV programme (7)
19 Neuter (a female cat, for example) (4)
21 Yield to another's wish or opinion (6)
22 Seller (6)
23 Pertinent (3)
24 Tiny fastener with a threaded shank and no head (4,5)

Down

1 Direction of the rising sun (4)
2 Is unable to (6)
3 Sun umbrella (7)
4 Words used to refer to people, places or objects (5)
5 Abnormally deficient in colour (6)
6 Be of different opinions (8)
9 Cook rapidly over a high heat while mixing briskly (4,3)
12 Body of water to the east of Great Britain (5,3)
14 Secures, fixes (7)
15 Opening move in chess (6)
16 Row of unravelled stitches in a stocking (6)
18 Deviating from the truth (5)
20 Become larger (4)

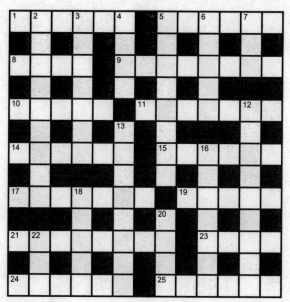

Across

1 Hind portion of a side of bacon (6)
5 Releases (4,2)
8 Hard fruits (4)
9 Unaware of (8)
10 Oddment (5)
11 Science subject taught at school (7)
14 Motorless plane (6)
15 Clockwork model of the solar system (6)
17 Increased threefold (7)
19 Aqualung (5)
21 Psychological disorder characterised by delusions of persecution (8)
23 Employs (4)
24 Breaks with established customs (6)
25 Appraisal of the value of something (6)

Down

2 Like an uncle in kindness or indulgence (9)
3 Popular hot condiment (7)
4 Carpentry pin (4)
5 Midday meal (8)
6 Wheel coverings (5)
7 Alcoholic spirit flavoured with juniper berries (3)
12 Arm of the Atlantic Ocean (9)
13 Causing fear by threatening great harm (8)
16 Recently enlisted soldier (7)
18 Strong flame that burns brightly (5)
20 Travelling show (4)
22 Large monkey (3)

496

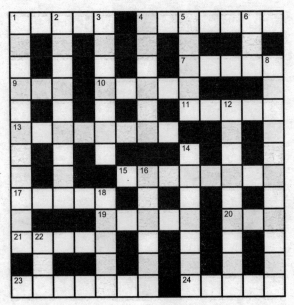

Across

1 Product of an oyster (5)
4 Tube-shaped structure of the inner ear (7)
7 Agent which assists colonic irrigation (5)
9 Twosome (3)
10 Male deer (5)
11 Bushy plant (5)
13 Headlight reflectors set into a road (4-4)
15 Mayfly (8)
17 Burn with steam (5)
19 Jordan's only port (5)
20 Alcoholic brew (3)
21 Clean with hard rubbing (5)
23 Greek mythological flying horse (7)
24 Grass border along a road (5)

Down

1 Dies earlier than (11)
2 Concentrated bitters for food and beverages (9)
3 Oil extracted from the flax plant (7)
4 Bring into existence (6)
5 Green salad vegetable (5)
6 Deciduous tree (3)
8 Mixed feelings or emotions (11)
12 Scented liquid used as a perfume (4,5)
14 City in western Israel (3,4)
16 Keyboard instruments (6)
18 Repairs a worn or torn hole (5)
22 Sebastian ___, former athlete (3)

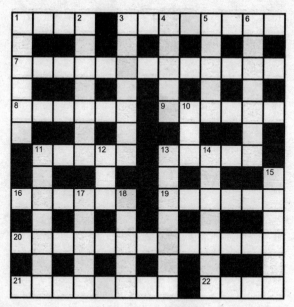

Across

1 Flexible containers (4)
3 Anyone below the rank of peer (8)
7 Preference that comes from considerable experience (8,5)
8 Very hot, tapering pepper (6)
9 Fidel ____, former Cuban socialist leader (6)
11 Mountain call (5)
13 Built-up areas (5)
16 Flings up, as with a coin, for example (6)
19 Sir Malcolm ____, English composer and trumpeter (6)
20 Inadvertent (13)
21 Deserter (usually of an oppressive regime) (8)
22 Exchanged for money (4)

Down

1 Cook (vegetables) briefly (6)
2 Sordid (7)
3 Showing warmth and friendliness (7)
4 Doctor in the armed forces (5)
5 Semi-transparent gemstones (5)
6 Obtains by coercion or intimidation (7)
10 Flurry (3)
11 Capital of Cameroon (7)
12 Biblical first woman (3)
13 Farm vehicle (7)
14 Microsoft operating system (7)
15 Woolly-headed (6)
17 On account of (5)
18 Endearing (5)

498

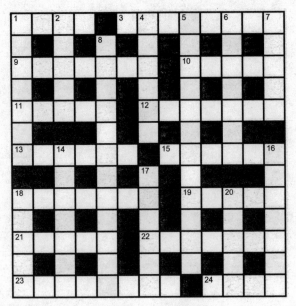

Across

1 Have to (4)
3 Shipwrecked person (8)
9 Of great consequence (7)
10 Spirit dispenser (5)
11 Largest of Jordan's cities (5)
12 Existing as an essential characteristic (7)
13 Arouse or elicit a feeling (6)
15 Distance end to end (6)
18 Lacking professional skill (7)
19 State in north-eastern India (5)
21 Joint in the leg (5)
22 More impoverished (7)
23 Meal accompaniment (4,4)
24 Long fishes (4)

Down

1 Knead (7)
2 Watery fluid of the blood (5)
4 Descend by rope (6)
5 Someone who deliberately stirs up a problem (12)
6 Applying moisture (7)
7 Sailing vessel (5)
8 Crazy, insane (coll) (5,3,4)
14 Snapped (7)
16 Upper-arm bone (7)
17 Dried plums (6)
18 Collect or gather, hoard (5)
20 Derogatory, sneering (5)

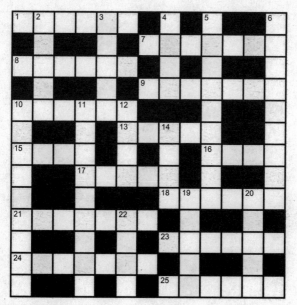

Across
1 Fairness (6)
7 Supplier of refreshments (7)
8 Bicycle for two riders (6)
9 Julia ___, actress (7)
10 Small carnivore with short legs and an elongated body (6)
13 In many cases or instances (5)
15 Racing sled for one or two people (4)
16 Inactive (4)
17 Moving or extending horizontally on (5)
18 Borne on the water (6)
21 Pleasure trips (7)
23 Inaccessible and sparsely populated (6)
24 Reverberating (7)
25 Notice for sale (abbr) (6)

Down
2 Tremble with seismic vibrations (5)
3 Melodic subject of a musical composition (5)
4 Palm starch used in puddings (4)
5 Plant lasting for more than two or three seasons (9)
6 Elected head of a republic (9)
10 Self-discipline (9)
11 Tool used to press clothes (5,4)
12 Company emblem (4)
14 Roman cloak (4)
19 Demon (5)
20 Sacred table in a church (5)
22 Unit of heredity found on a chromosome (4)

500

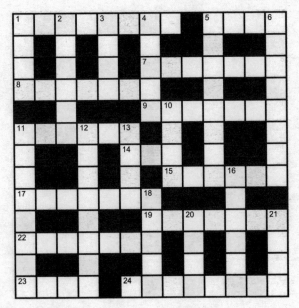

Across

1 Taking pleasure (8)
5 Blemish, defect (4)
7 Junior diplomat (7)
8 Beatles song, ___ Rigby (7)
9 Russian artificial satellite, the first to orbit the Earth (7)
11 Avoiding waste (6)
14 Ancient (3)
15 Treeless Russian plain (6)
17 Explosive device attached to a vehicle (3,4)
19 Stretchy fabric (7)
22 Type of refrigerator (7)
23 Mouth parts (4)
24 Crystalline rock that can be cut for jewellery (8)

Down

1 Fourth largest of the Great Lakes (4)
2 State capital of Alaska (6)
3 Involuntary intake of breath through a wide open mouth (4)
4 Approaches (5)
5 Crack in a bone (8)
6 Debris (8)
10 Stuffs with soft material (4)
11 Emphatic (8)
12 Joseph ___, propaganda minister in Nazi Germany (8)
13 Rich soil (4)
16 Root vegetable (6)
18 Capital of Switzerland (5)
20 Kingsley ___, 20th century author (4)
21 Informal restaurant (4)

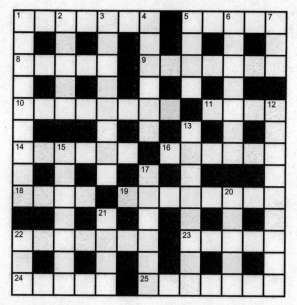

Across

1 Watch attentively (7)
5 Contest between opposing teams (5)
8 Register formally as a participant (5)
9 Cumbersome (7)
10 Came into view (8)
11 Moved very fast (4)
14 Country that shares a border with Egypt (6)
16 Say again (6)
18 Pleasant (4)
19 Think back (8)
22 Extremely old (7)
23 Fruit, an important source of oil (5)
24 Item of bed linen (5)
25 Look up to, esteem (7)

Down

1 Surgical procedure (9)
2 Thick sugary liquid (5)
3 Let go of (8)
4 Substance covering the crown of a tooth (6)
5 Create (4)
6 Tread on and crush (7)
7 Owned (3)
12 Cleansing agent (9)
13 Willing to give, charitable (8)
15 Use again after processing (7)
17 Liquid produced by a flower (6)
20 Salt water (5)
21 Retained (4)
22 Beast of burden (3)

502

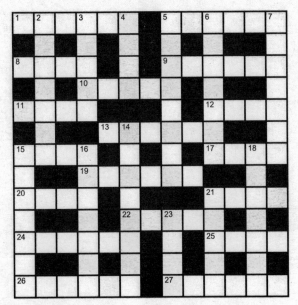

Across

1 Silver-white element (6)
5 Empower (6)
8 Establishments where alcohol is served (4)
9 Occupation, job (6)
10 End in a particular way (5)
11 Restrict one's food intake (4)
12 Gumbo (4)
13 Shooting star (6)
15 Abounding with fog (4)
17 Hardwood (4)
19 Real (6)
20 Metal food containers (4)
21 Bulk (4)
22 Jewish scholar (5)
24 Norway lobsters (6)
25 In one's sleeping place (4)
26 Employee (6)
27 Light tanker for supplying water or fuel (6)

Down

2 Egg-shaped and flutey-toned musical instrument (7)
3 Thing of value (5)
4 Bathroom fixtures (4)
5 And so on (Latin) (2,6)
6 Aerodrome (7)
7 Set aside (7)
14 Outer surface (8)
15 Tool used to cut metal (7)
16 Face veil worn by Muslim women (7)
18 Morally strict (7)
21 Sound made by a cat (5)
23 Aggressive remark directed like a missile at a person (4)

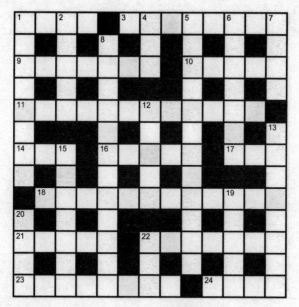

Across

1 Infrequent (4)
3 Insignia used by the medical profession (8)
9 Filled with bewilderment (7)
10 Bus garage (5)
11 Belonging to the present time (12)
14 Negative word (3)
16 Crisp bread (5)
17 Cane spirit (3)
18 Contest in which intelligence rather than violence is used (6,2,4)
21 Bingo (5)
22 Motionlessness (7)
23 Social activities and entertainment following a day on the piste (5-3)
24 Australian term for a young kangaroo (4)

Down

1 Having a ruddy complexion (8)
2 Resident of the capital of Italy (5)
4 Append (3)
5 Having insufficient employees (12)
6 Male ruler (7)
7 Satisfy completely (4)
8 Intended to attract notice and impress others (12)
12 Location, whereabouts (5)
13 Diplomatic messenger (8)
15 Betrayer of one's country (7)
19 Presentation, briefly (5)
20 Primitive chlorophyll-containing, mainly aquatic organism (4)
22 Gall (3)

504

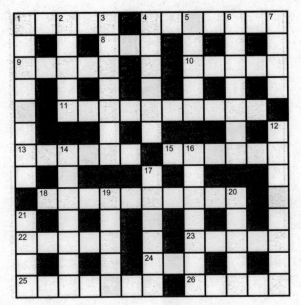

Across

1 Has in mind (5)
4 Heavy material used to ensure stability (7)
8 Also (3)
9 Low humming sound (5)
10 Discontinue (5)
11 Learner (10)
13 Sickness (6)
15 Wax drawing implement (6)
18 Expecting the best (10)
22 Level betting (5)
23 Blood pump (5)
24 Expert (3)
25 Lax (7)
26 Grooved surface of a pneumatic tyre (5)

Down

1 Substance taken to alleviate the symptoms of disease (8)
2 Hawaiian greeting (5)
3 Church tower (7)
4 Corpses (6)
5 Lawful (5)
6 Lawlessness (7)
7 Tall perennial woody plant (4)
12 Turned inside out (8)
14 Innumerable but many (7)
16 Move by degrees in one direction only (7)
17 Lion or tiger, for example (3,3)
19 Bring out an official document (5)
20 Make sore by rubbing (5)
21 Hollow metal device that rings when struck (4)

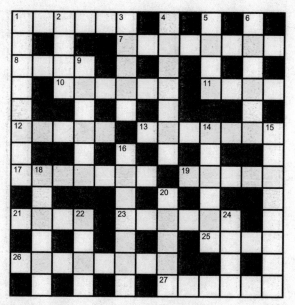

Across

1 Plant similar to the rhododendron (6)
7 Carry on (8)
8 Cast off (4)
10 Walk unsteadily (6)
11 Hyphen (4)
12 Lone Star State of the USA (5)
13 Depending on free oxygen or air (7)
17 Contempt (7)
19 Motorcycle rider (5)
21 Estimation (4)
23 Terminal section of the alimentary canal (6)
25 Cylindrical store-tower (4)
26 Impetus (8)
27 Person authorised to conduct religious worship (6)

Down

1 Mixed haphazardly (8)
2 Assist in doing wrong (4)
3 Extremely sharp (5)
4 Underwater breathing device (7)
5 William ____ , Scottish pirate (4)
6 Breakfast food (6)
9 One whose age has impaired his intellect (6)
14 Abominable (6)
15 Haggard, drawn (8)
16 Move from one country to another (7)
18 Not outside a building (6)
20 One who is playfully mischievous (5)
22 Not many (1,3)
24 Fail to hit (4)

506

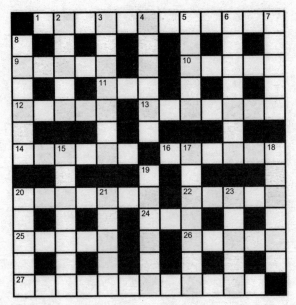

Across

1 Meat-based delicacy (5,7)
9 Fountain nymph (5)
10 Flexible twig of a willow (5)
11 Carbon dioxide, for example (3)
12 Latin American dance (5)
13 Autumn month (7)
14 Pinned down (6)
16 Act against an attack (6)
20 Enfold (7)
22 Arm joint (5)
24 Bow (3)
25 Panorama (5)
26 Abrupt (5)
27 Carefree and happy (12)

Down

2 Mode of expression (5)
3 Final stages of an extended process of negotiation (7)
4 Lend flavour to (6)
5 German submarine in World War II (1-4)
6 Diffusing warmth and friendliness (7)
7 Departure from what is ethically acceptable (5)
8 Coincidence, accord (6)
15 Floe (7)
17 Device that causes something to be removed (7)
18 One who uses a divining rod to find water (6)
19 Former parish official (6)
20 Fibre used for making rope (5)
21 Act of stealing (5)
23 Canal boat (5)

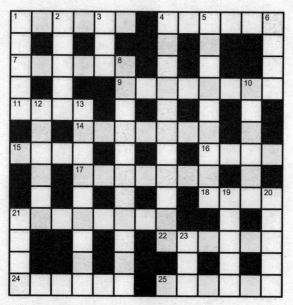

Across

1 Marked by hard-headed intelligence (6)

4 Decorated the surface of by inserting wood, etc (6)

7 Language of Israel (6)

9 Fruit extract used for cooking (5,3)

11 Bobbin (4)

14 Moving toward a centre (7)

15 Deep prolonged loud noise (4)

16 Chief port of Yemen (4)

17 Voter (7)

18 Abominable snowman (4)

21 Large bottle with small handles at the neck (8)

22 Country, capital Banjul (6)

24 Conformed to some shape or size (6)

25 In a state of expectant irritability (2,4)

Down

1 Detest (5)

2 Item of dining room furniture (5)

3 Definite article (3)

4 Intimating (11)

5 Celebrated in fable (9)

6 Distribute playing cards (4)

8 Australian musical instrument, played by holding in both hands and flexing (6,5)

10 To set in from the margin (6)

12 Develop (6)

13 Focus of public attention (9)

19 Flowed back (5)

20 Extremely angry (5)

21 Unable to hear (4)

23 Beard found on a bract of grass (3)

508

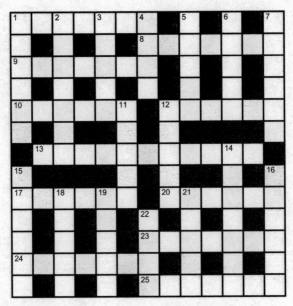

Across

1 Bag that fills with air or liquid (7)
8 Submit or live through (7)
9 Accuse of a wrong (7)
10 Asiatic wild ass (6)
12 Hard-cased arthropod (6)
13 Road construction vehicle (11)
17 Accompany (6)
20 Paper handkerchief (6)
23 Transparent type of cellulose film (7)
24 Experiencing motion nausea (7)
25 Ask earnestly (7)

Down

1 Bonfire signal (6)
2 Alongside each other (7)
3 Ambition (5)
4 Ladder step (4)
5 Condensed but memorable saying (5)
6 Slang of thieves and vagabonds (5)
7 Discuss, talk about (6)
11 Send (payment) (5)
12 Swell, puff up (5)
14 Bring into servitude (7)
15 Television receiver (6)
16 Vast, sandy region (6)
18 Framework of a military unit (5)
19 Overzealous (5)
21 Chemically inactive (5)
22 Cook in an oven (4)

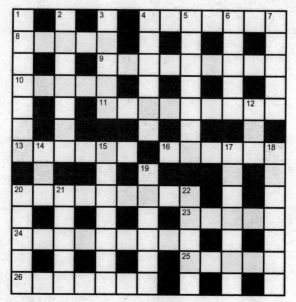

Across

4 One who imputes guilt or blame (7)
8 Relating to sound (5)
9 Heavenly (9)
10 Mexican comrade (5)
11 Fit to fly (9)
13 Rope or canvas headgear for a horse (6)
16 Blazing (6)
20 British statesman who served as Prime Minister four times (9)
23 Close-fitting (5)
24 Shiite religious leader (9)
25 Fill with high spirits (5)
26 Present for acceptance or rejection (7)

Down

1 Phlegm (7)
2 Commander of a fleet (7)
3 Bedtime beverage (5)
4 Tempt (6)
5 Shed, slough (4,3)
6 Canonised person (5)
7 Automobile race run over public roads (5)
12 Stitch back (3)
14 Be unwell (3)
15 Let up (4,3)
17 Word of transposed letters (7)
18 Former province of northern Ethiopia (7)
19 Tree that bears catkins (6)
20 Clench, clutch tightly (5)
21 Famous Mexican-American battle (5)
22 Gas formerly used as an anaesthetic (5)

510

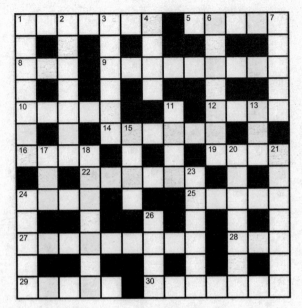

Across

1 Diffusing friendliness (7)
5 Deflect, fend off (5)
8 Branch of the British armed forces (inits) (3)
9 Person who undertakes various small tasks (3-3,3)
10 Mixture of rain and snow (5)
12 Gives assistance (4)
14 Child without parents (6)
16 Come to earth (4)
19 Strap with a crosspiece on the upper of a shoe (1-3)
22 At the tail of a ship (6)
24 Bellow (4)
25 In the middle of (5)
27 Mountainside cable railway (9)
28 Weeding tool (3)
29 Lament for the dead (5)
30 In the direction of (7)

Down

1 Spray can (7)
2 Number represented by the Roman XV (7)
3 Very drunk (slang) (6)
4 Small whirlpool (4)
6 Vigorous and active (7)
7 Hinged lifting tool (5)
11 Partially burn (4)
13 Chemical that carries genetic information (inits) (3)
15 Speed of progress (4)
17 In the past (3)
18 Sweetheart (7)
20 Male sibling (7)
21 Return to a former state (7)
23 Constricted (6)
24 Type of firearm (5)
26 Coagulate (4)

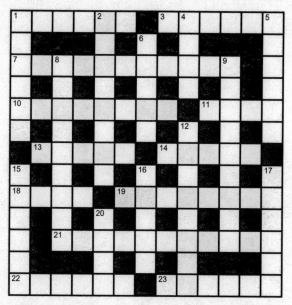

Across

1 Opening in the rear of the barrel of a gun (6)
3 Circa, close to (6)
7 Country, capital Riyadh (5,6)
10 One who is not a member of a group (8)
11 Woven into a thread (4)
13 Relative by marriage (2-3)
14 Vegetable used as a substitute for spinach (5)
18 Stare at lustfully (4)
19 Narrow, pointed shoe heel (8)
21 Ill-fated (4-7)
22 Reprimand (6)
23 Pressure line on a weather map (6)

Down

1 Confer, grant a right or title (6)
2 Scientifically detached, unemotional (8)
4 Deep red gemstone (4)
5 Rectangular, dotted playing piece (6)
6 Shed tears (5)
8 Removes a knot (9)
9 Equipment designed to serve a specific function (9)
12 Stretches of not very deep water (8)
15 Stiff straw hat with a flat crown (6)
16 Twig (5)
17 Wallet for storing loose papers (6)
20 Errand (4)

512

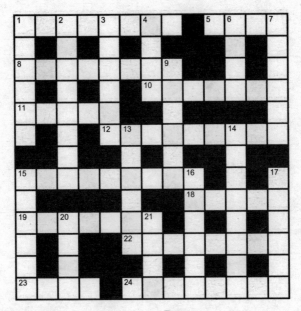

Across

1 Valuable fodder and
lawn plant (8)
5 Humble request for help (4)
8 Substance used for
colouring fabrics (8)
10 Passage (7)
11 The Devil (5)
12 Abundant wealth (9)
15 Retrace one's course (9)
18 Improve, correct a text (5)
19 Combat vessel (7)
22 Race between candidates
for elective office (8)
23 Basic unit of currency
in Germany (4)
24 Bald (8)

Down

1 Red salad vegetable (6)
2 Operated by generated
power (8)
3 Light-sensitive membrane
at the back of the eye (6)
4 Filter (4)
6 Young, unmarried
woman (4)
7 Uncle's wife (6)
9 Caper, cavort (6)
13 Relating to or
containing iron (6)
14 Steep descent by
an aircraft (8)
15 Be on one's guard
against (6)
16 Custodian (6)
17 Handsome youth loved
by Aphrodite (6)
20 Bring up (4)
21 Daddy (4)

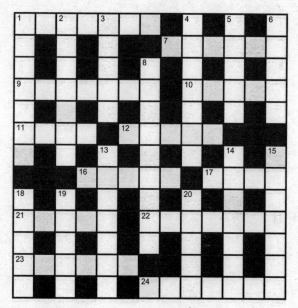

Across

1 Formal charge of wrongdoing (7)
7 Preposterous (6)
9 Type of bet for a win and a place (4,3)
10 Daughter of a sibling (5)
11 Professional cook (4)
12 Projectile intended to be shot from a bow (5)
16 Groom's partner (5)
17 Extinct bird of Mauritius (4)
21 Plenty (5)
22 Small, dark-coloured British bird (4,3)
23 Conventional (6)
24 Financial obligation unlikely to be repaid (3,4)

Down

1 It's said to make the heart grow fonder (7)
2 J D Salinger novel, The ___ in the Rye (7)
3 Expression of dislike (5)
4 Desert, leave (7)
5 Hand tool for boring holes (5)
6 Mammary gland of bovids (5)
8 Spin-off (2-7)
13 London football club (7)
14 Country dwelling (7)
15 Get in touch with (7)
18 Lose consciousness momentarily (5)
19 Gush (5)
20 Cooked in an oven (5)

514

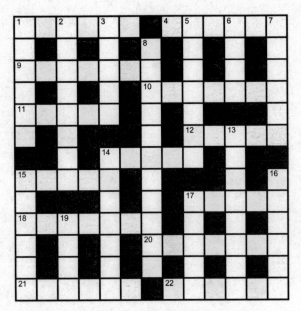

Across

1 Try to locate (6)
4 Leave a job voluntarily (6)
9 Animated film (7)
10 Shattered, broken into pieces (7)
11 Orders (5)
12 Platform (5)
14 Fully developed person (5)
15 More senior in years (5)
17 Territory occupied by a nation (5)
18 Mode (7)
20 Highest in stature (7)
21 Alternative – this or that (6)
22 Water boiler (6)

Down

1 Safe (6)
2 Placed in a particular order (8)
3 Cuts into pieces (5)
5 Gases ejected from an engine as waste products (7)
6 One-twelfth of a foot (4)
7 Knitting tool (6)
8 Contrivances for producing musical sounds (11)
13 Obvious to the mind or senses (8)
14 Newspaper feature (7)
15 Bureau, place of work (6)
16 Sofa, couch (6)
17 Find the answer to (5)
19 Condiment, sodium chloride (4)

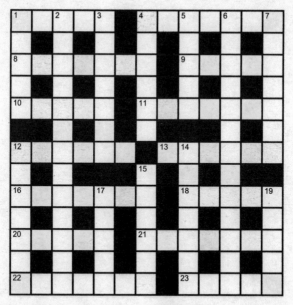

Across

1 Church passage (5)
4 Imaginary sea nymph (7)
8 Animal skin (7)
9 Drivers' stopover (5)
10 ___ Mulroney, former Canadian prime minister (5)
11 Feeling self-conscious (7)
12 Horse's pace between a trot and a gallop (6)
13 Made happen (6)
16 Man devoted to the pursuit of pleasure (7)
18 Misgiving (5)
20 Provide food for an event (5)
21 Personal belief or judgment (7)
22 Flat area in a series of slopes (7)
23 Construct (a building) (5)

Down

1 Off the cuff (2-3)
2 Person in charge of a railway stop (13)
3 Make more attractive (7)
4 Masonry bond (6)
5 Dance of Cuban origin (5)
6 Medicine used to treat allergies and hypersensitive reactions (13)
7 Misled (7)
12 One who imitates the behaviour of another (7)
14 Obtain (7)
15 Well in the past (6)
17 Loose garment worn by Muslim women (5)
19 Claude ___, French painter (1840–1926) (5)

516

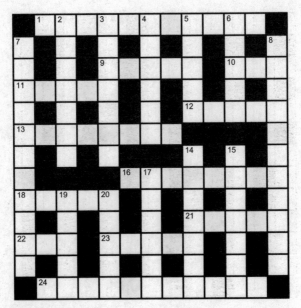

Across

1 Heedful of potential consequences (11)
9 Bamboo-eating mammal (5)
10 Grow old (3)
11 Connected series or group (5)
12 Battleground (5)
13 Honour, award (8)
16 Acute insufficiency (8)
18 Deep serving spoon (5)
21 Acted out without words (5)
22 Hollow, flexible structure resembling a bag (3)
23 Harmless tropical house-lizard (5)
24 Extreme or irrational fear of water (11)

Down

2 Not accurate (7)
3 Gelatinous container with medicine inside (7)
4 Having a crew (6)
5 Pedestrianised public square (5)
6 Lifting machine (5)
7 Tape used to clean between the teeth (6,5)
8 Banknotes or coins considered as an official medium of payment (5,6)
14 Musical effect produced by rapid alternation of tones (7)
15 Type of long-grained rice (7)
17 Symptom of indigestion (6)
19 Corrode (5)
20 English composer (1857–1934) (5)

Across

1 Capital of Venezuela (7)
6 Part of a curve (3)
8 Atomic exploding device (1-4)
9 Leaves dried and prepared for smoking (7)
10 Alcove (5)
11 Thrown into a state of intense fear (8)
13 Guts, intestines (6)
15 Ludicrous failure (6)
18 Ribbon-like intestinal parasite (8)
19 Projection shaped to fit into a mortise (5)
21 Small cucumber pickled whole (7)
22 Foxhole (5)
23 Angry (3)
24 Tax imposed on ships (7)

Down

2 Pear-shaped fruit (7)
3 Proprietary trademark of a popular soft drink (4-4)
4 Tool similar to a spade (6)
5 Midday (4)
6 Localised sore (7)
7 Bye-bye (7)
12 Number denoted by the Roman XIX (8)
13 Christening (7)
14 Suffering from physical injury (7)
16 Cutting up (meat) into slices (7)
17 Captured (6)
20 Standard (4)

518

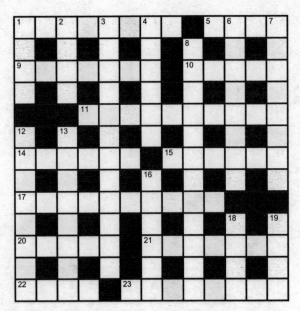

Across

1 Scaremonger (8)
5 Shed bodily fluid (4)
9 Protection (7)
10 Eagle's nest (5)
11 Position of ease and luxury (coll) (3,2,5)
14 Jungle man who was raised by apes (6)
15 Come back (6)
17 City in southern Ohio, USA (10)
20 Former model and ex-wife of Donald Trump (5)
21 Native of Rangoon, for example (7)
22 Short intake of breath (4)
23 Areas set aside for sleeping (8)

Down

1 Domed recess (4)
2 Afresh (4)
3 Having the ability to work with numbers (12)
4 Discourse (6)
6 Common flower also known as a delphinium (8)
7 Putting on clothes (8)
8 Lotion that reduces the effect of balding (4,8)
12 Heaping, piling (8)
13 Natives of Teheran, for example (8)
16 Incapable (6)
18 Courageous man (4)
19 Folds over and sews together (4)

Across

1 Seedless raisin (7)
5 Favourite pursuit followed as an amusement (5)
7 Gesture involving the shoulders (5)
8 Without a trace of moisture (4-3)
9 Harsh or corrosive in tone (7)
10 Scrutinise accounts (5)
11 Computerised system for trading in securities (inits) (6)
13 North American tribe (6)
18 Bicker (5)
20 Fluid agent (gas or liquid) that reduces heat (7)
21 Burn bubble (7)
22 Representative (5)
23 Role player (5)
24 Keep out (7)

Down

1 Provide with nourishment (7)
2 Pantries (7)
3 Branch of mathematics (7)
4 Period of office of a chief monk (6)
5 Red dye (5)
6 Polish to a high sheen (7)
12 Synthetic fabric (7)
14 Lacking wit or imagination (7)
15 French castle (7)
16 Give the right to (7)
17 Accumulate (6)
19 Come in (5)

520

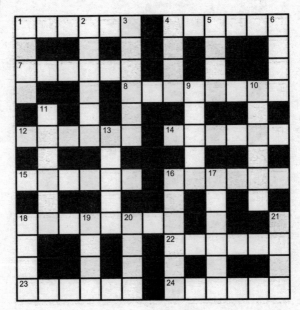

Across

1 Muscle that flexes the forearm (6)
4 Scribble (6)
7 Look around a shop casually and randomly (6)
8 The world of scholars (8)
12 Shelters from light (6)
14 Marked by injustice (6)
15 Provide a favour for someone (6)
16 Corrupt morally (6)
18 Part of a bed (8)
22 Coiffure (6)
23 Entangle or catch in (6)
24 Provide with choice food or drink (6)

Down

1 Infant (4)
2 English king, 1004–66 (6)
3 Perspires (6)
4 Heroic tale (4)
5 Contest of speed (4)
6 Tibetan or Mongolian priest (4)
9 Move to music (5)
10 Frozen spike of water (6)
11 Disorder characterised by fear (6)
13 Avid (5)
16 One of Santa's reindeer (6)
17 Looking directly towards (6)
18 Spice made from the covering of the nutmeg (4)
19 Remove (4)
20 Individually (4)
21 Give medicine to (4)

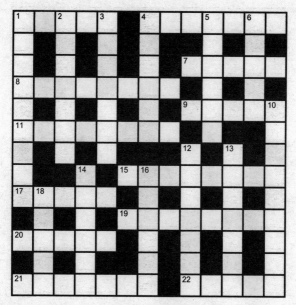

Across

1 Ordered series (5)

4 Island country, capital Nassau (7)

7 Acute abdominal pain (5)

8 In a cheerless manner (8)

9 Trick (5)

11 Give up the throne (8)

15 Garment extending from the waist to the ankle (8)

17 Quick, fast (5)

19 Of sound (8)

20 Coat with fat during cooking (5)

21 Welfare (7)

22 Backless chair (5)

Down

1 Abrasive medium used to remove paint from wood (9)

2 Prior to a specified time (7)

3 Clasp another person in the arms (7)

4 Vote (6)

5 Exist in large quantities (6)

6 Defence plea of being elsewhere (5)

10 Something achieved by a narrow margin (5,4)

12 Type of cloud (7)

13 Nazi secret police force (7)

14 Largest digit of the foot (3,3)

16 Space vehicle (6)

18 Humble (5)

522

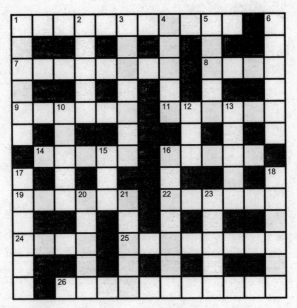

Across

1 Detrimental to physical or moral well-being (11)
7 Cadaverous (8)
8 Appellation (4)
9 Put into cipher (6)
11 Bowed, curved (6)
14 Buenos ____, capital of Argentina (5)
16 Intended (5)
19 Central American canal (6)
22 Strong alcoholic drink (6)
24 Receptacle for a coin (4)
25 Small nocturnal mammal with protective spines (8)
26 Enormous gorge in northern Arizona (5,6)

Down

1 Division of Ireland (6)
2 Expression of greeting (5)
3 Alphabetic characters (7)
4 Patty Bouvier's twin sister in TV's *The Simpsons* (5)
5 Frenzied (5)
6 Order of business (6)
10 Mound of stones piled up as a memorial (5)
12 Strong-scented perennial herb (3)
13 Follower of a major religion (5)
15 Forest tree (3)
16 Tuneful (7)
17 Muscular cramps (6)
18 Root from which something starts (6)
20 Modify (5)
21 Anaemic-looking (5)
23 Female monarch (5)

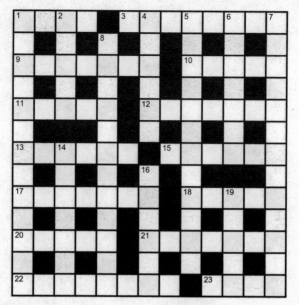

Across
1 Informal farewell remark (2-2)
3 Exercise that increases the need for oxygen (8)
9 Style of design popular in the 1920s and 1930s (3,4)
10 Plant life (5)
11 Group of islands, capital Apia (5)
12 Inaudible (7)
13 Pulsates (6)
15 Severe or trying experience (6)
17 Sharp-cornered (7)
18 Statement of beliefs (5)
20 Salmon-like fish (5)
21 Message informing of danger (7)
22 Units of heat, often applied to a foodstuff (8)
23 Norse thunder god (4)

Down
1 Crossing the sea between Britain and the USA (13)
2 ___ pole, tribal emblem (5)
4 Second book of the Old Testament (6)
5 Not for quotation (3,3,6)
6 Prehistoric metalworking period (4,3)
7 Person who spreads malicious gossip (13)
8 Vehicle with four wheels in which a baby is pushed around (12)
14 Plaything made from pieces of cloth (3,4)
16 Snooze (6)
19 ___ Piaf, French cabaret singer (1915–63) (5)

524

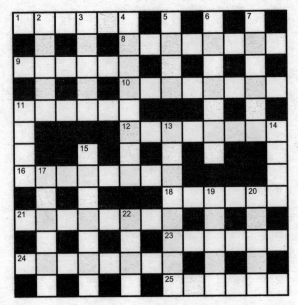

Across

1 Arch of the foot (6)
8 Worthy of trust (8)
9 Residential district, often run-down (6)
10 Price reduction (8)
11 Writing desk (6)
12 Novelties pulled at Christmas (8)
16 Competitor who finishes second (6-2)
18 Aircraft shed (6)
21 Type of neuralgia that affects the hips (8)
23 Kept out (6)
24 Recipient of a university degree (8)
25 In accord with the latest fad (6)

Down

2 Prime minister of India from 1947 to 1964 (5)
3 Name of a book (5)
4 Manufacturer (8)
5 In addition (4)
6 Portable rocket launcher (7)
7 Two-dimensional (6)
11 Ursine mammal (4)
13 Basis of written language (8)
14 Heavenly body (4)
15 Advancing to the front (7)
17 Open, a bottle of wine for example (6)
19 Impudent aggressiveness (5)
20 Set straight or right (5)
22 Muslim prayer leader (4)

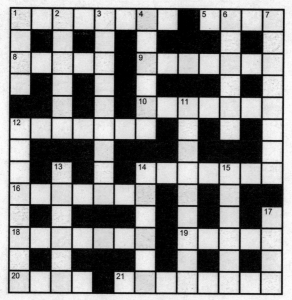

Across

1 Financially ruined (8)
5 Region bordering Israel and Egypt (4)
8 Passions (5)
9 Having a secret or hidden meaning (7)
10 Look that is believed to have the power to inflict harm (4,3)
12 Without any attempt at concealment (7)
14 Great joy (7)
16 Greek goddess of fertility (7)
18 Impartial (7)
19 Depression scratched into a surface (5)
20 Dull pain (4)
21 Hired murderer (8)

Down

1 Lacking hair (4)
2 US state in which Las Vegas is located (6)
3 Discipline in personal and social activities (9)
4 Pouch (6)
6 Song of devotion or loyalty (6)
7 Attribute an action, saying, or quality to (8)
11 Acute highly contagious viral disease (9)
12 Brightly coloured handkerchief often worn about the neck (8)
13 Surprise attack (6)
14 Boring tools (6)
15 Reduces to small shreds (6)
17 Part of the lower jaw (4)

526

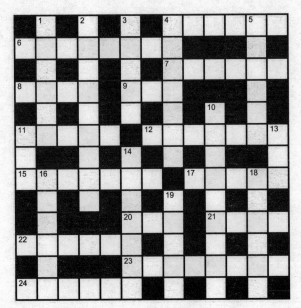

Across

4 Keg, cask (6)
6 Casserole of aubergine and ground lamb in a sauce (8)
7 Formula for cooking (6)
8 Number indicated by the Roman V (4)
9 Appropriate, seize (3)
11 Skinny, underweight (5)
12 Freedom (7)
15 Stroll (7)
17 Paved surface where aircraft stand (5)
20 Son of Noah (3)
21 Book of the Old Testament (4)
22 Place where films are shown (6)
23 Maintain in unaltered condition (8)
24 Make certain of (6)

Down

1 Part of a dress above the waist (6)
2 Rising in power (9)
3 Perhaps (5)
4 Cheap purchase (7)
5 Specialist (6)
10 Cooked by immersing in fat or oil (4-5)
11 Had existence (3)
13 Japanese currency unit (3)
14 Form differently (7)
16 Deed (6)
18 Set of eight notes (6)
19 Fossilised resin (5)

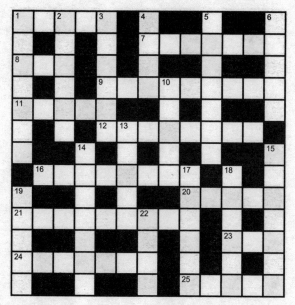

Across

1 Jelly based on fish or meat stock (5)
7 Native of Lhasa, for example (7)
8 Mown grass used as fodder (3)
9 The act of leaving (9)
11 Message sent from one computer to another (5)
12 Grace, style (8)
16 Woven picture (8)
20 Person who does no work (5)
21 Respectful awe (9)
23 Grandmother (3)
24 Daybreak (7)
25 Perfume (5)

Down

1 Gain with effort (7)
2 Regular date on which wages are received (6)
3 Stick of wax with a central wick (6)
4 At the peak of (4)
5 Allowing (7)
6 Extension to a main building (5)
10 Annoyance (5)
13 Strong, tightly twisted cotton thread (5)
14 Comes into view (7)
15 Small crown (7)
17 Gives way (6)
18 Woman with fair skin and hair (6)
19 Newly made (5)
22 Requirement (4)

528

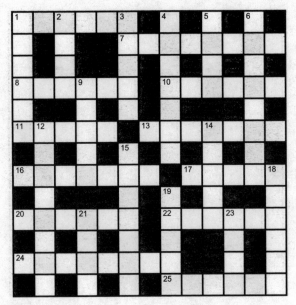

Across

1 Archer (6)
7 Higher than average (5,3)
8 Compositor (6)
10 Conquer (6)
11 Cause anxiety or alarm (5)
13 Reproduction (7)
16 It begins after 31 December (3,4)
17 Articles of commerce (5)
20 Move restlessly (6)
22 No particular person (6)
24 Income (8)
25 Resist separation (6)

Down

1 Animals (6)
2 Compass point at 270 degrees (4)
3 Mother-of-pearl (5)
4 Member of an army (7)
5 Hinged section of a table (4)
6 In equilibrium (8)
9 After the expected time (5)
12 Relating to office work (8)
14 Dotty, mentally irregular (slang) (5)
15 Cocktail of vermouth and gin (7)
18 Involuntary expulsion of air from the nose (6)
19 Strong, lightweight wood (5)
21 Association of criminals (4)
23 On a single occasion (4)

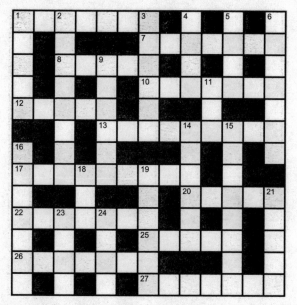

Across

1 Rectangular stones with curved tops (7)
7 Teach (7)
8 Bedroom on a ship (5)
10 Restrain with fetters (7)
12 First stomach of a cow (5)
13 Concord (9)
17 Ruthless pursuit of one's own interests (3-3-3)
20 Deciduous conifer (5)
22 Stuffy (atmosphere) (7)
25 Paved area that adjoins a house (5)
26 Green vegetable (7)
27 Migratory grasshoppers of warm regions (7)

Down

1 Group of singers (5)
2 Developing into (8)
3 Detection device (6)
4 State parliament of Russia (4)
5 Poorly lit (4)
6 At a lower place (7)
9 Crescent-shaped yellow fruit (6)
11 English river (3)
14 Young bird of prey (6)
15 Massive (8)
16 Move forward (7)
18 Long and slippery fish (3)
19 Chase away (6)
21 Is suspended (5)
23 Loose flowing garment (4)
24 Mild yellow Dutch cheese (4)

530

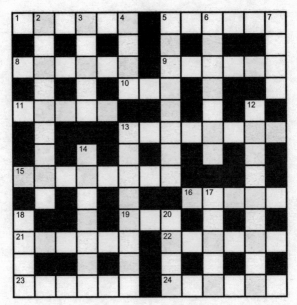

Across

1 Fielding position in cricket closest to the bowler (3-3)
5 Acid found in milk (6)
8 Moral principles (6)
9 Improved, mended (6)
10 Australian running bird (3)
11 Lay out in a line (5)
13 In an opposing direction (8)
15 Band of colours, as seen in a rainbow (8)
16 Thin meat soup (5)
19 Mischievous little fairy (3)
21 Disperse (6)
22 Maltreater (6)
23 Ship's officer who keeps accounts (6)
24 Live on, persist (6)

Down

2 Seize a thing on its way (9)
3 Board used with a planchette (5)
4 Coalesce (4)
5 Tree with pendulous, bright yellow flowers (8)
6 Implements for eating food (7)
7 Birthday missive (4)
12 Constellation of Ursa Major (5,4)
13 Passageway (8)
14 Female stage performer (7)
17 Ball-shaped (5)
18 Request on an invitation (inits) (4)
20 Gait (4)

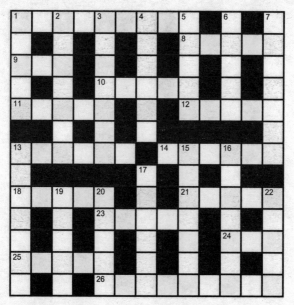

Across

1 French part of the Riviera (4,5)
8 Decorate (5)
9 Fruiting spike of a cereal plant (3)
10 Leave or strike out, as of vowels (5)
11 Thoroughly unpleasant (5)
12 Detection and location device (5)
13 Next to (6)
14 Dazed state (6)
18 Foundation (5)
21 Far beyond the norm (5)
23 Wading bird (5)
24 Egg cells (3)
25 British snake (5)
26 Bulbous spring-flowering plant (9)

Down

1 Dirt-free (5)
2 Lunges (7)
3 Free from tears (3-4)
4 Point in the sky directly above the observer (6)
5 One who drives cars at high speeds (5)
6 Globe, planet (5)
7 Underwriter (7)
13 Looked after a small child in the absence of a parent (7)
15 Huge destructive wave (7)
16 Inciting sympathy and sorrow (7)
17 Stocking support (6)
19 Sleazy or shabby (5)
20 Fleeced (5)
22 Victoria Beckham's former surname (5)

532

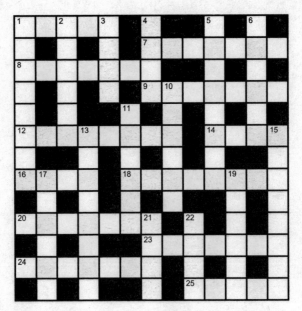

Across

1 Breakfast rasher (5)
7 Breathe (7)
8 Raise in value or esteem (7)
9 Feed (7)
12 Again (4,4)
14 Man-eating giant (4)
16 On the house (4)
18 Put off, evade (8)
20 Disease transmitted by the mosquito (7)
23 Implement, tool (7)
24 Russian tea urn (7)
25 Cut finely (5)

Down

1 Curt or disdainful rejection (5-3)
2 French brandy (6)
3 Indian bread, baked in a clay oven (4)
4 Tiny, common UK bird (4)
5 Plausible but false (8)
6 Pencil mark remover (6)
10 Exaggerate to an excessive degree (6)
11 Tiny Japanese tree (6)
13 Lifting device (8)
15 Excluded from, forced to leave (8)
17 40th President of the USA (6)
19 Perplexing riddle (6)
21 Halo of light (4)
22 Professional charges (4)

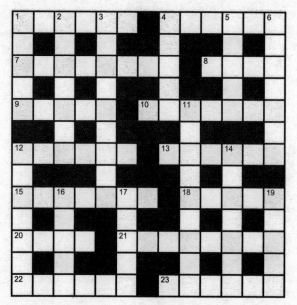

Across

1 Single-celled, water-living protozoon (6)
4 Pantry (6)
7 Pre-dinner drink (8)
8 Presidential assistant (4)
9 Island located south of Sicily (5)
10 Medical instrument used to inject (7)
12 Serviette made of cloth (6)
13 Less tight (6)
15 Hosni ___, former Egyptian president (7)
18 Wireless (5)
20 Cry loudly and without restraint (4)
21 Marine crustacean (8)
22 However (6)
23 Vehicle for carrying a coffin (6)

Down

1 Clock that wakes a sleeper at a preset time (5)
2 Partly coincide (7)
3 Army officer rank (9)
4 Of imposing height (5)
5 Condescend (5)
6 Graceful woodland animal (3,4)
11 River, the boundary between Mexico and Texas, USA (3,6)
12 Country, capital Windhoek (7)
14 Conveyance attached to a motorcycle (7)
16 Humorously vulgar (5)
17 Church associated with a convent (5)
19 Abnormally fat (5)

534

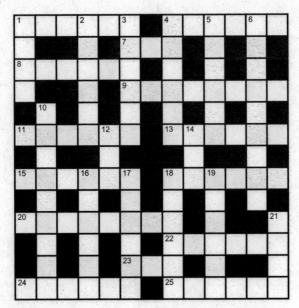

Across
1 Material (6)
4 Accident, fate (6)
7 Sleeveless outer garment worn by Arabs (3)
8 Medicine that induces vomiting (6)
9 Wooden board or platter (8)
11 Any leafy plants eaten as vegetables (6)
13 Astonished (6)
15 Playing card suit (6)
18 ___-Herzegovina, European country (6)
20 Popular frozen dessert (3,5)
22 Ensign (6)
23 Consciousness of one's own identity (3)
24 Breakfast food made from grains (6)
25 Forceful military attack (6)

Down
1 Feast upon (4)
2 Baby's plaything (6)
3 Prickly desert plant (6)
4 Equipment for taking pictures (6)
5 Tree with sharp thorns (6)
6 Self-service restaurant (9)
10 Bag with a handle used to carry papers, files, etc (9)
12 Hard-shelled fruit of a tree (3)
14 Sound made by a cow (3)
16 Elongated cluster of flowers (6)
17 Israeli monetary unit (6)
18 Woody tropical grass (6)
19 Black eye (slang) (6)
21 Curved gateway (4)

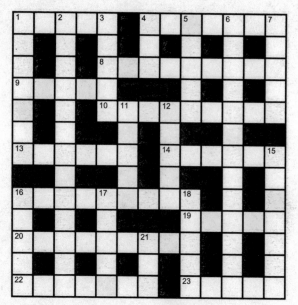

Across

1 Protective secretion of bodily membranes (5)
4 Shored up (7)
8 Thistle-like flower head with edible fleshy leaves (9)
9 Blessed with good fortune (5)
10 Expletive (5,4)
13 Popular beverage (6)
14 Country, capital Paris (6)
16 Venetian traveller who explored Asia in the 13th century (5,4)
19 Tailed heavenly body (5)
20 Man-made (9)
22 Less clouded (7)
23 Hear a court case anew (5)

Down

1 Shellfish (7)
2 Perimeter of a circle (13)
3 Murders (5)
4 Cherry stone (3)
5 ___ Wilde, playwright (5)
6 Authoritative declaration (13)
7 Fearful expectation (5)
11 Give birth to puppies (5)
12 Dreadful, terrible (5)
15 Rapture (7)
16 Harmonious sounds (5)
17 Alternative (5)
18 Happen (5)
21 Pitch (3)

536

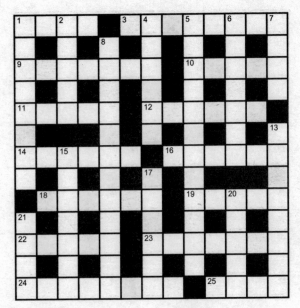

Across

1 Crust-like surface of a healing wound (4)
3 Former British colony in the West Indies (8)
9 Aural pain (7)
10 Fall out of date (5)
11 American raccoon (5)
12 Lacking a sense of security (6)
14 Without effort (6)
16 Newspaper chief (6)
18 Russian soup, with a beetroot juice base (6)
19 Care for sick people (5)
22 Undefined (5)
23 Attendant on an aeroplane (7)
24 Innkeeper (8)
25 Watery part of milk separated from the curd in making cheese (4)

Down

1 Made a preliminary drawing (8)
2 Largest artery of the body (5)
4 Wide street or thoroughfare (6)
5 Graceful stage performer (6,6)
6 Money put into a bank (7)
7 Thin part of a wine glass (4)
8 Seemingly small but actually mortal weakness (8,4)
13 Amicable (8)
15 Double-barrelled firearm (7)
17 One in pursuit (6)
20 Get to (5)
21 Extremely wicked (4)

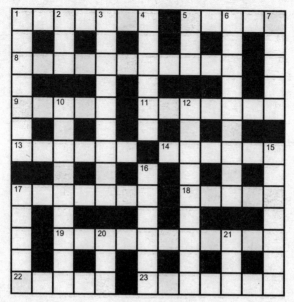

Across

1 Pierced with a sharp tool (7)

5 Throws away as refuse (5)

8 Meeting arranged in advance (11)

9 First letter of the Greek alphabet (5)

11 Field of study (7)

13 Frogmen (6)

14 Desired (6)

17 Act of God (7)

18 Imperial measures of capacity (5)

19 Leader in a campaign or movement (5-6)

22 Hold on tightly (5)

23 Lever operated with the foot (7)

Down

1 In the direction of the ocean (7)

2 High mountain (3)

3 Miscellaneous curios (4-1-4)

4 Dislike intensely (6)

5 Mature female deer (3)

6 Showing signs of wear and tear (4-5)

7 Commence (5)

10 Luciano ____, Italian tenor who died in 2007 (9)

12 Utter obscenities or profanities (9)

15 Be worthy of (7)

16 Glowing with heat (3-3)

17 Wizardry (5)

20 Fireside mat (3)

21 Fishing implement (3)

538

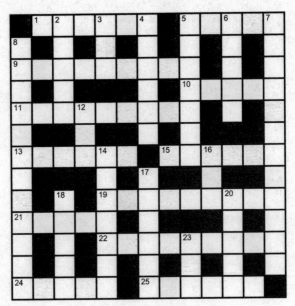

Across

1 Smoked herring (6)

5 Distinctive spirit of a culture (5)

9 Subdued (9)

10 Give qualities or abilities to (5)

11 Formidable task or requirement (4,5)

13 Bracelet (6)

15 Get around, circumvent (6)

19 Alternately to a higher and lower level (2,3,4)

21 Foreigner, stranger (5)

22 Flowers with a trumpet-shaped central crown (9)

24 Void of content (5)

25 Mission (6)

Down

2 Urge or force to an action (5)

3 Food in a pastry shell (3)

4 Live, dwell (6)

5 Getting on in years (7)

6 Convenient (5)

7 The entertainment industry (4,8)

8 Something that bulges out (12)

12 Fall behind (3)

14 Dirty washing (7)

16 Seedcase (3)

17 Flummox, confuse (6)

18 Confuse (3,2)

20 Aromatic, edible bulb (5)

23 Belonging to us (3)

Across

- **4** Fruit resembling a small peach (7)
- **7** Talk about in detail (7)
- **8** Gives a clue (5)
- **9** Greenfly, for instance (5)
- **10** Epoch, age (3)
- **11** Imbecile (5)
- **12** Boundary (9)
- **14** Of a quantity that can be counted (9)
- **17** Deceiver (5)
- **18** Ventilate (3)
- **19** Roman prophetess (5)
- **21** Evenly matched (5)
- **22** Tapering stone pillar (7)
- **23** Cowboy's hat (7)

Down

- **1** Collection of ancient Scandinavian poetry (4)
- **2** Book of the Old Testament (6)
- **3** Basic, essential (11)
- **4** Upward movement (6)
- **5** Frank and direct (6)
- **6** Glass cylinder closed at one end (4,4)
- **8** Coiffeuse (11)
- **12** Gland located behind the stomach (8)
- **13** Rubbish, waste (6)
- **15** Dark brownish-red colour (6)
- **16** Reel, spool (6)
- **20** Body of water (4)

540

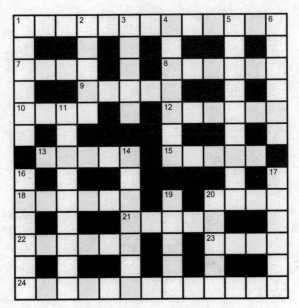

Across

1 Questioned minutely (5-8)
7 Roman emperor 54–68 AD (4)
8 Venom (6)
9 Control board (5)
10 Double-reed woodwind instrument (4)
12 Series of arches supported by columns (6)
13 Emblem worn like a brooch (5)
15 Australian wild dog (5)
18 Fisherman (6)
20 Bundle of straw or hay (4)
21 Feather worn as an ornament (5)
22 Deadly (6)
23 Went on horseback (4)
24 Arrangement of parts or elements (13)

Down

1 Deep gorge (6)
2 Ambit (5)
3 Hard blackish wood (5)
4 Clap one's hands (7)
5 Feeling of longing for something past (9)
6 Performer who moves to music (6)
11 Large reddish-brown ape (5-4)
14 Noise excluder (7)
16 Aromatic bulb used as seasoning (6)
17 Belittle (6)
19 Purchaser (5)
20 Cap made of soft cloth (5)

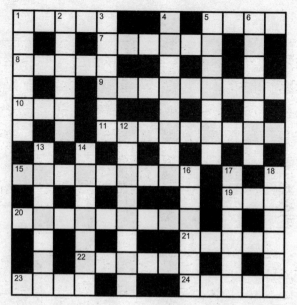

Across

1 Confusion, disarray (5)
5 Cattle reared for their meat (4)
7 Three times (6)
8 Grin (5)
9 Essential (9)
10 Science workshop (abbr) (3)
11 Act of mass destruction and loss of life (9)
15 Instrument that measures the height above ground (9)
19 Container for ashes (3)
20 Well-ordered (9)
21 Painting stand (5)
22 Lime tree (6)
23 Branch of the armed forces (4)
24 Divisions of the school year (5)

Down

1 Fortress, stronghold (6)
2 Bent outwards with the joint away from the body (6)
3 Unpleasant odour (6)
4 Tedious (8)
5 Animal product used as a furniture polish (7)
6 Wholly occupy (7)
12 Responsive to orders (8)
13 Sunshine State of the USA (7)
14 At last (7)
16 Rat or mouse, for example (6)
17 Treasurer at a college (6)
18 Joints between the legs and feet (6)

542

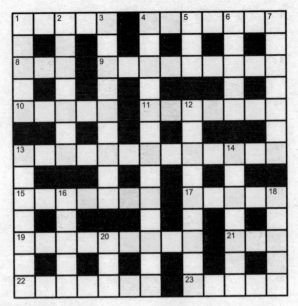

Across

1 Picture puzzle (5)
4 Emerges from an egg (7)
8 Awkward, stupid person (3)
9 Entertainment (9)
10 Disreputable wanderer (5)
11 Ultimate client for which a thing is intended (3,4)
13 Force of fluid on the walls of the arteries (5,8)
15 Loss of memory (7)
17 Fertile tract in the desert (5)
19 Worship (9)
21 Little insect (3)
22 Hole, aperture (7)
23 Hank of knitting wool (5)

Down

1 Fowl's perch (5)
2 Large shaggy-haired brown bison (7)
3 Rushes wildly in a sudden mass panic (9)
4 Burglary (13)
5 Stand for a golf ball (3)
6 Takes notice (5)
7 Release (3,4)
12 Capital of Iowa, USA (3,6)
13 Swaggering show of courage (7)
14 Steal the show (7)
16 Not a single person (2-3)
18 Glossy fabric (5)
20 Muhammad ____, former boxer (3)

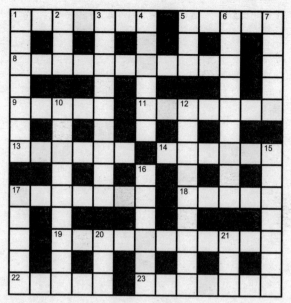

Across

1 Ceremonial dinner party (7)

5 Military trainee (5)

8 Being everywhere at once (11)

9 Spring-flowering plant (5)

11 Distinctly (7)

13 Hindu Festival of Lights (6)

14 Skin disorder (6)

17 Lover, suitor (7)

18 Consumed (5)

19 Part of England that includes Devon, Cornwall and Somerset (4,7)

22 Contrite (5)

23 Banded with pieces of contrasting colour (7)

Down

1 Swollen, distended (7)

2 Convent sister (3)

3 Not widely liked (9)

4 Deep ditch (6)

5 Billiards stick (3)

6 Preventative measure (9)

7 Delicious (5)

10 Tool used to cut the grass (9)

12 Funds of a government (9)

15 Vexed (7)

16 Elastic straps that hold up trousers (6)

17 Bottomless gulf or pit (5)

20 Pigs' home (3)

21 Bathroom fixture (3)

544

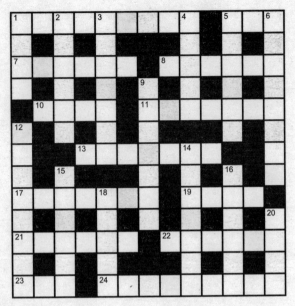

Across

1 Word that qualifies a noun (9)
5 Melancholy (3)
7 Fungal, mossy growth (6)
8 Dairy product (6)
10 Part of the body containing the brain (4)
11 Thin varnish used to finish wood (7)
13 England, Scotland and Wales (7)
17 Body of water between Israel and Jordan (4,3)
19 Lie adjacent to another (4)
21 Referee (6)
22 Loose Japanese robe (6)
23 At a great distance (3)
24 Condiment often served with roast lamb (4,5)

Down

1 Gifted, competent (4)
2 Short coat (6)
3 Popular British cheese (7)
4 Dodge (5)
5 Take up residence (6)
6 Without deviation (8)
9 Receptacle used by smokers (7)
12 Restrain with a manacle fastened around the wrist (8)
14 Slanted letters (7)
15 Covered picnic basket (6)
16 Puzzle in which numbers must fit into a 9x9 grid (6)
18 Scarper (5)
20 Bird symbolising peace (4)

Across

1 Guide (6)
5 Request for a repeat performance (6)
8 Land force of a nation (4)
9 Drink (8)
11 Punctuation mark : (5)
12 Filled pasta cases (7)
14 Wide-mouthed cup (6)
15 Canine film star (6)
18 Painkiller developed in Germany in the 1890s (7)
20 Young dog (5)
22 Organised collection of related information (8)
24 Child of Adam and Eve (4)
25 Group of countries with one ruler (6)
26 Apprehension (6)

Down

2 Fleshy pendulous part of the hearing organ (7)
3 Area used for repairing a ship below its waterline (3,4)
4 Causes friction (4)
5 Likely to provoke jealousy (8)
6 Welsh breed of dog (5)
7 Boisterous practical joke (3)
10 Group considered superior (5)
13 Supply with water (8)
14 Facial hair (5)
16 Highly seasoned meat stuffed in a casing (7)
17 Make an impact on (7)
19 Native of Baghdad, eg (5)
21 List of dishes available (4)
23 Limb (3)

Solutions

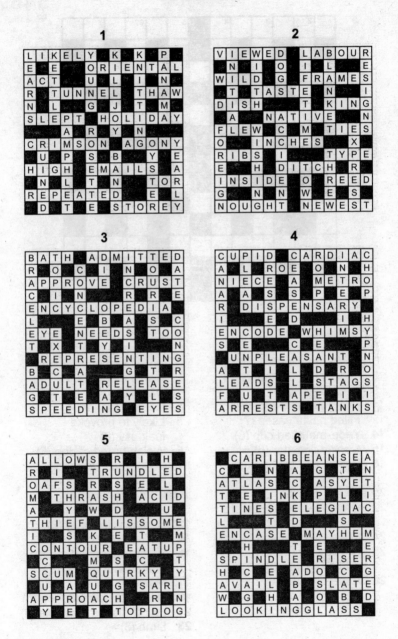

1

L	I	K	E	L	Y		K		K		P	
E		E				O	R	I	E	N	T	A	L
A	C	T			U		L		I		N	
R		T	U	N	N	E	L		T	H	A	W
N		L		G		J		T		M	
S	L	E	P	T		H	O	L	I	D	A	Y
		A		R		Y		N	
C	R	I	M	S	O	N		A	G	O	N	Y
	U		P		S		B			Y		E
H	I	G	H		E	M	A	I	L	S		A
	N		L		T		N			T	O	R
R	E	P	E	A	T	E	D			E		L
	D		T		E		S	T	O	R	E	Y

2

V	I	E	W	E	D		L	A	B	O	U	R
	N		I		O		I		L			E
W	I	L	D		G		F	R	A	M	E	S
	T		T	A	S	T	E		N			I
D	I	S	H			T			K	I	N	G
	A		N	A	T	I	V	E				N
F	L	E	W		C		M		T	I	E	S
O		I	N	C	H	E	S				X	
R	I	B	S		I			T	Y	P	E	
E		H		D	I	T	C	H			R	
I	N	S	I	D	E		O		R	E	E	D
G		N		N		W		E			S	
N	O	U	G	H	T		N	E	W	E	S	T

3

B	A	T	H		A	D	M	I	T	T	E	D
R		O		C		I		N		O		A
A	P	P	R	O	V	E		C	R	U	S	T
C		I		N			R		R			E
E	N	C	Y	C	L	O	P	E	D	I	A	
L			E		B		A		S		C	
E	Y	E		N	E	E	D	S		T	O	O
T		X		T		Y		I			N	
	R	E	P	R	E	S	E	N	T	I	N	G
B		C		A			G		T		R	
A	D	U	L	T		R	E	L	E	A	S	E
G		T		E		A		Y		L		S
S	P	E	E	D	I	N	G		E	Y	E	S

4

C	U	P	I	D		C	A	R	D	I	A	C
A		L		R	O	E		O		N		H
N	I	E	C	E		A		M	E	T	R	O
A		A		S		S		P		E		P
R		D	I	S	P	E	N	S	A	R	Y	
I			E		D				I		H	
E	N	C	O	D	E		W	H	I	M	S	Y
S		E		C		E			C		P	
	U	N	P	L	E	A	S	A	N	T		
A		T		I		L		D		R		O
L	E	A	D	S		L		S	T	A	G	S
F		U		T		A	P	E		I		I
A	R	R	E	S	T	S		T	A	N	K	S

5

A	L	L	O	W	S		R		I		H	
R		I		T	R	U	N	D	L	E	D	
O	A	F	S		R		S		E		L	
M		T	H	R	A	S	H		A	C	I	D
A			Y		W		D			U		
T	H	I	E	F		L	I	S	S	O	M	E
I		S		K		E		T			M	
C	O	N	T	O	U	R		E	A	T	U	P
	C		M		S		C			T	
S	C	U	M		Q	U	I	R	K	Y		Y
	U		A		U		G		S	A	R	I
A	P	P	R	O	A	C	H			R		N
	Y		E		T		T	O	P	D	O	G

6

	C	A	R	I	B	B	E	A	N	S	E	A
C		L		N		A		G		T		N
A	T	L	A	S		C		A	S	Y	E	T
T		E		I	N	K		P		L		I
T	I	N	E	S		E	L	E	G	I	A	C
L			T		D			S				
E	N	C	A	S	E		M	A	Y	H	E	M
		H			T		E					E
S	P	I	N	D	L	E		R	I	S	E	R
H		C		E		A	D	O		C		G
A	V	A	I	L		B		S	L	A	T	E
W		H		A		O				B		D
L	O	O	K	I	N	G	G	L	A	S	S	

Solutions

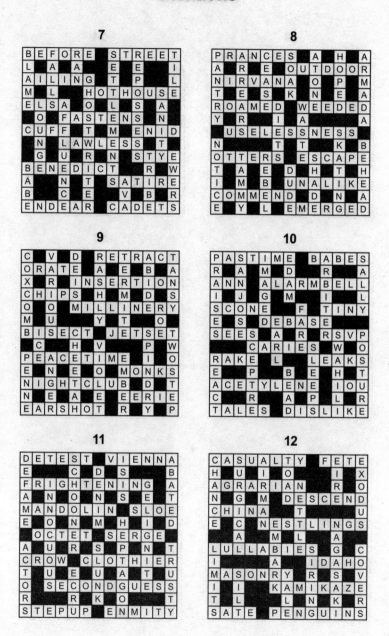

7

B	E	F	O	R	E		S	T	R	E	E	T
L		A		A			E		E			I
A	I	L	I	N	G		T		P			L
M		L			H	O	T	H	O	U	S	E
E	L	S	A		O		L		S		A	
	O		F	A	S	T	E	N	S		N	
C	U	F	F		T		M		E	N	I	D
	N		L	A	W	L	E	S	S		T	
G		U		R		N		S	T	Y	E	
B	E	N	E	D	I	C	T			R		W
A		N		T			S	A	T	I	R	E
B		C		E			V		B			R
E	N	D	E	A	R		C	A	D	E	T	S

8

P	R	A	N	C	E	S		A		H		A
A		R		E		O	U	T	D	O	O	R
N	I	R	V	A	N	A		O		P		M
T		E		S		K		N		E		A
R	O	A	M	E	D		W	E	E	D	E	D
Y		R		I		A						A
	U	S	E	L	E	S	S	N	E	S	S	
N				T		T		K			B
O	T	T	E	R	S		E	S	C	A	P	E
T		A		E		D		H		T		H
I		M		B		U	N	A	L	I	K	E
C	O	M	M	E	N	D		D		N		A
E		Y		L		E	M	E	R	G	E	D

9

C		V		D		R	E	T	R	A	C	T
O	R	A	T	E		A		E		B		A
X		R		I	N	S	E	R	T	I	O	N
C	H	I	P	S		H		M		D		S
O		O		M	I	L	L	I	N	E	R	Y
M		U		Y		T		T		O		
B	I	S	E	C	T		J	E	T	S	E	T
	C		H		V			P				W
P	E	A	C	E	T	I	M	E		I		O
E		N		E		O		M	O	N	K	S
N	I	G	H	T	C	L	U	B		D		T
N		E		A		E		E	E	R	I	E
E	A	R	S	H	O	T		R		Y		P

10

P	A	S	T	I	M	E		B	A	B	E	S
R		A		M		D		R				A
A	N	N		A	L	A	R	M	B	E	L	L
I		J		G		M		I				L
S	C	O	N	E			F		T	I	N	Y
E		S		D	E	B	A	S	E			
S	E	E	S		A		R		R	S	V	P
			C	A	R	I	E	S		W		O
R	A	K	E		L			L	E	A	K	S
E			P		B		E		H			T
A	C	E	T	Y	L	E	N	E		I	O	U
C			R		A		P		L			R
T	A	L	E	S		D	I	S	L	I	K	E

11

D	E	T	E	S	T		V	I	E	N	N	A
E			C		D		S					B
F	R	I	G	H	T	E	N	I	N	G		A
A		N		O		N		S		E		T
M	A	N	D	O	L	I	N		S	L	O	E
E		O		N		M		H		I		D
	O	C	T	E	T		S	E	R	G	E	
A		U		R		S		P		N		T
C	R	O	W		C	L	O	T	H	I	E	R
T		U		E		U		A		T		U
O		S	E	C	O	N	D	G	U	E	S	S
R				R		K		O				T
S	T	E	P	U	P		E	N	M	I	T	Y

12

C	A	S	U	A	L	T	Y		F	E	T	E
H		U		I		O				I		X
A	G	R	A	R	I	A	N			R		O
N		G		M		D	E	S	C	E	N	D
C	H	I	N	A			T					U
E		C		N	E	S	T	L	I	N	G	S
		A		M		L		A				
L	U	L	L	A	B	I	E	S		G		C
I				A			I	D	A	H	O	
M	A	S	O	N	R	Y		R		S		V
I		I		K	A	M	I	K	A	Z	E	
T		L		L		N		K				R
S	A	T	E		P	E	N	G	U	I	N	S

Solutions

13

```
H U N C H E S   A   U   I
E   E   O     E D I S O N
N   A   O   A   H   E   G
P A T C H U P   E Q U A L
E   E   A   P   R   P   E
C A N E   F L I E S
K   S   B   A   S   G   G
    R E C U R   E A S E
B   F   E   D   W   L   N
A C I D S   E A R P L U G
N   S   W   D   O   O   H
J E T L A G   N   P   I
O   S   X   D I G E S T S
```

14

```
B L A N C H   E S T E E M
R   B   H   E   P   L   O
E M O T I O N   A   S   U
A   V   L   C O N F E S S
S I E G E   A   N     S
T   P     P E E R A G E
    A   O   S   R   B
B I R D F L U   L     D
O   F   L   S H A M E
R E B E C C A   O   S   S
D   A   U   T E A T I M E
E   R   T   E   V   V   R
R O B U S T   R E J E C T
```

15

```
L A P I S   C O M P A C T
U   I   T   O   O   P   I
C E N T A U R   L O P E D
I   H   T   P   A   R   I
D R O N E   S I R L O I N
    L   L   E     P   G
B Y E B Y E   C H O R U S
I   C     D   O   I
C H A M B E R   S P A W N
Y   M   A   A   T   T   U
C H E F S   P R E M I E R
L   R   I   E   S   O   S
E T A I L E R   S E N S E
```

16

```
  H O N E Y S U C K L E
T   C   M   K   H   E   H
O   T   P L A Z A   M O O
N O O S E   T   R   U   R
S   B   R   E   T Y R E S
I C E H O U S E       E
L   R   R     H   M   E
L     P A N O R A M A
I N T R O   B   L   N   D
T   E   L   J   S C I F I
I M P   I N E P T   A   S
S   I   V   C   E   C   H
  A D V E N T U R I S M
```

17

```
D R E S S E D   B   R O T
    O   C   A D A G E   E
E M B L E M S   R   V   S
    A   N   H   S W E A T
I N T R A N E T     N   I
    C   R   R   W   U   F
D E C E I T   B A K E R Y
I   O   O   L   V     E
S   R     D I V E R T E D
T E R M S   N   B   L
E   O   P   G L A D D E N
N   D R A P E   N     C
D I E   T   R A D I A T E
```

18

```
S U S P E N S E   I C E S
I   O   L   U   C   R   T
T R A D E I N   O M E G A
E   K   V   D   N   D   R
      R E T R O G R E S S
T   C   N   Y   L   N   H
O W L E T S   B O R Z O I
A   E   H   L   M   A   P
N O R T H K O R E A
D   I   O   S   R   L   A
F I C H U   S H A V I N G
R   A   R   E   T   N   E
O G L E   A S B E S T O S
```

552

Solutions

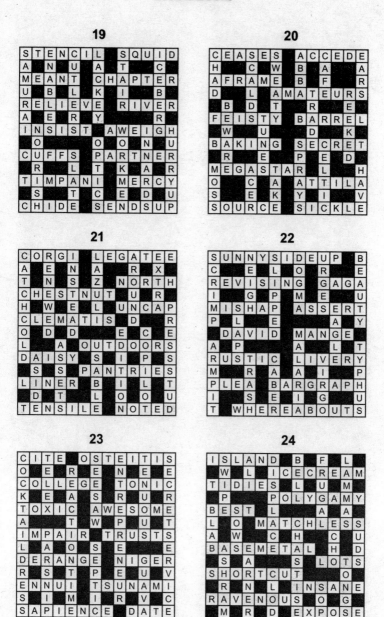

553

Solutions

25

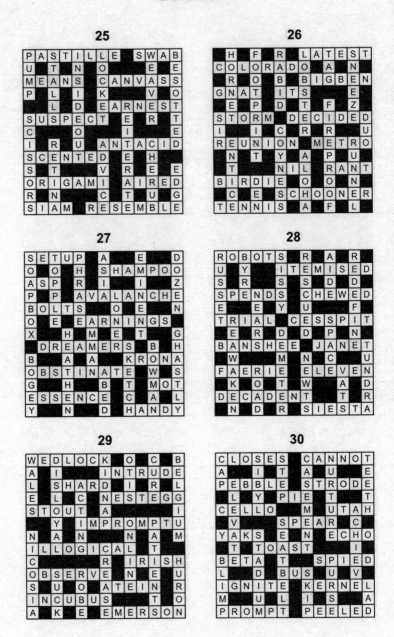

26

27

28

29

30

Solutions

31   32

33   34

35   36

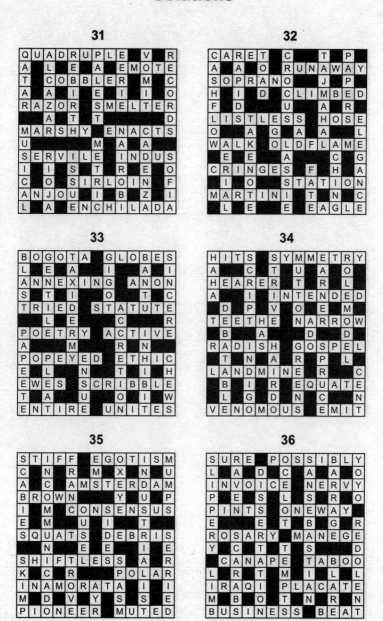

Solutions

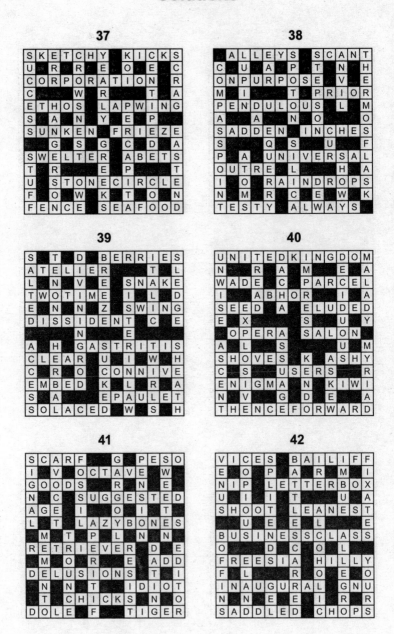

37

S	K	E	T	C	H	Y		K	I	C	K	S
U		R		R	E		O		E			C
C	O	R	P	O	R	A	T	I	O	N		R
C			W		R			T				A
E	T	H	O	S		L	A	P	W	I	N	G
S		A		N		Y		E		P		
S	U	N	K	E	N		F	R	I	E	Z	E
		G		S		G		C		D		A
S	W	E	L	T	E	R		A	B	E	T	S
T		R			E		P					T
U		S	T	O	N	E	C	I	R	C	L	E
F		O		W		K	T		O			N
F	E	N	C	E		S	E	A	F	O	O	D

38

	A	L	L	E	Y	S		S	C	A	N	T
C		U		A		P		T		N		H
O	N	P	U	R	P	O	S	E		V		E
M		I		T			T		P	R	I	O	R
P	E	N	D	U	L	O	U	S		L		M
A		A		N		O					O
S	A	D	D	E	N		I	N	C	H	E	S
S				Q		S		U			F
P		A		U	N	I	V	E	R	S	A	L
O	U	T	R	E		L			H		A
I		O		R	A	I	N	D	R	O	P	S
N		M		R		C		E		W		K
T	E	S	T	Y		A	L	W	A	Y	S	

39

S		T		D		B	E	R	R	I	E	S
A	T	E	L	I	E	R			T			L
L		N		V		E		S	N	A	K	E
T	W	O	T	I	M	E		I		L		D
E		N		N		Z		S	W	I	N	G
D	I	S	S	I	D	E	N	T		C		E
			N				E				
A		H		G	A	S	T	R	I	T	I	S
C	L	E	A	R		U		I		W		H
C		R		O		C	O	N	N	I	V	E
E	M	B	E	D		K		L		R		A
S		A			E	P	A	U	L	E	T	
S	O	L	A	C	E	D		W		S		H

40

U	N	I	T	E	D	K	I	N	G	D	O	M
N			R		A		M			E		A
W	A	D	E		C		P	A	R	C	E	L
I			A	B	H	O	R			I		A
S	E	E	D		A		E	L	U	D	E	D
E		X			S		U			U		Y
	O	P	E	R	A		S	A	L	O	N	
A		L		S				U		M
S	H	O	V	E	S		K		A	S	H	Y
C		S		U	S	E	R	S			R
E	N	I	G	M	A		N		K	I	W	I
N		V		G		D		E			A
T	H	E	N	C	E	F	O	R	W	A	R	D

41

S	C	A	R	F		G		P	E	S	O
I		V		O	C	T	A	V	E		W
G	O	O	D	S		R		N		E	
N		C		S	U	G	G	E	S	T	E	D
A	G	E		I		O		I		T	
L		T		L	A	Z	Y	B	O	N	E	S
	M		T		P		L		N		N
R	E	T	R	I	E	V	E	R		D		E
	M		O		R		E		A	D	D
D	E	L	U	S	I	O	N	S		T		I
	N		N		T			I	D	I	O	T
	T		C	H	I	C	K	S		N		O
D	O	L	E		F			T	I	G	E	R

42

V	I	C	E	S		B	A	I	L	I	F	F
E		O		P		A		R		M		I
N	I	P		L	E	T	T	E	R	B	O	X
U		I		I		T			U		A
S	H	O	O	T		L	E	A	N	E	S	T
		U		E		E		L			E
B	U	S	I	N	E	S	S	C	L	A	S	S
O			D		C		O		L		
F	R	E	E	S	I	A		H	I	L	L	Y
F			L		R		O		E		O
I	N	A	U	G	U	R	A	L		G	N	U
N		N		E		E		I		R		R
S	A	D	D	L	E	D		C	H	O	P	S

556

Solutions

43

O	C	T	O	P	U	S			C	A	M	E	L
P		A		R		E		U		O			U
P	E	R	P	E	T	R	A	T	O	R			R
O			V		I		T			T			C
S	U	P	R	A		A	N	G	U	I	S	H	
E		L		L		L		R		C			
D	E	A	D	E	N		D	E	V	I	L	S	
		T		N		F		A		A		P	
T	H	I	S	T	L	E		T	O	N	G	A	
U		T			R		B					T	
N		U	N	D	E	R	W	E	I	G	H	T	
I		D		I		I		A		O		E	
S	H	E	E	P		C	O	R	S	A	I	R	

44

S	U	R	F	B	O	A	R	D			T	I	P
C		O		R			R		O				L
A	Z	A	L	E	A		F	E	L	I	N	E	
M		D		V		S		A		L			C
	H	I	F	I		C	O	M	M	E	N	T	
N		E		T		I			T			R	
O			T	Y	P	E	S	E	T			U	
V		E			N		N	G				M	
E	L	A	S	T	I	C		S	E	E	R		
M		R		R		E		N		N		E	
B	O	W	L	E	D		B	A	R	I	U	M	
E		I		E			R		U			I	
R	I	G		S	U	C	C	E	S	S	O	R	

45

B	A	B	I	E	S		S	U	B	W	A	Y
	P		D		T		E		O		P	
E	P	E	E		I	R	R	I	G	A	T	E
	L		A		R		G		I			
B	E	L	L	E		B	E	S	E	E	C	H
	T		L		P		A			O		
A	R	G	Y	L	E		N	I	M	B	U	S
	E			C		T		A		N		
P	E	R	S	E	U	S		B	R	O	T	H
		M		L		O		A		L		
V	A	C	A	T	I	O	N		B	L	E	D
	H		C		A		U		O		S	
T	A	L	K	E	R		S	Q	U	A	S	H

46

M	A	R	T	I	A	L	A	R	T	S		I
U		H		S		U			P	A	N	
S	E	L	E	C	T	I	O	N		O		H
T			O		G		R			R		A
Y	O	K	O	O	N	O		S	T	E	A	L
		V		I		W		I				E
E	Q	U	A	L	S		A	T	T	E	N	D
M		T		H		I		L				
E	X	C	E	L		A	T	H	E	I	S	T
R		A		L		R						U
A		R		A	P	P	E	R	T	A	I	N
L	E	O		N		S		I				E
D		B	L	O	O	D	S	U	C	K	E	R

47

S	E	M	I		S	A	S	H	C	O	R	D
H		C		P		W		A		O		
A	L	O	E	V	E	R	A		R	U	B	Y
P		D		E		T		R		B		
E	L	A	T	E	D		H	O	Y	D	E	N
D		E		U						R		
	S	T	A	M	P		D	I	T	T	Y	
E			I		R		A					
M	A	N	I	A	C		S	N	A	K	E	S
S		S		O		P		C				S
B	I	L	L		P	R	O	V	I	N	C	E
	D		E		R		S		N			N
P	E	R	S	U	A	D	E		G	A	I	T

48

S	O	D	A		E	L	L	I	P	S	I	S
A		R		L		O		N		T		I
T	S	A	R	I	N	A		C	R	U	S	T
C		W		T		T		O		D		E
H	O	L	S	T		H	U	R	R	I	E	D
E			L		E		R		E			
L	I	M	P	E	T		B	I	D	D	E	R
	A		F		W		G				E	
C	A	S	T	I	L	E		I	N	P	U	T
A		T		N		B		E			R	
G	R	I	E	G		P	A	L	E	T	T	E
E		F		I		E		I		A		A
D	E	F	O	R	M	E	D		C	L	A	D

Solutions

49

50

51

52

53

54

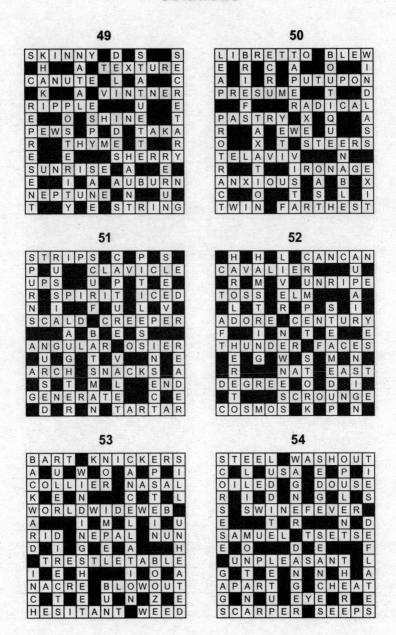

Solutions

55

56

57

58

59

60

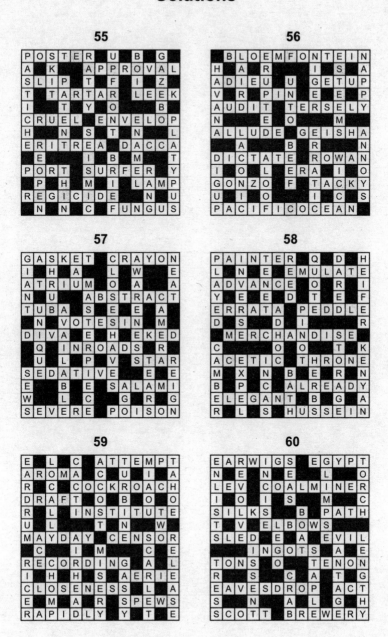

Solutions

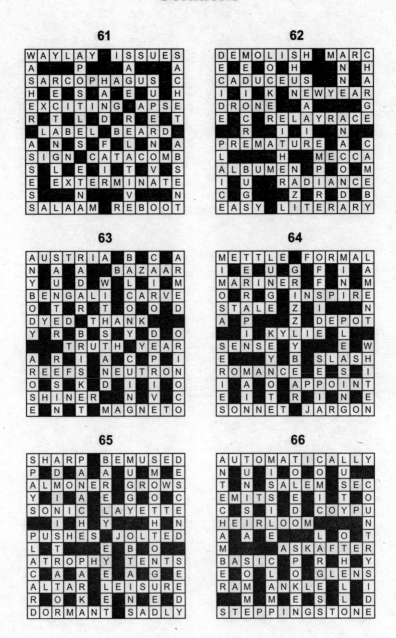

61 • **62** • **63** • **64** • **65** • **66**

Solutions

67

```
A S E P T I C . K . M U G
. P . E . A L I V E . O
G A T H E R S . S . L . N
. T . N . T . S H A R E
S U I T A B L E . N . B
. L . G . E . O . G . A
S A C R E D . S P R E A D
Y . L . R . P . E . . V
S . E . . F O U N T A I N
T R A P S . N . I . . A
E . N . A . D E N S I T Y
M . S U R G E . G . . O
S H E . K . R E S P I R E
```

68

```
P R A C T I C E . C A N S
I . Y . R . H . A . L . A
C H A R A D E . C R A W L
K . H . V . A . Q . C . U
. . R E S T A U R A N T
C . P . L . S . A . R . A
L A R V A E . V I C T O R
E . O . G . N . N . E . Y
A B B R E V I A T E
R . A . N . E . A . L . S
C U B I C . C O N S O L E
U . L . Y . E . C . G . N
T I E R . A S T E R O I D
```

69

```
C A C K L E D . A B B E Y
L . H . E . E . U . . N
A R A B S . N E G L E C T
S . T . S . O . U . . L
S E E K O U T . R A D O N
I . A . N . E . . . S
C O U R S E . F A S T E N
. R . . U . R . W . O
B O G U S . P U C C I N I
. T . H . B . H . N . S
F U R N A C E . I N T R O
. N . L . A . V . U . M
I D Y L L . T R E M B L E
```

70

```
T O O B A D . B U C K E T
I . I . E . O . O . . Y
E Q U A L S . B . M . R
S . S . I N S T A N C E
. H . E . R . I . L
C U R D L E . C A R E E R
. B . A . . R . V
U R S I N E . P A S T E L
. I . G . R . E . R
E S P R E S S O . L . A
P . O . A . P A D D E D
I . T . L . E . O . Z
C L I E N T . R A M B L E
```

71

```
C O S T S . R E C E I P T
A . H . P . E . V . A
F . R . U . M . B E A N S
E V I C T I O N . N . I
T . V . N . T . P E A C H
E Y E L I N E R . D . O
R . L . K . . F . B . R
I . . J . B A S E L E S S
A L O O F . G . R . D . E
. I . S . N E U R I T I S
A L P H A . N . O . I . H
. A . U . . C . U . M . O
S C R A W N Y . S I E G E
```

72

```
S O L A R S Y S T E M . B
U . D . C . A . X . . A
T I R A M I S U . A B E T
U . M . E . N . L . . H
R E A S O N . A S T U T E
E . L . C . . . N . R
. A D D L E . P A N T S
P . E . . A . I . A
R A R E F Y . S E R E N E
I . C . U . S . E . R
M E M O . C R I T E R I A
E . L . C . N . V . T
D . V I N A I G R E T T E
```

Solutions

73

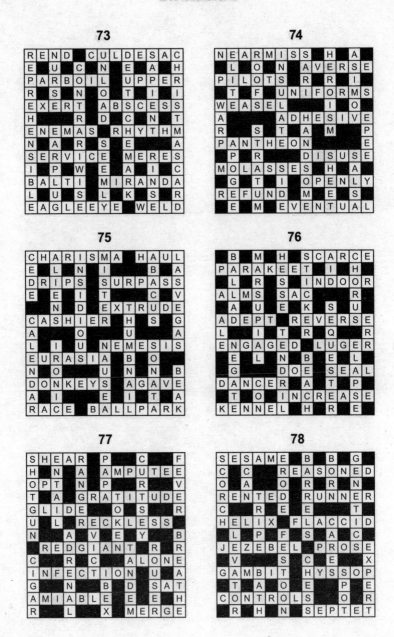

```
R E N D . . C U L D E S A C
E . U . C . N . E . A . H .
P A R B O I L . U P P E R .
R . S . N . O . T . I . I .
E X E R T . A B S C E S S .
H . . R . D . C . N . T . .
E N E M A S . R H Y T H M .
N . A . R . S . E . . A . .
S E R V I C E . M E R E S .
I . P . W . E . A . I . C .
B A L T I . M I R A N D A .
L . U . S . L . K . S . R .
E A G L E E Y E . W E L D .
```

74

```
N E A R M I S S . H . A . .
. L . O . N . A V E R S E .
P I L O T S . R . R . I . .
. T . F . U N I F O R M S .
W E A S E L . . I . O . . .
A . . . A D H E S I V E . .
R . S . T . A . M . . P . .
P A N T H E O N . . . E . .
. P . R . . D I S U S E . .
M O L A S S E S . H . A . .
. G . T . I . O P E N L Y .
R E F U N D . M . E . S . .
. E . M . E V E N T U A L .
```

75

```
C H A R I S M A . H A U L .
E . L . N . . . B . A . . .
D R I P S . S U R P A S S .
E . E . I . T . . C . V . .
. N . D . E X T R U D E . .
C A S H I E R . H . S . G .
A . . O . . U . . . A . . .
L . I . U . N E M E S I S .
E U R A S I A . B . O . . .
N . O . . U . N . N . B . .
D O N K E Y S . A G A V E .
A . I . . E . I . T . A . .
R A C E . B A L L P A R K .
```

76

```
. B . M . H . S C A R C E .
P A R A K E E T . I . H . .
. L . R . S . I N D O O R .
A L M S . S A C . . R . . .
. A . U . E . K . S . U . .
A D E P T . R E V E R S E .
L . I . T . R . Q . R . . .
E N G A G E D . L U G E R .
. E . L . N . B . E . L . .
. G . . D O E . S E A L . .
D A N C E R . A . T . P . .
. T . O . I N C R E A S E .
K E N N E L . H . R . E . .
```

77

```
S H E A R . P . C . F . . .
H . N . A . A M P U T E E .
O P T . N . P . R . V . . .
T . A . G R A T I T U D E .
G L I D E . O . S . R . . .
U . L . R E C K L E S S . .
N . A . V . E . Y . B . . .
. R E D G I A N T . R . R .
C . R . C . A L O N E . . .
I N F E C T I O N . U . A .
G . N . B . D . S A T . . .
A M I A B L E . E . E . H .
R . L . X . M E R G E . . .
```

78

```
S E S A M E . B . B . G . .
C . C . R E A S O N E D . .
O . A . O . R . R . N . . .
R E N T E D . R U N N E R .
C . R . E . E . . T . . . .
H E L I X . F L A C C I D .
. L . P . F . S . A . C . .
J E Z E B E L . P R O S E .
V . S . C . E . X . . . . .
G A M B I T . H Y S S O P .
. T . A . O . E . P . E . .
C O N T R O L S . O . R . .
. R . H . N . S E P T E T .
```

562

Solutions

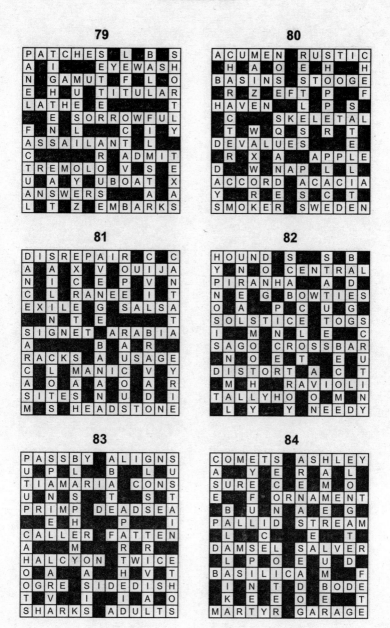

79

P A T C H E S L B S
A I E Y E W A S H
N G A M U T F L O
E H U T I T U L A R
L A T H E E T
E S O R R O W F U L
F N L C I Y
A S S A I L A N T L
C R A D M I T
T R E M O L O V S E
U A Y U B O A T X
A N S W E R S A A
L T Z E M B A R K S

80

A C U M E N R U S T I C
H A O E H H
B A S I N S S T O O G E
R Z E F T P F
H A V E N L P S
C S K E L E T A L
T W Q S R T
D E V A L U E S E
R X A A P P L E
D W N A P L L
A C C O R D A C A C I A
Y R E S C T
S M O K E R S W E D E N

81

D I S R E P A I R C C
A A X V O U I J A
N I C E P V N
C L R A N E E I T
E X I L E G S A L S A
N T E T
S I G N E T A R A B I A
A B A R
R A C K S A U S A G E
C L M A N I C V Y
A O A A O A R
S I T E S N U D I
M S H E A D S T O N E

82

H O U N D S S B
Y N O C E N T R A L
P I R A N H A A D
N E G B O W T I E S
O A P C U G
S O L S T I C E T O G S
I M N L E C
S A G O C R O S S B A R
N O E T E U
D I S T O R T A C T
M H R A V I O L I
T A L L Y H O O M N
L Y Y N E E D Y

83

P A S S B Y A L I G N S
U P L B L U
T I A M A R I A C O N S
U N S T S T
P R I M P D E A D S E A
E H P I
C A L L E R F A T T E N
A M R R
H A L C Y O N T W I C E
O A A H V T
O G R E S I D E D I S H
T V I I A O
S H A R K S A D U L T S

84

C O M E T S A S H L E Y
A Y E R A L
S U R E C E M O
E F O R N A M E N T
B U N A E G
P A L L I D S T R E A M
L C E T
D A M S E L S A L V E R
L P O E U D
B A S I L I C A M F
I N T D B O D E
K E E O E T
M A R T Y R G A R A G E

563

Solutions

85

B	A	S	I	L			F	L	A	T	T	E	N
O		C		U		O		F		R			A
N		H		R	E	P	R	I	M	A	N	D	
A	L	I	C	E				R		N			I
N		Z		D	I	S	P	E	N	S	E	R	
Z		O		G		I			A				
A	P	P	E	A	L		E	D	I	T	E	D	
		H		O		R			L			I	
W	O	R	K	H	O	U	S	E		A		N	
E		E		A			S	I	N	C	E		
I	G	N	O	R	A	M	U	S		T		O	
G		I		S		A		A		I		U	
H	E	A	T	H	E	R		Y	A	C	H	T	

86

B	E	S	T		C	O	M	P	O	S	E	R	
A		A	R		N		R		U			E	
S	O	L	D	I	E	R		E	A	S	E	L	
I		V		C		U		S		P		Y	
L	E	E	C	H		S	Y	S	T	E	M		
I			T		H		G		N		D		
S	E	A	B	E	D		D	A	W	D	L	E	
K		B		R		A		L				R	
	D	A	M	S	O	N		L	A	N	A	I	
Z		N		C		I		E		O		S	
I	N	D	I	A		M	A	R	T	I	N	I	
N		O		L		U		Y		S		V	
C	O	N	D	E	N	S	E		B	Y	T	E	

87

S	N	A	F	F	L	E		B	U	C	K	S	
H		R		A		Y		O		H		T	
I	N	C	A	R	C	E	R	A	T	E		I	
M			M		L			V				N	
M	E	A	T	S		I	N	S	T	A	N	T	
E		N		T		D		H		L			
R	E	A	P	E	R		F	A	D	I	N	G	
		L		A		I		N		E		R	
B	A	G	H	D	A	D		G	A	R	B	O	
A		E			I	R						W	
N		S	U	P	P	O	S	I	T	I	O	N	
N		I		A		T		L		L		U	
S	W	A	M	P		S	C	A	L	L	O	P	

88

	A	S	L	E	E	P		P	A	N	I	C	
H		I		G		L		R		A		U	
I	N	T	E	G	R	A	T	E		O		T	
P		A			C			C	O	M	M	A	
P	E	R	S	E	V	E	R	E			I		
O			A		S		D			D		D	
P	A	W	P	A	W		D	E	P	A	R	T	
O			V		R		A			A		H	
T		D		A	L	A	B	A	S	T	E	R	
A	I	R	E	R		D				E		U	
M		A		I	S	I	N	G	L	A	S	S	
U		M		C		U		U		S		T	
S	T	A	G	E		M	A	N	G	E	R		

89

A		F		T		S	C	A	L	P	E	L	
F	L	O	R	I	S	T			H			I	
A		E		M		O		A	L	O	N	G	
R	E	T	I	E		L	A	P		B		N	
		U		C		I		P	O	I	S	E	
B	Y	S	T	A	N	D	E	R		A		O	
O			P			O		O		U		U	
T		A		S	O	Y	A	B	E	A	N	S	
S	A	D	H	U		I		A		D			
W		J		L	I	P		T	O	R	S	O	
A	M	U	S	E		P		I		O		X	
N		S			E	M	O	T	I	V	E		
A	C	T	U	A	T	E		N		T		N	

90

S	T	S	W	I	T	H	I	N	S	D	A	Y	
H		A		I		M		A		A		A	
A	K	I	N		B		P	E	N	N	O	N	
R			L	I	E	G	E			G		K	
E	D	G	Y		R		R	E	C	E	D	E	
D		A			I		R		R		D		
	T	R	A	W	L		L	E	M	O	N		
H		I		I				U			A		
O	R	B	I	T	S		B		A	S	I	F	
W		A		T	H	O	R	N			L		
D	E	L	U	X	E		W		T	I	N	A	
A		D		N		E		E			M		
H	A	I	L	E	S	E	L	A	S	S	I	E	

564

Solutions

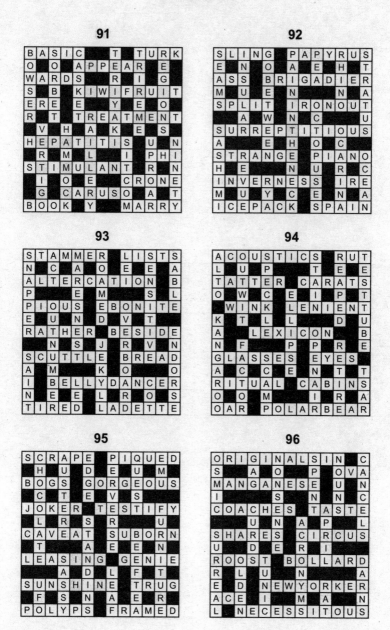

91

B	A	S	I	C		T		T	U	R	K
O		O		A	P	P	E	A	R		E
W	A	R	D	S		R		I		G	
S		B		K	I	W	I	F	R	U	I	T
E	R	E		E		Y		E		O	
R		T		T	R	E	A	T	M	E	N	T
	V		H		A		K		E		S	
H	E	P	A	T	I	T	I	S		U		N
	R		M		L		I		P	H	I
S	T	I	M	U	L	A	N	T		R		N
	I		O		E			C	R	O	N	E
	G		C	A	R	U	S	O		A		T
B	O	O	K		Y			M	A	R	R	Y

92

S	L	I	N	G		P	A	P	Y	R	U	S
E		N		O		A		E		H		T
A	S	S		B	R	I	G	A	D	I	E	R
M		U		E		N			N		A	
S	P	L	I	T		I	R	O	N	O	U	T
		A		W		N		C			U	
S	U	R	R	E	P	T	I	T	I	O	U	S
A			E		H		O		C			
S	T	R	A	N	G	E		P	I	A	N	O
H		E		N		U		R		C		
I	N	V	E	R	N	E	S	S		I	R	E
M		U		Y		C		E		N		A
I	C	E	P	A	C	K		S	P	A	I	N

93

S	T	A	M	M	E	R		L	I	S	T	S
N		C		A		O		E		E		A
A	L	T	E	R	C	A	T	I	O	N		B
P		E		M			S		L			L
P	I	O	U	S		E	B	O	N	I	T	E
E		U		N		D		V		T		
R	A	T	H	E	R		B	E	S	I	D	E
		N		S		J		R		V		N
S	C	U	T	T	L	E		B	R	E	A	D
A		M			K		O			O		O
I		B	E	L	L	Y	D	A	N	C	E	R
N		E		E		L		R		O		S
T	I	R	E	D		L	A	D	E	T	T	E

94

A	C	O	U	S	T	I	C	S		R	U	T
L		U		P			T		E		E	
T	A	T	T	E	R		C	A	R	A	T	S
O		W		C		E		I		P		T
	W	I	N	K		L	E	N	I	E	N	T
K		T		L		L			D		U	
A			L	E	X	I	C	O	N			B
N		F			P		P		P		R	E
G	L	A	S	S	E	S		E	Y	E	S	
A		C		C		E		N		T		T
R	I	T	U	A	L		C	A	B	I	N	S
O		O		M		I		I		R		A
O	A	R		P	O	L	A	R	B	E	A	R

95

S	C	R	A	P	E		P	I	Q	U	E	D
	H		U		D		E		U		M	
B	O	G	S		G	O	R	G	E	O	U	S
	C		T		E		V		S			
J	O	K	E	R		T	E	S	T	I	F	Y
	L		R		S		R			U		
C	A	V	E	A	T		S	U	B	O	R	N
	T			A		E		E		N		
L	E	A	S	I	N	G		G	E	N	I	E
		A		D		L		F		T		
S	U	N	S	H	I	N	E		T	R	U	G
	F		S		N		A		E		R	
P	O	L	Y	P	S		F	R	A	M	E	D

96

O	R	I	G	I	N	A	L	S	I	N		C
S		A		O		P			O	V	A	
M	A	N	G	A	N	E	S	E		U		N
I			S			N		N		N		C
C	O	A	C	H	E	S		T	A	S	T	E
		U		N		A		P			L	
S	H	A	R	E	S		C	I	R	C	U	S
U		D		E		R		I				
R	O	O	S	T		B	O	L	L	A	R	D
R		L		U		N					A	
E		D		N	E	W	Y	O	R	K	E	R
A	C	E		I		M		A			N	
L		N	E	C	E	S	S	I	T	O	U	S

565

Solutions

97

D	A	I	S		T	E	S	T	C	A	S	E
A		L		H		I		H		E		
R	E	V	I	S	I	O	N		A	G	A	R
K		T		R		E		I		L		
E	T	C	H	E	S		W	A	R	D	E	R
N		E		T		D		G				
	S	U	R	L	Y		F	O	C	U	S	
	H		E			A		Y		A		
C	A	N	C	E	R		R	E	C	T	U	M
	C		O		A		R		L		I	
O	K	R	A		B	L	A	Z	O	N	E	D
	L		S		B		G		P		S	
N	E	U	T	R	I	N	O		S	C	U	T

98

D	A	M	E		N	A	U	T	I	L	U	S
Y		O		B		T		A		I		H
N	U	P	T	I	A	L		R	O	T	O	R
A		E		O		A		T		H		U
M	U	S	I	C		S	P	A	R	I	N	G
I			H		T		R		U			
C	A	R	V	E	D		H	E	L	M	E	T
	A		M		L		S			R		
S	U	I	C	I	D	E		A	L	P	H	A
I		N		S		S		U		L		G
R	E	B	U	T		S	E	C	L	U	D	E
E		O		R		E		E		T		D
N	E	W	L	Y	W	E	D		B	O	D	Y

99

B	A	L	S	A	M		R		R			B
	M		D		S	O	M	E	O	N	E	
B	O	B	B	I	N		S		P			D
	U		O		C	A	L	L	O	U	S	
D	R	E	S	S	Y			E			P	
E		P		A	D	O	P	T			R	
M	O	R	E		R		V		I	D	L	E
I		C	A	N	O	E		O			A	
T		U			R	A	N	C	I	D		
A	N	A	L	Y	S	T		B		D		
S		A		C		C	A	M	P	E	R	
S	A	L	T	P	A	N		S			A	
E			E		B		B	E	A	G	L	E

100

S	H	E	E	P	I	S	H		S	W	A	P
O		R		A		I			C			O
U		R		C		N	O	M	I	N	A	L
P	L	A	T	E	A	U		M			I	
	N			S	L	E	I	G	H	T		
S	A	D	I	S	M		E		T			I
Y		D		I		A		A			C	
N		E		D		F	O	R	C	E	S	
O	R	G	A	N	I	C			A			
P		L			A	S	S	U	R	E	D	
S	H	R	I	M	P	S		U		B		I
I		S			T		E		O		E	
S	W	O	T		D	E	S	T	I	N	E	D

101

S	A	T	Y	R	S		M		R		D	
C		O			O	P	E	N	E	Y	E	D
O	A	T		B		A		P		C		
O		T	A	V	E	R	N		A	M	O	K
P		E		R		D		R		Y		
S	P	R	A	Y		D	E	N	T	I	S	T
		T		K		R		E				
F	I	T	T	I	N	G		G	E	N	U	S
	N		A		O		A		E		T	
B	L	O	C		C	A	M	P	U	S		A
	A		H		K		I			T	N	T
T	W	E	E	Z	E	R	S		L		E	
	S		D		R		S	T	R	E	S	S

102

D	E	A	F	E	N		C	O	M	I	N	G
	M		E		O		L		O			E
S	P	A	R	E		A	C	R	O	S	S	
	O		R	I	L	E	S		T			T
A	W	A	Y			S		I	O	T	A	
	E			A	N	T	I	C	S			P
C	R	E	W		A		F		E	R	G	O
A			A	R	R	O	Y	O			R	
T	H	I	S		C			K	E	E	L	
E		P		O	F	T	E	N		N		
R	U	B	I	E	S		O		O	K	A	Y
E		S		I		M		W		D		
R	I	C	H	E	S		B	A	N	K	E	R

566

Solutions

103

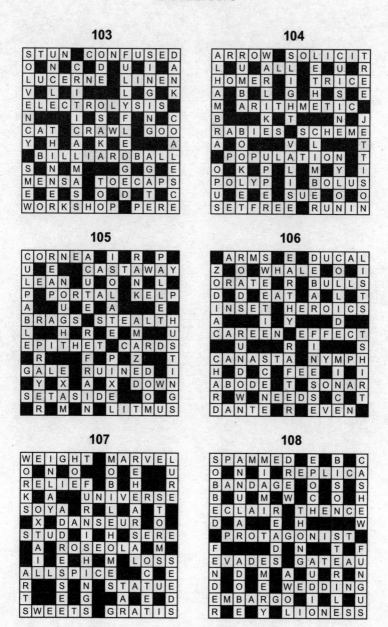

```
S T U N   C O N F U S E D
O   N   C   D   U   I   A
L U C E R N E   L I N E N
V   L   I       L   G   K
E L E C T R O L Y S I S
N       I   S   F   N   C
C A T   C R A W L   G O O
Y   H   A   K   E       A
  B I L L I A R D B A L L
S   N   M       G   G   E
M E N S A   T O E C A P S
E   E   S   O   D   T   C
W O R K S H O P   P E R E
```

104

```
A R R O W   S O L I C I T
L   U   A L L   E   U   R
H O M E R   I   T R I C E
A   B   L   G   H   S   E
M   A R I T H M E T I C
B       K   T       N   J
R A B I E S   S C H E M E
A   O       V   L       T
  P O P U L A T I O N   T
O   K   P   L   M   Y   I
P O L Y P   I   B O L U S
U   E   E   S U E   O   O
S E T F R E E   R U N I N
```

105

```
C O R N E A   I   R   P
U   E     C A S T A W A Y
L E A N   U   O   N   L
P   P O R T A L   K E L P
A   U   E   A     E
B R A G S   S T E A L T H
L   H   R   E   M     U
E P I T H E T   C A R D S
  R   F   P   Z     T
G A L E   R U I N E D   I
  Y   X   A   X   D O W N
S E T A S I D E   O     G
  R   M   N   L I T M U S
```

106

```
  A R M S   E   D U C A L
Z   O   W H A L E   O   I
O R A T E   R   B U L L S
D   D   E A T   A   L   T
I N S E T   H E R O I C S
A   I   Y       D
C A R E E N   E F F E C T
  U   R   I         S
C A N A S T A   N Y M P H
H   D   C   F E E   I   I
A B O D E   T   S O N A R
R   W   N E E D S   C   T
D A N T E   R   E V E N
```

107

```
W E I G H T   M A R V E L
O   N   O   O   E       U
R E L I E F   B   H     R
K   A   U N I V E R S E
S O Y A   R   L   A   T
  X   D A N S E U R   O
S T U D   I   H   S E R E
  A   R O S E O L A   M
  I   E   H   M   L O S S
A L L S P I C E   C   E
R   S   N   S T A T U E
T   E   G   A   E   D
S W E E T S   G R A T I S
```

108

```
S P A M M E D   E   B   C
O   N   I   R E P L I C A
B A N D A G E   O   S   S
B   U   M   W   C   O   H
E C L A I R   T H E N C E
D   A   E   H       W
  P R O T A G O N I S T
F       D   N       T   F
E V A D E S   G A T E A U
N   D   M   A   U   R   N
D   O   E   W E D D I N G
E M B A R G O   I   L   U
R   E   Y   L I O N E S S
```

567

Solutions

109

B		R		M		C	O	H	A	B	I	T
A	R	E	N	A		H		A		L		E
T		B		S	T	A	I	R	C	A	S	E
T	H	E	T	A		P		P		C		N
L		C		I	C	E	H	O	C	K	E	Y
E		C			L		O			K		
D	E	A	L	E	R		U	N	U	S	E	D
	D		N		C			I		O		
H	O	M	E	G	U	A	R	D		L		S
E		O		O		N		U	N	I	T	S
N	O	T	O	R	I	O	U	S		C		I
N		E		G		E		T	H	O	S	E
A	C	T	R	E	S	S		Y		N		R

110

P	O	R	K	P	I	E		B	A	S	R	A
A		E		A		L		N			F	
N	O	D		T	R	A	N	S	I	E	N	T
A		T		O		N		S			E	
C	O	A	T	I		A			E	M	I	R
E		P		S	T	I	F	L	E			
A	L	E	C		A		R		D	A	M	P
		A	N	C	H	O	R		G			I
M	A	L	T		K		O	V	E	R	T	
A		S		B		L		L		L		E
F	R	E	E	W	H	E	E	L		E	C	O
I			Y		E	E		S		S		U
A	C	H	E	S		P	A	R	E	S	I	S

111

S	A	F	E	T	Y		S	L	A	C	K	S
E			A		A		A					H
A	E	R	O	N	A	U	T	I	C	S		O
R		E		G		G		D		N		V
C	O	N	F	I	N	E	D		C	A	R	E
H		D		B		R		L		K		L
	Y	I	E	L	D		B	A	B	E	L	
B		T		E		O		X		B		S
R	A	I	N		S	T	E	A	D	I	L	Y
A		O		K		H		T		T		N
H		N	O	N	R	E	S	I	D	E	N	T
M			O		R		V					A
S	C	R	I	B	E		R	E	F	L	E	X

112

E	M	B	L	A	Z	O	N		B	O	Y	S
X		L		P		B			N		U	
O	V	E	R	L	O	O	K		C		I	
C		S		O		E	N	T	R	E	A	T
E	P	S	O	M		E			I			O
T		Y		B	L	U	E	P	E	T	E	R
		O		A		L		I				
S	O	U	T	H	W	E	S	T		T		M
N				Y		A	M	I	T	Y		
I	N	B	R	I	E	F		T		V		S
P		I			R	A	G	T	R	A	D	E
E		T			R		L		T			L
R	A	S	H		T	O	N	E	D	E	A	F

113

S	Y	R	I	N	G	E		M		B		S
U		H		A		R	O	D	E	N	T	
R		O		D		E		O		A		A
M	U	D	P	I	E	S		R	U	R	A	L
I		I		R		C		H		D		E
S	C	U	D		M	A	K	E	R			
E		M		M		L		N		D		J
		R	E	L	A	X			H	I	R	E
G		A		A		T		E		V		A
R	O	O	T	S		O	I	L	W	E	L	L
A		R		L		R		D		R		O
B	A	T	T	E	R		E		S		U
S		A		S		C	A	R	P	E	T	S

114

M	I	N	I	O	N		H	U	B	B	U	B
I		O		B		D		N		A		A
S	U	R	V	E	Y	I	N	G		R		N
U		M		S		S		O	N	S	E	T
S	C	A	L	E		E	N	D				E
E		L				N		L	E	P	E	R
		L		G	O	T	B	Y		A		
B	U	Y	E	R		A			R		N	
U			I	N	N		G	R	A	T	E	
D	U	C	T	S		G		N		S		W
G		E		T	A	L	K	A	T	I	V	E
E		L	L		E		S		T		S	
T	I	L	L	E	R		T	H	R	E	A	T

568

Solutions

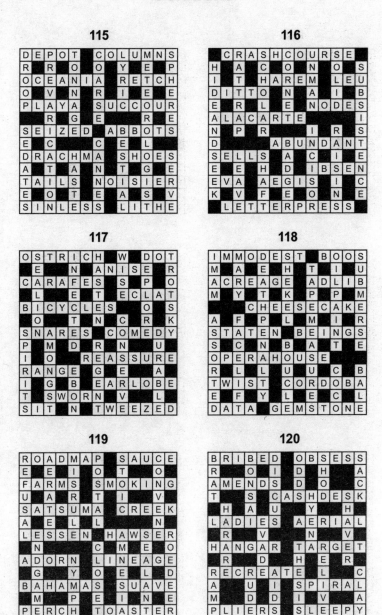

115

D	E	P	O	T		C	O	L	U	M	N	S
R		R		O		O		Y		E		P
O	C	E	A	N	I	A		R	E	T	C	H
O		V		N		R		I		E		E
P	L	A	Y	A		S	U	C	C	O	U	R
		R		G		E				R		E
S	E	I	Z	E	D		A	B	B	O	T	S
E		C				C		E		L		
D	R	A	C	H	M	A		S	H	O	E	S
A		T		A		N		T		G		E
T	A	I	L	S		N	O	I	S	I	E	R
E		O		T		E		A		S		V
S	I	N	L	E	S	S		L	I	T	H	E

116

	C	R	A	S	H	C	O	U	R	S	E	
H		A		C		O		N		O		S
I		T		H	A	R	E	M		L	E	U
D	I	T	T	O		N		A		I		B
E		R		L		E		N	O	D	E	S
A	L	A	C	A	R	T	E					I
N		P		R			I		R		S	
D			A	B	U	N	D	A	N	T		
S	E	L	L	S		A		C		I		E
E		E		H		D		I	B	S	E	N
E	V	A		A	E	G	I	S		I		C
K		V		F		E		O		N		E
	L	E	T	T	E	R	P	R	E	S	S	

117

O	S	T	R	I	C	H		W		D	O	T
	E		N		A	N	I	S	E		R	
C	A	R	A	F	E	S		S		P		O
	L		E		T		E	C	L	A	T	
B	I	C	Y	C	L	E	S		O		S	
	O		T		N		C		R		K	
S	N	A	R	E	S		C	O	M	E	D	Y
P		M		D		R		N		U		
I		O		R	E	A	S	S	U	R	E	
R	A	N	G	E		G		E		A		
I		G		B		E	A	R	L	O	B	E
T		S	W	O	R	N		V		L		
S	I	T		N		T	W	E	E	Z	E	D

118

I	M	M	O	D	E	S	T		B	O	O	S
M		A		E		H		T		I		U
A	C	R	E	A	G	E		A	D	L	I	B
M		Y		T		K		P		P		M
			C	H	E	E	S	E	C	A	K	E
A		F		P		L		M		I		R
S	T	A	T	E	N		B	E	I	N	G	S
S		C		N		B		A		T		E
O	P	E	R	A	H	O	U	S	E			
R		L		L		U		U		C		B
T	W	I	S	T		C	O	R	D	O	B	A
E		F		Y		L		E		C		L
D	A	T	A		G	E	M	S	T	O	N	E

119

R	O	A	D	M	A	P		S	A	U	C	E
E		E		I		O		T		O		
F	A	R	M	S		S	M	O	K	I	N	G
U		A		R		T		I		V		
S	A	T	S	U	M	A		C	R	E	E	K
A		E		L		L				N		
L	E	S	S	E	N		H	A	W	S	E	R
		N		C		M		E		O		
A	D	O	R	N		L	I	N	E	A	G	E
	G		Y		O		E		L		D	
B	A	H	A	M	A	S		S	U	A	V	E
	M		P		E		I		N		E	
P	E	R	C	H		T	O	A	S	T	E	R

120

B	R	I	B	E	D		O	B	S	E	S	S
R		O		I		D		H			A	
A	M	E	N	D	S		D		O		C	
T		S			C	A	S	H	D	E	S	K
	H		A		U		Y				H	
L	A	D	I	E	S		A	E	R	I	A	L
R			V			N			V			
H	A	N	G	A	R		T	A	R	G	E	T
R			D		H		E		R			
R	E	C	R	E	A	T	E		L			C
A		U		I		S	P	I	R	A	L	
M		D		D		I		V			A	
P	L	I	E	R	S		S	L	E	E	P	Y

Solutions

121

```
S P R E E . C A T C H E R
U . E . G . H . . L . J .
P . Y . O . O . H A Z E L
P O N Y T A I L . R . C .
O . A . R . C . D E L T A
S T R A I N E R . T . . C
I . D . P . . H . N . . C
N . . T . E S C A P A D E
G A V E L . L . N . T . S
. L . N . D O L D R U M S
S O U N D . W . L . R . O
. H . I . . L . E . A . .
F A L S I F Y . S A L T Y
```

122

```
D O W N T O E A R T H . C
R . O . B . D . O . . . R
I R I S H S E A . T O G A
E . E . C . M . A . . . V
S U B D U E . S I L A G E
T . R . N . . I . . . . N
. B A D G E . P L U M S .
S . W . . O . . E . . . A
C A L V E S . S A N D A L
Y . I . W . T . A . . . I
T A P S . A D E Q U A T E
H . O . R . R . R . . . N
E . P R O M I S C U O U S
```

123

```
A H O Y . D I S T A S T E
R . U . B . N . A . . . L
T A N T R U M . P E N C E
S . C . O . A . E . . . C
A G E N T . T O R R E N T
N . H . E . E . A . . . R
D A S H E D . S C A M P I
C . H . R . S . O . . . C
R E U N I O N . R E L I C
A . T . N . A . D . . . O H
F A T A L . I N E R T I A
T . E . A . L . R . T . I
S H R E W I S H . B O A R
```

124

```
U S E S U P . G . D . B
. T . W . A W A K E N E D
K A Y A K S . P . C . L
. V . Y . T A S M A N I A
L E S S O R . . D . Z
U . . . A N S W E R E D
G . W . M . P . S . . A
E S P E C I A L . . M
. U . A . . A S S I G N
P R O T E S T S . Y . E
. R . H . N . H A R D E N
D E L E G A T E . I . S
. Y . R . P . S C A L E D
```

125

```
S U I T C A S E . T A X I
A . N . O . P . . I . N
N Y L O N . R E F U S E D
K . A . T . A . L . U
. N . A . N U C L E U S
P U D D I N G . O . S . T
R . N . M . . . R
O . H . E . S U M M A R Y
D I A G R A M . I . D
U . W . E . T . V . A
C H A N N E L . T H E I R
E . I . . L . E . R . M
S P I N . A S S E M B L Y
```

126

```
. D . I . B . A B D U C T
B E A N B A G S . U . H
. C . T . D . T A B L E T
F A M E . L E O . . E
N . G . Y . U . R . R
S T A R E . U N L E A S H
A . I . H . D . M . I
C H A T T E R . V A U L T
O . Y . A . I . I . O
U . . R A T . N A A N
B R A C E S . C . D . N
L . R . A C H I E V E R
S Y R U P Y . Y . R . D
```

Solutions

127

M	O	S	E	S		U		S		N		
I		A		Q		S	T	A	T	U	R	E
L	O	T		U		E		R		W		
K		E		A	G	R	E	E	A	B	L	E
S	T	E	P	S			T		Y		L	
O		N		H	I	G	H	N	E	S	S	
P			T		M		E		D		S	
	B	E	R	I	B	E	R	I		G		A
B		I		U			C	O	A	T	I	
O	R	A	N	G	E	A	D	E		T		N
A		I		P		A			H	U	T	
S	P	I	T	T	L	E		G		E		L
T		Y		X		E	A	R	L	Y		

128

B	E	A	R	E	R		C		C		I	
A		L		A	N	A	T	H	E	M	A	
N		G		C		N		I		P		
A	R	A	B	L	E		D	E	N	I	A	L
N		L		R		I			I			
A	S	K	E	D		P	E	P	P	E	R	Y
	E		A		M		D		R		E	
R	A	T	T	R	A	P		M	E	N	D	S
W			T		A		S			H		
H	A	M	L	E	T		S	E	S	A	M	E
T		I		H		S			B		L	
K	E	R	O	S	E	N	E			E		V
	R		N		W		T	U	R	T	L	E

129

C	H	E	K	H	O	V		B		N		R
A		M			E	X	E	C	U	T	E	
R		P	A	I	R	S		A		D		F
D		L		N		S	Q	U	E	E	Z	E
S	L	O	E	S		E					R	
		Y		I	L	L	A	T	E	A	S	E
R		E		T			O		L		E	
U	N	D	A	U	N	T	E	D		L		
N				A		D	O	T	E	D		
I	N	J	U	R	E	S		L		H		A
N		E		O		T	H	E	S	E		T
T	R	E	A	C	L	E			R		E	
O		R		K		R	I	C	K	E	T	S

130

S	U	N	S	E	T		F	A	C	A	D	E
	N		H		A		A		L		C	
M	A	S	O	N	S		S	N	A	T	C	H
	D		V		K	I	T		M		O	
H	O	T	E	L			F		B		P	
	R			C	L	O	S	E	S	E	T	
	N		C		O		O		R		N	
D	E	T	A	I	L	E	D				E	
	D		P		O			A	B	A	T	E
P		S		S	I	N		A		R		
R	E	M	I	S	S		O	U	T	L	A	Y
O			Z		U		R		O		T	
P	O	W	E	R	S		M	I	N	C	E	D

131

D	E	D	I	C	A	T	E	D		H		W
U		R		R		A		R	O	U	G	H
N	E	O		O		K		I		M		E
E		W		S	L	I	C	E		A		T
S	E	N	D	S		N		R	A	N	C	H
		E		E		G				E		
W	I	D	E	S	T		B	A	T	T	E	R
I				F		B		R				
Z	E	B	R	A		O		S	H	A	P	E
A		R		L	A	R	G	E		I		A
R		U		L		C		N	O	R		
D	I	S	C	O		E		C		E		L
S		H		W	E	D	N	E	S	D	A	Y

132

L	A	P	E	L		U		T		B		
A		O		E		R	E	S	I	D	U	E
C	O	T	T	A	G	E			M		R	
R		T		D		A	N	G	E	L	I	C
O		E		P		E		L		E		
S	U	R	P	L	I	C	E		E	N	D	S
S		R		Q		D		S		E		
E	U	R	O		U	N	L	I	S	T	E	D
	N		P		E		E		E		I	
A	T	L	E	A	S	T		V		R		M
	R		R		S	C	O	U	R	G	E	
S	U	L	T	A	N	A		T		O		N
	E		Y		R		E	G	R	E	T	

Solutions

133

```
A D V I S E   E U R O P A
M   E   E     R   K   I
P A R A N O I A   B A L M
L   B   T     T   P   L
E L E M I   C O D E I N E
    N   M     I       S
B L A M E D   E R R O R S
I       N     E   C
O R B I T A L   C O U N T
M   L   S     T   L   U
A C I D   S E D I T I O N
S   N   A     V   S   E
S T I C K Y   N E A T E R
```

134

```
S U B M I T   P E D A L O
L   A   I O   R   I
A M O S   S   G   I M
G   K   S P R I N T E R
  L   E   U   O   K   L
P A D D L E   M Y S T I C
  T   E       E       G
S E P S I S   S W A T H E
  C   L   H   H   F   T
C O C A C O L A   F     G
  M   L   O   M   A U R A
  E   O   T   E   I     V
C R U M B S   S T R I D E
```

135

```
S O L I D   A C C L A I M
C   E   R   X   R   N   I
A   A   O P E R A T I O N
T I R E S     P   M   C
T   N   S H I P S H A P E
E   I   U   O   L
R A N D O M   L I N K U P
    G   U   I   I   A
S E C E S S I O N   N   R
E   U   H   O U G H T   I
C A R P E N T E R   D   I
T   V   L   A   T   O   E
S T E L L A R   H Y M N S
```

136

```
P I S A   O P E R A T O R
O   W   T   I   O   A   A
S U I T I N G   M U F T I
S   L   T   S   A   F   D
I S L E T   T A N N E D
B   L   Y   C   T   F
L I T T E R   P A R A D E
E   E   T   B   N   A
  B A M A K O   D O W E R
O   R   T   N   L   A   L
T I G H T   S H E A T H E
I   A   L   A   S   E   S
C O S M E T I C   E R O S
```

137

```
S H O T P U T   S Y L P H
M   N   R   R   K   O   A
A B O M I N A T I O N   I
S     V   G     G     R
H A N O I   I T A L I C S
E   U   L   C   R   T
S U M M E R   I M M U N E
    E   G   S   I   D   M
T O R M E N T   S L E E P
O   I     R   T     R
N   C E R T I F I C A T E
E   A   A   C   C   L   S
R E L A Y   T R E L L I S
```

138

```
  I S O B A R   C L A W S
N   A   A   H   O   B   C
A F T E R N O O N   O   A
I   E     D   D I V E R
L   D E P L E T E   E   L
S   L   S   M       E
C L U M S Y   K N I G H T
I       E   S   C   F
S   S   S H A R P E N   E
S W A T S   Y     O   V
O   U   I M I T A T I V E
R   N   O   N   I   S   R
S L A I N   G U L L E T
```

572

Solutions

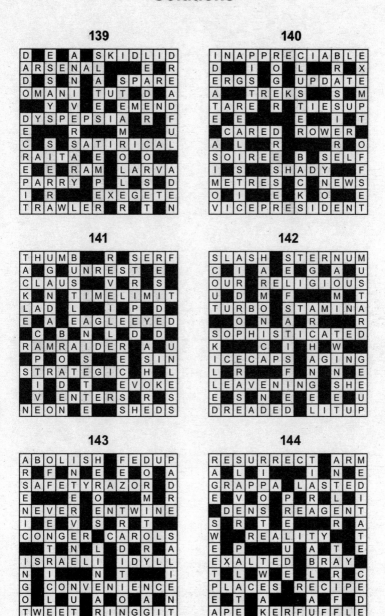

139

D		E		A		S	K	I	D	L	I	D
A	R	S	E	N	A	L			E		R	
D		S		N		A		S	P	A	R	E
O	M	A	N	I		T	U	T		D		A
	Y		V		E		E	M	E	N	D	
D	Y	S	P	E	P	S	I	A		R		F
E			R			M					U	
C		S		S	A	T	I	R	I	C	A	L
R	A	I	T	A		E		O		O		
E		E		R	A	M		L	A	R	V	A
P	A	R	R	Y		P		L		S		D
I		R			E	X	E	G	E	T	E	
T	R	A	W	L	E	R		R		T		N

140

I	N	A	P	P	R	E	C	I	A	B	L	E
D			I		O		L			R		X
E	R	G	S		G		U	P	D	A	T	E
A			T	R	E	K	S			S		M
T	A	R	E		R		T	I	E	S	U	P
E		E					E			I		T
	C	A	R	E	D		R	O	W	E	R	
A		L		R				R			R	O
S	O	I	R	E	E		B		S	E	L	F
I		S			S	H	A	D	Y			F
M	E	T	R	E	S		C		N	E	W	S
O		I			E		K		O			E
V	I	C	E	P	R	E	S	I	D	E	N	T

141

T	H	U	M	B			R		S	E	R	F
A		G		U	N	R	E	S	T		E	
C	L	A	U	S			V		R		S	
K		N		T	I	M	E	L	I	M	I	T
L	A	D		L		I		P		D		
E		A		E	A	G	L	E	E	Y	E	D
	C		B		N		L		D		D	
R	A	M	R	A	I	D	E	R		A		U
	P		O		S		E		S	I	N	
S	T	R	A	T	E	G	I	C		H		L
	I		D		T			E	V	O	K	E
	V		E	N	T	E	R	S		R		S
N	E	O	N		E			S	H	E	D	S

142

S	L	A	S	H		S	T	E	R	N	U	M
C		I		A		E		G		A		U
O	U	R		R	E	L	I	G	I	O	U	S
U		D		M		F			M		T	
T	U	R	B	O		S	T	A	M	I	N	A
	O		N		A		R				R	
S	O	P	H	I	S	T	I	C	A	T	E	D
K			C		I		H		W			
I	C	E	C	A	P	S		A	G	I	N	G
L		R			F		N		N		E	
L	E	A	V	E	N	I	N	G		S	H	E
E		S		N		E		E		E		U
D	R	E	A	D	E	D		L	I	T	U	P

143

A	B	O	L	I	S	H		F	E	D	U	P
R		F		N		E		E		O		A
S	A	F	E	T	Y	R	A	Z	O	R		D
E			E		O			O		M		R
N	E	V	E	R		E	N	T	W	I	N	E
I		E		V		S		R		T		
C	O	N	G	E	R		C	A	R	O	L	S
		T		N		L		D		R		A
I	S	R	A	E	L	I		I	D	Y	L	L
N		I		N		T				I		I
G		C	O	N	V	E	N	I	E	N	C	E
O		L		U		A		O		A		N
T	W	E	E	T		R	I	N	G	G	I	T

144

R	E	S	U	R	R	E	C	T		A	R	M
A		L		I			I		N		E	
G	R	A	P	P	A		L	A	S	T	E	D
E		V		O		P		R		L		I
	D	E	N	S		R	E	A	G	E	N	T
S		R		T		E			R		A	
W		R	E	A	L	I	T	Y		T		T
E		P			U		A		T		E	
E	X	A	L	T	E	D		B	R	A	Y	
T		L		W		E		L		R		C
P	L	A	C	E	S		R	E	C	I	P	E
E		T		A			A		F			D
A	P	E		K	E	R	F	U	F	F	L	E

Solutions

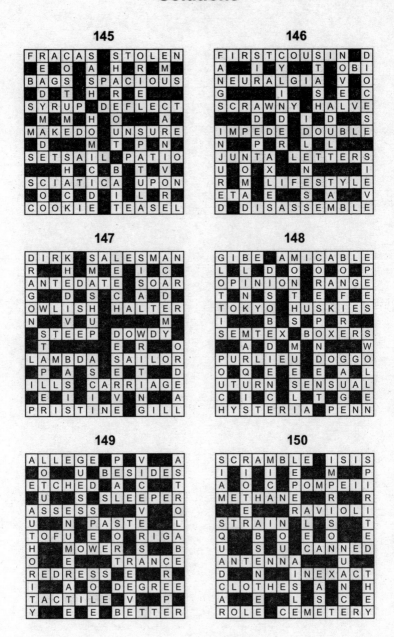

145

```
F R A C A S   S T O L E N
  E   O   A   H   R   M
B A G S   S P A C I O U S
  D   T   H   R   E
S Y R U P   D E F L E C T
  M   M   H   O       A
M A K E D O   U N S U R E
  D       M   T   P   N
S E T S A I L   P A T I O
    H   C   B   T   V
S C I A T I C A   U P O N
  O   C   D   I   L   R
C O O K I E   T E A S E L
```

146

```
F I R S T C O U S I N   D
A     I   Y     T   O B I
N E U R A L G I A   V   O
G       I     S   E   C
S C R A W N Y   H A L V E
      D D   I   D     S
I M P E D E   D O U B L E
N     P   R   L   L
J U N T A   L E T T E R S
U   O   X     N         I
R   M   L I F E S T Y L E
E T A   E     S   A     V
D   D I S A S S E M B L E
```

147

```
D I R K   S A L E S M A N
R   H   M   E   I   C
A N T E D A T E   S O A R
G   D   S   C   A   D
O W L I S H   H A L T E R
N   V   U       M
  S T E E P   D O W D Y
  T       E   R       O
L A M B D A   S A I L O R
  P   A   S   E   T   D
I L L S   C A R R I A G E
  E   I   I   V   N   A
P R I S T I N E   G I L L
```

148

```
G I B E   A M I C A B L E
L   L D   O   O   O   P
O P I N I O N   R A N G E
T   N   S   T   E   F E
T O K Y O   H U S K I E S
I   B   S   P   R
S E M T E X   B O X E R S
    A   D   M   N       W
P U R L I E U   D O G G O
O   Q   E   E   E   A   L
U T U R N   S E N S U A L
C   I   C   L   T   G E
H Y S T E R I A   P E N N
```

149

```
A L L E G E   P   V   A
  O   U   B E S I D E S
E T C H E D   A   C   T
  U   S   S L E E P E R
A S S E S S       V   O
U   N   P A S T E   L
T O F U   E   O   R I G A
H   E   M O W E R S   B
O   E     T R A N C E
R E D R E S S   E   R
I   A   O   D E G R E E
T A C T I L E   V   P
Y   E   E   B E T T E R
```

150

```
S C R A M B L E   I S I S
I   I   I   E   M     P
A   O   C   P O M P E I I
M E T H A N E   R   R
    E     R A V I O L I
S T R A I N   L   S   T
Q   B   O   E   O   E
U   S   U   C A N N E D
A N T E N N A   U
D   N   I N E X A C T
C L O T H E S   A   N H
A   E   L   S   C   E
R O L E   C E M E T E R Y
```

Solutions

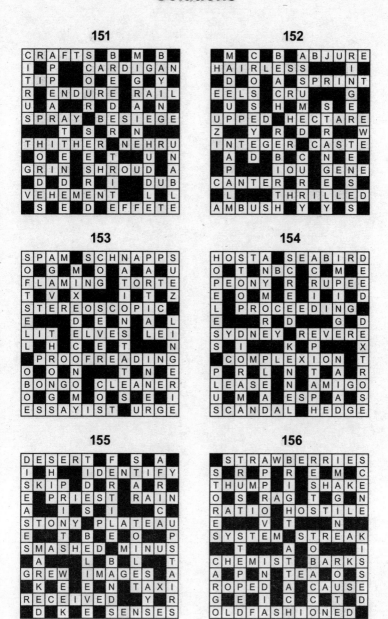

151

```
C R A F T S   B   M   B
I P     C A R D I G A N
T I P   O   E   G   Y
R   E N D U R E   R A I L
U   A   R   D   A   N
S P R A Y   B E S I E G E
    T   S   R   N
T H I T H E R   N E H R U
  O   E   E   T   U   N
G R I N   S H R O U D   A
  D   D   R   I   D U B
V E H E M E N T   L   L
  S   E   D   E F F E T E
```

152

```
  M   C   B   A B J U R E
H A I R L E S S       I
  D   O   A   S P R I N T
E E L S   C R U     G
  U   S   H   M   S   E
U P P E D   H E C T A R E
Z   Y   R   D   R     W
I N T E G E R   C A S T E
  A   D   B   C   N   E
  P     I O U   G E N E
C A N T E R   R   E   S
  L     T H R I L L E D
A M B U S H   Y   Y   S
```

153

```
S P A M   S C H N A P P S
O   G   M   O   A   A   U
F L A M I N G   T O R T E
T   V   X     I   T   Z
S T E R E O S C O P I C
E     D   E   N   A   L
L I T   E L V E S   L E I
L   H   C   E   T   N
  P R O O F R E A D I N G
O   O   N     T   N   E
B O N G O   C L E A N E R
O   G   M   O   S   E   I
E S S A Y I S T   U R G E
```

154

```
H O S T A   S E A B I R D
O   T   N B C   C   M   E
P E O N Y   R   R U P E E
E   O   M   E   I   I   D
L   P R O C E E D I N G
E     R   D     G   D
S Y D N E Y   R E V E R E
S   I   K   P     X
  C O M P L E X I O N   T
P   R   L   N   T   A   R
L E A S E   N   A M I G O
U   M   A   E S P   A   S
S C A N D A L   H E D G E
```

155

```
D E S E R T   F   S   A
I   H     I D E N T I F Y
S K I P   D   R   A   R
E   P R I E S T   R A I N
A   I   S   I       C
S T O N Y   P L A T E A U
E     T   B   E   O   P
S M A S H E D   M I N U S
  A     L   B   L     T
G R E W   I M A G E S   A
  K   E   E   N   T A X I
R E C E I V E D     Y   R
  D   K   E   S E N S E S
```

156

```
  S T R A W B E R R I E S
S   R   P   R   E   M   C
T H U M P   I   S H A K E
O   S   R A G   T   G   N
R A T I O   H O S T I L E
E     V   T     N
S Y S T E M   S T R E A K
  T     A   O     I
C H E M I S T   B A R K S
A   P   N   T E A   O   S
R O P E D   A   C A U S E
G   E   I   C   C   T   D
O L D F A S H I O N E D
```

Solutions

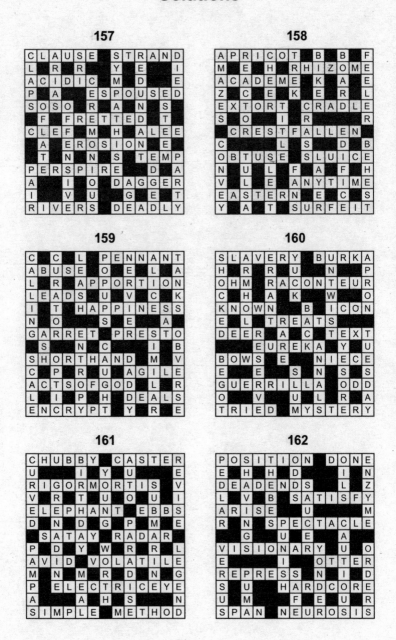

157

C	L	A	U	S	E		S	T	R	A	N	D
L		R		R			Y		E			I
A	C	I	D	I	C		M		D			E
P		A		E	S	P	O	U	S	E	D	
S	O	S	O		R		A		N		S	
	F		F	R	E	T	T	E	D		T	
C	L	E	F		M		H		A	L	E	E
	A		E	R	O	S	I	O	N		E	
	T	N	N		S		T	E	M	P		
P	E	R	S	P	I	R	E		D		A	
A		I		O		D	A	G	G	E	R	
I		V		U			G		E		T	
R	I	V	E	R	S		D	E	A	D	L	Y

158

A	P	R	I	C	O	T		B		B		F
M		E		H		R	H	I	Z	O	M	E
A	C	A	D	E	M	E		K		A		L
Z		C		K		K		E		R		L
E	X	T	O	R	T		C	R	A	D	L	E
S		O		I		R						R
	C	R	E	S	T	F	A	L	L	E	N	
C				L		S		D			B	
O	B	T	U	S	E		S	L	U	I	C	E
N		U		L		F		A		F		H
V		L		E		A	N	Y	T	I	M	E
E	A	S	T	E	R	N		E		C		S
Y		A		T		S	U	R	F	E	I	T

159

C		C		L		P	E	N	N	A	N	T
A	B	U	S	E		O		E		L		A
L		R		A	P	P	O	R	T	I	O	N
L	E	A	D	S		U		V		C		K
I		T		H	A	P	P	I	N	E	S	S
N		O		S		S		E		A		
G	A	R	R	E	T		P	R	E	S	T	O
	S		N		C			I			B	
S	H	O	R	T	H	A	N	D		M		V
C		P		R		U		A	G	I	L	E
A	C	T	S	O	F	G	O	D		L		R
L		I		P		H		D	E	A	L	S
E	N	C	R	Y	P	T		Y		R		E

160

S	L	A	V	E	R	Y		B	U	R	K	A
H		R		R		U			N			P
O	H	M		R	A	C	O	N	T	E	U	R
C		H		A		K			W			O
K	N	O	W	N		B		I	C	O	N	
E		L		T	R	E	A	T	S			
D	E	E	R		A		C		T	E	X	T
			E	U	R	E	K	A		Y		U
B	O	W	S		E		N	I	E	C	E	
E		E		S		N		S		S		S
G	U	E	R	R	I	L	L	A		O	D	D
O		V		U		L		R				A
T	R	I	E	D		M	Y	S	T	E	R	Y

161

C	H	U	B	B	Y		C	A	S	T	E	R
U			I		Y		U					E
R	I	G	O	R	M	O	R	T	I	S		V
V		R		T		U		O		U		I
E	L	E	P	H	A	N	T		E	B	B	S
D		N		D		G		P		M		E
	S	A	T	A	Y		R	A	D	A	R	
P		D		Y		W		R		R		L
A	V	I	D		V	O	L	A	T	I	L	E
M		N		M		R		D		N		G
P		E	L	E	C	T	R	I	C	E	Y	E
A			A		H		S					N
S	I	M	P	L	E		M	E	T	H	O	D

162

P	O	S	I	T	I	O	N		D	O	N	E
E		H		H		D				I		N
D	E	A	D	E	N	D	S			L		Z
L		V		B		S	A	T	I	S	F	Y
A	R	I	S	E			U					M
R		N		S	P	E	C	T	A	C	L	E
	G		U		E		A					
V	I	S	I	O	N	A	R	Y		U		O
E		I				I		O	T	T	E	R
R	E	P	R	E	S	S		N		I		D
S		U		H	A	R	D	C	O	R	E	
U		M		F		E		U				R
S	P	A	N		N	E	U	R	O	S	I	S

Solutions

163

C	O	R	A	C	L	E		P		W		C
O		E		O			G	A	L	A	X	Y
N		M		V		R		S		L		C
T	R	A	P	E	Z	E		S	M	E	L	L
A		R		N		P		K		S		E
C	U	R	L		A	L	T	E	R			
T		Y		B		E		Y		H		P
			B	E	I	N	G		G	A	Z	A
S		A		A		I		M		B		C
O	C	C	U	R		S	E	A	S	I	C	K
U		R		D		H		T		T		A
T	H	E	M	E	D			H		A		G
H		S		D		R	O	S	E	T	T	E

164

S	E	T	O	U	T		D	E	B	T	O	R
N		E		S		S		A		A		O
A	D	A	M	A	N	T		R		R		B
P		P		G		I	N	T	E	N	S	E
P	H	A	S	E		C		H				R
Y		R			K		E	I	G	H	T	
		T		A	L	I	E	N		R		
S	T	Y	E	S		N			E		O
H			K		S		S	H	E	E	R	
R	E	T	R	A	C	E		T		T		W
E		E		N		C	H	A	L	I	C	E
D		N		C		T		R		N		L
S	U	D	D	E	N		F	R	U	G	A	L

165

P	I	Q	U	E		S	A	D	N	E	S	S
A		U		V		T		I		M		I
G	L	A	Z	I	E	R		G	L	E	A	N
E		L		L		E		I		R		G
S	E	I	N	E		S	E	N	E	G	A	L
		F		Y		S		E		E		E
B	O	I	L	E	R		G	A	R	N	E	T
A		C			A		N		C			
C	H	A	R	T	E	R		T	R	Y	S	T
K		T		O		R		O		E		E
L	Y	I	N	G		A	N	N	E	X	E	S
O		O		A		Y		Y		I		T
G	E	N	E	S	I	S		M	O	T	H	S

166

	D	E	N	T	A	L	F	L	O	S	S	
N		S		O		A		O		C		C
O		C		N	I	N	N	Y		O	A	R
T	R	A	P	S		D		A		R		O
I		P		U		A		L	A	N	E	S
C	H	E	E	R	F	U	L					S
E		S		E			V		T		S	
B			G	A	T	E	P	O	S	T		
O	P	E	R	A		B		N		O		I
A		D		L		B		I	N	L	E	T
R	I	G		P	R	E	S	S		K		C
D		E		H		S		O		I		H
	A	S	S	A	S	S	I	N	A	T	E	

167

K	A	T	Y	D	I	D		C		D	I	P
	S		O		A	P	A	C	E		R	
F	A	T	U	O	U	S		T		V		O
	R		R		H		S	M	A	R	T	
T	U	N	G	S	T	E	N		L		E	
	L		T		D		H	U	C			
J	E	S	T	E	R		F	O	R	E	S	T
I		E		P		D	M		T			
T		C		L	I	C	E	N	S	E	E	
T	A	R	T	S		G		T		A		
E		E		P		E	C	O	N	O	M	Y
R		C	H	A	T	S		W		E		
S	H	Y		R		T	A	N	K	A	R	D

168

C	A	P	A	C	I	T	Y		B	O	S	S
O		A		A		I		F		U		E
P	E	N	G	U	I	N		L	A	T	H	E
E		E		S		K		U		S		D
			C	E	R	E	M	O	N	I	A	L
S		C		C		R		R		D		E
K	E	R	N	E	L		B	E	R	E	T	S
I		I		L		S		S		R		S
T	E	M	P	E	R	A	N	C	E			
T		I		B		G		E		D		P
I	N	N	E	R		G	O	N	D	O	L	A
S		A		E		E		C		V		N
H	A	L	E		A	D	H	E	R	E	N	T

577

Solutions

169

S	U	P	E	R	B		C	U	T	O	F	F
U		O		A	G	A		U				I
B	U	T	T	I	N		P	A	R	T	E	D
U		I		J		R		C			D	
R		O		T	O	P	I	C		R		L
B	O	N	G	O		L		L	A	Y	B	Y
	L		O	M	E	G	A			A		
A	D	U	L	T		A		M	E	R	R	Y
F		N		H	O	T	U	P		E		A
R		Z		N		N		C		W		
E	L	I	C	I	T		I	N	B	O	R	N
S		P		O	P	T		I			E	
H	Y	S	S	O	P		Y	E	L	L	E	D

170

B	Y	P	A	S	S		S	P	Y	I	N	G
U			C		M		A					R
T	H	E	R	A	P	E	U	T	I	C		U
T		G		R		S		H		A		B
E	X	O	R	C	I	S	E		S	T	A	B
R		M		E		Y		F		A		Y
	R	A	L	L	Y		Q	U	I	L	L	
C		N		Y		A		G		O		D
A	V	I	D		A	L	L	I	A	N	C	E
N		A	K		G		T		I		T	
N		C	O	N	T	A	M	I	N	A	T	E
E			E		E		E		V		E	S
D	I	N	N	E	R		H	E	L	M	E	T

171

S	T	E	E	P	L	E		S	K	U	L	L
E		N		U		A		I				E
N	A	G		R	E	C	Y	C	L	I	N	G
A		R		I		H		L		L		G
T	O	A	D	S		H		J	U	L	Y	
O		V		T	U	X	E	D	O			
R	E	E	F		R		N		Y	A	L	E
			I	N	G	E	S	T		L		S
H	E	R	S		E			R	E	B	E	C
A		H		B		E		E		E		A
P	I	P	E	D	R	E	A	M		R	A	P
P		Y		R		R		O		T		E
Y	O	K	E	L		G	A	R	L	A	N	D

172

S	C	U	F	F	E	D		B	O	M	B	S
	O		L		B		S		W		R	
A	N	N	A		B	U	L	L	E	T	I	N
	G		T		I		U		S		D	
C	A	T	T	I	N	E	S	S		P	L	Y
			E		G		H		L		E	
S	C	A	R	S			G	I	L	D	S	
	R		S		S		P		A			
F	U	G		T	H	E	O	R	I	S	E	S
	S		S		O		T		S		X	
W	H	I	T	E	O	U	T		I	T	C	H
	E		A		T		E		N		O	
U	S	U	R	Y		B	R	I	G	A	N	D

173

P	E	A	R		B	A	T	H	R	O	O	M
R		R		C		M		A		U		I
O	R	E	G	A	N	O		B	A	T	E	D
C		N		S		E		E		S		L
R	E	A	C	H		B	E	R	N	I	N	I
A			R		A		D		Z			F
S	C	A	R	E	S		R	A	C	E	M	E
T		W		G		A		S				C
I	N	K	L	I	N	G		H	Y	P	E	R
N		W		S		R		E		A		I
A	D	A	P	T		E	R	R	A	N	D	S
T		R		E		E		Y		D		I
E	L	D	O	R	A	D	O		J	A	W	S

174

V	E	R	G	E	S		P		D		B	
	X		E		A	C	A	D	E	M	I	A
P	I	C	N	I	C		S		C		C	
	L		O		R	E	S	E	R	V	E	D
N	E	P	A	L	I			I			P	
O					S	U	R	C	E	A	S	E
V		B		T		E		D			L	
A	N	T	O	N	Y	M	S					S
	E		T			O	B	L	A	T	E	
T	E	E	T	O	T	A	L		A		E	
	D		L		B		V	E	R	B	A	L
S	E	R	E	N	A	D	E		G		L	
	D		D		R		D	R	O	W	S	Y	

578

Solutions

175   **176**

177   **178**

179   **180**

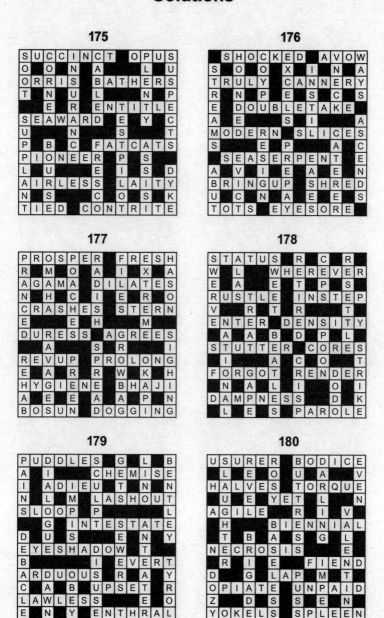

Solutions

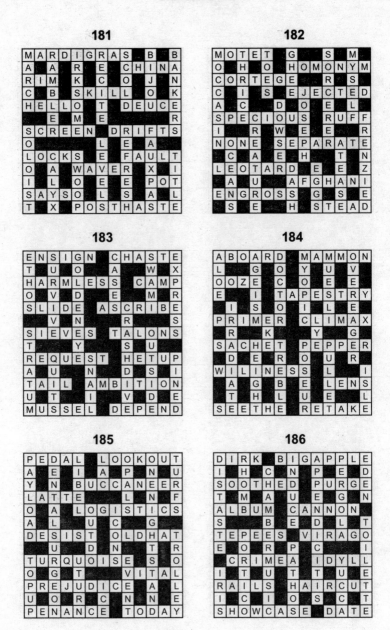

Solutions

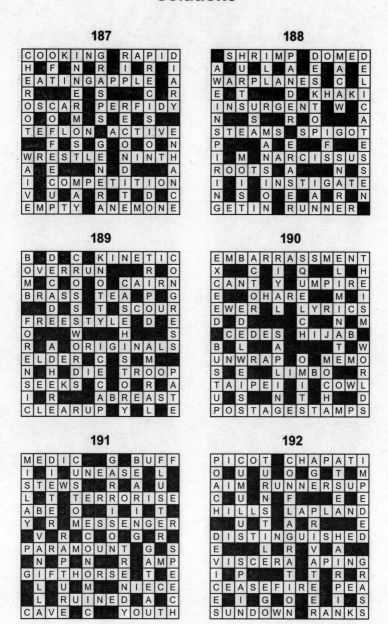

187
```
C O O K I N G   R A P I D
H   F   N   R   I   R   I
E A T I N G A P P L E   A
R     E   S       C   R
O S C A R   P E R F I D Y
O   O   M   S   E   S
T E F L O N   A C T I V E
    F   S   G   O   O   N
W R E S T L E   N I N T H
A   E       N   D   A
I   C O M P E T I T I O N
V   U   A   R   T   D   C
E M P T Y   A N E M O N E
```

188
```
  S H R I M P   D O M E D
A   U   L   A   E   A   E
W A R P L A N E S   C   L
E   T       D   K H A K I
I N S U R G E N T   W   C
N   S   R   O       A
S T E A M S   S P I G O T
P   A   E   F       E
I   M   N A R C I S S U S
R O O T S   A       N   S
I   I   I N S T I G A T E
N   S   O   E   A   R   N
G E T I N   R U N N E R
```

189
```
B   D   C   K I N E T I C
O V E R R U N       R   O
M   C   O   C A I R N
B R A S S   T E A   P   G
    D   S   T   S C O U R
F R E E S T Y L E   D   E
O   W       H       S
R   A   O R I G I N A L S
E L D E R   C   S   M
N   H   D I E   T R O O P
S E E K S   C   O   R   A
I   R   A B R E A S T
C L E A R U P   Y   L   E
```

190
```
E M B A R R A S S M E N T
X   C   I   Q   L   H
C A N T   Y   U M P I R E
E   O H A R E   M   I
E W E R   L   L Y R I C S
D   D       C   N   M
    C E D E S   H I J A B
B   L   A       T   W
U N W R A P   O   M E M O
S   E   L I M B O   R
T A I P E I   I   C O W L
U   S   N   T   H   D
P O S T A G E S T A M P S
```

191
```
M E D I C   G   B U F F
I   I   U N E A S E   L
S T E W S   R   A   U
A   T   T E R R O R I S E
A B E   O   I   I   T
Y   R   M E S S E N G E R
  V   R   C   O   G   R
P A R A M O U N T   G   S
  N   P   N   R   A M P
G I F T H O R S E   T   E
  L   U   M   N I E C E
  L   R U I N E D   A   C
C A V E   C   Y O U T H
```

192
```
P I C O T   C H A P A T I
O   U   U   O   G   T   M
A I M   R U N N E R S U P
C   U   N   F   E   E
H I L L S   L A P L A N D
    U   T   A   R   E
D I S T I N G U I S H E D
E   L   R   V   A
V I S C E R A   A P I N G
I   P   T   T   R   R
C E A S E F I R E   P E A
E   I   G   O   E   I   S
S U N D O W N   R A N K S
```

Solutions

193

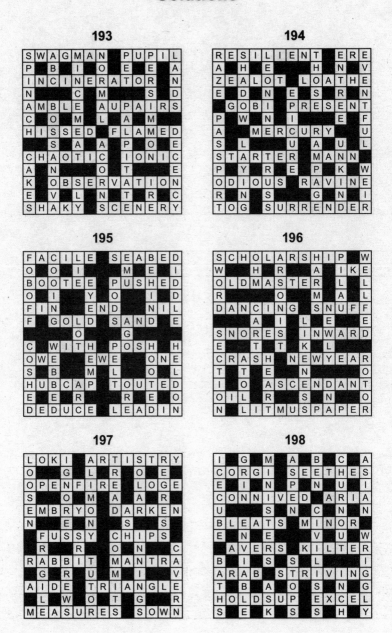

S	W	A	G	M	A	N		P	U	P	I	L
P		B		I		O		E		E		A
I	N	C	I	N	E	R	A	T	O	R		N
N			C		M				S		D
A	M	B	L	E		A	U	P	A	I	R	S
C		O		M		L		A		M	
H	I	S	S	E	D		F	L	A	M	E	D
		S		A		A		P		O		E
C	H	A	O	T	I	C		I	O	N	I	C
A		N			O		T					E
K		O	B	S	E	R	V	A	T	I	O	N
E		V		L		N		T		R		C
S	H	A	K	Y		S	C	E	N	E	R	Y

194

R	E	S	I	L	I	E	N	T		E	R	E
A		H		E			H		N		V
Z	E	A	L	O	T		L	O	A	T	H	E
E		D		N		E		S		R		N
	G	O	B	I		P	R	E	S	E	N	T
P		W		N		I			E		F
A		M	E	R	C	U	R	Y			U
S		L			U		A		U		L
S	T	A	R	T	E	R		M	A	N	N
P		Y		R		E		P		K		W
O	D	I	O	U	S		R	A	V	I	N	E
R		N		S			G		N		I
T	O	G		S	U	R	R	E	N	D	E	R

195

F	A	C	I	L	E		S	E	A	B	E	D
O		O		I			M		E		I
B	O	O	T	E	E		P	U	S	H	E	D
O		I		Y		O		I		D
F	I	N		E	N	D		N	I	L
F		G	O	L	D		S	A	N	D		E
			O			G				
C		W	I	T	H		P	O	S	H		H
O	W	E		E	W	E		O	N	E
S		B		M		L		O		L
H	U	B	C	A	P		T	O	U	T	E	D
E		E		R			R		E		O
D	E	D	U	C	E		L	E	A	D	I	N

196

S	C	H	O	L	A	R	S	H	I	P		W
W		H		R		A			I	K	E
O	L	D	M	A	S	T	E	R		L		L
R			O		M		A	L
D	A	N	C	I	N	G		S	N	U	F	F
		A		I		L		E			E
S	N	O	R	E	S		I	N	W	A	R	D
E		T		T		K		L
C	R	A	S	H		N	E	W	Y	E	A	R
T		T		E		N					O
I		O		A	S	C	E	N	D	A	N	T
O	I	L		R			S		N		O
N		L	I	T	M	U	S	P	A	P	E	R

197

L	O	K	I		A	R	T	I	S	T	R	Y
O		G		L		R		O		E
O	P	E	N	F	I	R	E		L	O	G	E
S		O		M		A		A		R
E	M	B	R	Y	O		D	A	R	K	E	N
N		E		N		S		S		S
	F	U	S	S	Y		C	H	I	P	S
	R		R		O		N			C
R	A	B	B	I	T		M	A	N	T	R	A
	G		R		U		I			I		V
A	I	D	E		T	R	I	A	N	G	L	E
	L		W		O		T			G		R
M	E	A	S	U	R	E	S		S	O	W	N

198

I		G	M		A		B		C		A
C	O	R	G	I		S	E	E	T	H	E	S
E		I		N		P		N		U		I
C	O	N	N	I	V	E	D		A	R	I	A
U			S		N		C		N		N
B	L	E	A	T	S		M	I	N	O	R
E		N		E			V		U		W
	A	V	E	R	S		K	I	L	T	E	R
B		I		S		S		L			I
A	R	A	B		S	T	R	I	V	I	N	G
T		B		A		O		S		N		G
H	O	L	D	S	U	P		E	X	C	E	L
S		E		K		S		S		H		Y

Solutions

199

200

201

202

203

204

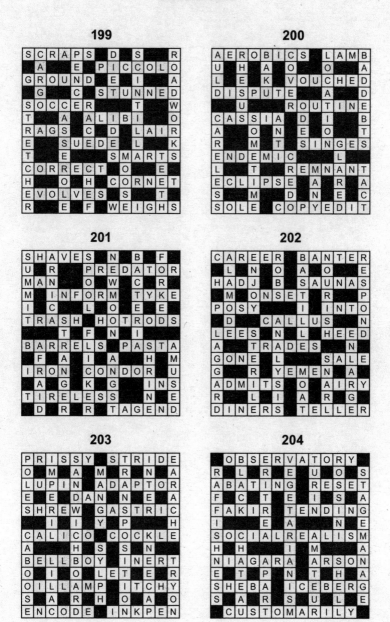

Solutions

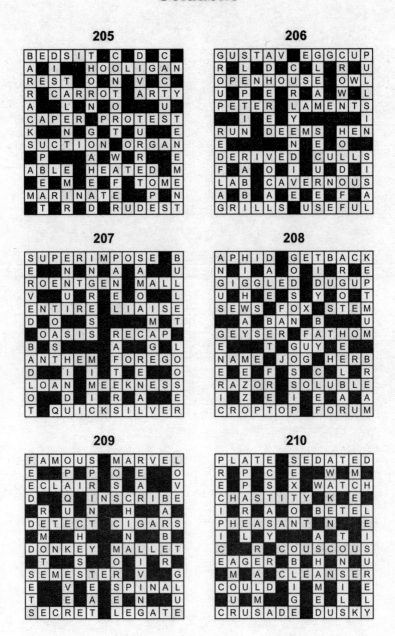

205

B	E	D	S	I	T		C		D		C
A		I			H	O	O	L	I	G	A	N
A	R	E	S	T		O		N		V		C
R		C	A	R	R	O	T		A	R	T	Y
A			L		N		O			U		
C	A	P	E	R		P	R	O	T	E	S	T
K			N		G		T		U			E
S	U	C	T	I	O	N		O	R	G	A	N
	P			A		W		R			E	
A	B	L	E		H	E	A	T	E	D		M
	E		M		E		F		T	O	M	E
M	A	R	I	N	A	T	E			P		N
	T		R		D		R	U	D	E	S	T

206

G	U	S	T	A	V		E	G	G	C	U	P
R		L		D		C		L		R		U
O	P	E	N	H	O	U	S	E		O	W	L
U		P		E		R		A		W		L
P	E	T	E	R		L	A	M	E	N	T	S
		I		E		Y						I
R	U	N		D	E	E	M	S		H	E	N
E				N		E		O				
D	E	R	I	V	E	D		C	U	L	L	S
F		A		O		I		U		D		I
L	A	B		C	A	V	E	R	N	O	U	S
A		B		A		E		E		F		A
G	R	I	L	L	S		U	S	E	F	U	L

207

S	U	P	E	R	I	M	P	O	S	E		B
E		N		N		A		A		A		U
R	O	E	N	T	G	E	N		M	A	L	L
V		U		R		E		O		L		L
E	N	T	I	R	E		L	I	A	I	S	E
D		O		S				M		T		
	O	A	S	I	S		R	E	C	A	P	
B		S		A		G			L			
A	N	T	H	E	M		F	O	R	E	G	O
D		I		I		T		E			O	
L	O	A	N		M	E	E	K	N	E	S	S
O		D		I		R		A			E	
T		Q	U	I	C	K	S	I	L	V	E	R

208

A	P	H	I	D		G	E	T	B	A	C	K
N		I		A		O		I		R		E
G	I	G	G	L	E	D		D	U	G	U	P
U		H		E		S		Y		O		T
S	E	W	S		F	O	X		S	T	E	M
		A		B	A	N		B		U		
G	E	Y	S	E	R		F	A	T	H	O	M
E			T		G	U	Y		E			
N	A	M	E		J	O	G		H	E	R	B
E		E		F		S		C		L		R
R	A	Z	O	R		S	O	L	U	B	L	E
I		Z		E		I		E		A		A
C	R	O	P	T	O	P		F	O	R	U	M

209

F	A	M	O	U	S		M	A	R	V	E	L
E			P		P		O		E			O
E	C	L	A	I	R		S	A				V
D		Q		I	N	S	C	R	I	B	E	
	R		U		N		H			A		
D	E	T	E	C	T		C	I	G	A	R	S
	M		H			N			B			
D	O	N	K	E	Y		M	A	L	L	E	T
	T		S			O		I		R		
S	E	M	E	S	T	E	R		V		G	
E		V		E			S	P	I	N	A	L
T		E		A		E		N			U	
S	E	C	R	E	T		L	E	G	A	T	E

210

P	L	A	T	E		S	E	D	A	T	E	D
R		P		C		E		W		M		
E		P		S		X		W	A	T	C	H
C	H	A	S	T	I	T	Y		K		E	
I		R		A		O		B	E	T	E	L
P	H	E	A	S	A	N	T		N			E
I		L		Y			A		T			I
C			R		C	O	U	S	C	O	U	S
E	A	G	E	R		B		H		N		U
	M		A		C	L	E	A	N	S	E	R
C	O	U	L	D		I		M		I		E
	U		M			G		E		L		L
C	R	U	S	A	D	E		D	U	S	K	Y

584

Solutions

211

```
S A D D L E . . A L L I E D
O . . O . D . I . . . . A
U N C O N C E R N E D . M
G . O . G . A . E . O . P
H A R D S E L L . F L E E
T . K . H . S . M . C . N
. A S C O T . B A B E L .
H . C . T . M . N . V . S
A C R E . G O L D F I S H
Z . E . O . U . I . T . A
A . W O B B L E B O A R D
R . . O . T . L . L . E
D A G G E R . C E N S U S
```

212

```
D I S C L O S E . F E E S
E . I . I . C . . D . C
C A D U C E U S . G . R
I . E . H . M A C H E T E
D O W S E . M . . . W
E . A . N O T O R I O U S
. . Y . O . S . B .
C U S T O D I A N . D . R
R . . L . A B U S E . E
I N S U R E D . T . R . S
S . O . S A L I V A T E
I . N . N . V . T . N
S A S H . R E V E R E N T
```

213

```
S I R O C C O . L . B . R
E . E . A . F A C A D E
V . D . B . T . U . S . A
E N D L E S S . N O T E D
N . E . R . E . D . E . Y
T E E M . S T E E R .
Y . R . P . S . R . R . L
. . E A S E L . C E D E
S . B . I . F . P . P . T
M E A N S . L E A F L E T
I . C . L . Y . G . A . E
L O O T E R . A . C . R
E . N . Y . B A N G E R S
```

214

```
S A F E L Y . H A T R E D
C . O . E . N . C . O . E
A I R F A R E . E . D . P
N . E . S . A R T D E C O
T E M P T . R . A . . S
Y . O . . S . T E R S E
. . S . S U I T E . E .
C A T C H . G . . L . B
A . . E . H . S C A L E
R A M P A R T . H . T . H
E . A . T . E X A M I N E
S . C . H . D . K . V . S
S T E R E O . R E L E N T
```

215

```
C R A B S . P O S S E S S
L . U . T . O . A . X . U
A T T R A C T . U S H E R
S . H . R . A . N . I . G
S C O U T . S H A M B L E
. R . L . H . . I . O
G A I T E R . B A T T E N
U . T . . T . B . I .
A N A L O G Y . S P O O R
R . R . V . P . T . N . I
A M I G O . H E A T I N G
N . A . L . U . I . S . I
I G N E O U S . N O M A D
```

216

```
. W A T E R C O U R S E .
N . C . L . L . D . C . N
E . C . A M E N D . A D O
W O R K S . R . E . R . N
Y . U . T . I . R E E V E
E Y E P I E C E . D . X
A . . C . . H . . I
R . M . E D G E W A Y S
S C A L P . I . A . D . T
D . T . A . S . D R A K E
A R T . C H A O S . G . N
Y . E . K . R . E . I . T
. P R E S U M P T I O N .
```

585

Solutions

217

```
H A C K S A W . T . M O B
. V . T . A R O M A . E
T E R R I E R . B . C . E
. R . L . R . Y E A S T
C A T H E T E R . . B . L
. G . T . N . D . R . E
P E S E T A . R E C E S S
R . A . O . G . M . . U
O . R . . T A P E W O R M
M U C U S . N . N . F
O . A . C . N A T U R A L
T . S C A R E . I . . C
E L M . B . T E A C H E R
```

218

```
S E T P I E C E . F A I R
A . H . D . O . C . P . E
I T A L I C S . L A P E L
D . I . O . M . O . E . I
. . . A S S I S T A N C E
S . P . Y . C . H . D . V
N Y L O N S . P E T I T E
O . A . C . B . S . X . D
W A T E R T I G H T . . .
D . F . A . G . O . M . C
R I O T S . T O R N A D O
O . R . Y . O . S . G . S
P O M P . H E R E D I T Y
```

219

```
C H A S S I S . C H A P S
H . N . U . U . R . . R
O N A I R . S H A R P E N
P . G . P . S . S . F
P A R T A K E . S A L A D
E . A . S . X . . C
D E M I S E . Q U E B E C
. M . . S . K . L . A
B A L L S . P E R T A I N
. N . H . O . A . T . D
B A S M A T I . I R A Q I
. T . D . L . N . N . E
B E A D Y . S C E N T E D
```

220

```
J O Y O U S . A V O W A L
O . S . I . F . U . . A
E T H I C S . A . Z . C
Y . R . T O R T O I S E
. N . I . E . I . K
B O W S E R . B A C K E R
. M . V . . R . W
B A R T E R . C A S K E T
. D . N . O . H . R
A S S E S S O R . E . B
G . K . A . P I A Z Z A
E . E . L . U . R . K
S U N S E T . S E S A M E
```

221

```
S U S H I . S T A M I N A
L . U . N . E . A . E
I . R . S . C . B I D E T
N I N E T E E N . D . D
G . A . O . D . D E N S E
S O M E R S E T . N . X
H . E . E . . M . G . T
O . . B . E S C A L A T E
T H R O W . C . D . Z . N
. E . R . P R I N C E S S
E A V E S . I . E . L . I
. V . A . P . S . L . O
C Y C L I S T . S K E I N
```

222

```
B A R B I T U R A T E . B
E . A . R . U . A . . O
A V E R S I O N . S P E W
U . O . C . U . E . . Y
T R A N C E . P U R S U E
Y . M . . P . . . L . R
. W A G E S . A B B E Y
B . S . . . T . . D . J
A S S E S S . T O U S L E
N . Q . A . E . T . T
T H O U . L U N A T I C S
A . A . V . D . E . . A
M . B L O O D S T R E A M
```

Solutions

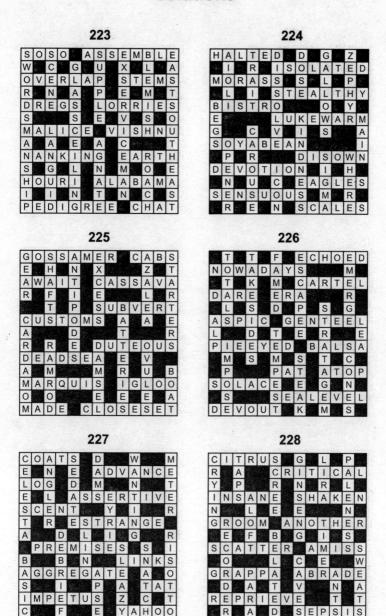

223 **224**

225 **226**

227 **228**

Solutions

229

```
S E R I O U S . B . C . A
H . E . . . E Y E B A L L
O . S I M O N . A . V . L
R . E . I . S A T I A T E
T E R M S . O . . . . . G
. . V . F O R E T A S T E
R . E . I . . O . T . D .
U N S E T T L E D . A . .
N . . . . . E . D U M P S
A B S C E S S . L . P . A
W . N . P . S W E D E . L
A C A D E M E . . . D . E
Y . G . E . R E D R E S S
```

230

```
H I C C U P . H E C K L E
. D . R . E . O . H . . W
R E B E L S . P R A I S E
. N . E . T E E . M . . R
I T A L Y . . L . B . S .
. I . . . O P E R E T T A
. C . C . V . S . R . . A
R A S H N E S S . . . . L
. L . O . R . . L A S E R
D . C . S A D . G . M . .
A T T I R E . A V A T A R
M . C . A . I . I . T . .
E G R E S S . S I N G E R
```

231

```
C A M P S . D E S C A N T
R . . H . U . T . . Y . .
E X P L A I N . A D D L E
W . . D . D . Y . . O . .
N O W H E R E . S T U N G
E . I . . E . . U . L . .
C Y G N E T . A S T H M A
K . G . A . . T . . D . .
S I T E S . C O P I O U S
. R . I . R . U . . T . .
L O D G E . O N T H E G O
. N . V . S . U . . N . .
U S E L E S S . P A D R E
```

232

```
G A S P S . F . . P . I .
R . A . H . R A I L I N G
A C H I E V E . . E . S .
F . A . D . E G O T R I P
F . R . D . N . H . T . .
I N A C T I V E . O V U M
T . A . L . I . R . . I .
I B I S . U P S T A I R S
. O . S . T . S . M . T .
S W E E T E N . B . M . R
. L . T . E R A S U R E .
L E N T I L S . R . N . S
. R . E . . T . S E E P S
```

233

```
P A P A C Y . S P I T E S
E . I . O . E . . E . T .
A E R O N A U T . M A M A
K . A . D . T . L . T . .
S I N A I . F O R E S E E
. . H . M . . E . . L . .
G R A V E L . S C U R R Y
L . . N . . E . U . . . .
A P O S T L E . P A N T S
S . X . I . T . R . I . .
S W I M . S T R I K I N G
E . D . T . . V . O . H .
S N E E R S . B E A T I T
```

234

```
S O R T E D . S P E N D S
O . . I . U . A . L . O .
A R I D . R . L . A . W .
R . Y . E X A C T I N G .
. N . U . S . A . E . R .
R U M P U S . M Y S T I C
. M . R . . E . . G . . .
P E D A N T . S W A T H E
. R . G . R . C . B . T .
C A R R I A G E . U . . V
. B . E . S . N . S O Y A
. L . E . H . I . E . T .
J E R S E Y . C I R R U S
```

588

Solutions

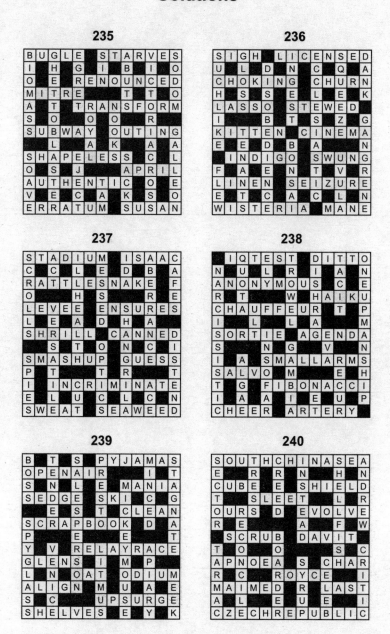

235

236

237

238

239

240

Solutions

241

```
S H I R T     P   S A R I
U G   A S S A I L   E
B A N N S     R   I   O
T   I   T   S A L T I R E
L I T R E     B   H   D
E   E   R E C O V E R E D
  Q   V   P   L   R   R
N U M E R I C A L   C   S
  I   H   L     A L I V E
D E C I B E L   N   N   N
  T   C   P   C A D E T
  L   L U S T R E   E   R
L Y R E     Y     T A R R Y
```

242

```
J A C O B   C H A R N E L
A   A   A   A   I   O   A
D A M   R E S E R V O I R
E   B   B   H     N   D
D E R M A   R E P L E T E
    I   R   E   R     R
R O C K I N G H O R S E S
H     A   I   G   A
O F F E N D S   N E W E L
M   L   T   O   M   A
B O U N D L E S S   I T S
U   I   O   R   I   L   T
S E D A T E S   S E L L S
```

243

```
C O N F I R M   L O C H S
H   O   N   I   O   H   I
A G R I C U L T U R E   E
N     L   L     V   G
C O P S E   E N S L A V E
E   I   M   R   N   L
L A N D E D   B O R I N G
    E   N   T   W   E   O
S H A T T E R   W O R L D
E   P     Y   H     D
N   P R E D O M I N A T E
D   L   R   U   T   L   S
S P E A R   T R E L L I S
```

244

```
T E S T P I L O T   H E M
A   H   R     O   O   O
S T A R E D   I N D O O R
K   M   C   S   E   P   T
  G A M E   E A R P L U G
U   N   D   T     A   A
N     L E E T I D E   G E
D   B     L   E   P   E
E X A M P L E   S O A P
R   B   E   R   P   E   S
S L O W E R   B A R L E Y
E   O   V     I   L   N
A W N   E X P U R G A T E
```

245

```
U P K E E P   S K A T E S
  E   N   E   U   V   E
B R U T   A N N U A L L Y
  C   R   R   B   I
B O G E Y   G A L L O W S
  L   A   M   T     H
M A R T H A   H O B N O B
  T     V   E   R   L
B E T W E E N   P A G E S
  A   R   G   V   S
D I S G U I S E   U P O N
  N   E   C   M   R   M
A N O R A K   S T A M E N
```

246

```
S H O W O F H A N D S   B
A   E   O   E   C A R
M E T E O R I T E   U   E
B   C   D   B   A
A B R A D E D   S C A N T
    B   F   S   U   H
A R G Y L E   A R R I V E
M   S   D   L   S
A B A S H   C A Y E N N E
T   Z   E   R     V
O   T   M A N I F E S T O
R O E   I   E   A   K
Y   C O N S I D E R A T E
```

590

Solutions

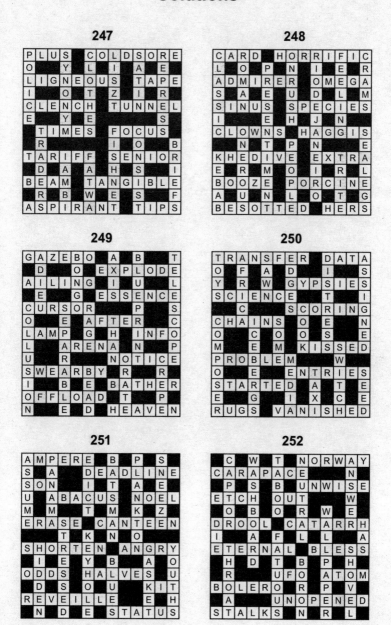

247

```
P L U S   C O L D S O R E
O   Y   L   I   A   E
L I G N E O U S   T A P E
I   O   T   Z   I   R
C L E N C H   T U N N E L
E   Y   E           S
  T I M E S   F O C U S
  R       I   O       B
T A R I F F   S E N I O R
  D   A   A   H   S   I
B E A M   T A N G I B L E
  R   B   W   E   S   F
A S P I R A N T   T I P S
```

248

```
  C A R D   H O R R I F I C
  L   O   P   N   I   E   R
  A D M I R E R   O M E G A
  S   A   E   U   D   L   M
  S I N U S   S P E C I E S
  I   E   H   J   N
  C L O W N S   H A G G I S
    N   T   P   N       E
  K H E D I V E   E X T R A
  E   R   M   O   I   R   L
  B O O Z E   P O R C I N E
  A   U   N   L   O   T   G
  B E S O T T E D   H E R S
```

249

```
G A Z E B O   A   B     T
  D   O   E X P L O D E
A I L I N G   I   U     L
  E   G   E S S E N C E
C U R S O R   P       S
O   E   A F T E R     C
L A M P   G   H   I N F O
L   A R E N A   N     P
U   R       N O T I C E
S W E A R B Y   R     R
I   B   E   B A T H E R
O F F L O A D   T   P
N   E   D   H E A V E N
```

250

```
T R A N S F E R   D A T A
O   F   A   D     I     S
Y   R   W   G Y P S I E S
S C I E N C E     T     I
  C       S C O R I N G
C H A I N S   O   E     N
O   C   O   O   S     E
M   E   M   K I S S E D
P R O B L E M       W
O   E   E N T R I E S
S T A R T E D   A   T   E
E   G   I   X   C   E
R U G S   V A N I S H E D
```

251

```
A M P E R E   B   P   S
S   A   D E A D L I N E
S O N   I   T   A   E
U   A B A C U S   N O E L
M   M   T   M   K   Z
E R A S E   C A N T E E N
    T   K   N   O
S H O R T E N   A N G R Y
  I   E   Y   B   A   O
O D D S   H A L V E S   U
  D   S   O   U   K I T
R E V E I L L E   E   H
  N   D   E   S T A T U S
```

252

```
  C   W   T   N O R W A Y
C A R A P A C E       N
  P   S   B   U N W I S E
E T C H   O U T       W
  O   B   O   R   W   E
D R O O L   C A T A R R H
I   A   F   L   L     A
E T E R N A L   B L E S S
H   D   T   B   P   H
R   U F O   A T O M
B O L E R O   R   P   V
A   U N O P E N E D
S T A L K S   N   R   L
```

591

Solutions

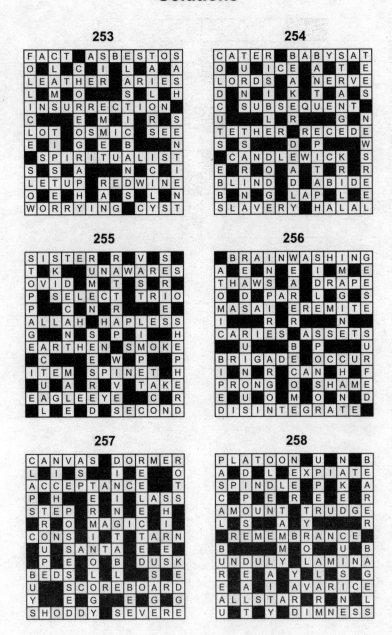

253

F	A	C	T		A	S	B	E	S	T	O	S
O		L		C		I		L		A		A
L	E	A	T	H	E	R		A	R	I	E	S
L		M		O				S		L		H
I	N	S	U	R	R	E	C	T	I	O	N	
C				E		M		I		R		S
L	O	T		O	S	M	I	C		S	E	E
E		I		G		E		B				N
	S	P	I	R	I	T	U	A	L	I	S	T
S		S		A			N		C		I	
L	E	T	U	P		R	E	D	W	I	N	E
O		E		H		A		S		L		N
W	O	R	R	Y	I	N	G		C	Y	S	T

254

C	A	T	E	R		B	A	B	Y	S	A	T
O		U		I	C	E		A		T		E
L	O	R	D	S		A		N	E	R	V	E
D		N		I		K		T		A		S
C		S	U	B	S	E	Q	U	E	N	T	
U				L		R		G				N
T	E	T	H	E	R		R	E	C	E	D	E
S		S			D		P					W
	C	A	N	D	L	E	W	I	C	K		S
E		R		O		A		T		R		R
B	L	I	N	D		D		A	B	I	D	E
B		N		G		L	A	P		L		E
S	L	A	V	E	R	Y		H	A	L	A	L

255

S	I	S	T	E	R		R		V		S	
T		K			U	N	A	W	A	R	E	S
O	V	I	D		M		T		S		R	
P		S	E	L	E	C	T		T	R	I	O
P		C		N		R		E			E	
A	L	L	A	H		H	A	P	L	E	S	S
G		N		S		P		I				H
E	A	R	T	H	E	N		S	M	O	K	E
	C		E		W		P		P			P
I	T	E	M		S	P	I	N	E	T		H
	U		A		R		V		T	A	K	E
E	A	G	L	E	E	Y	E			C		R
	L		E		D		S	E	C	O	N	D

256

	B	R	A	I	N	W	A	S	H	I	N	G
A		E		N		E		I		M		E
T	H	A	W	S		A		D	R	A	P	E
O		D		P	A	R		L		G		S
M	A	S	A	I		E	R	E	M	I	T	E
I				R		R			N			
C	A	R	I	E	S		A	S	S	E	T	S
		U			B		P					U
B	R	I	G	A	D	E		O	C	C	U	R
I		N		R		C	A	N		H		F
P	R	O	N	G		O		S	H	A	M	E
E		U		O		M		O		N		D
D	I	S	I	N	T	E	G	R	A	T	E	

257

C	A	N	V	A	S		D	O	R	M	E	R
L		I		S			I		E			O
A	C	C	E	P	T	A	N	C	E			T
P		H		E		I		L	A	S	S	
S	T	E	P		R		N		E		H	
	R		O		M	A	G	I	C		I	
C	O	N	S		I		T		T	A	R	N
	U		S	A	N	T	A		E		E	
	P		E		O		B		D	U	S	K
B	E	D	S		L		L		S		E	
U			S	C	O	R	E	B	O	A	R	D
Y		E		G			E		G		G	
S	H	O	D	D	Y		S	E	V	E	R	E

258

P	L	A	T	O	O	N		U		N		B
A		D		L		E	X	P	I	A	T	E
S	P	I	N	D	L	E		P		K		A
C		P		E		R		E		E		R
A	M	O	U	N	T		T	R	U	D	G	E
L		S		A		Y						R
	R	E	M	E	M	B	R	A	N	C	E	
B			M		O		O		U		B	
U	N	D	U	L	Y		L	A	M	I	N	A
R		E		A		Y		L		S		G
E		A		I		A	V	A	R	I	C	E
A	L	L	S	T	A	R		R		N		L
U		T		Y		D	I	M	N	E	S	S

Solutions

259

```
B . C . R . D W A R F E D
A D A G E . O . N . I . E
L . P . B O T A N I C A L
L I T H E . I . U . H . V
A . I . L O N G I T U D E
D . V . . G . T . . U .
S H E K E L . H Y S S O P
. U . R . P . . T . E
O B S E R V A N T . R . R
R . E . A . T . A D I O S
I M P E T U O U S . P . I
O . I . I . I . T E E N S
N U A N C E S . Y . D . T
```

260

```
S I N C E R E . A E G I S
H . O . L . D . N . . U
A I M . A N I M A T I O N
L . I . P . T . H . . N
L U N G S . . H . U G L Y
O . E . E N V I E S .
T H E E . I . F . E P I C
. . . N U N C I O . L . I
P A S S . A . . F L A I R
O . . N . B F . C . C
A L B A T R O S S . A I L
C . R . . A . E . T . E
H A V E N . R E T R E A T
```

261

```
C L A R E T . B R O O M S
R . B . . E . A . . . T
A S S O C I A T I O N . A
F . T . A . R . D . E . B
T O R T I L L A . S E A L
Y . A . M . Y . C . D . E
. . C H A P . O R A L .
D . T . N . N . E . E . K
O P A L . S A U C E P A N
C . R . B . V . H . O . I
K . T H R E A T E N I N G
E . . A . L . . . N . H
T I M B E R . S E P T E T
```

262

```
C H A S T I S E . A M E N
L . . A . T . . . E . U
A F F E C T E D . . D . G
W . U . T . M O O R I N G
E N N U I . . R . C . E
D . A . C O N S T R I C T
. . N . L . A . N .
I N D E L I B L E . E . J
S . G . V . . M A M B A
S T A N L E Y . P . A . I
U . M . . R E G I O N A L
E . E . . T . R . . . O
D U S T . S I L E N C E R
```

263

```
S T E P S O N . W . P . C
T . X . A . P O T A T O
A . C . L . I . U . N . M
P O I N T E R . N O I S E
L . T . Y . R . D . C . T
E V E N . F I X E D .
R . D . P . T . D . R . A
. . . M A D A M . B O W S
S . I . R . B S S . S . H
C O S T S . L E N I E N T
O . L . L . E . O . T . R
P L A Y E R . . O . T . A
E . M . Y . P E P P E R Y
```

264

```
A B R U P T . S T R A Y S
L . E . E . B . I . F . E
B U L L S . U . P . R . T
I . A . T . R A P P O R T
N E T W O R K . I . . . L
O . I . . . I G N O B L E
. . O . P . N . G . R .
C A N T A T A . . O . B
H . . I . F I A N C E E
A M M O N I A . L . C . L
L . O . T . S . P H O T O
E . W . E . O . H . L . N
T U N D R A . W A V I N G
```

593

Solutions

265

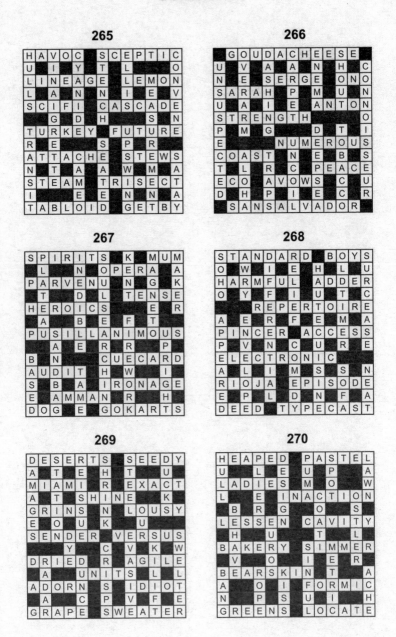

H	A	V	O	C		S	C	E	P	T	I	C
U		I		Y		T		L			O
L	I	N	E	A	G	E		L	E	M	O	N
L		A		N		N		I		E	V
S	C	I	F	I		C	A	S	C	A	D	E
		G		D		H			S		N
T	U	R	K	E	Y		F	U	T	U	R	E
R		E			S		P		R		
A	T	T	A	C	H	E		S	T	E	W	S
N		T		A		A		W		M	A
S	T	E	A	M		T	R	I	S	E	C	T
I			E		E		N		N		A
T	A	B	L	O	I	D		G	E	T	B	Y

266

		G	O	U	D	A	C	H	E	E	S	E	
U	V	A		A		N		H			C
N	E		S	E	R	G	E		O	N	O
S	A	R	A	H		P		M		U		N
U		A		I		E		A	N	T	O	N
S	T	R	E	N	G	T	H					O
P		M		G			D		T		I
E				N	U	M	E	R	O	U	S
C	O	A	S	T		N		E		B		S
T		L		R		C		P	E	A	C	E
E	C	O		A	V	O	W	S		C		U
D		H		P		I		E		C		R
	S	A	N	S	A	L	V	A	D	O	R	

267

S	P	I	R	I	T	S		K		M	U	M
	L			N		O	P	E	R	A		A
P	A	R	V	E	N	U		N		G		K
	T			D		L		T	E	N	S	E
H	E	R	O	I	C	S			E		R
A			B	E		F	T				
P	U	S	I	L	L	A	N	I	M	O	U	S
	A		E		R		R			P	
B		N			C	U	E	C	A	R	D
A	U	D	I	T		H		W			I
S		B		A		I	R	O	N	A	G	E
E		A	M	M	A	N			R		H
D	O	G		E		G	O	K	A	R	T	S

268

|S|T|A|N|D|A|R|D| |B|O|Y|S|
|O| |W| |I| |E| |H| |L| |U|
|H|A|R|M|F|U|L| |A|D|D|E|R|
|O| |Y| |F| |I| |U| |T| |C|
		R	E	P	E	R	T	O	I	R	E
	A		E		R		F		E		M	A
P	I	N	C	E	R		A	C	C	E	S	S
P		V		N		C		U		R		E
E	L	E	C	T	R	O	N	I	C		
A		L		I		M		S		S		N
R	I	O	J	A		E	P	I	S	O	D	E
E		P		L		D		N		F		A
D	E	E	D		T	Y	P	E	C	A	S	T

269

D	E	S	E	R	T	S		S	E	E	D	Y
A		T		E		H		T			U
M	I	A	M	I		R		E	X	A	C	T
A		T		S	H	I	N	E			K
G	R	I	N	S		N		L	O	U	S	Y
E		O		U		K		U			
S	E	N	D	E	R		V	E	R	S	U	S
		Y		C		V		K		W
D	R	I	E	D		R		A	G	I	L	E
	A		U	N	I	T	S		L		L
A	D	O	R	N		S		I	D	I	O	T
A			A		C		P		V		F	E
G	R	A	P	E		S	W	E	A	T	E	R

270

H	E	A	P	E	D		P	A	S	T	E	L
U		L		E		U		P			A
L	A	D	I	E	S		M		O		W
L		E		I	N	A	C	T	I	O	N
	B		R		G		O			S
L	E	S	S	E	N		C	A	V	I	T	Y
	H		U			T			L
B	A	K	E	R	Y		S	I	M	M	E	R
V		O			I		E		R
B	E	A	R	S	K	I	N		T			A
A		O		I		F	O	R	M	I	C
N		P		S	U		I				H
G	R	E	E	N	S		L	O	C	A	T	E

594

Solutions

271

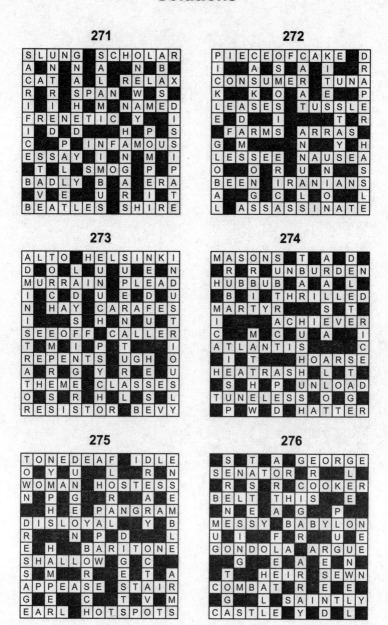

S	L	U	N	G			S	C	H	O	L	A	R
A		N		N			A		N			B	
C	A	T		A		L		R	E	L	A	X	
R		R		S	P	A	N			W		S	
I		I		H		M		N	A	M	E	D	
F	R	E	N	E	T	I	C			Y			I
I		D		D				H		P			S
C			P		I	N	F	A	M	O	U	S	
E	S	S	A	Y		I		N		M			I
	T		L		S	M	O	G		P		P	
B	A	D	L	Y		B		A		E	R	A	
	V		E			U		R		I		T	
B	E	A	T	L	E	S		S	H	I	R	E	

272

P	I	E	C	E	O	F	C	A	K	E		D
I		A		S		A		I				R
C	O	N	S	U	M	E	R		T	U	N	A
K		K		O		A		E				P
L	E	A	S	E	S		T	U	S	S	L	E
E		D		I				T				R
	F	A	R	M	S		A	R	R	A	S	
G		M			N			Y				H
L	E	S	S	E	E		N	A	U	S	E	A
O			O		R		U		N			S
B	E	E	N		I	R	A	N	I	A	N	S
A			G		C		L		O			L
L		A	S	S	A	S	S	I	N	A	T	E

273

A	L	T	O		H	E	L	S	I	N	K	I
D		O		L		U		U		E		N
M	U	R	R	A	I	N		P	L	E	A	D
I		C		D		U	E	D		D		U
N		H	A	Y		C	A	R	A	F	E	S
I			S		H		N		U		T	
S	E	E	O	F	F		C	A	L	L	E	R
T		M		I		P		T		I		I
R	E	P	E	N	T	S		U	G	H		O
A		R		G		Y		R		E		U
T	H	E	M	E		C	L	A	S	S	E	S
O		S		R		H		L		S		L
R	E	S	I	S	T	O	R		B	E	V	Y

274

M	A	S	O	N	S		T		A		D	
	R		R		U	N	B	U	R	D	E	N
H	U	B	B	U	B		A		A		L	
	B		I		T	H	R	I	L	L	E	D
M	A	R	T	Y	R		S		T			
I			A	C	H	I	E	V	E	R		
C		M		C		U		A				I
A	T	L	A	N	T	I	S					C
	I		T			H	O	A	R	S	E	
H	E	A	T	R	A	S	H		L		T	
	S		H		P		U	N	L	O	A	D
T	U	N	E	L	E	S	S		O		G	
P		W		D		H	A	T	T	E	R	

275

T	O	N	E	D	E	A	F		I	D	L	E
O		Y		U		L			I		R	N
W	O	M	A	N		H	O	S	T	E	S	S
N		P		G		R		A			A	E
		H		E		P	A	N	G	R	A	M
D	I	S	L	O	Y	A	L			Y		B
R			N		P	D						L
E		H		B	A	R	I	T	O	N	E	
S	H	A	L	L	O	W		G		C		
S		M		R			E		T		A	
A	P	P	E	A	S	E		S	T	A	I	R
G		E		C			T		V		M	
E	A	R	L		H	O	T	S	P	O	T	S

276

	S		T		A		G	E	O	R	G	E
S	E	N	A	T	O	R		R			L	
	R		S		R		C	O	O	K	E	R
B	E	L	T		T	H	I	S			E	
	N		E		A		G			P		
M	E	S	S	Y		B	A	B	Y	L	O	N
U		I		F		R		U			E	
G	O	N	D	O	L	A		A	R	G	U	E
		G		E		A		E		N		
	T		H	E	I	R		S	E	W	N	
C	O	M	B	A	T		R		E		E	
G			L		S	A	I	N	T	L	Y	
C	A	S	T	L	E		Y		D		L	

595

Solutions

277

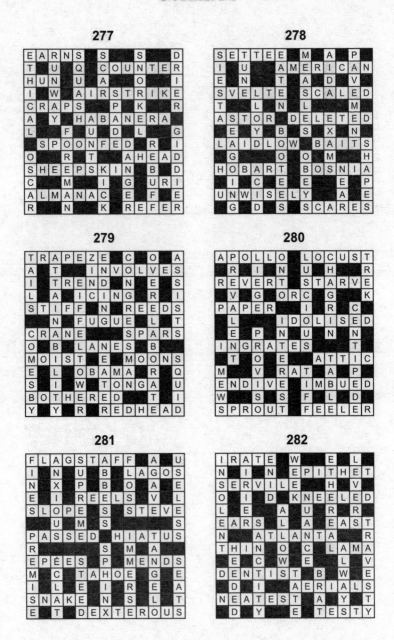

E	A	R	N	S		S		S		D
T		U		Q		C	O	U	N	T	E	R
H	U	N		U		A		O		I
I		W		A	I	R	S	T	R	I	K	E
C	R	A	P	S			P		K		R
A		Y		H	A	B	A	N	E	R	A
L			F		U		D		L		G
	S	P	O	O	N	F	E	D		R		I
O			R		T			A	H	E	A	D
S	H	E	E	P	S	K	I	N		B		D
C			M			I		G		U	R	I
A	L	M	A	N	A	C		E		F		E
R			N			K		R	E	F	E	R

278

S	E	T	T	E	E		M		A		P
I		U			A	M	E	R	I	C	A	N
E		N		T		A		D		V
S	V	E	L	T	E		S	C	A	L	E	D
T		L		N		L				M
A	S	T	O	R		D	E	L	E	T	E	D
	E		Y		B		S		X		N
L	A	I	D	L	O	W		B	A	I	T	S
	G			O		O		M			H
H	O	B	A	R	T		B	O	S	N	I	A
	I		C		E		E			E		P
U	N	W	I	S	E	L	Y			A		E
	G		D		S		S	C	A	R	E	S

279

T	R	A	P	E	Z	E		C		O		A
A		T			I	N	V	O	L	V	E	S
I		T	R	E	N	D		N		E		S
L	A		I	C	I	N	G		R		I
S	T	I	F	F		N		R	E	E	D	S
	N		F	U	G	U	E		L		T
C	R	A	N	E			S	P	A	R	S
O		B		L	A	N	E	S		B
M	O	I	S	T		E		M	O	O	N	S
E		L		O	B	A	M	A		R		Q
S		I		W		T	O	N	G	A		U
B	O	T	H	E	R	E	D			T		I
Y		Y		R		R	E	D	H	E	A	D

280

A	P	O	L	L	O		L	O	C	U	S	T
	R		I		N		U		H			R
R	E	V	E	R	T		S	T	A	R	V	E
	V		G		O	R	C		G			K
P	A	P	E	R			I		R		C
	L			I	D	O	L	I	S	E	D
	E		P		N		U		N		N
I	N	G	R	A	T	E	S			T
	T		O		E			A	T	T	I	C
M			V		R	A	T		A		P
E	N	D	I	V	E		I	M	B	U	E	D
W			S		S		F		L		D
S	P	R	O	U	T		F	E	E	L	E	R

281

F	L	A	G	S	T	A	F	F		A		U
I		N		U		B		L	A	G	O	S
N		X		P		B		O		A		E
E		I		R	E	E	L	S		V		L
S	L	O	P	E		S		S	T	E	V	E
		U		M		S						S
P	A	S	S	E	D		H	I	A	T	U	S
R			S		M		A
E	P	É	E	S		P		M	E	N	D	S
M		C		T	A	H	O	E		G		E
I		L		E		I		R		E		A
S	N	A	K	E		N		S		L		T
E		T		D	E	X	T	E	R	O	U	S

282

I	R	A	T	E		W		E		L
I	N		I		N		E	P	I	T	H	E	T
S	E	R	V	I	L	E		H		V
O		I		D		K	N	E	E	L	E	D
L		E		A		U		R		R
E	A	R	S		L		A		E	A	S	T
N		A	T	L	A	N	T	A			R
T	H	I	N		O		C		L	A	M	A
	E		C		W		E		L		V
D	E	N	T	I	S	T		B		W		E
	D		I			A	E	R	I	A	L	S
N	E	A	T	E	S	T		A		Y		T
	D		Y		E		T	E	S	T	Y

Solutions

283

284

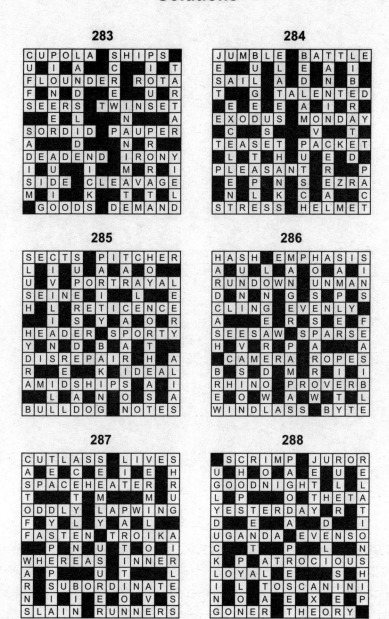

285

286

287

288

Solutions

289

```
B . M . S . S A D N E S S
A D A M A N T . . . Y . A
C D F I . O V E R T . T
H O R S E . G A B . F . C
. A D M . S H U S H . E
D E S P E R A D O . L . E
O . . P . . L . . . L
L D . O U R S E L V E S
D I E T S . A . S . E
R . T . I M P . C O R P S
U B O A T . I . E M . P
M . U . D E N T I N E
S C R O L L S . T . N . D
```

290

```
R A G A N D B O N E M A N
E . P . E . F . . I . U
P E E P . A . F A B L E D
E . . L A T E R . L . G
A W A Y . H . O F F I C E
L . L . . . A . N . S
. B A N D S . D A T E D
A . R . O . . R . S
L A M B D A . B . C Y A N
K . B . N A I R A . U
A G E O L D . R . P A N G
L . L . . S . D . R . L
I S L E S O F S C I L L Y
```

291

```
F R A N C . . T R E N C H
L . B . O U S E . N . A
A R A B S . . R . T . S
M . T . S U M M A R I S E
I . E . E . I . O . I
N O D . T R A N S P O S E
G . A . E . U . Y . M
O N P U R P O S E . R A M
. I . D . T . R . E . E
O B L I V I O U S . B . N
. B . B . L . A B O R T
. L . L . E M I T . R . A
L E V E R S . . Z O N A L
```

292

```
S E E D S . T W O S T E P
C . M . A . R . P . H . I
R A P . F L A T T E R E R
A . E . E . N . . E . A
M E R I T . S U S P E C T
. . O . Y . P . T . . E
S T R E P T O C O C C U S
I . . I . R . P . H
C O R O N E T . P L A I D
K . U . . C . R . R . A
P U N C T U A T E . M E N
A . I . I . F . S . E . C
Y A N G T Z E . S U R G E
```

293

```
F A R A W A Y . B R I E F
O . O . H . I . A . L . R
C O N T I N E N T A L . O
U . . T . L . . G . . N
S E R V E . D I A M O N D
E . E . H . S . L . T
D E A D E N . E D I T O R
. R . A . T . E . E . E
S T R E T C H . B A N K S
A . A . R . A . . . . P
I . N E W Y E A R S E V E
L . G . A . A . A . G . C
S H E E R . T O N I G H T
```

294

```
W I S E C R A C K . G A S
A . E . L . . O . . O . P
S E A L E D . C A R A F E
P . S . A . T . L . T . C
. B O R N . R E A G E N T
M . N . S . O . . E . R
A . . L E T D O W N . . U
S . S . . D . E . S . M
T R A I P S E . S O A K
O . Y . L . N . T . L
D R I V E N . V E R O N A
O . N . A . . R . N . Y
N A G . D I A G N O S I S
```

Solutions

295

```
O U T P U T   M A S T E R
  N   I   A   O   L   G
I D E A   N A R R A T O R
  E   N   G   T   N
B R A I D   B U N T I N G
  T   S   T   A       A
R A F T E R   R A C E M E
  K   U   Y   A   E
F E A T H E R   I N E P T
  W   L   B   V   L
R E M E D I A L   A S A P
  A   A   F   E   S   T
B U C K L E   W A S H E R
```

296

```
D A R E S S A L A A M   F
I   X   T   B   I O U
S P I T   A L S O   A   N
C   E   C   M   O   E
O L D N I C K   B O W E R
    S   A   A   W       A
S A D I S T   L E N T I L
E   V   O   T   E
C A G E Y   T E R R A I N
R   E   I   R   S   E
E   T   K A L E   H A L E
C R U   E   G   I   D
Y   P A S S I O N P L A Y
```

297

```
H A S P   C O N D O N E D
E   E   R   I   F   Y
A L A R M I N G   F O E S
R   B   M   H   E   W
T A I N T S   T H R E A D
H   R   O   A   S
  O D E O N   S Y L P H
  B   I   H   R   P
S T A L L S   U N R E A L
  R   I   T   T   S   A
B U C K   E N T R A I L S
  D   E   R   E   D   M
R E I N D E E R   B E T A
```

298

```
T A C K   E L L I P S I S
A   H   S   A   N   A   P
P R E T E N D   T O W E R
I   S   C   L   E   F   I
O U T D O   E A R R I N G
C   N   S   M   S
A L L U D E   N E P H E W
  I   F   L   D       I
C H A L I C E   I N S E T
A   I   D   M   A   H   H
B A S E D   O A T C A K E
I   O   L   N   E   V   R
N O N S E N S E   L E G S
```

299

```
C H A N C E   O   D   E
  I   R   S L O E G I N
O N A G E R   I   X   J
  D   E   P O R T I C O
T U M B L E   E   Y
I   R   L O V E R   M
G O B I   B   I   I D L E
H   C R A V E   T   N
T   K   S L Y E S T
E E L W O R M   A   H
N   O   I   B U R I A L
E M E R A L D   D   D
D   K   L   O S P R E Y
```

300

```
S E C U R E S T   H A N S
O   O   O   O   O   I
F   R   M   U M P T E E N
T E N S E S T   W   I
  I       H E R A L D S
D U S T   R   D   T   T
A   H E S I T A T E D   E
F   S   D   M   R E A R
F O R T I E S   V
O   C   U N C O I L S
D E B A T E S   A   A T
I   S   I   F   T   U
L O S E   R E V E R E N D
```

Solutions

301

M	A	S	S	E	S		A		M		G	
E		U			M	A	R	M	O	S	E	T
A	R	C		I		S		U		N		
D		K	I	R	T	L	E		S	K	I	N
O		L		H		N		S		U		
W	R	E	S	T		M	A	L	A	I	S	E
		I		I		L		K				
S	L	A	T	I	N	G		E	A	T	U	P
	E		U		H		V		A		O	
V	E	G	A		A	W	A	I	T	S		L
	W		T		L		U			S	E	A
H	A	R	E	B	E	L	L		E		N	
	Y		D		R		T	I	T	L	E	D

302

Z	A	M	B	I	A		E	L	E	V	E	N
	L		E		C		S		X			E
A	B	B	E		E		C	I	C	A	D	A
	A		C	O	S	T	A		I			R
A	N	K	H			P		S	O	L	E	
	I			E	S	T	A	T	E			S
B	A	R	B		H		D		S	O	R	T
A			A	L	E	X	E	I			E	
T	A	M	P		L			P	U	S	H	
I			T		T	U	R	B	O		H	
S	A	L	I	N	E		O		I	M	A	M
T			S		R		L		N		P	
E	A	S	E	L	S		E	S	T	H	E	R

303

M	A	L	T		P	A	S	S	W	O	R	D
A		E		I		C		A		C		A
R	E	A	D	M	I	T		N	E	A	R	S
K		V		P			T		R			H
S	T	E	R	E	O	S	C	O	P	I	C	
M			R		P		D		N			F
A	L	B		I	M	A	G	O		A	D	O
N		L	S		W		M					R
	A	U	T	H	E	N	T	I	C	A	T	E
U		S		A			N		M			C
S	A	H	I	B		A	L	G	E	B	R	A
E		E		L		S		O		E		S
D	I	S	P	E	R	S	E		G	R	I	T

304

S	A	B	L	E		F	R	E	T	F	U	L
C		L		N	I	L		L		O		A
R	H	E	U	M		A		E	R	R	O	R
A		E		A		R		M		E		D
T		D	I	S	B	E	L	I	E	V	E	
C			S		D			E		S		S
H	A	L	T	E	R		D	R	Y	R	O	T
Y		O		K		A						U
	A	N	T	H	R	A	C	I	T	E		R
S		G		U		Y		M		N		G
T	H	R	U	M		A		E	L	A	T	E
A		U		U		K	E	N		C		O
G	E	N	E	S	I	S		T	I	T	A	N

305

A	B	S	E	N	T		A		B		S	
B		H		H	E	N	P	A	R	T	Y	
D	R	A	T	E		T		L		U		
U		H	A	I	R	D	O		D	U	C	K
C		K		E		N				C		
T	I	B	E	R		E	Y	E	B	R	O	W
E		U		S		M		L				A
D	A	P	P	L	E	D		J	A	M	E	S
	R			A		F		Z				T
A	C	N	E		L	O	O	T	E	D		R
	T		W		I		Y		R	I	F	E
T	I	R	E	S	O	M	E			M		L
	C		S		N		R	A	V	E	N	S

306

	D	E	S	C	R	I	P	T	I	O	N	S
B		R		A		N		A		V		C
L	E	A	D	S		B		L	H	A	S	A
I		T		T	W	O		E		T		B
N	A	O	M	I		R	U	S	T	I	C	S
K			L		N				O			
S	T	Y	L	E	S		S	E	A	N	C	E
		A			R		X				R	
D	O	R	M	I	C	E		C	R	E	D	O
U		D		N		T	A	U		L		D
B	L	A	N	C		I		S	P	A	R	E
A		G		U		N		E		N		S
I	C	E	C	R	E	A	M	S	O	D	A	

600

Solutions

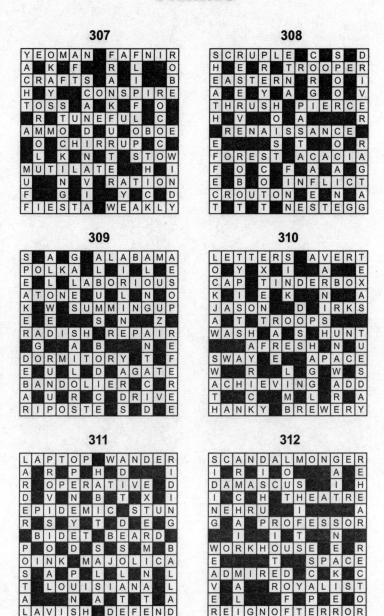

307

Y	E	O	M	A	N		F	A	F	N	I	R
A		K		F			R		L			O
C	R	A	F	T	S		A		I			B
H		Y			C	O	N	S	P	I	R	E
T	O	S	S		A		K		F		O	
	R		T	U	N	E	F	U	L		C	
A	M	M	O		D		U		O	B	O	E
	O		C	H	I	R	R	U	P		C	
	L		K		N		T		S	T	O	W
M	U	T	I	L	A	T	E		H		I	
U		N		V		R	A	T	I	O	N	
F		G		I		Y		C		D		
F	I	E	S	T	A		W	E	A	K	L	Y

308

S	C	R	U	P	L	E		C		S		D
H		E		R		T	R	O	O	P	E	R
E	A	S	T	E	R	N		R		O		I
A		E		Y		A		G		O		V
T	H	R	U	S	H		P	I	E	R	C	E
H		V		O		A						R
	R	E	N	A	I	S	S	A	N	C	E	
E				S		T			O		R	
F	O	R	E	S	T		A	C	A	C	I	A
F		O		C		F		A		A		G
E		B	O		I	N	F	L	I	C	T	
C	R	O	U	T	O	N		E		N		A
T		T		T		N	E	S	T	E	G	G

309

S		A		G		A	L	A	B	A	M	A
P	O	L	K	A		L		I		L		E
E		L		L	A	B	O	R	I	O	U	S
A	T	O	N	E		U		L		N		O
K		W		S	U	M	M	I	N	G	U	P
E		E		S		N		Z				
R	A	D	I	S	H		R	E	P	A	I	R
	G		A		B		N		E		F	
D	O	R	M	I	T	O	R	Y		T		F
E		U		L		D		A	G	A	T	E
B	A	N	D	O	L	I	E	R		C		R
A		U		R		C		D	R	I	V	E
R	I	P	O	S	T	E		S		D		E

310

L	E	T	T	E	R	S		A	V	E	R	T
O		Y		X		I		A				E
C	A	P		T	I	N	D	E	R	B	O	X
K		I		E		K		N		A		
J	A	S	O	N		D		I	R	K	S	
A		T		T	R	O	O	P	S			
W	A	S	H		A		S		H	U	N	T
			A	F	R	E	S	H		N		U
S	W	A	Y		E			A	P	A	C	E
W		R		L		G		W		S		S
A	C	H	I	E	V	I	N	G		A	D	D
T		C		M		L		R		R		A
H	A	N	K	Y		B	R	E	W	E	R	Y

311

L	A	P	T	O	P		W	A	N	D	E	R
A		R		P		H		D				I
R		O	P	E	R	A	T	I	V	E		D
D		V		N		B		T		X		I
E	P	I	D	E	M	I	C		S	T	U	N
R		S		Y		T		D	E		G	
	B	I	D	E	T		B	E	A	R	D	
P		O		D		S		S	M		B	
O	I	N	K		M	A	J	O	L	I	C	A
S		A		P		L		L	N		L	
T		L	O	U	I	S	I	A	N	A		L
A			N		A		T	T		T		A
L	A	V	I	S	H		D	E	F	E	N	D

312

S	C	A	N	D	A	L	M	O	N	G	E	R
I		R		I		O				A		E
D	A	M	A	S	C	U	S			I		H
I		C		H		T	H	E	A	T	R	E
N	E	H	R	U		I				I		A
G		A		P	R	O	F	E	S	S	O	R
	I		I		T		N					
W	O	R	K	H	O	U	S	E		E		R
E			T			S	P	A	C	E		
A	D	M	I	R	E	D		C		K		C
V		A		R	O	Y	A	L	I	S	T	
E		L		F		P		E		O		
R	E	I	G	N	O	F	T	E	R	R	O	R

Solutions

313 **314**

315 **316**

317 **318**

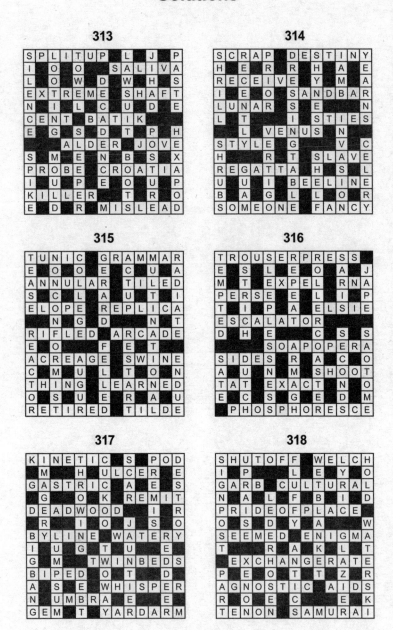

Solutions

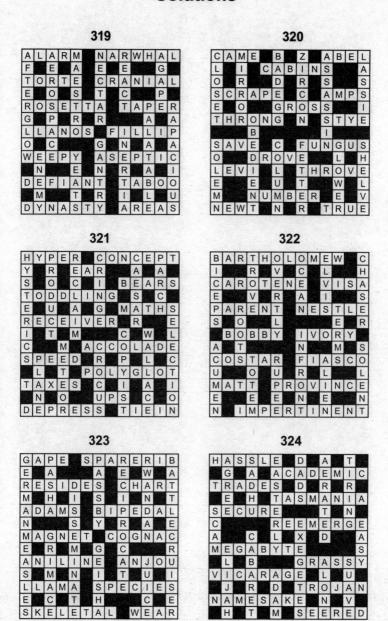

319

A	L	A	R	M		N	A	R	W	H	A	L
F		E		A		E		E		G		
T	O	R	T	E		C	R	A	N	I	A	L
E		O		S		T		C		P		
R	O	S	E	T	T	A		T	A	P	E	R
G		P		R		R			A		A	
L	L	A	N	O	S		F	I	L	L	I	P
O		C		G		N		A		A		
W	E	E	P	Y		A	S	E	P	T	I	C
	N		E		N		R		A		I	
D	E	F	I	A	N	T		T	A	B	O	O
	M		T		R		I		L		U	
D	Y	N	A	S	T	Y		A	R	E	A	S

320

C	A	M	E		B		Z		A	B	E	L
L		I		C	A	B	I	N	S			A
O		R		D		R		S		S		S
S	C	R	A	P	E		C		A	M	P	S
E		O		G	R	O	S	S				I
T	H	R	O	N	G		N		S	T	Y	E
			B						I			
S	A	V	E		C		F	U	N	G	U	S
O		D	R	O	V	E			L			H
L	E	V	I		L		T	H	R	O	V	E
E		E		U		T		W				L
M		N	U	M	B	E	R		E			V
N	E	W	T		N		R		T	R	U	E

321

H	Y	P	E	R		C	O	N	C	E	P	T
Y		R		E	A	R		A		A		
S		O		C		I		B	E	A	R	S
T	O	D	D	L	I	N	G		S		C	
E		U		A		G		M	A	T	H	S
R	E	C	E	I	V	E	R		R		E	
I		T		M		C		W		L		
C		M		A	C	C	O	L	A	D	E	
S	P	E	E	D		R		P		L		C
	L		T		P	O	L	Y	G	L	O	T
T	A	X	E	S		C		I		A		I
	N		O		U	P	S		C		O	
D	E	P	R	E	S	S		T	I	E	I	N

322

B	A	R	T	H	O	L	O	M	E	W		C
I		R		V		C		L				H
C	A	R	O	T	E	N	E		V	I	S	A
E		V		R		A		I				S
P	A	R	E	N	T		N	E	S	T	L	E
S		O		L					E			R
	B	O	B	B	Y		I	V	O	R	Y	
A		T			N		N		M		S	
C	O	S	T	A	R		F	I	A	S	C	O
U		O		U		R		L			L	
M	A	T	T		P	R	O	V	I	N	C	E
E		E		E		N		E		E		N
N		I	M	P	E	R	T	I	N	E	N	T

323

G	A	P	E		S	P	A	R	E	R	I	B
E		A		A		E		W		A		
R	E	S	I	D	E	S		C	H	A	R	T
M		H		I		S		I		N		T
A	D	A	M	S		B	I	P	E	D	A	L
N			S		Y		R		A		E	
M	A	G	N	E	T		C	O	G	N	A	C
E		R		M		G		C			R	
A	N	I	L	I	N	E		A	N	J	O	U
S		M		N		I		T		U		I
L	L	A	M	A		S	P	E	C	I	E	S
E		C		T		H			C		E	
S	K	E	L	E	T	A	L		W	E	A	R

324

H	A	S	S	L	E		D		A		T	
	G		A		A	C	A	D	E	M	I	C
T	R	A	D	E	S		D		R		R	
	E		H		T	A	S	M	A	N	I	A
S	E	C	U	R	E			T			N	
C				R	E	E	M	E	R	G	E	
A		C		L		X		D			A	
M	E	G	A	B	Y	T	E				S	
	L		B		G	R	A	S	S	Y		
V	I	C	A	R	A	G	E		L		U	
	J		R		D		T	R	O	J	A	N
N	A	M	E	S	A	K	E		N		V	
	H		T		M		S	E	E	R	E	D

603

Solutions

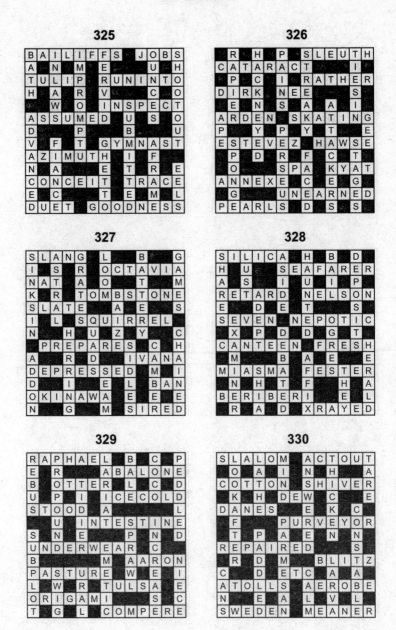

325

B	A	I	L	I	F	F	S		J	O	B	S
A		N		M		E		U			H
T	U	L	I	P		R	U	N	I	N	T	O
H		A		R		V		C			O
		W		O		I	N	S	P	E	C	T
A	S	S	U	M	E	D		U		S		O
D				P			B				U
V		F		T		G	Y	M	N	A	S	T
A	Z	I	M	U	T	H		I		F
N		A				E		T		R		E
C	O	N	C	E	I	T		T	R	A	C	E
E		C				T		E		M		L
D	U	E	T		G	O	O	D	N	E	S	S

326

	R		H		P		S	L	E	U	T	H
C	A	T	A	R	A	C	T					I
	P		C		I		R	A	T	H	E	R
D	I	R	K		N	E	E					S
	E		N		S		A		A			I
A	R	D	E	N		S	K	A	T	I	N	G
P			Y		P		Y		T			E
E	S	T	E	V	E	Z		H	A	W	S	E
	P		D		R		F		C			T
	O				S	P	A		K	Y	A	T
A	N	N	E	X	E		C		E			G
	G			U	N	E	A	R	N	E	D
P	E	A	R	L	S		D		S		S	S

327

S	L	A	N	G		L		B			G
I		S		R		O	C	T	A	V	I	A
N	A	T		A		O		T			M
K		R		T	O	M	B	S	T	O	N	E
S	L	A	T	E		A		E			S
I		L		S	Q	U	I	R	R	E	L
N			H		U		Z		Y		C
	P	R	E	P	A	R	E	S		C	H
A		R		D			I	V	A	N	A
D	E	P	R	E	S	S	E	D		M	I
D		I		E		L		B	A	N
O	K	I	N	A	W	A		E		E	E
N		G		M		S	I	R	E	D

328

S	I	L	I	C	A		H		B		D
H		U			S	E	A	F	A	R	E	R
A		S		I		U		I		P
R	E	T	A	R	D		N	E	L	S	O	N
E			D		E		T			S
S	E	V	E	N		N	E	P	O	T	I	C
	X		P		D		D		G		T
C	A	N	T	E	E	N		F	R	E	S	H
	M			B		A		E			E
M	I	A	S	M	A		F	E	S	T	E	R
	N		H		T		F			H		A
B	E	R	I	B	E	R	I			E		L
	R		A		D		X	R	A	Y	E	D

329

R	A	P	H	A	E	L		B		C		P
E		R				A	B	A	L	O	N	E
B		O	T	T	E	R		L		C		D
U		P		I		I	C	E	C	O	L	D
S	T	O	O	D		A				L
		U		I	N	T	E	S	T	I	N	E
S		N		E		P		N		D
U	N	D	E	R	W	E	A	R		C
B			M			A	A	R	O	N
P	A	S	T	U	R	E		W		E		I
L		W		R		T	U	L	S	A		E
O	R	I	G	A	M	I			S		C
T		G		L		C	O	M	P	E	R	E

330

S	L	A	L	O	M		A	C	T	O	U	T
	O		A		I		N		H			A
C	O	T	T	O	N		S	H	I	V	E	R
	K		H		D	E	W		C			E
D	A	N	E	S			E		K		C
	F				P	U	R	V	E	Y	O	R
	T		P		A		E		N			N
R	E	P	A	I	R	E	D					S
	R		D		M			B	L	I	T	Z
C		D		E	T	C		A				A
A	T	O	L	L	S		A	E	R	O	B	E
N		E		A		L		V				L
S	W	E	D	E	N		M	E	A	N	E	R

Solutions

331

```
T I D A L W A V E . G . C
O . E . A M . N O R T H
K . A . P L U G S . E . I
Y . D L . L . U . A . C
O P E R A T E . E X T R A
. . N . N . T . . . . N
I N S I D E . G A U C H E
N . . . . F . R . A
C O M I C . I N T E R I M
I . U . H L . I . B . O
S . Z . A T L A S . I . O
O N A I R . I . T . N . D
R . K . M O N A S T E R Y
```

332

```
T H R O B . S . . R . W
A . O . A . L I B E R A L
S I B E R I A . . T . P
T . B . T . B A H R A I N
E . E . D . R . A . T
F O R S W E A R . C O I N
U . H . A . I . T . A
L A M E . F I V E S T A R
. L D . E . E . . I . C
S E A L A N T . B . T . O
V . O . . R E A L I S T
V E R A N D A . L . A . I
. L D . P . M A N I C
```

333

```
L O N D O N . B U T T E R
U . I . S . E . A . E
R I G A T O N I . A B L E
E . E . E . G . L . L
S A L T O . S E C R E T E
. L . L . O . . C
T E A P O T . T R Y O U T
A . G . . U . P
N U R E Y E V . S P A N S
G . A . S . C . L . I
L A N D . S E D A T I O N
E . E . E . T . N . A
S T E V E N . Y E M E N I
```

334

```
V I C T O R . D E S E R T
A . H . E L I . T . I
S U R E . O . E . A . G
E . B . P A S T I C H E
. R . E . E . N . T
C O U S I N . L I S T E N
. Q . C . . A . O
G U S S E T . U N P L U G
. E . M . H . P . U . S
O F F I C I A L . N . M
. O . L . R . O . J U D O
. R . E . T E A . A . W
S T O D G Y . D E B R I S
```

335

```
G A S E S . R E A D I N G
E . T . I . I . B . M . A
N . R . R E D C A R P E T
E V A D E . O . . R . E
T . N . N E F A R I O U S
I . G . A . L . B
C A U G H T . I M P A C T
. L . E . K . B . R
G U A R A N T E E . I . I
U . T . A . A L L E N
S W I N G W I N G . I . K
T . O . E . N . L . T . E
S I N G L E T . E G Y P T
```

336

```
L O B E . C O L U M B U S
I . A . P . U . N . E . O
M A K E O U T . S I N K S
E . E . S . W . Y . G . O
R E S A T . I N S T A L
I . . M O T E T . L . C
C A M P E D . A E R I A L
K . O . R E A R M . . U
. I N F I R M . A N E L E
S S . D . U . T . X . L
P E T R I . S E I Z U R E
O . E . E . E C . D . S
T I R A M I S U . L E S S
```

Solutions

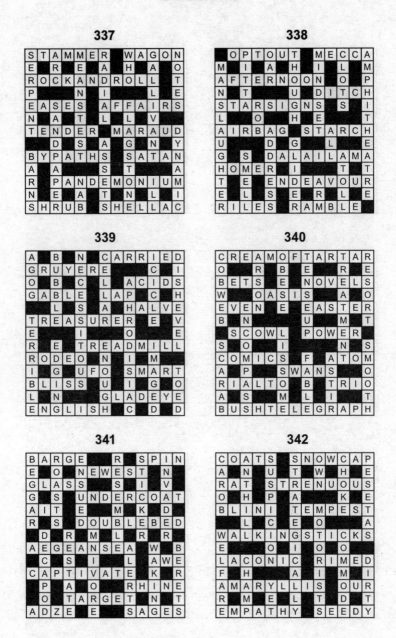

337

338

339

340

341

342

Solutions

343

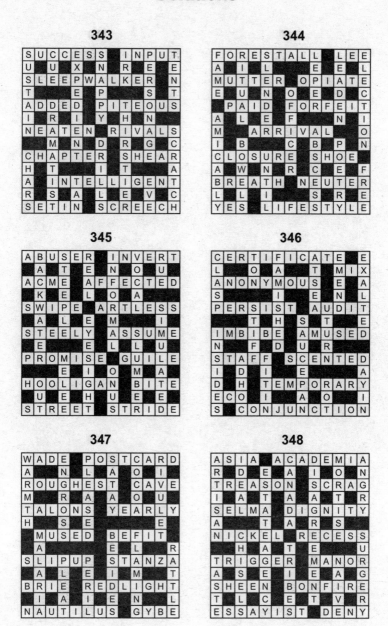

S	U	C	C	E	S	S		I	N	P	U	T
U		X		N		R		E			E	
S	L	E	E	P	W	A	L	K	E	R		N
T			E		P			S			T	
A	D	D	E	D		P	I	T	E	O	U	S
I		R		I		Y		H		N		
N	E	A	T	E	N		R	I	V	A	L	S
		M		N		D		R		G		C
C	H	A	P	T	E	R		S	H	E	A	R
H		T		I		T				A		
A		I	N	T	E	L	L	I	G	E	N	T
R		S		A		L		E		V		C
S	E	T	I	N		S	C	R	E	E	C	H

344

F	O	R	E	S	T	A	L	L		L	E	E
A		I		L				E		E		L
M	U	T	T	E	R		O	P	I	A	T	E
E		U		N		O		E		D		C
	P	A	I	D		F	O	R	F	E	I	T
A		L		E		F			N		I	
M			A	R	R	I	V	A	L			O
I		B			C		B		P		N	
C	L	O	S	U	R	E		S	H	O	E	
A		W		N		R		C		E		F
B	R	E	A	T	H		N	E	U	T	E	R
L		L		I				S		R		E
Y	E	S		L	I	F	E	S	T	Y	L	E

345

A	B	U	S	E	R		I	N	V	E	R	T
	A		T		E		N		O		U	
A	C	M	E		A	F	F	E	C	T	E	D
	K		E		L		O		A			
S	W	I	P	E		A	R	T	L	E	S	S
	A		L		E		M			I		
S	T	E	E	L	Y		A	S	S	U	M	E
	E			E		L		L		U		
P	R	O	M	I	S	E		G	U	I	L	E
		E		I		O		M		A		
H	O	O	L	I	G	A	N		B	I	T	E
	U		E		H		U		E		E	
S	T	R	E	E	T		S	T	R	I	D	E

346

C	E	R	T	I	F	I	C	A	T	E		E
L		O		A			T		M	I	X	
A	N	O	N	Y	M	O	U	S		E		A
S			I			E		N		L		
P	E	R	S	I	S	T		A	U	D	I	T
		T		H		S		T		E		
I	M	B	I	B	E		A	M	U	S	E	D
N		F		D		U		R				
S	T	A	F	F		S	C	E	N	T	E	D
I		D		I		E				A		
D		H		T	E	M	P	O	R	A	R	Y
E	C	O		I		A		O			I	
S		C	O	N	J	U	N	C	T	I	O	N

347

W	A	D	E		P	O	S	T	C	A	R	D
A		N		L		A		O		I		
R	O	U	G	H	E	S	T		C	A	V	E
M		R		A		A		O		U		
T	A	L	O	N	S		Y	E	A	R	L	Y
H		S		E				E				
	M	U	S	E	D		B	E	F	I	T	
A				E		L		R				
S	L	I	P	U	P		S	T	A	N	Z	A
	A		L		E		I		M		T	
B	R	I	E		R	E	D	L	I	G	H	T
	I		A		I		E		N		L	
N	A	U	T	I	L	U	S		G	Y	B	E

348

A	S	I	A		A	C	A	D	E	M	I	A
R		D		E		A		I		O		N
T	R	E	A	S	O	N		S	C	R	A	G
I		A		T		A		A		T		R
S	E	L	M	A		D	I	G	N	I	T	Y
A			T		A		R		S			
N	I	C	K	E	L		R	E	C	E	S	S
	H		A		T		E				U	
T	R	I	G	G	E	R		M	A	N	O	R
A		S		E		I		E		A		G
S	H	E	E	N		B	O	N	F	I	R	E
T		L		C		E		T		V		R
E	S	S	A	Y	I	S	T		D	E	N	Y

607

Solutions

349
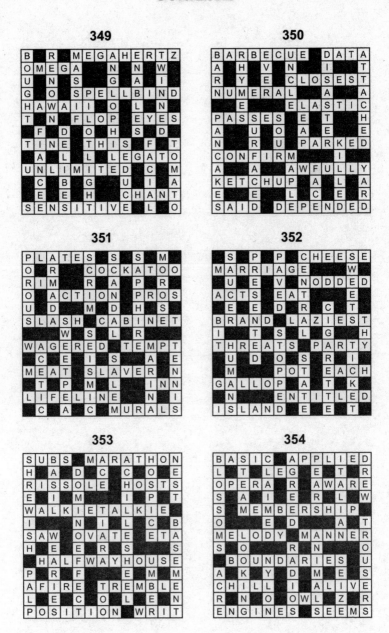

B	R		M	E	G	A	H	E	R	T	Z
O	M	E	G	A			N		N		W
U		N		S		G		A		I	
G		O		S	P	E	L	L	B	I	N	D
H	A	W	A	I	I		O		L		N
T		N		F	L	O	P		E	Y	E	S
	F		D		O		H		S		D
T	I	N	E		T	H	I	S		F		T
	A		L		L		L	E	G	A	T	O
U	N	L	I	M	I	T	E	D		C		M
	C		B		G		U		I		A
	E		E		H		C	H	A	N	T
S	E	N	S	I	T	I	V	E		L		O

350

B	A	R	B	E	C	U	E		D	A	T	A
A		H		V		N			I			T
R		Y	E		C	L	O	S	E	S	T
N	U	M	E	R	A	L		A			A
		E			E	L	A	S	T	I	C
P	A	S	S	E	S		E		T		H
A			U		O		A		E		E
N		R		U		P	A	R	K	E	D
C	O	N	F	I	R	M			I
A		A		A	W	F	U	L	L	Y
K	E	T	C	H	U	P		A		L	A
E		E		L		C	E	R
S	A	I	D		D	E	P	E	N	D	E	D

351

P	L	A	T	E	S		S		S		M
O		R			C	O	C	K	A	T	O	O
R	I	M		R		A		P		R
O		A	C	T	I	O	N		P	R	O	S
U		D		M		D		H		S
S	L	A	S	H		C	A	B	I	N	E	T
		W		S		L		R
W	A	G	E	R	E	D		T	E	M	P	T
	C		E		I		S		A		E
M	E	A	T		S	L	A	V	E	R		N
	T		P		M		L			I	N	N
L	I	F	E	L	I	N	E			N		I
	C		A		C		M	U	R	A	L	S

352

	S		P		P		C	H	E	E	S	E
M	A	R	R	I	A	G	E				W
	U		E		V		N	O	D	D	E	D
A	C	T	S		E	A	T			E
	E		E		D		R		C		T
B	R	A	N	D		L	A	Z	I	E	S	T
I		T		S		L		G			H
T	H	R	E	A	T	S		P	A	R	T	Y
	U		D		O		S		R		I
	M			P	O	T		E	A	C	H
G	A	L	L	O	P		A		T		K
	N			E	N	T	I	T	L	E	D
I	S	L	A	N	D		E		E	T

353

S	U	B	S		M	A	R	A	T	H	O	N
H		A		D		C		C		O		E
R	I	S	S	O	L	E		H	O	S	T	S
E		I		M		I		I		P		T
W	A	L	K	I	E	T	A	L	K	I	E
I			N		I		L		C		B
S	A	W		O	V	A	T	E		E	T	A
H		E		E		R		S			S
	H	A	L	F	W	A	Y	H	O	U	S	E
P		R		F			E		M		M
A	F	I	R	E		T	R	E	M	B	L	E
L		E		C		O		L		E		N
P	O	S	I	T	I	O	N		W	R	I	T

354

B	A	S	I	C		A	P	P	L	I	E	D
L		T		L	E	G		E		T		R
O	P	E	R	A		R		A	W	A	R	E
S		A		I		E		R		L		W
S		M	E	M	B	E	R	S	H	I	P
O		E		D		D			A		T
M	E	L	O	D	Y		M	A	N	N	E	R
S		O			R		N				O
	B	O	U	N	D	A	R	I	E	S		U
A		K		Y		D		M		E		S
C	H	I	L	L		I		A	L	I	V	E
R		N		O		O	W	L		Z		R
E	N	G	I	N	E	S		S	E	E	M	S

608

Solutions

355

```
M E R I N O   W   P   B
E   E     C H A R A D E S
D E E P   T   S   L   S
I   F O M E N T   M A I N
A     E   T   R       D
T E S T S   R E F I N E D
O     I   V   L   R     E
R A T C H E T   G O O D S
  B     R   H   N       I
L O R E   S P I R I T   R
  U   Y   I   V   C I A O
A N T E L O P E     D   U
  D   D   N     S T R E S S
```

356

```
  F E R R I S W H E E L S
R   X   E   T   A   X   I
A T T I C   R   V I P E R
P   O   L E I O   R   E
P I L A U   N U C L E U S
E     S   G       S
L A T H E R   A L A S K A
    R     D   I       E
C L I M A T E   S O B E R
O   C   D   B U T   R   A
Y I E L D   T   E D I C T
P   P   E   O   N   A   E
U N S U R P R I S I N G
```

357

```
D O C K E D   P A S T R Y
R   L   E     R   A     A
O R A C L E   E   F     R
O   S     F L O W E R E D
P U S S   F   C   T   U
  T   T W I T C H Y   R
G O Y A   C   U   N E E D
  P   T R A M P L E   K
  I   U   C   I   T S A R
B A K E L I T E   W   E
U   T   O   D A R I N G
S     T   U     I   F   A
H A V E R S   B R U T A L
```

358

```
W A S H T U B   L   B   A
R   T   U   A G E L E S S
E Q U A T O R   D   A   T
T   M   O   D   G   C   E
C Y B O R G   T E T H E R
H   L   R   W         N
  S E N T I M E N T A L
A       L   E     B   P
C A S U A L   D A M S E L
C   O   C   A   N   O   A
E   L   U   R I V A L R Y
P L A S T I C   I   V   E
T   R   E   H A L B E R D
```

359

```
O   P   S   I N F I D E L
F A U N A   N   L   O   A
F   R   L E T H A R G I C
I S S U E   I   T   G   E
C   U   S U M P T U O U S
E   E     E   E       S
S H R I M P   P R O P E R
  E     O   S     L   O
C R E D U L O U S   U   B
L   X   N   R   T I N G E
A D A P T A B L E   D   R
M   L   I   E   E R E C T
P A T I E N T   P   R   S
```

360

```
A U D I T O R   F J O R D
N   R   A   E   A     R
A G A   I C E H O C K E Y
L   C   L   D   K     A
Y A H O O     P   A B E D
S   M   R O G E R S
T E A R   N   G   S C O T
      E X C U S E   H   R
S O W S   E     R O U G E
W   P   Z   A   C   A
A N X I E T I E S   K I D
R   T   N   E   L   L
M O W E R   C O R T E G E
```

Solutions

361

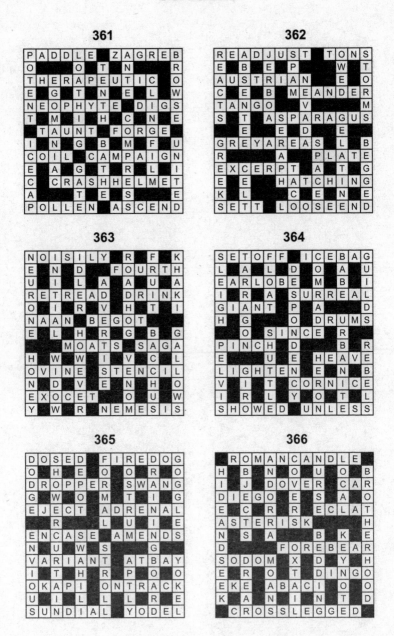

```
P A D D L E . Z A G R E B
O . . O . T . N . . . R
T H E R A P E U T I C . O
E . G . T . N . E . L . W
N E O P H Y T E . D I G S
T . M . I . H . C . N . E
. T A U N T . F O R G E .
I . N . G . B . M . F . U
C O I L . . C A M P A I G N
E . A . G . T . R . L . I
C . C R A S H H E L M E T
A . . T . E . S . . . E
P O L L E N . A S C E N D
```

362

```
R E A D J U S T . T O N S
E . B . E . P . . W . T
A U S T R I A N . . E . O
C . E . B . M E A N D E R
T A N G O . V . . . M
S . T . A S P A R A G U S
. E . E . D . E .
G R E Y A R E A S . L . B
R . . A . . P L A T E
E X C E R P T . A . T . G
E . E . H A T C H I N G
K . L . . C . E . E
S E T T . L O O S E E N D
```

363

```
N O I S I L Y . R . F . K
E . N . D . F O U R T H
U . I . L . A . A . U . A
R E T R E A D . D R I N K
O . I . R . V . H . T . I
N A A N . B E G O T .
E . L . H . R . G . B . G
. M O A T S . S A G A
H . W . W . I . V . C . L
O V I N E . S T E N C I L
N . D . V . E . N . H . O
E X O C E T . O . U . W
Y . W . R . N E M E S I S
```

364

```
S E T O F F . I C E B A G
L . A . L . D . O . A . U
E A R L O B E . M . B . I
I . R . A . S U R R E A L
G I A N T . P . A . . D
H . G . . O . D R U M S
. O . S I N C E . R .
P I N C H . D . . B . R
E . U . E . H E A V E
L I G H T E N . E . N . B
V . I . T . C O R N I C E
I . R . L . Y . O . T . L
S H O W E D . U N L E S S
```

365

```
D O S E D . F I R E D O G
O . H . E . O . O . R . O
D R O P P E R . S W A N G
G . W . O . M . T . I . G
E J E C T . A D R E N A L
. R . . L . U . I . E
E N C A S E . A M E N D S
N . U . W . S . . G
V A R I A N T . A T B A Y
I . T . H . R . P . O . O
O K A P I . O N T R A C K
U . I . L . L . L . R . E
S U N D I A L . Y O D E L
```

366

```
. R O M A N C A N D L E .
H . B . N . O . U . O . B
I . J . D O V E R . C A R
D I E G O . E . S . A . O
E . C . R . R . E C L A T
A S T E R I S K . . . H
N . S . A . . B . K . E
D . . . F O R E B E A R
S O D O M . X . D . Y . H
E . R . O . T . D I N G O
E K E . A B A C I . O . O
K . A . N . I . N . T . D
. C R O S S L E G G E D .
```

610

Solutions

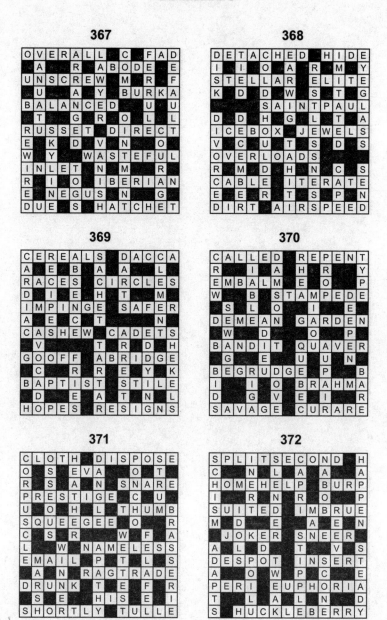

367 368

369 370

371 372

Solutions

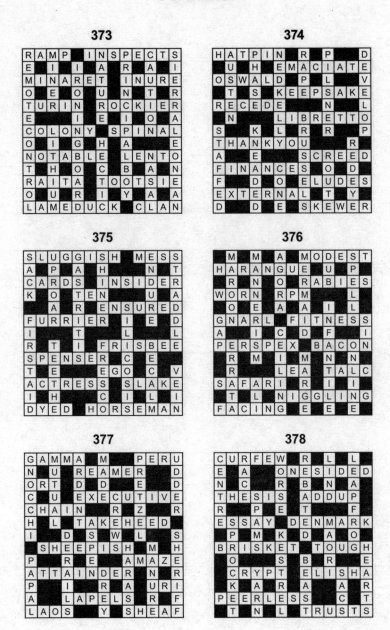

373

```
R A M P   I N S P E C T S
E   I   I   A   R   A   I
M I N A R E T   I N U R E
O   E   O   U   N   T   R
T U R I N   R O C K I E R
E     I   E   I   O   A
C O L O N Y   S P I N A L
O   I   G   H   A     E
N O T A B L E   L E N T O
T   H   O   C   B   A   N
R A I T A   T O O T S I E
O   U   R   I   Y   A   A
L A M E D U C K   C L A N
```

374

```
H A T P I N   R   P     D
  U   H   E M A C I A T E
O S W A L D   P   L     V
  T   S   K E E P S A K E
R E C E D E       N     L
  N     L I B R E T T O
S     K   L   R   R     P
T H A N K Y O U       R
A     E       S C R E E D
F I N A N C E S   O   D
F     D   O   E L U D E S
E X T E R N A L   T   Y
D     D   E   S K E W E R
```

375

```
S L U G G I S H   M E S S
A   P   A   H     N   T
C A R D S   I N S I D E R
K   O   T E N     U   A
  A   R   E N S U R E D
F U R R I E R   I   E   D
I     T     L     L
R   T I   F R I S B E E
S P E N S E R   C   E
T   E     E G O   C   V
A C T R E S S   S L A K E
I   H     C   I   L   I
D Y E D   H O R S E M A N
```

376

```
  M   M   A   M O D E S T
H A R A N G U E   U   P
  R   N   O   R A B I E S
W O R N   R P M     L
O   E   A   A   I   L
G N A R L   F I T N E S S
A   I   C   D   F     I
P E R S P E X   B A C O N
  R   M   I   M   N   N
  R     L E A   T A L C
S A F A R I   R   I   I
  T   L   N I G G L I N G
F A C I N G   E   E   E
```

377

```
G A M M A   M     P E R U
N   U   R E A M E R     D
O R T   D   D     E     D
C   U   E X E C U T I V E
C H A I N     R   Z     R
H   L   T A K E H E E D
I     D   S   W   L     S
  S H E E P I S H   M   H
P   R   E     A M A Z E
A T T A I N D E R   N   R
P   I     R   A   U R I
A   L A P E L S   R     F
L A O S     Y   S H E A F
```

378

```
C U R F E W   R   L   L
E   A     O N E S I D E D
N   C   R   B   N   A
T H E S I S   A D D U P
R   P   E   T       F
E S S A Y   D E N M A R K
P   M   K   D   A   O
B R I S K E T   T O U G H
O     S   B   R     E
  C R Y P T   E L I S H A
K   A   R   A     A   R
P E E R L E S S     C   T
  T   N   L   T R U S T S
```

612

Solutions

379

S	Y	M	P	T	O	M		R		B		U
O		I			A	M	A	D	E	U	S	
F		S	E	M	I	S		T		E		U
I		N		E		S	H	E	L	T	E	R
A	M	O	U	R		E						P
		M		E	N	D	O	S	C	O	P	E
O		E		L				T		B		D
F	O	R	S	Y	T	H	I	A		S		
F				A		T	I	E	U	P		
S	U	L	P	H	U	R		I		S		A
I		Y		A		M	O	C	K	S		R
D	E	N	T	A	T	E				E		I
E		X		R		D	E	C	A	D	E	S

380

	I	T	A	L	I	C		C	H	O	R	E	S
		H		O		R		O		A			T
B	E	L	I	Z	E		N	U	T	R	I	A	
		H		R		E	T	C		M			Y
B	A	B	E	L			R			E			E
		G			E	L	E	V	A	T	E	D	
		U		V		V		T		L		X	
R	E	L	E	G	A	T	E					T	
E		R		N			B	E	R	E	T	
L		B		E	L	I		A		R		
A	T	H	E	N	S		R	E	G	A	I	N
T		N		C		I		R		O		
E	F	F	A	C	E		S	H	E	R	R	Y

381

T	O	N	S	I	L	L	I	T	I	S		M
I		I		C		U		R		A	R	E
B	A	G		E	P		E		L		A	
I		G		C	H	I	D	E		V		S
A	G	A	M	A		N		S	W	E	L	L
		R		P	E						E
M	O	D	I	S	H		B	R	I	C	K	S
A			S		U		A				
R	U	R	A	L		A		B	A	H	T	S
I		E		A	D	L	I	B		O		H
N		V		D		M		I		O	B	I
E	M	U		L		O		S		T		N
R		P	I	E	I	N	T	H	E	S	K	Y

382

S	C	R	E	W		F			D		R	
Y		A		E		L	I	M	I	T	E	D
S	I	N	C	E	R	E			S		G	
T		G		D		D	R	A	S	T	I	C
E		E		C		A		E		N		
M	E	R	C	H	A	N	T		C	R	A	M
I			H		N		T		T			O
C	O	M	E		C	O	L	O	S	S	A	L
	P		N		A		E			N		A
S	A	P	I	E	N	T		E		O		S
	Q		L			I	M	P	I	O	U	S
G	U	I	L	D	E	R		I		Z		E
	E		E			E		C	H	E	S	S

383

S	C	R	U	B	S		T	I	S	S	U	E
C		E		O		U		T		L
A	L	A	R	M	I	S	T		B	O	L	D
M		D		B		T		I		E
P	I	E	R	S		S	I	D	E	C	A	R
		R		H			R			L
D	A	S	H	E	D		S	U	P	P	L	Y
W			L			M		R		
I	M	P	U	L	S	E		S	C	E	N	E
N		L		T		T		T		V		W
D	A	U	B		A	B	D	I	C	A	T	E
L		M		G			C		I		R
E	X	P	I	R	E		S	K	U	L	K	S

384

F	A	C	T	O	R		R	E	A	G	A	N
A		E		A		A		B		P	
T	U	F	T		N		R		L		P	
E		H		G	R	E	Y	A	R	E	A	
	F		Y		E		S		Z		R	
G	U	E	S	T	S		T	R	E	A	T	Y
N			E			E		A	
T	I	N	C	A	N		R	E	C	O	I	L
C		A		E		E		A		N
G	U	E	R	I	L	L	A		N		D
L		A		L		R		O	K	R	A
A		T		I		M	E		E		T
C	R	U	S	O	E		S	E	S	A	M	E

Solutions

385 386

387 388

389 390

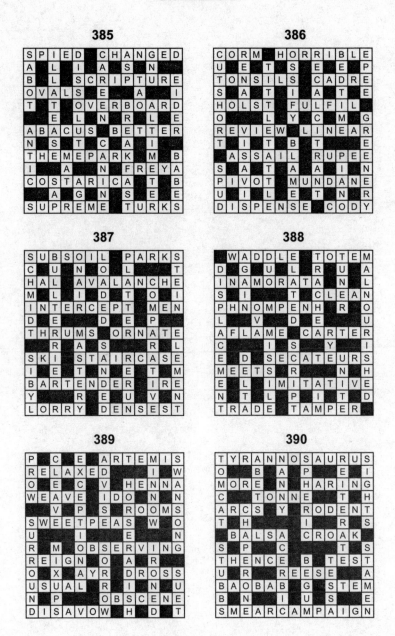

Solutions

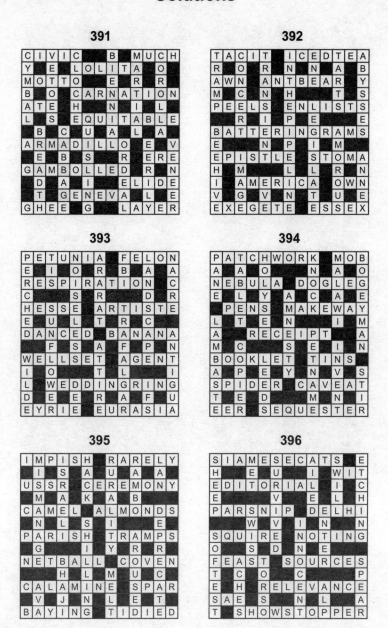

391

C	I	V	I	C		B		M	U	C	H
Y		E		L	O	L	I	T	A		O
M	O	T	T	O		E		R		R	
B		O		C	A	R	N	A	T	I	O	N
A	T	E		H		N		I		L	
L		S		E	Q	U	I	T	A	B	L	E
	B		C		U		A		L		A
A	R	M	A	D	I	L	L	O		E		V
	E		B		S		R		E	R	E
G	A	M	B	O	L	L	E	D		R		N
	D		A		I			E	L	I	D	E
	T		G	E	N	E	V	A		L		E
G	H	E	E		G			L	A	Y	E	R

392

T	A	C	I	T		I	C	E	D	T	E	A
R		O		R		N		N		A		B
A	W	N		A	N	T	B	E	A	R		Y
M		C		N		H				T		S
P	E	E	L	S		E	N	L	I	S	T	S
		R		I		P		E				E
B	A	T	T	E	R	I	N	G	R	A	M	S
E				N		P		I		M		
E	P	I	S	T	L	E		S	T	O	M	A
H		M			L		L		R		N
I		A	M	E	R	I	C	A		O	W	N
V		G		V		N		T		U		E
E	X	E	G	E	T	E		E	S	S	E	X

393

P	E	T	U	N	I	A		F	E	L	O	N
E		I		O		R		B	A		A	A
R	E	S	P	I	R	A	T	I	O	N		C
C			S		R			D		R		
H	E	S	S	E		A	R	T	I	S	T	E
E		U		L		T		R		C		
D	A	N	C	E	D		B	A	N	A	N	A
		F		S		A		F		P		N
W	E	L	L	S	E	T		A	G	E	N	T
I		O		T		L		L				I
L		W	E	D	D	I	N	G	R	I	N	G
D		E		E		R		A		F		U
E	Y	R	I	E		E	U	R	A	S	I	A

394

P	A	T	C	H	W	O	R	K		M	O	B
A		A		O				N		A		O
N	E	B	U	L	A		D	O	G	L	E	G
E		L		Y		A		C		A		E
	P	E	N	S		M	A	K	E	W	A	Y
L		T		E		N				I		M
A			R	E	C	E	I	P	T			A
M		C				S		E		I		N
B	O	O	K	L	E	T		T	I	N	S	
A		P		E		Y		N		V		S
S	P	I	D	E	R		C	A	V	E	A	T
T		E		D			M		N			I
E	E	R		S	E	Q	U	E	S	T	E	R

395

I	M	P	I	S	H		R	A	R	E	L	Y
	I		S		A		U		A		A	
U	S	S	R		C	E	R	E	M	O	N	Y
	M		A		K		A		B			
C	A	M	E	L		A	L	M	O	N	D	S
	N		L		S		I				E	
P	A	R	I	S	H		T	R	A	M	P	S
	G				Y		R		R		R	
N	E	T	B	A	L	L		C	O	V	E	N
		H		L		M		U		C		
C	A	L	A	M	I	N	E		S	P	A	R
	V		J		N		L		E		T	
B	A	Y	I	N	G		T	I	D	I	E	D

396

S	I	A	M	E	S	E	C	A	T	S		E
H		E		U		I			W	I	T	
E	D	I	T	O	R	I	A	L		I		C
E				V			E		L		H	
P	A	R	S	N	I	P		D	E	L	H	I
		W		V		I		N			N	
S	Q	U	I	R	E		N	O	T	I	N	G
O		S		D		N		E				
F	E	A	S	T		S	O	U	R	C	E	S
T		C		O		C						P
E	H		R	E	L	E	V	A	N	C	E	
S	A	E		S			N		L			A
T		S	H	O	W	S	T	O	P	P	E	R

Solutions

397

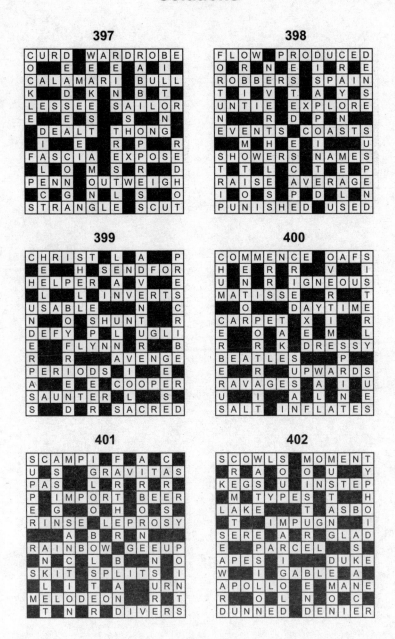

```
C U R D   W A R D R O B E
O   E   E   E   A   I
C A L A M A R I   B U L L
K   D   K   N   B   T
L E S S E E   S A I L O R
E   E   S   S   N
  D E A L T   T H O N G
  I   E   R   P   R
F A S C I A   E X P O S E
  L   O   M   S   R   D
P E N N   O U T W E I G H
  C   G   N   L   S   O
S T R A N G L E   S C U T
```

398

```
F L O W   P R O D U C E D
O   R   N   E   I   R   E
R O B B E R S   S P A I N
T   I   V   T   A   Y   S
U N T I E   E X P L O R E
N   R   D   P   N
E V E N T S   C O A S T S
  M   H   E   I   U
S H O W E R S   N A M E S
T   T   L   C   T   E   P
R A I S E   A V E R A G E
I   O   S   P   D   L   N
P U N I S H E D   U S E D
```

399

```
C H R I S T   L   A     P
  E   H   S E N D F O R  R
H E L P E R   A   V     E
  L   L   I N V E R T S
U S A B L E     N     C
N   O   S H U N T     R
D E F Y   P   L   U G L I
E   F L Y N N   R     B
R   R     A V E N G E
P E R I O D S   I   E
A   E   E   C O O P E R
S A U N T E R   L   S
S   D   R   S A C R E D
```

400

```
C O M M E N C E   O A F S
H   E   R   R   V     I
U   N   R   I G N E O U S
M A T I S S E   R     T
  O     D A Y T I M E   R
C A R P E T   X   I     R
E   O   A   E   M   L
R   R   K   D R E S S Y
B E A T L E S     P
E   R   U P W A R D S
R A V A G E S   A   I   U
U   I   A   L   N     E
S A L T   I N F L A T E S
```

401

```
S C A M P I   F   A   C
U   S   G R A V I T A S
P A S   L   R   R   R
P   I M P O R T   B E E R
E   G   O   H   O   S
R I N S E   L E P R O S Y
  A   B   R   N
R A I N B O W   G E E U P
  N   C   L   B   N   O
S K I T   S P L I T S   I
  L   I   T   A   U R N
M E L O D E O N   R   T
  T   N   R   D I V E R S
```

402

```
S C O W L S   M O M E N T
  R   A   O   O   U   Y
K E G S   U   I N S T E P
  M   T Y P E S   T   H
L A K E   T   A S B O
  T   I M P U G N   I
S E R E   A   R   G L A D
E   P A R C E L     S
A P E S   I   D U K E
W   I   G A B L E   A
A P O L L O   E   M A N E
R   O   L   N   O   C
D U N N E D   D E N I E R
```

Solutions

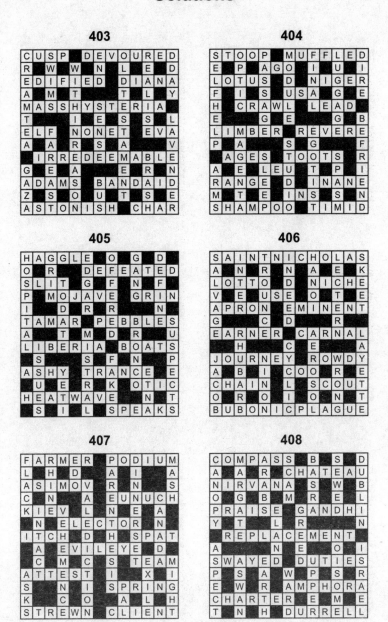

403

```
C U S P . D E V O U R E D
R . W . W . N . L . E . D
E D I F I E D . D I A N A
A . M . T . . T . L . . Y
M A S S H Y S T E R I A .
T . . I . E . S . S . L
E L F . N O N E T . E V A
A . A . R . S . A . . V
. I R R E D E E M A B L E
G . E . A . . E . R . N
A D A M S . B A N D A I D
Z . S . O . U . T . S . E
A S T O N I S H . C H A R
```

404

```
S T O O P . M U F F L E D
E . P . A G O . I . U . I
L O T U S . D . N I G E R
F . I . S . U S A . G . E
H . C R A W L . L E A D .
E . . G . E . . . G . B
L I M B E R . R E V E R E
P . A . . S . G . . . F
. A G E S . T O O T S . R
A . E . L E U . T . P . I
R A N G E . D . I N A N E
M . T . E . I N S . S . N
S H A M P O O . T I M I D
```

405

```
H A G G L E . O . G . D
O . R . D E F E A T E D
S L I T . G . F . N . F
P . M O J A V E . G R I N
I . D . R . R . . R . N
T A M A R . P E B B L E S
A . T . M . D . R . . U
L I B E R I A . B O A T S
. S . . S . F . N . . P
A S H Y . T R A N C E . E
. U . E . R . K . O T I C
H E A T W A V E . . N . T
. S . I . L . S P E A K S
```

406

```
S A I N T N I C H O L A S
A . N . R . N . A . E . K
L O T T O . D . N I C H E
V . E . U S E . O . T . E
A P R O N . E M I N E N T
G . . . C . D . . . R .
E A R N E R . C A R N A L
. . H . . C . E . . . A
J O U R N E Y . R O W D Y
A . B . I . C O O . R . E
C H A I N . L . S C O U T
O . R . O . I . O . N . T
B U B O N I C P L A G U E
```

407

```
F A R M E R . P O D I U M
L . H . D . A . I . . A
A S I M O V . R . N . S
C . N . . A . E U N U C H
K I E V . L . N . E . A
. N . E L E C T O R . N
I T C H . D . H . S P A T
. A . E V I L E Y E . D
C . M . C . S . T E A M
A T T E S T . I . X . I
S . N . I . S P R I N G
K . C . O . . A . L . H
S T R E W N . C L I E N T
```

408

```
C O M P A S S . B . S . D
A . A . R . C H A T E A U
N I R V A N A . S . W . B
O . G . B . M . R . E . L
P R A I S E . G A N D H I
Y . T . . L . R . . . N
. R E P L A C E M E N T .
A . . . N . E . O . . I
S W A Y E D . D U T I E S
P . S . A . W . P . S . R
E . W . R . A M P H O R A
C H A R T E R . E . M . E
T . N . H . D U R R E L L
```

Solutions

409

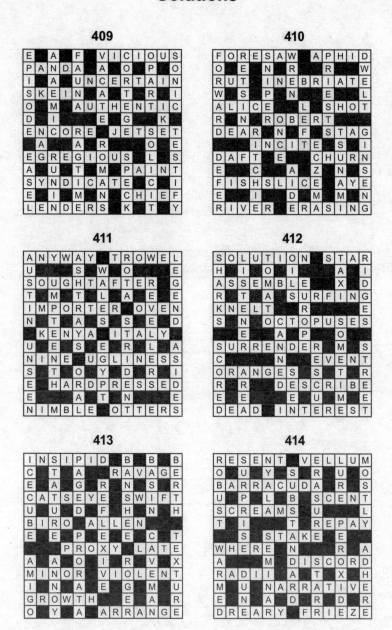

```
E . A F . V I C I O U S
P A N D A . A . O . P . O
I . A . U N C E R T A I N
S K E I N . A . T . R . I
O . M . A U T H E N T I C
D I . . E . G . . K
E N C O R E . J E T S E T
. A . A . R . . . O . E
E G R E G I O U S . L . S
A . U . T . M . P A I N T
S Y N D I C A T E . C . I
E . I . M . N . C H I E F
L E N D E R S . K . T . Y
```

410

```
F O R E S A W . A P H I D
O . E . N . R . . R . . W
R U T . I N E B R I A T E
W . S . P . N . . E . . L
A L I C E . . L . S H O T
R . N . R O B E R T
D E A R . N . F . S T A G
. . . I N C I T E . S . I
D A F T . E . . C H U R N
E . C . A . Z . N . . . S
F I S H S L I C E . A Y E
E . I . . D . M . M . . N
R I V E R . E R A S I N G
```

411

```
A N Y W A Y . T R O W E L
U . . S . W . O . . . . E
S O U G H T A F T E R . G
T . M . T . L . A . E . E
I M P O R T E R . O V E N
N . T . A . S . S . E . D
. K E N Y A . I T A L Y .
U . E . S . E . R . L . A
N I N E . U G L I N E S S
S . T . O . Y . D . R . I
E . H A R D P R E S S E D
E . . . A . T . N . . . E
N I M B L E . O T T E R S
```

412

```
S O L U T I O N . S T A R
H . I . O . I . . A . . I
A S S E M B L E . . X . D
R . T . A . S U R F I N G
K N E L T . . R . . . . E
S . N . O C T O P U S E S
. . . E . A . P . . O . .
S U R R E N D E R . M . S
C . . . N . . . E V E N T
O R A N G E S . S . T . R
R . R . D E S C R I B E
E . E . E . U . M . . . E
D E A D . I N T E R E S T
```

413

```
I N S I P I D . B . B . B
C . T . A . . R A V A G E
E . A . G . R . N . S . R
C A T S E Y E . S W I F T
U . U . D . F . H . N . H
B I R O . A L L E N
E . E . P . E . E . C . T
. . . P R O X Y . L A T E
A . A . O . I . R . V . X
M I N O R . V I O L E N T
I . N . A . E . G . M . U
G R O W T H . E . A . R
O . Y . A . A R R A N G E
```

414

```
R E S E N T . V E L L U M
O . U . Y . S . R . U . O
B A R R A C U D A . R . S
U . P . L . B . S C E N T
S C R E A M S . U . . . L
T . I . . T . R E P A Y
. . S . S T A K E . E
W H E R E . N . . R . A
A . . . M . D I S C O R D
R A D I I . A . T . X . H
M . U . N A R R A T I V E
E . N . A . D . R . D . R
D R E A R Y . F R I E Z E
```

Solutions

415

```
M A C A W   S L O B B E R
U   O   A   E U   L   O
C O N T R O L   G L O R Y
U   S   F   E   H   O   A
S U T R A   C I T A D E L
    E   R   T     P   T
G I R D E R   B L U R R Y
R   N       I   A   E
A M A L G A M   C A S T E
P   T   L   P K   S   V
H A I T I   E P I C U R E
I   O   D   L   N   R   R
C O N F E S S   G R E E T
```

416

```
  T R A D I N G P O S T
B   O   O   O   I   O   B
A   D   C R O W N   R Y E
T H E F T   D   U   T   N
H   N   O   L   P A S S E
I N T E R N E T           D
N   S   S       G   S   I
G       M A J E S T I C
S E V E R   T   N   R   T
U   E   O   O   E C O L I
I O N   D I N A R   K   O
T   U   E   E   A   E   N
  S E C O N D C L A S S
```

417

```
O R I N O C O   H   L A T
  A   P   K Y O T O   A
R I V I E R A   O   C   C
  D   N   P   P L A I T
M E C H A N I C S   L   I
  R   I   O     L   L
A S H O R E   G R O Y N E
F   E   W   E   E   E
F   X   S E N S A T I O N
L E A V E   O   C   L
I   G   O   B O H E M I A
C   O V U L E   E   T
T A N   L   L E S O T H O
```

418

```
C O M E D I A N   H I R E
O   A   I   B   S   N   N
P A R E S I S   U P S E T
Y   E   A   O   B   P   R
      A G G R E S S I V E
F   I   R   B   T   R   A
R A M M E D   P A L E S T
E   P   E   I   N   D   Y
S T A L A G M I T E
H   I   B   P   I   D   R
M O R A L   O C A R I N A
A   E   E   S   T   V   F
N O D E   R E L E V A N T
```

419

```
J A Y W A L K   M A C H O
A   O   S   A   A   Y
C H U M P   R U M M A G E
K   N   I   A   M   I
D O G T R O T   A R I E S
A   E   I   E       N
W I R I N G   S M I L E S
  R   F   I   E   E
P O L Y P   U N S L I N G
  N   I   N   S   S   M
S A L T P A N   I N U S E
  G   E   E   O   R   N
J E A N S   L O N G E S T
```

420

```
B I A S E D   C E M E N T
R   E   A   R   A   O
A T T A I N   O   L   G
N   A   I M P E T I G O
  P   I   E   X   R
P L U R A L   S T U P I D
I   I       R   S
F A R R O W   M A R B L E
N   L   O   A   Y
S T R A I N E R   P   G
U   M   A   R O T A T E
E   E   N   I   O   N
Z I N N I A   S H R O V E
```

Solutions

421

```
S E E D S     H I R S U T E
U   S   H O       Y   E
P   T   A N   F L A N K
P R A I R I E S   V   E
O   T   P   S A U T E
R E E L E C T I O N       A
T   S   Y     M   C   G
E     D E G E N E R A T E
R A T E D   M   T   M   R
    B   V   O B L I V I O N
M A R I E   O   M   L   E
    T   C   S   E   L   S
R E P E A T S     S P A T S
```

422

```
H A N D G R E N A D E     B
E     E   E     O   E     L
C H E E K I E R     M E S A
K     D   G     T   O     Z
L E S S O N     H O B B L E
E     A   E         L     R
  B U I L D     S H E E T
A     D         U     N   H
P R I S E S     B I R D I E
P     M   E     Z   O     R
L A C E   A P E R T U R E
E     A   R         O     B
S   A R I S T O C R A C Y
```

423

```
T O F F     L I F E S P A N
E   L   P   N   X   R   A
A B U S E R S     T S A R S
R   K   N   E   O   L   T
G L E A N   C E R T I F Y
A       Y   T   T   N
S C R A W L     W I D E S T
    E   H   T   O       R
D O S S I E R     N O R M A
O   I   S   I   A   O   P
M I D S T   F A T I G U E
E   U   L   L   E   U   Z
D E E P E N E D   P E R E
```

424

```
S U T U R E     P   D   P
  N   N   G U I D E D O G
I D L I N G   S   C   I
  E   O   S E A H O R S E
F R E N C H       R   O
I       E F F L U E N T
J   A   L   L   M   W
I C E L O L L Y       I
  L   I       P I P I N G
C I A B A T T A   L   I
  N   A   U   P R A Y E R
Z I M B A B W E   I   C
  C   A   A   R I N S E D
```

425

```
B A D L A N D S     S T A B
O   E   S   E       R   A
L O I N S   C Y C L I N G
A   F   E   R       L   U
    I   R   E N N O B L E
N E C K T I E     E   Y   T
A       I       G       T
R   L   O   F O L I A G E
C H I A N T I     I   U
O   N       A   G   N   E
S A D D E N S     E S T E R
I   E       C   N   I   O
S A N D   F O R T R E S S
```

426

```
  U   P E P Y S       L   U
B R A E   A   T A K E U P
  E   D   C   A       A   H
T A K E H E A R T     G O O
E     S   D   D       U   L
A R E T E   F O R C E P S
T   A   P   M   O   T
R A I L W A Y   O U N C E
O   N   L   P   N       R
L A D   R E P E R T O R Y
L   I   T   N   E       I
E A G L E T   N   S A F E
Y   O   E X I T S     T
```

620

Solutions

427

```
F E T E S . E . . B . . D
L . E . P . B I R E T T A
O A R . A . B . . C . . T
T . R . D O S S H O U S E
S W O R E . . L . M . . S
A . R . S H R I V E L S .
M . . M . A . C . S . . R
. R E A L I S E S . B . E
A . . S . K . . T O A S T
U N P O P U L A R . B . A
R . N . . A . A . I L K .
A N D R E W S . T . E . E
L . . Y . . H . A S S E S
```

428

```
G E N I U S . B . B . N .
R . O . . C L A R I N E T
I . O . . A . N . L . G .
L I N T E L . D O L L A R
L . R . P . S . . . . T .
E S T O P . L A N O L I N
. T . U . B . W . C . O .
M E N T I O N . B E I N G
. A . O . A . A . R .
A D R O I T . S U N D A E
. I . A . L . S . . A . A
A L L T H E R E . . D . S
. Y . H . G . T H R O N E
```

429

```
H O S T A G E . P . H . C
U . M . . . G O U L A S H
R . U S H E R . N . H . U
O . G . O . E N T R A N T
N I G H T . S . . . . N .
. . L . T A S K F O R C E
O . E . U . . I . E . . Y
S U R F B O A R D . T . .
T . . . C . G R A I N . .
M E L O D I C . E . I . E
A . U . I . E A T E N . P
R I C H A R D . . . E . A
K . K . Z . E N T H R A L
```

430

```
M E D L A R . E N S I G N
. L . A . O . N . E . . E
B E R T H S . S T E R E O
. G . T . A S H . T . . N
T A P E R . . R . H . P .
. N . . . T O I L E T R Y
. T . A . A . N . D . I .
C L A V I C L E . . . V .
. Y . A . T . . A S P I C
P . . R . L E D . T . L .
U N W I S E . A P O G E E
P . C . S . S . I . O . G
A F T E R S . S U D D E N
```

431

```
M A S O C H I S T . M . S
A . A . E . N . A B A F T
F . C . Z . M . L . Y . O
I . K . A B A C K . O . R
A V I A N . T . S P R E E
. . N . N . E . . . . . Y
P I G P E N . L A P S E S
I . . . B . L . C . . . .
P O S T S . E . L U R I D
E . E . A N D R E . A . R
T . D . V . L . G . P . U
T R A C E . A . R . E . I
E . N . S U M M O N S E D
```

432

```
C H O R D . A . . C . R .
H . L . E . L E G A T E E
A L D E N T E . . U . C .
R . M . S . C O N T A I N
I . A . H . P . I . P .
S Y N D R O M E . O V E R
M . . E . A . N . U . . E
A S I F . R H E O S T A T
. E . I . D . R . . I . I
T A R N I S H . B . R . C
. S . I . . I S O L A T E
B O W T I E S . S . D . N
. N . E . S . S M E L T .
```

621

Solutions

433

C	L	A	M	M	Y		C	R	I	T	I	C
R		N		E			E		O		L
A	S	T	E	R	O	I	D		S	K	Y	E
S		E		R		A			Y		A
S	I	N	A	I		D	R	A	G	O	O	N
		N		M			L				E
G	R	A	T	E	D		F	O	R	M	E	R
I			N			N		I	
N	I	G	H	T	L	Y		G	I	D	D	Y
G		R		A		S		W		A
H	O	O	F		R	E	V	I	S	I	O	N
A		W		G		D		F		K
M	A	N	A	G	E		R	E	C	E	S	S

434

| | | | | | | | | | | | |
|A|D|R|I|F|T| |C|A|M|E|B|Y|
|J| |M| |H| |O| |I| |A|
|A|T|O|P| |R| |B| |R| |L|
|R| |A| |I|N|W|A|R|D|L|Y|
	S		R		F		E		O		P
T	O	M	T	I	T		B	O	R	R	O	W
	L		L				U		I
H	U	M	B	L	E		O	R	I	E	N	T
T		I		X		P		S		T
R	I	C	O	C	H	E	T		O		T
O		P		A		I		B	E	T	A
N		I		L		N	A		A		L
P	S	Y	C	H	E		G	A	R	B	L	E

435

| | | | | | | | | | | |
|L|O|B|E|S| |K|N|E|E|P|A|D|
|A| |L| |M| |I| |D| |R|U|
|M| |O| |A|T|T|R|I|T|I|O|N|
|B|O|O|T|S| | |C| |M| |C|
|E| |D| |H|A|B|I|T|U|A|T|E|
N		R		N		B			R	
T	O	E	I	N	G		S	A	W	Y	E	R
		L		S		E		S		E
G	L	A	D	S	T	O	N	E		C	E
I		T		M			A	S	H	E	N
G	U	I	N	E	A	P	I	G		O	T
O		O		L		H		E		O	R
T	I	N	K	L	E	D		R	A	L	L	Y

436

| | | | | | | | | | | |
|D|E|C|K| |D|A|T|A|B|A|S|E|
|I| |A| |C| |N| |S| |D|U|
|S|I|R|L|O|I|N| |H|O|V|E|R|
|L| |D| |N| |U| |W| |A|O|
O	N	S	E	T		A	G	E	I	N	G
D			E		L		D		C		L
G	L	O	O	M	Y		S	N	E	E	Z	E
E		T		P		F		E			W
	S	T	A	T	U	E		S	O	U	N	D
B		O		U		E		D		M	N
L	I	M	B	O		B	R	A	M	B	L	E
O		A		U		L		Y		R	S
C	A	N	I	S	T	E	R		H	A	T	S

437

| | | | | | | | | | | |
|D|U|S|T|M|A|N| |T|R|A|I|L|
|E| |A| |A| |O| |O| |U|A|
P	A	L	I	N	D	R	O	M	E	S		M
O			G		W			C		B
S	E	P	I	A		A	L	I	G	H	T	S
E		A		N		Y		M		W
D	U	N	D	E	E		U	P	H	I	L	L
		O		S		S		R		T	A
T	O	R	R	E	N	T		O	O	Z	E	D
I		A		R		V			E
C		M	A	G	N	I	F	I	C	E	N	T
K		I		A		C		S		T	T
S	O	C	K	S		T	R	E	A	C	L	E

438

| | | | | | | | | | | |
| |C|L|O|S|E|S| |P|A|N|I|C|
|W| |E| |R| |E| |R| |O|O|
A	B	O	R	I	G	I	N	E		V	N
Y		T			Z		S	T	E	P	S
S	T	A	I	R	W	E	L	L		L		I
A		R			D		E			D
N	U	D	I	T	Y		B	Y	E	B	Y	E
D			Y		D			A		R
M		E		P	N	E	U	M	O	N	I	A
E	D	D	I	E		C			D		B
A		G		S	T	O	N	E	W	A	L	L
N		A		E		C		N		G	E
S	P	R	A	T		T	H	A	W	E	D

Solutions

439

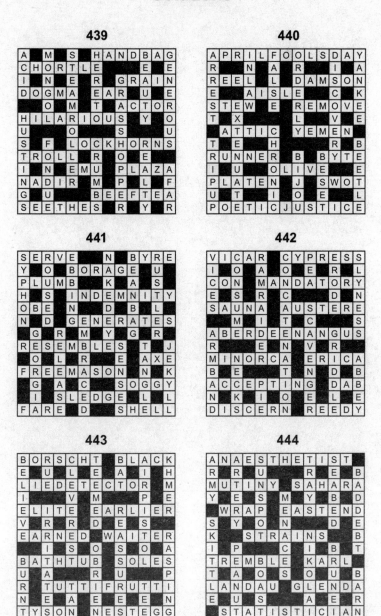

440

441

442

443

444

Solutions

445

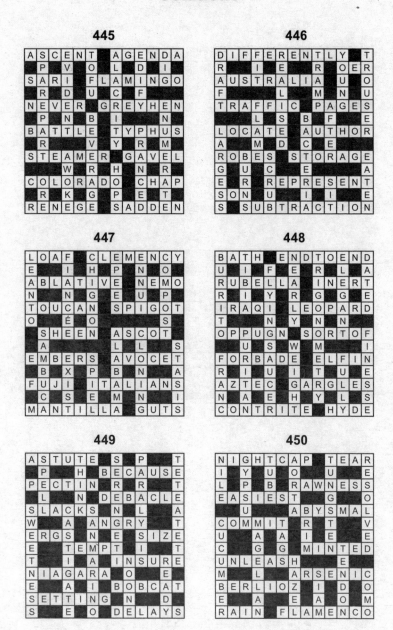

446

447

448

449

450

Solutions

451

```
C O F F I N . A . P . I
O . E . A P P A R E N T
P A N . V . P . E . D
I . C E R E A L . S W I G
E . E . L . I . E . A
D I S C O . H E A R I N G
. . O . C . S . V
W E A L T H Y . D E B T S
. C . L . E . W . A . T
S H O E . C O O L E R . A
. O . C . K . R . R A M
F E A T H E R S . E . P
. D . S . D . T A B L E S
```

452

```
. G . T . B . S H A N T Y
M O V E M E N T . . . Y
. D . A . A . A B D U C T
D I S C . T O N . . . O
. V . H . S . L . F . O
R A V E L . R E C L I N E
A . S . D . Y . Y . L
T A T T I E R . S A S S Y
G . S . B . E . G . I
A . . U L M . A D E N
A T H E N S . B . R . V
H . . S P E C I M E N
C A V I T Y . R . C . S
```

453

```
L A I D . S T A G N A N T
A . D . E . E . S . R
S H A N N O N . N O O S E
T . H . G . . E . C . E
P R O F I T M A R G I N
O . . N . O . A . A . W
S E E . E X P E L . L E I
T . P . D . U . S . D
. D I S R E P U T A B L E
S . G . I . . O . L . E
K I R O V . L A R C E N Y
I . A . E . I . E . A . E
M E M O R I E S . S T U D
```

454

```
S A W E D . I S T H M U S
U . H . I N N . I . E . T
P E A R S . D . D H A K A
P . R . L . E . E . N . Y
L . F R I E N D S H I P
I . . K . T . . N . A
E T C H E S . B A D G E R
D . O . P . N . . . K
. B R I D E S M A I D . A
A . S . O . A . R . E . N
L E A F Y . L . C O C K S
A . I . E . M P H . A . A
S T R A N D S . Y O Y O S
```

455

```
R A B B L E . A . G . H
E . E . R O L L O V E R
P R E P . R . G . N . A
U . F R E E Z E . G O R E
B . . I . D . B . . S
L A B E L . C R U M P E T
I . S . J . A . E . R
C U R T A I L . A R E N A
. P . T . D . G . . N
A R C H . T H A M E S . S
. O . I . E . M . R I C E
C O N V E R G E . . G . P
. T . E . Y . S I G N E T
```

456

```
. W O R L D W I D E W E B
B . B . U . O . O . A . R
O D E O N . R . P U R E E
F . S . A C T . E . R . V
F L E E T . H A Y W I R E
I . . I . Y . . . O
N U A N C E . D R Y R U N
. P . R . I . . . E
G O R I L L A . C O M E T
O . I . A . I N K . O . T
R A C K S . D . E Q U A L
G . O . E . E . T . R . E
E N T E R P R I S I N G
```

Solutions

457

```
C A S K E T   I N S I S T
L   U   R   S   T       I
A E R I A L   L   A     E
W   E     A B A T T O I R
S E R F   P   M   I   D
  N   I R A N     O   I
C O T S   Z   C   N O O K
  U   H     F R E E   T
  G   E   M   E   R I S K
S H O R T A G E     N   N
E     M   Y   P A G O D A
A     A   B     N   F   V
L O U N G E   S T I F L E
```

458

```
B L E S S E D   S   B   Z
E   X   W   R E T R A C E
M E T H A N E   A   L   P
U   R   M   W   L   L   H
S C U L P T   G L O S S Y
E   D   E   A         R
  C E M E N T M I X E R
A     E   M     D   B
L O C K E T   A D D U C E
P   R   E   C   E   C   A
A   O   R   U P S T A R T
C O N V I C T   K   T   E
A   Y   E   E A S T E R N
```

459

```
I   P   L   B O M B A R D
N A O M I   A   A   L   U
C   I   L A S E R B E A M
U L T R A   K   T   R   M
B   I   C H E M I S T R Y
U   E     T   N     U
S T R I V E   C I N E M A
  O   E   R     C   G
S O U T H W E S T   U   I
T   N   I   L   A D A P T
A D D I C T I O N   D   A
T   U   L   C   G R O U T
E Y E L E S S   Y   R   E
```

460

```
D E P O S I T   B R A S S
I   E   E   I   A       I
S U N   R E D P E P P E R
T   D   B   Y     T     E
A L I B I     A   U P O N
N   N   A N T L E R
T U G S   O   M   E V E N
      M O R O S E   E   A
T H A I   M     C O R G I
O   T   E   L   B     V
N O S T A L G I A   O B E
I   E   G   I   S     T
C A N N Y   S O R C E R Y
```

461

```
S A B B A T   P L O U G H
K     I   W   E       A
I M P E R M A N E N T   C
N   E   W   F   K   E   K
N A R R A T E D   K N E E
Y   C   V   R   W   N   R
  B A L E D   W A D E D
R   P   S   E   I   S   E
E D I T   F A N T A S I A
D   T   W   R   R   E   R
S   A C H I E V E M E N T
E     O   D   S       H
A U T U M N   A S T R A Y
```

462

```
O P P O S I T E   D A M N
L   U   O   W       N   O
D E R A N G E D     T   U
H   U   A   E V E N I N G
A L L O T     O       H
T   E   A S T R O N A U T
    N   C   A     R
A R T I C H O K E   M   F
N       E     S H A M E
D I P L O M A   C   T   W
R   A     E X P O S U R E
E   C   L   R   R   S
W H E T   S E A T B E L T
```

Solutions

463

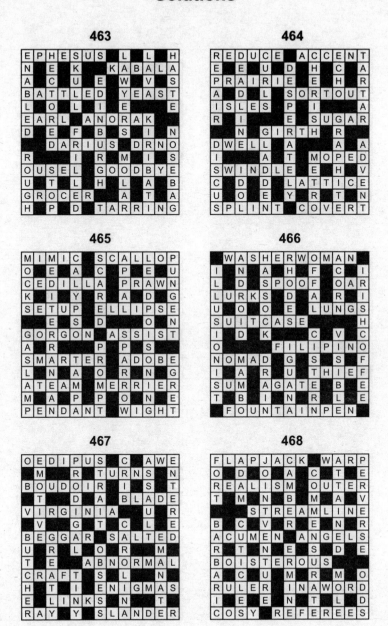

E	P	H	E	S	U	S		L		L		H
N		E		K			K	A	B	A	L	A
A		C		U		E		W		V		S
B	A	T	T	L	E	D		Y	E	A	S	T
L		O		L		I		E				E
E	A	R	L		A	N	O	R	A	K		
D		E		F		B		S		I		N
		D	A	R	I	U	S		D	R	N	O
R			I		R		M		I			S
O	U	S	E	L		G	O	O	D	B	Y	E
U		T		L		H		L		A		B
G	R	O	C	E	R			A		T		A
H		P		D		T	A	R	R	I	N	G

464

R	E	D	U	C	E		A	C	C	E	N	T
E		E		U		D		H		C		A
P	R	A	I	R	I	E		E		H		R
A		D		L		S	O	R	T	O	U	T
I	S	L	E	S		P		I				A
R		I			E		S	U	G	A	R	
	N		G	I	R	T	H		R			
D	W	E	L	L		A			A		A	
I			A		T		M	O	P	E	D	
S	W	I	N	D	L	E		E		H		V
C		D		D		L	A	T	T	I	C	E
U		O		E		Y		R		T		N
S	P	L	I	N	T		C	O	V	E	R	T

465

M	I	M	I	C		S	C	A	L	L	O	P
O		E		A		C		P		E		U
C	E	D	I	L	L	A		P	R	A	W	N
K		I		Y		R		A		D		G
S	E	T	U	P		E	L	L	I	P	S	E
		E		S		D			O		N	
G	O	R	G	O	N		A	S	S	I	S	T
A		R			P		P		S			
S	M	A	R	T	E	R		A	D	O	B	E
L		N		A		O		R		N		G
A	T	E	A	M		M	E	R	R	I	E	R
M		A		P		P		O		N		E
P	E	N	D	A	N	T		W	I	G	H	T

466

	W	A	S	H	E	R	W	O	M	A	N	
I		N		A		H		F		C		I
L		D		S	P	O	O	F		O	A	R
L	U	R	K	S		D		A		R		I
U		O		O		E		L	U	N	G	S
S	U	I	T	C	A	S	E					H
I		D		K			C		V		C	
O			F	I	L	I	P	I	N	O	
N	O	M	A	D		G		S		S		F
I		A		R		U		T	H	I	E	F
S	U	M		A	G	A	T	E		B		E
T		B		I		N		R		L		E
	F	O	U	N	T	A	I	N	P	E	N	

467

O	E	D	I	P	U	S		C		A	W	E
	M		R		T	U	R	N	S		N	
B	O	U	D	O	I	R		I		S		T
	T		D		A		B	L	A	D	E	
V	I	R	G	I	N	I	A		U		R	
V		G		T		C		L		E	
B	E	G	G	A	R		S	A	L	T	E	D
U		R		L		O		R		M	
T		E		A	B	N	O	R	M	A	L	
C	R	A	F	T		S		L		N	
H		T		I		E	N	I	G	M	A	S
E		L	I	N	K	S		N		T	
R	A	Y		Y		S	L	A	N	D	E	R

468

F	L	A	P	J	A	C	K		W	A	R	P
O		D		O		A		C		T		E
R	E	A	L	I	S	M		O	U	T	E	R
T		M		N		B		M		A		V
			S	T	R	E	A	M	L	I	N	E
B		C		V		R		E		N		R
A	C	U	M	E	N		A	N	G	E	L	S
R		T		N		E		S		D		E
B	O	I	S	T	E	R	O	U	S		
A		C		U		M		R		M		O
R	U	L	E	R		I	N	A	W	O	R	D
I		E		E		N		T		L		D
C	O	S	Y		R	E	F	E	R	E	E	S

Solutions

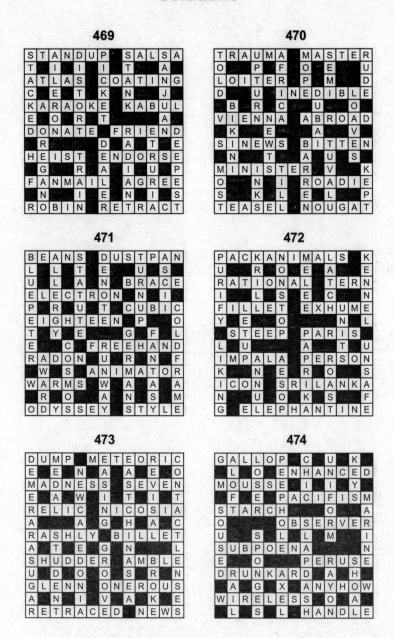

469

```
S T A N D U P   S A L S A
T   I   I   I   T     A
A T L A S   C O A T I N G
C   E   T   K   N     J
K A R A O K E   K A B U L
E   O   R   T       A
D O N A T E   F R I E N D
  R       D   A   T   E
H E I S T   E N D O R S E
  G   R   A   I   U   P
F A N M A I L   A G R E E
  N   I   E   N   I   S
R O B I N   R E T R A C T
```

470

```
T R A U M A   M A S T E R
O   P   F   O   E     U
L O I T E R   P   M   D
D   U   I N E D I B L E
  B   R   C   U     O
V I E N N A   A B R O A D
  K   E   E     A   V
S I N E W S   B I T T E N
  N   T   A   U   S
M I N I S T E R   V   K
O   N   I   R O A D I E
S   K   L   E   L   P
T E A S E L   N O U G A T
```

471

```
B E A N S   D U S T P A N
L   L   T   E   U   S
U   L   A   N   B R A C E
E L E C T R O N   N   I
P   R   U   T   C U B I C
E I G H T E E N   P   O
T   Y   E   G   F   L
E   C   F R E E H A N D
R A D O N   U   R   N   F
  W   S   A N I M A T O R
W A R M S   W   A   A   A
  R   O   A   N   S   M
O D Y S S E Y   S T Y L E
```

472

```
P A C K A N I M A L S   K
U   R   O   E   A     E
R A T I O N A L   T E R N
I   L   S   E   C     N
F I L L E T   E X H U M E
Y   E   O       N     L
  S T E E P   P A R I S
L   U       A   T   U
I M P A L A   P E R S O N
K   N   E   R   O     S
I C O N   S R I L A N K A
N   U   O   K   S     F
G   E L E P H A N T I N E
```

473

```
D U M P   M E T E O R I C
E   E   N   A   A   E   O
M A D N E S S   S E V E N
E   A   W   I   T   I   T
R E L I C   N I C O S I A
A   A   G   H   A   C
R A S H L Y   B I L L E T
A   T   E   G   N     L
S H U D D E R   A M B L E
U   D   O   O   S   R   N
G L E N N   O N E R O U S
A   N   I   V   A   K   E
R E T R A C E D   N E W S
```

474

```
G A L L O P   C   U   K
  L   O   E N H A N C E D
M O U S S E   I   I   Y
  F   E   P A C I F I S M
S T A R C H       O     A
O       O B S E R V E R
U   S   L   L   M       I
S U B P O E N A         N
E   O       P E R U S E
D R U N K A R D   A   H
  A   G   X   A N Y H O W
W I R E L E S S   O   A
  L   S   L   H A N D L E
```

Solutions

475

```
S E T A S I D E . . O S L O
I . O . P . E . . . T . B
C O B R A . C A R R I E D
K . A . G . A . . . G . U
. G . H . M Y A N M A R .
C L O S E U P . T . A . A
H . . T . . . O . . . T
E . G . T . M A N H O L E
S T A M I N A . E . R .
T . M . I . . M . A . F
N I B B L E D . E X C E L
U . L . E . N . L . E
T E E M . A N A T H E M A
```

476

```
. P . M . B O W . . A . B
C O Y O T E . E D I B L E
. R . Z . D . . S . H
O R A N G E A D E . E . E
. I . . L . I . N . A
O D O U R . K N I T T E D
. G . Z . W . G . N . N
P E L I C A N . S T U D Y
I . P . Y . B . . . A
G . L . E S C O R T I N G
E . A . I . O . A . G
O U T B I D . Z I P P E R
N . E . E K E . E . R
```

477

```
C L I M B . H . . P . S
A . N . R . A L B U M E N
R A N . E . L . B . . A
A . I . W H O S O E V E R
M A N G E . . C . R . L
E . G . R A D I A T O R .
L . C . D . O . Y . . F
. S L A M M I N G . D . R
L . D . I . A Z U R E . E
I N S E R T I O N . L . E
C . N . B . D . C O W
K N U C K L E . E . E . A
S . E . X . R A T T Y
```

478

```
N A C H O S . D . P . C
I . A . . P E R S O N A L
M . P . I . E . N . U
B U S H E L . S A D D L E
U . E . L . S . . D
S W E A T . R E S T O R E
. A . L . S O D . I . O
B R U S Q U E . B R I N E
P . . I . P . E . . R
A L B E R T . S I S T E R
. A . D . I . A . A . A
I N T E R N A L . . C . N
. E . N . G . M A R K E T
```

479

```
S M O K I N G . N . L . T
T . N . . A B O L I S H
O . C R U E L . D . E . I
V . E . N . O B S C U R E
E L O P E . R . . . . V
. . V . S P E C T A C L E
A . E . C . . A . A . S
C O R M O R A N T . L .
T . . . L . T H E R E
S W A L L O W . O . N . A
O . G . E . A L O U D . G
U N R E A D Y . . A . L
T . A . D . S C O U R G E
```

480

```
S T R E A K . H A L V E S
. E . L . E . I . E . O
T A V E R N . L E N T I L
. G . C . O I L . G . O
D A N T E . . S . T . U
. R . . . P H I S H I N G
. D . F . R . D . Y . A
F E A R S O M E . . . N
. N . I . P . . A C R I D
L . T . E N D . H . M
A V A T A R . R E A S O N
M . E . T . A . S . U
E N E R G Y . B R E A S T
```

629

Solutions

481

```
M I S T L E T O E . S . D
A . T . A . Y . M O W E R
N . O P T . P . B . A . O
G . O . E Z I N E . M . U
O R D E R . S . D Y I N G
. . I . A . T . . . . . H
B U N D L E . P L A N E T
E . . . B . O . A . . . .
S I N G S . E . R E I C H
I . E . W H A L E . R . A
E . P . E . R . L E O . R
G R A C E . D . E . B . E
E . L . P E S S I M I S M
```

482

```
S H A F T . B . . A . M .
H . L . R . A U C T I O N
A R C H E R S . . Y . V .
R . O . K . S T E P S I N
E . V . . P . H . I . N .
O V E R T A K E . C A G E
U . . E . N . L . A . . V
T O P S . T E M P L A T E
. B . T . R . A . L . R .
B E T R A Y S . R . K . Y
. Y . I . L E E W A R D .
M E C C A N O . I . L . A
. D . T . E . N O I S Y .
```

483

```
T R E M O R . S E P T I C
A . A . V . U . H . O .
M U R D E R E R . D U M B
E . D . R . G . G . B .
D O R I S . R E F U S A L
. . U . L . . R . . . E
C A M P E R . B A R B E R
R . E . . . C . E .
O C T O P U S . T U L L E
C . A . R . I . L . I
H U L L . B L O O M I N G
E . O . A . . U . N . H
T U N E I N . T S H I R T
```

484

```
B E H A L F . S I F T E D
I . L . R . Q . E . S .
R A N I . E U N T . T .
D . . C U S T A R D P I E
. R . I . C . L . E . M
P E D A L O . L A R I A T
. C . Y . . K . T .
T O S S E D . P A M P E R
. V . L . O . U . E . D
H E L I C O P T E R . . S
. R . C . M . O . L A S H
E . E . E . E . F . I . O
A D O R E D . F I N I T E
```

485

```
A D I E U . P R O F I L E
D . N . N . A . B . T .
E . T . I N T R I N S I C
P R E E N . T . E . . A
T . R . S W E E T T A L K
. P . T . R . A . R . E
T A R T A N . E S P I E D
O . E . L . I . T . S
P E T U L A N C E . . M
I . S . F . L O O S E . .
C E L E B R A T E . T . T
. . A . S . N . S . L . A
P A Y M E N T . S P E L L
```

486

```
P U C E . P L A T Y P U S
A . H . C . A . A . R . A
T E A C O S Y . P R E S S
I . I . N . M . E . V . H
E A R L S . A R M I E S
N . . E . N . E . N . D
C E L E R Y . M A N T R A
E . A . V . R . S . . Y
. I N V A D E . U P E N D
L . Y . T . V . R . X . R
O M A N I . E L E V A T E
G . R . V . A . S . C . A
S U D D E N L Y . I T E M
```

630

Solutions

487

```
R E N E W A L . . P R O O F
H . A . H . A . O . C . E
I M P R O V I D E N T . E
Z . . L . R . . A . . . L
O X E Y E . D R E D G E S
M . X . S . S . X . O . .
E N T R A P . L E A N E D
. R . L . S . M . A . R
P R E C E P T . P O L K A
A . M . . U . T . . . . W
P . I N G R A T I T U D E
A . S . A . R . O . F . R
W I T T Y . T E N U O U S
```

488

```
. E D W A R D . S C I F I
S . A . S . R . T . D . M
P A K I S T A N I . Y . M
A . A . . G . P I L A U .
C A R N I V O R E . L . N
E . O . N . N . . . . . E
S L O W L Y . I D E A L S
H . . A . B . T . . . . Y
U . S . W O R M C A S T S
T O W E L . E . . . P . T
T . I . E V E N T U A T E
L . N . S . D . A . D . M
E D G E S . S I M P E R .
```

489

```
S . A . F . S C O O T E R
C U S H I O N . I . . . H
A . L . D . A O . T O Y .
T R E N D . C A N A L . M
T . E . L . K . T . E Y E
E X P R E S S I O N S . .
R . U . K . C . O . . . I
. E N G I N E E R I N G .
F I X . O . E . U . N . N
E . P E A C E . R A T I O
T W O . T . D . O . E . R
C . R . . E X P E N S E .
H A T C H E D . E . D . D
```

490

```
E S T A B L I S H M E N T
X . P . O . P . . X . . H
P U M A . U . O R A T O R
E . . R I S E N . R . . E
C H I T . E . S I R E N S
T . N . . . O . . M . . H
. E V I S C E R A T E D .
S . E . O . . . . L . . H
H A R D E N . O . L Y R E
R . N . V O W E L . . . R
E M E R G E . I . A L S O
W . S . N . N . M . . . E
D I S I N T E G R A T E S
```

491

```
D O S E S . . R . A R I D
I . N . T H E I R S . N .
S T A L E . G . U . V . .
M . I . P I N O T N O I R
A L L . U . R . D . T . .
Y . S . P E D O M E T E R
. W . S . U . U . R . D .
F R E E P R E S S . C . A
. I . V . O . . K . R O B
I N T E N S I V E . A . A
. K . N . T . . T I T U S
. L . T R A G I C . E . E
V E R Y . R . . H E R O D
```

492

```
R O A R S . I N T E R I M
E . C . W . N . I . U . A
T I C . E C C E N T R I C
C . O . E . O . . A . . H
H A U N T . N E B U L A E
. . N . C . S . A . . . T
M O T I O N P I C T U R E
A . . R . I . K . P . . .
T I T A N I C . S T R O P
A . R . U . T . I . . . E
D I A R R H O E A . G E T
O . C . O . U . G . H . A
R O T A T E S . E X T O L
```

631

Solutions

493

```
D I S C A R D   T R U N K
O   T   M   A   A       N
O N O   B A L A L A I K A
R   C   E   L   L   N   V
M A K E R E A D Y   S H E
A   M       S   H   I
T H A T C H   H O T D O G
    R   A   H       E   A
W O K   S L A U G H T E R
I   E   H   B   E   R   O
P A T R I C I A N   A R T
E       E   T   C       T
S W E A R   S P E C K L E
```

494

```
E X C E P T I O N   P A D
A   A   A       O   A   I
S U N D R Y   Q U A L M S
T   N   A   S   N   L   A
  G O E S   T A S T I N G
N   T   O   I   D   R
O     G L O R I F Y     E
R   G       F   A   L   E
T R A I L E R   S P A Y
H   M   Y   Y   Y   D   G
S U B M I T   V E N D O R
E   I   N       N   E   O
A P T   G R U B S C R E W
```

495

```
G A M M O N   L E T S G O
  V   U   A   U   Y   I
N U T S   I G N O R A N T
  N   T   L   C   E
S C R A P   P H Y S I C S
  U   R   G   E       A
G L I D E R   O R R E R Y
  A   I   N   E   I
T R E B L E D   S C U B A
    L   V   F   R   B
P A R A N O I A   U S E S
  P   Z   U   I   I   A
R E B E L S   R A T I N G
```

496

```
P E A R L   C O C H L E A
R   N   I   R   R   L
E   G   N   E   E N E M A
D U O   S T A G S       M
E   S   E   T   S H R U B
C A T S E Y E S   O   I
E   U   D       T   S   V
A   R   E P H E M E R A
S C A L D   I   L   W   L
E     A Q A B A   A L E
S C O U R   N   V   T   N
  O   N   O   I   E   C
P E G A S U S   V E R G E
```

497

```
B A G S   C O M M O N E R
L   Q   O   E   P   X
A C Q U I R E D T A S T E
N   A   D   I   L   O
C H I L L I   C A S T R O
H   I   A   D   T
  Y O D E L   T O W N S
  A   V   R   I   A
T O S S E S   A R N O L D
U   I   W   C   D   D
U N I N T E N T I O N A L
  D   C   E   O   W   E
D E F E C T O R   S O L D
```

498

```
M U S T   C A S T A W A Y
A   E   R   B   R   E   A
S E R I O U S   O P T I C
S   U   U   E   U   T   H
A M M A N   I N B U I L T
G   D   L   L   N
E X C I T E   L E N G T H
    R   H   P   M       U
A M A T E U R   A S S A M
M   C   B   U   K   N   E
A N K L E   N E E D I E R
S   E   N   E   R   D   U
S I D E D I S H   E E L S
```

632

Solutions

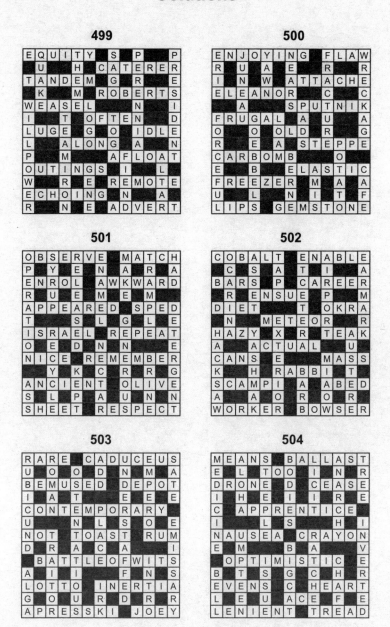

499 **500**

501 **502**

503 **504**

Solutions

505

A	Z	A	L	E	A		S		K		M
S		B			C	O	N	T	I	N	U	E
S	H	E	D		U		O		D		E
O		T	O	T	T	E	R		D	A	S	H
R		T		E		K				L
T	E	X	A	S		A	E	R	O	B	I	C
E		R		M		L		D		A
D	I	S	D	A	I	N		B	I	K	E	R
	N			G		S		O		E
I	D	E	A		R	E	C	T	U	M		W
	O		F		A		A		S	I	L	O
M	O	M	E	N	T	U	M			S		R
	R		W		E		P	A	R	S	O	N

506

	L	I	V	E	R	S	A	U	S	A	G	E
U		D		N		E		B		M		R
N	A	I	A	D		A		O	S	I	E	R
I		O		G	A	S		A		A		O
S	A	M	B	A		O	C	T	O	B	E	R
O			M		N				L
N	A	I	L	E	D		D	E	F	E	N	D
	C			B		J				O
S	H	E	A	T	H	E		E	L	B	O	W
I		B		H		A	R	C		A		S
S	C	E	N	E		D		T	E	R	S	E
A		R		F		L		O		G		R
L	I	G	H	T	H	E	A	R	T	E	D

507

A	S	T	U	T	E		I	N	L	A	I	D
B		A		H		N		E		E
H	E	B	R	E	W		S		G		A
O		L			O	L	I	V	E	O	I	L
R	E	E	L		B		N		N		N
	V		I	N	B	O	U	N	D		D
B	O	O	M		L		A		A	D	E	N
	L		E	L	E	C	T	O	R		N
	V		L		B		I		Y	E	T	I
D	E	M	I	J	O	H	N			B		R
E		G		A		G	A	M	B	I	A
A		H		R			W		E		T
F	I	T	T	E	D		O	N	E	D	G	E

508

B	L	A	D	D	E	R		A		A		C
E		B		R		U	N	D	E	R	G	O
A	R	R	A	I	G	N		A		G		N
C		E		V		G		G	O	O	F
O	N	A	G	E	R		B	E	E	T	L	E
N		S		S		E		L				R
	S	T	E	A	M	R	O	L	L	E	R
A			I		A			N		D
E	S	C	O	R	T		T	I	S	S	U	E
R		A		A		B		N		L		S
I		D		B		A	C	E	T	A	T	E
A	I	R	S	I	C	K		R		V		R
L		E		D		E	N	T	R	E	A	T

509

C		A		C		A	C	C	U	S	E	R
A	U	D	I	O		L		A		A		A
T		M		C	E	L	E	S	T	I	A	L
A	M	I	G	O		U		T		N		L
R		R		A	I	R	W	O	R	T	H	Y
R		A		E		F		E		E
H	A	L	T	E	R		A	F	L	A	M	E
	I		A	P			N		N		R
G	L	A	D	S	T	O	N	E		A		I
R		L		E		P		T	I	G	H	T
A	Y	A	T	O	L	L	A	H		R		R
S		M		F		A		E	L	A	T	E
P	R	O	F	F	E	R		R		M		A

510

A	F	F	A	B	L	E		A	V	E	R	T
E		I		L		D		I				O
R	A	F		O	D	D	J	O	B	M	A	N
O		T		T		Y		R				G
S	L	E	E	T			C		A	I	D	S
O		E		O	R	P	H	A	N		N
L	A	N	D		A		A		T	B	A	R
	G		A	S	T	E	R	N		R		E
R	O	A	R		E			A	M	O	N	G
I		L		C		R		T		T		R
F	U	N	I	C	U	L	A	R		H	O	E
L		N		O		O		E		E		S
E	L	E	G	Y		T	O	W	A	R	D	S

Solutions

511

B	R	E	E	C	H		A	R	O	U	N	D
E				L		C	U					O
S	A	U	D	I	A	R	A	B	I	A		M
T		N		N		I		Y		P		I
O	U	T	S	I	D	E	R		S	P	U	N
W		A		C		D		S		A		O
	I	N	L	A	W		C	H	A	R	D	
B		G		L		S		A		A		F
O	G	L	E		S	T	I	L	E	T	T	O
A		E		T		I		L		U		L
T		S	T	A	R	C	R	O	S	S	E	D
E				S		K		W				E
R	E	B	U	K	E		I	S	O	B	A	R

512

R	Y	E	G	R	A	S	S		P	L	E	A
A		L		E		I			A		U	
D	Y	E	S	T	U	F	F		S		N	
I		C		I			T	R	A	N	S	I	T
S	A	T	A	N		O						I
H		R		A	F	F	L	U	E	N	C	E
	I			E		I			O			
B	A	C	K	T	R	A	C	K		S		A
E				R				E	M	E	N	D
W	A	R	S	H	I	P		E		D		O
A		E			C	A	M	P	A	I	G	N
R		A			P		E		V			I
E	U	R	O		H	A	I	R	L	E	S	S

513

A	C	C	U	S	A	L		A		A		U
B		A		C			A	B	S	U	R	D
S		T		O		B		A		G		D
E	A	C	H	W	A	Y		N	I	E	C	E
N		H		L		P		D		R		R
C	H	E	F		A	R	R	O	W			
E		R		A		O		N		C		C
			B	R	I	D	E		D	O	D	O
F		S		S		U		B		T		N
A	M	P	L	E		C	O	A	L	T	I	T
I		U		N		T		K		A		A
N	O	R	M	A	L			E		G		C
T		T		L		B	A	D	D	E	B	T

514

S	E	A	R	C	H		R	E	S	I	G	N
E		R		H		I		X		N		E
C	A	R	T	O	O	N		H		C		E
U		A		P		S	M	A	S	H	E	D
R	A	N	K	S		T		U		L		
E		G			R		S	T	A	G	E	
		E		A	D	U	L	T		P		
O	L	D	E	R		M			P		S	
F				T		E		S	T	A	T	E
F	A	S	H	I	O	N		O		R		T
I		A		C		T	A	L	L	E	S	T
C		L		L		S		V		N		E
E	I	T	H	E	R		K	E	T	T	L	E

515

A	I	S	L	E		M	E	R	M	A	I	D
D		T		N		O		U		N		E
L	E	A	T	H	E	R		M	O	T	E	L
I		T		A		T		B		I		U
B	R	I	A	N		A	B	A	S	H	E	D
		O		C		R		R		I		E
C	A	N	T	E	R		C	A	U	S	E	D
O		M			B		C		T			
P	L	A	Y	B	O	Y		Q	U	A	L	M
Y		S		U		G		U		M		O
C	A	T	E	R		O	P	I	N	I	O	N
A		E		K		N		R		N		E
T	E	R	R	A	C	E		E	R	E	C	T

516

	C	I	R	C	U	M	S	P	E	C	T	
D		N		A		A		L		R		L
E		E		P	A	N	D	A		A	G	E
N	E	X	U	S		N		Z		N		G
T		A		U		E		A	R	E	N	A
A	C	C	O	L	A	D	E					L
L		T		E			T		B		T	
F					S	H	O	R	T	A	G	E
L	A	D	L	E		I		E		S		N
O		E		L		C		M	I	M	E	D
S	A	C		G	E	C	K	O		A		E
S		A		A		U		L		T		R
	H	Y	D	R	O	P	H	O	B	I	A	

635

Solutions

517

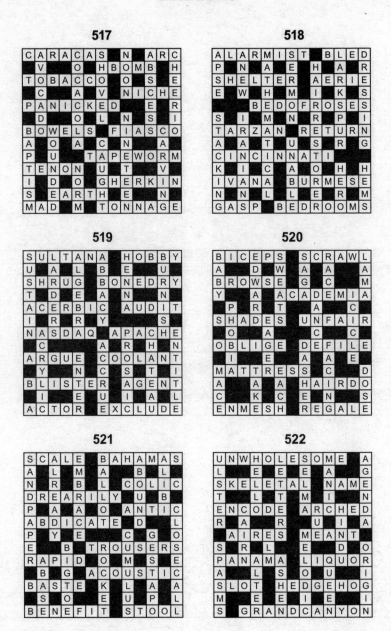

C	A	R	A	C	A	S		N		A	R	C
	V		O		H	B	O	M	B		H	
T	O	B	A	C	C	O		O		S		E
	C		A		V		N	I	C	H	E	
P	A	N	I	C	K	E	D		E		R	
	D		O		L		N		S		I	
B	O	W	E	L	S		F	I	A	S	C	O
A		O		A		C		N		A		
P		U		T	A	P	E	W	O	R	M	
T	E	N	O	N		U		T		V		
I		D		O		G	H	E	R	K	I	N
S		E	A	R	T	H		E		N		
M	A	D		M		T	O	N	N	A	G	E

518

A	L	A	R	M	I	S	T		B	L	E	D
P		N		A		E		H		A		R
S	H	E	L	T	E	R		A	E	R	I	E
E		W		H		M		I		K		S
				B	E	D	O	F	R	O	S	E	S
S		I		M		N		R		P		I
T	A	R	Z	A	N		R	E	T	U	R	N
A		A		T		U		S		R		G
C	I	N	C	I	N	N	A	T	I			
K		I		C		A		O		H		H
I	V	A	N	A		B	U	R	M	E	S	E
N		N		L		L		E		R		M
G	A	S	P		B	E	D	R	O	O	M	S

519

S	U	L	T	A	N	A		H	O	B	B	Y
U		A		L		E			U			U
S	H	R	U	G		B	O	N	E	D	R	Y
T		D		E		A		N			N	
A	C	E	R	B	I	C		A	U	D	I	T
I		R		R		Y			S			S
N	A	S	D	A	Q		A	P	A	C	H	E
	C			A		R		H		N		
A	R	G	U	E		C	O	O	L	A	N	T
	Y		N		C		S		T		I	
B	L	I	S	T	E	R		A	G	E	N	T
	I		E		U		I		A		L	
A	C	T	O	R		E	X	C	L	U	D	E

520

B	I	C	E	P	S		S	C	R	A	W	L
A		D		W		A		A		A		A
B	R	O	W	S	E		G		C		M	
Y		A		A	C	A	D	E	M	I	A	
	P		R		T		A			C		
S	H	A	D	E	S		U	N	F	A	I	R
	O		A			U		C		C		
O	B	L	I	G	E		D	E	F	I	L	E
	I		E		A		A		A		E	
M	A	T	T	R	E	S	S		C		D	
A			A		A		H	A	I	R	D	O
C		K		C		E		N			S	
E	N	M	E	S	H		R	E	G	A	L	E

521

S	C	A	L	E		B	A	H	A	M	A	S
A		L		M		A		B		L		
N		R		B		L		C	O	L	I	C
D	R	E	A	R	I	L	Y		U		B	
P		A		A		O		A	N	T	I	C
A	B	D	I	C	A	T	E		D		L	
P		Y		E			C		G		O	
E			B		T	R	O	U	S	E	R	S
R	A	P	I	D		O		M		S		E
	B		G		A	C	O	U	S	T	I	C
B	A	S	T	E		K		L		A		A
	S		O		E		U		P		L	
B	E	N	E	F	I	T		S	T	O	O	L

522

U	N	W	H	O	L	E	S	O	M	E		A
L		E		E		E		A		G		G
S	K	E	L	E	T	A	L		N	A	M	E
T		L		T		M		I		N		
E	N	C	O	D	E		A	R	C	H	E	D
R		A		R			U		I			A
	A	I	R	E	S		M	E	A	N	T	
S		R		L			E		D			O
P	A	N	A	M	A		L	I	Q	U	O	R
A		L		S		O		U		I		
S	L	O	T		H	E	D	G	E	H	O	G
M		E		E		I		E				I
S		G	R	A	N	D	C	A	N	Y	O	N

Solutions

523

T	A	T	A		A	E	R	O	B	I	C	S
R		O		P	X		F		R		C	
A	R	T	D	E	C	O		F	L	O	R	A
N		E		R		D		T		N		N
S	A	M	O	A		U	N	H	E	A	R	D
A			M		S		E		G			A
T	H	R	O	B	S		O	R	D	E	A	L
L		A		U		D		E				M
A	N	G	U	L	A	R		C	R	E	D	O
N		D		A		O		O		D		N
T	R	O	U	T		W	A	R	N	I	N	G
I		L		O		S		D		T		E
C	A	L	O	R	I	E	S		T	H	O	R

524

I	N	S	T	E	P		P		B		P	
	E		I		R	E	L	I	A	B	L	E
G	H	E	T	T	O		U		Z		A	
	R		L		D	I	S	C	O	U	N	T
B	U	R	E	A	U			O		A		
E					C	R	A	C	K	E	R	S
A		O		E		L		A				T
R	U	N	N	E	R	U	P					A
	N		W				H	A	N	G	A	R
S	C	I	A	T	I	C	A		E		M	
	O		R		M		B	A	R	R	E	D
G	R	A	D	U	A	T	E		V		N	
	K		S		M		T	R	E	N	D	Y

525

B	A	N	K	R	U	P	T		G	A	Z	A
A		E		E		O			N		C	
L	O	V	E	S		C	R	Y	P	T	I	C
D		A		T		K			H		R	
	D		R		E	V	I	L	E	Y	E	
B	L	A	T	A	N	T		N		M		D
A			I			F			I	
N		A	N		D	E	L	I	G	H	T	
D	E	M	E	T	E	R		U		R		
A		B			I		E		A		C
N	E	U	T	R	A	L		N	O	T	C	H
N		S			L		Z		E		I	
A	C	H	E		A	S	S	A	S	S	I	N

526

	B		A		M		B	A	R	R	E	L
M	O	U	S	S	A	K	A				X	
	D		C		Y		R	E	C	I	P	E
F	I	V	E		B	A	G		E			
	C		N		E		A		D		R	
W	E	E	D	Y		L	I	B	E	R	T	Y
A		A		R		N		E			E	
S	A	U	N	T	E	R		A	P	R	O	N
	C		T		S		A		F		C	
T			H	A	M		R	U	T	H	
C	I	N	E	M	A		B		I		A	
O				P	R	E	S	E	R	V	E
E	N	S	U	R	E			R		D		E

527

A	S	P	I	C		A			L			A
C		A		A		T	I	B	E	T	A	N
H	A	Y		N		O		T			N	
I		D		D	E	P	A	R	T	U	R	E
E	M	A	I	L			N		I			X
V		Y		E	L	E	G	A	N	C	E	
E			A		I		E		G			C
	T	A	P	E	S	T	R	Y		B		O
F		P		L			I	D	L	E	R
R	E	V	E	R	E	N	C	E		O		O
E		A		E		L		N	A	N	
S	U	N	R	I	S	E		D		D		E
H		S		D		S	C	E	N	T	

528

B	O	W	M	A	N		S		L		B	
E		E			A	B	O	V	E	P	A	R
A		S		C		L		A		L		
S	E	T	T	E	R		D	E	F	E	A	T
T			A		E		I			N		
S	C	A	R	E		R	E	P	L	I	C	A
	L		D		M		R		O		E	
N	E	W	Y	E	A	R		G	O	O	D	S
	R			R		B		N		N		
F	I	D	G	E	T		A	N	Y	O	N	E
	C		A		I		L			N		E
E	A	R	N	I	N	G	S			C		Z
	L		G		I		A	D	H	E	R	E

637

Solutions

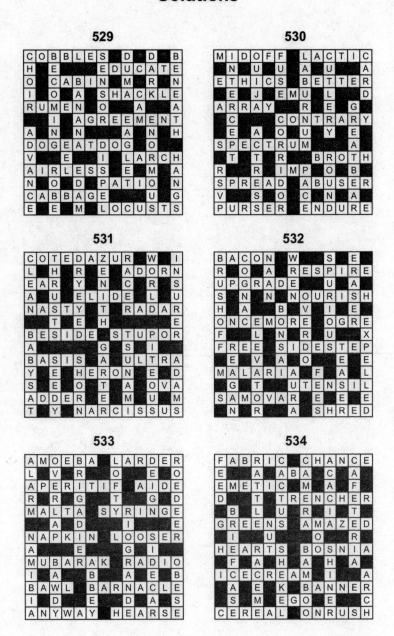

529

```
C O B B L E S   D   D   B
H   E       E D U C A T E
O   C A B I N   M   R   N
I   O   A   S H A C K L E
R U M E N   O   A     A
    I   A G R E E M E N T
A   N   N     A   N   H
D O G E A T D O G   O
V   E   I   L A R C H
A I R L E S S   E   M   A
N   O   D   P A T I O   N
C A B B A G E     U   G
E   E   M   L O C U S T S
```

530

```
M I D O F F   L A C T I C
  N   U   U   A   U     A
E T H I C S   B E T T E R
  E   J   E M U   L     D
A R R A Y   R   E   G
  C     C O N T R A R Y
  E   A   O   U   Y   E
S P E C T R U M     A
  T   T   R     B R O T H
R   R   I M P   O   B
S P R E A D   A B U S E R
V   S   O   C   N   A
P U R S E R   E N D U R E
```

531

```
C O T E D A Z U R   W   I
L   H   R   E   A D O R N
E A R   Y   N   C   R   S
A   U   E L I D E   L   U
N A S T Y   T   R A D A R
    T   E   H       E
B E S I D E   S T U P O R
A       G   S   I
B A S I S   A   U L T R A
Y   E   H E R O N   E   D
S   E   O   T   A   O V A
A D D E R   E   M   U   M
T   Y   N A R C I S S U S
```

532

```
B A C O N   W   S   E
R   O   A   R E S P I R E
U P G R A D E   U   A
S   N   N   N O U R I S H
H   A   B   V   I   E
O N C E M O R E   O G R E
F   L   N   R U   X
F R E E   S I D E S T E P
  E   V   A   O   E   E
M A L A R I A   F   A   L
  G   T   U T E N S I L
S A M O V A R   E   E   E
  N   R   A   S H R E D
```

533

```
A M O E B A   L A R D E R
L   V   R   O   E   O
A P E R I T I F   A I D E
R   R   G   T   G   D
M A L T A   S Y R I N G E
    A   D   I       E
N A P K I N   L O O S E R
A   E   G   I
M U B A R A K   R A D I O
I   A   B   A   E   B
B A W L   B A R N A C L E
I   D   E   D   A   S
A N Y W A Y   H E A R S E
```

534

```
F A B R I C   C H A N C E
E   A   A B A   C   A
E M E T I C   M   A   F
D   T   T R E N C H E R
  B   L   U   R   I   T
G R E E N S   A M A Z E D
  I   U       O   R
H E A R T S   B O S N I A
  F   A   H   A   H   A
I C E C R E A M   I     A
  A   E   K   B A N N E R
  S   M   E G O   E   C
C E R E A L   O N R U S H
```

638

Solutions

535

```
M U C U S . P R O P P E D
O . I . L . I . S . R . R
L . R . A R T I C H O K E
L U C K Y . . A . N . A .
U . U . S W E A R W O R D
S . M . . H . W . . U . .
C O F F E E . F R A N C E
. E . . L . U . . C . C .
M A R C O P O L O . E . S
U . E . T . . C O M E T .
S Y N T H E T I C . E . A
I . C . E . A . U . N . S
C L E A R E R . R E T R Y
```

536

```
S C A B . B A R B A D O S
K . O . A . V . A . E . T
E A R A C H E . L A P S E
T . T . H . N . L . O . M
C O A T I . U N E A S Y .
H . . L . E . T . . I . F
E A S I L Y . E D I T O R
D . H . E . C . A . . . I
. B O R S C H . N U R S E
E . T . H . A . C . E . N
V A G U E . S T E W A R D
I . U . E . E . R . C . L
L A N D L O R D . W H E Y
```

537

```
S T A B B E D . D U M P S
E . L . R . E . O . O . T
A P P O I N T M E N T . A
W . . C . E . . . H . R .
A L P H A . S U B J E C T
R . A . B . T . L . A . .
D I V E R S . W A N T E D
. A . A . R . S . E . E .
M I R A C L E . P I N T S
A . O . . D . H . . . E .
G . T O R C H B E A R E R
I . T . U . O . M . O . V
C L I N G . T R E A D L E
```

538

```
. K I P P E R . E T H O S
P . M . I . E . L . A . H
R E P R E S S E D . N . O
O . E . . I . . . E N D O W
T A L L O R D E R . Y . B
U . A . . E . L . . U . .
B A N G L E . B Y P A S S
E . . A . B . . O . . . I
R . M . U P A N D D O W N
A L I E N . F . . N . E .
N . X . D A F F O D I L S
C . U . R . L . U . O . S
E M P T Y . E R R A N D .
```

539

```
E . E . F . A P R I C O T
D I S C U S S . . A . E .
D . T . N . C . H I N T S
A P H I D . E R A . D . T
. . E . A . N . I D I O T
P E R I M E T E R . D . U
A . . E . . . D . . . . B
N . R . N U M E R A B L E
C H E A T . A . E . O . .
R . F . A I R . S I B Y L
E Q U A L . O . S . B . A
A . S . . O B E L I S K .
S T E T S O N . R . N . E
```

540

```
C R O S S E X A M I N E D
A . C . B . P . O . . . A
N E R O . O . P O I S O N
Y . . P A N E L . T . . C
O B O E . Y . A R C A D E
N . R . . . U . . L . . R
. B A D G E . D I N G O .
G . N . A . . . I . . . D
A N G L E R . B . B A L E
R . U . . P L U M E . . M
L E T H A L . Y . R O D E
I . A . . U . E . E . . A
C O N F I G U R A T I O N
```

Solutions

541

```
C H A O S . T . B E E F
A . K . T H R I C E . N
S M I L E . . R . E . G
T . M . N E C E S S A R Y
L A B . C . S . W . O .
E . O . H O L O C A U S T
. F . F . B . M . X . S
A L T I M E T E R . B . A
. O . N . D . O . U R N
O R G A N I S E D . R . K
. I . L . E . . E A S E L
. D . L I N D E N . A . E
N A V Y . T . . T E R M S
```

542

```
R E B U S . H A T C H E S
O . U . T . O . E . E . E
O A F . A M U S E M E N T
S . F . M . S . . D . F
T R A M P . E N D U S E R
. . L . E . B . E . . E
B L O O D P R E S S U R E
R . . E . E . M . P . .
A M N E S I A . O A S I S
V . O . . K . I . . T . A
A D O R A T I O N . A N T
D . N . L . N . E . G . I
O P E N I N G . S K E I N
```

543

```
B A N Q U E T . C A D E T
L . U . N . R . U . E . A
O M N I P R E S E N T . S
A . . O . N . . E . T
T U L I P . C L E A R L Y
E . A . U . H . X . R
D I W A L I . E C Z E M A
. N . A . B . H . N . N
A D M I R E R . E A T E N
B . O . . A . Q . . O
Y . W E S T C O U N T R Y
S . E . T . E . E . A . E
S O R R Y . S T R I P E D
```

544

```
A D J E C T I V E . S A D
B . A . H . . L . E . I
L I C H E N . B U T T E R
E . K . D . A . D . T . E
. H E A D . S H E L L A C
H . T . A . H . . E . T
A . . B R I T A I N . L
N . H . . R . T . S . Y
D E A D S E A . A B U T
C . M . C . Y . L . D . D
U M P I R E . K I M O N O
F . E . A . . C . K . V
F A R . M I N T S A U C E
```

545

```
L E A D E R . E N C O R E
. A . R . U . N . O . A
A R M Y . B E V E R A G E
. L . D . S . I . G . L
C O L O N . R A V I O L I
. B . C . I . B . . T
B E A K E R . L A S S I E
E . . R . E . A . M
A S P I R I N . P U P P Y
R . R . G . M . S . R
D A T A B A S E . A B E L
. R . Q . T . N . G . S
E M P I R E . U N E A S E
```